VIRGIL'S
EPIC TECHNIQUE

Current and forthcoming titles in the Bristol Classical Paperbacks series:

VIRGIL'S
EPIC TECHNIQUE

Richard Heinze

Translated by Hazel and David Harvey
and Fred Robertson
Preface by Antonie Wlosok

Second Edition with Index of Citations

Dedicated to the memory of Georg Kaibel

Cover illustration:
The Wooden Horse, detail from *The Siege of Troy*, by Biagio Di Antonio
[Fitzwilliam Museum, Cambridge]

First published in 1993 by
Bristol Classical Press
an imprint of
Gerald Duckworth & Co. Ltd
61 Frith Street
London W1V 5TA
E-mail: inquiries@duckworth-publishers.co.uk
Website: www.ducknet.co.uk

Second edition 1999

Reprinted 2000

A catalogue record for this book is available
from the British Library

ISBN 1-85399-579-7

Printed in Great Britain by
Booksprint

Contents

Foreword to the 1999 edition

The production of Heinze's classic work in paperback, which we hope will make it more accessible to undergraduates, has provided an opportunity to improve the text by eliminating some errors and also by including Heinze's own very helpful list of citations of passages from the *Aeneid* – thus making it easier for students to consult those sections of Heinze which apply to the particular passages they are studying. We should also like to acknowledge our indebtedness to Anastasios Nikolopoulos, formerly a student of Corpus Christi, Oxford, for a helpful list of misprints in the first edition.

Fred Robertson

Preface to the 1st edition

This book does not attempt to pass value-judgements but to establish historical facts. It does not ask what Virgil should or could have done, but what he wished to do; it tries to understand how the *Aeneid* came into being, in so far as it was the result of the poet's conscious and purposeful artistic actions. It is true that this method will also cast sidelights on the poet's personality, his view of the world, the intellectual currents of his time; I have touched upon these things when the questions which I have asked myself could be answered in no other way. I have completely ignored the language and metre of the *Aeneid*: both are of the greatest importance for the effect of the work, but not for the understanding of the work as an epic poem. My greatest desire was to further this understanding; if I have succeeded, the history of poetic technique will also have benefitted. I do not need to spell out how much remains to be done in this field; my work has necessarily suffered from the fact that there is as yet no adequate study of the technique of pre-Virgilian prose or verse narrative, and the post-Aristotelian theory of narrative art is also still totally obscure. I have only been able to fill these gaps to a very small extent for my own purposes; my main aim had to be to deduce from the work itself the artistic intentions of the *Aeneid*. There had not been many previous studies of this precise subject, but every contribution to the understanding of any single line was there for me to draw upon, and it goes without saying that I could not have written this book without the work of generations of commentators. I have made use of this common store of knowledge built up by their diligence without giving detailed references, or even checking to establish, for example, who was the first to discover the Greek original of one of Virgil's lines, or who first aired a now generally accepted explanation; for the rest I have tried to give honour where honour is due, although the extent of international literature on Virgil is so great that I cannot be sure that I have succeeded. Again and again I could have entered into controversies about points great and small; I refrained from this for the most part, only referring to a few very recent works which seem to me to be typical of certain directions taken by modern interpreters of Virgil.

The two halves of the book attempt to reach the same goal by different paths. In the first half I have analysed the technique of fairly long passages of the *Aeneid*. I hope that these chapters will, if used in conjunction with the existing commentaries, serve as an introduction to those wishing to learn to understand the work. For each passage I have tried to establish what the poet was trying to do, and reconstruct the considerations which led him to the existing solution; I have tried to establish what the poet found in his sources and what he borrowed from his models, thereby providing a basis for the examination of his own contribution as adaptor or new creator. At the same time I had to consider how the shaping of his whole work was influenced not only by his aesthetic goals but also by his political and moral standpoint. The second half summarizes the results gained from this examination and attempts to organize them into a systematic account of his epic technique. I could not always avoid repeating myself; I hope to have avoided this where possible by the use of plentiful cross-references.

Berlin, November 1902

Preface to the 2nd edition

For this new edition I have made grateful use of the corrections and additions that emerged in reviews of my book. I have had no reason to make any far-reaching changes. Where it seemed to be required I have indicated my agreement or disagreement with the literature on Virgil which has appeared since the first edition; in particular I was glad to be able to refer copiously to Norden's commentary on *Aeneid* Book VI (cited throughout by the author's name) in order to amplify or confirm my interpretations. In the first edition I refrained from discussing Book VI because of the imminent publication of Norden's work. Now that it is available I still refrain, since I should only be able to repeat, in all essential matters, what Norden has said, particularly in his summing-up on pp. 342ff.

Leipzig, February 1908

Preface to the 3rd edition

In this edition too, mostly thanks to the work of others, I have corrected, or attempted to offer further confirmation for, many interpretations, but the book remains essentially the same.

Leipzig, July 1914

Since the appearance of the third edition, a great deal has been written about Virgil, including much about matters discussed or touched upon in this book. To respond to everything, agreeing or disagreeing, would have taken up a great deal of time which I believe better spent on other work. I am therefore allowing the third edition to be reprinted as it stands, and do so the more readily since recent discussions have not made me retract my previous beliefs with regard to the more important individual questions, such as the genuineness of the Helen episode in Book II, or the relative date of composition of Book III, or Virgil's philosophical views.

Leipzig, October 1928
Richard Heinze

Translators' Note

As Heinze did not translate his numerous quotations from Greek and Roman authors, we have added translations in square brackets. For Virgil himself we have used W.F. Jackson Knight's Penguin version of the *Aeneid* (Harmondsworth, 1956); we are most grateful to Mr J.D. Christie, representing the estate of Jackson Knight, for permission to do so. We have occasionally modified this version slightly in order to make it clear how the Virgilian phrase illustrates Heinze's argument. We are responsible for translations from other authors.

We would like to thank the late I.R.D. Mathewson, who read the opening chapters, and suggested a number of improvements.

No attempt has been made to update Heinze's bibliography. For discussions of more recent work the reader should consult R.D. Williams, *Virgil* (*Greece & Rome New Surveys in the Classics* no. 1, Oxford [1967], with addenda); annual bibliographies in *Vergilius* from no. 19 (1973) onwards; A.G. McKay, *Classical World* 68 (1974) 1-92; V. Pöschl, *Abhandl. Akad. Wiss. Göttingen, philol.-hist. Klasse* 32 (1979) 1-29; *Arethusa* 14 (1981) 179-86; W. Suerbaum, *Gnomon* 56 (1984) 208-28. Marginal figures represent the page numbers of the third German edition.

It has taken several years longer than originally envisaged to bring this work to completion, and we are very grateful to Messrs Teubner and to Mr John Betts of the Bristol Classical Press for their patience. In particular, HMH and FDH are indebted to Mr Betts for his happy suggestion that FR should be brought in to expedite the conclusion of the work, and to FR for his willingness to do so. The translation up to p. 218 is basically the work of HMH and FDH; thereafter, of HMH and FR.

Hazel and David Harvey, Fred Robertson
1993

Preface to the present edition
by Antonie Wlosok

In 1903, when Richard Heinze's *Virgils epische Technik* first appeared, the poet's reputation was at a very low ebb. It had begun to sink in the eighteenth century, in the wake of the aesthetic concept of the 'genius', and declined even more rapidly in the nineteenth century. Works of reference and encyclopaedias, particularly in Germany, repeated the dismissive judgement that the *Aeneid* was merely the product of a clumsy and uninspired attempt to imitate Homer (and other poets).[1] It was generally felt that the writer of an epic that was so obviously derived from Greek models did not even deserve to be called a poet. In the eyes of such critics, the *Aeneid* lacked everything that prevailing opinion considered essential for true poetry: originality of poetic creation, spontaneity of emotion, liveliness, and a vivid and graphic representation of events. It was widely believed that Virgil was a writer who simply copied from his sources and had no artistic views of his own, but had merely cobbled together material from here, there and everywhere, with no overall plan, so that the final product could not even be regarded as an integral whole. Amongst classicists it was fashionable to draw attention to contradictions, inconsistencies, awkwardness, weaknesses and errors.[2]

It was against this background that Heinze's book raised the whole question of Virgil's artistic aims and his own individual achievement in relation to his literary predecessors and his sources. This approach to the question gave new direction to the study of Virgil; it also inaugurated a whole new era of Latin studies, which at that time were concerned almost exclusively with source-criticism (*Quellenforschung*). We might even go so far as to say that with this work Heinze was the first scholar to establish the study of Latin literature as a separate branch of literary criticism, conscious of its own special function within the field of classical scholarship.[3]

Heinze's method of research remains exemplary even today. By means of painstaking analysis of the whole poem[4] and patient interpretation of the text, constantly drawing comparisons with Virgil's model, Homer, and avoiding all value-judgements, Heinze skilfully pursued one central question: what were Virgil's intentions, and how did he achieve them?

By this method, Heinze succeeded in proving convincingly that Virgil followed clear ideas and effective artistic principles in the selection and shaping of his material, and that he created an epic style that was very much his own, characterized above all by its dramatic, ethical and emotional nature. By 'emotion' we mean that the feelings of the chief characters, both in their actions and in their sufferings, are brought to the forefront of Virgil's narrative, and that he often subordinates the description of external events and situations to the expression of emotional processes, states or moods.

It was Heinze himself who later, in a lecture delivered in 1918,[5] singled out 'the warmth and insight of its emotions' as the most important human quality of the *Aeneid*, and summed up the essential quality of Virgil's descriptive method thus: 'Virgil tells his story like a dramatist, and he portrays the emotions like a painter'; and this portrayal is not merely the result of perceptive observation, but involves entering into the very soul of his characters and showing us how things look from their point of view. Today we can see that in making observations of this kind, Heinze anticipated by many years modern methods of research into narrative.

Furthermore, his book also immediately stimulated scholars to undertake further research into the techniques of narrative and imitation. In particular, within the field of Virgilian scholarship, numerous studies on the theme of 'the art of Virgil' began to appear.[6] Before long, scholars also extended their investigations into areas that Heinze had chosen not to tackle when he restricted his study to Virgil's poetic 'technique', as he called it; they began to reveal the large number of echoes, correspondences and cross-references within the *Aeneid*, and, last but not least, the symbolic nature of Virgilian poetry.[7] Finally, Heinze's fresh approach to the author's artistic intentions – which required a readiness to understand such intentions – prepared the way for a veritable blossoming of interpretations of Virgil that concentrated on the proper understanding of the poet's text.

The significance of Heinze's book was immediately recognized by the academic world,[8] although, of course, classicists who were committed to the opposite way of thinking did not approve of it.[9] Friedrich Leo declared that it was the best thing yet written about Virgil.[10] A second edition (1908) was soon published, and then a third (1915), in which Heinze expanded some discussions and made a number of corrections. Its true value was appreciated in numerous reviews, and in tributes to Heinze at the time of his death,[11] and the majority of its conclusions accepted. Many are now commonplaces of Virgilian scholarship.

The two ideas that won the least acceptance were, first, the theory that Virgil composed the individual books of the *Aeneid* as self-contained poems intended for separate performance, and, secondly, Heinze's views on the relative chronology of the books. Equally controversial was his view that Aeneas' character underwent a development in the course of the work, in the sense of a gradual approach towards perfection and towards the Roman Stoic ideal that Heinze believed Aeneas to represent.[12] He firmly maintained this view even in the third edition of his book, in which he adduced further evidence to support it. Amongst its most influential adherents were C.M. Bowra[13] and K. Büchner,[14] and even today it has still not been totally refuted.

In later years, when further progress had been made in the study of Virgil's art, certain limitations in Heinze's work became apparent.[15] They arose from the fact that he had decided to restrict his study to Virgil's epic *technique* – in other words, to those principles which could be clearly established as guiding the way in which Virgil shaped his material, as opposed to, for example, the symbolic or ambivalent aspects of his poem. However, it is precisely this decision that resulted in the much-praised 'masterly clarity and precision' of the book,[16] and ensured its high standing as a 'classic in criticism'.[17] Nowadays the art of sound, scholarly literary criticism is all too frequently forgotten; here is a work that will provide an excellent introduction to that art for yet another generation.

Notes to the Preface

1. The most important examples are the entries on Virgil by W.S. Teuffel in his article in Pauly's *Realencyclopädie* [the earliest version] VI (1852) 2644-62, and in his own *Geschichte der römischen Literatur* I, first published in Leipzig in 1868-9; the fifth edition was revised by L. Schwabe in 1890 and has been frequently reprinted. The basis of his judgements, and his presuppositions, are revealed by statements such as : 'Virgil is not a natural poet, nor is he a folk-poet: he is a literary poet; and he is not a literary genius, merely a talented writer.... And most of the shortcomings in his work stem from this fact, that he is a literary poet' (Pauly 2650-1); or, from the first edition of his *Geschichte der römischen Literatur* (391): 'He is too little of a genius.... The extreme conscientiousness of his work cannot compensate for his lack of creative power and imagination and of originality, vividness and vivacity'.

These judgements reflect the aesthetic theories of the Romantic school, and the authority of a man such as Barthold Georg Niebuhr, whose frequently quoted opinion of Virgil (*Vorträge über römische Geschichte*, lectures delivered in Bonn in the winter semester of 1828/9, Isler [ed.] [Berlin, 1848] III 130) is apparent throughout. Before long, the influential Theodor Mommsen, who shared Niebuhr's aversion to Virgil, added the weight of his authority to Teuffel's views (cf. Wilamowitz, 'Theodor Mommsen: warum hat er den vierten Band der Römischen Geschichte nicht geschrieben?', in *Kleine Schriften* VI [1972] 31). Still more negative judgements by specialists on Virgil's *Aeneid* were gathered together by H.T. Plüss in *Virgil und die epische Kunst* (Leipzig, 1884) 1-4, which, despite its scholarly imperfections, must be regarded as a forerunner of Heinze's work.

2. A prime specimen of this type of criticism is W. Kroll, 'Studien über die Komposition der Aeneis', *Fleckeisens Jahrbuch* Suppl. 27 (1902) 135-69.

3. In his Leipzig inaugural lecture, 'Die gegenwärtigen Aufgaben der römischen Literaturgeschichte' (*Neue Jahrbücher* 19 [1907] 161-750), Heinze announced that he intended to pursue research into the literary technique of Roman authors. The significance of this remark was immediately perceived by E. Bickel (*Bursians Jahresbericht* 140 [1908] 244-7).

4. However, Heinze says little about Book 6 of the *Aeneid*, since Eduard Norden's commentary (*P. Vergilius Maro: Aeneis Buch VI* [Leipzig 1903]) appeared at approximately the same time.

5. Published posthumously under the title 'Virgil' by A. Körte in R. Heinze, *Die augusteische Kultur* (Leipzig, 1930; reprinted Darmstadt, 1960) 141-56; the quotations are from pp. 151 and 152.

6. An early example is H.W. Prescott, *The Development of Virgil's Art* (Chicago, 1927; reprinted New York, 1963), in which the first part of the 'epoch-making work of Richard Heinze' appears in a new guise, 'paraphrased, rearranged, condensed and expanded' (Preface viii-ix).

7. In this context, the most important discussions are the Virgilian studies of

F. Klingner, which are strongly influenced by Heinze, especially his article 'Virgil als Bewahrer und Erneuerer', in *Das humanistische Gymnasium* 42 (1931) 123-36 (see p. 131 for Heinze), and V. Pöschl's influential *Die Dichtkunst Virgils* (first edn Wiesbaden, 1950; third edn Berlin and New York, 1977; translated into English by Gerda Seligson as *The Art of Virgil* [Ann Arbor, 1962]).

8. Expressed in the reviews by R. Helm, *Berliner Philologische Wochenschrift* 15 (1903) 454-60, 489-93; F. Leo, *Deutsche Literaturzeitung* 10 (1903) 594-6; J. Ziehen, *Neue Jahrbücher* 13 (1904) 644-52 (a joint review of Heinze and of Norden's commentary on *Aeneid* VI); G.J. Laing, *AJP* 26 (1905) 330-42; E. Bickel, loc. cit. (n. 3 above).

9. Unsympathetic and, in some parts, petty criticism is to be found above all in P. Jahn, *Bursians Jahresbericht* 130 (1906) 61-70, in the reviews mentioned on p. 70 of his article, and in the works discussed in the pages that follow (71-7).

10. F. Leo, loc. cit. (n. 8 above) 596: 'To the best of my knowledge of the secondary literature, this book is the best thing yet written about Virgil. Furthermore, it has general significance in that it is a model of thorough analysis and scholarly appreciation of a great work of literature'.

11. The most important obituaries: A. Körte, 'Worte zum Gedächtnis an Richard Heinze', *Berichte der Sächsischen Akademie der Wissenschaften, philol.-hist. Klasse* 81.2 (1929) 11.30; F. Klingner, 'Richard Heinze†', *Gnomon* 6 (1930) 58-62; E. Norden, 'Richard Heinze: ein Gedenkblatt (1930)', *Das humanistische Gymnasium* 41 (1930) 21-4 = *Kleine Schriften* (Berlin, 1966) 669-73. A remarkable act of homage is the praise bestowed on the work in the year of Heinze's death by J. Vanheusden in his 'Over Virgilius' epische Techniek: een ontleding van Richard Heinze's *Virgils Epische Technik*', in *Philol. Studien* (Leuven) 2 (1929/30) 50-69. Later appreciations of his achievements in Virgilian studies may be found in F. Klingner, 'Virgil: Wiederentdeckung eines Dichters', *Das neue Bild der Antike* 2 (1942) 219-45 = *Römische Geisteswelt* (fifth edn Munich, 1965) 239-73, and in E. Burck's introduction to R. Heinze, *Vom Geist des Römertums* (third edn Darmstadt, 1960) 1-8. See also K. Büchner in *RE* VIIIA 2 (1958) s.v. P. Vergilius Maro, 1486; A. Wlosok, 'Vergil in der neueren Forschung', *Gymnasium* 80 (1973) 131-5; A. Perutelli, 'Genesi e significato della "Virgils epische Technik" di Richard Heinze', *Maia* 25 (1973) 293-316; id., *Enciclopedia Virgiliana* II (1985) 840-1 s.v. Richard Heinze and F. Serpa (ed.), *Il Punto su Virgilio* (Bari, 1987); for Heinze see pp. 10-22.

12. F. Leo, loc. cit. (n. 8 above) 595, immediately declared that he was convinced by Heinze on this point, and regarded this 'discovery' as one of the most important conclusions of the book; so too J. Ziehen, loc. cit. (n. 8 above). H.W. Prescott (n. 6 above) 479-80 also accepted Heinze's view, though his interpretation involved certain modifications of it.

13. C.M. Bowra, 'Aeneas and the Stoic ideal', *Greece and Rome* 3 (1933) 8-21; id. *From Vergil to Milton* (London, 1945) 58-9.

14. K. Büchner, *RE* VIII 2 (1958) *passim.*

15. They were pointed out very cautiously by F. Klingner in his review of Pöschl's book on Virgil (n. 7 above) in *Gnomon* 24 (1952) 138; cf. K. Büchner, loc. cit. 1337-9, and Brooks Otis, *Virgil: a Study in Civilised Poetry* (Oxford, 1963) 405.

In this context it is worth mentioning that H. Dahlmann (a pupil of Heinze's) used to say that Heinze had serious doubts about publishing his book, and even considered destroying the manuscript. It was not until Georg Kaibel encouraged him and urged him to publish that he was persuaded to change his mind. Hence the dedication.

16. F. Klingner, loc. cit. (n. 15 above).

17. E.T. Merrill, *Class. Jnl.* 11 (1915) 511.

PART I

1

The Fall of Troy

The fall of Troy had been depicted in literature and art for centuries; it was a subject 3
that no age, no genre had failed to use. The ancient epic was succeeded by lyric and
drama; Hellenistic poetry had plucked new fruit from this part of the saga in its own
distinctive manner; in the visual arts, too, the most moving scenes, from Laocoon's
ordeal to the flight of Aeneas, were familiar to all from the numerous different
versions created by the great masters. The task of retelling this well-known story
must have seemed particularly attractive to a poet who felt no compulsion to explore
untrodden paths, and who made it his ambition, not to astonish with novelties, but to
achieve greatness in the familiar. Indeed, it is precisely here, in this most frequently
trodden area, that Virgil's art is most apparent. It would be altogether easier for us to
evaluate the true meaning of this art of his, and to establish his unique intentions and
means, if only we possessed just one or other of the earlier versions in full; though
even the little that has survived will prove useful for our purpose. But first we must
gain a broad, general impression of the nature of Virgil's undertaking.

Ἰλιόθεν με φέρων ἄνεμος Κικόνεσσι πέλασσεν [the wind carried me from
Ilium and brought me to the Cicones]: this is how Odysseus begins his tale. That is
also the real beginning of the story of the *Odyssey*. The story of the *Aeneid* begins
with the destruction of Troy, for the hero's mission is to carry the Trojan Penates to
Latium, and here is the origin of the mission; therefore the *Iliu Persis* [sack of Troy]
had to be included in the poem. Putting the narrative into Aeneas' own mouth seems
to us nowadays a straightforward imitation of the technique of the *Odyssey*. But we 4
ought to be aware how new and bold this device must at first have appeared to the
poet. The events of Odysseus' homeward journey nearly all involved Odysseus
himself, and putting them into the first person instead of the third entailed few
changes in the presentation. But for Virgil it was a matter of presenting the ebb and
flow of the nocturnal battle through all the streets, palaces and shrines of Troy, and
the deeds and sufferings of a whole series of people, as the experiences of one single
man. It is easy to see what difficulties this caused; but it also offered the outstanding
artistic advantage of concentrating the action: in this way, and in this way only,
could a jumbled sequence of unconnected scenes be made into a unity that would
satisfy Virgil's ideals of poetic construction. And this conception of his task also
opened up a totally unexpected path, which no narrator of the Sack of Troy had ever
trodden before: these events had never previously been presented as a continuous
narrative by a *Trojan*. Admittedly the dramatists, notably Euripides in his plays
concerning the sack of Troy, had put themselves inside the minds of the vanquished,
but in a drama they could only portray single episodes, or give a general impression
of the night of terror. But Virgil gives us the story, not of just any Trojan, but of the
father of the Roman people. This fact immediately determined the ethos of the
narrative and the major values which it would enshrine. For straightaway there

3

emerged new rocks, that could only be avoided by careful navigation; rocks, it is true, which only existed for a Roman, and which it is difficult for us to envisage. The ancestors of the Romans are conquered and cave in; they renounce the chance of taking revenge and continuing the fight; Aeneas has survived the fall of his native city, has deserted its ruins in order to establish a new city in a strange land. A Roman would inevitably feel deeply ashamed at the thought of such behaviour. Rome for him is what Troy was for Aeneas: how could a Roman choose to turn his back on his own city in her hour of defeat, taking his wife, child and household with him, rather than stay and perish too? How could he think of carrying the gods of his city into a foreign land?

In order to understand the attitude of a Roman, we must read the speech which Livy puts into the mouth of Camillus in the debate about moving from the site of Rome to Veii (5.5lff.). I quote just a few sentences:

5   This, too, is a struggle for our fatherland, and, as long as life lasts, to withdraw
      from it would be a disgrace for others, but for Camillus an abominable
      impiety.... Our city was founded on the basis of good auspices and good
      auguries; there is not a place in it to which sacred duties are not attached, in
      which gods do not dwell; the solemn sacrifices have not only their set days but
      also their set localities. Do you intend to abandon all these gods of state and
      family?... We will be regarded not as conquerors who are leaving their city,
      but as defeated men who have lost their city; people will say that the defeat at
      the Allia, the conquest of the city, the siege of the Capitol drove us to desert
      our Penates and to flee into exile from a place that we are not able to
      defend.... Would it not be better to live in huts like shepherds and rustics
      among our sacred places and our Penates, than for the entire people to go into
      exile? Does the soil of our fatherland, and this earth that we call Mother, have
      no hold on us? Is our love for our fatherland merely an attachment to façades
      and roof-beams?

Later on in the course of the *Aeneid* the objections embodied in this attitude are removed in part. It turns out that the Penates are not migrating to some strange country but returning to their original home.[1] There is no such comfort in the *Ilioupersis*: there, Troy is the native land, and Aeneas is driven from it. Virgil had to make it his aim, above all, to avoid any sense of disgrace, to defend the Trojans in general, but above all his hero, from accusations of cowardice or weakness, timid

6   despondency or disloyalty towards his fatherland.[2] Sympathy for the vanquished grows when that for the conqueror is withdrawn, so his second concern had to be to strip the Greeks of the glory of victory, while taking the greatest care to avoid any appearance of malice. The outlines of the narrative were firmly fixed in tradition; the poet had to be very sparing in his invention of new episodes to serve his purpose, in case his readers should fail to recognize the *Fall of Troy*. Thus, as far as content was concerned, his art was necessarily one of *selecting* from the rich treasury of the traditional story whatever was suitable for his purpose and omitting all the rest unless it was impossible to do so.

These simple considerations clearly imply that it is highly unlikely that Virgil used only one of his predecessors as his sole or main source, for none of them had been pursuing the same aim as Virgil, either as regards content or form. Nor in writing the *Aeneid* did Virgil feel constrained in any way: there was no single earlier version of the *Sack of Troy* which was regarded as canonical to the extent that any deviation would meet with disapproval. Nor should we imagine that his knowledge of the tradition was in any way narrow or restricted. It is obvious that either personally or with the help of educated Greek friends he drew on all the relevant accounts that were available at that time.

Virgil's *Sack of Troy* consists of three parts: the introduction, during which the wooden horse is taken into the city (lines 13-249), the battle at night (250-558), and Aeneas' flight (559-803). As we can see, these sections are roughly equal in length, which suggests that the poet regarded them as of equal importance. Merely from the point of view of form, he would not have been happy with a type of composition such as we find in Tryphiodorus, where some 500 and 200 lines correspond with Virgil's first two sections. For the same reason he would have regarded it as totally inadmissible to devote a mere handful of lines to the departure of Aeneas, which for the Romans was the most important event of all. In drama, intensity of action can perhaps compensate for brevity of treatment, but not in epic.

We will follow the course of the narrative.

I. *The Wooden Horse* 7

1. Sources

Troy had been besieged by the Greeks for ten long years, to no avail. Finally they hid in a wooden horse, which the Trojans themselves pulled into their city. In the night, the soldiers left their hiding-place and overwhelmed the sleeping Trojans.... This ancient story must have given rise to adverse comment at a very early date: how could the Trojans be so unsuspecting and foolish as to pull the agent of their own destruction into the city? Some have believed it possible to trace the stages by which these criticisms resulted in increasingly elaborate versions of the story; however, it can be no more than a purely hypothetical exercise to arrange the versions according to this principle since most of the surviving versions cannot be securely dated. According to the narrative in the *Odyssey* (8.502ff.), which Proclus tells us corresponds with Arctinus' *Sack of Troy*, and which also forms the basis of the version in Apollodorus, the horse is pulled to the acropolis without a moment's thought: it is only then that they wonder what to do with it, and decide – according to Proclus – to dedicate it to Athena. Sinon is not mentioned in the *Odyssey*, and in the mythographers he is only the man who is assigned the task of giving the fire-signal to the Greek ships. In fact, in Apollodorus' version he does this from Achilles' tomb, in Proclus' from the city itself. Sinon must have known not only that the horse was in the city, but also that the Trojans were asleep. To discover this he must have crept in using some kind of disguise.[3] We learn from the *Tabula Iliaca* that he had a more important rôle in the *Little Iliad*: he enters the city walking in

5

front of the horse; from the later versions of the story we may draw the conclusion that he persuaded the Trojans to accept the treacherous votive offering. It is clear that in this version the Trojans' suspicions were aroused from the start, then lulled by the Greeks' falsehood and deceit; the *Little Iliad* gives an explanation of the actions taken by the Trojans, and their gullibility is contrasted with the cunning of their enemies. Sophocles may have written a play about Sinon, and Aristotle certainly lists Sinon as one of the subjects for tragedy drawn from the *Little Iliad*, and it is reasonable to suppose that Sinon's deception of the Trojans in fact formed the nucleus of this play. But later even this motivation seems to have been regarded as no longer sufficient. It

8 may well have seemed strange, judging ancient legends by the standards of their own time, that a common cheat was able to delude wise Priam and his wise elders. Some Hellenistic writer will then have taken the step of introducing the legend of Laocoon, and presenting it in a bold new version as the definitive explanation of how the Trojans had been deceived. It is true that it had already been associated with the fall of Troy, but not with the story of the horse. Laocoon is the embodiment of their justifiable mistrust. When the gods send the serpents to kill his sons, the Trojans take this to be divine confirmation of Sinon's words, and this is enough to make their decision quite comprehensible to any reader who believed in divine signs. This last, most elaborate form of the legend has also left traces in the accounts in the mythographers.[4] Quintus of Smyrna took it over wholesale, though in a form superficially contaminated with another version; his source was probably some mythographic work.[5]

Virgil must have had no hesitation in choosing this final version of the tradition. Not only was it the richest and artistically most rewarding, it was also the version in which the behaviour of the Trojans was shown in the most favourable light.

2. Sinon

Let us look at the Sinon scene, leaving aside for a moment its connection with the Laocoon scenes. We know from Tryphiodorus that Virgil's poem was not the first in which Sinon spoke to Priam himself and Priam listened graciously and even asked him to explain the significance of the gigantic horse. Moreover we learn from Quintus that Sinon's lie, that it was to be dedicated to the gods so as to ensure a safe voyage back to Greece, was not Virgil's invention either. Much of the manner in which this material is narrated also stems from Virgil's source. Quintus seems to have had only a bare outline before him. The whole construction betrays its late date by the way that it is pieced together from motifs that were already well known. Sinon plays the rôle that Odysseus himself plays in Euripides' *Philoctetes*. In order

9 to win the confidence of Philoctetes, who was suffering from a mortal wound on account of the behaviour of the Greeks, and above all of Odysseus himself, Odysseus pretended that he himself was a Greek who had been maltreated by his own people and exiled as a result of the machinations of Odysseus:[6] so in Euripides the deceiver blames himself, and this motif seems to have been invented for this context. But in both passages it is the unjust condemnation of Palamedes that is said to have led to the misfortune of the liar, who claims to have been a friend of the dead

Palamedes; and it has therefore been suggested that the echo of Euripides' lines can be heard in Virgil's.[7] But Virgil was not the first to make use of the device derived from Euripides. This can be seen from the fact that Quintus' version agrees in its main outlines with Virgil, suggesting that they had an earlier common source. Furthermore, Calchas' proposal, based on his interpretation of divine will, that Sinon should be sacrificed to ensure a safe journey home is, as Virgil himself reminds us (116f.), modelled on the sacrifice of Iphigenia; we will, of course, also recall Achilles' threat (Quintus 14.216) that he will send a storm to prevent the Greeks leaving unless Polyxena is sacrificed to him: Calchas was also involved in the sacrifice of Polyxena. On the other hand, we may consider that the rhetorical working-out of the ρῆσις [speech] as well as the ethos of the whole scene is Virgilian. Sinon's deception surely started life as a stratagem worthy of Odysseus himself, brilliantly revealing the superiority of the versatile Greek over the barbarian Priam. Now, in Virgil's hands, this famous exploit becomes a scandalous piece of behaviour, a despicable lie, corroborated by a false oath (154ff.; *periurus* [195] [perjured]), compounded by the abuse of a most noble trustfulness, helpfulness, sympathy, piety and hospitality, and designed to destroy those who practise such virtues. It is only because the Trojans themselves are so totally incapable of deviousness, indeed ignorant of it (106), that they do not even expect to meet it in an enemy. But Sinon is not the only crafty one: Aeneas now suddenly realizes that Sinon is only a typical 10 representative of the general depravity of the Danai: *crimine ab uno disce omnis* (65) [from this one proof of their perfidy you may understand them all], *scelerum tantorum artisque Pelasgae* (106) [to what length of wickedness Greek cunning could go], *dolis instructus et arte Pelasga* (152) [adept in deceit, and with all the cunning of a Greek]. This is the voice of Virgil the Roman; the conventional Roman ideal is the upright, sincere man of honour, incapable of any deviousness, who therefore easily falls victim to the deviousness of a foreigner. An excellent parallel with this Trojano-Roman view of Sinon's deception is provided by the patriotic view of the disaster at Cannae, as it appears in Valerius Maximus[8] (7.4 ext. 2): according to Valerius, before the battle 400 Carthaginians claiming to be deserters were welcomed by the Romans and then proceeded to draw their swords, which they had concealed, and to attack the army in the rear. The narrator concludes: *haec fuit Punica fortitudo, dolis et insidiis et fallacia instructa. quae nunc certissima circumventae virtutis nostrae excusatio est, quoniam decepti magis quam victi sumus* [this was the bravery of the Carthaginians, full of tricks and snares and deception: this is the most convincing excuse for the eclipse of our brave soldiers, since we were cheated rather than beaten].[9] So in fact it is to the credit of the Trojans to have been defenceless against the wiles of Sinon, that typical representative of his loquacious, cunning, perfidious race,[10]

quos neque Tydides nec Larisaeus Achilles, 11
non anni domuere decem, non mille carinae.

[men whom neither Tydeus' son nor Larissaean Achilles could subdue, for all their ten years of war and a thousand keels.] The reader's sympathy is mixed with admiration; the admiration which Sinon's artfulness might have aroused in him is swamped by indignation.

7

The more sophisticated Sinon's lying becomes, the more powerfully this effect is achieved. Virgil has done his utmost here. His main concern was to arrange his material so as to be convincing both artistically and in its content. Sinon's speech taken as a whole falls into three almost equal sections: the first narrates the events leading up to the proposal to kill him, the second the proposal itself and his flight, and the third reveals the secret of the votive offering. Corresponding with this, again in a truly Virgilian way, is an intensification of the emotions on the Trojan side. Sinon's introductory remarks had aroused their curiosity – he seems not to be a Greek – and they no longer feel any hostility towards him. The first part of his narrative with the reference to the prophet Calchas towards the end, awakens their burning curiosity; the second, pity; when it comes to the third part, they are no longer thinking of Sinon – it is a question of saving Troy (*servataque serves Troia fidem* [160]) [if Troy is preserved, may she honour her word]. Thus before our very eyes the arrogant lack of concern initially shown by the Trojans gradually changes to deep sympathy and earnest foreboding. I will not discuss the individual artful devices employed by Sinon since most of them were pointed out long ago by the ancient interpreters,[11] but will restrict myself to pointing out how in the course of the speech Sinon reveals himself, gradually and apparently quite unintentionally, as characterized by a whole range of the very noblest qualities, as well as caught up in circumstances that call for deep compassion: steadfastness in misfortune and unshakeable honesty (80), poverty (87), loyalty towards his friend (93), suffering and humiliation on his friend's account (92), an inability to cheat or deceive (94), revulsion against the war (110) which he had not become involved in of his own accord (87), isolation amongst his fellow Greeks (130), *pietas* (137) [a sense of duty] towards his home-country, his children and his father, *religio* (141) [reverence towards the gods]: he even seems to feel that he has somehow wronged the gods by escaping sacrifice (*fateor* [134] [I admit]). In spite of all the injustice he has suffered, he does not scorn his compatriots, the *impius Tydides* [sacrilegious son of Tydeus] and the *scelerum inventor Ulixes* [Ulysses, quick to invent new crimes], until he has gone over to the Trojan side and has solemnly dissociated himself from the Greeks, at which point he expresses pious revulsion from the wicked behaviour of these two. Only then does he wish for the destruction of those who intended to do him such mortal injury[12] (190). It is clear that all these devices arouse sympathy for Sinon, and strengthen the inclination of the Trojans to believe his story. This plausibility (πιθανότης) is also supported by the full and circumstantial nature of the account, which answers any sceptical questions before they are asked, and by the abundance of details which seem to well up from Sinon's excited memory, allaying any suspicion that it might all be a fiction.[13] In short, Virgil has aimed not merely at rivalling Homer in the art praised by Aristotle (*Poet.* 24), that of making one's heroes tell lies, but at outdoing him.

The inevitable consequence is that Sinon succeeds totally in convincing the Trojans. For all these skilful devices would be valueless if they did not achieve the fundamental and indeed the only aim of the speech, to convince the audience. It is essential that not even a shred of doubt should remain. That would mean that Sinon had made a poor speech. And so – *talibus insidiis periurique arte Sinonis credita res* [we gave Sinon our trust, tricked by his blasphemy and cunning]. How does this connect with the function which Laocoon had to fulfil in the version of the story outlined above?

3. Laocoon

A crowd of Trojans are standing around the wooden horse and arguing about what to do with it when Laocoon makes his first appearance:

Primus ibi ante omnis magna comitante caterva
Laocoon ardens summa decurrit ab arce.

[but there, in front of all, came Laocoon, hastening furiously down from the citadel with a large company in attendance.]   13

In highly emotional language he warns them of the cunning of the Greeks and flings a lance at the horse's belly, which resounds with a roar. Apollodorus tells us that Laocoon warned the Trojans, but, except for Virgil, only Tzetzes (*Posthom.* 713) says that he reinforced his words by hurling his spear. Since that is the only detail for which it would be necessary to assume that Virgil was Tzetzes' source, it is more likely that this too is derived from an earlier tradition.

The way in which Laocoon is introduced has been judged to be so ill-adapted to the context[14] that some have concluded that in lines 35-56 Virgil originally had in mind the earlier version in which it was only after the horse had been pulled into the citadel that Laocoon gave his advice; and that he later incorporated these lines into the new version, with some slight changes, which were not sufficient to obliterate their original character. The same problem arises with the second Laocoon scene: it has been argued that it presupposes the version of the story in which Laocoon was killed by the snakes during the joyful sacrifices in the city not as a punishment but as an omen sent by friendly gods in order to warn the Trojans. I am not convinced by any of the criticisms that have been made of the present position of the lines. Quite apart from practical considerations, it is the dramatic character of Virgil's narrative that is responsible for the way in which Laocoon is not envisaged as one of the group arguing around the horse, but is brought on purely to give a warning, and this is a technique which we shall notice again and again. Imagine the scene on the stage. First Thymoetes, then Capys would make his proposal; some of the citizens would support one, some the other. During the confusion Laocoon would come *rushing* onto the stage, just as he does in Virgil. This is the only way to give an audience the impression that he is not just another character with something to say, but that something with important consequences is happening. And – still in terms of our imaginary stage production – Laocoon would already have been briefed about what had been going on. A dramatist scrupulous about motivation would perhaps have sent one of those *quorum melior sententia menti* [who judged more wisely] to fetch him, to help his group to win the argument. But in fact an audience would hardly   14
notice if a motivation of this kind were omitted. The dramatist could make Laocoon enter without saying where he had come from. Virgil says not simply *accurrit* [rushes to them], but *summa decurrit ab arce* [rushes down from the citadel]. In

other words, he had remained in the city. Some have believed that this contradicts the earlier description *panduntur portae: iuvat ire* etc. (26ff.) [we flung the gates open, and we enjoyed going etc.]. But did Virgil give us his word that every Trojan, man, woman, child and mouse, had come out of the city? And even if he did say *omnes* [all], he could have left Laocoon in the city. He also says *nos abiisse rati ...ergo omnis longo solvit se Teucria luctu* [we thought they (i.e. the Greeks) had sailed...so *all* the land of Troy relaxed after its years of unhappiness]. But afterwards we hear that Laocoon does not believe that the enemy has sailed away (*creditis avectos hostis?* [Do you really believe that your enemies have sailed away?] he asks), that is, his anxiety is by no means totally allayed. Even the most recent and most acute commentators have not criticized the poet for any contradiction here; it would have been very pedantic to do so; in that case, they ought not to have objected to the other apparent difficulty that we have mentioned. Laocoon takes no part in the general rejoicing; he has his suspicions about the apparent retreat of the enemy; so it is quite reasonable that he would not be amongst the inquisitive crowds that come swarming out exultantly onto the plain that the Greeks have left empty. The poet tells us that Laocoon was not there with incomparable brevity: *summa ab arce* [from the height of the citadel]. But why *summa* [height]? We should translate 'coming down from the citadel on high',[15] where *summa* perhaps is intended only to indicate the long distance that Laocoon had to cover, and together with *ardens, primus ante omnis, d e c u r r i t*, and *procul* [furious in front of all, hastening down, far off] add to the effect of violent excitement. But perhaps the real reason why the poet had the idea of making Laocoon run down was because from the heights of the citadel, *unde omnis Troia videri*[16] *et Danaum solitae navis et Achaica castra* (461) [whence we used to look out over all Troy and see the Greek camp and fleet], he could have seen the excited crowds around the horse – he might also have looked across the sea to discover whether any suspicious sail was visible. But even so, how would Aeneas have known of it? Let us merely note that Virgil allows Aeneas to say something that, strictly speaking, he could not have known at the time and could hardly have discovered later. We shall find other places where Virgil does not stay scrupulously within the confines of the first-person narrative. When Laocoon is introduced in the older tradition, he is said to be a priest of Apollo; Virgil, however, does not characterize him in any such way. This omission is deliberate (Virgil names his own priest of Apollo, Panthus [319]), since the divine protector who guards Troy so faithfully cannot abandon his priest to such a gruesome death. So Laocoon is simply an aristocrat, like Thymoetes or Capys. We gather immediately from *magna comitante caterva* [with a large company in attendance] that he does not belong to the *vulgus* [ordinary people]: he is not accompanied by a random crowd of Trojans who, like him, happen to have remained in the city, but with a group of his *comites* [attendants];[17] driven by burning impatience, he has rushed on ahead of them. The rumbling echo from the horse's armoured load is not heard by the Trojans, whom the gods have stupefied (54); we are not told anything else about the effect produced by Laocoon's appearance. This is quite natural because – again in a very dramatic way – immediately after or even during his speech (*ecce...interea* [57] [suddenly...meanwhile]), the Trojans' attention is diverted. Sinon is dragged on, and at this point a captured Greek is understandably more

15

interesting than anything else.

Virgil is not quite as successful in the second Laocoon scene as in the first in overcoming the technical difficulties that arise from his method of composition. Sinon has finished his speech. As at the first break in the narrative (54), Aeneas, the narrator, interposes a few words from his own point of view (195ff.). The Trojans are convinced, and that seals their fate. It only remains for them to act on their conviction, to come to a decision and carry it out. Then something new, unexpected and ghastly happens: the serpents come across the sea, and Laocoon and his sons suffer a most excruciating death. And now, under the impression that this is an act of divine judgement, the decision is indeed made without further ado, and executed without the slightest hesitation.[18] The most recent critics are certainly right to say that, from a logical point of view, no further motivation was necessary. Once the Trojans had been convinced by Sinon, then they were bound to proceed to their decision and its execution, though perhaps not with so much haste and with such unanimous enthusiasm – that is, provided that nothing else happened to make them reconsider. But we have already seen that Virgil could not follow his source here, and we have also seen why. His source (as we may deduce from Quintus) had used Laocoon's death in order to dispel any reservations that the Trojans may still have had after Sinon's speech. Why did Virgil not omit Laocoon's death completely? In the first place, it would in that case have been necessary to omit the first appearance of Laocoon as well, and the whole scene centred on the wooden horse would have lost much of its dramatic impetus. But this technical problem is not the most important point. Laocoon's death would only be superfluous to the narrative if it were a second motivation that came from the same sphere as the first. But beside mortal deception, and at a higher level, comes the sign from the gods. And I would even say that if Virgil had not found this episode in the tradition, it would have been necessary for him to have invented a similar motive. For in the whole of the *Aeneid*, no great event ever occurs without Virgil reminding us that it is the will and work of the gods. And this is the greatest event of all, the act which brings about the destruction of Troy; is it to be the sole exception? Whenever Aeneas does anything for the salvation of his people, and for the Rome of the future, the poet piously gives the glory for it to the gods of Rome. The great men of this world are merely their tools. But the gods are also responsible for disaster: it is they who send storms and destruction upon ships, and enemies and death upon armies; it is they, not the Greek forces, who destroy Troy; therefore they too must have been responsible for allowing the fatal horse to enter the city. That is taken for granted by Virgil and by anyone who is in sympathy with his thought. And indeed there is also another reason to believe in the power of the gods: it is the only way to silence the reproach that the Trojans were stupid. Laocoon's death thus also serves the special viewpoint which, as I have explained above, Virgil had to keep in mind throughout his narration of the Sack of Troy.[19] And he achieves his aim for every impartial reader; everyone realizes that the Trojans are overcome by a higher power which no mortal could understand, for what good would it have done them if they had remained unconvinced by Sinon's lies? Now, in the light of this divine judgement they hesitate no longer.

I now wish to refer briefly to the purely artistic advantage which Virgil gained by

11

introducing the Laocoon scene; it is something quite distinct from the pathetic nature of the scene itself, and was not consciously sought after by the poet. I referred above to the very gradual intensification of the mood of the Trojans, and the skilful way in which it is represented. One must imagine them as being deeply impressed by Sinon's final words. It is only after the intervention of the terrifying and astonishing omen that the crowd is seized with enthusiasm: those whom we should imagine as having listened in silence up to this point, now eagerly set to work, everyone is busy, festive hymns fill the air. Thus begins the ecstatic festival of joy which is to lead Troy to destruction. In every drama, and in narrative too, it is much more effective when a significant change is brought about by a sudden violent action rather than by a gradual development.[20] It would have been extemely diffi-cult, in my view, to create the artistically necessary shock of excitement from Sinon's long-drawn-out narrative.

Enough on the justification for the whole scene. The motivation of details, for example the transition, is, however, open to criticism. We are told that Laocoon is performing a sacrifice on the shore, *mactabat* [was sacrificing]. We have to assume that this is already taking place during Sinon's speech. But how could Laocoon have
18   left before a decision had been reached about the fate of the horse? Had he, too, been convinced by Sinon? That is hardly credible, in view of the evidence we have already had of his farsightedness. And why should he be making a solemn sacrifice to Neptune before the horse had been pulled into the city – for that would appear to be the most urgent task? Admittedly, the sacrifice to Neptune seems to have been given a motivation in Virgil's source, or in his own mind, and this may lead to an answer to our other questions. There can only be one reason for sacrificing to Neptune at this point: to implore him to destroy the Greek fleet, which is now in his power. Here it seems to me that there is an undeniable point of contact with an incident invented by Euphorion. According to Servius *ad loc.*, Euphorion related that, before the beginning of the war, the Trojans had stoned their priest of Neptune to death because he had not performed any sacrifice or made any vow to the god to prevent the Greek expedition from crossing the Aegean to Troy. Now, the sanctuary of the gods was on the shore; during the war the cult had therefore lapsed[21] and there had been no need to replace the priest. I suggest that this explains Virgil's remark-able phrase *ductus Neptuno sorte sacerdos* [chosen by lot to be a priest of Neptune].[22] There was no time to lose if they were not to miss the opportunity to do
19   what they had failed to do at the beginning of the war. The enemy ships might already have completed the greater part of their short journey. Therefore – I am following the idea through in order to show that it entails nothing implausible – while Sinon was still telling his tale, Laocoon could have heard that the preparations for the sacrifice were complete. Chosen by lot to offer the sacrifice, he goes to perform his sacred duty, accompanied by his two sons.

No doubt you will ask in astonishment, 'Are we supposed to "understand" all this? Why does the poet say nothing about all this? Why is he satisfied with a brief allusion?' In my opinion, Virgil has not completely overcome the technical difficul-ties at this point. He could not allow Sinon's narrative to be interrupted with the apparently unimportant news that Laocoon had left; nor could he allow time to elapse after the end of the speech so that Laocoon could start the preparations for the sacrifice; nor, finally, could he weigh down the account of the appalling death of Laocoon with details that might well interest a conscientious critic who was scrutinizing the text from a logical point of view – for details of this kind would have interrupted the process of transporting the excited listener, involved heart and soul, to the scene at the point where everything is aimed at putting him into the frame of mind of the Trojans as they are carried from one astonishing event to another. So Virgil sacrificed absolutely correct motivation, and said only exactly as much as was necessary to allow the reader to gather what must have happened. He was relying on the fact that his reader, overcome by the pathos of the situation, would not painstakingly smooth out every fold of the story to see whether he could find any holes in it; in my view, the successful effect that he achieves proves once again that his instincts were right.

Virgil finds himself in all these difficulties only because he has separated the first Laocoon scene from the second. Why did he not do what Quintus does, and have Laocoon making his first appearance after the Sinon scene, so that his punishment follows immediately after? That would have made everything run smoothly, and there would be no problem about a transition. Nor would there be any difficulty from the point of view of the narrative; on the contrary, it is surely more natural for the punishment to come immediately after the crime, than for the serpents to wait until the precise moment that Sinon completes his lengthy speech. So Virgil must have been led to remodel the scene by considerations of a formal or artistic nature, and these can be easily reconstructed. First, the effect of Sinon's speech would have been weakened if Laocoon had expressed his doubts after it and it would inevitably have thrown the Trojans back into a state of indecision; whereas with the introduction of the Laocoon scene, the impression made by Sinon's speech is greatly enhanced. Secondly, the first Laocoon scene forms the artistic motivation for the entry of Sinon, because it has the greatest effect at this point: he appears at the very moment at which Laocoon's advice and action are on the point of exposing the cunning Greek ruse. At the height of the action the counter-action supervenes: that is characteristic of the structure of Virgil's narrative.

Quintus, writing a straightforward narrative, is able to say that Athena sent the serpents: the Muse has revealed it to the poet. In Virgil, Aeneas narrates as an eye-witness; we have to be told how he and his fellow-Trojans discovered who sent the punishment. Of course, there could be no doubt in anyone's mind in antiquity that it was a manifestation of divine anger; but Virgil wanted to indicate that it was specifically Athena who was responsible, and that the injury to her votive offering had injured her. He had come across a tradition in which the serpents, having accomplished their deed, disappeared into the sanctuary of Apollo,[23] and he transferred it to the temple and statue of Athena:

> *delubra ad summa dracones*
> *diffugiunt saevaeque petunt Tritonidis arcem*
> *sub pedibusque deae clipeique sub orbe teguntur.* (225-7)

[the pair of serpents now made their retreat, sliding up to the temple of heartless Minerva high on her citadel, where they vanished near her statue's feet behind the circle of her shield]. Although Aeneas narrates this, he does not do so as a direct witness. The Trojans on the plain could not see into the citadel, and it would be ridiculous to imagine that they ran along beside the serpents. They could only have seen what direction they took and, at most, have learnt from others afterwards where they had hidden. Virgil will hardly have thought all this through in detail in his mind, but this is another passage where he has not felt restricted by every implication of the first-person narrative, for two reasons: not to burden the narrative with wearisome diffuseness, and not to be obliged to lose the benefit of a motif which is so important for the story.

4. The horse enters Troy

21

In the description that follows, I single out Virgil's brevity for comment: he does not describe the journey to the city (Tryph. 304-35), nor does he give more than the bare fact of Cassandra's unheeded warning (Tryph. 358-445, Quintus 525-85), and this is simply to produce an effective contrast with the activity of the unheeding Trojans; it is clear that he avoids writing episodes just for the sake of it. Instead, he lingers over the moment at which the horse crosses the encircling wall: this fateful moment deserves emphatic treatment. This is not (as in Quintus and Tryphiodorus) followed by a detailed description of the joyful festivities, the music, dancing and general intoxication;[24] the narrator could not recall these hours without shame and remorse, nor could his audience hear about this infatuated celebration without feeling contempt and pity. Instead of a description we have only the lines:

> *nos delubra deum miseri, quibus ultimus esset*
> *ille dies, festa velamus fronde per urbem,* (248-9)

[...we, poor fools, spent this our last day decorating with festal greenery every temple in our town], two lines which are certainly calculated, but in which the art of calculation comes close to genius.

II. *The Battle*

1. Preliminaries

The second section, the Night Battle (*Nyktomachia*), opens with a short account of the events that occurred before Aeneas awoke: the Achaean fleet returns, Sinon opens the horse, which disgorges its occupants, who disperse through the sleeping city, slay the watchmen at the gates and open the city to their comrades. This is exactly the way in which Aeneas, at the beginning of the first part of his story (2.13-24) had spoken of the actions of the Greeks, before he started on his full account. At that stage, confining himself strictly to his own experiences, he was only able to say that the Greeks sailed away and left the wooden horse behind on the shore. It was only later that he discovered their destination and their plans. Now, however, when these events are mentioned a second time, we are also told, in its 22 proper place, how Aeneas learnt what he had anticipated in his first account: Panthus comes down from the citadel and tells him about what has happened (328ff.). Because this is narrated twice, it has been suggested that one of the two passages is a later addition;[25] but that is certainly not so. When, in the course of an action narrated by the hero himself, he has to deal with events which he did not hear about, or realize the importance of, until later, there are two possibilities open to the poet. He can make the narrator keep very strictly to the order in which he experienced the events, and that means that, for the time being, the audience will be as much in the dark about those events, or their significance, as he had been at the time. This technique can create a feeling of restless excitement of the kind that modern novelists are particularly eager to achieve, but which is alien to the aims and conventions of an ancient epic. The other possibility is that the narrator tells the events in the order in which they actually happened, drawing on his later knowledge: that is the naïve technique such as is used in the stories told by Odysseus. Odysseus narrates the experience of his companions in Circe's palace in complete disregard of the fact that he himself only learnt of them later, from Eurylochus, and some of them even later than that, from his other ship-mates; he tells us what his comrades did on Thrinacia while he was asleep, what Eurylochus said, etc., just as if it were not himself, Odysseus, but the poet speaking. When they come to Polyphemus' cave (*Od.* 9.187), he tells his audience what it was like and how it was laid out, instead of doing what a sophisticated narrator would do, start by arousing vague misgivings in his audience, and then make them share the feeling of horror which gripped the men waiting in the cave when they caught sight of the monster. Virgil proceeds in the same way, but he is just a little more sophisticated about it. He is not interested in creating tension, any more than Homer was; rather, he wants his audience to grasp the whole situation from the very start. This can only be achieved by a narrative that anticipates later knowledge. On the other hand, we also need to be told when and how the situation was explained to Aeneas: that is why Panthus' speech is essential. But Panthus certainly does not tell Aeneas everything that Aeneas has told us;[26] in fact, once our attention has been drawn to it, we might well ask where exactly 23 Aeneas has got all these details from: that it was the king's ship that gave the fire signal,[27] which heroes were inside the horse,[28] that they slid down on a rope,[29] and so forth, and the same is true of his first account, where he says that the heroes were picked by lot, etc. An ancient solver of literary problems (λυτικός) would perhaps have explained that Aeneas was told all this afterwards, years later, by Achaemenides, the companion of Odysseus. I am myself quite sure that Virgil never bothered himself with such possibilities, but once again was not confining himself strictly to the stand-point of the first-person narrative; he wanted to give his audi- 24 ence not merely a bare outline of the essential facts, but a vivid picture. Every Trojan must have got a general idea of what had happened only too soon; the details came along with it. Nevertheless, the description is sufficiently short and concise to give the effect of an actual spoken account, contrasting sharply with the return to Aeneas' own narrative, which is resumed with the phrase *tempus erat quo prima quies* [it was the time when rest first comes]. This is very different from Odysseus' account of the adventures on Thrinacia, where we still get a full and detailed narrative even when Odysseus himself was not present.

One detail of Panthus' account should be emphasized, since it is of some significance for the visual aspect of the scenes that follow: the Greek fleet sails towards the shore *tacitae per amica silentia lunae* (255) i.e. through the calm night by the friendly light of the moon.[30] The moon has played a role in depictions of the Fall of Troy from the earliest times: 'It was midnight, the bright moon rose', says the *Little Iliad*.[31] Understandably enough: if it had been a pitch dark night, it would have been necessary to provide some source of light for each scene. So Virgil, too, mentions the moonlight again when some of Aeneas' companions gather round him, *oblati per lunam* (340) [looming through the moonlight]. On the other hand, an impression of the darkness of the night is necessary for the Androgeus scene: the Greeks mistake Aeneas and his men for their own compatriots and only become suspicious when the expected answer to their greeting does not come (376); afterwards the Trojans make further use of the darkness when they put on the armour of the slain and are thus able to storm unrecognized amongst the enemy troops. That would have been impossible in daylight, when faces might be recognized. That is why Virgil mentions the 'shadows of the black night' several times in these scenes;[32] of course he can say this, in spite of the moonlight, because these scenes take place in the narrow streets of the city. There 'lights bright as day and dark night-shadows form great opposing masses'.[33]

2. Hector's appearance

Up to this point, Aeneas had been recounting events which he and his fellow-citizens had experienced together, in which he had not himself played a leading rôle. In the scene centred on the wooden horse and in those that follow, he is generally no more than just one of the Trojans, included whenever they are mentioned. During the night of terror, however, every man is thrown on his own resources, and now Aeneas embarks on the account of his own personal experiences, and does not digress from them thereafter.

The appearance of Hector to Aeneas in a dream (268-97) has no immediate consequence, and is never alluded to again. From a superficial point of view, it might therefore appear pointless; whereas in reality it is of great significance in preparing for the following scenes. This is not only because it begins the description of the night of slaughter with a scene full of pathos that graphically summarizes the essentials of what is to follow, and at one stroke puts the reader into the right frame of mind for hearing about these events.[34] Perhaps even more important than this artistic purpose is the need to present Aeneas' attitude to these events in the right light from the beginning. Even before the hero is in a position to act, he, and still more the reader, needs to be convinced that the fate of Troy has been decided, and therefore that not even Aeneas with all his energy and courage can avert this fate. It is also necessary to prepare the reader to accept the way in which Aeneas deserts his city, instead of staying to perish with it; and this desertion needs to be presented not as the faint-hearted flight of a man concerned only to save his own skin, but as a way of carrying out an act of pious duty towards the sacred images, the Penates of Troy, for whom he must provide a new, secure home. I am inclined to believe that Virgil started from this abstract requirement. It would be impossible to meet this requirement more successfully than Virgil has done by introducing the vision of Hector. Hector is able to fulfil this function better than any man alive, better than any other of the Trojan dead. If Hector advises Aeneas to give up all attempts at resistance, we know that resistance really is of no avail. If Hector urges flight, flight cannot be dishonourable. It is possible that Virgil was influenced by the memory of the appearance of Achilles in the Νόστοι, when he gave the opposite warning before the fleet set sail; moreover, it is certain that in the details of the description Virgil was purposely echoing the appearance of Homer at the beginning of Ennius' *Annals*, the most famous dream vision in Roman literature, and at the same time Paris' words to Hector's corpse in Ennius' tragedy; but these borrowings do not in any way mar the unity of his conception. And it is characteristic of Virgil's creative method that he was not satisfied with attaining the abstract goal that he had in mind, but that the scene has blossomed into a significance of its own, and developed   27 motifs not required by the action, but poetically valuable in themselves: the pathos in the appearance of Hector, intensified by the memory of his days of splendour, Aeneas' pity and the dream-like confusion of his thoughts. In this way the scene gains significance over and above its value within the context.[35]

Hector's words are short and clear, as befits the man. He releases Aeneas from his duty towards his former fatherland, points him towards his new duty and his new homeland; *fuge* [flee], the heart of the message, is practically his first word. But when this *fuge* is followed by *teque his eripe flammis* [and escape from these flames], then that too must somehow be significant. In the whole course of the narrative from now on, it is striking how deliberately Virgil emphasizes the burning of the city: the houses of Deiphobus and Ucalegon are already on fire (310), Panthus speaks excitedly of the *incendia* (327, 329) [fires], as does Aeneas (353) and the Greek Androgeus (374);[36] everywhere there are the flames as well as the enemy to terrify them (337, 431, 505, 566, 600, 632, 664, 705); scarcely have Aeneas and his family left their house when it flares up in a sheet of flame (758-9). In short, the reader's imagination is constrained again and again to envisage the conquered city of Ilium as a sea of flames: it is burning as soon as the Greeks have broken in, it collapses at the moment that the city is finally captured (624), and it is from the smoking rubble of the sanctuaries that the plunderers loot whatever is left for them to pillage. This does not correspond at all with the traditional version: in that, the Greeks do not set fire to the city until just before their departure;[37] in Euripides (*Tro.* 1260) Talthybius orders men to go into the city to start fires while the captured women make their way to the ships. This is comparable with Aeschylus' version, where Clytaemnestra imagines the victorious Greeks no longer starving in the damp, cold camp on the plain but resting their weary limbs in the comfort of the palaces of   28 Troy (*Agam.* 334). I do not know who was the first to paint this striking picture of the battle among the flames of Troy; it may have been the man who first made the flames retreat before Aeneas as he fled.[38] This was, in my opinion, invented merely for the sake of effect; the earlier version is the more probable, since, if you think about it, the Greeks had no reason to start a fire which might be as disastrous to themselves as to their enemies, and which would consume not only houses and temples but also the booty.[39] This innovation (probably Hellenistic) suited Virgil's purpose admirably; that is why he has deliberately emphasized it, preparing for it in Hector's words, not primarily for the sake of effect (although the splendid, terrifying picture of the burning city must have appeared vividly before his eyes)[40] but above all for the sake of the story. As a result the Trojans have to fight not only against mortal enemies but also the power of the elements, against which all resistance is in vain;[41] this means that it is not the sacred city of Pergamon, with its mighty towers, that Aeneas has to leave, but a smoking heap of rubble and ashes. That is why, when he returns to the conquered city, he has to see his own house, from which he rescues his father and son, in flames (757), and has to see the sacred *adyta* (764) [shrines], whose gods he carries with him, on fire. *Fuit Ilium* [Ilium is finished]: this is intended to make his departure easier, and to enable the patriotic reader to sympathize with his decision.

3. Aeneas in the battle

Aeneas survived the fall of Troy. That was a tradition that was established, and already to be found in the famous prophecy in the *Iliad* (20.307). However, when it comes to the detailed circumstances of his escape, the tradition splits into countless branches. The earliest, that used by Sophocles in his *Laocoon*, had Aeneas leave Troy before it was captured. Later, the view prevailed that he fled the captured city, rescuing his aged father and the gods of his household. Indeed, he succeeds in escaping only because he is protected by Aphrodite, who shields him from both the fire and the enemy's weapons. We do not know the source of this mythical version; Virgil makes use of it, as we shall see,[42] but cannot employ it in his account of the actual departure from Troy. For this, there were other versions available, which managed without any miraculous element and explained his escape as the result of natural means. Aeneas was said to have fallen into the hands of the Greeks, but to have been spared by them as a reward for betrayal, or, to use a kinder expression, in gratitude for offering guest-friendship to Odysseus, and for his efforts to restore Helen (Livy 1.1). But the most popular version seems to have been a legend which can be traced back to Timaeus, according to which Aeneas held the citadel to the last, and then capitulated on condition that he should be allowed to depart unharmed, and chose to take with him, not gold or silver, but his frail old father; granted a further choice in recognition of his virtue, he chose to take the images of the gods. At this, the Greeks, disarmed by such piety, not only allowed him to depart unharmed with all his worldly possessions and all his household, but even supplied him with ships in which to sail away.[43] Naturally Virgil retained the piety (εὐσέβεια) of Aeneas that is glorified in this version, but he could not make use of any of the rest of it: he could not allow Aeneas to be indebted in any way to the generosity of the hated enemy. And there was in fact another tradition which also had Aeneas holding the citadel, but had him departing without any help from the enemy.[44] Hellanicus, who narrated the fall of Troy as if it were an episode of contemporary military history, omitted those parts of the Aeneas tradition which were in any way legendary or difficult to believe. It is Aeneas who is credited with the rescue of most of the Trojans: he sees in good time that the Greeks have broken in, so that while the Greeks are swarming through the city he and his men can occupy its strong fortified citadel which offers shelter for the fugitives. When he realizes that it cannot be held 30 for ever, he resolves to rescue at least the people, sacred objects and as many possessions as possible, and so, while the enemy is devoting its entire attention to the attack on the citadel, he sends the whole baggage-train out along the road to Mount Ida. When that is safe, he and the others who have been occupying the citadel (part of which has already been captured by Neoptolemus) withdraw from it and catch up with those who have been sent on ahead, and are not pursued by the enemy, who are totally absorbed in looting.

It is perfectly possible that Virgil had this very pragmatic account in front of him,[45] when he was plotting Aeneas' adventures in the night of terror. In Virgil, too, Aeneas is warned in good time, so that he is not surprised by the enemy. His first thought is to occupy the citadel; he gathers a resolute band around him, then helps, successfully for a while, in the defence of the citadel, until Neoptolemus succeeds in forcing his way in. The rendezvous which he arranges with his household and comrades at a point on the road to the mountains may also have been taken by Virgil from Hellanicus, and in both versions a large group of men, women and children have gathered there (797-8). But there the resemblance ends. It is noticeable that Aeneas cuts a much more splendid figure in the historian's account than in Virgil, although the latter certainly had no desire to keep silent about the meritorious actions traditionally ascribed to his hero. Virgil, unlike Hellanicus, does not have a walled citadel rising up above the city like, for example, the Acropolis at Athens. In his version, the battle is concentrated on the palace of Priam, although this should be imagined as an extensive range of buildings, protected like a fortress by towers and battlements. But Aeneas and his men do not succeed in reaching this fortification and making defensive preparations before the enemy reaches it. The handful of fighting men that he has collected has been wiped out on the way. Almost *alone*, with only two men, both incapable of fighting, he reaches the palace, which has now 31 become the centre of the most furious part of the fighting. He takes part, certainly, in the defence of the palace, but he does not succeed in rescuing anyone or anything. Still *alone*, he returns to his own house, with divine help; and, not in any orderly military retreat with closed ranks, but in anxious flight, accompanied only by his closest relatives, he finally escapes from the city.

The warlike, heroic virtues of Aeneas, his swift and energetic resolve, his circumspect, tenacious courage, are certainly displayed much more splendidly in Hellanicus. But the stronger and more organized the resistance in that version, the more the reader gains the impression that it was armed force that decided the issue: a strong walled citadel is occupied by a considerable body of troops under Aeneas' command, but they cannot hold it against enemy attack; finally, most of the Trojans retreat unmolested by the enemy; only a minority fall during the attack. And that was just what Virgil was so anxious to avoid: giving the impression that there had been a serious battle with one side winning, the other losing. He wanted to present Troy as having fallen to Sinon's false oath, not to the sword of the enemy.[46] That is why it is emphatically brought to our attention, again and again, that Ilium's fate had been decided even before Aeneas awakes. And it is not in the course of the battle that the hero himself realizes this for the first time; Hector has already told him in his dream, and when, awakened by the noise of battle, he sees from the roof of the house the raging firestorm, he realizes with lightning speed that it is too late to rescue anything. When he nevertheless snatches up his weapons, it is not with the hope of being able to ward off destruction, but rather in the rage of despair and with certain death before his eyes:

32

> *arma amens capio, nec sat rationis in armis:*
> *sed glomerare manum bello et concurrere in arcem*
> *cum sociis ardent animi: furor iraque mentem*
> *praecipitant pulchrumque mori succurrit in armis.*[47]

[out of my senses, I grasped my arms: not that I had any plan for battle, but simply a burning desire to muster a band for fighting, and rally with my comrades at some position of defence. Frantic in my fury I had no time for decision; I only remembered that death in battle is glorious]. This mood would surprise us if we, and Aeneas too, had not already been prepared for it by the vision of Hector, which is still affecting Aeneas, though he is not conscious of the fact. And, before he can come to his senses, Panthus, too, runs up to him and confirms that things could not be worse. The will of the gods (*numine divom* [336]) is thus the only explanation for Aeneas' decision to plunge into the fighting after all; but to his companions who crowd around he cannot promise victory, only death, as the reward for the struggle (333);[48] so too the last defenders of the stronghold of Priam see death already before them (446f.), and although it is the desire to help them that drives Aeneas up onto the battlements, he knows very well that all he is doing is bringing reinforcements to men already vanquished (*vim addere victis* [452]). So there is no question of resistance by powerful, organized troops. It is only by chance that a few men gather round their leader Aeneas, and in other passages too the poet takes pains to make us see his hero as an isolated figure: standing as a helpless onlooker on the roof of the palace, he has to behold the murder of Priam; then he looks round in despair and sees that he is alone; at that moment the rage of despair seems to overwhelm him once again, and his divine mother has to save the lives of him and of his family. Aeneas' narrative mentions no heroic deeds; the only thing he boasts of is that he made no attempt to avoid death (431ff.). The tradition knew of no particularly spectacular deeds performed by Aeneas during the night-battle, and it would have been in bad taste to have introduced any invented ones. On the other hand, the first-person form of the narrative came as an advantage for the poet in this passage. When a narrator says nothing to his own glory, the reader can interpret this as modesty, and fill in the gaps out of his own imagination. For Virgil, more important than any successful feats of arms was the act of *pietas* which constituted Aeneas' chief claim to fame: his rescue of his father from the burning city. This might have been combined with Hellanicus' account, but not very easily: it would have been difficult to explain why the son was carrying his father on his own shoulders if they were leaving together with baggage-carriers, soldiers and a whole crowd besides. The transformation made by Virgil led quite naturally to the image which, more than anything else in the entire story of Aeneas, has imprinted itself deeply in every reader's mind.

33

4. Panthus and the Penates

Panthus is called *arcis Phoebique sacerdos*, that is, as commentators have rightly explained, the priest of the sanctuary of Apollo on the citadel.[49] We know from a tradition mentioned first by Servius *ad loc.* that Virgil was not the first to make him the priest of Apollo. Indeed, the *Iliad* already assumes a close connection between Panthus and Apollo, when the god (15.521) protects Polydamas, son of Panthus, and the poet explains 'Apollo did not allow the son of Panthus to fall amongst the fighters in the front rank'. It may have been this very line which generated the legend. In Virgil, Panthus comes down from the citadel and is thus able to give Aeneas the most reliable news; but that does not exhaust the significance of his entrance.

For Virgil there was no doubt that Aeneas rescued the Trojan Penates from the 34 vanquished city. They are the gods of the hearth of the Roman state, as they had previously been the gods of the states of Alba and Lavinium. Every Roman doubtless believed that they were also the Penates of the Trojan state, not simply the household gods of Anchises. Virgil, at any rate, does not allow us to doubt that this is his conception of them, from the moment that he first mentions them: *sacra suosque tibi commendat Troia penates* (293) [Troy entrusts to you her sanctities and her Guardians of the Home], said Hector to Aeneas in the dream, and, also in the dream, Aeneas saw him carry Vesta and the sacred flame from the *adyta penetralia* [inner shrine] as representatives of the *sacra penatesque* [sanctities and Guardians of the Home]: these *penetralia*[50] were the equivalent of the Roman *penus Vestae* [sanctuary of Vesta]. Furthermore, whenever the Penates are mentioned later in the poem, they are never spoken of as the family-gods of Aeneas, but only as the gods of Troy. If Aeneas is to rescue these national Penates from Troy, he must first get hold of them. Where were they? According to Hellanicus (Dion. Hal. 1.46) the ἱερὰ τὰ πατρῷα τοῖς Τρωσίν [the traditional sacred objects of the Trojans] were on the citadel; Virgil too accepts this as a traditional datum. Now, Aeneas could have carried these *sacra* [sacred objects] with him when he comes down again from the citadel, but this solution is prevented by the same religious considerations which later (717) make it necessary for Anchises to carry them, since Aeneas himself is bloodstained and must not touch them. So too the worst sacrilege committed by Diomedes and Odysseus was considered to be that they had dared to lay bloodstained hands on the image of the goddess (167). Thus one tradition, known to us only from the *Tabula Iliaca*, proved very convenient for Virgil. On this, a man whose name can unfortunately no longer be established,[51] gives Aeneas a casket, the sacred *aedicula* [small shrine], which is shown again later as they leave the city. Virgil transfers this rôle to Panthus the priest of Apollo: *sacra manu victosque deos parvumque nepotem ipse trahit* (320-1) [leading his little grandson by the hand and carrying his sacred vessels and figures of his defeated gods]. I believe that there can be no doubt that these *sacra victique dei* [sacred vessels and defeated gods] are not intended to be the single *simulacrum* [image] of Apollo but the very objects which Hector had described a few lines before as *sacra suosque penates*;[52] the two lines

21

35 even echo each other in their form, in that *sacra* comes in the same position in the line each time, and the *victi dei* are the same as the *victi penates*, as they are called at 1.68 and 8.11. Panthus rescues these *sacra* from the citadel and brings them down to Aeneas, in whose pious and courageous care he knows they will be safest. The dream is thus promptly confirmed. Panthus then follows Aeneas into the fight and falls (429);[53] there was no need for Virgil to state explicitly that he did not take the sacred objects and his little grandson with him, but left them in Aeneas' house. Consequently Aeneas takes over the duties of the priest: he asks his father to carry the *sacra patriosque penates* as they leave, and immediately afterwards calls them *Teucri penates* (747). It would be excessively pedantic, and an insult to the intelligence of his readers, if at this point the poet were to emphasize explicitly that these are the same as the *sacra Troiaeque penates* and the *sacra victique dei* that he had mentioned before.[54]

36

5. Coroebus

Virgil deliberately chose not to give a general description of the night of slaughter such as we read in Quintus and Tryphiodorus. His need to concentrate the action forbade any such attempt. All that we learn of the Night Battle is what Aeneas and his men experience on the way to the citadel and on the citadel itself, and this brings the events into sharper focus than if we saw the whole panorama from a bird's eye view. We go with Aeneas through the narrow streets of the ancient city, past the houses that have been forced open and the shrines that have been violated, and see the corpses of the slain strewn everywhere, lying where the enemy overtook them unaware (363ff.), and we become witnesses of what is perhaps the Trojans' only piece of good fortune, and then of its inevitable unfortunate outcome. It was probably Virgil himself who introduced into the story of the sack of Troy the stratagem of exchanging armour – though doubtless there were historical precedents;[55] it is also natural that the Trojan would be able to tell the story of an incident which does not appear in the Greek accounts of the victory; only an excess of invention would have been a misjudgement.

Virgil placed Coroebus in the foreground here, and to good effect. In the later tradition he is represented as a suitor of Cassandra, succeeding Othryoneus (*Iliad* 13.363) when he is killed by Idomeneus. The significance of his proverbial stupidity, allegedly invented by Euphorion (Serv. on 341), cannot be established.

37 Perhaps it developed from the foolish boasting of Othryoneus (13.366) and was transferred to him by Quintus (13.175); perhaps it was also based on the recklessness with which he cast his bride's warnings to the four winds. Virgil justifies him with a single word and calls on the listener's pity: *infelix, qui non sponsae praecepta f u r e n t i s audierit* (345) [it was disastrous for him that he had not heeded the wild warnings of his princess] – that was divine destiny. But it seems that he did not wish to obliterate his traditional characteristics altogether: it is Coroebus who, excited by his first lucky success, immediately feels renewed hope and attempts to stave off inevitable destiny by means of a ruse (unobjectionable in itself).[56] The younger men are caught up by his plan. Significantly, Aeneas here mentions only the others (*hoc*

omnis iuventus laeta facit [394] [all our company followed his example in high spirits]); he himself is not to be thought of in borrowed arms.

At first the trick has the desired success. It is a well-known dramatic device, which Sophocles is particularly fond of using, to make an apparently successful early achievement increase the effect of the subsequent disaster. At the same time, this successful phase of the battle serves to strengthen the emphasis of the whole narrative. Where before we saw only the Trojans conquering or dying, now we see the Greeks too, fleeing in masses; no wonder Aeneas dwells on the memory (399-40; 421). But Coroebus gives Virgil the opportunity he desired to weave the pathetic fate of Cassandra into the action (rather than mention it in a separate episode, which, as we have said, he generally avoids):[57] Coroebus falling in battle for the sake of his bride is a very happy invention which, in my opinion, we should credit to Virgil.[58] 38 The young hothead forgets the caution required by his disguise and flings himself upon her captors; his companions do not desert him; the noise of the fighting attracts the enemy, who gather from all directions; the ruse is discovered:[59] Coroebus falls,[60] and once again Cassandra has to see her own prophecy fulfilled before her very 39 eyes. But it is true tragic irony that it is the very attempt to avert the ruinous destiny that leads to ruin: the Trojans, disguised as Greeks, fall at the hands of their own compatriots.

6. On the citadel

During the fighting, which wipes out nearly all his followers,[61] Aeneas and two men unfit for battle who cling to him for protection are separated from the others. They hear the noise of the fighting raging around Priam's palace; one has to imagine it as being not far from the temple of Athena, which also stands on the *arx*. Now the last act of the drama begins: the fall of Troy culminates in the death of King Priam. This symbolic use of the poetic architecture appears so obvious to us now that, as far as I am aware, no interpreter has commented on this example of it in Virgil as being anything special. But here, as so often, it is one more triumphant success for the poet that he has made us take his innovation for granted. We know of no tradition which represented Priam's death as the crowning event of the sack of Troy. In Polygnotus' *Sack of Troy* at Delphi, Priam lies slain while Neoptolemus, striding over Elasos, whom he has just killed, swings a deadly blow at Astynoos; Pausanias informs us that, according to Lesches, Neoptolemus killed Priam 'in passing' (10.27.2). Thus, even in the accounts which give only the major episodes of the sack of Troy, in Apollodorus (*epit.* 5.10) and Tryphiodorus (634), the death of Priam is certainly not placed in the final, most emphatic position, and in Quintus, although it is shifted so that it comes last among Neoptolemus' deeds (13.220), it is followed not only by the death of Astyanax and other episodes but also by the fall of Deiphobus and general descriptions of the fighting. Indeed, narrative in early epic was essentially concerned with conveying information about events; from that point of view the death of Priam was certainly an important occurrence in its own right, and indeed it was one of the major episodes of the sack of Troy that were depicted in archaic art, but it was not 40 presented as being of particular significance for the fall of Ilium. The aged king was a weaker obstacle than Elasos and Astynoos, even though they were no more than ordinary soldiers. But for a poet arranging his material from an artistic viewpoint, it was impossible that Priam should be killed 'in passing'. Instead, his death becomes an image that represents the fall of Troy. It forms the chief climax of the book, and its effect is not to be weakened by the addition of trivial or less important material.[62] But Virgil's art is too discreet to compel us to feel this by the use of some high-sounding phrase. The best way to achieve this effect is for the final battle to take place around Priam's palace, and for the last opponent whom Neoptolemus encounters to be the king himself; and when Aeneas turns back at this point and abandons the struggle, this is not because he reasons 'now Priam is dead, so it is all over' (which might be artistically satisfying but would not be true); the *peripeteia* is motivated, again in an apparently very simple way: Aeneas, who has seen the ignominious death of the aged Priam, is suddenly seized with anxiety about the fate of his own aged father.

Aeneas' position during these last scenes is quite clear. The palace is under attack from the front. To help defend it, Aeneas needs to reach the roof by means of a rear entrance; but from the roof it is only the immediate threat that can be fought off, the attempt by the Greeks to storm the battlements by using a *testudo* [a shelter of shields, resembling a tortoise]. When Neoptolemus succeeds in breaking down the gate and forcing his way into the *vestibulum*, across it and then into the *atrium*, the defenders on the roof are reduced to the condition of helpless spectators. And, of course, from the roof they can see everything that is going on in the *atrium*. Virgil imagines it as having a large central opening, perhaps more in the style of a Greek αὐλή, but in any case large enough to allow the massive household altar with its Penates[63] to stand in its centre, *nudo sub aetheris axe* (512) [bare to the heavens], as Virgil expressly emphasizes. The women and Priam have taken refuge by this altar. While Neoptolemus and his men are rampaging inside the palace, the Trojans remaining on the roof disappear one by one. Some try to escape by jumping down from the roof onto the ground outside, others fling themselves in despair into the flames. When Aeneas looks round, he finds he is alone.

For the reasons given above, we might have expected Priam's death to have been described in some detail, with a formal speech and reply in accordance with the conventions of epic. There is something painful, almost comic, if one has to visualize Aeneas witnessing all these tragic happenings as an inactive spectator on the roof. Virgil has made use of an original device to tone down this effect. First Aeneas states quite briefly (499-502) that he has seen with his own eyes how Neoptolemus and the Atridae stormed through the palace, and how Priam fell at the altar; then the *thalami* [bed-chambers] collapse; wherever there is no fire stands the foe.[64] And now (506) the narrative makes a fresh start with the ultimate fate of Priam, *forsitan et Priami fuerint quae fata requiras* [you may also want to know how Priam met his end], but this is described in such a way that the narrator vanishes from our field of vision. We have no impression that we are listening to an eye-witness. Indeed we might be justified in doubting whether Aeneas himself could possibly have observed the whole sequence of events, as he describes Priam putting on his armour, what Hecuba said, etc. Thus here, too, Virgil does not adhere strictly to a first-person narrative, but sacrifices it to the higher artistic economy of the work.[65]

24

7. The death of Priam

The mythographic tradition says that Neoptolemus killed Priam at the altar of Zeus Herkeios. Quintus and Tryphiodorus appear to have had no other version in their sources. Quintus does not let the king perish in total silence but gives him one more speech pleading for death, which is welcome to him after all his sufferings,[66] to which Neoptolemus replies that he was going to kill him anyway and had no intention of sparing an enemy's life, 'since men love nothing so much as their own lives'. Tryphiodorus gives no details; he only stresses the cruelty of Neoptolemus, who would not allow himself to be moved either by pleas or by the white hairs of the king, which once moved Achilles himself to pity. Here the atmosphere surrounding Neoptolemus is quite Virgilian: both writers base their material on the Hellenistic poets.

In Virgil the scene is enriched with a series of subsidiary motifs: Priam arming himself, the presence of Hecuba, the death of Polites, the feeble attack by Priam. We know of no poetic version of the tale that corresponds to this; but can all of it be Virgil's invention, transforming the dry bones of the traditional narrative into a scene of dramatic movement? I think not, since more or less close analogies for almost all the individual incidents can be found elsewhere.[67] Priam's arming and his attempt to fight: Polygnotus painted a breastplate lying on the altar of Zeus (Paus. 10.26.5); Robert (*Die Iliupersis des Polygnot* 67) interprets this as showing that Priam was about to put on his armour when he was surprised by Neoptolemus. Robert also refers to a sarcophagus relief on which the aged king is dropping a sword with which he had been fighting. The presence of Hecuba: the *Tabula Iliaca* and other representations[68] show her sitting on the altar beside Priam; in Euripides she says that she was an eye-witness of his death (*Tro.* 481). Polites' death at the hand of Neoptolemus: Quintus 13.214, admittedly not related to Priam; but the death of the son before his father's eyes reminds us that on the earlier Attic vases the death of Astyanax was generally associated with that of Priam, in that they show the body of the slain child lying in the lap of his grandfather as his grandfather himself is put to death.[69] The poetic tradition does not associate them in this way. I do not dare to contradict Robert, who attributes the spontaneous appearance of this motif in archaic art to the desire to show as much as possible in one picture; but it would be strange if the poets had not taken up this effective motif once it had been created. But if, say in Hellenistic times, the son Polites was substituted for the grandson Astyanax,[70] that can easily be explained by the overwhelming importance that the tragic poets in particular had meanwhile conferred upon the version of Astyanax's death with which we are familiar.

In considering all these separate components, we have not yet touched on the most important thing: the action and the motivating mood; yet it is precisely this that will be Virgil's own, for the whole scene bears the unmistakeable imprint of his genius. Priam's death is not that of a passive victim of the fighting; nor does death come to him as a welcome release; nor again does he whine like a coward or plead for his life. He wished to die as a warrior, and although at first he yields to the prayers of his aged wife, his old herioc blood surges up when he sees the death of his son; and he does die a warrior's death. This arouses in the listener not simply pity but also respect and admiration, and tempers the dreadful anguish of the events with a trace of sublimity. From the point of view of technique, the old man's throw of the spear and his last angry speech are of the utmost significance. Blow follows upon blow, as required by the dramatic mode of composition, and each blow is motivated by the one that precedes it. If Priam had been murdered while he was just sitting there quietly, it would have seemed an unprepared, almost accidental occurrence, hanging in the air. Hecuba's intervention is necessary, so that she may become an active character instead of a passive one, and also to bring Priam to the altar in spite of the fact that he is armed. Finally, it is true that Neoptolemus is cruel and heartless, and also that he commits a most dreadful outrage against the gods, not only by killing a man at the altar, but because he himself drags the old man in the most brutal manner to the altar in the first place, as if to butcher him for a sacrifice (here Virgil goes further than any of our other accounts); however, he is not simply a bloodthirsty butcher who kills everything that stands in his way. He is inflamed by his aged opponent's scornful words and by his attack, and the brutal deed can thus be seen as the result of an upsurge of an angry desire for vengeance. He still commits a brutal act, but Virgil avoids giving the effect of an unmotivated atrocity.

The closing words with their reference to the contrast between Priam's former greatness and his pitiful death would seem superfluous if it were not that the style demands an epilogue of this kind, to underline as it were the significance of the narrated events. This is not the poet's objective account, but the speech, let us say the ῥῆσις, of the compassionate Aeneas;[71] these last lines lead us back to him.

III. *The Departure*

1. Helen and Venus

The death of Priam forms the turning-point. It puts an end to the battle for the city, and it instigates Aeneas' flight. For the first time, Aeneas is seized by shudders of fear. Up to this point he had been carried along by a wild fury of despair. Now the fate of the house of Priam and his family seems to him to be an image of what will happen, or has already happened, to his own household. He immediately looks around – he has been oblivious to his surroundings during the final grim drama – and finds himself alone.

This is where the Helen episode (567-88) begins. The lines survive only in Servius. In my opinion there cannot be the slightest doubt that they are not the work of Virgil. The facts concerning their transmission and the way that they offend against Virgilian linguistic usage would alone suffice to prove this.[72] There are also other reasons for doubting them. Two of them were pointed out as early as Servius, to explain why Varius and Tucca deleted the lines: *et turpe est viro forti contra feminam irasci, et contrarium est Helenam in domo Priami fuisse illi rei, quae in sexto dicitur, quia in domo inventa est Deiphobi, postquam ex summa arce vocave-*

rat Graecos [it is unbecoming for a brave man to be angry with a woman, and, besides, the presence of Helen in Priam's palace contradicts the statement in Book 6 that she was found in Deiphobus' house after she had summoned the Greeks from high on the citadel]. Both these reasons are valid although they require modification. It is not *irasci* which would dishonour Aeneas; but I am convinced that Virgil could never have allowed his pious hero to think even for a fleeting moment of killing a defenceless woman (it is not as if she were Camilla, exulting in battle), above all when it is a woman who has sought protection at the altar. How could such an idea be consistent with the deep revulsion with which he has just narrated the violation of the sanctity of an altar? And this time it is at the altar of Vesta, that is, of the very goddess who had been entrusted to Aeneas' protection together with the Penates. Moreover, it is only later that Aeneas learns of Helen's treachery, from Deiphobus in the Underworld; the events of the past few years might well give him reason to curse Helen as the cause of the whole war, but would hardly put into his head the insane notion of killing her. Moreover, the passage obviously contradicts the account in Book 6 on several points: a Helen who had given the fire-signal to the Greeks, who had delivered Deiphobus defenceless into their hands, did not need to fear their revenge. This contradiction, like so many others that occur in the *Aeneid*, might be attributed to the unfinished state of the work; but if my interpretation above (n. 27) is correct, Virgil had this episode of Book 6 in mind when he was composing Book 2, so that this explanation is impossible in this case. Moreover, if Venus' words *non tibi Tyndaridis facies invisa Lacaenae* etc. (601) [you must not blame the hated beauty of the Spartan Tyndarid] refer to this intention of Aeneas to attack Helen, what justification can there be for the following phrase, *culpatusve Paris* [nor is Paris to blame], for Aeneas cannot have given him a single thought during the whole of this scene? Finally a technical argument which, as far as I am aware, has not been advanced before. The words *scilicet haec Spartam incolumis patriasque Mycenas aspiciet* etc. ['So!', thought I, 'shall she unharmed, again see Sparta and Mycenae the land of her birth?'] would be the only soliloquy by Aeneas[73]   47 in his accounts of adventures in Books 2 and 3. It is obvious what an unnatural and frigid effect is created by any such soliloquies in a first-person narrative, let alone lengthy ratiocinations of the kind that occur in this example; they belong to the world of some mannered late Greek romance. We would have to accept this as a lapse of taste on Virgil's part if the passage were not open to objections on other grounds, but, in my view, Virgil would have been at pains to avoid anything of this kind, perhaps strengthened in his attitude by Homer's example. We should remember that Odysseus never once represents himself as delivering a soliloquy throughout the entire course of his adventures.[74] It is conceivable that the ancient commentators on the *Odyssey* pointed this out and showed how very different it was from the extended soliloquies in *Odyssey* 5 and 6; in that case, Virgil would have been aware of this contrast and it would have come naturally to him to adhere to the convention.

In short, I take the spuriousness of these lines to be proven. But I am inclined to believe that there was in fact a lacuna at the point where they were inserted. For, even if we are prepared to accept the fact that line 589 is connected by *cum* for no good reason, and that the allusion to Helen and Paris by Venus in her speech is not directly motivated or prepared by anything that has gone before – and that would not be totally impossible – yet when the goddess takes the hero by the right hand and restrains him, *dextra prehensum continuit* (592), we certainly ought to be told what he is being restrained from; but there is nothing at all about that in the lines of Virgil that have survived. That Virgil should have written Venus' speech without giving any explanation of what had led up to it, namely Aeneas' intentions, seems as incredible to me as it did to Thilo (loc. cit.); in that case we must agree with Thilo's conclusion, that Virgil did indeed originally write some lines, which are now missing because he struck them out and did not put anything in their place. What was in these lines? What decision had Aeneas taken?

In the first place, it can *not* have been the decision to return to his family. For in that case Venus' admonition would have been superfluous. The argument that she might not have known his unspoken intentions is not worth refuting. Moreover the 48 poet has made every effort to establish that it is only because of the goddess that Aeneas is reminded that he must turn back to look for his family. Not that he is deficient in love and piety; but we should remember the situation: Aeneas is standing alone on the roof of the palace; fire and foe all around; it seems impossible to get through, nor does there seem to be any hope that his forsaken household could have escaped the twofold raging death. His own escape and the safety of his household are both expressly attributed to the miraculous intervention of the deity. Since Aeneas cannot count on this in advance, it is understandable that he has no thoughts of flight when the reward if he succeeds in getting through – highly improbable in itself – would be to see the ghastly scene that he has just witnessed enacted even more horribly in his own house. This explains one part of Venus' exhortation: she has protected his household so far, she will lead Aeneas himself through unharmed; he may follow her commands without fear (606ff.). It is completely in character for Venus, who in Virgil, even in serious moments, is almost always something of a tease, that she did not go to the heart of the matter immediately, but pretends to be surprised that Aeneas is in a furious rage instead of worrying about his family (which is also her family, *quo n o s t r i tibi cura recessit* [how can your love for *us* have passed so far from your thoughts?]); it is as though she wishes to take pleasure in his astonishment first, before she gives him her comforting assurance.

Neither the goddess' allusion to Helen nor her revelation of the hostile gods has any direct connection with her exhortation. Both would obviously tend to dissuade him. Some ancient editor invented the Helen episode in order to motivate the dissuasion. He was not an uncultured man; not a poet, however, even if he did know how to imitate Virgil's style if need be; but he was familiar with epic tradition and poetry; it was the Menelaus and Helen episode in the *Iliu Persis* that gave him his idea – Menelaus, too, is prevented by Aphrodite from wreaking vengeance; in writing the scene he borrowed from the scene in Euripides' *Orestes*, in which Pylades incites Orestes to murder Helen.[75] Thus his technique of imitation is very 49 similar to Virgil's own; the whole conception, however, is un-Virgilian, as I have shown above. Furthermore, it is inconceivable that Aeneas should have considered taking up the fight again in the hope of achieving a victory. Indeed, the poet has made his despair clear from the beginning, with all the means at his disposal. Besides, this would not explain the reference to Helen.

Aeneas has come face to face with death, and there is only one decision that he can have considered: to go to meet death rather than remain passively waiting for it. His choice was between the quickest way, putting an end to his own life by his own hand,[76] and seeking death among the dense ranks of the enemy, perhaps in the hope of first wreaking his revenge on Neoptolemus for Priam's death. Although the first alternative would have provided splendid dramatic tension and a good motivation for the intervention of his divine mother, yet her own words[77] seem to recommend the latter. We can see why Virgil eventually rejected the idea. It would have developed into a repetition of what Aeneas had said at the beginning of the battle – *furor iraque mentem praecipitant pulchrumque mori succurrit in armis* (316) [frantic in my fury I had no time for decisions; I only remembered that death in battle is glorious] – and would have infringed a fundamental rule of Virgil's technique, that a climax should be approached gradually. But the second alternative would provide a complete explanation for Venus' intervention and her speech. She offers the despairing hero a means of escape by her divine assistance (note that at this stage she says nothing about fleeing from the city), she gives him the opportunity to fulfil the claims of *pietas* towards his family; but she does more than this, she shows him that his *furor* and *ira* (594f., cf. 316) [frenzy and anger] are directed not against the consequences of human action, but against a decree of the gods. That is the meaning of the lines

> *non tibi Tyndaridis facies invisa Lacaenae*
> *culpatusve Paris, divom inclementia, divom*
> *has evertit opes sternitque a culmine Troiam.*

[you must not blame the hated beauty of the Spartan Tyndarid, or even Paris. It was the gods who showed no mercy; it is they who are casting Troy down from her splendour and power]. Her revelation of the hostile gods serves the same purpose, and is not intended to show, for example, that further resistance is in vain. She mentions Helen and Paris, not Sinon and Neoptolemus, because Virgil is employing the well-known convention, of which the tragedians were particularly fond, whereby one refers back to the first causes of misfortune. In this case he follows the usage of tragedy very closely.[78] In Aeschylus the nuptials of Paris, 'destroyers of friends', are cursed (*Agam.* 1156), and in Sophocles Paris is cursed by Ajax's men. But it is Euripides who is particularly rich in gruesome imprecations and bitter accusations against Helen as the original cause of the war. Trojans[79] and Greeks[80] alike hate her, hold her responsible for all their miseries, and wish her to suffer and perish; the mood in which we have to imagine Aeneas is matched most closely by the words of the Trojan women (*Hec.* 943) as they go into slavery, 'cursing Helen, sister of the Dioscuri, and the shepherd of Ida, unfortunate Paris; for their wedding has driven us to miserable exile'. And yet she had been exonerated of all responsibility by the one who had most reason to curse her. In Homer, Priam spoke these immortal words in reply to her self-reproaches: 'I do not recognize you as guilty; it is the gods who are to blame. It is they who sent me the war which has caused so much weeping' (*Iliad* 3.164). That vexed Euripides; in order to counter this pious yet sacrilegious tolerance, he composed the debate between Helen and Hecuba in the *Troades*, and when

29

Helen puts the blame on the gods, he makes Hecuba tear her case to pieces with the utmost scorn. Virgil, of course, knew this scene. His own kind of piety causes him to take sides, and Aeneas hears from the mouth of his divine mother that Priam had spoken the truth. But if the gods desire Troy's fall, a pious man should behave with quiet resignation, not rebellion or despair. Aeneas is brought by Venus to this state of resignation.

It is probably, though in my opinion not absolutely necessarily, to be assumed that when Venus mentions Helen and Paris it is because Aeneas had blamed them either in words or in his thoughts. I do not know in what form Virgil gave, or intended to give these thoughts; a brief exclamation could have been enough, which need not have been expanded into a soliloquy; or there might have been simply a description of the emotions which made Aeneas wish to go to his death.

2. Vision of the gods

The vision which Venus unveils to Aeneas has a much more powerful effect on him than her mere words. He sees with his own eyes what is hidden from mortals, and no mortal had yet ever seen. Sometimes one deity grants a favoured mortal the privilege of seeing him or her with his own eyes. But in this vision the veil which screens from mortal sight the whole world of the gods and their sway on earth is pulled aside. The motif is borrowed from the *Iliad* (5.127) but it is developed very much more powerfully. In the *Iliad*, Athena gives Diomedes supernatural powers of sight, so that he can distinguish gods from men on the battlefield and avoid fighting with them; however, that means that he recognizes only those gods with whom he comes into contact himself. Virgil's inspiration, too sublime even for the poet's words to do it justice, almost too vast for the imagination to grasp, arouses misgivings for that very reason. We might easily believe it if the poet himself described it; but, as it is, it is narrated by Aeneas as an eyewitness. We therefore feel entitled to clear, tangible, concrete images. Neptune, for example, capable of uprooting the whole city from its foundations, is represented in a way that almost goes beyond our powers of visualization. Jupiter, who imbues the Greeks with courage and strength and incites the gods themselves to fight against Troy, is a figure that completely baffles any attempt that might be made to imagine him in physical terms, and even if in this case Virgil tactfully allows Venus not to draw Aeneas' attention to him explicitly, as she does with the other gods, yet Jupiter must be among the *numina magna deum* [giant powers of gods] that Aeneas sees.[81] Juno stands as πρόμαχος [defender] at the Scaean Gate and summons the Greeks from the ships – what, still? one asks in amazement; for it was long ago that Androgeos had rebuked the men he took to be his companions for coming so late from the ships; we had been under the impression that there were no more left to come by the time that Priam's citadel fell. If it were a matter of a panorama of the whole sack of Troy, we could understand what Juno was doing. She does not put her hand to the task herself, for that would hardly be seemly for the *regina deum*; but, as far as she is concerned, the city she hates cannot be overwhelmed by the enemy soon enough; so she stands at the gate and calls furiously across the plain, and her cry spurs on the Greeks to make haste with the destruction of the city.

The starting-point of Virgil's conception can be traced with the help of Tryphiodorus. He too depicts the participation of the gods (559ff.), but as part of his general description of the night of terror. Enyo rages through the streets all night, accompanied by the gigantic Eris who inflames the Argives to battle, and finally Ares arrives to grant them victory. From the citadel terrifying shouts are heard from Athena as she shakes her aegis. Hera's tread makes the aether rumble; the earth trembles, shaken by Poseidon's trident; Hades leaps up in horror from his throne. All this is simply a copy of the picture that introduces the Battle of the Gods in Homer,[82] with only a few changes in detail to fit the new situation: Ares too is on the Greek side now, Athena no longer stays on the shore but stands on the citadel as she does in Virgil, and as Ares does in Homer.[83] The other divergences from Homer, which Tryphiodorus and Virgil have in common, are unimportant. They both mention 53 Hera, both give Athena her aegis and Poseidon his trident. As we can see, there is no reason at all to suppose that Tryphiodorus knew Virgil's description and made use of it. In every essential he keeps closer to Homer than to the Roman poet, except that Zeus does not appear in his account, whereas in Homer he sends peals of thunder from on high, and Virgil shows him doing something altogether different. Everything that Virgil adds in order to make the scene more vivid and to present in visible symbols the enmity of the gods towards Troy is absent from Tryphiodorus. But surely no one will doubt that the scene in the *Iliad* is the direct or indirect model for Virgil's scene; indirect, in my view, since Tryphiodorus also made use of it, and both of them made the same minor changes. Any famous version of the Sack of Troy, we may assume, will have included a scene showing the hostile gods taking part in the final struggle of the great war, on the lines of Homer's Battle of the Gods; but now there is no god fighting on the side of the defeated. Virgil realized that this would make a magnificent finale for his Sack of Troy, and reshaped it for his own special purposes. First it had to be changed into narrative in the first person; consequently the scene had to become visible to Aeneas.

Virgil found a means of achieving this in Venus' intervention, and was thus able to make the thrilling scene into an integrating component of the entire action: it is indispensable in that it convinces Aeneas through the evidence of his own eyes. But the scene has not completely lost its original purpose, that of concentrating the mighty struggle into one magnificent symbol. In the case of Jupiter, Virgil does without the concrete representation of his actions required by the new context, and he is not afraid to introduce an anachronism into his portrayal of Juno. Other singularities can easily be explained by the particular nature of his poem. Mars, the ancestor of the Romans, cannot appear as one of the *inimica Troiae numina* [powers not friendly to Troy]. Athena does not shout – no goddess shouts in Virgil – and consequently there is something rather insipid about the simple phrase *summas arces insedit* [sits on the citadel's height]. Jupiter supplies the crowning touch: it is only when the Almighty himself supports the enemies of Troy that all hope is lost.

3. Venus' protection

54 Venus' warnings, instructions and promises refer only to the immediate problem, how Aeneas is to get from the citadel to his father's house. Perhaps this is not obvious at first hearing, but it is if you consider it carefully; we would expect Venus to say something about what is to be done after that: that Aeneas is to leave Troy, together with his household, that he will be able to leave it safely, and so forth. But the words *eripe nate fugam…nusquam abero* (619) [son, make your escape…. I will be near you everywhere] are not to be taken in this sense; that is made clear by the addition of the explicit *et tutum patrio te limine sistam* [and set you safe at your father's door]. The economy of the epic (one might almost say the economy of the drama) requires that the effect of the Venus scene should be limited to this much; otherwise the scenes that follow could not be presented as the poet intended. Venus could not promise her protection for the departure – for in that case the loss of Creusa and Aeneas' anxious confusion would be impossible; nor could she recommend the departure at all, since this would exclude in advance the possibility of Anchises' refusal and everything that goes with it. But there was a version of the story in which Aeneas and his family are guided out of Troy by Venus; it has survived in pictorial art,[84] it is in Tryphiodorus,[85] and was also known to Quintus (13.326ff.); indeed the detail mentioned both by him and by Virgil, that the fire retreated before Aeneas, and the enemy's missiles were unable to injure him, allows us to conclude that there was an established tradition about the nature of the goddess' guidance.[86] Sophocles, who in his *Laocoon* shows Aeneas and his family leaving Troy before it fell, cannot have said anything about divine guidance of this kind, but in his version Anchises, who urged the departure, acts in accordance with warnings from Aphrodite. Thus Virgil has made as much use of this tradition as he could without prejudice to his intentions for the rest of Book 2. It is only when we remember the original version that it seems remarkable that Venus should protect the way from the citadel to Aeneas' house, and then disappear, when, as she herself points out, the house was surrounded by swarms of enemy troops.

55 4. Anchises and the *auspicium maximum*

The scenes in Anchises' house before the departure are significant in several respects. The piety of the hero towards his father, the main feature of Aeneas in popular tradition, first comes to the forefront here. It is not enough that Aeneas should carry his father out of the burning city on his own shoulders: he is also faced with his father's refusal to allow himself to be rescued, and is prepared to lose his wife and child and his own life together with his father rather than abandon him to face the merciless enemy on his own. Anchises himself, Creusa and Iulus are introduced; this was particularly necessary in Creusa's case, since the listener has to know something about her if he is to feel any interest in the story of her miraculous disappearance. The artistic effect of Anchises' refusal is to hold up the action and create tension; immediately before Aeneas and his family succeed in escaping, there is serious doubt that they will ever manage to get away.

To all this Virgil added something new and absolutely essential. The departure from Troy, the beginning of their new life and their new foundation, had to proceed *auspicato* [after the auspices had been taken]. The usual view was that the whole system of augury on which the Roman state religion rested was based on the auspices of Romulus, the omen of the birds described by Ennius, which gave him the precedence over Remus; or on the prototype of all magistrates' auspices, the signs from heaven, which Romulus prayed for to confirm his right to the monarchy. However, another tradition went back even further and claimed that the *auspicium maximum* [greatest omen], lightning from the left out of a clear sky, first appeared in favour of Ascanius in his battle with Mezentius (Dion. Hal. 2.5.5); others mentioned not Ascanius but Aeneas himself in this context (Plutarch *Qu. R.* 78). Later on in the poem, Virgil mentions both traditions,[87] without giving any impression that the *auspicium* was something as yet unknown, or that belief in auspices began on these occasions. In his view, the decisive moment, which above all demanded an authoritative indication of the approval of the gods, is the turning-point which led to the foundation of the new Troy, and he introduces a sign here that corresponds to the *auspicium maximum*, but differs as much from all the later ones as an original does from its copies.[88] Instead of a flash of lightning, a star crosses the night sky, leaving a long, shining trail, but it comes with all the phenomena that accompany lightning, thunder on the left out of a clear sky, and sulphurous smoke. However, all the attendant circumstances correspond so closely with the rites of augury and yet arise so entirely from the situation that we may be justified in calling it an *aition* [traditional explanation]: for this is the nature of such *aitia*, that a practice, which is constantly repeated in later times, is explained in all its details by the particular circumstances of a unique situation. The gods send a sign: a flame plays around Iulus' head.[89] Aeneas and Creusa are terrified and hastily attempt to smother the flame. Only Anchises suspects that the sign may be a good omen. But it is perfectly understandable in this situation that he should ask the gods for an unambiguous confirmation; after all, until now he had believed that the destruction of Troy was a divine sign that meant that he should remain behind. He turns to Jupiter, for he was the god whose lightning, he thought, had indicated that he no longer had any right to live (648); we know that the Romans believed that all auspices were sent by Jupiter. However, to ask for an unambiguous sign is technically *impetrare auspicia*; the *auspicium impetrativum* [auspice in response to a request] serves to confirm the *auspicium oblativum* [an unsolicited auspice] or the *omen*, as Anchises says: *da deinde augurium, pater, atque haec omina firma* [give us now your message and confirm this sign], apparently using a solemn formula, since it tallies exactly with what Cicero says in the *De Divinatione* of the confirmation of the *auspicium oblativum* by the *impetrativum*, the lightning from the left: *sic aquilae clarum firmavit Iuppiter omen* [so Jupiter confirmed the clear omen of the eagle].[90] Moreover, it arises naturally from the situation that it is Anchises who prays and receives the sign at this point: just as here it is the head of the house, so later it is always the head of the state, that is, the magistrate, who takes the auspices. Furthermore, details of the rite are prefigured here. It is night time and already near dawn; that is the time

56

57

ordained for taking auspices.[91] Anchises, because he is lame, is seated; likewise the magistrate who watches the skies.[92] He rises after the appearance of the sign (699), because he now wishes to set out without delay; the magistrate had to do the same immediately after he had seen the sign, before another sign could cancel out the first: on *se tollit ad auras* [he rose] Servius explicitly says *verbum augurum, qui visis auspiciis surgebant e templo* [a word applied to augurs, who rose from the temple when they had seen the auspices]. Virgil, in my opinion, does not draw the parallel explicitly, as he does in similar cases elsewhere, since he could not put such an explanation in Aeneas' mouth here, but he could expect his reader to recognize the course of events as the original model for the whole rite of taking the auspices.

I need only add a brief word concerning the dramatic composition of the scene. Aeneas hardly behaves like a dramatic hero, in that he takes no initiative of his own, but acts merely as the central figure of the whole; action and counter-action come from Anchises and Creusa; their behaviour creates a knot which can only be untied by divine intervention, a veritable *deus ex machina*. It is Aeneas' men who take the part of the chorus in this scene; their presence is indicated briefly but very effectively by the words *arma, viri, ferte arma* (668) [quick comrades! Bring me arms]. We are like spectators: not only do we hear speeches, we also see action and movement: Anchises' words (651) are followed by the entreaties of the weeping household; Aeneas arms himself to go to his death, after announcing his decision; on the threshold of the house we see the pathetic group of parents and son, as Creusa beseeches her husband to stay. In a word, πρᾶξις [action], ἦθος [character], and διάνοια [intellect], all receive their equal due, and everything serves to arouse the hearer's πάθος [emotion] with a quick succession of emotions.

5. Creusa

In the ancient tradition, Aeneas is accompanied on his flight by his wife Eurydice.[93] In Virgil, Aeneas loses his wife Creusa[94] during the departure, while they are still within the city, and learns later from her shade that it was Jupiter's will that she should not accompany him to distant lands, nor did she have to suffer enslavement by the enemy either, for the mother of the gods was keeping her there in her native country (788). The representation on the *Tabula Iliaca*, taken together with a tradition recorded by Pausanias, makes it reasonably certain that Virgil's version of the story had existed in its essential outlines before him.[95] Why he chose it is obvious: otherwise Creusa would have had to die during the journey, and that would have produced a doublet of the death of Anchises. As it is, it gives him the opportunity to create an effective final scene for his Sack of Troy.

Virgil, apparently intentionally, has left us somewhat in the dark about the precise details of Creusa's disappearance. Aeneas only learns that the Great Mother *his detinet oris* (788) [is keeping (her) in this land]; this allows us to deduce that she is not dead (although the expressions *simulacrum, umbra* and *imago* are in fact appropriate to and commonly used only of the appearance of the departed, whose real self has perished) but has been removed to a higher and immortal existence – for which again *nota maior imago* (773) [in her ghostly form larger than life] is suitable[96] –

which means, no doubt, that she has become one of the attendants of the Mother of the Gods:[97] Creusa's fate is the fate that Diana intended for Camilla, when she wanted to take her up to become one of her attendants.[98] Aeneas can infer this, and so can we; Creusa herself does not mention it, as though she were afraid to reveal a mystery connected with the worship of Cybele; and certainly from the artistic point of view there is no need, nor indeed would it be desirable, for the veil of secrecy to be drawn back completely from miracles of this kind.

But there is one fact that the poet wishes to make clear beyond all doubt: that it had already been determined in advance, either by fate or by the decision of Jupiter, that Creusa was not to accompany her husband on his wanderings: *non haec sine numine divom eveniunt, nec te comitem hinc portare Creusam fas aut ille sinit superi regnator Olympi* (777-9) ['what has happened is part of the divine plan. For the law of right and the supreme ruler of Olympus on high forbid you to carry Creusa away from Troy']. These are the words of the shade of Creusa; she repeats the idea emphatically so as to allay Aeneas' 'senseless grief'.[99] This grief, she says, 60 should give way to quiet resignation, exactly the same kind of resignation that Venus had demanded when she revealed the destruction of Troy as the work of the gods. At the same time this exonerates Aeneas from any charge of guilt that he himself or anyone else might bring against him; even if it was his senseless flight that had resulted in the loss of Creusa, he had only been a tool in the hands of the gods. He is comforted by the thought that Creusa does not have to suffer as a captive of the Greeks, but remains in her native land, though removed to a higher existence; this is of secondary importance but it makes it easier for him to submit to the gods' will. But now a problem arises. In the previous scenes Virgil has done his utmost to motivate the loss of Creusa as naturally as possible: she has to be following her husband (with, it seems to us, an excess of caution) alone and at some distance; Aeneas, alarmed by his father's warning cry (733), has to turn off the road in his anxiety to escape the approaching enemy; later, and even when he is telling the story to Dido, he does not know whether Creusa went the wrong way, or had stopped (because she had lost sight of her husband and did not know which way to go) or was so exhausted that she had sat down because she could go no further – whichever of these she had done, she might easily have fallen into the hands of the enemy. We ask ourselves why the poet has motivated her disappearance in such a circumstantial way, when the Magna Mater could have simply taken Creusa to herself.

It might be thought that a satisfactory answer is that Virgil was simply following the tradition according to which Creusa was in danger of being taken captive, and was rescued by the Great Mother; there had to be some motivation for that danger. It is true that Virgil has introduced a new motif, that the separation of Creusa from Aeneas had been decreed by the gods from the start, and consequently he could have shaped the narrative in such a way that there was no mention of any danger or of the events connected with it. But imagine what the scene would have been like in that case. Creusa would have been walking in front of Aeneas (as she is often repre- 61 sented as doing in the visual arts) and would have suddenly disappeared ἀναρπασθεῖσα [spirited away], rather like Iphigenia at the altar at Aulis, or like a warrior who is taken away by the hand of a god out of the reach of an enemy spear. Aeneas, with Anchises on his shoulders, would have stood there dumbfounded and amazed; a voice from heaven would have explained what had happened, and the group fleeing from the city would have continued on their way. The whole scene would have been incomparably duller and poorer in content, not only because Aeneas would have had no opportunity to show his love for his wife: the meeting with the shade of Creusa would have been impossible; the position of Aeneas during her disappearance would have bordered on the ridiculous; the scene would have had no tension or dramatic movement. Thus it is easy to understand why Virgil adhered to the traditional version in spite of the fact that he was providing a new reason for what happened. It is true that Creusa's separation from Aeneas is now determined by fate, and Aeneas' frantic flight is caused by the gods so as to bring it about; but the poet has conceived it in such a way that the Great Mother alleviates the harshness of fate by taking Creusa to herself, out of the hands of her enemies – the danger is the opportunity for her helpful intervention, exactly as later in Book 9 (77ff.) the danger with which the Trojan ships are threatened gives her the opportunity to make use of Jupiter's permission to give them an immortal form. In order to carry out the new plan, the most important thing was that Creusa should be isolated so that Aeneas would notice only later that she was missing. Virgil took considerable pains over the motivation; the only thing which seems improbable is the excess of caution which we mentioned earlier. Furthermore, Virgil prepares the way for Aeneas' confusion by the description of how the hero, who a moment before was not afraid of the thick swarms of the Greek troops, is now startled by every breeze, every sound, full of anxiety about his son and his father (726-9): in this state, what an effect his father's cry of alarm must have had on him: *nate.. fuge, nate; propinquant* (733) [Son, you must run for it. They are drawing near]. The outward situation is perfectly clear: Anchises believes that he can see enemy troops advancing along the street towards them: Aeneas cannot go back; therefore he has to turn aside into a pathless, unfamiliar area. Since Creusa had been behind him, he is not immediately aware of her disappearance in the confusion of his flight; he does not know why she is not following him, but there are many possibilities: he lists them: *substitit – erravitne via – resedit* (739) [did she stop...or stray from the path...or just sink down in weariness?]. Finally, it makes perfectly good sense that Aeneas should tell the earlier part of the story as if he still knew nothing about the revelation that he received later; that is necessary from an artistic point of view, so that the scenes that follow will not be deprived of their effect, and it is justified in practice by the vividness with which the narrator relives the terror of the discovery and his own despair.

62

Creusa not only allays Aeneas' worries about what has happened; at the same time she also predicts the future to him and allows us to understand why Jupiter does not permit her to follow her husband: after a long journey to the land of Hesperia, he will find by the bank of the Tiber a new happiness, a new kingdom and a king's daughter for a wife. This prophecy is extremely suitable as a conclusion for Virgil's account of the sack of Troy: the reader learns in broad outlines the final result of the events which have passed before his eyes. There is something very similar in the poem about Oenone which Quintus introduced into his 10th Book, when Hera tells her handmaidens all the effects that the death of Paris will entail for Troy (344ff.). A conclusion of this kind was an artistic necessity as long as Virgil was composing his

Sack of Troy as a separate poem, intended to stand alone. As soon as this separate poem was incorporated into the larger context of the epic, there was no longer a need for any prophecy at this point, or at least no more than the prospect of a *regia coniunx* [royal bride] awaiting Aeneas in a distant land. Indeed, when Virgil later decided that Aeneas was to learn only gradually and step by step the destination of his travels, the precise references that Creusa had made to Hesperia and the Tiber created a contradiction and ought to have been deleted. This would not have affected the essential message of Creusa's speech.

6. Conclusion

Aeneas must not leave Troy as a solitary refugee, accompanied only by his father and son and a handful of servants. Creusa had prophesied a new kingdom for him, and for this reason he must be represented from the outset as leader of a host, capable of forming the nucleus of a new nation. In Hellanicus that was provided for by the course of events (see above pp. 18ff.). It is difficult to reconcile it with Virgil's new version. Aeneas' return to the city, together with the description of what he sees there, forms a very effective conclusion to the Sack of Troy,[100] and it is this that Virgil uses to conceal the resulting improbability: when Aeneas returns, he finds that a large crowd has gathered, ready to follow him wherever he goes. This gives him the rôle of the leader of a colony – he himself was not able to explain why this crowd has gathered (*invenio admirans* [797] [I was surprised to find them]), but this is not the time for detailed explanations. A rapid ending is necessary not only from the artistic point of view; it is also required by the course of events. The morning star has risen over Ida, and there is no time to lose. One more glance back at his native city: the gates are in the hands of the enemy, no help can be expected from any direction;[101] then start they must on their way into exile: *cessi et sublato montis genitore petivi* (804) [in resignation I lifted my father and moved towards the mountains].

63

EXCURSUS
Virgil, Quintus and Tryphiodorus

In the discussion above I have treated the versions of Quintus and Tryphiodorus as independent representatives of a tradition concerning the fall of Troy quite distinct from Virgil's. This conflicts with the widespread belief that they were both dependent on Virgil.[102] It is therefore necessary for me to justify my approach here. I admit in advance that there is nothing that can be said *a priori* against the assumption that the two Greek writers were familiar with the Roman epic, since we know nothing at all about them except that they lived at a time when a knowledge of Latin among educated Greek writers is a reasonable assumption. The verdict must depend on the comparison of parallel passages, and this is the method that I propose to follow.

64

I. *Quintus*

In Quintus the relevant passages in the Sack of Troy, if we disregard unimportant details, are the account of the wooden horse, Sinon and Laocoon, and the departure of Aeneas; also in Book 14 the description of the tempest and the scene with Aeolus that introduces it. I begin with the Sack of Troy.

1. The wooden horse

In Virgil, all that Aeneas knows about the wooden horse is that it was built *divina Palladis arte* (18) [with the divine craftsmanship of Minerva] by Epeos (264); Sinon says that it was built at the behest of Calchas (176f.), who had interpreted the omens sent by Minerva. In Quintus we find in great detail the version derived from the *Odyssey* (8.492ff.), which was also known to Virgil: Ἐπειὸς ἐποίησεν [Epeios made] the horse σὺν Ἀθήνῃ (12.104-56) [with the help of Athena], the instigator of the deception is Odysseus (25ff., 74f.); this, it is true, is not explicitly stated by Homer (he says only ὅν ποτ' ἐς ἀκρόπολιν δόλον ἤγαγε δῖος Ὀδυσσεὺς ἀνδρῶν ἐμπλήσας [which lord Odysseus once brought into the citadel as a trick, filling it with men] but it was interpreted in this way in the mythographic tradition also:

65 Apollod. *epit. Vat.* 5.14: ὕστερον δὲ ἐπινοεῖ δουρείου ἵππου κατασκευὴν καὶ ὑποτίθεται Ἐπειῷ [later he invented the building of the wooden horse and attributed it to Epeios]. At the same time Quintus has also given Calchas a role which is significant at least for the outward action: he gathers together the princes for the decisive assembly, advises them on the basis of a bird-omen to abandon the siege and to devise a trick, and finally announces that there are favourable omens which show approval of Odysseus' suggestion; when Neoptolemus and Philoctetes oppose the deception and want to fight on, Zeus' thunderbolt frightens them and confirms Calchas' words. There is no reason to believe that Calchas owes his rôle in Quintus to his prominence in Sinon's lying tale in Virgil, since Quintus frequently introduces him as a character elsewhere: in accordance with the tradition (Apollod. *epit. Vat.* 5.8) it is Calchas who announces that Philoctetes is indispensable (9.325); earlier he had prophesied the capture of Troy in the tenth year of the war (6.61); it is also he who urges that Neoptolemus should be fetched (6.64), so that Helenus loses his traditional rôle; and it is he who, in a passage which is certainly free invention on the part of Quintus, makes sure that Aeneas departs unharmed (13.333) and gives the order that Hecuba should be carried across the Hellespont after her metamorphosis (14.352).

2. Sinon

In the Sinon scene, the following is all that our two epics have in common: 'When the Greeks have sailed away, leaving Sinon behind, the Trojans rejoice and hasten to the shore.[103] They gaze in amazement at the huge horse. Sinon, who is not known to the Trojans, tells them in reply to their question that Odysseus had planned to sacrifice him to ensure the army's safe voyage home, but that he had escaped. The Greeks had been ordered by Calchas to dedicate the horse to Athena, to appease her anger.' In every other respect the treatment is as different as it could be. In Virgil, Sinon's story is that he has run away and hidden in the reeds. In Quintus (less happily) he says that he placed himself under the protection of the sacred votive offering. In Virgil, the unsuspecting Trojans are easily deceived by Sinon's lies, in Quintus they torture the Greek like a slave to extract the truth from him. In Virgil, all the emphasis is laid on Sinon's perjurious slyness, in Quintus on the steadfastness with which he sticks to his version despite all the tortures.[104] Virgil also gives us the 66 whole of the story that Sinon makes up about what had happened previously, Priam's part in the events,[105] the assertion that the fate of Troy depends on the horse and where it is to go, and that the Greeks will be returning soon; Quintus has nothing of all this. Despite that, could he have had Virgil's narrative before his eyes and deliberately changed it in this way, above all by abbreviating it? It is perhaps possible that Virgil, who narrated the events from the Trojan point of view, had directed all the light onto them and left the Greeks too much in the shadows for his taste, and that he was hoping to redress the balance by changing the sly deceiver Sinon into the hero, and representing the unsuspecting, pious Trojans as cruel and suspicious (although he does not take this line in, for example, the Laocoon story which follows, or indeed anywhere at all in his poem); but this would still leave unexplained his concision and brevity by comparison with the leisurely exposition in his model. Would he not have made full use of the rich material which lay before him, as is his custom in other parts of his poem? Above all, would he have passed over such an important motif as the significance of the horse for the destiny of Troy, thus deliberately dispensing with an admirable way of explaining why the Trojans actually pulled the horse into the city? He leaves this important point almost totally obscure.[106] I believe that this is a particularly clear indication that Quintus knows no 67 more than he tells us, in other words that those features which are common to Quintus and Virgil were ultimately derived from a common source; there is nothing among them that could not have been found in a prose epitome.[107]

The same applies to the last part of the story of the horse: a rope is flung around it, it is pulled into the city to the sound of singing or of the playing of flutes, part of the wall had to be torn down – none of these are things which Quintus need in fact have taken from Virgil.[108] On the other hand, Quintus says that Epeios had laid 'smoothly rolling logs' under the feet of the horse beforehand (425). Virgil, more thoughtful than Tryphiodorus (100), showed better judgement in omitting this detail from his version of Sinon's tale. What would be the point of the wheels if the builders intended the horse to stay where it was? So in Virgil the Trojans fetch the rollers later (235).

3. Laocoon

And now Laocoon. Quintus tells us the following about him: when Sinon had told

his lying tale, some believed him, others agreed with the advice given by Laocoon, who saw through the deception and suggested setting the horse on fire to see if there was anything hidden inside. And they would have followed his advice and escaped destruction if Athena had not been angry and made the earth shake under Laocoon; and dreadful pain and disease attacked his eyes; when he still persisted in giving the same advice, she blinded him. That was decisive: the Trojans pulled the horse into
68 the city. Laocoon persevered with his warning, but the Trojans took no notice of him, for fear of the gods' rebuke (says Quintus). Then Athena devised harm for the sons of Laocoon: she made two serpents come over the sea from Calydna; they devoured the two boys and disappeared beneath the earth; people still point out the place in the sanctuary of Apollo. The Trojans erected a cenotaph to the dead boys, at which the unhappy parents mourned.

How does this version stand in relation to the tradition? After the detailed analyses of the transmission of the story that have been made by Robert and Bethe, there is no need to go through the facts of the case at any great length. It seems clear to me that Quintus combined two versions of the tale. According to one version, Apollo sent the serpents; they came from the island of Calydna and killed the two sons of Laocoon in the temple of Apollo Thymbraeus. That was either as a punishment for an offence that the priest of Apollo had committed previously, or as a presage of the destruction that threatened Troy. According to the other version, which we find elsewhere only in Virgil, Laocoon had uttered a warning about the wooden horse; then two serpents come from Tenedos and kill Laocoon together with his sons on the sea-shore; the Trojans regard this as a divine punishment and proceed to pull the horse into the city. From the first version, Quintus has taken the island of Calydna, the location of the events inside the city, and the temple of Apollo Thymbraeus (which, however, is mentioned only as the place where the snakes disappear) the death of the sons only, and not of the father, and the time when the incident occurs, after the horse has been brought in. On the other hand, he agrees with Virgil on two points, that Laocoon warns the Trojans not to bring it in while they are still on the shore, and that the serpents are sent by Athena as a punishment for his warning. In order to combine the two versions he is obliged, first, to make Laocoon give his warning twice, and secondly, so that his punishment may lead to the decision about the horse, to invent a second punishment, which happens straight away, while they are still outside the city, the blinding, which he, like, for example, the seer Phineus, suffers because of his untimely prophecy. As usual, the author has to pay for combining the two versions: the death of Laocoon's sons has no consequences whatever and appears as pointless cruelty on the part of Athena, and why the serpents have to make for the sanctuary of Apollo is left totally unexplained.

Quintus, then, knew the Virgilian version of the story; but did he know it from Virgil? There are no important details on which they agree: no one will regard it as
69 significant that they both have the sea roaring, the serpents flicking their fangs and the Trojans running away in terror. On the other hand there is a large number of characteristic differences which show that Quintus is independent of Virgil. In Virgil Laocoon thrusts his spear into the side of the horse; in Quintus he contents himself with mere words, although one would think that an imitator must have realized how much more serious Laocoon's 'impiety' would seem if he actually

struck the horse. In Virgil the serpents pursue their course with terrifying determination, so that it is clear to everyone that they are obeying instructions from the gods; in Quintus everyone runs away, and only Laocoon and his sons stay behind – πέδησε γὰρ οὐλομένη Κὴρ καὶ θεός [for deadly doom and the goddess held them bound], says the poet, which shows that he was looking for a motive although a much better one was available to him in Virgil. The most important difference, however, is that in Virgil Laocoon's warning comes *before* Sinon appears, and his death occurs later so as to confirm Sinon's false story, for which the Trojans have already fallen (this order of events is not without its problems, but I have attempted to explain it above as the result of Virgil's particular standpoint). In Quintus Laocoon's punishment follows on the heels of his warning and serves to tip the scales, as after Sinon's story the Trojans were still not sure what to do, and Laocoon, who here enters the action for the first time, would otherwise have gained the upper hand in the argument. It is obvious, in my opinion, that Quintus has preserved the original version.

And do we really have no trace of the 'Virgilian' version anywhere else, other than in Virgil and Quintus, the version, that is, where the essential point is the connection of the miraculous serpents with Laocoon's warning? Indeed, Robert must have believed that it was only in Virgil's version that Laocoon had anything to do with the horse, and that was indeed so remarkable that we can understand how he arrived at his conclusions. But since then we have learnt from the epitome of Apollodorus (5.17) that Laocoon's warning about the horse does not appear only in Virgil. What might be the purpose of inventing this episode, which is a doublet of the old tradition whereby it was Cassandra who gave the warning?[109] I have already pointed out that Apollodorus mentions the warning: nevertheless the Trojans decide 70 not to destroy the horse, which they have already pulled into the citadel, and they turn their attention to sacrificing and feasting. 'But Apollo sends them a sign: two serpents…devour the sons of Laocoon'. Is it possible to combine both versions? Bethe has attempted to do so: 'During the sacrifice (or in Apollodorus rather during the εὐωχία [feasting] which follows the sacrifice) Apollo himself gives the final warning, after the voices of his prophets have fallen on deaf ears, by sending a sign from heaven'.[110] I consider that impossible. On what grounds? Is the prophet who gave the warning on Apollo's behalf now himself to serve as a terrible warning, by the loss of his sons and the extremely horrible nature of their death? Surely every ancient spectator would more probably have taken it as a condemnation of the warning. I am convinced that when the death of Laocoon's sons is reported *after* the warning, the *post hoc* must also be a *propter hoc*.[111] Why is it not in Apollodorus?[112] Because of the nature of our epitome, we are unable to come to a firm conclusion; but we should note how Laocoon is first introduced: Κασάνδρας δὲ λεγούσης ἔνοπλον ἐν αὐτῷ δύναμιν εἶναι, καὶ προσέτι Λαοκόωντος τοῦ μάντεως, τοῖς μὲν ἐδόκει κατακαίειν [when Cassandra, and also the seer Laocoon, claims that there is an armed contingent inside, some thought they should burn it]. In my opinion that is patched together very badly. Apollodorus, who is recounting Laocoon's death as a σημεῖον [sign] in accordance with one of his sources, must have taken from another source, which represented it as a punishment for the 71 warning, only the warning itself; or he may have simply combined the two versions from his mythographic sources; that would be characteristic of his method.[113] If that is so, we can reconstruct Quintus' mythographic source as follows: 'Laocoon's sons were killed, according to some authors, because he offended against Apollo; according to others it was a sign presaging the fall of Troy; others again say that he advised against taking in the wooden horse and that he, together with his sons, was therefore killed by serpents sent by Athena. Frightened by this, the Trojans trusted Sinon and pulled the horse into the city'.

4. Aeneas' departure

Aeneas' departure is narrated by Quintus (13.300ff.) as follows: Aeneas had fought bravely and killed many Greeks; now as he saw the city in flames, people and possessions being destroyed, wives and children being carried into slavery, he despaired at the fate of his ancestral city and thought of escaping, just as the steersman, when the ship is lost, climbs into the little lifeboat. Carrying his feeble old father, and leading his little son by the hand, he made his way over the corpses: Cypris guided him, protecting the husband, son and grandchild from harm (328):

> τοῦ δ' ἐσσυμένου ὑπὸ ποσσί
> πάντῃ πῦρ ὑπόεικε· περισχίζοντο δ' αὐτμαί
> Ἡφαίστου μαλέροιο, καὶ ἔγχεα καὶ βέλε' ἀνδρῶν
> πῖπτον ἐτώσια πάντα κατὰ χθονός, ὁππόσ' Ἀχαιοί
> κείνῳ ἐπέρριψαν πολέμῳ ἔνι δακρυόεντι.

[as he hurried along, the fire gave way under his feet everywhere: the blasts of strong Hephaestus parted around him, and the swords and javelins which the Achaeans hurled at him in the tearful war all fell harmlessly to the ground]. Then Calchas held his men back and ordered them to refrain from attacking them (338), for it was divinely decreed that by the Tiber this man should:

> τεύξέμεν ἱερὸν ἄστυ καὶ ἐσσομένοισιν ἀγητόν
> ἀνθρώποις, αὐτὸν δὲ πολυσπερέεσσι βροτοῖσι
> κοιρανέειν· ἐκ τοῦ δὲ γένος μετόπισθεν ἀνάξειν
> ἄχρις ἐπ' ἀντολίην τε καὶ ἀκαμάτου δύσιν ἠοῦς·
> καὶ μὰν οἱ θέμις ἐστὶ μετέμμεναι ἀθανάτοισιν,
> οὕνεκα δὴ πάις ἐστὶν ἐυπλοκάμου Ἀφροδίτης.

[found a holy city, a marvel to men of the future, and rule over far-scattered peoples: from him a race to come would rule as far as the rising and the setting sun. Indeed he is entitled to dwell with the immortals since he is the son of fair-tressed Aphrodite.] His life should be spared in any case because he had chosen to carry with him not gold and possessions, but his father and his son, which showed him to be an admirable son and father. The Greeks obeyed, and marvelled at him as at a god, but he went on, wherever his hastening feet should carry him.

It is clear that Quintus has combined two versions of the story with some degree of skill: according to one, Aphrodite rescued her own from the burning city; according to the other the Greeks were so impressed by Aeneas' piety that they allowed him and his family to depart unharmed. The first version is also the one used by Virgil, but he remodelled it to suit his purposes: Venus does not escort her son out of the city, but only from the citadel to his house.[114] Thus here, too, Quintus gives us the original version, not Virgil's remodelling. In the light of this, it proves nothing that the lines quoted above (328ff.) have an admittedly striking resemblance to the following lines in Virgil (632-3):

> *ducente deo flammam inter et hostis*
> *expedior, dant tela locum flammaeque recedunt.*

[with the goddess guiding me I won my way between the flames and the foes. The weapons let me through; the fires drew back from me.] This is an obvious way to make vivid the idea that they both had to express: 'to go in safety through the burning city and the enemy hosts'. In the second passage, Quintus has remembered *Odyssey* 22.255:

> οἱ δ᾽ ἄρα πάντες ἀκόντισαν ὡς ἐκέλευεν
> ἱέμενοι· τὰ δὲ πάντα ἐτώσια θῆκεν Ἀθήνη.

[they all threw their lances with all their might as he instructed: but Athena rendered them all fruitless].[115] But it has also been suggested that Calchas' prophecy must be derived from the *Aeneid*. There is in fact no doubt that it is based on Poseidon's famous prophecy at *Iliad* 20.307:

> νῦν δὲ δὴ Αἰνείαο βίη Τρώεσσιν ἀνάξει
> καὶ παίδων παῖδες, τοί κεν μετόπισθε γένωνται.

[but now the mighty Aeneas will rule over the Trojans and his children's children who will come after him]. This was amplified by Quintus to suit his context; he knew the story of the foundation of Rome and he knew of the apotheosis of Aeneas. He does not need to have had any further information; indeed one may say with certainty that he did not have the *Aeneid* before him as he wrote; of course he has Aeneas as the founder of Rome (for how can ἱερὸν ἄστυ καὶ ἐσσομένοισιν ἀγητὸν ἀνθρώποις [a holy city, a marvel for men of the future] be taken in any other way?); we might perhaps take this to be a vague utterance in the style appropriate to   73
prophecy, if we did not know that this tradition did in fact exist, and indeed persisted alongside the official Roman version until quite a late period.[116] Moreover, Quintus knows nothing about Anchises having been lamed by Zeus' lightning; he has to be carried πολυτλήτῳ ὑπὸ γήραϊ μοχθίζων [because he was wearied by a long- suffering old age]. Finally, the fact that Quintus (together with other accounts, see n. 95) mentions neither the rescue of the Trojan *sacra* and Penates nor Aeneas' wife cannot, in my opinion, be interpreted as a deliberate deviation from Virgil.

5. The Night Battle

The comparison of these individual episodes needs to be complemented by an overall comparison of the two accounts. If Quintus had indeed read Virgil's work, it left no impression on him. Unlike Virgil, he makes no attempt to bring any kind of unity to his depiction of the sack of Troy. All we find in Quintus is an attempt at a kind of grouping: general descriptions of battles and destruction (13.78-167 and 430-95) frame the individual episodes: the actual fighting is represented in these episodes by the deeds of Diomedes (168-210) and Neoptolemus (213-50), between which the Greek heroes are dealt with in a mere two lines; then comes an unconnected series of the five best-known scenes in the sack of Troy (251-429). The relatively broadly-drawn general descriptions and the rather feeble speeches that are inserted indicate that here too the poet is short of material. In that case would he have ignored the Androgeos scene, apparently invented by Virgil (370-401), and the fight for the citadel? Would he have discarded the link between the death of Coroebus and the rape of Cassandra, and the combination of the deaths of Polites and Priam into one effective episode?[117] That would have been a remarkable example of restraint on the part of a compiler who in other parts of the poem uses whatever comes his way!

6. Aeneas and the storm at sea

74 In Virgil (1.50ff.), Juno, wishing to destroy the Trojan fleet with a storm, goes to Aeolia, the home of the winds. Because they would otherwise carry away the land and sea with them in their violence, Jupiter has shut them away in dark caves, piled a huge mountain on top of them and given them Aeolus as their king, who sits there enthroned on a high citadel and rules over the raging winds. At Juno's request he thrusts his spear[118] into the mountain, and immediately all the winds come storming out and hurl themselves upon the sea and the land.

In Quintus (14.466ff.), Athena, wishing to punish the Greeks with a destructive storm, sends Iris to Aeolus, in Aeolia, where are the caves of the raging winds, enclosed all around with rugged cliffs, and close by, the home of Aeolus. There she meets him and his wife and his twelve children; at her request he goes outside, rips open the high mountain with a blow from his trident; the winds storm out, and hardly waiting to hear his instructions, they chase over the sea to the cliffs of Caphereus.

It is undeniable that there is a connection between these two accounts; so either Quintus drew on Virgil, or both go back to a common source. The latter possibility, in my view, can be raised to the status of a certainty.

The version which we find in Quintus is obviously derived from Homeric ideas and is still very close to Homer in many ways. According to Odysseus' account (10.1ff.), there lives on Aeolia, an island surrounded by a wall of bronze, rising up like a smooth cliff, Aeolus, a friend of the immortal gods, with his wife and their twelve children; Zeus has put him in charge of the winds, to lull them or to restrain them, whichever he wishes. This is precisely the picture of Aeolus and his powers which Quintus has in mind – but there is *one* new element in his version. The story in the *Odyssey* does not concern itself with the way in which Aeolus controls the winds. Perhaps they are held in by the bronze wall, or perhaps the leather bag which Odysseus is given is their usual container. Even in antiquity, literary critics found this leather bag too vulgar,[119] and possibly also too difficult to visualize. But other sources said that the winds lived in caves,[120] so it was an obvious move to transfer these caves to Aeolia, and since they have to be enclosed, to locate them in the depths of a mountain. To let the winds out all at once, Aeolus has to rip open the mountain, and to do this he is given a trident like Poseidon the earthshaker.[121] This sets the scene; the action, the despatch of Iris to the winds, comes from Book 23 of the *Iliad* (198). 75

In Virgil, the representations of the winds and of Aeolus are developed still further, in a very individual way. For artistic reasons, which will be discussed later, he is intent on arousing the listener's interest in the winds from the beginning; he therefore takes longer to describe them when they are introduced. Moreover, since the storm is to be depicted as one of supernatural violence, he wants to tell the listener beforehand just what it means to unleash the winds. Finally, since for the scene with Neptune he requires the winds to appear as *persons*, he needs to give an impression of them as powerful individuals from the beginning. He portrays them as prisoners, who have to be kept in a gaol, fettered, so that they will not destroy the whole world; who storm against their prison in violent rage, and who, as soon as a fissure is opened up, without needing any command, fling themselves with dreadful violence upon land and sea. Corresponding with this transformation of the material onto the grand scale, and this new personification of the winds, is the change in the rôle of Aeolus. He is no longer simply the 'friend of the immortals', put in charge of the winds, but a ruler and the governor of a prison, raised to this responsible position by Jupiter, who, as Guardian of the Universe, has to keep the powers of nature within bounds. As a king, Aeolus does not live in a mere 'house' as he does in Homer and Quintus, but sits on a lofty citadel and wields the sceptre as a sign of his rank. There is no more talk of his cosy family life; instead he is presented as a bachelor, as is shown by the fact that Juno offers him a pretty wife, *liberum procreandorum causa* [for the procreation of children]. His weapon is not the trident of a god in a folk-tale, but the lance of a hero. 76

If Quintus had derived his description from this description in Virgil, he would have been displaying a very delicate poetic tact in restoring the naïve Homeric traits without yielding even once to the temptation offered by the nature of his source to build up the scene in a heroic, grandiose and elevated manner. Those who know him will hardly think him capable of such an achievement; those who know Virgil will realize how characteristic of his art is the process of transformation that we have been able to identify here.[122]

A comparison of the descriptions of the sea-storm, which follow the Aeolus scene in Quintus and Virgil, confirms our conclusion and brings us one step nearer to their common source. The relationship of the two authors to Homer is reversed in this instance. Virgil's intention is not to give a depiction but a narrative of events,

and therefore he gives only a brief general description of the storm and the distress of the ships – just as he had previously used only two lines (34-5) to describe the safe part of the voyage – and narrates instead the progress and intensification of the destruction. For the details he relies as far as possible on Homer, the model for all such narratives, combining elements of the relevant descriptions in Homer in order
77   to make up his own.[123] The storm is chiefly modelled on the storm in Book 5 of the *Odyssey*, where the situation is closest to the present one; Apollonius has also supplied some details. Apart from the necessary changes in such details as the names of places and persons, there are only two lines which do not correspond with passages in Homer and Apollonius, namely 106-7:

hi summo in fluctu pendent, his unda dehiscens
terram inter fluctus aperit; furit aestus harenis.

[some hung poised on wave-crests; others saw the waves sink before them to disclose, below seething water and sand, the very bottom of the sea]. However, it is precisely these lines which correspond remarkably closely with Quintus' description of the storm, 14.492ff.:

νέας ἄλλοτε μέν που
ὑψηλὸν φέρε κῦμα δι᾽ ἠέρος, ἄλλοτε δ᾽ αὖτε
οἷα κατὰ κρημνοῖο κυλινδομένας φορέεσκε
βυσσὸν ἐς ἠερόεντα· βίη δέ τις ἄσχετος αἰεί
ψάμμον ἀναζείεσκε διοιγομένοιο κλύδωνος.

[now a high wave carried the ships through the air, and again they were carried rolling down a steep slope to the murky depths: and always an irresistible force belched up sand as the sea opened up.] Virgil's lines are distinguished by energetic brevity; the content of the two passages is identical, and even if the details are not exceptional in themselves[124] the fact that they occur in the same context indicates that there must be some connection. Otherwise, Quintus proceeds in a completely different way. After giving a detailed description of the departure of the Greeks and the safe earlier part of the voyage (370-418), he dwells at length on the general description of the storm and the distress of the ships (488-529), and then goes on to depict the shipwreck and the death of Ajax in just as much detail (530-89) and finally returns once more to the misfortunes of the other Greeks (590-610), culminating in Nauplius' revenge (611-28). Here we are miles away from the simplicity of the early epic. Quintus seems to have deliberately avoided any reminiscence of the well-known lines of the *Odyssey*; instead we are given an *ecphrasis* in the best style of Hellenistic and Roman poetry. It is quite obvious that in this passage Quintus is not expanding the narrative himself on the basis of brief mythographic memoranda, but is following a detailed description in an earlier poem: this is confirmed by comparing it with Seneca's description of the same sea-storm in his
78   *Agamemnon*, which, in spite of some major differences – Seneca was no mere translator – shares so many characteristic details with Quintus that it is quite clear that ultimately they reflect a common source.[125] There is not the slightest reason to

suppose that Quintus borrowed from Virgil the one short passage quoted above. We ought rather to conclude that both poets made use of one and the same description of the disastrous voyage home from Troy, and that Quintus took over the essentials, expanding them to some extent, whereas Virgil drew the inspiration for his Aeolus-scene from his source, but as far as the sea-storm was concerned, he borrowed only a single detail, while in other respects avoiding the mass of pictorial detail in his Hellenistic source in favour of the narrative simplicity of earlier epic. Who was the author of that common source I cannot say; we should not forget that more than one famous poet tried his hand at this very subject.[126] But Virgil himself has hinted at his source, as he tends to do elsewhere by means of his similes,[127] in that a description of the death of Ajax which he incorporates into Juno's speech (lines 39-45) is more detailed than is necessary for his immediate purpose.

II. *Tryphiodorus*

1. Helen

I can be considerably briefer in discussing Tryphiodorus. One important point, the participation of the gods in the destruction of Troy, has already been discussed above on p. 31, where I demonstrated that Virgil cannot have been Tryphiodorus' source. Another point can be settled by a different method: the detail that Helen summoned the Greeks with a torch, which, in all the accounts of the sack of Troy known to us, occurs only in Tryphiodorus (512-21) and Virgil (6.518), is not, as we might imagine, an invention of Virgil's, but is derived from Greek poetry,[128] and perhaps appeared already in Stesichorus.[129] Once we know that, it is easy to see that Virgil's account is a more elaborate version of the simple description in Tryphiodorus: so as to be able to raise the huge torch on the heights of the citadel without arousing suspicion, Helen persuades the women of Troy to form a chorus and perform a Bacchic dance, which she leads, carrying the torch like a maenad. It is clear that this detail was inserted to answer the question: how could Helen give the torch-signal without being noticed and without attracting attention to herself in the city? The earlier version, in which Sinon gave the torch-signal from Achilles' tomb outside the city, did not require special motivation.

2. Sinon

This leaves only the Sinon scene, and here there are similarities which at first sight might appear surprising. In Tryphiodorus, however, Sinon's entrance is quite different from the version in Virgil: naked and with his flesh torn by whip-lashes, he throws himself at Priam's feet; he pretends that his fellow countrymen have inflicted this punishment on him because he was unwilling to take flight with them and urged them to stay; then they left him behind in the enemy's land. Now he warns Priam not to offend Ζεὺς ἱκέσιος [Zeus, god of suppliants]: if he is slain by a Trojan, that will please the Greeks.[130] Priam reassures him:

ξεῖνε, σὲ μὲν Τρώεσσι μεμιγμένον οὐκέτ' ἔοικε
τάρβος ἔχειν· ἔφυγες γὰρ ἀνάρσιον ὕβριν 'Αχαιῶν.
αἰεὶ δ' ἡμέτερος φίλος ἔσσεαι, οὐδέ σε πάτρης
οὐδὲ πολυκτεάνων θαλάμων γλυκὺς ἵμερος αἱρεῖ

[Stranger, you need not be afraid any more, now that you are among Trojans: you have escaped the implacable violence of the Achaeans. You will always be our friend, and sweet longing for your country and its rich palaces will not seize you],
80   then he asks him what he is called and where he came from as well as about the significance of the horse. This is certainly very reminiscent of Priam's speech in Virgil:

quisquis es amissos hinc iam obliuiscere Graios,
  noster eris; mihique haec edissere vera roganti (147-8)

['Whoever you are, there are no Greeks here; forget them quickly and become one of us. Now answer my questions truthfully', etc.] But is there anything in Tryphiodorus that might lead us to suppose that his version is a derivative reworking of Virgil's? How simply and naturally the events unfold in Tryphiodorus! Sinon advised the Greeks not to leave – thus he deliberately shows himself to have been anti-Trojan, and this causes them to trust what he goes on to say; his fellow countrymen treated him badly and left him behind in enemy territory – with cruel irony, for that was just what he had wanted; because of this harsh treatment he turns to the enemy for protection – the old motif of the traitor who deserts, like Zopyrus et al. – and claims the right of a suppliant: Priam grants him this right and admits him to the community of the Trojans. In Virgil, Sinon is a prisoner, not a suppliant, and his reception is motivated to a lesser degree by Priam's compassion for him; so just before Priam's speech Sinon has to bewail the loss of his native country (137ff.): this makes the virtue of the Trojans appear greater – and that was part of Virgil's intention – but Tryphiodorus' version certainly seems closer to the original.
   Sinon then gives away the following information about the horse:

εἰ μὲν γάρ μιν ἐᾶτε μένειν αὐτοῦ ἐνὶ χώρῃ,
Τροίην θέσφατόν ἐστιν ἑλεῖν πόλιν ἔγχος 'Αχαιῶν·
εἰ δέ μιν ἁγνὸν ἄγαλμα λάβῃ νηοῖσιν 'Αθήνη,
φεύξονται προφυγόντες ἀνηνύστοις ἐπ' ἀέθλοις.

['If you allow it to remain here in your land, it is fated that the sword of the Achaeans will capture the city of Troy: but if Athena receives it as a sacred gift into her temple then the Greeks will flee with their task unaccomplished']. So here we have the Virgilian alternative that we found was missing from Quintus' version; but in Virgil all the motifs are developed and strengthened; we are aware of the trouble that he took to make the Trojans feel that it was absolutely essential to bring the horse into the city: the horse is the substitute for the stolen Palladium, and will protect the city in its place; the πόλεμος παλίνορσος Ἀχαιῶν (282) [renewed war with the Achaeans], which is only an alarming possibility in Tryphiodorus, is very much a reality in Virgil: the Greeks will return as soon as they have propitiated the 81 gods in their own country; instead of the promise in Tryphiodorus that if they take the horse into the city the Greeks will be put to flight again, Virgil makes Sinon offer a greater promise, that the descendants of the Trojans will themselves invade the country of the Greeks; finally, Tryphiodorus has only 'if you let the horse stand here'; whereas Virgil has 'if you should harm it'; that is just what Laocoon had already done, which makes it appear more urgent than ever to atone for his act and to pull the horse into the city. Everything, in my view, points towards the conclusion that Tryphiodorus' account is not a simplified and shortened version of Virgil's, but rather reflects the earliest source, and that Virgil's version is not an original creation, but an enhanced remodelling of an earlier source. And a little thought should show that it never was very likely that Virgil was the first to invent this alternative; if it is not to be found in the scanty mythographic epitomes that have survived, and Quintus did not find it either in his mythographic source, no one would wish to draw the conclusion that it did not exist before Virgil. What we have learnt from the story of Helen's torch-signal can, where necessary, serve as a warning against conclusions of such a kind.

Otherwise one looks in vain in Tryphiodorus' work for any echoes of Virgil which are not drawn from the common stock of the tradition; there is no trace in him of anything that may reasonably be claimed as Virgil's in the way of individual touches, motivation, ethos or composition. His artistic standpoint, diametrically opposed to Virgil's, is not one that is concerned with drama or pathos, and if he did know Virgil he certainly did not like him. Nor is he in the least interested in encyclopaedic completeness; what he enjoyed, and what he had a natural talent for, was decorating his grand material with graceful and interesting arabesques and original ornamentation. As a basis for this, all he needed was the traditional material that we may imagine was easily available to him and to his educated contemporaries.

Notes to Chapter 1

1. At 3.163ff. the Penates say: *est locus, Hesperiam Grai cognomine dicunt... hae nobis propriae sedes, hinc, Dardanus ortus Iasiusque pater, genus a quo* 5 *principe nostrum* [there is a region for which the Greeks use the name Hesperia... this is our true home: from here came Dardanus and Iasius, another chieftain of our blood, and founder of the Trojan nation]; cf. 7.205, 240. Thus Virgil (cf. G. Wissowa, *Gesammelte Abhandlungen zur römischen Religions- und Staatgeschichte* [Munich, 1904] 113 n. 3) has concluded from Dardanus' Italian origin that the *Phrygii penates* rescued by Aeneas are themselves Italian in origin. On this tradition see Thrämer in Pauly-Wissowa *RE* IV 2175, who is certainly right to regard Virgil as following it, not inventing it.

2. Ancient commentators often point this out, quite correctly: see H. Georgii, *Die antike Aeneiskritik* (Stuttgart, 1891) 46f., but note that he mistakenly concludes that their aim is to deflect a serious criticism of Aeneas' character. This is unfortunately one of numerous places in Georgii's book where references by the commentators to intentions of the poet that are not completely obvious are wrongly interpreted as forms of defence.

7   **3.** πρότερον εἰσελθὼν προσποίητος [having previously entered in disguise], Proclus; we are reminded of Odysseus disguised as a beggar (his πτωχεία).

8   **4.** Apollod. *epit. Vat.* 5.17.

   5. In what follows, I treat both Quintus and Tryphiodorus as representatives of a tradition independent of Virgil; for my reasons see the excursus (pp. 37f.) where there is also a fuller discussion of the mythographical tradition of the Laocoon story.

9   **6.** In Dio. Chrys. (*Or.* 59), Odysseus begins: εἰμὶ Ἀργεῖος τῶν ἐπὶ Τροίαν στρατησάντων [I am an Argive, one of those who took part in the expedition against Troy]: cf. Sinon, *neque me Argolica de gente negabo* [I will not deny that I am an Argive]. Odysseus has been grievously offended by the Greeks, ἐξ ὧν δικαίως σοὶ μὲν ἂν φίλος εἴην, κείνων δὲ ἐχθρός [because of which I should be justified in being your friend and their enemy]: cf. Virgil 2.158, *fas odisse viros* [it is right that I should hate them].

   7. *Fando aliquod si forte tuas pervenit ad auris Belidae nomen Palamedis et incluta fama gloria* [there may perhaps have come to your ears some mention of Palamedes, son of Belus, a king of great military renown]: cf. οἶμαι σε γιγνώσκειν τὸν Ναυπλίου παῖδα Παλαμήδην· οὐ γὰρ δὴ τῶν ἐπιτυχόντων οὐδὲ ὀλίγου ἄξιος συνέπλει οὔτε τῷ στρατῷ οὔτε τοῖς ἡγεμόσιν [I think you know of Palamedes, son of Nauplios. He was no ordinary or mean member of the expedition among the army and its leaders].

10   **8.** Based on Livy 22.48.

   9. Cf. Varro's definition of *victus* ('vanquished') quoted by Servius on 11.306. Punic treachery is well-known (*perfidia plus quam Punica* [treachery greater than Carthaginian]) (Livy 21.9, characterizing Hannibal); cf. 22.6.12; *Poeni foedifragi* [the Carthaginians breakers of treaties] (Cic. *De Off.* 1.38); *Afri gens periura* [the Africans, a perjured people] (Virg. *Catal.* 9.51); *ipse fons perfidiae...Karthaginienses* [the Carthaginians...the very originators of treachery] (Val. Max. 9.6 ext. 1); other examples in Otto, *Sprichwörter der Römer* s.v. *Punicus*; cf. also E. Wölfflin, *Archiv für latein. Lexicogr.* 7 [1892] 135-7; for example, a similar innocent faith in *fides Punica* [Carthaginian trustworthiness], according to highly coloured Roman accounts, betrayed the consul Cornelius Scipio Asina into the hands of his enemies (Münzer, Pauly-Wissowa *RE* IV 1486). But the Romans were also inclined to suspect perfidiousness in other enemies: *genus Numidarum infidum* [the faithless race of Numidians] (Sall. *Iug.* 46.3) cf. *fallacissima gens* [a most deceitful nation] (Cic. *Ad Att.* 11.7.3); the Ligurians are *insidiosi fallaces mendaces* [treacherous deceitful liars] according to Cato and Nigidius (Serv. on *Aen.* 11.700); Lucanians *ut pleraque eius generis ingenia sunt, cum fortuna mutabilem gerentes fidem* [like most of their race, changing their loyalty with their fortune] (Livy 8.24.6); *perfidus Samnis* [the perfidious Samnite] (Livy 9.3.2); the Sardinians *libertatem a servitute nulla re alia nisi mentiendi licentia distinguendam putant* [they believe the only thing that distinguishes freedom from slavery is the licence to tell lies] (Cic. *Pro Scaur.* 17.38); the Gauls are *suspecta gens ob infida multa facinora* [a nation which is suspect because of its many crimes of faithlessness] (Livy 21.52.7), the Germans *natum mendacio genus* [a nation born to lie] (Vell. 2.118); *Dacorum gens numquam fida* [the Dacian race is never to be trusted] (Tac. *Hist.* 3.46); the perfidy of the Parthians was also well-known: Hor. *Ep.* 2.1.112; *Odes* 4.15.23 cf. Tac. *Ann.* 13.38ff.; the Cappadocians as professional liars: *Schol. Pers.* 6.77; finally *pleraque barbarorum ingenia* [most barbarian characters] were thought to be unreliable: Livy 22.22.6.

10. *Graeci gens lingua magis strenua quam factis* [the Greeks, a race more energetic in speech than in action] (Livy 8.22.8); *gens ad fingendum parata* [a race ready to invent fictions] (Val. Max. 4.7.4); *Graecula cautio chirographi* [a Greek, i.e. unreliable, guarantee given by my own hand] known from Cic. *Ad Fam.: Ep.*   11
7.18.1, cf. *De Orat.* 1.47; *Pro Flacc.* 9ff. Otto, *Sprichwörter der Römer* s.v. *Graecus*.

11. More recent exegetes have contrived to find more subtleties: I am not convinced of the existence of the alleged ἀμφιβολίαι [ambivalences] in 154ff.

12. It is also not until this point that he divulges (*fas omnia ferre sub auras, si*   12
qua tegunt [158] [it cannot be sin for me to expose what the Greeks are hiding]), that the Greeks have only left in order to make a quick return and to renew the fighting (176-82), and have not, as he had maintained at 108ff., given up the struggle out of war-weariness. The contradiction between the two passages is entirely deliberate.

13. When people tell lies – for example, defendants in court cases – they can often be seen to invent a mass of apparently insignificant detail in order to give an appearance of verisimilitude.

14. E. Bethe, 'Vergilstudien I', *Rhein. Mus.* 46 (1891) 511ff. Followed by Sab-   13
badini, *Il primitivo disegno dell' Eneide* (Turin, 1900) 19ff.

15. There is no need to think that Virgil means the highest part of the citadel as   14
opposed to the lower part, any more than at 12.697 where Aeneas, storming Lavinium, *deserit et muros et summas deserit arces* [left the walls and the high citadel].

16. So too Dido (4.409) sees *arce ex summa* [from high on the citadel] the Trojans on the shore preparing to leave.

17. Similarly, Dido the *Queen* moves *magna iuvenum stipante caterva* (1.497,   15
4.136) [closely attended by a numerous, youthful retinue], King Helenus *multis comitantibus* (3.346) [with many attendants]; King Aeneas, it is true, *multis cum milibus* [with many thousands] but *magna medius comitante caterva* (5.76) [in the midst of a large crowd in attendance]; when Androgeos meets the Trojans in battle *magna comitante caterva* (2.370) [with a large crowd of attendants], this signifies that he is the leader of the company.

18. The poet clearly intended a development from *credita res* (196) [we believed   16
his story] to *ducendum ad sedes simulacrum conclamant* (232) [they shouted for the horse to be taken to its place]. Sabbadini fails to notice it when he writes (20): *allora i Troiani si persuadono che bisogna introdurre in città il cavallo. Ma come se già prima erano stati persuasi da Sinone?* [Then the Trojans decide that it is necessary to bring the horse into the city. But how can that be, if they had already been persuaded by Sinon?].

19. Goethe (*Über Laokoon* [*Werke*, 40-vol. edn] 30.317) laid emphasis on this in   17
interpreting the Laocoon episode in Virgil, too exclusively in my view, but correctly.

The objections of Plüss (*Vergil und die epische Kunst* [Leipzig, 1884] 42ff.) do not seem to me to get to grips with this interpretation. It is not a question of Virgil presenting an unforgivable act of stupidity by the Trojans in a kinder light, but of preventing their action from appearing as unforgivable stupidity. Otherwise I am in complete agreement with Plüss on many matters. I refer you to his own discussion of this.

20. Schiller likes to use this effect. I am thinking of such scenes as *Wallensteins Tod* III 16, after the long conversation between Wallenstein and the lance-corporal, when Buttler enters; or at the end of Act III after the scene between Max and Wallenstein when the cuirassiers storm in.

18   **21.** This is the reason, according to Bethe, why the phrase *s o l l e m n i s ad aras* [at the altar of the cult] is ill-adapted to the situation: the sanctuary would not have been able to survive the storm and stress of the ten years' war, or must at least have been out of use during those years. But why should the Greeks have destroyed the altar? And even if the altar had not been used, it remains the *ara sollemnis*, i.e. the place where sacrifice was offered according to established sacred custom, in contrast to a turf altar erected for a single sacrifice, of the kind that we often find in the *Aeneid*. Furthermore, the epithet is very suitable here, because this is the first time the sacrifice is being offered to Neptune again at his own sacred place (perhaps newly rededicated – does it make any difference?).

22. It might be objected that no reader would be aware of this connection unless he knew his Euphorion by heart. But do we know that Virgil could not assume this familiarity among the élite of his readership? Again, after Thymoetes' advice to pull the horse into the city, he continues *sive d o l o seu iam Troiae sic fata ferebant* (34) [perhaps out of treason or perhaps because Troy's fate was already fixed], and he must have assumed that this would mean something to one or another of his readers; but that would only be the case if they knew Euphorion's version (which we know from Servius *ad loc.*). It did not matter if the average reader missed these allusions; they were there for the connoisseur to enjoy.

20   **23.** Quintus 12.480: Τῶν δ' ἔτι σῆμα φαίνεθ' ὅπου κατέδυσαν ἐς ἱερὸν Ἀπόλλωνος Περγάμῳ ἐν ζαθέῃ [their memorial still can be seen where they entered the temple of Apollo in holy Pergamon]. This is probably derived from local tradition.

21   **24.** All of this, the *falsa gaudia* (6.513) [deluded joy], is indicated later by a single word, *urbem somno* vinoque *sepultam* (265) [a city buried in a sleep deepened by *wine*]. It goes without saying that the cup circulates at festivities (*festa fronde* [249] [with festal greenery]); this only needs to be mentioned to explain why the surprise attack succeeds so rapidly.

22   **25.** Sabbadini op. cit. n. 14 above, 22.

26. Similarly, Eurylochus' speech (*Od.* 10.251ff.) is much more concise than the earlier narrative of Odysseus.

23   **27.** *Flammas cum regia puppis extulerat, fatisque deum defensus iniquis...laxat claustra Sinon* (256ff.) [the king's ship displayed a fire-signal; and Sinon under the divine protection of an unjust destiny...released the Greeks from their confinement]. This is now usually understood not, with Heyne (referring to Sen. *Agam.* 427, *signum recursus regia ut fulsit rate* [when the signal for retreat shone from the

king's ship]), as the signal to depart, but as the signal to Sinon; correctly, in my opinion, for the former is a totally unimportant detail, and there is no need whatever for it be be mentioned here in close connection with Sinon's action. The other sources have only the fire-signal given by Sinon, or by Antenor instead of him (schol. Lycophron 340), or by Helen: this last version is followed byVirgil (6.518) in the speech of Deiphobus, and Virgil no doubt had this later passage in mind when he kept this motif in reserve for it. But he obviously feels the need to establish a connection between the fleet and Sinon, so as to explain the synchronization of their movements, and so he reverses the traditional motif. If one thinks about it, Sinon needs to have accurate information about the approach of the fleet, so as not to open the horse too soon.

28. Virgil names nine, not in the shapeless list of the mythographers, but arranged artistically in three groups of three. Of course this does not mean that there may not have been more; there were, for example, twenty-two in Tryphiodorus' list (152ff.), thirty plus in Quintus (12.314), while others even speak of a hundred, or thousands. Virgil could not omit the list, since it was a standard feature of any account of the fall of Troy. The names are in the tradition: we find Neoptolemus, Menelaus, Odysseus, Sthenelus, Thoas and Epeos in Quintus, Acamas in Tryphiodorus (cf. Paus. 1.23.8), Machaon is named as coming out of the horse in the pseudo-Hippocratic *Epistle* 27, p. 318 Herch. (already quoted by Heyne as *Thessalus* in πρεσβευτικῷ; I owe the identification to a timely communication from Marx); this leaves only Thessandrus unattested elsewhere. Tradition also plays a hand in making Epeos come last, as in Quintus (329) and Tryphiodorus (182): there the heroes are mentioned by name as they climb into the horse, and of course Epeos is the one who knows best how the fastening works.

29. That, too, is tradition, Apollod. *epit.* 5.20. Elsewhere it is a ladder, see Paulcke, *De Tabula Iliaca quaestt. Stesichoreae* (Diss. Königsburg, 1897) 81.

30. Ancient authors frequently transfer 'calmness' from the night to the moon, the ἄσυχος δαίμων [quiet divinity] (Theocr. 2.11), and the stars, the *taciturna noctis signa* [the silent night signs] (Hor. *Odes* 2.8.10); it is irrelevant in this passage that the new moon was called *luna silens* [the silent moon]; cf. Stat. *Theb.* 2.58: *per Arcturum mediaeque silentia Lunae* [by Arcturus and the silence of the moon at midnight]. The adjective *amica* [friendly] must refer to *luna*, the moon that shows them the way; if Virgil meant that they succeeded in remaining unnoticed because of the friendly silence of the night, it would hardly be consistent to mention the moonlight.

31. Schol. Eurip. *Hec.* 910: νὺξ μὲν ἔην μέσση, λαμπρὰ δ᾽ ἐπέτελλε σελήνη [it was midnight, and the bright moon was rising], quoted by Callisthenes as proof that the poet sets the destruction of Troy on the eighth day of the waning of the moon in the month of Thargelion; F. Marx (*Rostocker Prog.* [1889/90] 13) also refers to the representation on the Etruscan mirror IV 2.CCCXCIX Gerh. of the rape of Cassandra by Ajax, where, however, the identification of Selene is not completely certain. Hellanicus set the event on a night when the moon was full (Clem. Alex. *Strom.* I p. 139 Sylb.; for this and other evidence cf. Müller, *Fr. Hist. Gr.* I 568; Usener, *Arch. für Religionswissenschaft* VII [1904] 313f.), but we do not know whether he was following an earlier tradition. Among later writers only Petronius in his *Troiae Halosis* 54 has a full moon: *iam plena Phoebe candidum extulerat iubar* [now the full moon had shown her bright light].

25   **32.** *nox atra cava circumvolat umbra* (360) [black night surrounds us in hollow darkness], *per caecam noctem* (397) [in the utter darkness], *si quos obscura nocte per umbram fudimus insidiis* (420) [those whom in the darkness we had sent hurrying away in the night-shadows]. Otherwise only at 621, when the bright, heavenly vision of Venus suddenly disappears, *spissis noctis se condidit umbris* [she vanished into the dense shadows of the night] which gives a splendid effect of contrast; also during the flight, *ferimur per opaca locorum* (725) [on we went, keeping to the shadows].

33. In just the same way, Virgil juxtaposes the darkness of the night and the brightness of the moon in the Nisus episode: Euryalus' helmet betrays him to the enemy *sublustri noctis in umbra...radiisque adversa refulsit* (9.373) [gleaming in the night-shadows...it reflected rays of light], and the moon then shows Nisus his destination (403); in the dense wood *rara per occultos lucebat semita calles* (383) [only here and there was there a glimmer of a path among the hidden pathways]; on the other hand, Nisus is hidden from his enemy by the dark shadows (411, 425). The references to light in the account of the fall of Troy have often been criticized (probably first by Wagner, *Quaestt. Virg.* XXXX 2) but the correct interpretation was first given I think by Kviçala, *Neue Beiträge zur Erklärung der Aeneis* 22.

26   **34.** *Vit-on jamais de mieux amené ni qui prépare un plus vif sentiment que ce songe d'Énée...peut-on lire cet endroit sans être ému?* [Did you ever see anything which is better introduced or which gives rise to a more intense emotion than this dream of Aeneas...can anyone read this passage without being deeply moved?]. Fénelon, *Lettre sur les occupations de l'Académie* V. Chateaubriand called the scene *une espèce d'abrégé du génie de Virgile* [a kind of encapsulation of Virgil's genius] (*Génie du christianisme* II 4.11). A hint of the right interpretation is given by Weidner, whose commentary on *Aeneid* I and II (Leipzig, 1869) is unsatisfactory in other respects but does at least have the merit of attempting to come to a deeper understanding of Virgil's artistic intentions.

27   **35.** Cf. Otto Ludwig, 'Handlungsszenen als Zustandsbilder', *Studien* I (1891) 454.

36. *Alii rapiunt incensa feruntque Pergama* [Troy is afire and the rest are looting and pillaging]: however, this is the only reference to flames in the scene involving Androgeos and Coroebus. Virgil has no need of the bright light of the flames here, and the Trojans are looking for shadowy parts of the city to practise their stratagem.

37. Apollod. *epit.* 5.23; Procl. *Iliup.*, cf. Tryph. 680.

28   **38.** As in Quintus' version, as well as in Virgil (and Ovid). See the excursus at the end of this chapter. Quintus also makes the fire start during the battle: 13.82, 304, 316, 431ff., 442, 452, 458, 461.

39. Of course it is a completely different matter when in 12.569ff. Aeneas throws fire into the still unconquered city of Laurentum, to force it to surrender.

40. *Sigea igni freta lata relucent* (312) [the wide straits of Sigeum are lit up by the burning]: a painter's touch, without significance for the story.

41. *Succurritis urbi incensae* (352) [the city which you would rescue is already ablaze].

42. Chapter III, section 3 below.   29

43. Timaeus: Wissowa, *Hermes* 22 (1887) 41. The legend with slight differences also appears in Lycophron 1263ff.; Varro ap. schol. Veron. *Aen.* 2.717; Diod. 7.2; ps-Xen. *De Venatione* 1.15; and, in a very abbreviated form, Apollod. *epit.* 5.21.

44. Dion. Hal. 1.46ff.

45. He need not, of course, have read Hellanicus himself; it is hard to believe   30
that Dionysius did either. Here too, both may have made use of a common source.

46. Hence the very deliberate phrase *victor Sinon* (329) [Sinon victorious]; the   31
Trojans and their gods are already *victi* [defeated] at the beginning of the battle (320, 354, 367; cf. 452); the enemy's sword is drawn not for battle but for murder (*parata neci* [334] [ready for killing]). Here too, it is parallels from Roman historiography that can throw most light on Virgil. Cicero still knows of a battle lost at Caudium (*De Offic.* 3.109; *Cato maior* 41); Livy will not allow anything of the kind, but expressly denies that swords were drawn (9.5.10): everything was decided by the ambush and the stupidity of the generals. At the Allia, in exactly the same way, the blame is laid on the incompetence of the generals and the surprise attack of the enemy: it does not amount to a real battle (5.38). 'Both nations and individuals feel shame at a failure which reveals the limitation of their strength, greater than even the greatest sense of shame that they feel when through laziness and cowardice they have not bothered to make any effort at all: in the former case their highflown pretensions are shattered, in the latter they remain intact' (Niebuhr, *Römische Geschichte* III 248): *mutatis mutandis* this may be applied to the situation here.

47. To understand this passage, we should recall that very similar expressions   32
are used in the description of the battle-fury of Turnus when he is maddened by Allecto (7.460-2): *arma amens fremit, arma toro tectisque requirit, saevit amor ferri et scelerata insania belli, ira super* [out of his wits, he roared for weapons and hunted for them by his bedside and all through the house. In him there rioted the bloodthirsty lust of the blade, the accursed lunacy of war, and, above all, anger]. It is significant that Aeneas, in the grip of mindless fury, has no thought whatever for his family here. Further discussion of this later.

48. It is wrong to take the pointed *sententia una salus victis, nullam sperare salutem* (354) [nothing can save the conquered but the knowledge that they cannot now be saved] as meaning that Aeneas hoped that desperate courage might yet be rewarded (commentators have cited as parallels for this meaning Justin 20.3: *dum mori honeste quaerunt feliciter vicerunt, nec alia causa victoriae fuit quam quod desperaverunt* [while they sought to die honourably, they were fortunate enough to conquer, and the only reason for their victory was their despair], or Hannibal's words in Livy 21.44: *nullum contemptu vitae telum ad vincendum homini ab dis immortalibus acrius datum est* [no sharper weapon for conquering has been given to man by the immortal gods than contempt for life]; the notion is rather 'in defeat, a man who hopes to save his life will either flee or surrender; but for me and you, these means of escape are not possible: for us nothing remains but death'.

49. However, this particular expression may have been chosen to suggest that   33
Panthus held the office of chief priest, since Apollo is the special protecting deity of Troy.

50. *Pergameumque larem et canae penetralia Vestae...veneratur* (5.744) [he   34 paid reverence in prayer to the God of the Homes in Troy's citadel, and to the inner shrine of Vesta the silver-haired].

51. Only the last two letters, ων, are preserved, which excludes Anchises and Panthus; it seems hopeless to try to guess the name (Paulcke op. cit. 70).

52. The ancient commentators understood this correctly: see Servius on 320f. It is idle to ask why a priest of *Apollo* should rescue the *sacra* from the shrine of Vesta. In Rome there was no separate *sacerdos Vestae*. During the sack of Rome by the Gauls it is the Flamen Quirinalis who, together with the Vestal Virgins, rescues the *sacra publica* (Livy 5.36ff.); I doubt whether we should conclude from this that there were close connections between this Flamen and the cult of Vesta.

53. *Nec te tua plurima, Panthu, labentem pietas nec Apollinis infula texit* (429) [and you, Panthus, even all your holiness and Apollo's own emblem on your brow could not save you in your falling], a clear reference to the incident in the *Iliad* (15.521) referred to above, where the priestly status of Panthus even saved his son from death.

54. Wissowa, in the article in which he elucidated the tradition concerning the Roman Penates (*Hermes* 22 [1887] 29ff. [= *Gesamm. Abhandl. z. röm. Religions- u. Stadtgesch.* 94ff.]; cf. also his article in Roscher's *Lexikon der Mythologie* III 1897ff.) mentions the 'vague' nature of Virgil's references, implying that he failed to give a clear and consistent picture of them. Virgil was right not to do so: it was difficult or even impossible to represent the mysterious Penates in such a way. Virgil clearly follows Varro in this, as he nearly always does in sacred matters. The double expression *sacra patriique penates* which (*vel sim.*) is used most frequently in the second book (but also simply *sacra Troiae* [293, 717]) allows the imagination a great deal of freedom. Vesta and the sacred flame (297) which Varro also connects closely with the cult of the Penates, can also be thought of as included with them; since it was hardly possible not to mention the sacred flame, but since it was also difficult to imagine it being transported, it finds its place in Aeneas' dream-vision. Virgil makes use of the identification of the Penates with the *magni dei* (which is also Varronian) when he wants to emphasize their power: 3.12, cf. 8.679; the figure of epexegesis with copula (*penates et magni di*: cf. E. Norden, *Antike Kunstprosa²* [Leipzig, 1909] 127) appears for the third time in the expression *effigies sanctae divom Phrygiique penates* (3.148): if the Penates (following the traditional version: Dion. Hal. 1.67) are to appear to Aeneas himself in a dream, they must be thought of as *statues* of gods, naturally miniature ones, since they are carried around; so they must be something like the *sigilla* [statuettes] honoured in the Roman household cult. Varro (schol. Varron. *Aen.* 2.717) also calls them *sigilla*, and, in view of the established use of this word, Wissowa can hardly have been right in suggesting that he was referring to aniconic symbols (whatever Timaeus understood by his κηρύκια). Virgil refrained from indicating specific divinites, as did Varro in the *Antiquitates*. The poet was right not to embark on the speculations which Varro put forward in other passages.

55. For example, Frontinus *Strat.* 3.2.4: the Arcadians suddenly attack a fortress of the Messenians *factis quibusdam armis ad similitudinem hostilium...admissi per hunc errorem* [they made some weapons to look like those of the enemy...they were admitted as a result of this confusion]. Ibid. 3.11: *Timarchus Aetolus occiso Char-*

made Ptolemaei regis praefecto clamide interempti et galeari ad Macedonicum ornatus est habitum: per hunc errorem pro Charmade in Saniorum portum receptus occupavit [Timarchus the Aetolian, after killing Charmades, King Ptolemy's general, dressed himself up in Macedonian fashion in the cloak and helmet of the dead man. Through this deception he was admitted in Charmades' place into the harbour of the Sanii and took posession of it].

56. It is as if Virgil wished to contrast the wicked *perfidia* [treachery] of Sinon   37
with the *dolus* [deception] sanctioned by martial law; although it is true that Servius (on 381) believes that Coroebus' words *dolus an virtus, quis in hoste requirat?* [against an enemy, what does it matter whether it is deception or valour?] character-ize him as *stultus: cum sit turpis dolo quaesita victoria.* [foolish, since a victory won by deception is disgraceful]. Valerius Maximus (7.4.1) gives the ancient view of stratagems: *illa pars calliditatis egregia et ab omni reprehensione procul remota* [that kind of cunning is splendid. and far removed from any blame]; but the ruse must not develop into betrayal or the abuse of a noble trust as in the case of Sinon or the similar case of Sex. Tarquinius, who overcame Gabii *minime arte Romana, fraude et dolo* [by that most un-Roman of arts, trickery and deception] (Livy 1.53.4).

57. Understandably, Virgil follows the version of the story in which Cassandra is merely dragged from the altar, *trahitur* [is dragged] (cf. Eur. *Tro.* 71: ἡνίκ' Αἴας εἷλκε Κασάνδραν βίᾳ [when Ajax dragged Cassandra by force] [Paus. 10.26.3 etc.]: Töpffer in Pauly-Wissowa *RE* I 938); Aeneas could not mention her rape, which was invented in Hellenistic times to make Ajax's crime seem greater. On her chains, see Leo, *Hermes* 37 (1902) 44ff.; cf. also Eur. *Ion* 1403.

58. At least, it is only in Virgil that we hear of a fight over Cassandra. Even the   38
representation on the Vivenzio vase (a hydria by the Kleophrades Painter in Naples, *ARV²* 189.74) does not necessarily presuppose it (a dead man lies at the feet of Ajax, who is seizing Cassandra).

59. It has been objected that the discovery is reported (*illi etiam si quos... fudimus insidiis...apparent; primi clipeos mentitaque tela adgnoscunt* [420] [we were even confronted by some of those whom we had routed by our strategem: they were the first to see through our deceptive weapons and shields]) only after the account of how the Greeks, provoked by the rescue of Cassandra and reinforced by companions who come storming up from all around, have pressed in on the Trojans. I do not believe that one should assume (with Weidner, Conington and Deuticke) that Virgil intended to describe two stages of the struggle: (1) Ajax and his compan-ions fight over Cassandra in the belief that it is their fellow-Greeks who are contesting their prey (413-9); (2) the Greeks who had previously fled reassemble and uncover the ruse (420-3). In that case, Virgil would have had to reserve the terrible violence of the attack, which is made vivid by the simile (416-9), for the climax of the second stage of the struggle; and why should the *Danai undique collecti* [Greeks gathering from all around], the *Atridae Dolopumque exercitus omnis* (413-15) [Atridae and all the Dolopian army], side so decisively with Ajax and against the group whom they took to be their compatriots? Clearly Virgil is thinking of those who had previously been deceived as being among the *Danai undique collecti* (413); we should note that even in 413-9 nothing is said of the actual fighting (which is not mentioned until 424) but only of hostile crowds storming in.

The disguise is not said to have been penetrated until the end of this description. This is so that the defeat of the Trojans should appear to be the direct result of their being recognized. One only has to imagine lines 420-3 inserted after 412 (as L. Müller suggested) to see how *ilicet obruimur numero* (424) [weight of numbers bore us down] will then hang in the air; quite apart from the fact that the return of those who have previously been driven away will appear to be a mere coincidence. On the other hand, it is, strictly speaking, true to say that, in the text as it now stands, the explanation of the furious attack by the united Greeks appears too late (Schiller remedied this in his German version by boldly paraphrasing *gemitu* [groaning] in 413 as 'the screams of the dying have already long betrayed us'); here, too, the poet thought it more important to put an energetic emphasis on the dramatic *peripeteia* than to produce an absolutely faultless motivation.

60. *Penelei dextra* (425) [by the hand of Peneleus], whereas the tradition (Paus. 10.27.1) said Neoptolemus or Diomedes. Neoptolemus is not allowed to appear until more time can be devoted to him (469); Diomedes is not mentioned at all in the *Iliu Persis*; is Virgil perhaps protecting the reputation of the later Italian settlers (cf. 11.225ff.)? Virgil probably simply took over Peneleus from a catalogue of heroes in the horse (Tryph. 180).

39   **61.** That there were more than the seven named is implied by *confertos audere in proelia vidi* (347) [I saw them shoulder to shoulder, dauntless for battle], cf. *socia agmina credens* (371) [mistaking us for some of his own troops]; and one does not necessarily have to assume that the incomplete line 346 indicates that Virgil intended to name any more. Similarly in 6.773ff. a few names of Latin cities are listed to stand for the thirty, and likewise the names mentioned at 261ff. are only the most important ones: see above, n. 28.

40   **62.** Virgil might have drawn his inspiration from Priam's words *Iliad* 22.60ff.: αὐτὸν δ' ἂν πύματόν με κύνες...ἐρύουσιν (66) [myself, last of all, dogs...will tear apart].

63. The tradition had been unanimous in speaking of Ζεὺς Ἑρκεῖος; Virgil deliberately replaces him with the Penates (514; 517) because he was presenting them

41   as the ancestors of Rome (according to Dion. Hal. 1.67.3 Penates can also be translated Ἑρκεῖοι) and he locates this altar of the Penates, according to the old Roman custom, in the *atrium*. Scholars have rightly reminded us that Augustus transplanted a wild palm growing outside his house *in compluvium deorum Penatium* [into the courtyard of the Penates]. The *penetralia* (485) are the same as the *atria* (484), as is shown by 7.59: *laurus erat tecti medio in penetralibus altis* [there was a laurel in the centre of the palace, within the high-roofed innermost part]; moreover it is obvious that the Penates would be located in the *penetralia: penates...etiam penetrales a poetis vocantur* [the Penates are also called 'gods of the interior' by poets], Cic. *De Nat. Deorum* 2.68; μύχιοι, Dion. Hal. *ad loc.; Iuppiter Herceus...quem etiam deum penetralem appellabant* [Jupiter Herceus...whom they also called the god of the interior] [Paulus 101]; cf. Wissowa, *Religion der Römer*, 104.8.

64. On this type of concise *propositio* of the theme, followed by a fuller development, see Norden 275.

65. It is a different matter in lines 483ff., *apparet domus intus et atria longa patescunt* [the interior stood revealed. A long vista of galleries was exposed] etc.

(i.e. to Neoptolemus, after he has broken down part of the door). Here, certainly, Aeneas is narrating from the viewpoint of others, but this is acceptable since he has 42 clearly imagined himself in their position. While the fighting is still raging at the door, the women wander through the halls, and bid farewell to their beloved old home (489f.); when the enemy break in, they take refuge at the altar; it is only then that Aeneas can see *Hecubam centumque nurus* [Hecuba and her hundred princesses] from above.

66. To be fair, it should be said that Quintus clearly intended to make the brief preceding speech of old Ilioneus, in which he pleads as a suppliant for his life, a foil for Priam's words: that is to say, he did have the beginnings of an artistic purpose.

67. Whether the tree shading the altar on the Naples hydria by the Kleophrades Painter is intended to represent a laurel (as e.g. Baumeister, *Denkm.* I 742 asserts), which would imply that here too Virgil is following a tradition, I am unable to decide.

68. Cf. Paulcke loc. cit. n. 29 above, 39, 51.   43

69. See Luckenbach, *Verhältnis der griechischen Vasenbilder zu den Gedichten der epischen Cyclen* 632; Robert, *Bild und Lied* (Berlin, 1881) 74.

70. Cf. Robert op. cit. 60.

71. We may compare the closing words of the narrative of the *paidagogos* in 44 Sophocles *Electra* (757), of the messenger in *Andromache* (1161), the *Bacchae* (1151), *Heracles* (1013) etc.; on the ἐπιφωνεῖν διηγήσει [concluding narrative] suited to the style of drama, see Theon *Prog.* II 91 Sp. Aeneas concludes (557) *iacet ingens litore truncus, avolsumque umeris caput et sine nomine corpus* [his tall body was left lying headless on the shore, and by it the head hacked from his shoulders: a corpse without a name]. In Pacuvius (Serv. on 557 and 506) Neoptolemus captured Priam in his palace and killed him at Achilles' tomb; *tunc eius caput conto fixum circumtulit* [then he carried his head around fixed to a pole]. Virgil wanted to use this version of the tradition, in so far as it could be reconciled with his principal source, as it suited his anti-Greek viewpoint (cf. on combining different versions in this way, the excursus on sources at the end of this chapter, and Norden 255f.). Admittedly, Aeneas could not have known the facts that he narrates here (see above p. 10) but could only visualize them from his knowledge of Neoptolemus: for it was a most barbarous custom for an enemy to display as a trophy the head of a man he 45 has slain: cf. 9.465, the Rutuli; 12.511 Turnus. The corpse was not even allowed to burn where it was, amidst the blazing ruins of the king's palace, but was thrown onto the desolate shore; this completes the picture of an inhuman hatred that persists beyond death (Seneca seized on this: *magnoque Iovi victima caesus Sigea premis litora truncus* [*Tro.* 140] [slain as a victim to great Jupiter you lie headless on the shore of Sigeum], cf. *ibid.* 55: *caret sepulcro Priamus et flamma indiget ardente Troia* [Priam lacks a tomb and has no pyre though Troy is burning]).

72. This has been shown conclusively by, among others, Thilo (preface to his edition XXXIff.) and Leo (*Plaut. Forschungen*[2] [Berlin, 1912] 42.3); now Norden (443, 447) demonstrates that the handling of *synaloiphe* also betrays the non-Virgilian origin of the lines. The language not only contains very obvious mistakes (some of which had already been pointed out by Peerlkamp) but displays throughout an inability to use Virgilian diction: I would point to *servantem, aspicio, erranti, sibi*

infestos, praemetuens, invisa, exarsere ignes animo, subit ira...ulcisci, parto trium-pho, Iliadum turba, exstinxisse nefas, ferebar: all these are echoes of Virgilian diction but are un-Virgilian in choice of word, meaning or combination, and there are too many examples in a few lines to be explicable by chance. The most recent defenders of the authenticity of the passage (H.F. Fairclough, *Class. Phil.* 1 [1906] 221ff.; Gerloff, *Vindiciae Vergilianae* [Diss. Jena, 1911]) are no more convincing than their predecessors; how, for example, can one justify the expression *sceleratas poenas* by referring to *sceleratum limen* at 6.563 (see Norden *ad loc.*)? The 'paral-lel' scene at the beginning of *Odyssey* 20 where the hero cannot decide whether to kill the impudent slave-girls now or later and then Athena assures him of her help, seems to me to bear so slight a resemblance to it that I find it hard to believe that it

46   would have occurred to Virgil's interpolator – though of course it may have done. Gerloff's main error is his mistaken conclusion concerning the facts of the trans-mission of this passage (see now also Leo's remark, *Monolog in Drama*, 5.1), moreover he does not discuss the diction. Hartmann's article in favour of the lines, *Mnemosyne* (1905) 441ff. is so rhetorical that there is no way of refuting it.

47   **73.** *Talia iactabam* (588) [such were my wild words] i.e. not simply thoughts.

   74. The groan of shock at *Odyssey* 12.371: Ζεῦ πάτερ ἠδ' ἄλλοι μάκαρες θεοί [Father Zeus and ye other blessed gods] etc. (οἰμώξας δὲ θεοῖσι μετ' ἀθανάτοισι γέγωνον [370] [I groaned and cried aloud to the immortal gods]) should not be regarded as a soliloquy.

48   **75.** This has already been observed by Emmenessius; the borrowing is quite clear: *Or.* 1137: εἰ μὲν γὰρ εἰς γυναῖκα σωφρονεστέραν ξίφος μεθεῖμεν, δυσ-κλεὴς ἂν ἦν φόνος· νῦν δ' ὑπὲρ ἁπάσης Ἑλλάδος δώσει δίκην, ὧν πατέρας ἔκτειν', ὧν τ' ἀπώλεσεν τέκνα...ὀλολυγμὸς ἔσται, πῦρ τ' ἀνάψουσιν θεοῖς, σοὶ πολλὰ κἀμοὶ κέδν' ἀρώμενοι τυχεῖν, κακῆς γυναικὸς οὕνεχ' αἷμ' ἐπράξαμεν [if

49   we were putting to the sword a good woman, that would be an infamous murder: but instead the woman who killed their fathers and ruined their children will pay the penalty on behalf of all Greece...there will be shouting, they will light fires to the gods, praying that many blessings should come to you and me because we *shed the blood of an evil woman*...] (that is what is intended by *sceleratas sumere poenas*) ...οὐ δεῖ ποτ' οὐ δεῖ Μενέλεων μὲν εὐτυχεῖν, τὸν σὸν δὲ πατέρα καὶ σὲ κἀδελφὴν θανεῖν, δόμους τ' ἔχειν σούς, δι' Ἀγαμέμνονος δόρυ λαβόντα νύμφην [it surely must not come about that Menelaus should thrive while your father and you and your sister die; that he should have your home after taking his bride by Agamemnon's spear]. The questions *occiderit ferro Priamus* [shall Priam have fallen by the sword?] etc. are very clumsily substituted for Euripides' pattern of clauses, and are weak imitations of such passages as 4.590: *pro Iuppiter! ibit hic et nostris inluserit advena regnis?* [Ah, Jupiter! Is this stranger to make a mock of my realm, and calmly go?] (where *ire* and *inludere* have not yet taken place) and 9.783: *unus homo...tantas strages i m p u n e per urbem ediderit? iuvenum primos tot miserit Orco?* [will a single man have dealt such slaughter all over your town, unpunished? Will he have sent so many of your finest youth to Orcus?]. νυμφόκλαυτος Ἐρινύς [an avenging deity, a bride bringing woe] at Aesch. *Ag.* 749 has been cited as a parallel for *Troiae et patriae communis Erinys* (573) [an aveng-ing deity, a curse alike to Troy and to her homeland], but the source is clearly *Or.*

1388: ξεστῶν Περγάμων 'Απολλωνίων 'Ερινύν [the avenging deity of Apollo's well-built citadel of Troy] (referring to Helen's beauty), and the *Phrygii ministri* [Trojan servants] of 581 may also derive from the *Orestes*.

76. Conington, following Ti. Donatus, also considered this.

77. *quis indomitas tantus dolor excitat iras...non prius aspicies ubi...liqueris Anchisen?* [what great bitterness rouses such ungovernable fury?...ought you not first to see where you have left Anchises?].

78. Already in Homer (*Od.* 14.68) Eumaeus says ὡς ὤφελλ' Ἑλένης ἀπὸ φῦλον   50 ὀλέσθαι πρόχνυ, ἐπεὶ πολλῶν ὑπὸ γούνατ' ἔλυσεν [would that Helen's whole tribe had perished utterly, since she has loosened the knees of many warriors].

79. Andromache: ὦ Τυνδάρειον ἔρνος, οὔποτ' εἶ Διός...ὄλοιο· καλλίστων γὰρ ὀμμάτων ἄπο αἰσχρῶς τὰ κλεινὰ πεδί' ἀπώλεσας Φρυγῶν [O child of Tyndareus, you are no child of Zeus...may you perish, since you have destroyed the glorious plains of Troy because of your beautiful eyes] (*Tro.* 766; cf. *Androm.* 105, 248); Hecuba (*Tro.* 1213).

80. For example, Pylades in *Orestes*, see n. 75 above; Peleus (*Androm.* 602); the chorus in *Electra* (479); Iphigenia (*Iph. Taur.* 356; the chorus at 439f.); Teucer (*Hel.* 72) ἐχθίστην ὁρῶ γυναικὸς εἰκὼ φόνιον ἥ μ' ἀπώλεσε πάντας τ' 'Αχαιούς. [I see the hateful image of the woman, the murderess who killed me and all the Achaeans]. Virgil's *Tyndaridis facies invisa* [the hated image of the Tyndarid] is strongly reminiscent of this.

81. The difficulties in presenting this whole scene are admittedly alleviated by   52 the fact that it is Venus who describes the activities of the individual gods, while Aeneas himself uses only words of a very general nature to describe his vision (*apparent dirae facies inimicaque Troiae numina magna deum* [622] [there were revealed the shapes of dread, the giant powers of gods not friendly to Troy]).

82. *Iliad* 20.47ff., beginning with Eris; Ares and Athena shout, each urging their own side on to battle; Poseidon makes the earth tremble, so that Hades is frightened and starts up from his chair; Zeus sends great peals of thunder from on high.

83. ὀξὺ κατ' ἀκροτάτης πόλιος Τρώεσσι κελεύων, ἄλλοτε πὰρ Σιμόεντι θέων ἐπὶ Καλλικολώνη· [calling in shrill tones to the Trojans from the topmost citadel, and again, speeding along Simois over Callicolone].

84. Wörner in Roscher's *Lex.* I 185.   54

85. Tryph. 651: Αἰνείαν δ' ἔκλεψε καὶ 'Αγχίσην 'Αφροδίτη οἰκτείρουσα γέροντα καὶ υἱέα, τῆλε δὲ πάτρης Αὐσονίην ἀπένασσε [Aphrodite, taking pity on the old man and his son, stole away Aeneas and Anchises, and took them far from their homeland to Ausonia].

86. The words *miraculo magis* [more by a miracle] in Cassius Hemina's account of the departure (schol. Veron. 2.717), and ὅστις πυρὸς ἔσχισεν ὁρμήν [who parted the flames] in the Sibylline Oracle (5.9, 12.9) probably also belong to this tradition. When Ovid says (*Ex P.* 1.1.33) *cum foret Aeneae cervix subiecta parenti dicitur ipsa viro flamma dedisse viam* [when Aeneas bore his father on his shoulders, the very flames, they say, made a path for the hero], this can no longer be regarded as a vague echo of Virgil, in the light of the other examples.

87. 8.524, 9.630.   55

88. The early commentators called it an *auspicium maximum*, Serv. on 693; we   56

61

know that any signs from heaven, not only lightning, counted as auspices.

89. Servius points out that in the case of the youthful Servius Tullius this sign was interpreted by Tanaquil as foretelling his future glory, *perita caelestium prodigiorum mulier* [a woman skilled in heavenly portents] (Livy 1.34.9); and again in the case of Iulus' great descendant, Augustus, *Aeneid* 8.680.

90. *De Div.* 1.47, 106. Cf. also the prayer of the augurs in Livy 1.18: *Iuppiter pater: si est fas hunc Numam Pompilium...regem Romae esse, uti tu signa nobis certa adclarassis...* [Father Jupiter, if it is fated that this Numa Pompilius should be king in Rome, grant us a clear and certain sign].

57   **91.** Mommsen, *Staatsrecht* I 102.1.

92. Mommsen op. cit. 105.4.

93. The earliest evidence is probably a coin from Aineia (sixth century; Baumeister, *Denkm.* Fig. 1015); then, apart from numerous pictorial representations,

58   Hellanicus (Dion. Hal. 1.46.4); also Naevius, who includes Anchises' wife as well in the group leaving Troy: Servius on 3.10.

94. She was called Eurydice in early epic (Paus. 10.26.1) and still in Ennius (*Ann.* 37V). We do not know when or by whom Creusa was substituted; there was a Creusa among the prisoners in Polygnotus' picture in the Lesche at Delphi (Paus. loc. cit.; Robert, *Iliupersis* 8); Apollodorus knows her as a daughter of Priam (3.12, 5.6: Hellanicus? Robert 62); Livy names her as Aeneas' wife (1.3), as do Dion. Hal. (3.31.4), Pausanias loc. cit., schol. Lycophron 1263 etc. Our epitome of Apollodorus does not mention Aeneas' wife in the departure scene (5.21), nor does Tryphiodorus (651), nor significantly, since he gives such a wealth of detail in his narrative, Quintus (13.300-52).

95. The *Tabula Iliaca* depicts the departure at two moments, at the city gate and at the ship. At the city gate a woman can be seen between Ascanius and Aeneas, in an attitude of mourning; she is unnamed but can surely be none other than Aeneas' wife. Below, at the ship, this woman is no longer there: in other words she has been lost between the two scenes (Paulcke op. cit. n. 29, 41.73f.). Pausanias (10.26.1) records a tradition in which Creusa, as Aeneas' wife, was saved from slavery by Aphrodite and the Mother of the Gods. If we combine the two traditions we come close to Virgil; it is quite possible that Stesichorus had already shown Creusa,

59   unable to follow quickly enough and in danger of being taken captive, being saved by a well-disposed divinity, just as he showed Hecuba being rescued by Apollo, who carried her off to Lycia. According to a later tradition, Priam's daughter Laodice also escapes captivity by a miracle: the earth swallows her up (Lycophron, probably also Euphorion). Euripides uses this motif in the *Orestes*: Helen, just at the moment when she is about to be put to death, ἐκ θαλάμων ἐγένετο διαπρὸ δωμάτων ἄφαντος...ἤτοι φαρμάκοισιν ἢ μάγων τέχναισιν ἢ θεῶν κλοπαῖς (1494f.) [she vanished from the chambers through the house, whether by magic potions or the arts of magicians or stolen by the gods]. In later stories it is not uncommon for a divinity to rescue a person from death or some other misfortune by carrying them off: Leucippus (Parthen. 15), Britomartis (Antonin. 40); Byblis saved from suicide by nymphs and turned into their συνδίαιτος ἑταιρίς [companion living with them] (Antonin. 30). For similar beliefs in a later period see Rohde, *Psyche* II² 375ff. Whether the Great Mother already plays a rôle in Stesichorus is doubtful; for

the early epic Robert rightly rejects the possibility (op. cit. n. 69, 62); but in any case her intervention was not a motif created by Virgil.

96. In the same way the god Romulus-Quirinus appears to Julius Proculus καλὸς ὀφθῆναι καὶ μέγας ὡς οὔποτε πρόσθεν [fine to behold and bigger than ever before] (Plut. *Rom.* 28). Similarly in Ovid, who however may have had the Virgil passage before him, *pulcher et humano maior...'prohibe lugere Quirites'...iussit et in tenues oculis evanuit auras* ['handsome and larger than a human... 'do not let the Romans grieve', he said, and vanished from their sight into thin air] (*Fast.* 2.503).

97. Since female θαλαμηπόλοι [maidservants] and πρόπολοι [attendants] serve the goddess on earth, the same is naturally true in her divine abode, and her servants there enjoy immortality; by chance, we even know one of the ὀπαδοὶ τῆς Κυβέλης νύμφαι [nymphs attendant on Cybele], Sikinnis (Arrian in Eustath. on *Iliad* 12 p. 1078). Aphrodite abducts Phaethon καί μιν ζαθέοις ἐνὶ νηοῖς νηοπόλον μύχιον ποιήσατο, δαίμονα δῖον [and made him keeper of the inner shrine in her sacred temple, a divine spirit] (Hesiod, *Theog.* 990). Galinthias becomes Hecate's ἱερὰ διακονός [sacred attendant] (Antonin. 29).

98. 11.586 *cara mihi comitumque foret nunc una mearum* [she could have been one of my companions still, and still dear to me].

99. We might well believe that Virgil was thinking of the account of the rape of Ganymede in the Homeric hymn to Aphrodite: Τρῶα δὲ πένθος ἄλαστον ἔχε φρένας, οὐδέ τι ᾔδει ὅππη οἱ φίλον υἱὸν ἀνήρπασε θέσπις ἄελλα· τὸν δὴ ἔπειτα γόασκε διαμπερὲς ἤματα πάντα...εἶπεν δὲ ἕκαστα Ζηνὸς ἐφημοσύνῃσι διάκτορος Ἀργειφόντης, ὡς ἔοι ἀθάνατος καὶ ἀγήρως ἴσα θεοῖσιν (207) [inconsolable grief filled the heart of Tros: he did not know whither the heaven-sent wind had caught up his dear son. Thereafter he mourned him always, unceasingly: but the guide, slayer of Argus, told him everything on Zeus' orders, how his son would be deathless and ageless like the gods]. Apart from this information, Tros is also compensated with ἄποινα [spoils], in the form of the divine steeds, so that his grief turns to joy. **60**

100. Leo, *Deutsche Litt. Ztg.* (1903) 595. **63**

101. *nec spes opis ulla dabatur* [no hope of assistance remained]: Sabbadini is of the opinion (op. cit. n. 14, 24) that this originally meant that there was no possibility of helping Creusa: 747-800 would then be a later addition as a result of which these words now have the inappropriate meaning that Aeneas was considering resuming the fight, something that was quite out of the question in the circumstances. I do not see why we should not take *spes opis* quite literally ('hope for aid or support'): Aeneas and his men have done what they could, no help is to be expected from man or god, there is nothing left to do but make a final withdrawal. It is perfectly natural that at this decisive moment he should think yet again 'supposing by some miracle we could still be saved!', and yet be convinced at the same time that there was no further spark of hope. Sabbadini's other alleged contradictions (Aeneas speaks of *portae* at 730 and 803, but of *porta* at 752; 748 *curva vallis*, whereas previously a *tumulus* had been named as the meeting-place) are even less persuasive.

102. Set out in detail by Kehmptzow, *De Quinti Smyrn. fontibus et mythopoeia* (Diss. Kil. 1891), and in the review of this work by Noack, *Gött. Gel. Anz.* (1892) 769-812. On Tryphiodorus see Noack, *Hermes* 27 (1892) 457-63; *Rhein. Mus.* 48

(1893) 420-32. Since this excursus was written, the commonly held view mentioned above has been contested by Kroll, *Studien über die Komposition der Aeneis* in *Festschrift C.F.W. Müller zum 70. Geburtstag gewidmet* (= *Fleckeisens Jahrbuch* Suppl. 27 [1900]) 161-9; similarly Norden, *Neue Jahrbücher* 7 (1901) 329 n. 1. Both authors have, in my opinion, interpreted the relationship correctly, but for the purpose of their argument they only refer briefly to the decisive factors. Since the question is of such importance I thought it necessary to present my own more detailed discussion none the less. Recently, P. Becker (*Rhein. Mus.* 68 [1913] 68-90) has argued again for Quintus' dependence on Virgil; I have taken his main arguments into account in what follows in so far as they refer to the passages under consideration; Becker has also attempted to show that Quintus' account of the duel between Achilles and Memnon (2.396ff.) makes use of the duel between Aeneas and Turnus, and that his account of the boxing match (4.284ff.) draws on the corresponding scene in *Aen.* 5. I do not refute that here, since I believe that any unbiased reader will realize that Becker fails in his attempt.

103. At this point Virgil is closer in the details to the version of Apollodorus than Quintus is: ἔρημον δὲ Τρῶες τὸ τῶν Ἑλλήνων θεασάμενοι στράτευμα καὶ νομίσαντες πεφευγέναι [the Trojans, seeing the Greek camp deserted, and thinking they had fled], *nos abisse rati et vento petiisse Mycenas...iuvat ire et Dorica castra desertosque videre locos litusque relictum* (25-8) [we thought they had sailed for Mycenae before the wind...we enjoyed going to look at the Greek camp and the deserted space and the shore they had left].

104. Quintus' narrative is clumsy, but that is what he means (cf. 39f., where it would be bold to take εἰς ὅ κε as introducing a final clause, and 420), not that Sinon does not utter a word until he is tortured (cf. Koechly, *Prolegomena* p. xxxi); if that was what he meant, Quintus' narrative would be even clumsier, for he would have failed to mention what according to this interpretation is the main point, that Sinon is *silent* until he pretends that the cruel tortures have forced him to speak; lines 370ff. and 387f., which say that he spoke as he did *despite* the torture, would then be the height of clumsiness.

105. This is not Virgil's invention, see p. 6 above; nevertheless it could of course have been missing in the outline of the plot used by Quintus. It is certainly not to be concluded from the absence of Priam that Quintus took an anti-Trojan position.

106. He gives no explanation at all in the narrative itself, although, as Becker has pointed out to me, in Odysseus' preceding speech we read μιμνέμεν εἰς ὅ κεν ἄμμε ποτὶ πτόλιν εἰρύσσωσι δήιοι ἐλπόμενοι Τριτωνίδι δῶρον ἄγεσθαι (12.236) [wait until our enemies drag us into the city, thinking they are bringing an offering to Tritonis]: though of course they could not rely on this. In Apollodorus the horse is pulled into the city before they discuss what to do with it.

107. There is a verbal echo: in Virgil, Sinon has remained behind *in utrumque paratus, seu versare dolos seu certae occumbere morti* (61-2) [ready for either outcome, whether success in his deceptions or certain death]; in Quintus he says τὸ γὰρ νύ μοι εὔαδε θυμῷ, ἢ θανέειν δηΐοισιν ὑπ' ἀνδράσιν, ἢ ὑπαλύξαι Ἀργείοις μέγα κῦδος ἐελδομένοισι φέροντα (12.250) [this is fixed in my heart, either to die at the hands of the enemy or to escape, bringing great glory to the hopes of the Argives]. It is not an unusual idea, and it could easily have occurred to the two

authors independently. Tryphiodorus gives the same remark to Odysseus: ἀλλὰ χρὴ ζώοντας ἀοίδιμον ἔργον ἀνύσσαι ἢ θανάτῳ βροτόεντι κακοκλεὲς αἶσχος ἀλύξαι (126) [we must either survive and accomplish a famous deed or escape infamous disgrace by a bloody death]; cf. also e.g. Eurip. *Or.* 1149ff. Nor is anything proved by the comparison of *undique visundi studio Troiana iuventus circumfusa ruit certantque inludere capto* (63-4) [anxious to look at him, the young Trojans came hastening up and gathered round, outdoing each other in mockery of the captive] with καί μιν ἀνειρόμενοι Δαναῶν ὕπερ ἄλλοθεν ἄλλος μέσσον ἐκυκλώσαντο περισταδόν (361) [and questioning him about the Greeks they surrounded him from all sides, standing round him].

108. Nor is the change, that Sinon was not, as he perhaps was shown on the *Tabula Iliaca* (the interpretation of the scene leaves room for a good deal of doubt), led into the city *in chains*; the version of the story that he had taken from his epitome had itself already made this impossible.

109. This warning was not given until the horse was already standing on the 69 citadel; Apollodorus, Virgil and Tryphiodorus are all agreed on this (although in Apollodorus the debate about what to do with the horse also comes afterwards; and only in his version does Cassandra interrupt this debate, and in Tryphiodorus the most that may be doubted is whether he is referring to the moment when the horse was pulled in; but in any case it is already inside the city); in Hygin. *Fab.* 108 Priam has already given the command to bring the horse in and declared a joyous festival. 70 On the *Tabula Iliaca* Cassandra meets the procession at the city gate; this does not necessarily imply the existence of another version: the matter has obviously already been decided here too. Quintus selects an even later moment when the festival is already in full swing. He had to make this change, because he had put the renewal of Laocoon's warnings and the miraculous serpents at the other point, as we have seen. He and Tryphiodorus have some features in common, but hardly enough to suggest a common source. These considerations tell against Becker's interpretation (op. cit. n. 64, 86), which is factually incorrect in some parts and incomplete in others.

110. *Rhein. Mus.* 46 (1891) 517.

111. Becker (op. cit. 85) disputes this: 'The god has given his first warnings *through the mouth* of his priest to no effect, now he gives a clearer warning *through punishing him*'. Becker does not adduce any analogies for a warning in the form of the *punishment* of a faithful servant through whose mouth the god has spoken; it would, I think, be hard to find one.

112. Nor did the ancient commentators on Virgil know anything of it; they simply contrast the *historia* and the Virgilian version. Anyone who is familiar with the mythological capabilities of these scholiasts will not wish to draw conclusions here based on their silence.

113. For a different attempt at a solution, which I find unsatisfactory, see Wag- 71 ner, *Apollod. epit. Vat.* 233.

114. See above p. 32. 72

115. Cf. also *Iliad* 20.344, ἦ μέγα θαῦμα τόδ᾽ ὀφθαλμοῖσιν ὁρῶμαι...ἔγχος μὲν τόδε κεῖται ἐπὶ χθονός, οὐδέ τι φῶτα λεύσσω τῷ ἐφέηκα [surely this is a great marvel that I see with my eyes...here lies my spear on the ground, and I see no sign of the man at whom I threw it].

73   **116.** Cf. Wörner in Roscher *Lex*. I 182.

117. Becker (op. cit. 87) is however quite wrong to think that in his description of the death of Priam Quintus, writing from a point of view directly opposite to that of Virgil, 'carefully avoided anything that might arouse sympathy, indignation or revulsion'; that is exactly what the description at 244ff. is intended to do. Nor does Pyrrhus believe what Priam says, but exults that he is taking away his enemy's dearest possession, his life (239f.); Becker has obviously overlooked this.

74   **118.** *conversa cuspide* (81) [he swung his lance round], by which Virgil cannot have meant a trident. The only example in the *Thesaurus* where *cuspis = tridens* is Ovid's *deus aequoreas qui cuspide temperat undas* [the god who controls the waves of the sea with his trident] (*Met*. 12.580); that is a completely unambiguous metonymy, quite unlike the use of *cuspis* in our passage.

75   **119.** [Longinus] *On the Sublime* 9.14.

120. Τηλεπόροις δ' ἐν ἄντροις τράφη θυέλλαισιν ἐν πατρῴαις Βορέας [daughter of Boreas, she was reared in distant caves among her father's stormwinds] (Soph. *Antig*. 983); ἑπτάμυχον Βορέαο παρὰ σπέος [by the seven-chambered cave of Boreas] (Callim. *Del*. 65).

121 This trident and its purpose are known to Lucan also: *si rursus tellus pulsu laxata tridentis Aeolii tumidis inmittat fluctibus eurum* (2.456) [even if the earth, opened again by Aeolus with his trident, let loose the East wind on the swollen waves]; it would be a remarkable coincidence if he had substituted it for Virgil's lance on his own initiative.

76   **122.** There are no significant correspondences in the details in Virgil and Quintus. When he describes the mountain of the winds, Quintus lays emphasis on the sounds they make: ἔνθ' ἄνεμοι κελαδεινὰ δυσηχέες ἠυλίζοντο ἐν κενεῷ κευθμῶνι· περίαχε δ' αἰὲν ἰωὴ βρυχομένη ἀλεγεινά [there dwelt the winds howling noisily in their hollow cave, and ever the dreadful roaring din echoed around], whereas Virgil emphasizes the character of the personified winds: *vasto rex Aeolus antro luctantis ventos tempestatesque sonoras imperio premit ac vinclis et carcere frenat; illi indignantes magno cum murmure montis circum claustra fremunt* (52-6) [in the great spaces of a cavern they wrestle, and hurricanes roar: but Aeolus, the king who rules them, confines them in their prison, disciplined and curbed. They race from door to bolted door, and all the mountain reverberates with the noise of their resentment]. Virgil could have drawn the inspiration for this portrayal of Aeolus from a word of Apollonius, in whose epic Hera sends Iris to Aeolus ὅστ' ἀνέμοις αἰθρηγενέεσσιν ἀ ν α σ σ ε ι (4.762) [who rules over the winds born in the clear sky] and tells him to hold back the winds except for Zephyrus (ἀνέμων ἀικας ἐρύξειν [818, cf. 5.383] [to curb the rushing of the winds]).

123. 85f. ~ *Od*. 5.295f.; 87 ~ *Od*. 10.122; 88f. ~ *Od*. 5. 293f.; 90 ~ *Od*. 12.415; 91 ~ *Od*. 5.305, *Il*. 15.628, Apollon. 2.580; 92-101 ~ *Od*. 5.297, 306-10; 102 ~ *Od*. 5.313; 103 ~ *Il*. 15.627; 105 Apollon. 2.583; on 106f. see above; 113ff. ~ *Od*. 12.411ff.; 118f. ~ *Od*. 12.67f.

77   **124.** *furit aestus harenis* [the billows are seething with sands] can be paralleled, for example, in Sophocles *Antig*. 585 πόντιον οἶδμα...κυλίνδει βυσσόθεν κελαινὰν θῖνα [the swelling sea rolls black sand from its depths] similarly Virgil, *Geo*. 3.240: *ima exaestuat unda verticibus nigramque alte subvectat harenam* [the bottom

of the sea seethes and swirls and spews up black sand from its depths].

125. Liedloff (*De tempestatis...descriptionibus quae apud poetas Romanos saec.* 78
I post Chr. leguntur [descriptions of storms in Roman poets of the first century BC],
Diss. Leipzig [1884] 17 n. 1) long ago pointed this out, and listed details from the
description of the peaceful part of the voyage; comparable passages from the *ecphrasis* [description] of the storm are: *undasque miscent imber et fluctus suas* [the
rain and the waves mingle their waters] (Seneca, *Ag.* 490), θαλάσσης καὶ Διὸς
ὕδωρ μισγόμενον [the water of Zeus mingling with the sea] (Quintus 14.599), *ipsa
se classis premit et prora prorae nocuit et lateri latus* [the fleet crushes itself, one
prow damages another, one ship's side another] (*Ag.* 497), αἱ γὰρ ῥα συνωχαδὸν
ἀλλήλῃσιν αἰὲν ἐπερρήγνυντο [and the ships were constantly shattered against one
another] (Quintus 517), *nil ratio et usus audet...remus effugit manus* [reason and
practice are of no avail...the oar slips from their hands] (*Ag.* 507, 509), οἱ δ' ἄρ'
ἀμηχανίῃ βεβολημένοι οὔτ' ἐπ' ἐρετμῷ χεῖρα βαλεῖν ἐδύναντο τεθηπότες
[thrown about helplessly, in their confusion they could not lay their hand on the oar]
(Quintus 497), *terraque et igne victus et pelago iacet* [he lies overcome by land and
fire and the sea] (*Ag.* 556), γαίῃ ὁμῶς δμηθέντα καὶ ἀτρυγέτῳ ἐνὶ πόντῳ [over-
whelmed at once by the land and in the barren sea] (Quintus 589).

126. See Liedloff op. cit. 4; it is only by chance (Athen. 8.338a) that we know
that the description of this storm by Timotheus in his *Nauplius* was famous. We may
add Philetas, in whose poem Odysseus tells Aeolus τὰ περὶ Τροίης ἅλωσιν καὶ ὅν
τρόπον αὐτοῖς ἐσκεδάσθησαν αἱ νῆες κομιζομένοις ἀπὸ τῆς Ἰλίου [all about the
capture of Troy and how their ships were scattered while they journeyed from Ilium]
(Parthen. 2), and Callimachus, who included the story in the first book of his *Aitia*
(schol. *Iliad* 13.66). We should also remember the extravaganza *Nauplius* in
Heron's mechanical theatre.

127. Ehrwald, *Philol.* 53 (1894) 729.

128. Schneidewin indicated this in his observation on Hippolytus (*Refutat. omn.* 79
haeres. ed. Duncker-Schneidewin, 252) and on Epiphanius *Adv. Haer.* vol. II Book
I.21.3, as Knaack has opportunely reminded us: *Rhein. Mus.* 48 (1893) 632; see now
also Norden 254.

129. Immisch, *Rhein. Mus.* 52 (1897) 127.

130. χάρμα γὰρ Ἀργείοισι γενήσομαι [I shall become a source of joy to the
Argives]; Homeric χάρμα = *Schadenfreude* [delight at another's misfortunes]; for
then the Trojans will have to pay for their impious act. This is a long way from
Virgil's *iamdudum sumite poenas: hoc Ithacus velit et magno mercentur Atridae*
(2.104-5) [it is more than time for you to be taking vengeance on me: how that 80
would please the Ithacan, and what would the sons of Atreus not give in return for
it!], because in that case their evil intention is carried out by an enemy's hand.

2

The Wanderings of Aeneas

It has often been felt, and stated, that Book 3 of the *Aeneid* is a work of considerably less artistic merit than Book 2. The reason for this cannot be that Book 2 recounts only one single great event, whereas Book 3 deals with a loose sequence of adventures; this is also true of the books of the *Odyssey* in which Odysseus narrates his adventures, and they have never been accused of having less poetic value for that reason. But it is precisely this obvious comparison that has had a fatal effect on Virgil's narrative. Indeed, the reader almost feels that, for once, Virgil has set out to rival Homer without much pleasure or self-confidence. This may explain why he kept postponing work on this book; it is, as we shall see, among the last parts of the *Aeneid* to have been written. Whereas the abundance of poetic material that was already in existence for the sack of Troy proved an invaluable advantage to the poet, here he found himself in precisely the opposite position: he had, as far as we know, not a single poetic predecessor. There was no shortage of source-material for the actual events, but this took the form not of a tradition that had grown up over the centuries, but of artifically cobbled-together history; his sources were not poets but antiquarians; it was all wretchedly monotonous. We are fairly well informed about the nature of the traditional material that was available to Virgil, because it is obviously the same as that which formed the basis for Dionysius of Halicarnassus' account (*Antiquities* 1.48ff.); we may therefore attempt to trace the way in which Virgil transformed this intractable material into poetry so as to make it into a work of art.

1. Unity of the narrative: foundations of cities

The historian who first assembled the numerous traditions about settlements, cults and temples founded by Aeneas along the coasts of the Mediterranean into a co-
herent and connected narrative must have been at a loss to motivate the frequent interruptions of his voyage and the innumerable foundations of cities. For the former, as we gather from Dionysius, he generally used one of two motives: either Aeneas lingers to renew old friendships – for example in Delos (1.50), Arcadia, Zacynthos – or adverse winds force him to wait or to take another course (49.3: παρ' οἷς διατριβὴν ἀπλοίας ἕνεκεν ἐποιήσαντο [they stayed among them because the weather was unsuitable for sailing]: thus he waits in Thrace until the season is suitable for sailing (49.4), is forced to wait longer than he had intended in Zacynthos (50.3) and is forced to sail around Sicily (52.1). A city is founded in Thrace (49.4) to provide a dwelling-place for those who do not wish to travel any further; similarly in Sicily (52.4) – here, according to other sources, because some of the ships had been burnt, and the diminished fleet could no longer carry all the Trojans. The direction of the voyage, towards the west, was either revealed to them by the Sibyl of

Erythrae before they left their native land, or else only when they reached the oracle at Dodona; they will recognize the end of their journey, when it comes, by the omen of 'eating their tables' (55.4). Anything that does not fit into this westward journey Dionysius either omits completely, as in the case of the episode on Crete, or explains by one of the causes that we have mentioned.

Hence it is only the direction of the voyage that gives this narrative any unity; all the individual episodes are only chance interruptions to the journey, delays to their final arrival – some welcome, some unwelcome – that are unrelated to one another; some of them could easily be omitted, or others added, without the course of the action being affected. To give some inner unity to the action, to make the component episodes seem necessary to it, was the first task that faced Virgil. A loose series of landfalls and foundations of cities, friendly encounters and ἄπλοιαι [confinements to the safety of a harbour] was, in his view, no ἕν [unity]; it was neither worthy nor capable of representation in poetry. Virgil chose for his narrative thread the gradual, progressive revelation of the destination of his voyage.[1]

This revelation takes place in five stages: (1) Aeneas leaves his native land because of auguries that tell him to seek a new home abroad. (2) In Delos he receives the oracle that refers to the *antiqua mater* [ancient mother]. (3) In Crete he learns from the Penates that this means Italy. (4) On the Strophades he receives from Celaeno the prophecy of the portent of the tables. (5) In Buthrotum he receives from Helenus directions on how to reach the west coast of Italy, and the prophecy of the portent of the sow, together with the advice that he should ask the Sibyl at Cumae for further information about the future. This indicates the place where the new settlement is to be founded as clearly as can be without actually mentioning the name of the place, and Aeneas would now have followed the course prescribed by Helenus, and reached his goal without any more mistakes or wandering – if Juno in her anger had not prepared a new obstacle for him on the coast immediately opposite the promised land, an obstacle that combines the two motifs that are familiar from Dionysius: adverse winds and seductive hospitality. Most of the individual components of this development in the story existed already in the tradition, either actually or potentially: the oracle in their Trojan homeland, the two *prodigia*, the Sibyl, the encounter with Helenus combined with the oracle of Dodona, the prophecy by the Penates. Virgil's contribution lay in arranging them in a progressive development, above all by the gradual disclosure of Fate, and in the major role that he allots to Apollo. In both cases Virgil was using themes suggested to him by Greek foundation-legends.

Apollo is not mentioned in any of the pre-Virgilian accounts of Aeneas' wanderings, or in any of the later ones that are independent of Virgil; he has only an indirect influence on the Trojans' travels in so far as the Sibyl is his prophetess. At the same time, there was a tradition mentioned by Varro, according to which Venus guided the voyage by her star (Serv. on 2.801). Virgil says nothing of this, but sets Apollo very emphatically in the central position. Virgil not only stresses that it is Apollo who inspires the Cumaean Sibyl; it is Apollo to whom Aeneas addresses his prayer for an oracle (6.56); how Apollo's priestess is possessed by the god is described in detail at 6.77ff.; Aeneas is honoured at Delos, by hearing Apollo's very own voice; it is at Apollo's command that the Penates speak (3.155); it is from

84

Apollo that the Harpy has obtained her knowledge (251); it is in Apollo's temple that he hears Helenus, the priest of the god, tell him that Apollo will protect him in the future too (395). The decisive stimulus for this emphasis on the services performed by Apollo may have been Augustus' predilection for him as the god of the

85 Julian family; but the idea comes originally, as I have said, from Greek foundation-legends. The rôle played by Apollo, and particularly by his Delphic oracle, in the sending out of colonies is well known;[2] more significant still than the numerous surviving accounts of the consultation of the oracle is the great number of colonies that bear the name Apollonia. Amongst the foundations in which Apollo played an important rôle were two of the most important cities on the west coast of Italy: Rhegium[3] and Cumae.[4] Virgil represents the ἀποικία [colony] of Aeneas as a third city alongside these two.

The initial obscurity of the oracle, and its gradual clarification, also has its origin in Greek ways of thinking. Of the foundation-legends known to me, it is that of Cyrene which provides the closest parallels (Herod. 4.150). The king of Thera is advised by the Pythia at Delphi to found a colony in Libya. However, he does not know where Libya is, and therefore fails to send out a colony. Thera then suffers a severe drought (analogous with the crop failure that afflicts the Trojans in Crete [3.141f.]), and when the oracle is asked for help, it tells them again to go to Libya. So they decide to risk the attempt, and a Cretan called Korobios, who promises to show them the unknown land of Libya, leads them to the island of Platea, which is situated off Libya. They settle on this island, but without success. And they hear again from the Pythia that they are still not in Libya. Then they finally cross over onto the mainland.[5] Just as in this case a drought reminds the Therans of their instructions, so too drought and infertility are elsewhere often the reason for sending out a colony, or are a sign that the god's plan has not been fulfilled by the settlement: the foundation of Rhegium goes back to an ἀφορία [crop-failure] in Chalcis (Strab. 6.257); and μεγάλων αὐχμῶν γενομένων [after a great drought] the men of Ainos, at the command of the oracle, leave Kirrha where they have just settled (Plut. *Qu. Gr.* 26).

86 Finally, with regard to the two portents that indicate the end of the journey, Virgil was able simply to follow the tradition. Even if we accept that these stories are based on local legends, their connection with Aeneas doubtless goes back to Greek historians, who in turn were constructing their narratives on the analogy of Greek foundation-legends. To mention only a few examples, I recall the Etruscan children from Brauron, who were to settle where they lost their goddess and their anchor (Plut. *Virt. Mul.* 247e), or the Spartan Phalanthus, who was promised a permanent residence by the Delphic oracle 'when he felt rain' ὑπὸ αἴθρα [under a clear sky] (Paus. 10.10.6) where the double meaning of αἴθρα – both a proper name (his wife's name was Aithra) and 'blue sky' – corresponds with that of *mensae*; even more frequent, as is well-known, are the cases where an animal, such as the sow in this case, indicates the site for a new foundation.

Thus Virgil has turned the story of Aeneas' wanderings into a unified Ῥώμης κτίσις [founding of Rome], comparable to Greek foundation-legends, but uniting all the motifs of these legends much more comprehensively than can have been the case in any one of these legends, either genuine or spurious.

2. Relationship to the other books

The idea of drawing the wanderings of Aeneas into the tightly organized form that we have described came to Virgil only after much of the *Aeneid* had been written in the form in which we have it.[6] It is worth devoting some time to this matter, as it 87 leads to valuable insights into Virgil's working methods. Let us first examine what we are told outside Book 3 about the plan of the voyage and the Trojans' knowledge of their destination.

According to 2.781, before Aeneas left Troy he was told by Creusa that he will come to the 'Hesperian land, where through rich pastures with gentle current the Lydian Thybris flows.'

According to 4.345, 'Grynean Apollo and Lycian oracles' have commanded him to go to Italy.

According to 1.382, he put to sea because of an oracle, in which 'his divine mother showed him the way.'

According to 1.205 and 554, 4.432, 5.731 and 6.67, the Trojans know Latium to be the destination of their journey; at 5.83 Thybris is mentioned by Aeneas and again at 6.87 by the Sybil.

Thus when Virgil was writing 1, 2, 4 to 6, he imagined Aeneas as knowing the name of the land and its river during his journey, and according to the references in 2 and 4, which are not contradicted by anything in the other books listed above, he already had this knowledge before he sailed. It is uncertain what rôle Virgil had intended the two portents to play in all this; it is quite conceivable that he had not made any firm decision about it; on the other hand, 5.82f.

> *non licuit finis Italos fataliaque arva*
> *nec tecum Ausonium, q u i c u m q u e est, quaerere Thybrim,*

[it was not granted to me to have you at my side as I quested for Italy's boundaries where fate has given us lands, or for Ausonian Tiber, *wherever that river may be*]. This seems to suggest that Virgil considered, at least in passing, the possibility of using the motif from Greek foundation-legends that we have discussed above, in which the name of the destination is known but not its whereabouts;[7] in that case, 88 one or both portents might serve to let them know that they had come to the end of their journey.

This conception is totally inconsistent with the basic idea of the composition of Book 3 that we have outlined above: the only question is which version is the result of *curae posteriores* [afterthoughts]. If we assume that Virgil wrote Book 3 first, it is very difficult to see any reason at all that might have prompted him at a later stage to ruin the unity that characterized his version, by which the whole book stands or falls. This would not only have invalidated the individual prophecies, but, more importantly, Virgil would have had to invent some entirely new motivation for the foundations in Thrace and Crete, unless he scrapped them altogether, or else have reverted to a disconnected narrative of the kind that we get in Dionysius. However, there is no indication in the other books of any new unified plan which might have replaced the old one; there are three successive episodes – the guidance by Venus, Creusa's prophecy, and the 'Lycian' oracle – that would need to be brought together in some context: but they would not have produced material for the new Book 3; these episodes however had obviously been invented not as parts of a single unified conception, but because of the immediate requirements of each situation; and none of them is in itself so important that Virgil might reasonably have altered his original plan for their sake.[8] On the other hand, if we think of Book 3 as still to be written, each reference is quite plausible in its context as a provisional explanation; and furthermore it is quite natural that before Virgil had decided on the plan of Book 3 he might find it more congenial to work with specific names, such as Latium and Thybris, rather than with some unknown destination: however, these names are nowhere essential to his purpose.[9]

The conclusion that Book 3 was composed at a later stage will become even clearer if we go on to examine the treatment of the two portents in Books 7 and 8.

The portent of the tables is, according to tradition, the fulfilment of a prophecy which was given to Aeneas by the Sibyl of Erythrae or the oracle at Dodona, and will indicate to Aeneas and his men that they have reached the end of their journey. This is exactly the purpose it serves Virgil in Book 7; here the prophecy is traced back to Anchises, who bequeathed it to his son (*fatorum arcana reliquit* [123] [he left the secret of destiny]) – apparently not in the underworld, but during his life-time, perhaps on his deathbed, when the power of prophecy is usually enhanced. It is clear from the manner in which it is introduced, and above all from the fact that it is quoted *verbatim*, that Virgil is not referring to some earlier passage in which it was mentioned: the oracle is introduced without any preparation, just like Apollo's promise at 6.343 and Venus' at 8.534; when Aeneas says *nunc repeto* (7.123) [now I remember] we may assume, as so often when oracles are introduced, that he has suddenly remembered something long forgotten; the prophecy of Lycophron's Cassandra, which refers to this portent, μνήμην παλαιῶν λήψεται θεσπισμάτων [he will remember ancient oracles] (*Alexandra* 1252), is fulfilled in exactly the same way. We might expect that, continuing the motif hinted at earlier, Aeneas would now joyfully realize that this is the promised land of Latium and the promised Thybris; but this is not what Virgil does: instead, Aeneas prays to the *adhuc ignota flumina* (137-8) [the rivers which as yet they did not know], and the next day when he learns the names Numicius, Thybris and Latium, it does not seem that they come as an answer to any existing expectations. This is not completely outweighed by the fact that in Ilioneus' speech to Latinus, just as in the earlier books, Virgil seems to assume some previous knowledge of the localities which they seek.[10] It may be that Virgil came to realize during the composition of his work that if the names are known the portent becomes basically meaningless: the names might be identified with the localities in perfectly natural ways. To sum up: the version of the portent of the tables in 7 is derived almost entirely from tradition; it is in no way tied up with a unified plan of Aeneas' wanderings, but is quite independent of it.

In Book 3 we find instead a highly individual new version, probably invented by Virgil: the portent is not a sign promised by a friend or a benevolent divinity to show them when they have reached the end of their wanderings, but a punishment

announced by their enemy Celaeno; not a favourable sign, but a horror which seems to cast doubt on the happy outcome of the enterprise. Not only is there a threat of terrible starvation, but the apparently unambiguous and negative words, 'You will not establish a city until hunger forces you to eat your tables' (255-7), seem to lay down an impossible condition. Phalanthus, who was to found Tarentum when he felt rain ὑπ' αἴθρᾳ [from a clear sky], also despaired in much the same way, and believed that the god had imposed an impossible condition on him.[11] However, Celaeno's prophecy does not only come as the splendid climax of the adventure of   91 the Harpies; it also plays an important part in the plot of the book: after the Penates seem at last in Crete to have indicated their destination, and the Trojans are steering westwards full of hope, this comes as a severe setback. The unexpected threat seems to throw everything into uncertainty again. Then Aeneas meets Helenus and questions him with renewed anxiety about the future; not only does he receive reassurance from him, but he is saved from another vain attempt to found a settlement, this time on the nearest part of the coast of Italy, which otherwise he surely would have done.

Thus the appearance of the portent has been prepared for; the reader is waiting for it, and the effect of the happy solution is immeasurably increased by the anxiety which has prevailed from the start. If we compare this version with that in Book 7, there cannot, in my opinion, be any doubt as to which was intended to supersede the other.[12]

According to the older traditions, the portent of the sow indicated either the site   92 of Alba Longa and the period of thirty years which will elapse before its foundation,[13] or the site of Lavinium together with the name and foundation-date of Alba.[14] Understandably, Virgil was unwilling to reject a firmly established part of the tradition, but he was unable to make the portent indicate any specific site, either for Alba, that is perfectly clear, or for Lavinium, whose foundation lies outside his narrative, since, in contrast to the versions of Dionysius and others, it was not to take place until after the agreement with Latinus. This meant that it was only possible for the portent to refer to the name and foundation-date of Alba; and it is these, therefore, that Virgil kept in the narrative of Book 8. As a result, the introduction of the portent had to be remodelled, and Virgil resorted to an expedient that is not altogether satisfactory: Aeneas, anxious about the coming battle, has fallen asleep on the bank of the Tiber; the god Tiberinus appears to him and gives him courage: he really has arrived at the place where he is destined to found his city, and he need not fear the battle. 'And', he continues, 'so that you will not think when you awake that you have been deceived by an idle dream (let this be a sign to you): beneath the oaks   93 on the riverbank you will find an enormous sow with thirty newborn piglets' (8.45-8):

alba, solo recubans, albi circum ubera nati
ex quo ter denis urbem redeuntibus annis
Ascanius clari condet cognominis Albam.

[a white sow, stretched on the ground, with her white piglets at her teats; within thirty circling years from this time, Ascanius shall found a city of illustrious name, Alba].

He goes on to advise him to ask Evander for help. Thus, as in the tradition, Aeneas receives the information about the foundation of Alba from a vision in a dream;[15] what is new in Virgil is the context in which the information is given. The immediate rôle of the portent here is only to corroborate the words of Tiberinus; the foundation of the city is mentioned only in passing without any intrinsic connection with the purpose in hand; the portent has no significance whatever as a means of identifying the site.[16] And if we were given the impression in the case of the portent of the tables in Book 7 that the reader was hearing of it for the first time, so here it is absolutely impossible that it had been prepared for in earlier parts of the narrative or that it had played any rôle in the scheme of Aeneas' wanderings.

In Book 3 Helenus predicts the portent, and here it is firmly embedded in the scheme of the wanderings. Because the name of the promised land is not disclosed to Aeneas until the very last moment, he has to be given a sign by which he can recognize it: this sign will be the portent of the sow. That is why here in Book 3, after the description of the portent, which is word for word identical with that in Book 8, it is explicitly stated that *is locus urbis erit, requies ea certa laborum* (393) [this spot shall be the place for your city, and there you shall find sure rest from your toils]. This does not mean that the city is to be founded exactly where the sow will be resting – for neither Lavinium nor Alba lies *secreti ad fluminis undam* [by the waters of a secluded stream], where according to 3.389 they will find the sow, nor can the camp by the river be termed *requies certa laborum* [a sure resting-place from their toils] – but only that the promised *land* will be recognized by this sign; previously, too, in Helenus' speech, the prophecy was concerned only with this land (*ante...quam tuta possis urbem componere terra: signa tibi dicam* [387-8] [before you can settle your city on safe soil: I shall give you a sign]). Thus the portent of the sow is given the significance which the portent of the tables had had in the tradition: the latter is given a new meaning in its turn: it no longer indicates the site, but the time; it becomes a *condicio sine qua non* [necessary pre-condition]. From this we may divine how Virgil intended to combine the fulfilment of the two prophecies: after landing on the bank of the Tiber, Aeneas would find the sow and thus recognize the promised land; however, he still anxiously awaits the starvation predicted by the Harpy; before he realizes it, at their very first meal, this prophecy too is fulfilled.

In the case of the portent of the sow too the version in Book 3 is the later one; this could in any case be deduced from the fact that it is not introduced here, as it is in Book 8, without any preparation and with awkward motivation, but has a firm place in the arrangement of the whole. However, it is clear that the identical lines that appear in both books (3.390-2 = 8.43-5) were originally written for Book 8: there the exact description of where and how makes good sense, for the more precisely the details are predicted, the more convincingly their literal fulfilment proves that the vision was trustworthy. For the oracle in Book 3 the circumstantial details have no significance and are quite uncharacteristic of such prophecies. Above all, the heavy emphasis on the colour white is important in Book 8, since the reference to Alba follows, but not important in Book 3, where Alba has not yet come into the picture. From the situation in Book 8 the detail *sollicito secreti ad fluminis undam* [in an anxious time, by the waters of a secluded stream] has crept into Book 3. On the

assumption that Book 3 was written first, such a precise description of a situation in the distant future would be quite uncharacteristic of Virgil's style.

Because of all this, I am convinced that the unified plan of the wanderings presented in Book 3 was not created until at least two-thirds of the poem had been 95
written. Thus, instead of starting by erecting the scaffolding, as it were, Virgil put this off until a much later stage and began to work on separate sections, making provisional assumptions as the situation called for them, without letting them have much influence on the general outlines of each section; he introduced the two portents in Books 7 and 8 without any presuppositions whatever, so that the two books could be read as an independent work, without the reader feeling that anything was missing. It was only later, when he was filling in the gap between Troy and Carthage, that he created the unified structure of prophecies and portents, without considering what he had already written, primarily because it was necessary to impose some unity and progressive development on Book 3. He never got as far as working out the consequences of his new conception: he would have had to delete much in the other books, and change many details, and in Book 7 he would have had to rewrite the whole story of the landing. It is indeed possible that a few traces of the earlier version might have escaped his notice; but I have no doubt that he would have achieved a unity as far as the essentials were concerned.

There is no reason to doubt that, right until the end, Virgil regarded the scheme of the wanderings, in the form in which we have it, as the definitive version. It is true that in Book 10 (67ff.) there is yet another motif that one might be tempted to regard as an indication that Virgil intended to make a further change: according to this passage, Aeneas sought Italy *Cassandrae impulsus furiis* [actuated by Cassandra's raving]. But these are the words of Juno, which contradict Venus' statement that the Trojans had sought their new homeland *tot responsa secuti quae superi manesque dabant* (34ff.) [led by all those oracles from the High Gods and the Nether Spirits]; and it is clear that Juno is spitefully trying to devalue the significance of these *responsa* [oracles] by mentioning only one prophecy, that given by a crazed woman: in fact, according to 3.183, a passage already composed, which the poet doubtless had before him when writing Book 10, it was from Cassandra that Anchises – though he had not believed her – had first heard of Hesperia and the kingdom in Italy.

3. Juno and Venus

No ancient reader will have asked the impertinent question, why Aeneas was subjected to these years of wandering: for Apollo, who certainly had Aeneas' interests 96
very much at heart, might surely have spared him a lot of trouble by giving him an unambiguous oracle before his departure; but who would dare to call the god to account for what he sees fit to reveal to mortals or to conceal from them, when every message, even when it is wrapped in the desperately ambiguous obscurity of oracular language, deserves most humble thanks as an act of the purest grace, condescension and compassion.

However, anyone who has read the opening of the *Aeneid* before reading Book 3 will perhaps expect to find a particular motivation for Aeneas' lengthy wanderings.

For the proem suggests that they are to be blamed on Juno's thirst for vengeance: it was she who drove the pious hero into so many travails and dangers, she who pursued the Trojans over all the seas and kept them away from Latium, as the poet says;[17] indeed the queen of the gods herself speaks of the plan she embarked on to turn the Trojan king away from Italy, a plan which she does not wish to abandon,[18] and of the war which she has been waging for so many years with that one race.[19] In fact from this moment onwards she is active enough: the tempest which drives Aeneas to Carthage is her work, she causes the union with Dido; later it is her intervention that leads to the burning of the ships, which results in the foundation of Segesta; she stirs up war in Latium by means of Allecto and never ceases to support the enemies of the Trojans. But until that moment we have just mentioned, in other words during the years between the departure from Troy and the departure from Sicily, throughout the events treated in Book 3, we hear nothing of Juno's intervention; and yet this period covers by far the greatest part of the *errores* [wanderings] and *labores* [toils]. The contradiction seems blatant, and yet I do not believe that it is a case of an inconsistency arising from different plans, or that Virgil would have smoothed over this contradiction. When he wrote the proem to Book 1, he had most

97 probably not yet created the scheme for Book 3 as it now stands, and it is conceivable that at that stage he was intending to allot an active role to Juno in the period that preceded the beginning of the action of Book 1. In my view it is more probable that he was thinking only of the events that followed and, with these in mind, proceeded to model his proem on that of the *Odyssey*. Then, when he composed Book 3, there was no opportunity for an open and obvious intervention by Juno; but if the poet had any doubts about whether this was compatible with the words of the proem he would have been able to feel reassured by the precedent of his model, Homer. For in the proem to the *Odyssey*, even less ambiguously than in the *Aeneid*, the exhausting wanderings of the hero are blamed on an angry deity (Poseidon in this case); and yet here, too, as far as we know, Poseidon plays no part in Odysseus' destiny until after the beginning of the action, during the sea-storm in Book 5; in Odysseus' own narrative we hear nothing in his various unhappy adventures of anything that might have been caused by Polyphemus' prayer to his father; and in the case of Odysseus' longest sojourn, the seven years spent with Calypso, it is even clearer than in the *Aeneid* that it cannot have been the result of the work of Poseidon. Any reader who noticed this would have to assume that Odysseus had never been told that his sufferings were due to the enmity of the god, and Virgil could count on the same assumption. It is clear from the single passage in Book 3 which points to Juno's enmity that he was well aware of the parallel: Helenus urgently advises Aeneas (435ff.) that the most important thing is to win Juno's favour by prayers, vows and sacrificial offerings: only if he succeeds in this will he reach Italy

98 safely from Sicily.[20] Aeneas acts according to this advice at the time of the first landing in Italy (3.546), and this single mention of his obedience to it must also count *instar omnium* [on behalf of all] for the future. Nevertheless he did not succeed in calming the wrath of Juno, as is shown by the fact that the crossing from Sicily to Italy does not go smoothly: thus Helenus' words of warning refer to the sea-storm narrated in Book 1. However this is itself clearly modelled on the words of Teiresias, *Odyssey* 11.100ff.: he too warns of Poseidon's future anger, and pro-

ceeds (121ff.) to point out the way to appease him: he says no more of the earlier results of this anger than Helenus says of Juno's previous hostile activities.

Just as the hostile goddess remains in the background, so too does the goddess who favours him. According to Aeneas' own narrative, Venus seems never to have appeared to him, either to guide him, or to advise or to assist him, throughout the greater part of the period of his wanderings. Yet Virgil must have had different intentions about this matter when he was writing Book 1, since he makes Aeneas say to Venus that he had begun his journey *matre dea monstrante viam* (382) [shown the way by my divine mother], and makes him complain at her departure *quid natum totiens, crudelis tu quoque, falsis ludis imaginibus* (407-8) ['Ah, you too are cruel! Why again and again deceive your own son with your mocking disguises?']. But there is no reason to suppose that at that stage this intention had taken any particular form, and when he was writing Book 3 Virgil left Venus completely out of the picture; here too there is an analogy with the *Odyssey*. Odysseus in his own account of his adventures knows nothing of Athena's protection and support, and is still complaining about this neglect after he has landed in Scheria (*Od*. 6.325, cf. 13.318), without realizing that it was Athena who had made this very landing possible for him, providing him with active help at this point for the first time as far as we know: the poet himself felt it necessary to explain her previous absence on the grounds that she had been unwilling to oppose her father's brother (13.341, cf. 6.329). When Virgil was creating the relationship between Venus and Aeneas he clearly had the relationship between Odysseus and Athena in his mind, though he may not always have been aware of it, and I venture to suggest that in the phrase *totiens falsis ludis imaginibus* [again and again you deceive with mocking disguises] he was not thinking of particular appearances of Venus, but of the changing forms in which Athena manifested herself to Odysseus, who for his part, though admittedly without Virgilian pathos, half-reproachfully complains to his divine protectress σὲ γὰρ αὐτὴν παντὶ ἐίσκεις ['you assume all kinds of disguises'] (*Od*. 13.313). After the definitive reshaping of Book 3, Aeneas' complaint would admittedly seem meaningless to the reader, and we must assume that Virgil would have excised it once he realized that it was now irrelevant.

4. Compression of the material

If we compare Virgil's version with other accounts of the wanderings of Aeneas, it is immediately obvious that Virgil has greatly condensed the material. Instead of aiming at academic exhaustiveness, he picked out the incidents that suited his artistic purpose. His positive criterion for selection is the one that we have already discussed: the landmarks of the journey were to be the points at which he is granted further knowledge of his final destination. The most important negative criteria were, first, avoidance of tedious repetition of motifs, and, secondly, avoidance of all material that was of merely scholarly interest and could not somehow be made to appeal to the listener's feelings. The material is much more severely abridged in Book 3, and particularly in the parts that precede the arrival in Italy, than in the later sections of the journey that are spread over Books 5 to 8. There was more room in these books for fuller treatment of the available material, since the details were not crowded together in a small space and, above all, since the books were dealing with localities well-known to every person in the audience, places in which Virgil himself took a greater interest, and which he could assume had a greater interest for others.

100   Only six stops in Greek waters are mentioned: Thrace, Delos, Crete, the Strophades, Actium and Buthrotum. With the single exception of Actium, they are all harnessed to Virgil's new scheme. The first, the failure to found a settlement in Thrace, leads Aeneas to turn to Apollo on Delos for further directions. He has learnt that the gods do not approve of just any site for the new Troy; they must therefore have a definite destination for him in mind.[21] In Crete the second negative expression of divine will is immediately followed by another positive one: the adventure with the Harpies on the Strophades brings a third gloomy prediction, apparently the worst of all, since it applies to all future time. As a counterweight, Helenus' prediction provides the clearest and strongest positive assurance. Thus hindrance and assistance appear alternately until the very moment that the coast of the promised land comes into view for the searchers. For the *prodigia* [portents], Virgil has only once, in the case of Crete, made use of a traditional motif; the other two give the impression of being traditional but are in fact original inventions. For the prophecies, Virgil again went his own way. The tradition knew of a prediction by the Sibyl of Erythrae and a consultation of the oracle at Dodona. The Sybil had to be omitted so that the Cumaean Sibyl should not have a rival; the oracle at Dodona

101   was unsuitable because it had no connection with Apollo and would therefore have destroyed the unity of Virgil's new conception. Instead, we have Helenus, whom, according to tradition, Aeneas met in Dodona; he was all the more suitable because, like Teiresias-Circe and Phineus, as an inspired mortal exegete of the god, he was in the best position to give the detailed and careful instructions that were necessary for this stage of the journey; it is easy to understand why Virgil shifted the meeting from Dodona to the coast, at Buthrotum, since the tradition had Aeneas stopping there in any case. There were also sources for the visit to Delos and the guest-friendship of Anius; since the latter appears in the tradition as a reliable prophet, Virgil must at least have considered giving him the prediction, but this would have duplicated the Helenus motif. So Virgil has Apollo himself speaking from his holy of holies to Aeneas when he asks for an oracle – it is, to say the least, very doubtful whether Apollo of Cynthus had an oracle, and Virgil's words do not suggest that a regular oracle was established there: *da pater augurium atque animis inlabere nostris* (3.89) [grant us an augury, father, and come into our hearts] seems to be asking for some inspiration that is not precisely definable, and when in response the inner shrine opens, and the sound of the god's voice comes from the tripod within, this seems to be an unexpected and therefore an all the more valuable favour. Apollo's words are interpreted as referring to Crete and so Aeneas attempts to found a settlement there. Here too Virgil connects his narrative with traditional material, for the foundation of Pergamos on Crete was not only attributed to Trojans but also linked with Aeneas himself (Serv. on 3.133). Admittedly, it did not feature among Aeneas' most famous foundations, and Dionysius does not mention it at all; but it suited Virgil's purpose because it gave ambiguity to the oracle's statement and also

because it made the wanderers turn southwards, right away from the direction of their journey, just as the Libyan sea-storm does later, whereas the voyage as described by, for example, Dionysius, apart from the detour to Thrace, keeps more or less to the normal route from Troy to Italy, and therefore does not really correspond to the concept of 'wandering around'. In Crete it is the Penates who speak in Apollo's name, appearing to Aeneas as an image in a dream or a vision. Thus Virgil has changed the location of this episode, since in the traditional version it comes at a later point: in Latium, when the army of the Latins lay encamped opposite the Trojans, the Penates are said to have advised Aeneas in a dream not to fight but to come to a peaceful agreement.²² This had been omitted in Virgil's treatment of the story in Book 7, so that the motif was available for him to use at this point, where it fits the situation quite naturally; after all, on the matter of the new homeland the Penates are the ones who can speak with the greatest authority. Finally, Virgil has put the prophecy of the *prodigium* of the tables into Celaeno's mouth, which was surely his own original idea, as we have already said. In addition to these four prophecies there are prophecies by Creusa, the Sibyl, and Tiberinus in other books; and in a wider sense the 'pageant of heroes' in the underworld and the description of the Shield also belong in this context; we can see how careful Virgil was to vary the way in which the motif was presented.

    The stop at Leucas-Actium is the only one that is not connected with the main scheme.²³ The tradition knows of sanctuaries of Aphrodite founded by Aeneas on Leucas, at Actium, and in Ambracia. Virgil mentions none of these; just as, out of all the ἱερὰ τῆς Ἀφροδίτης [sanctuaries of Aphrodite] attributed to Aeneas, he selected just the one, the one that was most important to Rome, that of Venus Erycina (5.760), here, too, he is careful to avoid duplication. In the case of Actium, in total conformity with the standpoint of the whole narrative, Apollo is named, even though it is not explicitly stated that it is in his honour that Aeneas orders the games to be celebrated on the Actian shore as a thanksgiving for the safe voyage through a hostile region.²⁴ It is obvious that the whole episode is inserted because of the significance which Actium had gained for Virgil's generation. That is why it is only here that Virgil mentions a dedicatory gift by Aeneas, although according to the tradition he offered them in many places. For example, Aeneas is said to have dedicated a shield at Samothrace (Serv. on 287), as he does here.

    The passages that I have cited are the sum total of the material that Virgil took from the tradition for his narrative of this part of the journey. It is only a small part of what was available to him; he was able to draw on a richer tradition than is known to us from Dionysius, and even he tells us a great deal that Virgil disdained to use: apart from numerous stopping-points and foundations of temples, there are Aeneas' relationship with Launa, the daughter of Anius; the death of Cinaethus, who was buried on the promontory now called after him; the sojourn in Arcadia, where Aeneas left behind two daughters; the games established in honour of Aphrodite on Zacynthus; and the detour to Dodona, which we have already discussed. It would have been necessary to give all these events their own significance by inventing motivation, which would have expanded the narrative out of all proportion and would have overshadowed the principal theme in a most undesirable way, or, narrated in Apollonius' annalistic style, it would have been of merely academic interest,

102

103

which had no value for Virgil. We can readily understand why he simply dispensed with this surplus material. Nor does he record with antiquarian precision the local traditions of South Italian cities which claimed traces of a visit by Aeneas.[25] Aeneas puts in only at Castrum Minervae, to fulfil the vow which he made for a safe crossing; for the rest, the reference in Helenus' prophecy to Greek settlements along the coast explains why the Trojans do not put in to land at any point; this maintains the impression that the voyage is perilous and like a flight. The only omission that we might find surprising is the meeting with Diomedes, which, according to a respectable legend, took place in Calabria. Of course, Virgil could not use the story that Diomedes took Anchises' bones from the tomb and returned them to Aeneas; but there was another tradition, according to which Diomedes came up to Aeneas while he was sacrificing, to return the Palladium of Troy, possession of which had brought him misfortune. In order not to interrupt the sacrifice, Aeneas turned away

104   with his head covered, and so Nautes received the sacred object instead, which explains why the cult remained in the hands of his descendants, the Nautii.[26] Virgil retained the αἴτιον [traditional explanation] for covering the head during a sacrifice, and he also knows of Nautes as a favourite of Pallas (5.704); but he motivates the covering of the head as being due to fear of seeing an enemy while sacrificing, and omits Diomedes completely; and yet one would have thought that Virgil would have welcomed the opportunity for Aeneas to take the Palladium, and thus complete the number of *pignora imperii* [tokens of empire] in his care; as it is, the Palladium is mentioned only in Sinon's account of its theft (2.166). It is possible that he believed that this tradition was open to objections on factual grounds;[27] it is also possible that he considered it too novelistic that Aeneas and Diomedes should meet in person, and therefore chose to refashion the motif so as to create a new episode, which we now read in Book 11, the unsuccessful attempt by the Latins to obtain help from Diomedes: here, too, Diomedes comes to realise that the misfortune that dogs him is due to the fact that his fight against Troy was a fight against gods.

5. Poetic re-shaping

When Virgil selected material from the tradition and arranged it to accord with the dominant theme of his new scheme, he always started with the bare bones of the action. For all the rest, for the clothing of these bones with the flesh of living poetry, he had to rely on free invention. But his free invention is not a matter of new creation, it is a reshaping of existing motifs, working in features borrowed from other legends. He used three cycles of legends: the various versions of the tale of the destruction of Troy; the *Odyssey*; and the voyage of the Argonauts.

105   The legend of Polydorus comes immediately after the sack of Troy. Virgil used it in a highly original way, to motivate the Trojans' abandonment of their first attempt to found a city in Thrace. The spears which the treacherous Thracians rained down upon Polydorus grew roots and now cover his burial-mound with a thicket of myrtle and cornel cherry. When Aeneas tears a young tree out of the earth, blood flows from the roots; this happens again when he tries a second time; at the third attempt Aeneas hears from the grave the pitiful groan of the dead man and learns for the first

time that he had been murdered. For the account of Polydorus' fate which Aeneas proceeds to give, Virgil seems in all probability to have used Euripides' *Hecuba*;[28] but his version of the way in which Polydorus was killed, and the fate of his corpse, is completely different from that of Euripides. The ancient commentators were not able to identify any source for Virgil here.[29] Servius felt that it was necessary to defend Virgil against the charge of having invented an implausible falsehood by reminding us of the cornel cherry which had grown out of Romulus' spearshaft on the Palatine, but it is a far cry from that story to Virgil's invention. I prefer to believe that Virgil transferred to Polydorus something which he found in a narrative about someone else.[30] Given the nature of the relationship between Polydorus and Polymestor, it is highly improbable that he died in the manner narrated here. It is more likely that it was some hero who could not be beaten in close combat who was overcome from a distance by a shower of spears.[31] I do not believe that Virgil   106 invented the whole episode, primarily because there is no motivation in the present context for the miraculous transformation of the spearshafts into live saplings, whereas it would be easy to imagine that in the original story some god who was favourably disposed towards the murdered man covered the corpse in this way and thus made sure that it received a kind of burial. The idea that blood could still flow from the wounds of a man murdered long before will have been modelled on legends where bleeding from damaged plants and trees reveals that a metamorphosis has taken place. This motif may have been more common than it is possible for us to establish; the only example that I can recall is the metamorphosis of Lotis (Ovid *Met.* 9.344).[32] But it may have been precisely this detail of bleeding which led Virgil to take over the whole motif in the first place; as the expression *monstra deum*[33] (59) [divine omen] clearly shows, the gruesome event is intended to serve as a *prodigium*, warning the Trojans that the gods forbid the new foundation. However, it is well known how frequently blood plays a role in *prodigia*: sometimes it rains blood, sometimes blood appears in wells, rivers and lakes, or on images of gods; sometimes too – and this is closest to our example – the corn bleeds when it is reaped (Livy 22.1; 28.11).

More important than the question of Virgil's source, which cannot be answered with certainty at present, is the manner in which he narrates the whole episode. This deserves careful attention. The foundation of the city, which for an Alexandrian poet would be something of considerable importance, is dismissed in two lines; the name Aeneadae leaves us in doubt whether Virgil means Aineia in Macedonia or Ainos in Thrace;[34] indeed, Aeneas' account actually implies that no settlement took place, since all the Trojans depart again from the *scelerata terra* (60) [wicked land].   107 Moreover, we are not told anything about their relations with the Thracians who own the territory, or the *hospitium* mentioned in line 61; similarly we are left completely in the dark about what Aeneas believed concerning the fate of Polydorus, until the moment that the *prodigium* tells him the truth. We might easily assume that Aeneas had landed on a desolate coast, as in Latium, had immediately marked out the lines of the city walls, and that the sacrifice on the shore was the first to be offered by the Trojans in their new home, and that they then left again as quickly as they could – except that other phrases[35] seem to indicate that the Trojans spent the winter on the Thracian coast, which agrees with the tradition known to us from Dionysius. In a word, the poet deliberately puts all this to one side, perhaps salving his conscience with the thought that Aeneas, as narrator, would not expect his listeners to be interested in it, whereas the real reason was that the poet himself did not think it worth including. The only thing that he does think important is the emotional episode at the burial-mound, and while a writer more attracted by the gruesome than Virgil might have put all the emphasis on this aspect of the incident, Virgil imbues it with a different emotion: pity for the poor victim, who is still suffering pain even after death, and whose body is still being torn as if he were still alive.

108 The encounter with Helenus was one of the few motifs capable of poetic development which Virgil was able to take from the tradition (Dion. Hal. 1.32). We have already discussed the prediction. Virgil treated the scenes of greeting and departure in great detail, so as to develop all the pathos which the situation contained, especially that created by the presence of Andromache. The poet's interest is centred on her rather than on Helenus, who remains a colourless figure. Here, too, he took his inspiration from tragedy: he has Euripides' *unhappy* Andromache in mind; not the mother worrying about her little son (Molossus, son of Neoptolemus, does not appear; he would have destroyed the concentration of the interest on a single figure, and just imagine how Aeneas would have regarded the son of the man he loathed so much!), but the uncomforted, endlessly sorrowing widow of Hector and mother of Astyanax: Virgil does not permit the comparatively happy situation in which she now finds herself to have any effect on her nature. Thus her sorrow for her past losses is not tempered by joy in her living son and her Trojan husband, but only increased by the tormenting shame that she has had to share the bed of the arrogant victor. When she catches sight of Aeneas, her first thought is of Hector; she turns all her attention to Ascanius, overwhelms Aeneas with a host of questions about him, gives him parting gifts, for she seems to see Astyanax in him; this is one of the most moving passages in Virgil's poem.[36] Just as she is reminded of the death of

109 Astyanax, so too Andromache thinks of the sacrifice of Polyxena. Thus two of the most important episodes of the sack of Troy, of which Aeneas himself could not give an eye-witness account, are treated to some extent at this later point.[37]

110 Virgil made use of the *Odyssey* in many ways. First, as we have already observed in many instances, he has transferred the situations of Odysseus to Aeneas: this includes Helenus' prediction, which combines Teiresias' prediction with the instructions of Circe;[38] also the sojourn at Dido's court, which reminds us in more than one respect of the reception of Odysseus by the Phaeacians, and in another way of the Calypso story, although its main motif is borrowed from elsewhere; the slaughter of the cattle of the Harpies, in which he plays around very freely with the motif of the cattle of the Sun; the tempest in Book 1, where not only are the whole situation and important details in the description borrowed from the *Odyssey*, but also the words of the hero, though they are characteristically remodelled;[39] and finally, the Nekyia.

111 Secondly, Virgil introduced into his poem the places mentioned by Odysseus, together with their fabulous inhabitants. In doing so, he had a predecessor in Apollonius, who brought the Argo back home along the whole of the same route as Odysseus, most of this of course not by his own invention. The dangerous voyage through the Planktai (4.922) had already been mentioned in the *Odyssey* itself (12.59ff.); Scylla and Charybdis are also mentioned (Ap. 4.823, 920). The tradition

followed by Apollonius also included the purification by Circe (659) and the visit to the Phaeacians (980); and the Sirens (889) had also already been given their place in the tale of the Argonauts through the introduction of the story of Butes. For erudite philological and geographical reasons, Apollonius links Calypso's island, about which he tells us nothing except its location (572) and the cattle of the Sun which they see and hear as they sail by (963), with Thrinacia. Finally, Aeolus is ruler of the winds but does not come into direct contact with the Argonauts, a role similar to that which he plays in Virgil (762, 775, 817). Virgil's task was considerably more difficult: the legend had not covered the same ground before, and if he wanted his hero to undergo any experiences in the wake of Odysseus, he was obliged to depend entirely on his own free invention; and in so doing, in order to remain true to his principles, he had to avoid an episodic style as far as possible. The *Phaeacum arces* (291) [citadels of the Phaeacians] are mentioned only in order to indicate the locality, and so too is the Sirens' island (5.864), where the poet refers to its former terrors with the utmost brevity. Aeolus had been dealt with in the scene in Book 1: and only in this instance does Virgil depart from Homeric tradition and follow a different source.[40] Scylla and Charybdis however are given greater prominence; they are not an episodic addition, but the reason for the detour round Sicily. Aeneas does not see them himself, but only hears the mighty roar of Charybdis from afar (3.555ff.); but he has heard about the horrific creatures from Helenus (420ff.), in whose speech there is an excellent reason for their detailed description: it is the only way to give his warning the emphasis that is required. In the case of Circe, too, the Trojans only sail past (7.10-24): it is night, the reflection of moonlight trembles on the surface of the sea; a fire is blazing there on the shore in front of the enchantress' lofty palace; the roaring of wild beasts sounds through the stillness of the night. This is the last danger which threatens Aeneas and his men before they reach their destination; Neptune is merciful, and carries them past. The poet lingers rather 112 longer over this descriptive passage; not only because Circe alone of all these fabulous creatures was also involved in Latin legend; Monte Circeo, familiar to every Roman, had to be mentioned as a landmark, quite apart from its significance in legend; even today, anyone describing a voyage along that coast mentions it. There remains the only purely episodic insertion in Book 3, the scene on the shore of the Cyclopes. Virgil wanted to depict Polyphemus in all his frightfulness,[41] but without exposing Aeneas to the same kind of danger that Odysseus had to undergo, since he was taking care not to create an episode in rivalry with the incomparable adventure in Homer. That is why he introduces Achaemenides, whom he can use as a mediating figure to link the voyage of Aeneas directly with the most famous of all voyages: tradition did tell of a meeting between Aeneas and Odysseus himself,[42] but here Odysseus is replaced by one of his companions. However, Virgil was able to imbue this invented figure[43] and his fate with an emotional interest which transcends the monstrous element in the adventure: the unfortunate man who has to beseech his mortal enemy to rescue him from a fate that is even worse than dying – this is an invention that is entirely typical of Virgil's art.[44] Virgil emphasizes rather than conceals the similarity with the Sinon scene. Indeed, the Trojans' humanity cannot 113 be better demonstrated than here in this scene, where those who had once themselves been plunged into disaster because they trusted and took pity, nevertheless

83

show mercy again towards a suppliant enemy. And here, where no divine power is plotting misfortune for the pious, the nobility of their nature is rewarded: they owe their own rescue to the man they have rescued. Thus the bold cunning of Odysseus is implicitly matched by the *pietas* of the Trojans.

In the adventure with the Harpies on the Strophades various legendary motifs have been fused together. Apollonius had recounted in detail how the Boreads free Phineus from the Harpies and, at Iris' command, cease pursuing them at the islands which for this reason are known as the Strophades; the Harpies then disappear into a cave on Crete. In Virgil they continue to live on the Strophades, which are even called their *patrium regnum* (249) [hereditary kingdom]; he also gives them rich herds of cattle and goats, which hardly accords with their reputation as creatures that are always hungry and stealing food (in Virgil they still have *pallida semper ora fame* [217-18] [faces always pallid with hunger]). This device serves to introduce an adventure which is analogous with that of Odysseus on the Island of the Sun: the Trojans, like the companions of Odysseus, steal from herds which belong to immortals. When Aeneas' men proceed to fight the monstrous creatures, this may be a reminiscence of the Argonauts' fight with the birds of Ares, although the outcome is different (2.1035ff.). But the purpose of all this is only to provide the poet with the groundwork for his restructuring of the *prodigium* of the tables, which was an established part of the Aeneas legend. We have already discussed (p. 72 above) what was new in Virgil's interpretation of the oracle. The artistic value of the scene lies principally in the steady increase in tension; here the aim of the poet is to arouse not pity but terror, to raise an incident that is merely gruesome and repulsive and to invest it with grandeur and terror: the poet's intention is that Celaeno, as *Furiarum maxima* [greatest of the Furies] and the one who delivers Apollo's prophecy, shall appear as a mythically heroic creature instead of an eerie monster.

The Trojans do not actually run into any danger on the Strophades, but at least they have an opportunity to reach for their weapons; in the other adventures they do not even do that. They run away from Polyphemus before he can get hold of them; Scylla and Charybdis, like Circe, are only seen and heard from a distance; so too with the Sirens, and from them there is nothing else to fear. It is only in the sea-storm in Book 1 that Aeneas is in any real danger of losing his life; and even there he is rescued without any effort on his part. But even though Aeneas' trials during his wanderings do not demand the boldness, energy and endurance that were required of Odysseus, who again and again had to overcome difficulties at risk to life and limb, Virgil certainly did not intend to give the impression that his hero had an easier lot. What he has to suffer is emotional pain, with which the poet can involve himself to a much profounder degree than with physical pain and mortal danger: the loss of his native land, the bitterness of exile, hopes dashed again and again, the years of seeking an unknown destination: these are the sufferings of Aeneas; his fame, and his heroism, lie in his perseverance, in spite of everything, in the task which a god has imposed on him, and which he owes to the gods of his native land. Such emotional suffering and activity are of course much more difficult to depict than visible, physical events, and particularly difficult when they are described by the voice of the hero himself;[45] the poet is relying on the reader identifying so closely with the hero that he will himself feel the emotions which must have engulfed Aeneas. It is this, perhaps, rather than the impact of the individual adventures, which provides the emotional effect that Virgil strives after in his account of the wanderings of Aeneas.

Notes to Chapter 2

1. Cf. also Sabbadini, *Studi critici sulla Eneide* (Lonigo, 1889) 107.   83

2. W.H. Roscher, *Studien zur vergleichenden Mythologie der Griechen und*   85
Römer I: *Apollo und Mars* (Leipzig, 1873) 82ff.; *Ausführliches Lexikon der gr. und röm. Mythologie* (Leipzig, 1884-1937) I.440f.

3. Strabo 6.257.

4. This is clear from Statius *Silv.* 4.8.47 *tu, ductor populi longe migrantis, Apollo* [thou, Apollo, leader of a people migrating far].

5. A similar idea seems to underlie Euripides *Helen* 147, where Teucer wishes to learn from the prophetess Theonoe ὅπῃ νεὼς στείλαιμ' ἄν οὔριον πτερὸν εἰς γῆν ἐναλίαν Κύπρον, οὗ μ' ἐθέσπισεν οἰκεῖν 'Απόλλων [how I might steer my winged ship with a favourable wind to sea-girt Cyprus, where Apollo decreed that I should found a city].

6. So Schüler, *Quaestiones Vergilianae* (Diss. Greifswald, 1883) 8ff., rightly,   86
even though he does not support his conclusions with adequate reasoning; *contra*, Conrads (*Quaest. Vergil.*, Trier, 1863) and Georgii (*Über das dritte Buch der Aeneide* in *Festschrift zur 4. Säkulärfeier der Univ. Tübingen* [Stuttgart, 1877] 65ff.) had previously argued that it was the earliest of the books; similarly Kroll (op. cit. [in ch. 1 n. 102] 157ff.). Sabbadini, who agreed with Schüler in *Studi Critici* 105ff., later modified his view in *Il primitivo disegno dell'Eneide* (Turin, 1900) 30ff., in which he argues that Book 3 was written at the very beginning, in a simple narrative form, but was re-worked at a later stage and put into the mouth of Aeneas; I do not need to add anything to what Helm has said against this hypothesis (*Bursians Jahresberichte* 113 [1902] 50). For the rest, I hope that the exposition of my own view will make it unnecessary to engage in polemic against other individuals – for this reason too I do not defend my view against Karsten, *Hermes* 39 (1904) 259f.; I will only say that he has unfortunately more than once misunderstood me and argued against statements which are far removed from my own position. Gercke in his book   87
Die Entstehung der Aeneis (Leipzig, 1913) has recently revived Conrads' thesis and suggests that Book 3 was written after 7 and 8, and indeed after the whole of the second half of the *Aeneid*, while still being the earliest of the books in the first half (apart from a preliminary sketch for 4). In my view, not only is Gercke's interpretation of individual details highly debatable, but I also believe that the method which he uses in this case and throughout the whole of his book is wrong. It is futile to argue step by step when his standpoint is so completely different from my own (Gercke almost entirely ignores the artistic considerations, whereas I consider them to be of essential importance); I therefore refrain here as elsewhere from arguing with him, and refer to my detailed review of his book which will shortly appear in the *Anzeigen der Göttinger Gesellschaft der Wissenschaften* (117 [1915] 153-71).

88   **7.** It is worth mentioning that the same idea occurs in Ovid's letter from Dido: *certus es...quaeque ubi sint nescis Itala regna sequi* ['are you determined...and to seek the Italian kingdoms, when you do not know where they are'] (*Heroides* 7.9); *non patrium Simoenta petis, sed Thybridas undas...utque latet vitatque tuas abstrusa carinas vix tibi continget terra petita seni* ['it is not the Simois of your homeland you seek, but the waters of the Tiber...and the land you seek is so hidden, so remotely avoiding your ships, that you will hardly reach it as an old man'] (ibid. 145). In Book 3 Aeneas also once (500) mentions Thybris as his destination; at that point, his knowledge of the name is totally inconsistent with the plan of the book; for it cannot be merely by chance that Helenus mentions neither Thybris (which does not appear at all elsewhere in Book 3) nor Latium nor Laurentum in his prophecy: at 389 he says mysteriously *secreti ad fluminis oram* [by the shore of a remote river]. Of course there can be no question of the information being deliberately conveyed κατὰ τὸ σιωπώμενον [by a 'passing over in silence'] in this instance: that device is used to avoid tiresome narration or recapitulation of earlier events, which cannot be the case here. Thus when Thybris is mentioned at line 500 I can only regard it as an oversight on the part of the poet, who had not completely cleared his mind of his earlier idea. I am not convinced that the passages in Books 1, 4 and 6 which mention Latium and the Tiber are the result of the same oversight, since in those books there is no indication that Aeneas does not know the whereabouts of his new home.

89   **8.** In Creusa's speech the definite indication of the distination could easily have been omitted; *matre dea monstrante viam* [with my goddess mother showing the way] in Book 1 is a piquant addition to the scene, but does not affect its essential content; in Book 4 Apollo of Delos might just as well have appeared.

   9. Comparison of the similar lines 1.530-3 and 3.163-6 also shows that Book 3 was written after Book 1; the reference to *fama* is as suitable in the mouth of Ilioneus as it is awkward in the mouth of the prophesying Penates; therefore the lines in Book 3 were taken from Book 1, which had already been composed. I do not agree that the reverse can be proved by the line *terra antiqua, potens armis atque ubere glebae* (1.531 = 3.164) [an ancient land with might in her arms and in her fertile soil] (Kroll, *Neue Jahrbücher* vol. 11 [1908] 522 n. 3): in order to ward off the suspicion that the Trojans have planned a raid on Libya (527f.), Ilioneus is anxious to make Dido understand their real destination, and so has good reason to praise the land in which they hope to gain a new kingdom (this contrast with the *sedes paratae* [a place awaiting us] in Sicily is hinted at in line 557 and would probably have been made explicit when the half-line 534 was completed).

90   **10.** *Hinc Dardanus ortus, huc repetit iussisque ingentibus urget Apollo Tyrrhenum ad Thybrim et fontis vada sacra Numici* (240) [in it Dardanus was born, and to it we are recalled by Apollo who presses us onwards by his peremptory decrees towards Etruscan Tiber and the holy spring-water of Numicus]: these lines are fully consistent with the references in Books 2, 4, 5 and 6.

   11. Paus. 10.10.6: ἀδύνατα ἐνόμιζεν οἱ τὸν θεὸν χρῆσαι [he thought the god had answered him with an impossibility].

91   **12.** It is true that an attempt has been made (by Fulda, *Fleckeisens Jahrbuch* 155 [1897] 213f.) to reconcile the versions in Books 3 and 7: he argues that Aeneas, not

completely reassured by Helenus' comforting words about Celaeno's oracle, turned to Anchises, who, on his deathbed, gave him the true and undeceptive oracle of Apollo; the poet leaves the reader to deduce this from his narrative, in other words κατὰ τὸ σιωπώμενον [by a passing over in silence]. I thought that I would be able to pass over this suggestion in silence, but since not only Karsten (op. cit. n. 6, 262f.) but also the author of a recently published Würzburg dissertation (V. Henselmanns, *Die Widersprüche in Vergils Aeneis* [Aschaffenburg, 1914]) accepts Fulda's interpretation, I will explain why I find it completely untenable: (1) there is no point or meaning in the alleged addition: Helenus' prophecy loses its value and importance if Aeneas does not believe in every word of it but continues in doubt and 'in this difficulty' turns to his father. Moreover, this does not get him any further: the enigma, how devouring ones tables could possibly be a precondition for founding a city, remains unsolved. The fear of starvation remains, and even if Anchises speaks positively (*tum sperare domos...* [then you may hope for a home]) and Celaeno negatively (*non ante quam...* [not until]) this takes him no further forward than Helenus, who had said clearly enough (*nec tu mensarum morsus horresce futuros: fata viam invenient* [394-5] [and be not appalled by the fear of gnawing your tables: Destiny will find a way] that Celaeno's condition will not stand in the way of his reaching the end of his journey. (2) The cases of Virgilian σιωπώμενον [passing over in silence] which I cite in Part II ch. 3.11 and to which Karsten appeals, are quite different from this: there, the fact which has not been mentioned can be inferred *in toto* from the narrative itself; whereas here the most important thing, that Aeneas remained anxious despite Helenus' reassurance, and that Anchises finally calmed him down, is only a hypothesis based on a combination of this passage with the narrative in Book 3, and no reader who does not know Book 3 is going to imagine in Book 7 that something has happened previously without being mentioned. (3) From the artistic point of view it would be impossible to understand why, if Celaeno's prophecy had already been composed, Virgil did not return to it in Book 7 instead of introducing Anchises: there can be no doubt that the portent is much more effective when it proves that the enemy's threat is hollow than when it fulfils the prediction of a friend. That is why Helenus' speech deliberately leaves the meaning of Celaeno's threat unexplained: it only assures them that *fata viam invenient* [Destiny will find a way].

92

13. So Fabius Pictor: Cauer, *Die römische Aeneassage von Naevius bis Vergil* (*Fleckeisens Jahrbuch* Suppl. 15 [1887] 104ff.).

14. Thus Dion. Hal. 1.56. Varro *De Ling. Lat.* 5.144 *hinc post XXX annos oppidum conditum Alba; id ab sue alba nominatum; haec e navi Aeneae quom fugisset Lavinium, XXX parit porcos* [hence after 30 years the town of Alba was founded: this was given its name from a white sow which after fleeing from Aeneas' ship to Lavinium, bore 30 piglets] (cf. *Res Rust.* 2.4.18): *ex hoc prodigio post Lavinium conditum annis XXX haec urbs facta propter colorem suis et loci naturam Alba Longa dicta* [as a result of this portent this city was built 30 years after the foundation of Lavinium and called Alba Longa because of the colour of the sow and the character of the place]. Here *quom fugisset Lavinium* [after fleeing to Lavinium] should perhaps be interpreted in accordance with Dionysius, 'the place where Aeneas subsequently founded Lavinium'; in which case Dionysius follows the version

of the tradition represented by Varro.

93   **15.** In Fabius Pictor; according to Dionysius op. cit. it was φωνή τις ἐκ τῆς νάπης ἀφανοῦς ὄντος τοῦ φθεγγομένου [a voice of an unseen speaker from the glade] or according to others μεγάλη τις καὶ θαυμαστὴ ἐνυπνίου τῶν θεῶν τινι τῶν πατρίων εἰκασθεῖσα ὄψις [a great and wondrous vision in a dream representing one of his country's gods]. The situation with these ἕτεροι [others] is also the same as in Virgil: Aeneas, overcome by anxiety, has gone to sleep in the open air on the future site of Lavinium, to which the sow has led him.

    16. Line 46, *hic locus urbis erit, requies ea certa laborum* [this spot shall be the place for your city, and there you shall find sure rest from your toils] (= 3.393, as 43-45 = 3.390-392) is lacking in M and P, and in R and later MSS it is doubtless interpolated from Book 3, as is shown by the sense, quite apart from these facts concerning the textual tradition. R and later MSS are inclined to insert interpolations from parallel passages, as can be demonstrated elsewhere: cf. 2.76, 4.273, 528, 9.121, 10.278, 872, 12.612f., but this particular interpolation may also have been prompted by the way in which line 47 is loosely attached to the previous line by *ex quo*, which can easily be taken as temporal in sense [from which time], as by Heyne and Norden 197, or as *ex hoc prodigio* [from this portent] by analogy with Varro's words cited in n. 14 above.

96   **17.** *His accensa super iactatos aequore toto Troas...arcebat longe Latio, multosque per annos errabant acti fatis maria omnia circum* (1.29-32) [such were the causes of her fury: and so it was that the Trojans were tossed in storm over all the ocean; and still she kept them far from Latium, wandering for years at the mercy of the fates from sea to sea about the world].

    18. *Mene incepto desistere victam nec posse Italia Teucrorum avertere regem?* (37-8) ['I, vanquished? I, to abandon the fight? Lacking even the strength to keep Troy's prince from making Italy?'].

    19. *Una cum gente tot annos bella gero* (47) [I have been making war for all these years on a single clan]: this, however, also includes the Trojan war.

97   **20.** Sabbadini (op. cit. 27) considers these lines to be a later interpolation spun out of 8.60ff.: he has not produced any convincing arguments on this point, nor indeed for his entire hypothesis that the prophecy should be reduced to an original nucleus (374 to 395; 410 to 413; 429 to 432; 462ff.). The landing at the Promunturium Minervae 531ff. is alleged to be inconsistent with the command of Helenus at 381-3: surely far more so with lines 396ff., which Sabbadini 28 strangely misunderstands. He says that the 89 lines of the prophecy do not agree with its description as *pauca* [a few] at 377: but what he says there is *pauca e multis, quo tutior hospita lustres aequora* [only a few of many truths, that you may voyage the more safely over foreign seas], and in fact Helenus does omit a lot, e.g. Polyphemus, the burning of the ships, the death of Palinurus. He speaks only of *things which it is useful for*

98 *Aeneas to know in advance*, so that he can act on them. Therefore he says nothing, for example, of the death of Anchises or, consequently, of the visit to the Underworld, which is closely connected with Anchises' death according to Book 6 as we have it: and when Aeneas says *nec vates Helenus, cum multa horrenda moneret, hos mihi praedixit luctus, non dira Celaeno* (3.712) [Helenus the seer never foretold this grief to me among all his many dread warnings, nor did foul Celaeno], his words do

not express surprise that he had not been told of it, but simply say that the loss of his father was a greater sorrow than all those that had been prophesied. Helenus also says nothing of the sea-storm and the forced landing in Africa – not, as Karsten (op. cit. 289) suggests, because when Virgil was writing Book 3 he had not yet planned the narrative of Book 1 and Book 4, but because Aeneas can do nothing to avert that disaster, except to appease Juno where possible, as Helenus advises him to (433f.); in this advice and in the reason that Helenus gives for it I see an unambiguous reference to the sea-storm. That Helenus is not more explicit at this point is quite sufficiently motivated by lines 379f. as far as the content is concerned, and artistically simply by the fact that it would only spoil the effect of the narrative in Book 1 not to imagine Aeneas and his men as surprised by events.

21. Henselmanns (in the dissertation referred to in n. 12 above, 30f.) argues that 100 Aeneas and his men did not really want to settle in Thrace: 'Thrace was visited by their neighbours the Trojans only as a *hospitium* [a 'stop-over'] (cf. 3.15.61), and Book 3 (18ff.) says that a city was founded there merely to provide a historical explanation for Aenos in Thrace or for Aenea in Chalcidice.' How can it be *only* 'as a *hospitium*' (which Virgil does not say) and at the same time the foundation of a city? Why should Aeneas found a city, since he can hardly have done it to provide a historical explanation for the Thracian Aenea? When, after the discovery of Polydorus' murder, Aeneas consults the Trojans, like a consul asking the senate for its *sententia* [opinion], their verdict is *scelerata excedere terra* (3.60) [to leave this wicked land], showing that they had previously intended to remain there. Henselmanns' objection 'that for such a nearby and familiar country to be the promised land lies clearly outside the range of such (!) prophecies, which generally refer to some distant, unknown locality' only holds good on the assumption that Creusa's prophecy has already been made: but the whole plan of Book 3 excludes this possibility. In what follows I shall disregard the misunderstandings and errors of this dissertation.

22. Serv. on 3.148. Dion. Hal. 1.67.   102

23. The geographical details are as vague here as for the foundation in Thrace, for which see below. *mox et Leucatae nimbosa cacumina montis et formidatus nautis aperitur Apollo* (274-5) [presently there appeared the cloud-capped headland of Leucate, and Apollo's temple which seafarers hold in dread] – that can only be the temple of Apollo on the southernmost tip of Leucas – *hunc petimus fessi et parvae succedimus urbi* (276) [being weary, we head for this place and go up to the little city]: by *urbs* (a) Virgil either meant the city of Leucas, or else (b) he assumed the existence of a city of Actium and thought it was controlled by Apollo Leucatas, or else (c) he meant Anactorium; in any case, even if he had a clear picture of it in his own mind, he did not think it important to create such a picture in the reader's mind. Servius' interpretation of it as Ambracia is improbable in the extreme.

24. This motivation (and *de Danais victoribus* [taken from the victorious Greeks] on the dedicatory inscription) relies on the reader's awareness of the contrast, that at the very place where Aeneas celebrates with games *medios fugam tenuisse per hostes* [that they had safely escaped their enemies], his greatest descendant set up the Agon [games] in memory of his greatest victory.

25. Dion. Hal. 1.51.   103

104   **26.** Varro (*de familiis Troianis*) in Serv. on 2.166.

27. According to Varro's account, the cult statue of the Nautii (the *simulacrum aeneum Minervae, cui postea Nautii sacrificari soliti sunt* [the bronze statue of Minerva, to which the Nautii subsequently used to sacrifice], Festus 178 ed. Mueller [Leipzig, 1880] 166) would have to be the Palladium, although the official view, also represented by Varro himself in the *Antiquitates* (Wissowa, *Hermes* 22 [1887] 40), was that the Palladium was among the *sacra Vestae* [sacred objects of Vesta]. If Virgil had followed the former account, he would have been denying the existence of the *Palladium Vestae*. On the other hand, it is obvious that he could hardly accept the notion that there were two Palladia, which was plainly an emergency explanation invented by those who included the Palladium among the *sacra* rescued from Troy. The only course open to him was to say nothing about it.

105   **28.** Πολύδωρος...ὃν ἐκ Τροίας ἐμοὶ πατὴρ δίδωσι Πρίαμος ἐν δόμοις τρέφειν, ὕποπτος ὢν δὴ Τρωικῆς ἁλώσεως [Polydorus, whom his father Priam gave to me to bring up in my palace, fearing that Troy would be taken] *Hecuba* 1133 = *hunc Polydorum...infelix Priamus furtim mandarat alendum Threicio regi, cum iam diffideret armis Dardaniae cingique urbem obsidione videret* (49ff.) [when the hapless Priam, realizing that Troy was condemned to a long siege, had begun to lose faith in Trojan arms, he had secretly entrusted Polydorus...to the care of the King of Thrace]; *furtim* [secretly] and *auri cum pondere magno* [with a heavy store of gold] echo *Hecuba* 10: πολὺν δὲ σὺν ἐμοὶ χρυσὸν ἐκπέμπει λάθρᾳ πατήρ [and with me my father secretly sent much gold]; *dum fortuna fuit* (16) [in the days of her prosperity] = 1208 ὅτ' ηὐτύχει Τροία [while Troy prospered].

29. In recent works one occasionally reads that Lutatius Catulus had an account of the foundation in Thrace similar to Virgil's; this error goes back to Heyne, who quoted (excursus 1 to Book 3) as from the *Historiae* of Q. Lutatius what comes in the *Origo gentis Romanae* 9 shortly after a quotation from 'Lutatius', but is actually of course from Virgil.

30. See also Norden 166.

31. There is, for example, the murder of Pyrrhus by the Delphians in Eurip. *Andr.* 1128ff., or that of Achilles himself by the Trojans (schol. Eurip. *Tro.* 16), or of Leucippus by the companions of Daphne, Parthen. 15.

106   **32.** A more distant parallel is the metamorphosis of the Heliades (Ovid, *Met.* 2.359f.) where bleeding results from an attempt to free their bodies from the bark during the transformation. In the story of Eurypylus (ibid. 8.762), the only parallel known to Servius, the bleeding of the tree is probably a detail added by Ovid; it does not appear in Callimachus.

33. At 7.81 and 270 *monstra* is used of the *prodigia*, which at 58 are called *portenta deum*.

34. For an account of Aeneas as founder of Aineia and Ainos see Schwegler, *Römische Geschichte* (Tübingen, 1853-8) I.301 n. 7. Virgil is apparently thinking of Ainos, because that is where Polydorus' burial-mound was to be seen (Plin. *N.H.* 4.11, 43); but *procul* [far off] in line 13, the mention of Lycurgus and the name
107   Αἰνειάδαι, which is attested by Theon as a poetic name for Aineia (Steph. Byz. s.v.) might lead one to think rather of Aineia. Against Ainos, Servius (on line 16) objects that it already occurs in Homer (*Iliad* 4.520), and therefore it cannot have been

founded by Aeneas, which is why Virgil avoids the name. The Aeneas legend had been linked with Chalcidice since very ancient times, whereas Aeneas as the founder of Ainos is known only to Pomponius Mela (2.2.8); one should not rely on Servius' *Aenum constituit ut multi putant* [he founded Aenus, as many people believe], and it is not impossible that he was influenced by Virgil, just as Virgil is indubitably the source for Ammian. Marc. 22.8 (*Aenus qua diris auspiciis coepta moxque relicta ad Ausoniam veterem ductu numinum properavit Aeneas* [Aenus which was started under dire auspices and presently abandoned, and Aeneas under divine guidance hastened to ancient Ausonia] and the *Origo gentis Romanae* 9.4.

35. 69ff.: they depart *ubi prima fides pelago placataque venti dant maria et lenis crepitans vocat auster in altum* [as soon as we could trust the ocean, when winds offered us smiling seas and the whisper of a breeze invited us onto the deep]: this is most naturally taken as referring to the beginning of the sailing season in the spring, since there has not been any mention of a previous storm which has now calmed down (as at 5.763). Also *litora complent* [they crowd to the beach] in 71 shows that the Trojans are thought of as living in the new city.

36. There are many individual phrases that are clearly reminiscences of the Greek, most of them already noticed. In Aeneas' first speech *quis te casus d e i e c - t a m   c o n i u g e   t a n t o   excipit* (317) [what has fate done to you since you fell from the high estate of such a great husband] reminds us of Hector's words to Andromache (*Iliad* 6.462) σοὶ δ' αὖ νέον ἔσσεται ἄλγος χήτεϊ τοιοῦδ' ἀνδρὸς ἀμύνειν δούλιον ἦμαρ [and you will experience new grief at the lack of such a husband to ward off the day of slavery]. Andromache begins by saying how fortunate Polyxena is, to have escaped slavery by death: similarly in Euripides *Tro.* 630 she says of Polyxena: ὄλωλεν ὡς ὄλωλεν, ἀλλ' ὅμως ἐμοῦ ζώσης γ' ὄλωλεν εὐτυχεστέρῳ πότμῳ [she has died as she has died: nevertheless she has died by a happier fate than mine, although I live] and 677: ναυσθλοῦμαι δ' ἐγὼ πρὸς Ἑλλάδ' αἰχμάλωτος εἰς δοῦλον ζυγόν. ἆρ' οὐκ ἐλάσσω τῶν ἐμῶν ἡγεῖ κακῶν Πολυξένης ὄλεθρον [but I am carried by ship, a prisoner, to Greece to become a slave. Don't you think the death of Polyxena a lesser evil than mine?]; in his account of her fate Virgil may have had in mind the account that Andromache herself gives in the prologue to Euripides' play of that name (see Conington on 328); *me famulo famulamque Heleno transmisit habendam* (329) [he passed me on to be mate to Helenus, two house-slaves together], differs on a point of fact: this is to characterize Pyrrhus as the man who disposes of his slave-girl with the total arbitrariness of a master. With the question *ecqua tamen puero est amissae cura parentis* (341) [can the child remember the mother whom he lost?] compare Hecuba's question about Polydorus εἰ τῆς τεκούσης τῆσδε μέμνηταί τι μου [if he has any memory of me his mother] (Eurip. *Hec.* 92). Reminiscences of Telemachus' visit to Sparta (*Od.* 4.130, 149; 15.125f.) are woven into her parting words at 486ff.: see the commentators.

37. There are clear indications in the Andromache scene and the subsequent meeting with Helenus that these episodes were unfinished, quite apart from the half-lines at 316 and 340 – the latter is the only one in the *Aeneid* in which the sentence is even left incomplete. Thus Virgil certainly wrote line 348, *et multum lacrimas verba inter singula fundit* [talking with many tears at every word], and was of course able to do so despite *laetus* [joyful] in 347, but on the other hand I doubt

108

109

whether the line would have remained in this form if it was to follow immediately after 344f. Again, the reception and hospitality given to the *Teucri* (which Virgil writes at 352 instead of the usual *socii* [my men], because *socia urbe* [a city of friends] follows) might perhaps have been revised, although there is no justification for the objections raised against *illos* [them] in 353, since Aeneas is here indeed speaking of the *populus* [people], to whom Helenus gives a great feast *porticibus in amplis* [in a spacious colonnade], just as at the reception in Dido's palace only the *proceres* [leaders] are present, while the *populus* feasts on the shore (1.633). In general, as so often happens, scholars have used the established fact that the scenes have not received their final polish to make quite unjustified criticisms that greatly overshoot the mark (for example, Georgii op. cit. 76ff.). *Hector ubi est?* (312) ['where is Hector?'] has been criticized, but it is magnificent; after all, if the dead are appearing, Andromache thinks, then it is Hector above all that she may expect to see. (Dante felt the beauty of this passage, as is shown by his imitation in *Inferno* 10.58f.) Equally unobjectionable are the questions that Aeneas asks at 317ff. He says explicitly – *incredibilis fama* (294) [an incredible rumour] – that at first he could not believe the rumour that Helenus and Andromache were ruling in Chaonia; and the assertion that he would not have landed on Pyrrhus' shores unless he *had* believed it is quite arbitrary: it is clearly stated that he heard this rumour only after he had landed. The assumption that Aeneas gave an account of Creusa's fate which has fallen out of the text (Ribbeck) is just as mistaken as the assumption that Virgil on revision would have given a better reason for Andromache's knowledge of Creusa (Georgii); we have seen again and again in Book 2 that Virgil was no pedant in these matters. It is also obvious that Virgil does not mean that Andromache put one question after another without waiting for an answer, as 337ff. implies if we take it literally; but who would seriously expect the poet to give us Aeneas' answers? In the departure scene, Helenus' speech to Anchises comes very awkwardly in the middle of the list of gifts; I should be surprised if nobody has yet suggested putting lines 472-81 before 463: this would at least be preferable to the violent surgery that others have inflicted on the whole of this passage. The warning at 477-9 has quite rightly been criticized: Helenus had already said all this in much greater detail. Or should Anchises be supposed not to have been present when the prediction was delivered in the temple of Phoebus? In fact, Virgil has completely ignored Anchises throughout the whole of this scene, just as he remained in the background during the questioning of Apollo on Delos. That is perfectly understandable: Anchises, the crippled old man, never acts independently, but only advises or commands, or prays as the head of the family (265, 528), here *stans celsa in puppi* [high on the quarter-deck], as at 2.699: *se tollit ad auras adfaturque deos* [raising himself and looking upwards he prayed to the gods]. But Virgil felt that, since he was after all the head of the family, he should not be completely ignored throughout the extended Helenus scenes, and he therefore inserted lines 472-81 as an afterthought; in fact Helenus did not actually have anything important to say to Anchises, and so the advice in 477ff. is, in my view, merely temporary padding. Virgil introduced Anchises again as the supreme commander, without realizing that after 356ff. special arrangements for the departure were no longer necessary. 482 should follow 471, or even better 469 – perhaps 470f. were inserted only to provide

110

92

a basis for what follows: the guest-gifts are given at the moment of departure, whereas the provision of men (the *duces* are, as Wagner has already perceived, the ἡγεμόνες [1.32] [guides] mentioned by Dionysius, not, as Servius thought, *agasones* [lackeys], who could not be called *duces*), horses, sailing equipment and weapons had probably been seen to earlier. The arms of Neoptolemus are reserved for Aeneas; it is a kind of compensation for the defeated hero that he is now able to wear the armour of his enemy.

38. Virgil was also thinking of Phineus' prediction in Apollonius 2.311: hence *prohibent nam cetera Parcae scire Helenum farique vetat Saturnia Iuno* (379-80) [the rest the Fates do not allow Helenus to know, and Saturnian Juno forbids his prophesying] = οὐ μὲν πάντα πέλει θέμις ὔμμι δαῆναι ἀτρεκές· ὅσσα δ᾽ ὄρωρε θεοῖς φίλον, οὐκ ἐπικεύσω ['not everything is it lawful for you to know clearly: but whatever is pleasing to the gods, I will not conceal']. Apollonius gives a more personal reason for the withholding of information by the prophesier (see Hensel, *Weissagungen in der alexandr. Poesie* [Diss. Giessen, 1908] 27): Phineus is still being punished for having once revealed too much of Zeus' decrees to mankind. Virgil could not accept the idea that Zeus begrudged mankind full knowledge of the future, ἵνα καί τι θεῶν χατέωσι νόοιο [so that they may still have some lack of knowledge of the will of the gods] (Ap. Rhod. 2.316); he prefers to motivate it mythically, on the grounds of Hera's enmity.

39. See above p. 46.

40. See above p. 45.

41. To a certain extent, the ground for Achaemenides' description of Polyphemus has been prepared by the description of a natural horror: all through the night after they have landed, Aeneas' men hear the roaring of Etna and see its fires, without realizing where these terrifying phenomena come from.

42. Dion. Hal. 12.22. We need not discuss here whether the Lycophron scholia are right to see Odysseus in the Nanos mentioned at *Alexandra* 1244, with whom Aeneas forms an alliance in Etruria (cf. Geffcken, *Timaios' Geographie des Westens, Phil. Untersuch.* 13 [Berlin, 1892] 44).

43. It is clear from the name Achaemenides that he did invent him: a Greek writer – and any source would necessarily have been Greek – would hardly have given a companion of Odysseus this characteristically Persian name; the Roman poet may have been led astray by its similarity to Achaeus.

44. This emotional interest sharply differentiates the scene from the narrative in Apollonius 2.1092ff., the rescue of the sons of Phrixus by the Argonauts. On the surface the resemblance is unmistakable, and Virgil may have received the initial impulse for his creation from this passage: like Achaemenides, the sons of Phrixus are helplessly marooned on an island which is haunted by dangerous creatures (the birds of Ares); the dialogues also run very similarly to those in Virgil. But there is no connection between the birds of Ares and the shipwrecked men – the encounter might just as well have taken place on any other island – nor does Apollonius attempt to extract any pathos from the situation in which the sons of Phrixus find themselves. Furthermore, the dramatic effect is spoilt by the fact that the reader is told in detail beforehand what the Argonauts later learn from Argus. Compare in particular Virgil's description of Achaemenides' arrival with the dry words of

111

112

113

93

Apollonius τάχα δ' ἐγγύθεν ἀντεβόλησαν ἀλλήλοις, Ἄργος δὲ παροίτατος ἔκφατο μῦθον (2.1121-2) [soon they drew near and met each other, and Argus spoke first].

114   **45.** The ethos of Aeneas' parting words to Helenus and Andromache is indeed the ethos of the whole book: *vivite felices, quibus est fortuna peracta iam sua; nos alia ex aliis in fata vocamur* (493-4) [live, and prosper, for all your adventures are past. We are called ever onwards from destiny to destiny].

3

Dido

History told of the voluntary suicide of Queen Dido, whereby she kept faith with her husband Sicharbas beyond the grave. When she saw no other escape from an enforced marriage with Iarbas, she mounted the funeral-pyre. Some poet, perhaps Naevius,[1] freely reworked this story in the style of Hellenistic love-poetry, and sent to the funeral-pyre not the ever-faithful widow but the woman that Aeneas has loved and abandoned. Virgil has adopted this version, and consequently it has become famous, but the consciousness that it is a poetic fiction has not been lost; no historian, as far as we know, has granted it so much as a mention.[2] Even in Virgil the original picture of Dido shines through beneath his new over-painting; not only in the importance that Virgil still assigns to the motif of her loyalty to her dead husband: when Dido laments that she has allowed her sense of shame to die and has ruined her reputation, the one thing by which she had been hoping to gain immortality (4.322), there is a memory – no doubt unconscious – of that Dido who went to her death for the sake of loyalty, and so won for herself immortal fame.

Thus when Virgil incorporated Dido into his epic, it was certainly not because he was forced to do so by the strength of established tradition.

Nor was he constrained to do so for technical reasons, such as the need to provide someone to listen to Aeneas' story; Acestes, for example, could have fulfilled this function. It was simply that Virgil regarded a love story as an integral part of an epic. Circe and Calypso, Hypsipyle and Medea urgently demanded a counterpart if Aeneas' experiences were not to look jejune in comparison with those of Odysseus and Jason; moreover, Virgil's ideal was the greatest possible richness and the utilization of all possible epic motifs. As soon as Virgil's attention was drawn, by some earlier poetic version, to the woman who founded Carthage, we can imagine how his gaze will have lingered on her, spellbound; she was indeed ideally suited to the poet's purpose. History knew, of course, of other liaisons of Aeneas: he is said to have fathered a son by the daughter of Anius (Serv. on 3.80), and in Arcadia they knew of two daughters born to him by Codone and Anthemone (Agathyllus cited by Dion. Hal. 1.49); but what were these unknown girls compared with the most powerful queen known in the history of the west, the founder of the only city which was to threaten Rome? And what a perspective this struggle between Rome and Carthage, a struggle that was to affect the history of the entire world, gave to the encounter, first friendly, then hostile, of their two founders! But as soon as Virgil had envisaged the possibility of including Dido, then she was the obvious person to listen to Aeneas' tale – possibly Naevius suggested this idea too.[3] Virgil was doubtless proud of having discovered new and fruitful developments of the Homeric device of recounting adventures: Dido's burgeoning love impels her to her urgent questioning, and Aeneas' narrative of his deeds and disasters vastly intensifies her love, which thus becomes the motivation of the action.[4]

The tragic outcome of this love was taken over by Virgil from his predecessor. If it was Naevius, he can hardly have provided more than the barest skeleton of events;

118   the treatment is entirely Virgil's. There is probably no part of his epic where he stands at a further remove from Homer than here; and he seems to have been fully aware of what he was doing. If it was indeed his ideal to come as close as possible to early epic without losing those improvements and new developments of later times which he valued, then here he was entering a world which had really only been discovered since Homer's time: the portrayal of love as a passion which both floods the soul with rapture and at the same time destroys it. Homer does not say much about love; goddesses may not send their beloved hero on his way gladly, but nevertheless they do so with the carefree spirit that is characteristic of Homer's divinities: Calypso provides food for the journey, Circe gives directions for the journey, there are no fond words of farewell.[5] Apollonius, who is quite modern in his portrayal of Medea's vain struggle against overwhelming passion, nevertheless does not go far beyond the restrained tone of the ancient epic in his account of the episode on Lemnos, even though in itself it is analogous to the tale of Dido. We are given the farewell words of Hypsipyle and Jason, it is true, and there is talk of tears and the clasping of hands; but the couple seem to understand each other perfectly. Hypsipyle never counted on holding her beloved guest captive for ever; it does not occur to her to chide him for leaving her. The essential thing here is the event; Apollonius hardly even touches on the emotions involved. Virgil had chosen to use the form of the epic because he valued it above all for the opportunity that it gave him to create strong emotional effects. There was no lack of models and precedents: in no area was the last flowering of Greek poetry more inventive than in searching out all the dangers and misfortunes of consuming passion, love unknown or love deceived or unlawful love, which drove its victim through sorrow, shame and despair to suicide. Such themes, admittedly, had hardly ever yet formed the subject of an epic: the Hellenistic period had created for itself a new vehicle, the epyllion,

119   that was ideally suited to the new material. Virgil's poem about Dido, complete and self-contained, certainly had some kinship with that classical miniature form of narrative: but it is quite clear that, despite the subject-matter, the poet was striving to achieve and maintain the heroic tone of the epic. In this he was given invaluable help by drama: there he could learn how to treat his material in an elevated style, and he did not scorn this help.[6] The analysis which follows is an attempt to unravel the technique of Virgil's tragic epyllion into its component parts.

1. Scene setting: love

The fourth book is devoted to Dido. She dominates the scene to such an extent that the epic hero plays a secondary role. At the beginning of the book we find her caught in the toils of love. She attains her heart's desire; then comes the *peripeteia* of the drama, leading to a rapid plunge from the heights of happiness and to the fatal conclusion. The ground for this tragedy is laid in Book 1 in the full detail which is one of the advantages that an epic poet has over a dramatist.

Dido's entrance is prepared in two ways. First, Aeneas hears about her from

Venus; the narrative is ingeniously contrived so that it not only informs us but also wins our sympathies.[7] The listener is moved first to pity, then to admiration: here is a princess wounded to the depths of her soul, who pulls herself together, and whose misfortune gives her the strength to overcome her feminine frailty, to perform deeds of masculine daring – *dux femina facti* [the enterprise was led by a woman] – and, a mere woman, to venture to found a city amongst barbarian tribes, a city whose beginning prefigures its future greatness. Secondly, Aeneas sees Dido's achievement, the city itself, and is astonished by its magnificent lay-out and the swarming activity of the builders, in which the spirit of their queen is reflected (1.420-36); her humanity, which honours the greatness of another race, and pities their sufferings, is shown by the paintings in the temple, which also tell him that his own name and achievements are not unknown to the queen (456ff.).

Only now does Dido herself appear, and her appearance fully lives up to the expectations that Virgil has aroused in us: she enters in regal majesty with a royal retinue, with royal dignity.[8] So far, Aeneas has only admired her works, but now he sees her in action; so far, he has been hoping that she will show a sense of humanity and nobility, and now these hopes are fulfilled by the reception which she accords to the Trojan suppliants. Thus everything conspires to prepare the ground most propitiously for the long-awaited personal encounter between Aeneas and the queen, which now ensues.

All this is a piece of scene-setting which I believe to be without parallel in ancient narrative literature. Individual details are borrowed from Odysseus' reception by the Phaeacians: just as Venus tells Aeneas about Dido, so Athena tells Odysseus about Arete; Aeneas is astonished by the sight of Carthage, as Odysseus is by the harbours and ships, squares and walls in the city of the Phaeacians (*Od.* 7.43ff.). But it is easy to see how much more significant the two motifs have become in Virgil, since they both prepare the way for what is to come: Aeneas is to fall in love with the princess whom Venus praises so highly to him, and he is to take up and continue her work of building the city whose greatness and progress he so admires. Everything that he sees and experiences in the temple of Juno is calculated to make Aeneas, and with him the reader, admire Dido more and more, and this has no parallel in the *Odyssey*; Virgil's inspiration is a truly dramatic one: the poet transforms everything that he has to tell us about his heroine into action, which is carried forward by Aeneas. Thus not only has he already been won over to Dido before he has even exchanged a single word with her; the reader, too, receives an impression at her first entrance comparable to the impression that we experience in a drama at the first entrance of a principal character, about whom intense expectations have been aroused by an ingenious exposition – think for example of *Tartuffe* or *Egmont* – and Virgil can count on the reader's ready acceptance of what the Fates have in store for Dido in Book 4, since they have already begun to spin their thread.

Dido, too, for her part, has long and gradually been prepared for the appearance of Aeneas. It was from Teucer, after the fall of Troy, that she had first heard his name, and it had been from the lips of an enemy that she had first heard his praises (1.619ff.); she knows that he is the son of Venus. The battles around Troy and the part that Aeneas played in them are known to her in every detail. She has used a representation of them to adorn the principal temple of her new city, the temple in

120

121

which she herself is accustomed to sit upon the throne. And now she hears the king praised by his own men, and hears of their unconditional trust in him; no wonder that she is moved to wish to see him for herself. Scarcely has she uttered this wish than he is suddenly standing before her like some divine apparition,[9] in a state of exaltation brought about by his pride in what he has just heard, his joy that his companions and he himself have escaped death, and his admiration for Dido's regal manner: 'his divine mother had breathed the splendour of youth over him' is how Virgil, in truly Homeric fashion,[10] explains this enhancement of his nature at that moment, and the effect which his appearance will have on Dido.

Since the ground has been prepared on both sides, we might expect that mutual love will flare up at first glance. In Hellenistic love poetry, the sudden arousal of a passion, as quick as lightning, is actually a 'rule of artistic representation',[11] and this rule is also obeyed by the narrative of Apollonius' epic, at least as far as Medea's passion is concerned: she is struck by Eros' arrow as soon as she sets eyes on Jason, and her whole being is immediately overwhelmed by love (3.275ff.), while Jason ignores her completely at first, and it is only much later, during their secret conversation, that he himself is inflamed by the tears of the woman (1077f.). Medea is won over by the mere sight of him, by the heroic beauty of the man; indeed, in all the Hellenistic love poets that is the only reason why people fall in love. We have seen how Virgil has prepared the way for the mutual attraction of Dido and Aeneas by much subtler psychological means; similarly he does not ascribe the power to ignite a brilliant flame to a mere glance, despite the careful way in which he has assembled the flammable materials. It is true that these two are not to be compared with those youths and maidens who know nothing of Eros and, unprepared, fall victim to an unfamiliar passion. Virgil has completely avoided all mention of Aeneas' feelings of love. It is only at their separation that we are explicitly shown by means of small touches how deeply in love he has been. For the rest, the poet allows the facts to speak for themselves, after he has prepared the emotional ground as thoroughly as possible: Aeneas' feelings of admiration, and his sympathy and pity for Dido's former sufferings are combined with gratitude, which he expresses in extravagant words (597ff.). Dido's subsequent behaviour, her heartfelt and obvious attraction to the supposed Ascanius, and her passionate involvement with Aeneas' own fortunes are enough to do the rest. Later, there is no longer any need to state explicitly that her love is reciprocated: if a hero like Aeneas can forget his divine mission for the sake of a woman, even for a short time, how overwhelming his passion must be![12] Dido, too, has to forget, before she can open her heart to the new emotion: she is still attached to Sychaeus, the husband of her youth, and feels that it is her duty to remain faithful to him, and she fears that if she forms a new attachment she will be doing wrong to her first husband. So it would be inappropriate for her, too, to be suddenly pierced by an arrow shot at her by Eros, in the way that many other poets,[13] including Apollonius, had depicted the onset of love. Virgil follows the traditional technique of Hellenistic love-poetry in so far as he characterizes overwhelming love as the result of an intervention by Amor in person; but he chooses a form which contrives to portray the rapid but gradual invasion of this new love;[14] throughout the first night, while Aeneas talks of his deeds and sufferings, and, as we saw above, talks his way into Dido's heart, Amor lingers between the two in the guise of

Ascanius. But Virgil has also taken care that this intervention by the divinity appears necessary. It is not only a matter of conquering a woman's heart, which would probably not have withstood the heroic appearance of an Aeneas in any case, but it is a matter of Venus taking precautions against Juno's wiles (1.671ff.), since Juno could have used Dido as a means of expressing her hatred: and the only sure defence against the hatred that springs from the will of one god is love that is sent by another.[15]

2. Dido's guilt: Anna: passion

Dido's love has first to fight against her sense of duty. Her conversation with her sister (4.9ff.) allows us to witness that struggle, and the victory of love. Virgil has used her traditional faithfulness to her first husband to create a conflict within Dido herself which is of the greatest importance for the action. If Dido's death is to give the impression of poetic justice, she must be burdened with some form of guilt. This guilt lies in her deliberately violating the duty of fidelity which she herself regards as binding.[16] It is *pudor* [a sense of shame] which makes the new marriage impossible for her, and which, only too easily persuaded by Anna's specious arguments, she proceeds to disregard. Similarly, in Apollonius, it is αἰδώς [a sense   126
of shame] that at first restrains Medea; but in her case it is only maidenly decorum that prevents her from entering into a relationship with a strange man without her parents' knowledge; when she has freed herself after a long struggle, she says of it ἐρρέτω αἰδώς (3.784) [away with any sense of shame!]. Dido's *pudor*, on the other hand, is something very different: it is a power which she acknowledges to be divine and under divine protection. This is a specifically Roman way of thinking: a woman's *pudicitia* corresponds as a moral ideal to a man's *virtus*, and of all our evidence of the high regard in which the *univira* [a woman faithful to one husband] was held,[17] none is more characteristic than the information that only 'matrons of known modesty in their first and only marriage'[18] could make sacrifices at the altars of Pudicitia. We know very well how far practice in Virgil's time fell short of this ideal, but we may deduce from Virgil that, at least in the circles which still upheld something of the old Roman values, the requirement as such was maintained. One would dearly like to know the feelings with which Augustus heard these lines; he was Livia's second husband and had been Scribonia's third;[19] but to judge by the general tendency of his politics, and the way in which he kept his politics distinct from his own private life, it is not at all unlikely that he took a sympathetic view of a requirement which could only promote the reinstatement of the sanctity of marriage which he strove after so passionately. In any case, Virgil intended to show that Dido was a woman of the highest moral character by making her feel that this requirement was a moral and religious duty; she fails in this duty after its basis, her *love* for her first husband, has disappeared; but she does not escape the torture of a repentant conscience (4.552) and she pays for her guilt by her death (457ff.); and she is reunited with Sychaeus in the Underworld (6.474).

Tradition provided Dido with a sister, Anna. Virgil entrusts her with an important role, important, however, for his narrative technique rather than for the development   127 of the action: the rôle of confidante. At first one is inclined to make comparisons with Medea's sister, Chalciope, in Apollonius' poem, but she is a character who is required by the action, and Medea does not confide in her: on the contrary, she hides her personal feelings from her, and at the decisive moment, when she flees from her country, she acts quite independently, without consulting her sister. Here, too, Apollonius adheres strictly to the epic style. The confidante is a technical device, invented for the purposes of the theatre, taken over as a stock figure by classicizing tragedy from ancient tragedy (*Medea, Phaedra* etc.). Her function is to allow the audience to discover things which only one character can and does know; in this way the author can share her hidden feelings with the spectator, and create and overcome objections, without continually falling back on the device of the monologue.[20] The epic poet can use narrative instead of monologue, or alternate the two, a technique which Apollonius himself uses with great success. Virgil reserves monologue for the emotional climaxes of his narrative; in the earlier stages of the Dido episode he makes use of the confidante to transform epic narrative into dramatic action. Virgil's confidante is not the trusty nurse or maidservant who stands at the heroine's side in drama and who so often acts as the go-between in the romantic literature of the Hellenistic age,[21] serving her mistress' passion with blind obedience, taking no heed of duty or honour. There is usually something rather vulgar about this figure, and anything of that kind would be inconsistent with Virgil's concept of the elevated style that epic demands. He may on one occasion send the *nutrix* [nurse] (Barce 4.632) on an errand, but her status is too inferior to that of the queen for her to have any influence on her decisions, or to receive her humiliating confessions and convey her requests to Aeneas: but Anna, the *unanima soror* [likeminded sister], is ideal for all these purposes. Virgil also makes use of her to raise the emotional level of the final scene, and to portray the *effect* of the terrible event, something that he regarded as very important in every emotional scene: here the grief of the deceived and forsaken sister (675ff.), in whose arms Dido is dying, intensifies the effect that her death has on the reader. Of course, it is possible to imagine what Book 4 would be like without the figure of Anna; it would not affect the action to any great extent; but from an artistic point of view she is of great importance, and it can hardly be true that it was only at a later stage that Virgil added the scenes in which Anna appears;[22] since Virgil envisaged the action in dramatic form from the very beginning, the confidante too had a place in it from the very beginning.

Dido has confided in her sister in order to unburden her anxious heart. She feels the power of new love growing within her; but she feels that it is wrong to yield to it, and with a fearful oath she affirms her apparently steadfast resolve to resist it, as if to give herself something to cling to; thus she herself pronounces judgement on herself in advance. Anna, the *unanima soror*, knows very well what is really going on in her sister's mind, and seeks to dispel her scruples, principally by representing the fulfilment of her heart's desire as politically advantageous, indeed her royal duty. But in view of Dido's religious scruples, she first suggests that she should assure herself of Juno's approval by seeking her *venia* [pardon], or *pax* [peace], as Virgil calls it a few lines later;[23] this then becomes the sisters' first concern. Once the favourable outcome of the sacrifice has released Dido from *religio* [religious scruple], she is freed from her doubts and scruples, and is able to work with a clear conscience towards the fulfilment of her desires, and in the first place to seek to gain time: then the rest will come about of its own accord. We now hear (56ff.) that Dido follows her sister's advice with the utmost eagerness, and is insatiable in her praying and sacrificing; she turns above all to Juno, *cui vincla iugalia curae* [who is concerned with the bonds of marriage], who is able to dissolve the bonds of a former marriage and validate a new one. She tries to read the will of the gods in the entrails of the sacrificial animals.[24] But what is the result of these sacrifices? Are the entrails favourable or unfavourable? Virgil does not tell us, and so his interpreters have maintained both views with equal conviction and with equal justification. The fact is that Virgil has evaded a difficulty at this point in a rather radical way. We know from the final outcome that the sacrifices cannot have been favourable; otherwise the gods would have been deceiving Dido, or the seer must have been mistaken. On the other hand, if Juno is prepared to go straight ahead and ratify the marriage about which they were consulting her, then the poet cannot possibly say that she refused to accept the sacrifice. So he deliberately leaves the question unresolved. It does not 130 matter what the *vates* [seers] announce; they have no idea what is really agitating Dido's mind,[25] and they no doubt believe that prayers and vows can calm her down, when in fact she has been seized by the frenzy of love, and the flames of love are consuming the marrow of her bones (65-7).

The symptoms of this passion, which are described in lines 68ff., are familiar to us from the romantic literature of the Hellenistic period: torment and restlessness; pretexts for being at least in the company of her beloved;[26] she stammers in his presence;[27] she cannot hear enough of his voice; even when he is absent she still sees and hears no-one but him;[28] even at night she can find no rest;[29] and all the time she neglects the completion of her newly-founded city, to which her days have previously been devoted.[30] But Virgil is careful to avoid anything which might reduce this heroic passion to the level of the sentimental and bourgeois, and he scorns details which are better suited to the miniature technique of the epyllion than to the broad strokes of the epic. Nor does the action stand still while Dido's symptoms are 131 described, for we hear what else is taking place in Carthage, how Dido's subjects cannot remain unaware of her passion, and how her reputation is beginning to be sullied (91); Juno therefore, in order to prevent anything worse and at the same time to serve her own purposes, forms the plan of ratifying the marriage.[31]

The cave in which Aeneas and Dido seek shelter from the storm had its predecessor in the famous cave on Corcyra, which served Jason and Medea as a bridal chamber. There, too, according to Apollonius 4.1141ff., the nymphs sent by Hera enhanced the glory of the celebration. This passage may have been the source of Virgil's inspiration;[32] his mastery can be seen in the natural way in which he motivates what comes about because of the will of the gods, in the vivid descriptions of the splendid hunt and of the storm, and above all in the few lines (166-8) devoted to the fateful wedding, at which flashes of lightning serve as torches and the joyful cries of the nymphs high up on the wooded mountains serve as the wedding song. As Virgil describes the hunt in detail and in magnificent colours, we might imagine that he is merely using the resources of epic style, which glories in description for its own sake; but the passage also has a deeper meaning: the pair are riding forth as if in

101

a wedding-procession, regally attired, glowing as though with youthful desire, with a splendid retinue, and Virgil has sensed the tragic contrast, that Dido appears to us in radiant happiness for the last time on the day which will fulfil her heart's desire but which will also prove to be 'the first day of her death' (169).

132 ## 3. Dido's journey towards death: her character: conclusion

Virgil describes Dido's journey towards death with all the artistry at his command.[33] The *peripeteia* occurs immediately after the climax of the narrative which we have just dealt with; the poet passes rapidly over the period during which the two lovers live peacefully together, as though he were afraid of showing his hero neglecting his duty. We only hear what Fama says (173ff.): she distorts the truth when she depicts the pair as indulging in a life of luxury, unmindful of their duty as rulers; it is only later that we discover that this is untrue, when Mercury finds Aeneas busy with the work of building the city. The gossip reaches Iarbas, Jupiter listens to him and dispatches Mercury, Aeneas immediately obeys his command; Dido hears about his first secret arrangements for departure again from Fama, who thus completes her fatal work. From this point onwards, we accompany Dido along the short path she has yet to tread, which leads her to her death by way of every torment of the soul.[34]

133 Virgil had no need, nor did he consider it his duty, to display originality in the way in which Dido expresses her feelings. Despite the fact that much ancient literature has not survived, there is hardly a single essential feature in Virgil's depiction of her emotions that we cannot find in his predecessors. Here, too, the poet was borrowing his material; his personal contribution was the art by which he transformed it, and this art was so great that Dido is the only figure created by a Roman poet who was destined to have a place in world literature.

The material that was available to Virgil was rich enough. The grief of a forsaken woman had again and again been the subject of Greek poetry of every genre and style. From this mass of material, Virgil from the very first rejected anything which was inconsistent with the dignity of his style as being either too realistic or not realistic enough. Tragedy supplied the earliest example of the figure of the forsaken woman in Medea. During the Hellenistic period there were many such characters of the more dignified love-poetry, more at any rate than we know of today; but we can name Ariadne, whose lament at the loss of her love had been made familiar to the Roman public by Catullus;[35] Phyllis, well-known through Callimachus' poem; Oenone, whose unhappy fate is certainly known to us at any rate from a Hellenistic version (that of Quintus of Smyrna), to say nothing of numerous other comparable poems whose artistic merits have been totally obliterated because of the inadequate information that we have about them. Of these, two, like Dido, committed suicide: Phyllis hangs herself all alone (Ovid *Rem. Am.* 591), Oenone throws herself in the flames of the funeral-pyre which is consuming the body of Paris. But Greek poetry had also often enough recounted the story of unfortunate characters who commit suicide for reasons other than disappointment in love, and Virgil drew upon at least one of these figures, perhaps the most famous of all, the Ajax of Sophocles.

Virgil has made as much use as possible of the abundance of available motifs, intent as ever on the enrichment of his portrayal. But he does not describe a gloomy, irregular oscillation of the emotions: his Dido is not tossed this way and that by the conflict of her passions. On the contrary, the tragedy strides to its conclusion in a clear and controlled fashion. Here too, Virgil strives as far as possible for dramatic effect. He narrates only the observable action; he does not describe emotions but almost always lets the heroine herself express them. Indeed, he always directs his attention above all to linking the progressive heightening of these emotions closely with the development of the observable action. Each new phase in the outward course of events leads to a new phase in her inner development; and each of these phases represents as purely as possible one particular state of mind, uncontaminated by any other. Her first words to Aeneas (305ff.) express *painful surprise* at his lack of loyalty;[36] she has not yet entirely given up all hope of awakening his pity and sense of obligation towards her. When she realizes from his words that everything is now over, she says farewell in words of *scornful hatred*.[37] She cannot maintain this iron façade for long. When Aeneas' preparations for departure begin to be made openly, she abandons her pride – and the poet makes us realize what this means to someone like Dido – she gives way to *humble renunciation* and begs for at least a short delay so that she will not collapse in the pain of parting (429ff.).[38] This extreme measure does not work: Aeneas remains unmoved; horrifying omens of all kinds appear and Dido decides on death. The preparations for it begin; Dido herself takes part in them; we hear the thoughts that torture her on a sleepless night as her hard-won repose is lost in the storm of her emotions, and these thoughts lead her to the conclusion that death is really the only way out of her sorrow: she has finally come to *despair* about her future.[39] And now, in the grey light of dawn, she sees her fate sealed: the fleet is sailing away. The sudden sight rouses her to extreme *anger*, which is accompanied by a *thirst for revenge*:[40] what her vengeful hand cannot achieve, the curse shall do. But Dido cannot end her life like this, in demented fury. She makes her last arrangements, ensures that her sister will be the first to find her body,[41] and mounts the pyre. Gazing at the silent witnesses of her shortlived happiness she discovers the sublime *peace* of renunciation and takes stock of her life:[42] in full consciousness of her own greatness and of the height from which she has fallen, she takes her leave, unreconciled with her murderer, but reconciled with death.

All this is presented to us as vividly as possible in Dido's own words; only the linking text is supplied by the poet. From the point of view of technique, it is worth noting how Virgil has sought (deliberately, it seems) to avoid, or disguise, the monotony of constant monologues. She confesses her love to her sister. The *peripeteia* is followed by her two speeches to Aeneas, then she entrusts the mission to her sister. The considerations which lead to her final decision (534ff.) are presented not in a monologue but as an account of her thoughts (*secum ita corde volutat* [she communed with herself in her heart]). The sight of the ships sailing away throws her into a demented fury, in which she breaks out into wild cries. She comes to herself, horrified to find that she is talking to herself: *quid loquor? aut ubi sum? quae mentem insania mutat?* (595) ['What am I saying? Where am I? What mad folly is distorting my mind?']. The monologue develops into the prayer and *mandata* [orders], which are naturally spoken aloud. Her final monologue also begins with an apostrophe, as in tragedy.[43]

Virgil will hardly have found individually characterized female characters in his Hellenistic sources; nor can his heroine be compared in this respect with her great tragic predecessors, Deianeira, Medea or Ajax. She is not depicted with any realistic touches that might lead us to think that she was modelled on some living person, nor does she have any peculiar trait of character. On the other hand she is certainly not like some inert musical instrument from which, although it has no feeling, the poet can coax sounds full of pathos. The listener is expected not only to be interested in the state of her emotions, but also to feel personal sympathy for her, as the poet himself unmistakably did. In short, Dido is an ideal portrait of a heroic woman as conceived by Virgil. She therefore has to be portrayed in a way that is essentially negative: she must not be represented as girlishly naïve or timorous;[44] or humble (like so many of Ovid's portrayals of women), or sly, spiteful or barbarically savage

139   (the idea of physically attacking Aeneas to punish him for his faithlessness only occurs to her when she is in a demented state of delirium);[45] moaning and lamentation, sentimental wallowing in her own misfortune, useless regrets that things have happened like this and not turned out differently – Virgil uses all these standard features of tragic monodies and melodramatic Hellenistic scenes extremely sparingly;[46] only at one point, as we have seen, does Dido forget her pride. In contrast to these negative characteristics, Dido is given what seemed to Virgil a truly regal attitude: the deepest *humanitas* [sense of humanity] combined with *magnanimitas* [greatness of soul], displayed magnificently in her last words. Otherwise he dispenses altogether with devices that might have appealed to a poet striving to characterize his heroine – for instance, he could have transformed the masculine firmness of purpose and energy which she had displayed after Sychaeus' death into a dominating trait which she still possessed even in her misfortune; or he could have developed her *humanitas* in accordance with contemporary[47] ethical ideas into a generous forgiveness which would put her enemy to shame; or yet again, he could have brought her consciousness of her royal duty, to which Anna appeals, into the centre of her existence, so that everything else would seem unimportant by comparison: as it stands, we find, somewhat to our surprise, that the dying queen has no concern at all for the future of her city.

Virgil's renunciation of detailed characterization is consistent with the way that he does not attribute Dido's voluntary death to one single motive, but heaps up every imaginable one; sorrow at the loss of her beloved is by no means the motive that predominates. Here Virgil, whether consciously or unconsciously, is under the spell of tradition. For, strangely enough, although poets, particularly of the Hellenistic period, frequently described the suicide of young people who are unhappy in love,[48] and although on the other hand Greek epic and Greek poetry in general

140   frequently described the faithful wife who voluntarily followed her husband to death,[49] there are very few examples of girls or women inflicting an injury on themselves purely because they are disappointed in love, or their love is unreciprocated.[50] Rather, in the majority of cases, the hero or heroine suffers from a sense of shame because of some wrongful or humiliating deed: the threat of dishonour, or horror at their own action makes life unendurable.[51] We have seen that Virgil also introduced a motive of this kind: *non servata fides cineri promissa Sychaei* (522) [the vow which I made to the ashes of Sychaeus is broken] is the thought which sets

the seal on Dido's decision. But that is not all: there is also shame at the insult she has suffered (500ff.), the loss of her reputation for chastity, her greatest claim to fame (322); fear of being abandoned to the enemies who surround her, now that she has even lost the trust of her own subjects (320ff., 534ff.); the horrifying omens of every kind, which increase her fear (452ff.) the voice of her dead husband (457ff.). All these rage within her, and she succumbs to their combined onslaught, not to one single sorrow. Was Virgil seduced here too by the sheer richness of the motives available to him? Or did he think that it was impossible to accumulate too many causes to account for the death of his heroine, to outweigh such a heroic life? Here, too, he has taken care to preserve unity within this multiplicity: the whole of this disaster arises from *one* deed, and it is one man who has turned this deed from a blessing to ruin. We can only admire the skill with which we are made to see the far-reaching consequences of Aeneas' act, one after the other, without being wearied by any longwinded narrative. And this very skill, which allows a *situation* which has been brought about by a single deed to unfold in every direction like some growing plant – this skill irresistibly but imperceptibly convinces the listener of the necessity   141
of the tragic ending, whereas other great poets achieve this effect by letting it emerge from the growth of a deeprooted and individually depicted *character*.

It still remains for us to look at the way in which Dido prepares and accomplishes her death. There was a traditional version of the final scene, which Virgil must have had in his mind's eye:[52] Dido has had a funeral pyre constructed for her on the pretext that she intended to dissolve her former ties by means of a sacrifice to the dead; and on this pyre she kills herself by the sword.[53] Virgil needed only to substitute another pretext that was connected with Aeneas in order to make it convincing. He replaced the sacrifice to the dead with a magic one, that was still suited to the Underworld, so that it could serve as a preparation for her own descent   142
into that realm.[54] But, to the Roman mind, there was something mean and vulgar about magic; they knew of the old witches and wizards who carried on their disreputable trade with love-charms.[55] Virgil must therefore have felt it necessary to transform the whole scene into something great and heroic. The *maga* [witch] is no common witch, but one who has 'guarded the temple of the Hesperides,' and knew how to tame the dragon (483-5);[56] this helps to convince us that she also possesses   143
the other powers of which she boasts: love-magic comes first, but this is followed by magical powers which go beyond those that are normally mentioned and begin to suggest an almost divine omnipotence. The magic ceremony is then performed in a style that is correspondingly elevated: for this occasion no ordinary altar will suffice, but a funeral-pyre, surrounded by altars, is constructed; Erebus and Chaos are invoked, as well as Hecate, the goddess of magic; 'in a voice like thunder' she calls up three hundred gods from the depths. And the sacrifice is so sacred that Dido herself is not too proud to participate as the servant of the gods.[57] For the rest, the magic rite brings about exactly what Dido intends: a death amidst all the mementos of the brief period of joy that her love had brought her.

In tragedy we do not normally witness a death on the stage, but are only affected, like the hero's nearest and dearest, by the impact of the terrible event. So too in Virgil.[58] We do not see Dido plunge the sword into her breast.[59] Virgil's narrative passes over the decisive moment: her handmaidens see her collapse under the mortal   144 blow. Lamentation resounds throughout the halls, and spreads like a raging fire through the streets and houses of the city: we are made to feel the full significance of the death of a woman like Dido, and it is made explicit in Anna's words: *exstinxti te meque, soror, populumque patresque Sidonios urbemque tuam* ['Sister, you have destroyed my life with your own, and the lives of our people and Sidon's nobility, and your whole city too'].[60]

Notes to Chapter 3

115   1. I should not, however, wish to assert this as confidently as the majority of recent scholars have done. Of course, all that we know about Naevius in this connection is preserved in Servius' comment on 4.9: *cuius filiae fuerint Anna et Dido Naevius dicit* [whose daughters, Naevius says, were Anna and Dido]. We might well assume *a priori* that when Naevius first mentioned Carthage he also told the story of its foundation. And it is certainly worth observing that Macrobius states (6.2.31) that Virgil borrowed the tempest, Venus' lament and Jupiter's reassurance in Book 1 from Naevius, but says nothing at all about Dido in this context, whereas at 5.17.4 he makes Virgil responsible for distorting the Dido tradition and spoiling the popular image of her purity, without mentioning any predecessor. But these arguments *ex silentio* are not strong enough to prove that Naevius did not recount the story (as Lucian Müller, assumed: see L. Müller, *Q. Ennius, Eine Einleitung in das Studium der röm. Poesie* [St Petersburg, 1884] 147, and *Q. Ennii carminum reliquiae* [St Petersburg, 1884] XXIII). From Servius' comment on 4.682: *Varro ait non Didonem sed Annam amore Aeneae impulsam se supra rogum interemisse* [Varro says it was not Dido but Anna who was driven by love of Aeneas to kill herself on the pyre] it does not follow with absolute certainty that Varro was correcting the version that appears in Virgil; however, the most likely explanation for his remarkable statement is that Varro, in an attempt to reconcile the historical tradition with the poetical, asserted that, since Dido had killed herself for another reason, then the woman whom Aeneas loved, if indeed he did leave any such person behind in Carthage, can only have been Dido's sister Anna; this expedient would be rather like his favourite method of assuming homonyms in order to reconcile two mutually exclusive versions of a legend. If so, then Varro must have believed that the tradition was more than mere poetic fiction. Unfortunately, it is impossible to establish whether Ateius Philologus in his essay *An amaverit Didun Aeneas* [Whether Aeneas loved Dido] (Charisius I p. 127 K cites this title from Pliny) dealt

116   with this alternative version, or whether he investigated the historical basis of the tradition of Aeneas' and Dido's love (which in my view is more likely). But if the tradition did already exist in the Republican period, then certainly Naevius is the poet most likely to have created it (so too Meltzer – following Niebuhr and others – in Roscher's *Lex.* I.1013); bold and shaky hypotheses of another kind are found in E. Wörner, *Sage von den Wanderungen des Aeneas* (Leipzig, 1882) 17ff. E. Maass implausibly traces Ovid's story of Anna (*Fast.* 3.545ff.) back to Naevius (*Commentatio mythographica* [Greifswald, 1886] XVII), although Naevius had no reason to

mention Anna's eventual fate, and furthermore, if he had used this story, the episode would hardly have suited the purpose which we may assume lay behind his version, that of presenting the Punic War to some extent as the revenge of Dido's people for Aeneas' cruel behaviour. In Ovid, Dido's heiress makes peace with Aeneas, and Dido's people are not mentioned.

2. Apart from Malalas (ed. Dindorf [Bonn, 1831]) 162 and Cedrenus (ed. Bekker, [Bonn, 1838]) 1.246, who both depend on Virgil. The story has been attributed to Timaeus, wrongly, as shown by Geffcken, *Timaios' Geographie des Westens*, 47f., and others.

3. If Dido was the subject of the sentence *blande atque docte percontat quo*   117 *pacto Troiam urbem reliquerit* [persuasively and artfully she asks how he left the city of Troy]; against this, see F. Leo, *Geschichte der römischen Literatur* (Berlin, 1913) 1.82 n. 8. There is no possibility that Aeneas then told his story in reply: we know from the fragments that the passage was in the third person (F. Noack, *Hermes* 27 [1892] 437).

4. Did Virgil perhaps have in Philetas a predecessor in this innovation? He had narrated in his *Hermes* (Parthen. 2), taking his cue from *Odyssey* 10.14, how Aeolus τὰ περὶ Τροίης ἅλωσιν καὶ ὃν τρόπον αὐτοῖς ἐσκεδάσθησαν αἱ νῆες κομιζομέ- νοις ἀπὸ τῆς Ἰλίου διεπυνθάνετο [learned the story of the capture of Troy and how their ships were scattered as they voyaged from Ilium] from Odysseus, and how Aeolus' daughter Polymele had fallen in love with the hero. We do not know what Naevius made of the narrative-device (see above). Ovid (*Ars Am.* 2.127) has Odys- seus narrating *Troiae casus* [the fortunes of Troy] to Calypso: apparently his own invention (on the model of Virgil; compare his *iterumque iterumque* [again and again] with *Aen.* 4.19ff.) for the sake of the very Ovidian punchline.

5. A great contrast to this is Propertius 1.15.11: *multos illa (Calypso) dies in-*   118 *comptis maesta capillis sederat iniusto multa locuta salo* [for many days she (Calypso) sat there sadly, with hair unkempt, making many a complaint to the cruel sea] etc. Propertius takes this behaviour for granted, and there is no need to postulate any specific Hellenistic model for him. Some wretched late author, however, in a stupid attempt to parallel the Dido story, made the goddess Calypso herself commit suicide for love (Hygin. *Fab.* 243).

6. Cf. Norman Wentworth de Witt, *The Dido Episode in the Aeneid of Virgil*   119 (Diss. Chicago, 1907), where (38ff.) there is a good discussion of the dramatic character of the episode.

7. Comparison with the detailed narrative in Justin 18.4 is instructive, in that Justin provides evidence which shows how consciously Virgil strives here to pro- duce an emotional effect, to arouse pity for Dido and indignation against Pygmalion. Hence the repeated emphasis on Dido's love for Sychaeus and Pygmalion's cruel deception after he had killed him, which is revealed to Dido only by the pitiful appearance of his ghost (1.343-56); similarly, the intensification of the crime: *ante aras* [before the altar], *incautum superat* [he caught him off his guard], *inhumati coniugis* [her unburied husband], and Pygmalion's epithets: *scelere ante alios imma- nior omnis* [a monster of unmatched wickedness], *impius* [impious], *securus amorum germanae* [not concerned for his sister's love], *multa malus simulans* [with many cruel pretences]; the tyrant is hated or feared by his own people (361). That the victim himself discloses the crime is hardly Virgil's own invention: ἐξ ἐνυπνίου τὸν φόνον ἐπέγνω [she learned of the murder from a dream] (Appian *Pun.* 1); cf. the appearance of the murdered Polydorus in Euripides' *Hecuba*. Justin's narrative runs: *Elissa diu fratrem propter scelus aversata ad postremum dissimulato odio mitigatoque interim vultu fugam tacita molitur* [for a long time Elissa hated her brother because of his crime; but finally she concealed her hatred and while putting on a calm expression she silently planned her flight]; in a much more dramatic way Virgil allows the unhappy woman to be deceived at first by the apparition into

120 believing that her lost husband is still alive, and then the apparition itself suddenly destroys the illusion, whereupon she immediately prepares for flight. The flight itself is described very briefly; *navis quae forte paratae corripiunt onerantque auro* (362-3) [they hastily seized some ships which happened to be ready for sailing, and loaded them with the gold], whereas, in Justin, Dido deceives first her brother and then his messenger – which also involves playing an impious trick with the *manes* of her husband; if Virgil found that in his source (cf. Conington, introduction p. xl, although his interpretation is not entirely correct), he has deliberately omitted the sly deception and we can easily see why: it would have been a jarring note in his description of the heroic wife. If Sychaeus is given a prominent rôle, it is because this is προπαρασκευή [preparation] for the part that he is to play in Book 4; for the same reason it is also emphasized that he was Dido's first husband (345), which is not particularly relevant to Venus' narrative at this point.

8. Virgil has borrowed Homer's comparison of Nausicaa with Artemis leading the nymphs in their dance (1.498ff. cf. *Od.* 6.102ff.); this is a miscalculation, as Probus clearly explains in a well-known passage of sharp criticism (Gellius 9.9); contrast the skilful adaptation of the comparison by Apollonius in 3.875ff.

121 **9.** The mist that has veiled him like Odysseus in the city of the Phaeacians and like Jason until he reaches the palace of Aietes (Ap. Rhod. 3.210) now melts away. Incidentally, it is a misinterpretation of *iamdudum erumpere nubem ardebant* [they had long felt eager to break free from the cloud] at 580 to paraphrase it as 'the two men, burning with eagerness to make themselves visible, but incapable of doing so before the magic has disappeared of its own accord' as Cauer does (P. Cauer, *Grundfragen der Homerkritik* 2 [Leipzig, 1909] 341). We have already been told at

122 line 514 that Aeneas and Achates had wanted to become visible, *avidi coniungere dextras ardebant* [they were in burning haste to clasp their comrades' hands]: they cannot do so, because *res incognita animos turbat* [the mystery of it all perturbs them]. As soon as Achates says at lines 582ff. that there is no longer any danger, the mist disappears. It is clear from the question *quae nunc animo sententia surgit?* ['What are the feelings that now arise in your mind?'] that it depends only on their free will. Tasso's imitation, *Gerus. Lib.* 10.48f. is very instructive for understanding this passage of Virgil.

10. His model is of course *Od.* 6.229f., although in Homer natural means (bathing, oiling, clothing) enhance Odysseus' physical appearance, and these, so to speak, merely make Athena's influence visible. Virgil, as so often, makes the detail more abstract and therefore less immediately convincing, refined and carefully considered though it is. Apollonius 3.918ff. is not as good.

11. E. Rohde, *Der griechische Roman und seine Vorläufer* 3 (Leipzig, 1914)

159. So Virgil himself earlier: *ut vidi ut perii* [as I saw her so I was lost] (*Ecl.* 8.41), an effect spoilt by the author of the *Ciris* 429f. Also Catullus 64.86: *hunc simulac cupido conspexit lumine virgo regia...non prius ex illo flagrantia declinavit lumina* [as soon as the royal maiden saw him with desirous eyes,...she would not turn her burning eyes away from him until...] etc. Hellenistic love poetry was in its turn following the example of comedy: Terence, *Phormio* 111, *Eunuch.* 2.3 etc.

12. The fact that Virgil only hints allusively at Aeneas' love and says very little   123
about his sorrow at parting arises primarily from his fear of dwelling on the weakness of his hero. At the same time the artistic consideration of carefully preserving
the unity of the narrative means that Dido must be kept firmly in the foreground: cf.
'Composition' in Part II, ch. 4. I admit that this restraint causes the poet to make
sacrifices (see Drachmann's criticism of my arguments: *Nordisk tidskrift for filol.* 14
[1905] 64): the reader is not explicitly informed about Aeneas' own feelings, and
learns about them in less detail than he might wish. But I cannot agree with Drachmann's view that the entire narrative is absurd and lacking in motivation. 'Aeneas
cannot become involved in a cheap liaison simply to pass the time, nor can he fall
seriously in love and then refuse to marry, nor can he possibly leave a broken
marriage behind him. All this was quite clear to Virgil; nevertheless there were
important reasons why he could not omit the episode...knowing this, we can understand why Virgil is silent where he should have spoken, and why he uses his gods
instead of natural psychology.' But Virgil's Aeneas really is sincerely in love; the
poet states this clearly enough, in my view, to anyone sensitive to his hints, although
he does show consideration for his hero, since this is not a heroic deed but a
weakness: for Aeneas forgets his mission because of love, and furthermore does
wrong to Dido. According to de Witt (op. cit. n. 6 above, 28ff.) Virgil settled for the
'cheap liaison': 'Aeneas did not love Dido...it only makes matters worse that he felt   124
and confessed a certain affection for her.' But it is Virgil, not one of his characters,
who calls Aeneas and Dido *amantes* [lovers] at 4.221; the phrase *quando optima
Dido nesciat et tantos rumpi non speret amores* (291) [for in her ignorance and
goodness of heart Dido would never suspect that so deep a love could possibly be
broken] is part of Aeneas' own thoughts; in the Underworld Aeneas still speaks to
Dido *dulci amore* (6.455) [with tender love]; and I see no reason whatever in all
these cases to understand *amor* as anything other than 'love', totally sincere love.
When Juno confides her plan to Venus before the hunt, *tua si mihi certa voluntas*
(4.125) [if I may be sure of your compliance], Venus agrees: *non adversata petenti
adnuit* [to this proposal she raised no objection]: this is not a case of 'using the
goddess instead of natural psychology' – in this respect my conception of the
Virgilian gods differs radically from Drachmann's – but symbolizes the psychological process which a realistic narrator would describe in everyday language. To the
sensibilities of a modern reader, Aeneas' behaviour may easily seem heartless and
unchivalrous, particularly if his parting words at 333ff. are not understood as Virgil
intended: Aeneas, *obnixus curam sub corde premebat* [straining to master the agony
within him] forces himself with difficulty to suppress his feelings and to allow only
his reason to speak, because he knows that this is the only way that he can remain in
control of himself. Aeneas' mastery of his deepest emotions for the sake of the will
of the gods is expressed succinctly but, provided that we take Virgil's words

seriously, perfectly adequately in 345f. and 440ff. In any case, it is clear that Aeneas' feelings are nothing like as intense as Dido's. A woman can be overwhelmed by a love that verges on madness, but, in Virgil's view, it is not possible for this to happen to a man worthy of the name; reason, or duty, will always prevail in the end. In this Virgil can follow the literary tradition with a clear conscience, for, as de Witt rightly explains, there can be *insanus amor* [mad love] on the man's part in comedy, pastoral and elegy, but not in heroic poetry. I should add that Virgil certainly does not wish to make Aeneas appear innocent; but his guilt lies in beginning, not in ending, the affair. For further discussion see the section on 'Characters', Part II, ch. 2.1a below.

    13. E. Rohde, op. cit. 159 n. 4.

    14. *paulatim abolere Sychaeum* (720) [began gradually to dispel all thought of Sychaeus].

    15. It has often been remarked what a great difference there is between the emotional scene involving Venus and Amor in Virgil and the gaudy and flirtatious piece of miniature painting that is its equivalent in Apollonius: see for example Sainte-Beuve, *Etude sur Virgile* (Paris, 1857) 306ff.; we shall return to this in another context.

    16. I do not understand why this emphasis on her fidelity to her first husband should be regarded as 'arbitrary' (Drachmann op. cit. 65); perhaps because not all widows in a similar position would take this attitude? But Dido is not like everyone else, either in this matter or in any other. If we may discuss another passage at this point, this also applies to Drachmann's remark about Dido's thoughts of revenge (see above p. 104): 'Virgil has presented the whole course of events in a way that would make a wish for personal revenge on Dido's part seem completely natural and justifiable. Virgil's rejection of this motive is another example of his arbitrariness.' But Virgil has portrayed Dido in such a way that the *inhumanitas* involved in, for example, killing Ascanius and serving his dismembered limbs to his father as a Thyestian meal, would not appear natural, however justifiable or not one might consider such an act to be.

    17. Cf. J. Marquardt, *Privatleben der Römer²* (Leipzig, 1886) 42.

    18. Livy 10.23.9; further evidence in G. Wissowa, *Religion und Kultur der Römer* 2 (Munich 1912) 258 n. 2.

    19. It is true that he had separated from her, allegedly *pertaesus morum perversitatem eius* [tired of her shrewish disposition] (Suet. *Aug.* 62), and Ovid explains Livia's second marriage by saying that she alone was worthy of Augustus, and no other man was worthy of her – i.e. not even her first husband (*Trist.* 2.161, cf. *Fast.* 1.65).

    20. This point has now been developed by H. Ahlers, *Die Vertrautenrolle in der griechischen Tragödie* (Diss. Giessen, 1911), although he offers little more than a chronological survey of the material.

    21. For example, the τροφός [nurse] of Peisidice (Parthen. 21); of Ctesylla (Antonin. Liberalis 1.4); of Smyrna (id. 34.2), of Arsinoe (id. 39.3); in every case she acts as a go-between. An extended example in the neo-Hellenistic style is Carme in the *Ciris*, which, if we follow Sudhaus' happy conjecture (*Hermes* 42 [1907] 491), is largely based on the Smyrna of Helvius Cinna.

22. The first conversation between Dido and Anna (6-55) was explained as a 128
later addition by C. Schüler, *Quaest. Virgil.* (Diss. Greifswald, 1883) 24ff.; Sabbadini took up this idea and extended Schüler's conclusions to other scenes (*L'Eneide commentata* libri IV, V, VI [Turin, 1898] ixff.). His chief objection to that conversation is that the *pax* [peace] which they seek at the altars in lines 56ff. is something quite different from the *venia* [pardon] for which Dido is to beseech the gods in line 50: it is release from the torments of love. This cannot be right: the *pax* that Virgil mentions here is part of the established terminology of Roman religion and could never be understood as anything other than the *pax deorum* [peace of the gods]. For lines 65ff. see below; for the chronological framework see Part II, ch. 2.III.c) 'Time and Place'; it is not worth discussing the argument that in their second conversation (416ff.) Dido does not reproach Anna for her exhortations.

23. To secure a friendly relationship with the gods, to gain their *pax ac venia* [peace and their pardon], is the purpose of every prayer and sacrifice, if a god has 129 shown by *prodigia* or the like that he is angry (during a pestilence *unam opem aegris corporibus relictam, si pax veniaque a diis impetrata esset, credebant* [they believed the only hope left for their ailing bodies was if they secured peace and pardon from the gods] [Livy 1.31.7]; similarly *iussi cum coniugibus ac liberis supplicatum ire pacemque exposcere deum...matres crinibus templa verrentes veniam irarum caelestium finemque pesti exposcunt* [3.7.7] [they were ordered to go and pray with their wives and children, and to ask for the peace of the gods...the matrons, brushing the temples with their hair, asked for pardon from the divine anger and an end to the plague]; cf. 4.30.10, 7.2.1 etc.; cf. *Aen.* 3.261), or if a person fears that he may arouse divine anger by a future action *pacem veniamque precata deorum dearumque, si...silenda enuntiasset* [praying for the peace and pardon of the gods if she had proclaimed what should have been left unsaid] (Livy 39.10), or if some danger threatens, for which people wish to assure themselves of divine assistance, for example in battle (Cic. *pro Fonteio* 13.30: *illae* [i.e. *ceterae gentes* as opposed to the Gauls] *in bellis gerendis ab dis immortalibus pacem ac veniam petunt* [they (i.e. other nations) in waging war ask for peace and pardon from the immortal gods]: the *litatio* [the obtaining of favourable omens] during a sacrifice is a guarantee that it will be granted [Livy 6.1.12]: *quod non litasset...neque inventa pace deum...abiectus hosti exercitus Romanus esset* [since he had not obtained favourable omens, and a Roman army had been thrown to the enemy without the peace of the gods being obtained]; 12.7; 41.9 etc.). So too Cicero in the solemn prooemium of his speech *pro Rabirio* 2.5: *ab Iove optimo maximo ceterisque dis deabusque immortalibus...pacem ac veniam peto* [I ask for peace and pardon from Iuppiter Optimus Maximus and from all the other immortal gods and goddesses]. Similarly, and finally, in the prayer of the whole Roman people to the new god Romulus: *pacem precibus exposcunt, uti volens propitius suam semper sospitet progeniem* [by their prayers they ask for peace, so that he may always safeguard his own progeny willingly and propitiously] (Livy 1.16.3); cf. also *Aen.* 3.144, 370.

24. *spirantia consulit exta* [she consults the still breathing vitals], line 64; they are called *vates* [seers] in the following line; thus it is a question of *hostiae consultatoriae* [victims for religious consultation], as Servius correctly explains in his comment on 56 (cf. Wissowa 419), and the *vates* correspond to the *haruspices*.

130   25. *heu vatum ignarae mentes* (65) [how ignorant are the minds of seers!] is
explained by Servius as *ignarae amoris reginae* [ignorant of the queen's love], and
in my view that is the only correct interpretation. That is also how the words were
understood by other authors in antiquity, as shown by the imitations observed by
Forbiger on Silius' *Punica* 8.100: *heu sacri vatum errores* [oh, the accursed delu-
sions of seers] (in his version of the story of Dido) and Apuleius *Metam.* 10.2: *heu
medicorum ignarae mentes* [oh, the ignorant minds of doctors]: in both cases, those
involved have no idea of what it is really all about. In Virgil, the *vates* must believe
that Dido is only anxious to overcome some religious scruple, and that is indeed the
reason for her sacrifice, but it is not the true cause of the torment and agitation in
Dido's emotions, which have already been described in lines 1-9 and which become
more and more intense independently of the acts of sacrifice.

   26. Terence, *Eun.* 636ff.

   27. *mediaque in voce resistit* (76) [she checked herself with the words half-
spoken]: cf. Ap. Rhod. 3.686: φθογγῇ δ' οὐ προύβαινε περαιτέρω [she could not
continue speaking].

   28. Ap. Rhod. 3.453: προπρὸ δ' ἄρ ὀφθαλμῶν ἔτι οἱ ἰνδάλλετο πάντα,
καὐτός θ' οἷος ἔην...ἐν οὔασι δ' αἰὲν ὀρώρει αὐδή τε μῦθοί τε μελίφρονες οὓς
ἀγόρευσεν [and before her eyes she saw it all, what sort of man he was...and always
his voice rang in her ears, and the honeyed words which he spoke].

   29. E. Rohde, op. cit. n. 3, 168.

   30. Longus 1.13.6: τῆς ἀγέλης κατεφρόνει [she neglected her flock], Theocr.
11.73: αἴκ' ἐνθὼν ταλάρως τε πλέκοις [you should go and weave baskets] etc.
Virg. *Ecl.* 2.70: *semiputata tibi frondosa vitis in ulmo est* [your vine is half-pruned
on the leafy elm] (cf. already Sappho fr. 102 Lobel-Page; Hor. *Odes* 3.12.3).

131   31. Juno's attempt to override the decrees of fate in order to help Dido and
Carthage drives Dido to her death and in the end causes the destruction of Carthage;
it is quite possible that, as Conway says in his lecture *The teaching of Virgil*
(London, 1912) (of which he kindly sent me a copy), the careful reader is intended
to notice this; but surely this would only make him realise how wrong it is to oppose
fate in this way. Conway attempts to find references to the marriages which Augustus forced on his family and friends for political reasons, but I am not convinced.

   32. Conway op. cit. rightly draws attention to the strong contrast, which seems to
be deliberately emphasized, between the narratives of Apollonius and Virgil; this
brings out the tragic aspect of their night of love more clearly.

132   33. See now E. Penquitt (*De Didonis Vergilianae exitu* [Diss. Königsberg,
1910]) with good discussions of details, particularly the sacred objects. However, I
cannot say that I agree with his 'rhetorical' analyses of Dido's speeches; see the
section 'Rhetoric' in Part II, pp. 330f.

   34. The attempts to prove that this entire passage has been thoroughly revised,
and to reconstruct an earlier version (Schüler op. cit. 27ff., Sabbadini op. cit. x ff.
and *Il primitivo disegno dell'Eneide* [Turin, 1900] 43ff., F. Vivona, *Riv. di. Filol.* 26
[1898] 428ff.) seem to me to be totally misconceived. It is only the chronology of
the events against which valid objections can be made: on this see 'Time and Place'
in Part II, pp. 265f.). As for the other objections, there are some apparent oversights
on the part of the poet that are open to criticism, e.g. after *decrevit mori* (475) [she

decided to die] Dido takes the same decision again at 534ff. (although I consider that this is sufficiently motivated by lines 531ff., and from the technical standpoint it is easy to understand why Virgil places this recapitulation of Dido's motives immediately before she commits suicide). We might ask why Dido did not kill herself as soon as the funeral-pyre was built (although to my mind it is quite clear that, however firm her resolve, she only proceeds to carry it out after Aeneas' departure, which irrevocably extinguishes every hope): the second intervention of Mercury might be criticised as superfluous (which it may well be as far as the narrative is concerned, but not from a technical point of view, see below 'The structure of the action' (Part II, pp. 261f.). But even if all these objections were justified, they do not prove anything at all about the original form of the book and its re-writing; all these hypotheses are based on the presupposition that there was at least some stage at which the poet must have arranged his material in exactly the way that the critic   133
concerned would have wished.

35. Reitzenstein's article (*Hermes* 35 [1900] 86ff.) has made it impossible to doubt that the original of Catullus 64 was an Alexandrian poem.

36. Her first reaction is to feel that the cruellest thing is his apparent intention to   134
leave her secretly: cf. Eur. *Med.* 575f.: χρῆν σ᾽ εἴπερ ἦσθα μὴ κακός, πείσαντά με γαμεῖν γάμον τόνδ᾽, ἀλλὰ μὴ σιγῇ φίλων ['if you were not a coward you ought to have persuaded me first, before making this marriage, instead of keeping it secret from your friends']. The reference to the *data dextera quondam* [your right hand once given to me] at 307 is not adequately motivated by the earlier narrative, at least not as well as ἀνακαλεῖ δὲ δεξιᾶς πίστιν μεγίστην [she calls to witness the great pledge of the right hand clasped] in *Medea* 22. Her pleas are reminiscent of Tecmessa's words of entreaty and the general sense of her whole speech ἐμοὶ γὰρ οὐκέτ᾽ ἔστιν εἰς ὅ τι βλέπω πλὴν σοῦ [I no longer have recourse to anything but you] (Soph. *Ajax* 514); with *fuit aut tibi quicquam dulce meum* [if anything about me gave you pleasure] cf. ibid. 520: ἀνδρί τοι χρεὼν μνήμην προσεῖναι, τερπνὸν εἴ τί που πάθοι [a husband ought to remember if he ever had any pleasurable experience]. *infensi Tyrii* (321) [the Tyrians are hostile] – why? surely because she has set foreigners above her compatriots, rather like Ovid's Phyllis in *Heroides* 2.82: *quod ferar externum praeposuisse meis* [because I am said to have preferred a foreigner to my own people] etc.; cf. also *Medea* 495: τοῖς μὲν οἴκοθεν φίλοις ἐχθρὰ καθέστηκα [I have incurred the hatred of my friends from home]: all Dido's questions are modelled on those of Medea in that passage. Her rhetorical point *hospes, hoc solum nomen quoniam de coniuge restat* (323-4) ['Guest, since this is the only name left instead of husband'] seems to be developed from the famous pointed phrase of Callimachus' Phyllis (fr. 556, Loeb edn): νύμφιε Δημοφόων, ἄδικε ξένε [my bridegroom Demophoon, unjust guest] (see Rohde, op. cit. n. 2, 483). Her concluding words are reminiscent of Hypsipyle, who lets Jason leave since she has confident hope of a son (Apollonius 1.888ff.).

37. The Homeric phrase γλαυκὴ δέ σε τίκτε θάλασσα πέτραι τ᾽ ἠλίβατοι ['the shining sea and steep crags gave you birth'] had been used again and again in so many forms (even by Virgil himself in *Ecl.* 8.43), but Virgil had no qualms about using the formula again because he was achieving a different effect by contrasting it with *diva parens Venus* [Venus your divine parent]; for similar passages see Riese on Cat. 64.155: Ariadne says the same of Theseus. *num lumina flexit?* (369) [did he turn his eyes?]; cf. *Med.* 470: φίλους κακῶς δράσαντ᾽ ἐναντίον βλέπειν [to look your friends in the face when you have wronged them], though in a different sense.

135 *nusquam tuta fides* [nowhere is faith secure]; cf. *Med.* 492: ὅρκων φρούδη πίστις [faith in your oaths is gone]. The complaint that the gods are not giving any support, which was originally based on the fact that a broken oath had gone unpunished (*quamquam nil testibus illis profeci* [*Ecl.* 8.20] [although their witness has benefitted me not at all], cf. Asclepiades *AP* 5.52: κενὰ δ᾽ ὅρκια...ἡ δὲ θεῶν οὐ φανερὴ δύναμις [oaths are empty...the power of the gods is nowhere to be seen], *Med.* 412: θεῶν οὐκέτι πίστις ἄραρε [there is no longer any firm reliance on the gods]) appears in a different form here, since there is no oath to appeal to. It is only at this point, when she is no longer expecting any gratitude, that Dido first explicitly mentions all her services to Aeneas; previously she had only alluded to them in the phrase *si quid de te merui* (317) [if I ever did you a service] cf. *Med.* 476: ἔσωσά σε etc. [I rescued you]; Ariadne in Cat. 64.149: *certe ego te in medio versantem turbine leti eripui* etc. [surely I rescued you when you were swirling in a whirlpool of death]; Phyllis, Ov. *Heroides* 2.107: *quae tibi...longis erroribus acto Threicios portus hospitiumque dedi* etc. [I who gave you a harbour in Thrace and hospitality after your long wanderings]. The ethos of the proud *neque te teneo...i, sequere Italiam* ['I am not holding you...go, quest for Italy'] is that of *Iliad* 1.173: φεῦγε μάλ᾽, εἴ τοι θυμὸς ἐπέσσυται· οὐδέ σ᾽ ἔγωγε λίσσομαι εἵνεκ᾽ ἐμεῖο μένειν ['Run away by all means, if that is what you want: I am not pleading with you to stay for my sake']. The threat at 385ff. resembles Ap. Rhod. 3.704: ἢ σοίγε φίλοις σὺν παισὶ θανοῦσα εἴην ἐξ Ἀΐδεω στυγερὴ μετόπισθεν Ἐρινύς [or may I die with my dear children and be your hateful Fury hereafter, come from Hades], but is even closer to Medea's words at 4.383: μνήσαιο δὲ καί ποτ᾽ ἐμεῖο, στρευγόμενος καμάτοισι· δέρος δέ τοι ἶσον ὀνείροις οἴχοιτ᾽ εἰς ἔρεβος μεταμώνιον. ἐκ δέ σε πάτρης αὐτίκ᾽ ἐμαί σ᾽ ἐλάσειαν Ἐρινύες ['May you some day remember me when you are worn out by toils: may the fleece, borne on the winds, go down to nether darkness as insubstantial as a dream: and may my avenging Furies drive you forthwith from your homeland']. Moreover, in Virgil's lines, the two concepts, that the dead walk the earth (there is no allusion here to violent deaths, cf. Ovid *Ibis* 141ff.) and that they inhabit the underworld (Lucr. 4.41: *ne forte animas Acherunte reamur effugere aut umbras inter vivos volitare* [lest we happen to think that souls may escape from Acheron or that ghosts hover about among the living]), are not regarded as incompatible. The words *sequar atris ignibus absens* [though far away, I shall pursue you with flames of blackest pitch] at 389 refer, as Penquitt (op. cit.) rightly says, to the living Dido, but there is certainly no reference to magic here (if Virgil had intended that he would have expressed it more explicitly and in some better way); the first of the explanations that Servius gives (*alii 'furiarum facibus' dicunt, hoc est 'invocatas tibi immittam diras'* [some explain 'with the torches of the Furies' that is, 'I shall summon the Furies and send them to attack you']) is the correct one: Dido identifies herself (*sequar* [I shall pursue you]) with her curses, and thinks of these as Furies (Erinyes), who certainly do not restrict their vengeance to cases of murder (many examples in Rapp's article in Roscher's *Lex.* I.1322ff.).

38. Dido does not however humble herself as much as Ariadne in the Alexandrian poem which can be reconstructed from Cat. 64.158ff. and Nonnus *Dion.* 46.386ff., who would have gone with her lover as his servant if she could not go with him as his wife (Euripides' Medea only pretends to humble herself at 312ff.). It is also obvious why Dido does not make this last attempt herself, but sends her sister, and the passage in which she tries to persuade herself that this ploy is likely to be successful – *solam nam perfidus ille te colere, arcanos etiam tibi credere sensus; sola viri mollis aditus et tempora noras* (421-3) [for that traitor was never really attentive to anyone but you; you alone had his full confidence, and only you ever knew just how and when to approach this hard man tactfully] – is one of great beauty. We can also hear her bitter awareness that she herself can never have possessed Aeneas' full trust; otherwise how could he deceive her so cruelly now? The poet leaves it to our imagination to decide how much of Dido's statement is true: that, too, is the technique of drama. Dido's words at the end of her speech – *quam (veniam) mihi cum dederit cumulatam morte remittam* (436) [and when he has granted it (this indulgence) to me, I shall repay the debt, with the interest, in death] – cannot mean that she has already taken the decision to kill herself, nor that she expects to die of love after Aeneas' departure (as Penquitt suggests, 24ff.); she motivates her request for a delay by saying that she would not be able to survive the sudden separation (419ff.) and must first get used to the idea (*dum mea me victam doceat fortuna dolere* [until my fortune can teach me submission and the art of grief]). The meaning of her obscure words would have been quite clear if Virgil had written *cumulatam vel morte remittam* [i.e. even in death]; I believe the meaning to be 'I will reward it in good measure, even with my life' – although a precise situation in which Aeneas (or Anna, if Virgil wrote *dederis* [you have granted], which I do not believe) could ask for Dido's life is not envisaged. Cf. Terence, *Phormio* 165: *ut mihi liceat tam diu quod amo frui, iam depecisci morte cupio* [in order to be allowed to enjoy my love for so long, I am prepared to trade my death for it].

136

39. The way in which Virgil shows that death is the only possibility is derived from Soph. *Ajax* 460: I am hated by all, gods, Greeks, Trojans. πότερα πρὸς οἴ-κους...περῶ; καὶ ποῖον ὄμμα πατρὶ δηλώσω φανεὶς Τελαμῶνι;...ἀλλὰ δῆτ' ἰὼν πρὸς ἔρυμα Τρώων...; οὐκ ἔστι ταῦτα κτλ ['shall I go to my home? And how shall I face my father Telamon when I come before him?...but shall I go to the Trojan walls...? This cannot be...' etc.]. Then Medea (admittedly in a different context) νῦν ποῖ τράπωμαι; πότερα πρὸς πατρὸς δόμους;...ἢ πρὸς ταλαίνας Πελιάδας; κτλ (502f.) ['Now where am I to turn? To my father's house?...or to the wretched daughters of Pelias?' etc.]. And hence Ariadne in Cat. 64.177: *nam quo me referam?...Idaeosne petam montes?...an patris auxilium sperem?...coniugis an fido consoler memet amore?* ['For where am I to go?... To the Idaean mountains? Can I hope for help from my father?... Or can I console myself with the loyal love of my husband?']. The rhetorical use of the formula by C. Gracchus (Cic. *De Orat.* 3.214) *quo me miser conferam, quo vertam?* [Where can I go in my distress, where can I turn?] etc. was famous; strangely enough, he is borrowing from the no doubt widely known words of Ennius' Medea (fr. 231 Ribbeck): *quo nunc me vertam? quod iter incipiam ingredi* etc. ['Where can I turn now? what road can I start to take?...'].

40. The idea in 604ff. comes from Apollonius 4.391: ἴετο δ' ἥγε νῆα καταφλέξαι διά τ' ἔμπεδα πάντα κεάσσαι, ἐν δὲ πεσεῖν αὐτὴ μαλερῷ πυρί [she longed to set fire to the ship and to cut up everything completely and to fall herself into the raging fire]. The curses (the form *si tangere portus...necesse est et sic fata Iovis poscunt...at* etc. [if he must reach harbour and that is required by Jupiter's ordinances... nevertheless] is modelled on *Od.* 9.522: ἀλλ' εἴ οἱ μοῖρά ἐστι φίλους τ' ἰδέειν καὶ ἱκέσθαι...ἐὴν ἐς πατρίδα γαῖαν, ὀψὲ κακῶς ἵκοι etc. ['but if it is his fate to return home to his own land and see his friends, may he come late']) again occur first in Soph. *Ajax* 835: καλῶ δ' ἀρωγοὺς...σεμνὰς Ἐρινῦς τανύποδας κτλ [I call to my aid the stern, long-striding Furies...]. In Apollonius they take the form of a threat cf. Cat. 64.193: *Eumenides...huc huc adventate, meas audite querellas* etc. [you Eumenides, come here, come here and listen to my complaints] and Phyllis ἀρὰς θεμένη κατὰ Δημοφῶντος ἑαυτὴν ἀναιρεῖ [kills herself after calling down curses on the head of Demophoon] (Apollod. *epit.* 6.16). A similar suicide is that, for example, of Euopis, πολλὰ πρότερον λυπηρὰ καταρασαμένη τῷ αἰτίῳ τῆς συμφορᾶς [after first making many dreadful curses against the man responsible for her misfortune]; (Parthenius 31; quoting Phylarchus). These deathbed curses are always fulfilled; so here: the reader who half knows, half suspects this, will sense that Dido's death is an important event not only in the story of Aeneas, but in the history of the Roman empire, and his reactions will go far beyond sympathy for Dido as an individual. On the significance of the curse (for which see Conway, op. cit. 17, whose criticisms of my earlier comments are entirely justified) for the understanding of Aeneas' attitude see below in Part Two, the section of 'Characters' (Part II, pp. 223f.); for its place in the whole work see the section on 'Composition', Part II, ch. 4.

41. This corresponds with Ajax's prayer in Sophocles (827) that Zeus will let Teucer be the first to find his body: the only difference is that Dido is not concerned about burial, but wants to ensure that her eyes will be closed by her nearest and dearest.

42. *Incubuitque toro* (650) [she cast herself down on the bed], *os impressa toro* (659) [burying her face in the bed]; this is how Deianeira dies too: ἐπενθοροῦσ' ἄνω καθέζετ' ἐν μέσοισιν εὐναστηρίοις...'ὦ λέχη τε καὶ νυμφεῖ' ἐμά, τὸ λοιπὸν ...ἤδη χαίρετε κτλ. [she jumped up and sat in the middle of the bed – 'Oh bed, my bridal couch, goodbye for ever'] (*Trach.* 917). Euripides provided the precedent for this in Alcestis' farewell θάλαμον εἰσπεσοῦσα καὶ λέχος...'ὦ λέκτρον, ἔνθα παρθένει' ἔλυσ' ἐγώ, χαῖρ'· οὐ γὰρ ἐχθαίρω σ'· ἀπώλεσας δέ με μόνην' κτλ (175) [rushing into the bedroom and falling upon the bed... 'O bed on which I gave up my maidenhood farewell. I do not hate you. I am the only one you have destroyed']. Virgil had already recalled this last phrase at 496: *lectumque iugalem quo perii* [the bridal bed which was my ruin]. The situation however is close to that in the *Trachiniae*: as Hyllus is fetched by the τροφός [nurse] in Sophocles, so is Anna here: ὁρῶμεν αὐτὴν ἀμφιπλῆγι φασγάνῳ...πεπληγμένην (930) [we saw her struck by the two-edged sword], *illam..ferro conlapsam aspiciunt comites ensemque cruore spumantem* (663-5) [her servants saw her where she had fallen on the blade, with blood foaming about the sword]; then come the lamentations of the close relative who rushes to the scene: *sinu germanam amplexa fovebat cum gemitu* (686-7) [she clasped her sister to her breast and fondled her, sobbing], πλευρόθεν

137

116

Dido

πλευρὰν παρεὶς ἔκειτο πόλλ' ἀναστένων (938) [he lay with his side against hers groaning and groaning]. The magnificent *vixi et quem dederat cursum fortuna peregi, et nunc magna mei sub terras ibit imago* (653) [I have lived my life and finished the course which Fortune allotted me. Now my wraith shall pass in state to the world below] is a touch of purely Roman heroism; Virgil perhaps got the idea from its opposite: κάτειμι, πρίν μοι μοῖραν ἐξήκειν βίου [I shall go below the earth before it is my fate to leave this life] (Soph. *Antig.* 896, cf. 916ff.). It is well known that the wish *si litora tantum* etc. (657) [if only the Dardan ships had never reached my coast], which seems natural here, is almost formulaic: εἴθ' ὤφελ' Ἀργοῦς μὴ διαπτάσθαι σκάφος Κόλχων ἐς αἶαν κυανέας Συμπληγάδας [would that the ship Argo had never skimmed across the blue Symplegades to the land of Colchis] (*Med.* 1f.) cf. Ap. Rhod. 4.32; Cat. 64.171: *utinam ne...Gnosia Cecropiae tetigissent litora puppes* [would that the Athenian ships had never touched the shores of Cnossos] is taken over by Virgil practically *verbatim*. Sabbadini's view, that the speeches 607-29 and 651-62 cannot both have appeared in the original version because their dominant moods are different, has already been discussed on n. 34 above, 109.   138

43. On the use of monologue in the *Aeneid* see the section on 'Speech' below, Part II, ch. 3.III.

44. *Vultum demissa* (1.561) [with lowered eyes] (modelled on Apollonius' Hypsipyle, ἐγκλιδὸν ὄσσε βαλοῦσα (1.790) [she turned her eyes aside] and similarly his Medea, 3.1008) may therefore be regarded as an error of judgement.

45. See above n. 16 above, 110.   139

46. Lamentation 548-51. Then a touch of regret, 596ff.

47. Cic. *De Off.* 1.25.88: *nec vero audiendi qui graviter inimicis irascendum putabunt idque magnanimi et fortis viri esse censebunt; nihil enim laudabilius, nihil magno et praeclaro viro dignius placabilitate atque clementia* [nor must we listen to those who may think that one ought to be very angry with one's enemies and consider that appropriate to a great-hearted and good man; nothing is more praiseworthy, nothing more worthy of a great and outstanding person than clemency and a willingness to be placated].

48. Arceophron in Hermesianax (Antonin. Liberalis 39), Iphis (Ovid *Met.* 14.696ff.), the ἐραστής [lover] in Theocritus 23, cf. the threat in 3.25, imitated by Virgil in *Ecl.* 8.59; Narcissus (Conon 24). Rohde, *Gr. R.* 80f. collects these passages. Cf. the suicides, successful or unsuccessful, in the ancient novel, *Hermes* 34 (1899) 497 n. 2.

49. Rohde, op. cit. n. 2, 121.   140

50. Perhaps Phyllis in Callimachus, although in this case it also seems to have been the result of a feeling that she had been unbearably insulted: *et amoris impatientia et quod se spretam esse credebat* [both because of impatience with her love, and because she felt she had been spurned] (Serv. on *Ecl.* 5.10).

51. I cite a few of the many examples: Oenone allowed Paris to go to his death. Byblis (Parthen. 11 [= Apollonius] ὑπὸ τοῦ πάθους μὴ ἀνιεμένη, πρὸς δὲ καὶ δοκοῦσα αἰτία γεγονέναι Καύνῳ τῆς ἀπαλλαγῆς [having no relief from her suffering, and also feeling she was responsible for Caunus' desertion of her]; Cleoboea: ἐννοηθεῖσα ὡς δεινὸν ἔργον ἐδεδράκει, καὶ ἄλλως δὲ καιομένη

117

σφοδρῷ ἔρωτι [considering what a terrible thing she had done, and also burning with excessive love] (Parthen. 15); Euopis: διὰ τὸ δέος καὶ αἰσχύνην [because of fear and shame] (Parthen. 31; quoting Phylarchus).

141   **52.** We may well ask why all these complicated preparations for Dido's death are necessary. Could she not simply sit on the *lectus iugalis* [marriage-couch], like Deianeira, and plunge the sword into her heart? We might put the same question to the historical Dido, and will have to answer it on her behalf: she wanted to die not in secret and alone, as though she had something to be ashamed of, but in a way that would show all her people that Dido knew how to keep faith. This (hypothetical) motivation does not, however, appear in Virgil: Dido builds the pyre secretly *penetrali in sede* [right inside the palace], and there is nothing particularly glorious about suicide in this context. I believe that the traditional, arresting picture of Dido offering herself to Hades with all the pomp and magnificence of a sacrifice to the dead haunted Virgil's imagination, and it was only later that he discovered the concepts which would motivate the effect that he was aiming at, summarised in the phrase *sic sic iuvat ire sub umbras* (660) [this, this is the way I wish to go beneath the earth]: the fire shall consume with her all the *exuviae* [relics] of her faithless lover and (since Dido's palace naturally stands high up on the citadel) the flames will be seen by Aeneas from the sea as he sails away and abandons her, *secum ferat omina mortis* (662) [may he take with him the evil omens of my death]. Sabbadini excludes everything connected with the magic ceremony (474-503, 509-21) from his hypothetical 'first draft', because in his view Anna did not originally take part in the construction of the pyre: 'Everything that Dido asks Anna to do in lines 494-7, she does herself in lines 504-8.' But that is not true of the main task, the construction of the pyre; besides, it is obvious that neither Dido nor Anna would have personally carried up the *lectus iugalis* [marriage-couch]: Anna would have instructed slaves to do it. In that case, Dido can have seen to the *exuviae* [relics] personally, laying them on the *torus* [couch]; and even on the strictest interpretation this is compatible with others having actually placed all these objects on the pyre.

   53. σκηψαμένη τελετὴν πρὸς ἀνάλυσιν ὅρκων ἐπιτελέσειν [pretending that she will perform a rite to dissolve her vows] (Timaeus 566 fr. 23 Jacoby); *placatura viri manes inferiasque ante nuptias missura* [professing to placate the ghost of her dead husband and to make a sacrifice to his shade before her marriage (sc. to Iarbas)] (Justin. 18.6).

142   **54.** Hence the ambiguous phrase *sacra Iovi Stygio quae rite incepta paravi perficere est animus* (638) ['It is my intention to complete certain rites to Stygian Jupiter, which I have formally prepared and begun']. It is not clear whether in the mind of the *sacerdos* [priestess] the magic sacrifice is intended to arouse love in Aeneas or to destroy it in Dido: this obscurity has been discussed by Dedo, *De antiquorum superstitione amatoria* (Diss. Greifswald, 1904) 47ff. and by Penquitt op. cit. 38ff., 51ff. Lines 480 and 487ff. mention both alternatives; the burning of the *exuviae* [relics] and *effigies* [portrait] seems to refer only to the latter, but the mention of the love-charm ἱππομανές [hippomanes] at 515 refers equally clearly to the former. It is hardly a case of simple confusion arising from carelessness: preparations for the burning of the *exuviae* and *effigies* were essential to Dido's purpose (see p. 105); the other alternative is mentioned to Anna so as to make her believe in

Dido

it – only the possibility of keeping Aeneas in Carthage could really justify such mighty preparations and such haste. Lines 512-16 seem to have been added as an afterthought: *quaeruntur* [are sought] and *quaeritur* [is sought] are out of place in this context, and *ipsa* [she herself] in line 517 follows on from 509-11 more naturally than from 513-16: Virgil later expanded the passage about the magic rites, no doubt because he wanted these other alternatives to play their full part, without being any more concerned about the resulting lack of clarity than in the passage discussed above on p. 101. It is highly unusual, in my view, to divide the magic sacrifice into two: the action in lines 509ff., which according to line 638 is preparatory (*sacra rite incepta perficere est animus* [I intend to complete the rites formally begun]), and the main action at which the *hostiae* (639-40) [victims] are actually to be sacrificed: here it is very clear why Virgil has departed from normal practice.

55. It is also worth noting that Barce and Anna apparently believe in the power of magic, but not Dido: otherwise she could have attempted to use it in earnest. This shows that Virgil himself did not believe in it, any more than Horace did.

56. The concept of Medea the magician, who was the only person who could render harmless the dragon who guarded the Golden Fleece, has become fused in Virgil's mind with the Hesperides, a connection which Apollonius (4.1399) had already made; Virgil uses the past forms *dabat* and *servabat* because he is thinking of the death of the dragon described by Apollonius. It is easy to see why the μελιττοῦτα [honey-cake] and the soporific poppy given to Cerberus (4.421) should also be given to serpents so as to render them harmless (Herzog, *Hermes* 29 [1894] 625); however, this does not answer Ribbeck's objection, that this particular dragon's task is to stay awake, and so he ought not to be put to sleep. But Virgil's intention was to emphasize the power of the priestess; like the *maga* [witch] in Tibullus who *dicitur sola feros Hecatae perdomuisse canes* (1.2.52) [is reputed to be the only one to have tamed the dogs of Hecate], the *maga* here too could control the dragon just as well as Medea could. Remember that Apollonius (3.532) said of her καὶ ποταμοὺς ἵστησιν ἄφαρ κελαδεινὰ ῥέοντας ἄστρα τε καὶ μήνης ἱερῆς ἐπέδησε κελεύθους [she instantly stops the rivers which flow noisily along and she has checked the stars and paths of the sacred moon] = *sistere aquam fluviis et sidera vertere retro* (489) [to stay the current of a river and reverse the movement of stars], where the final climax spoils the sense of the magic (a divine power may stop the passage of time – as for example in the case of Zeus and Alcmene – but it is hardly possible to make it run backwards). For the same reason Virgil also adds *mugire videbis terram et descendere montibus ornos* (490-1) [you will see the earth bellowing and rowan trees marching down from the mountains]: this is not an actual magical practice, but the phrase credits the witch with the effect of the arrival of Hecate herself, *sub pedibus mugire solum et iuga coepta moveri silvarum* (6.256) [the ground bellowed beneath their feet and the slopes of the forest-clad mountains began to move]. One may contrast this description with the magic effects in another passage of Virgil, those mentioned by the country girl in *Ecl.* 8, the invocation of snakes in Marsus, the werewolf, the *excantatio frugum* [the removal of crops by enchantment]: those belong to the everyday magic of the peasants as opposed to heroic magic.

57. She strews the *mola* (517) [sacred meal] on the fire herself: in Theocritus

143

119

(2.18, cf. Virgil *Ecl.* 8.82) this is done by a serving-girl.

58. This was already observed by the ancient commentators: see Servius *ad loc.*

59. It is Aeneas' sword: so Ajax kills himself with Hector's sword. *Ensem...non hos quaesitum munus in usus* (647) [his sword...a gift not sought for such a use as this] has been thought to be irreconcilably incompatible (see Conington *ad loc.*) with *exuvias ensemque relictum* (507) [the clothes and the sword he had left behind] for the hypercritical reason that, in one passage, the sword 'belongs' to Aeneas, and, in the other, to Dido, and this leads to the further objection that a sword is not a suitable gift for a lady. It will not have been formally handed over; Aeneas hung up his weapons in their bedchamber at Dido's request (*quaesitum*), a pledge, as it were, of his love (cf. *Ecl.* 8.94) – it is difficult to imagine a clearer symbol of the total surrender of a warrior – and received from Dido in return a richly decorated sword and Tyrian garment (261).

60. *Ajax* 901 (chorus): κατέπεφνες ἄναξ τόνδε συνναύταν ['you have killed us, O King, your fellow-sailors']. With the preceding words compare *Ajax* 910: οἷος ἄρ' αἱμάχθης, ἄφρακτος φίλων· ἐγὼ δ' ὁ πάντα κωφός, ὁ πάντ' ἄϊδρις κατημέλησα ['you met a bloody death all on your own, unprotected by your friends: and I so stupid, so completely unknowing, noticed nothing'].

4

The Games

1. Introduction and motivation

The funeral games in honour of Patroclus are generally recognized to be one of the finest parts of the *Iliad*; the Greeks' obsession with competition would have ensured the popularity of this Book even if it were not such a splendid piece of poetry. There were many descriptions of similar games elsewhere in ancient epic. The late epics of Quintus and Nonnus represented a return to this tradition; in the same way, Virgil intended from the start that his work should include a description of funeral games that would be comparable with Homer's, since the *Aeneid* was to be a treasury containing every jewel of the epic and, at the same time, it would supply an ancient precedent for an important Roman institution, the *ludi funebres* [funeral games]. Obviously, it had to be Aeneas who held the games. But this still left the question, in whose honour they were to be performed; and again, where should they occur in the work, at what time and at what place; finally they had to be fitted into the action so that, in spite of the fact that they would have to form an episode within the narrative, they would still appear to be an integral part of it and not a piece of decoration arbitrarily stuck on to it afterwards. We can reconstruct with some confidence the considerations that must have led Virgil to the solution of these problems that we find in the poem as we read it today.

The person in whose honour the games are to be held must be someone of considerable importance, who has already appeared in the poem, and who stands close to the hero. These requirements stem from the nature of the institution. For Virgil, it was Anchises, and Anchises alone, who satisfied all these requirements. A casualty of the Latin war, Pallas for example, was out of the question, since this would have seriously disrupted the sequence of the final events as they gathered momentum towards the end of the epic. Anchises on the other hand, the ancestral head of the house of Aeneas, famous not only because he had been the beloved of Venus, but also because his son had rescued him from Troy, was ideally suited to provide the focus for a magnificent ceremony, which would at the same time also serve as yet another proof of Aeneas' filial *pietas*. Chronologically, Virgil had to place the ceremony after the Carthaginian episode, once he had decided that the events preceding the arrival of the Trojans in Sicily should be narrated by Aeneas himself in Carthage. The alternative would have been to put this episode at the very beginning of his work; this would have had a highly unfortunate effect, since it would have deflected attention away from the hero and on to subsidiary characters, and as a result, the opening of the poem would not have been lively, full of emotion, and fast-moving, but completely static. Moreover, what poet, conscientious and mature in his technique, would ever begin his poem with an interlude? And it is

146

121

equally unlikely that it ever occurred to Virgil to make Aeneas give an account of these games to Dido, not even a moderately detailed one; these peaceful activities would not have fitted very well into the framework of *casus* [events] and *errores* [wanderings]. They might have been mentioned very briefly, if, as in the case of the Actian games at 3.280ff., they involved something that was important for its own sake and for historical reasons, but they were not at all suitable for detailed description in Aeneas' speech to Dido, least of all at the end of his narrative, where they would have had to appear.[1]

147   However, if Aeneas has to celebrate games in honour of Anchises after the episode in Carthage, this leads to the rather awkward consequence that it is not an actual funeral ceremony at the grave of a man who has just died as in the *Iliad*, but a memorial service. For Anchises has to have died before Aeneas reaches Carthage; if his father had still been with him, his love-affair and the neglect of his divine mission would have been unthinkable. I call this consequence rather awkward because it inevitably weakens the motivation of the ceremony. It no longer arises directly from the context, nor is it a unique occasion, since it might be repeated at any time. In order to make the motivation slightly less weak, it is necessary that the ceremony should at least take place at the grave itself, where Aeneas happens to find himself exactly a year after the funeral, a fact which can be interpreted as a sign from the gods (5.56).[2]

148   This question of momentum was decisive when it came to the choice of the place where Anchises should die. There were various traditions: his grave was shown to visitors in Aineia, in Arcadia and in Epirus; Roman legend said that he came to Latium with the others and was buried there by Aeneas. Let us suppose that Virgil had placed his death in Epirus. In that case, the story could have unfolded exactly as we now have it; the funeral ceremony and the games in his memory could still have taken place in Sicily – indeed, Aeneas himself says that he will commemorate the date of his father's death wherever he finds himself, but it is obvious how much this would have weakened the motivation. So it is a question of finding somewhere that Aeneas could visit twice with some degree of plausibility. Geographically, the most convenient place was the western point of Sicily, and there were many other important considerations which made it suitable. For artistic reasons Virgil could not celebrate the games at just any point on the coast between, say, Calabria and Lucania; it had to be a place of some significance. And, in fact, of all the many places visited by Aeneas in his westward wanderings, the sojourn in Sicily was by far the most important from a Roman point of view. The Aeneas legend played an integral part in the beginnings of Roman rule in Sicily, and the sanctuary of Aphrodite Aineias on Mount Eryx, the cradle of the Roman cult of Venus, must have been regarded as a place of the greatest sanctity, especially during the Augustan period. It is therefore easy to understand why Virgil, who deals with the large number of other settlements founded by Aeneas by omitting some and passing quickly over others, should spotlight this one place, which was important because of Rome's relations with Sicily, the foundation of Segesta, and the sanctuary on Eryx. He used the traditional version to explain the reasons for landing there and founding the city: the storm, and the burning of the ships.[3] But as far as we know, it was his own idea to give a new reason for Aeneas' assocation with this sanctuary, a tie of

kinship, by situating Anchises' grave there. The unity of place and time thus created enabled Virgil to combine into a single narrative two quite separate incidents, the historically important fact of Aeneas' sojourn in Sicily and the foundation of a city, with the artistically important description of the funeral games. But, not content with this, he wanted to establish an inner link as well. In order to achieve this, he had to create an organic connection between the games and the burning of the ships by the Trojan women, which was the cause of the foundation of the city. This presented   149 him with no difficulties at all. The games are just what is required to allow the women to perform their action, so much so in fact that the reader might well suspect – though he would certainly be wrong – that this was why they were introduced. The women have to be left alone, and not merely for a short time, since in that case the fire would not have developed into a real danger. Therefore the men must be given some occupation that will keep them well away from the ships. Naturally, all the men would have been eager to attend the games; the *lusus Troiae* [Game of Troy] means that the adolescent boys leave the camp as well; only the women remain behind, as decent Roman women were expected to do.[4] This provides an occasion better suited to Juno's intrigue and Iris' mission than perhaps any other in the whole of the voyage. It is now or never that an attempt must be made to destroy the Trojan fleet, and thereby obstruct once again the fulfilment of *fatum* [destiny].

2. Composition

The description of the Games themselves is of exceptional importance for our purposes, since it is an obvious imitation, not to say re-working, of a book of Homer. It should therefore provide us with a great deal of information about Virgil's own artistic principles. Taken as a whole, the major difference between Virgil's narrative and Homer's is the greater attention paid to the proportions of the composition, and the smaller number of competitions. Homer describes eight, one after the other, apparently without arranging them according to any kind of artistic principle that might have bound them all together in some kind of unity; when the last competition is over, the spectators simply disperse. Virgil restricts himself to half the Homeric number, and finishes with an event which is not really a contest at all, the *lusus Troiae*. In Homer, more lines are devoted to the first contest, the chariot race, than to all the other games put together; some of these are described in more detail than others, but the accounts generally get shorter and shorter as they go on. The last description takes up only 14 lines, as opposed to 389 for the first. Virgil, too, describes the first contest in the greatest detail, as befits its importance; but the   150 third is also treated at considerable length, whereas the second and the fourth are about half as long, so that, twice, a long section is followed by a short one. This creates an impression not of a mere succession of a series of separate events, but of a structured whole.[5] In Homer, the interest falls off more and more towards the end; the last competition is not even held: Agamemnon rather than Meriones is given the first prize, on the grounds that everyone knows that he is the best at javelin-throwing. We may assume that this event is placed last so as to give it special emphasis, and because it sets the final seal on the reconciliation between Achilles and

Agamemnon; but the poet fails to do justice artistically to the importance of this occasion. In Virgil, the fourth and final event is clearly distinguished from the others by the miraculous sign that occurs when the last shot leaves the bow. This imbues the final contest with the highest possible aura.

In other ways, too, Virgil sought to avoid the weakening effect of frequent repetition, by making the descriptions of the contest as different as possible. First, he varied the nature and the numbers of the competitors. There is only one contest that involves two persons; there is only one in which a large number of men (some named and some not) take part; four heroes compete for the prize in the first and the last event, but in the first they do so together with their ships' crews. These four are the ancestors of Roman *familiae Troianae* [Trojan families], and commanders of ships; in other words, they are next in rank to Aeneas. The next competition, the foot-race, is for young boys (*pueri* [349]) who have not yet achieved fame, and it is won by the youngest of all; the veteran Entellus wins the boxing-match; the fourth event is distinguished from the first, which in other ways it resembles, by the fact that Acestes takes part in it; the *lusus Troiae* is performed by the boys and youths who are still too young to bear arms.

In Homer, each event is introduced in a stereotyped manner: first the kind of contest is specified, then the prizes; Achilles στῆ δ' ὀρθὸς καὶ μῦθον ἐν 'Αρ-γείοισιν ἔειπεν [stood upright and spoke these words among the Argives], and then, after the speech: ὣς ἔφατ' [so he spoke], ὦρτο δ' ἔπειτα [then upsprang] or ὄρνυτο δ' αὐτίκα [immediately arose] followed by the names of the contestants. This is repeated every time with only a few slight variations, except that in the case of the last event the introduction is considerably shortened. In the introductions, too, Virgil varies the treatment as much as possible; in the first contest the event is mentioned and then the contestants are enumerated; the prizes are not named until they are distributed after the contest. In the second event, we are told in reported speech of Aeneas' announcement of a foot-race; after the contestants have been listed, the prizes are described in direct speech. For the third event, he uses direct speech to announce the boxing match; we are then informed about the prizes and the contestants in reported speech. For the fourth, Virgil again resorts to reported speech for the announcement of the contest; we discover the names of the contestants as they draw lots for the order in which they are to compete; Aeneas says nothing in direct speech until after the event; and only the first of the prizes is described, by Aeneas himself.

The results of the contests also show the same striving to achieve variety. Only in the first does everything go according to rule (as in most of the competitions in Homer); in the second there is a dispute about the result because of Nisus' unfair trick (as in the chariot-race in Homer); in the third, the contestants are separated before the final decision (as in Homer's wrestling-match and armed combat); in the last one, the result is unexpectedly decided by the divine omen. This is the only new element added by Virgil; in other respects his artistic principles are revealed by the fact that he uses the possibilities provided by Homer once each.

3. Characters

It is clear that Book 23 of the *Iliad* is a late addition to the poem, because of the author's careful use of characterization, something that is alien to the earliest epic poetry. Next to the technical description of the competitions, this is his main aim: to show the Greek heroes displaying in ceremonial games the same skills that bring them success on the battle-field. The sharp light thrown in this book on, for example, Odysseus and the younger Ajax, by means of careful little touches; the characterization of Achilles by means of a wealth of detail; the allusions that reach out beyond the frame of the *Iliad* in the descriptions of people who are important in post-Homeric epic, such as Epeius; and above all Antilochus, who is given quite exceptional treatment and built up into a three-dimensional figure with the highest degree of artistic skill – all these are extremely attractive characteristics individual to this poet, and the significance of their contribution to the effect of the whole book could not fail to be observed by a perceptive reader such as Virgil; yet at the same   152
time it must have made it very much more difficult for Virgil as his follower to rival the achievements of his model. The enormous advantage that the Homeric poet possessed was that his readers already knew his characters. He makes use of well-known individual traits or endows well-known characters with new traits. In both cases he can be certain that the listener will happily follow. Virgil, on the other hand, first of all has to create the characters who take part in the games, and make us interested in their rivalry. During the actual contests he has to compensate for the advantages already possessed by the Homeric poet, and if he fails in this he has failed altogether to compete with him.

The commanders of the ships who take place in the naval race are shown to be men of importance, for, as they are introduced, three of them are explicitly said to be ancestors of well-known Roman families. In this way, Virgil built a bridge between the remote past and his own time, which brought the proceedings closer to the Roman reader; but it did not do anything to help him visualize them as individual persons, since, even leaving aside Gyas, whose Roman descendants are not mentioned at all (Servius tells us that he was the ancestor of the Geganii), neither the *gens Memmia* nor the *gens Cluentia* played such an outstanding role in Roman history that the reader's imagination would immediately have been able to supply the characteristic features of their ancestors, as it could have done for the ancestors of the Fabii or Appii, and which may indeed have been true in the case of Sergestus as the representative of the *gens Sergia*: in so far as L. Sergius Catilina was by far the most notorious member of this family, then every Roman who heard its name would immediately have thought of him. And indeed it may well be that Virgil intended to underline this connection when he depicts Sergestus as the man who is wrecked in the fury of the race: *furens animi* [wild with excitement] he tries to take the shortest course near the cliffs and runs his ship aground on the rocks[6] (202ff.). As in this case, so also in others: the decisive factor is not so much the quality of the ships as the character of their commanders. Gyas would have won if he had not thrown his own steersman overboard in a mad fit of anger (172ff.); Mnestheus,

153   himself driven on by burning ambition, knows how to make an energetic speech to his men so as to inspire them to make the greatest possible effort (189ff.), and he very nearly snatched the victory from Cloanthus, who had overtaken the rest by skilful steering, even though his ship was clumsier; but at the last moment (153-4) Cloanthus persuades the gods of the sea to help him, and with their assistance his ship the Scylla glides like an arrow into the harbour (225ff.). In the races in Homer, as in reality, the decisive factor is above all the quality of the horses; in second place, again as in reality, comes the element of chance, or as the poet prefers to say, the intervention of the gods, each of whom helps his own favourite and hinders his rival; the character of the hero himself comes only third in importance. It is only Antilochus who owes his victory over Menelaus to his own unaided human skill and audacity. Virgil, however, keeps this third factor well to the fore; and here we have a clear example of something that can be observed time and time again in his work, his predilection for giving an inner meaning to the action. This is one of the most important differences between the later, more reflective poet and the naïve nature of his Homeric model, which deals only with the perceptible world. However, the result is that this contest becomes not a description of a single historical event, but a 'typical' contest, something that transcends the individual event and takes on a universal significance. Not that I believe that Virgil consciously had this intention. He was not intending to create an allegory, but a straightforward narrative. But his whole way of thinking is grounded in a universal morality, and it follows inevitably that the individual event carries the mark of the universal, and very easily adapts itself to a universalizing viewpoint. Thus, this narrative is a typical one, which expresses the general truth that leaders and commanders come to grief because of blind, reckless audacity and because of passionate immoderation and wilfulness, whereas well-considered, steady effort, combined with skilful leadership, brings a man to the front; but that, in the end, the highest prize goes to the man who remembers to ask the gods to help him. We have only to think of the generals and statesmen of the Republic as they appear in the well-established tradition used by Livy to realize the truly Roman nature of this whole way of thinking.

     In the foot-race, the Homeric poet again makes the result depend on 'luck', which depends on the gods: Ajax slips and falls, so that he is overtaken by Odysseus, to

154   whom, moreover, Athena has given extra strength (*Iliad* 23.758ff.). Furthermore, considerable importance is assigned to the ability of the contestants: Antilochus comes in last despite Ajax's accident. Virgil takes over this fall from Homer, and assigns it, as Homer does, to the runner who is winning; but more important than the fall itself is what follows, where Virgil again makes the really decisive factor a psychological one: Nisus, in spite of his sudden accident, remembers his tender friendship with the youthful Euryalus and assures him of victory by a really very unsporting manoeuvre (334ff.). These two main characters reappear in Book 9, where the strength of their friendship is attested by the dangerous enterprise and by the death that they share. However, in Homer the games are a lighthearted epilogue to the serious fighting; but in Virgil the games form a prelude to it: and this order undermines the effect.[7]

     The *lacrimae decorae* (342) [appealing tears] which Euryalus sheds when his victory is disputed – he does not complain in words – are a very compact way of telling us that he is still little more than a child; though the half-lines 294 and 322 suggest that Virgil intended to add further detail eventually. As for Nisus, it is clear from his performance in the race and from his act of friendship, and again by his behaviour after Aeneas' decision, that he is a clever, cheerful character, rather like Antilochus, but with a greater skill and ingenuity in speaking.[8]

Virgil took over from Homer the way in which the contestants for the boxing-match are presented (368ff., cf. *Iliad* 23.664ff.). First, the acknowledged champion steps forward and defiantly claims the prize. Only after some delay does anyone challenge him. The self-confident boasting of Homer's Epeius – 'that's what I say and that's what I'll do: I'll tear his skin to shreds and I'll break his bones' – is toned down in Virgil: Dares is less brutal, in keeping with Virgil's sense of propriety, but this makes him less vivid as a character. On the other hand, the role of the challenger 155 is considerably enriched and goes much more deeply psychological: it is neither ambition nor desire for the prize that prompts the aged Entellus to enter the apparently unequal match; Acestes' words and his own feelings have roused his sense of honour; in the name of the god Eryx, of whom he is proud to have been a pupil, and to show that he is not lying and merely boasting of a reputation that he does not actually possess, and finally as a representative of Sicily against Troy (417), he dares to fight against an opponent much stronger than himself; a fall early in the match rouses his spirits still further, and his sense of shame, and his consciousness of what he had been and still is (*pudor et conscia virtus* [455]) doubles his strength and brings him a splendid victory.

In describing the final event, Virgil dispenses with all characterization. Mnestheus, already familiar to the reader from the ship-race, appears again; Eurytion is introduced as brother to Pandarus, who is already familiar to us; Hippocoon is a mere name; but the reader's attention is immediately aroused when Acestes appears. We already know enough of Virgil's artistic principles to expect that something special is going to happen; and our expectations are fulfilled, for his bow-shot provides the climax not only of this contest but of the whole games.

The individual characters have not been assigned arbitrarily to the various competitive events. Augustus is known to have taken an extremely lively interest in every type of contest (*agon*); apart from the fact that he personally enjoyed them, and wished to satisfy the appetite of the plebs for displays, it is possible that more idealistic reasons were involved. It is clear that he made an attempt to revive something of the noble agonistic spirit of the ancient Greeks. He founded a new 'sacred' contest (on Greek soil, admittedly), the Actian Games, and this inspired the institution of regular games in a great number of provincial cities (Suetonius *Aug.* 59). In Rome itself the *ludi pro salute divi Augusti* [games for the well-being of the divine Augustus], dedicated to Actian Apollo, were celebrated regularly from the year 28 BC, and, as in the great Greek games, men and youths from noble families entered the arena as contestants;[9] on other occasions, too, Augustus had youths from the most noble families driving chariots and horses in the Circus, or fighting against 156 animals (Suet. *Aug.* 43); thus, in the games which he instituted when the temple to Caesar was dedicated in 29 BC, patricians competed for prizes in chariot-racing (Dio 51.22). That must have seemed just as much *prisci decorique moris* [an example of ancient and glorious custom] to the emperor as the public appearance of noble youths in the *lusus Troiae* (Suet. *Aug.* 43); after all, according to learned tradition, in ancient times the citizens themselves took part in competitions in the circus (Pliny *N.H.* 21.7). But the appearance of respectable men in an athletic contest was still felt to be incompatible with Roman notions of propriety. Already under Augustus, it was necessary for the Senate to pass decrees forbidding senators and *equites* to appear as actors, or even as gladiators; but there seems to have been no need for decrees to discourage respectable men from pummelling each other naked in front of the plebs.[10] These attitudes are reflected in Virgil. If there is nothing disgraceful about respectable men driving chariots in public, it is even less shocking for the ancestors of Roman families to race their ships in order to gain a prize. But it would never have occurred to Virgil to present Mnestheus and Sergestus as boxers. On the contrary, he is careful to avoid any historical implications, and strongly emphasizes the mythical aspect: Dares has already beaten the Bebrycian Butes at Hector's funeral games; Entellus has learnt his skill from the deified Eryx, who once fought against Hercules on the Sicilian shore; also, the boxing-leathers made from the hides of seven oxen (404) are intended to strengthen the impression that in this contest the shadow of a bygone semi-divine age still looms over the present. It would have been just as unsuitable for men of the upper class to take part in the foot race as in the boxing, but it is no disgrace for youths, even respectable youths (*regius egregia Priami de stirpe Diores* [297] [Diores, sprung from the blood royal of Priam's exalted line]) to match their strength by taking part in a foot race before a crowd of spectators; Augustus himself once not merely permitted this, but actually arranged it himself (Suet. *Aug.* 43). An amusing accident, such as that of Nisus, can be taken lightly by the young, for they can bear being laughed at; but if it had happened to a hero comparable in stature to Homer's Ajax (*Iliad* 23.774), Virgil and his public would have perceived it as detracting from his dignity. On the other hand, there was no need for even the aged Acestes, the offspring of a god, to hesitate to take part in the – entirely mythical – archery competition.

157

Virgil's gaze lingers with exceptional tenderness on the youngest surviving generation of ancient Troy, the *Troianum agmen* [Trojan regiment], the contemporaries of Aeneas' own son, Iulus. A cheerful, splendid spectacle, a juvenile prelude to the serious battles in which the boys will take part when they reach maturity – there could be no better finale to the serious adult contests, bringing them to a close on a note of peace. Certainly Virgil was consciously writing with an eye to Augustus' own tastes – the emperor was known to be particularly fond of the *lusus Troiae*; the book was written before a series of accidents and the bitter complaints of the peevish Asinius Pollio, whose grandson was injured in this ceremonial procession, spoilt the emperor's pleasure in this spectacle, so that it was eventually discontinued (Suet. *Aug.* 43). But the passage gives a powerful impression that when Virgil was writing it, he was not merely doing so as a loyal member of Augustus' court, but had thrown himself heart and soul into the spectacle which he paints with such cheerful colours. And this is true not only of this scene; the same joy in the growing maturity of boys pervades the whole of the *Aeneid*: it is one of the most individually Virgilian features of the work. It is not only Iulus whose portrayal is enriched in this way. The idea of making Amor appear in his form, his child-like pleasure at the splendour of the hunt, and his boyish desire to match himself against really wild animals; his

extravagant gratitude towards Nisus and Euryalus, who want to fetch his father for him, and to whom, with the generosity of a child offering everything under the stars, he promises every imaginable magnificent gift (9.252-80); his abundant delight in battle, inflamed by his opponent's scornful speech (9.598-620): all these features are splendid innovations, and peculiarly Virgilian too; there is very little to match it in his characterization of grown men.[11] It is clear that in this passage he was also endeavouring to give Iulus as important a role as possible, since he was destined to   158
become the ancestor of the Julian *gens*, and the allusions that Jupiter makes to Iulus' destiny in his first great prophecy (1.267ff.) are part of this same endeavour.[12] But it is more than a matter of the official glorification of a genealogical fiction: it is   159
Virgil's love of youth that has created the life-like figure of Iulus. And beside Iulus stand those boys, somewhat older, already capable of bearing arms, but still imbued with all the first flush of youth, who go to meet their death: Euryalus, Pallas and Lausus. The pain felt at their premature passing comes like an echo of the grievous and genuine pain that was felt at the early death of M. Claudius Marcellus; these are figures the like of whom were not found by Virgil in Homer, nor in all probability anywhere else. Nor is it a coincidence that here too Virgil reflects Augustus' attitude. Numerous features of the emperor's private life as well as his public measures indicate how deeply he cared about the moral and physical welfare of adolescents, and how deeply he cared about the youth of Rome as a means of perpetuating his life's work.[13] This is very understandable: he yearned so passionately to see a new generation spring up from the blood-sodden battlefields of the civil wars, a generation which, innocent of the guilt of their fathers, would be able to reap the fruits of decades of slaughter. This longing should not be underrated simply because it was not destined to be fulfilled. This is the frame of mind in which Virgil had once written his poem to celebrate the birth of the little son of the consul Pollio; it is also the frame of mind which underlies the description of the *lusus Troiae*.

Aeneas himself appears in the foreground far less than Achilles in the games in the *Iliad*; there are no particular little touches of characterization of the kind that the Homeric poet employed to ensure that the hero who organizes the games should not be overshadowed by the contestants. His ingenuous boasting about his own horses (*Iliad* 23.276ff.), his unconcealed pleasure at Antilochus' praise of him as the best runner (795ff.), and the way in which he extols the prizes that he himself is offering   160
(832ff.) – all this is out of keeping with the more refined sense of what was proper that was characteristic of Virgil's time, as indeed it would be with our own. Achilles quickly and decisively calms down the outbreak of a quarrel (492ff.), whereas Aeneas has no opportunity to do so: Virgilian heroes do not quarrel.

Again, Virgil was unable to devise anything corresponding to the magnanimity of Achilles, when he praises his erstwhile opponent Agamemnon most generously (890ff.), or the delicate attention that he pays to the aged Nestor (616ff.): in place of this latter episode Virgil describes the honours given to Acestes, though this incident is of course treated in quite a different manner, and is motivated by considerations external to the games. The princely generosity of Aeneas radiates with a similar light; like Achilles, he is impelled by his sense of justice to make allowances for undeserved mishaps, though unlike Achilles (536ff.) this does not make him overlook all other considerations; but it means that the poet misses the opportunity to make use of the characteristic touch whereby his hero momentarily yields to justi-fied objections. Aeneas' intervention in the boxing match (465), which is motivated by his anxiety that the game is developing into a deadly combat, combines the intervention by the Achaeans in the hoplomachy [fight in armour] when they are anxious about what will happen to Ajax (822), and the ending of the wrestling-match by Achilles, who allows it to remain undecided so that there will be time for other competitions (735). We can see that in this episode Virgil has essentially merely sifted through the material provided by Homer, accepting what he could use, changing the emphasis in some places, and omitting what did not suit his narrative or his taste. The result in this case is that Aeneas comes across as a much weaker character than Achilles.

4. Structure of the action

Virgil himself may perhaps have felt that his characters were not as interesting as Homer's, and that he had not wholly succeeded in compensating for those advan-tages of the Homeric poet that we have already mentioned. On the other hand, he could rest assured that he had surpassed his predecessor in the construction of the book as a whole, above all in his *handling of the action*. We may summarize the improvement for which Virgil was aiming as *the achievement of concentrated dra-matic effect*.

In Homer, the chariot-race is preceded by the detailed instructions given by Nestor to Antilochus. This brings out the character of the old, experienced man, and will please any of the audience who have been trained in competitive sports and can appreciate his good advice. However, it has no significance for the action that follows; we are not told whether Antilochus made any attempt to follow Nestor's advice, and Nestor's prediction that the race will be decided by the driver's skill at managing the turning-post (344ff.) is not borne out by events. During the race, our attention is drawn away from the contestants to the spectators, with the interlude involving Ajax and Idomeneus. Virgil felt that both these episodes were disruptive, and omitted them. The chariot-race in Homer falls into two distinct sections: first Diomedes overtakes Eumelus, who drops out when his yoke breaks; then Antilochus overtakes Menelaus. No link is made between the two pairs; it is as though two separate races were being described. Finally, the fifth contestant, Meriones, hardly gets a look in; there is nothing to be said about him except that his horses are very slow and he himself is the least competent driver. Virgil's treatment is entirely different. Five competitors are too many to cope with; he therefore restricts himself to four. But our attention is on all four until the decisive point, which in this case really is the *meta*, the turning point. First we are told their relative positions as they approach the turning-post: Gyas in front, then Cloanthus; then Mnestheus and Ser-gestus, either neck and neck or alternately getting ahead of each other. Then, by means of a skilful manoeuvre, Cloanthus pulls ahead of Gyas, and the latter loses his steersman, so that the two behind begin to have hopes of overtaking him: Sergestus is less than one length ahead of Mnestheus, while the latter, in last place, urges his oarsmen to do their utmost: and before they have caught up with Gyas, Sergestus runs onto the rocks, Mnestheus gets ahead, first of him, then of Gyas, and only Cloanthus is still in front. Now the second part begins: two ships are completely out of the race, and the two others have to compete against each other over the rest of the course: the rowers increase their efforts, and the spectators become more excited. The tension mounts right up to the very end; it is only just before the harbour that Cloanthus' promise to the gods gives him the decisive victory. Homer, as we have seen, shifts our attention for a while from the chariots to the spectators' benches; to move from place to place is the epic poet's privilege. In Virgil the spectators are part of the overall scene; we do not lose sight of them when we are watching the competitors: at the start, each shouts encouragement to his favourite, at the climactic moment of reversal of fortune they laugh merrily at the steersman's 162 accident; they shout encouragement to Mnestheus as he makes his final effort, and pour scorn on the shipwrecked Sergestus when he eventually limps home with broken oars. This is not the first time[14] that we have observed Virgil's skill in making the reader feel that he is experiencing the events himself, and achieving the maximum ἐνάργεια [vividness] by portraying the effect of an event on those who witness it, a technique derived from drama. It is worth drawing attention to one almost imperceptible deviation from Homer, since it is another consequence of Virgil's vivid presentation of the event. In Homer the prizes are not distributed until all the competitors have assembled. A considerable amount of time has to pass before Eumelus, pulling his broken chariot himself, catches up with the others at the finishing-line; but we are aware of this interval only on subsequent reflection. Homer possibly hints at it with πανύστατος [last of all]. By contrast, Sergestus gets back after the victor has been proclaimed and crowned, and after the prizes have been distributed to the captains and their crews; they are all decorated with purple ribbons and rejoicing in their prizes; this emphasizes Sergestus' disgrace much more strongly.

For the foot-race there are three prizes: Homer has three runners, and again the real contest is between only two, Ajax and Odysseus; Antilochus is left a long way behind. The two former are almost evenly matched: Odysseus is always just at Ajax's heels, and finally wins the race, with the help of Athena; in other words, there is only *one* decisive moment. The equivalent in Virgil is Nisus' fall, but this leads to a second decisive event, the fall of Salius; and the completely unexpected result is that the third runner, Euryalus, is the winner; the spectators express their joyful surprise by applause and shouts of admiration (338). Thus, instead of a decision between two competitors, in which victory would *inevitably* have gone to one or the other, there is an unforeseen *peripeteia* [reversal of fortune].

Boxing matches had been described often enough in post-Homeric literature: there are the accounts of the famous fight between Polydeuces and Amycus in 163 Apollonius (2.1ff.) and Theocritus (22), both known to Virgil and both used by him as sources for some of his details. Homer's account is very straightforward. Victory goes to Epeius, who confidently challenges all comers, and not to Eurylus, who has to be encouraged by Diomedes to enter the competition; this is just how we would expect things to turn out. The fight is described very briefly; with one quick blow Epeius catches his opponent off guard and knocks him out. Apollonius gives a very much longer account, but avoids technical details, since he was not particularly interested in such things; the preparations for the fight are narrated at greater length than the fight itself; and again in the actual account similes play an important part, to compensate for the comparative lack of action. However, Apollonius gives an unexpected and individual version of the conclusion of the match: Polydeuces skilfully avoids a violent blow and then immediately takes advantage of the fact that his opponent is momentarily off his guard to strike him so violently on the temple that he collapses. Theocritus tried to improve on this: if we are going to have a description of a boxing-match, then it should be a real one, just like those that could be seen in the stadium. He therefore describes the various blows and feints, the spitting of blood and the ripping off of the skin and so forth, with great technical expertise, and he presents his account of the final stage, which takes the same course as in Apollonius, in full and faithful detail just as a sports reporter would. Theocritus' version was available to Virgil, and it would have been easy for him to have imitated it; he decided not to, but to give an overall picture of the whole course of the fight instead, much as Apollonius had done, which would allow him to contrast the characteristic attitudes of the two fighters. But Virgil's own contribution, in which he differs from all his predecessors, is the introduction of an unexpected *peripeteia*, which changes the simple straight line into a broken one, and gives the narrative a dramatic momentum. Entellus, who is aware that he is less agile than his opponent, and until now has stayed put in the same place to resist the swift attacks of his opponent, tries to punch him, misses, falls, and gets up a changed person: irresistible in his rage, driven to the extreme of fury by shame and anger, he now rains blow upon blow on his opponent, forcing him backwards, and would have done him serious injury if Aeneas had not intervened. It is extremely unlikely that in real life a boxer who starts as the equal, or in many respects the superior, such as Dares, could ever allow himself to become so helpless and defenceless against a sudden outburst of fury on the part of his opponent. This did not worry Virgil; he was more concerned with increasing the excitement, and, in fact, in his version the decisive factor is not greater muscle-power but the psychology of Entellus.

164

There is no such psychological motivation in the last contest, the archery competition; nevertheless, this passage also displays features that are characteristic of Virgil's art. Homer gives us the entertaining story of two archers: the first misses the dove, but by chance he cuts through the cord by which it is tied – which would be more difficult to do deliberately but still counts as a miss; everyone thinks that the bird has got away and that there is no winner; but with a swift, sure shot the other competitor hits the bird as it flies free. It is clear that the Homeric poet did not invent this story himself, since he spoils it by making Achilles say beforehand that the second prize will go to anyone who cuts the cord, a most unlikely eventuality. Virgil very sensibly discarded the speech.[15] In other respects, once again he surpasses his predecessor by building up excitement[16] – at the beginning he inserts a third shot, which only hits the mast of the ship, and at the end a fourth, apparently a mere display shot; but, amazingly, this has the greatest effect of all, since it is singled out for a miraculous sign from the gods, which we will discuss in more detail in a moment.

165

The reason for placing the miracle at this point is to raise the spectators' excitement to its highest point at the very end of the whole competition. It is obvious that it could not have been followed by a wrestling-match, or anything of that kind, without producing a sense of anticlimax. However, after the extreme tension, some sort of relief is required for artistic reasons, to allow the accumulated floods of emotion to run off in a different direction by diverting the reader's interest. This artistic effect is achieved by the *lusus Troiae*, and that is why it runs its course without any exciting incidents, an uninterrupted delight for the hearts and eyes of the assembled crowds. Now at last the atmosphere is sufficiently calm for an exciting new event to make its full impact – the Trojans learn that the ships are on fire.

5. The supernatural

The significance of the miracle of the burning arrow is by no means immediately clear; in recent years many have accepted Wagner's interpretation, according to which it is an allusion to the comet which appeared in the year 43 BC during the games held by Octavian in honour of Venus Genetrix, and was hailed by the people as the star of the deified Caesar (Pliny *N.H.* 2.94). This interpretation is highly implausible, in my view, for a number of reasons.[17] First, Virgil describes unambiguously a meteor shooting across the sky and immediately disintegrating in the air, whereas the comet appeared on seven consecutive days, and remained visible on each occasion for a considerable time. The resemblance between the two is thus much less specific than is required. The essential thing about the comet is that a new star appears in the heavens, which increases their total number – just as Caesar, the new god, increases the total number of immortals. Yet this essential factor is precisely what is lacking in the case of Virgil's meteor. The comet was itself a sign from heaven; when has one sign ever been heralded by another? Certainly, if Virgil had described something that really was analogous to the phenomenon of his own times, such as for example the appearance of a new star representing the apotheosis of Anchises, it would have been immediately obvious that it was intended to allude to it and to prefigure it. As it is, however, we would have to suppose that Virgil has deliberately obscured his meaning. He calls the seers who prophesy the fulfilment of the omen in years to come *terrifici* [arousing terror]; yet Caesar's comet brought no terror. Virgil connects the sign closely with Acestes and makes Aeneas link it exclusively with Acestes; but Acestes has nothing whatever to do with Caesar's comet. This brings us to my strongest objection, an objection on artistic grounds. The apotheosis of Caesar, or in more general terms, the elevation of the Julian *gens*, has no connection with the person most closely concerned with the miracle, and similarly it has no essential connection with the time at which the miracle occurs. It could equally well have occurred at any moment in the whole course of the *Aeneid*, and would have been smuggled in at this point by Virgil merely on the superficial grounds that games were in progress both now and when the omen is fulfilled. He would have based his decision only on the formal and technical consideration that this part of the story should have a splendid and effective finale. In that case it would merely be a device on the artistic level of the sunrise in Meyerbeer's *Le Prophète* which Richard Wagner used so aptly as an illustration of the nature of operatic effect.

Any interpretation that is to do justice to Virgil's artistic principles must in my

166

133

opinion be based on the character of Acestes and the time at which the miracle takes place. Aeneas accepts the extraordinary phenomenon as a sign from heaven[18] and treats it as such when he grants Acestes the honour of victory: *te voluit rex magnus Olympi talibus auspiciis exsortes ducere honores* (533-4) [for the supreme Olympian king had surely ordained, when he sent this potent sign, that you must carry away special honours]. However, we are intended to think not only of this immediate result, but also of the future: that is what the poet tells us in the lines that introduce the sign. What then is the chief significance of these games for Acestes? Immediately after the games comes the burning of the ships; and the immediate result of the

167 burning of the ships, which occurred in accordance with the will and command of Jupiter (726, 747), is kingdom and kingly power for Acestes. Too little attention has been paid to the fact that the events portrayed in 746ff. signify more than merely the foundation of one more city just like all the others. Virgil has taken great care throughout the book to avoid calling Acestes 'king', or to speak of a city of Acestes.[19] That is why we hear nothing of where the Trojans are accommodated when they arrive in Sicily; apparently they simply camp on the shore (43). We are intended to envisage Acestes and his people as country folk, living in the mountains (35), without any advanced urban culture,[20] and Acestes is not their king – they do not constitute a state – but merely one of their number, though famous and distinguished by his divine descent (38, 711). But now a city is founded, and Acestes becomes ruler of the new kingdom: *gaudet r e g n o Troianus Acestes* (757) [Trojan Acestes, who welcomed the thought of this *kingdom*]. This immediately endows him with *exsortes honores* [especial honours] far more substantial than those that he had won in the games, and the omen could be regarded as fulfilled; but when the seers *sera omina cecinerunt*[21] (524) [prophesied the late-fulfilled omens] they must have

168 looked even further into the future. The poet must be intending us to think of the future of Acestes' kingdom. Any Roman who heard this would inevitably be reminded of the time when Segesta played a role in the history of Rome; and that was during the first Punic War, when Segesta was the first of all the cities of Sicily to come over to the side of Rome, on the grounds of their common descent from Troy, and consequently to fight doggedly in the struggle against Carthage side by side with their new allies. Those were terrifying but great and glorious days; and it is to these, in my view, that the seers' prediction referred. The miracle occurs while the Sicilians and the Trojans are taking part as brothers in joyful games; it occurs on the day on which a new Trojan kingdom is founded in Sicily; it points to the man who is to become the first ruler of that kingdom; it presages, in a way that is simultaneously frightening and comforting, the distant times when the curse that the dying queen of Carthage called down on the departing Trojans will be fulfilled. In my opinion, this meets all the requirements necessary for the interpretation of a miracle which is a good deal more than a mere operatic effect.

From an artistic point of view, it is entirely right that the most manifest example of divine intervention should come here, at the end of the whole episode. The way in which the supernatural is handled reveals another difference between Virgil and Homer. In the latter, Apollo and Athene take an active part: Apollo strikes Diomedes' whip from his hand, Athene immediately gives it back to him and breaks Eumelus' yoke in revenge; in answer to Odysseus' prayer, Athena strengthens his feet and knees, and causes Ajax to slip in the dung (this clearly forshadows the disaster which the goddess is later to bring down upon Ajax); in the archery contest, Teucer forgets to promise a hecatomb to Apollo, which so infuriates the god that he makes him miss the target and gives the victory to the more pious Meriones instead. Virgil could not reconcile these actions with his conception of the majesty of the gods: at Actium, Apollo might stand on Augustus' flag-ship, and, in the slaughter of combat, the gods might ensure that no harm comes to their favourites; but to trip up a runner in a race is an act that is beneath their dignity. That is why even in the most important competition, the boat-race, where the prayer to the gods is answered and produces a real, and almost unfair, effect, it is not Neptune who intervenes, but the 169 lesser deities of the sea; the successful archer Eurytion addresses his brief prayer not to Apollo but to the hero Pandarus, who was both his brother and a master of the bow; the boxer Entellus fights and wins in the name of Eryx, the deified son of Venus (391, 412, 467, 488). But the accidents which befall Sergestus and Gyas and Nisus are caused by their own errors, not by the malevolence of a divine opponent.

6. Atmosphere

One last and very important difference between Virgil's account of the games and that of Homer can perhaps best be summed up in one short phrase: Virgil is interested in *emotional moods*. The poet has steeped himself in the feelings of his characters, and strives to convey to the reader the emotional frame of mind in which each of them finds himself. It is difficult to know to what extent this is a question of conscious effort, and to what extent it arises spontaneously from the poet's own mood. But every reader who allows the book to make its full impact on him will undoubtedly feel that he is taking part in a joyful celebration: joy is the keynote of the whole description.[22] The mood of the festival itself is prepared for by the happiness of both sides when the Trojans return unexpectedly to Acestes (34, 40) and the obviously favourable omen during the libation at Anchises' grave, which turns the offering to the dead into a joyful sacrifice (100). In joyful mood (107) the people gather on the shore in the bright light of dawn on the festive day, and this mood remains unbroken throughout the celebrations, rising to a climax during the last spectacular event, the splendid procession of youths, radiant with happiness (555, 575, 577). Virgil lingers lovingly over the depiction of the bright splendour of this procession, and seizes every opportunity to enliven his picture with bright, cheerful colours: the green of the boughs and garlands (110, 129, 246, 309, 494, 539; cf. 134, 556), and of the grass-clad natural amphitheatre (388) and the grassy stadium (287, 330); the purple of the victory ribbons (269), the gold on the edges of the commanders' mantles (132) and the prize garments (250), the gleam of the costly weapons and ornamented pieces (259 etc.) – all this forms the visible counter- 170 part, so to speak, of the happy mood of the joyful and excited spectators, the richly rewarded contestants and proud victors (269, 473), of Aeneas who celebrates the games, and of his guest-friend Acestes who quite unexpectedly wins the highest prize with the final shot. Virgil does his utmost to create the mood that he desires, not only through the events that he selects and the way in which he depicts them, but also by straightforward description of the feelings of his characters: *laetus* is the word which recurs time and time again,[23] so that the note, once struck, resounds again and again. Monotony is avoided by the more serious developments of the boxing-match; the moral motivation which Virgil introduces into this episode mitigates the effect of the bloody outcome and prevents the mood from being broken.

Mood-painting of this kind is quite alien to the spirit of the ancient epic. The bard who relates the funeral games takes more care than most of his fellows to tell us what effect each event had on the spirits of the competitors, and we hear a great deal about emotions both joyful and sad, but all these touches of local colour are not brought into relationship with each other or fused into any kind of predominant tone; and the poet makes no attempt to produce any overall emotional effect on the mind of the listener. We need only look at the prosaic and matter-of-fact way in which the games are introduced – αὐτὰρ Ἀχιλλεὺς αὐτοῦ λαὸν ἔρυκε καὶ ἵζανεν εὐρὺν ἀγῶνα [but Achilles kept the army there, and made them sit down in a broad arena] (*Iliad* 23.257-8) – and compare it with the elevated mood in which Virgil introduces his festival; or contrast the abrupt conclusion of the *agon* [contest] in Homer with the brilliantly-lit tableau in which Virgil unites the mood of all the participants so as to create a resounding finale. So far we have only been concerned to establish what is peculiarly Virgilian in his narrative. It is particularly easy to do this in the case of the Funeral Games, as they can be compared with their model. In the systematic section of our investigation (Part II), we will set this individual example in its context.

Notes to Chapter 4

146   **1.** It would require much more convincing arguments to prove that Virgil even for a moment contemplated such a gross misjudgment as those advanced by Kettner ('Das fünfte Buch des Aeneis', *Zeitschr. für den Gymnasialw.* 33 [1879] 641-53; his views, which develop those of Conrad and Ribbeck, are criticized by Schaper), who actually believes that the essential content of Book 5 – the games, and the burning of the ships – originally formed a separate book which contained the end of Aeneas' narrative, and that Book 6 followed immediately on from Book 4. Furthermore, Aeneas could not have narrated the burning of the ships in the form in which it now stands, with Iris' speech in her own words – that would have been a serious infringement of the technical conventions of first-person narrative which Virgil always strictly observes – and yet one phrase of Iris' (*septima post Troiae excidium iam vertitur aestas* [5.626] [it is now the close of the seventh summer since Troy's overthrow] compared with 1.755: *nam te iam septima portat...aestas* [for it is now the seventh summer of your travels]: on which see the section on 'Time and Place' below Part II, ch. 2.III.c) constitutes one of Kettner's main arguments for what he believes to be the original setting of the narrative. Two other objections have already been met by H.T. Plüss (*Vergil und die epische Kunst*, Leipzig [1884] 160 n. 1, 165 n. 1). There is another passage which might be of some importance in this connection: at 6.338 there is a reference to Palinurus *qui Libyco nuper cursu...exciderat*

puppi [who had lately fallen from the ship's stern during the voyage from Libya]. It has been suggested that this can only have been written when Virgil intended that the Trojans should sail direct from Carthage to Cumae, without stopping again in Sicily. For my part, I agree with the view of Conrad, that the version of the Palinurus scene in Book 6 shows that Virgil wrote Book 5 later; not because the narratives of Books 5 and 6 are not entirely consistent with each other (that would not in itself entail any conclusion about the chronology) but because the account in Book 6 does not presuppose that Palinurus' death has already been mentioned in Book 5. Virgil wrote Book 6 without taking into account what would have to be included in Book 5, just as he introduced the *prodigia* in Books 7 and 8 as something completely new, without thinking of the preparation for them which he subsequently provided in Book 3. We must always bear in mind that Virgil originally composed his books to be recited separately. When Virgil, as Suetonius tells us (p. 61, 17ff. Reifferscheid; cf. Serv. on 6.861), first recited Books 2, 4 and 6 to Augustus and his family, his audience would have known about Aeneas' visit to Libya, but not about his visit to Sicily: hence *Libyco cursu* [on the journey from Libya].

2. It is easy to see how important it is from an artistic point of view that Aeneas, despite his original intention, is forced by the storm to take refuge in Sicily, and how much clumsier it would have been if he had had to say to Palinurus at the beginning of Book 5: 'Steer towards Drepanum; I would like to celebrate funeral-games in honour of my father'. Virgil avoided anything as awkward as this; instead he took care to introduce the idea gradually. From the point of view of narrative it is just as important that Aeneas, who must have been anxious to complete his journey as quickly as possible after the long delay at Carthage, does not interrupt the voyage of his own free will. Finally, it would be impossible to improve on the way that the storm is motivated: after Dido's warning of the winter storms and her prophecy of the dangers of the sea it would have been artistically impossible for Aeneas to be given a smooth voyage to Cumae.

3. Dion. Hal. 1.52.

4. Augustus did not permit women to watch boxing matches at any rate: Suet. *Aug.* 49.

5. Virgil places the foot-race (which Homer brings in after the boxing and wrestling matches) first among the contests on dry land. Leo, *Deutsche Litt. Zeitung* 24 (1903) 595, points out that by making this change, Virgil is putting the foot-race in the position that it occupied in the Olympic Games and those modelled on them.

6. H.T. Plüss, *Neues Schweizer Museum VI* (1867) 41.

7. In Book 9 Virgil introduces Nisus and Euryalus with a great amount of detail, without reminding the reader that they have already appeared. This is perhaps the most striking example of a technique which we often find him using: see Part II, ch. 3.1.6 'Exposition of the characters'. I no longer believe that this shows that Virgil had not yet conceived, or at least not yet completed, the scene in Book 5 when he was writing Book 9; at any rate, another motif from Book 5, the *matres* [mothers] who stay behind in Acestes' city, had already reached its final form when he wrote the episode in Book 9: see 9.216ff., 285, 492.

8. 353ff. His words are intended to be lighthearted, but they conceal a number of rhetorical tricks: *si tanta sunt praemia victis* [if there are such prizes for the losers] – but not for all – *et te lapsorum miseret* [and you have pity on those who fall] – but only the competitor who fell because he was tripped; *ni me quae Salium fortuna inimica tulisset* [except that I was involved in the same bad luck as Salius] – but in a very different way.

155 9. This had already occurred at Sulla's victory celebrations, Asconius (ed. A.C. Clark 93) but it seems to have been so incompatible with contemporary Roman
156 *mores* that Cicero was able to pour bitter scorn on his rival Antonius for participating in them (*In Toga Candida* fr. 14.26 Müller).

10. Tac. *Ann.* 14.20: *quid superesse, nisi ut corpora quoque nudent [proceres Romani] et caestus adsumant easque pugnas pro militia et armis meditentur* [this was the limit, unless they (the Roman nobility) were to strip and put on boxing gloves and practise this type of fighting instead of warfare and military training].

157 11. Recent critics (who however cannot appeal to the authority of Heyne, who concludes his discussion [III⁴ 857] *absolvendus itaque in hoc Maro crimine neglecti temporum ordinis* [therefore Virgil should be acquitted of the charge of neglecting chronology in this episode]) have suggested that Virgil had no definite idea of Iulus' age and had only the vaguest conception of his character generally. In fact, at the time of the fall of Troy, Ascanius is a small boy; his mother can still just manage to pick him up, but he is quite capable of walking a considerable distance; we may
158 therefore conclude that Virgil thought of him as between four and five years old. If we calculate that the Trojans spend exactly seven years wandering over the seas, then in Carthage he will be between eleven and twelve years old, and in Latium one year older. Is there any detail that actually contradicts this scheme? Can a boy, the son of a hero, not ride at this age? Can he not be taken hunting (always under careful supervision, of course, since he is a royal child; the poet also mentions a guardian in passing at 5.546 and 9.649)? Can he not wish that he might encounter a boar? Can he not shoot an enemy (with divine help, as Virgil is careful to point out)? Or is he too old for a lady like Dido to decently take him on her lap? I must say that I see nothing whatever in all this that is incompatible with poetic truth. 'But', it may be objected, 'if he attends the council of leaders in Book 9 and gives instructions himself to the messenger who is sent to his father, he must surely be wiser than his years'. Precisely: that is just what Virgil himself says: *ante annos animumque gerens curamque virilem* (9.311) [he bore beyond his years the mind and responsibility of a man]. Virgil had seen for himself how a nineteen-year-old could put the most experienced and mature to shame when it was a matter of presence of mind and common sense.

12. Iulus, says Jupiter, will found Alba Longa and move the royal capital to that site, where it will remain for three hundred years *gente sub Hectorea* [under a dynasty of Hector's kin], as Virgil puts it, avoiding any such phrase as *sub Iuli gente* [under a dynasty descended from Iulus]. Iulus never appears in Virgil as the ancestor of the Alban kings, though admittedly he never expressly denies him that rôle either. Virgil follows that geneaology which we may assume was regarded as the standard one during the reign of Augustus, since Verrius Flaccus, too, amongst others (Festus 340 = Lindsay [Teubner] 460), argued for it. According to this version, the Alban kings were descended from Silvius, the son of Aeneas and Lavinia (*Silvius...unde*

genus Longa nostrum dominabitur Alba [6.766] [Silvius...founder of our dynasty which shall rule from Alba Longa]; *unde* is of course not temporal but goes closely with *genus*), not from Iulus, who did in fact found Alba but was not the ancestor of the genealogical line of Alban kings. Virgil does not mention that Iulus (or his son of the same name) had to give place to Silvius, or why he did so, or what compensation they received (though there is a hidden allusion for the well-informed reader at 12.189ff.; see E. Norden, *Neue Jahrbücher* 7 [1901] 281), nor does he need to. We know how the official version of the legend came to accept this account (Schwegler, *Röm. Gesch.* 1 337); but this somewhat artificial fabrication, which on any interpretation would imply that Iulus was displaced, was quite unsuitable for Virgil's poem, and if Iulus is 'suppressed' in the parade of heroes in Book 6 (to use A. Gercke's phrase, *Neue Jahrbücher* 7 [1901] 110), that is because he can hardly be mentioned together with Silvius without at least some reference to their relationship: on a practical level this silence is justified by the fact that it is both impossible and unnecessary for Iulus to be shown to his father in the underworld. Furthermore, to the best of my knowledge, the Iulii are *never* said to be descendants of the Alban   159 kings, nor therefore of Romulus (who ever heard of a son of Romulus?). Ovid, who says that the family of Silvius was descended from Iulus (*Fasti* 4.39ff.) clearly assumed that this was through a collateral line, as his expression *unde* (i.e. a *Iulo*) *domus Teucros Iulia tangit avos* [through whom (i.e. Iulus) the Julian house goes back to Trojan ancestors] makes clear; again, he never calls Romulus the ancestor of Augustus, although he not only had plenty of opportunity to do so in the *Fasti*, but also plenty of inducement on account of the well-known tradition that traced Augustus' ancestry back to the founder of Rome. One member of the Julian family, Proculus, appears in the Romulus legend; but he is not related to the kings, only πιστὸς καὶ συνήθης [a trusted friend] to Romulus; Plutarch, *Romulus* 28.

13. Cf. also Norden op. cit. in the previous note, 263.

14. The spectators are also referred to in the following passages: during the foot   162 race (338, 343), during the boxing match (369, 385, 450), during the archery contest (491, 529) and finally during the *lusus Troiae* (555, 575f.): this means that the vivid picture of the excited and interested crowd of spectators is maintained throughout. However, in this respect Virgil has done no more than his Homeric model: cf. *Iliad* 23.728, 766, 784, 815, 822, 840, 847, 869, 881.

15. Perhaps he was influenced by critics of Homer. The scholia on 23.857 say ἡ   164 διπλῆ ὅτι βέλτιον ἦν τοῦτο μὴ προλέγεσθαι ὑπὸ Ἀχιλλέως, ὥσπερ προγιγν-ώσκοντος τὸ ἀπὸ τύχης συμβησόμενον [scholars have marked this passage as spurious because it would be better if Achilles did not say this beforehand, as though he knew in advance what was going to happen by chance].

16. According to H. Georgii, *Die antike Aeneiskritik* 259, Virgil only wished to surpass his predecessor in the number, four instead of two: 'though the result amounts to no more than a miss for the first competitor and a shot in the air together with a miracle for the fourth'. As though the important thing there was the number of shots, rather than the increase in excitement from the first competitor to the second to the third, and then the unexpected shot by which the third is surpassed by the fourth. Georgii thinks that it is ridiculous, childish and absurd, that Acestes shoots into the air, *ostentans artem arcumque sonantem* (521) [proving that he

might have skill yet, and could make a strong bow twang]; but the Virgiliomastix who denied the possibility of *artem in vacuo aere ostentare* [showing off ones skills by shooting into thin air] had already been refuted by the ancient experts (Servius' *periti*): *posse ex ipso sagittariorum gestu artis peritiam indicari* [it is possible to assess the technical skill of archers simply on the basis of their bodily posture]; against *arcum sonantem* [make a strong bow twang] even the Virgiliomastix had no objection, for, as every child knows, you can shoot higher with a good bow than with a feeble one.

165   17. It has been attacked by Plüss, *Virgil und die epische Kunst* 125ff.; however, I cannot agree with his own interpretation, either in general or in detail; what he regards as a matter of minor importance, its connection with Acestes and Sicily (135f.) seems to me (as it did to Ribbeck, *Gesch, d. röm. Dichtung.* II 96) the only thing that really matters.

166   18. *nec maximus omen abnuit Aeneas* (530-1) [but their exalted prince Aeneas accepted the omen]: that does not mean that he relates it to himself; just as the other spectators recognize it as a divine sign – hence *superos precati* [they sent up a prayer to the holy gods] – so does Aeneas; it is he who is celebrating the games, and is, as we might say, the presiding magistrate of the games, and in that capacity there was no need for him to give the sign an official interpretation; and he could have ignored it in deciding the outcome of the contest.

167   19. Contrast the frequency with which the title of king which is absent in Book 5 is used in, for example, Book 8 of Evander: 53, 102, 126, 185f. etc. When Virgil was writing Book 1, he envisaged a Sicilian kingdom ruled by Acestes, and Sicilian towns (549, 558): this shows that at that stage he had not yet planned the way in which events develop in Book 5 as we now have it.

20. As Virgil says explicitly, *gaza l a e t u s agresti excipit* (40) [he gave them a joyous welcome with his *rustic* treasure]; Acestes' outward appearance, *horridus in iaculis et pelle Libystidis ursae* (37) [looking wild in his African bearskin and with his cluster of javelins] is in keeping with this. The *comites Acestae* (301) [comrades of Acestes] are *adsueti silvis* [from woodland homes]. According to Dion. Hal. 1.9 this is how the aborigines of the very earliest times used to live: ἐπὶ τοῖς ὄρεσιν ἄνευ τειχῶν κωμηδὸν καὶ σποράδες [on the mountains, without city walls, in villages, and scattered].

21. The obvious model for this passage, Calchas' interpretation of the omen at Aulis, should be enough to prevent us from taking these words to mean 'it was only later that the seers discovered the meaning', i.e. after the *exitus ingens* [great outcome] had taken place. *Sera omina* is the Homeric τέρας ὄψιμον ὀψιτέλεστον (*Iliad* 2.324), which Cicero too (*De Div.* 2.30.64) translates as *portenta sera*. Interpretation *ex eventu* [after the event] is certainly not the business of the *vates;* anyone can do that; conversely, *vates canunt* is the technical term for prophecy, and in particular for the interpretation of an omen by seers who are summoned for that specific purpose: see e.g. Livy 1.45.5; 55.6; 2.42.10; 5.15.4; 7.6.3 etc. Virgil's hysteron proteron *docuit...cecinere* does not constitute an obstacle to this interpretation; the poet mentions first what matters most to him. Similarly, we should take *magno futurum augurio monstrum* (522-3) as 'which *was to* prove extremely significant'; this does not refer to any later repetition of the omen.

22. I refer the reader to Plüss 148f. for a good discussion of this.   169
23. 34, 40, 58, 100, 107, 210, 236, 283, 304, 515, 531, 577.   170

5

Aeneas in Latium

The first part of Virgil's work deals with the events that begin with the capture of Troy and lead up to Aeneas' arrival in Latium. The second part covers the events that begin with that arrival and end with the moment when he finally secures his kingdom in Italy. The two parts might appear to be equal in importance, but the poet considered the second half to have greater spiritual significance, as he says in the second proem: *maior rerum mihi nascitur ordo, maius opus moveo* (7.37f) [a graver sequence of events open before me, and I now begin a grander enterprise]. The predominantly peaceful experiences of the first half contrast with the predominantly warlike ones of the second – *dicam horrida bella* [I shall tell of a ghastly war]; to describe such things is the noblest task of the epic poet, in the same way that war is the most important thing in the life of the individual and of the nation, and – we should add – in the same way that the ancients regarded the *Iliad* as Homer's outstanding masterpiece. And it was with the *Iliad* that Virgil had to compete in this part of his epic.

I. *General Survey*

1. Condensation of the material

Virgil's first task was to construct from the traditional material an overall scheme of events, and to divide them into books. We have already discussed the form which he gave to the story of the *prodigia* (ch. 2.2 above); now we must deal with his main theme, the relations between Aeneas and the native population, and the battles. First, however, we must briefly remind ourselves of the traditional version[1] so that we can establish the principles according to which Virgil reshaped, developed and arranged it.

Of the older versions of the story only that of Cato has survived to any extent. In his account the events unfold as follows: (1) Latinus allots a portion of land to the newcomers (Serv. on *Aen.* 11.316; fr. 8 Peter). (2) Trojan encroachment leads to war, in which the Rutulians under Turnus are allied with the Latins; Latinus is killed during the first encounter. (3) Turnus revives the war with the support of Mezentius; Aeneas vanishes, Turnus is killed. (4) During a third battle, Ascanius kills Mezentius in a duel (Serv. on 1.267; 4.620; 9.745; frr. 9, 10 Peter). In the later versions, the Latins and Rutulians do not unite to fight the Trojans, nor is Latinus killed as an enemy of Aeneas; rather, they stress the marriage of Aeneas with Lavinia[2] and play down the opposition between the Trojans and the Latins as much as possible. The most extreme example of this tendency is represented by the tradition which is followed by such as Dionysius of Halicarnassus: this is his schema (1.57f.):[3] (1) Aeneas settles without Latinus' permission on what is to become the site of Lavinium, but makes friendly alliance with him, marries his daughter, and helps him and his native troops to vanquish the Rutulians; the city of Lavinium is completed. (2) After two years the Rutulians rise up again under the leadership of the Latin aristocrat Turnus; they are beaten, but both Turnus and Latinus are killed in the battle so that Aeneas now becomes sole ruler of the Trojans and the native population. (3) After another three years comes a second war against the Rutulians, who are supported this time by the Etruscans under Mezentius: Aeneas is killed, Ascanius succeeds as ruler. (4) Ascanius successfully continues the war, Mezentius makes peace after the death of his son Lausus. Livy's account (1.1-2) is very much the same: (1) Latinus, full of admiration for Aeneas' nobility and spirit, allies himself with him (there is a brief mention of a variant, that the alliance was preceded by a battle); Aeneas marries his daughter, and Lavinium is founded. (2) Turnus, King of the Rutulians, who is betrothed to Lavinia, attacks the allies and is beaten, but Aeneas is killed; from then on, peace reigns; nothing is said of what becomes of Turnus and Mezentius. And there may have been other historians and antiquaries who put the scanty events that had become established in tradition into a somewhat different pattern and order; the essentials will have remained basically unchanged.

The first thing that Virgil needed to do was to condense his material. He combines the three or four battles of the traditional version into one battle, which does however include several clashes, and he compresses the events of several years into a few days. The events follow closely one upon another without any interruption that might divert the reader's attention. In the same way the author of the *Iliad* had compressed a great deal of material which had originally been spread over several years into the few days of the μῆνις [wrath of Achilles].

Unity of time involved unity of action. In the traditional versions, the Trojan successes are sporadic: first the Latins are won over and Lavinium is built, then the Rutulians are beaten and Turnus is killed, then finally the Etruscans are beaten, and Mezentius is either killed or surrenders; only then is the safety of the new settlement assured. Virgil concentrates all this: Aeneas faces the Latins, Rutulians and Mezentius simultaneously; the death of Mezentius, which in defiance of tradition occurs before that of Turnus, is only a prologue to the duel in which Turnus is killed and whereby all resistance is extinguished; Virgil takes care to let us know that from now on the Latins too will be submissive to Aeneas' rule. Only at this point, that is after Turnus' death, does Aeneas marry Lavinia and found his city: here too Virgil's account is unique. This new chronology was the result of the need for concentration, as was Virgil's conversion of the Latins into allies of the Rutulians, a detail in which he departs from later tradition and returns to Cato; so, too, the alliance with the native population occurs at the same time as the final consolidation of Trojan gains; both are the prizes of the victory of Aeneas in the duel which brings the epic to its end.

Thus on the relationship of the Latins with the Rutulians and the Trojans Virgil agrees with Cato; he differs from him in that he separates King Latinus from his subjects and does not involve him in the fighting. He needed to do this because, unlike Cato, he made everything culminate in the marriage of Aeneas to Lavinia. Virgil did not want Aeneas to drag his bride from her father by force of arms, let alone make his way to her over her father's dead body. Instead, the king himself gives his daughter to Aeneas in marriage, in obedience to a divine command, and Aeneas is defending a just claim when he insists on the fulfilment of this contract. Nor could Latinus be shown to break his word; but despite this Aeneas had to win his bride in battle. That presented a real problem, and even if the solution which Virgil chose is not perfect, we should at least realize that it is the result of careful and mature consideration.

When the passionate lust for war runs amok and rages all around the aged king Latinus so that he can no longer control it, he calls the gods to witness that he is only yielding to force (7.591ff.); he allows the wild hordes to have their will, but he himself refuses to have anything to do with the crime, foreseeing the vengeance that it will bring: *saepsit se tectis rerumque reliquit habenas* [he barred himself within his palace and resigned the reins of government]; Juno herself has to fling open the gates of war, since the king refuses to do so, although it is normally his function. Of course this does not mean that he totally abdicates his power – in that case he would have had to appoint a successor, but there is no mention of this; nor does he withdraw from his own people when he speaks to Aeneas, so Aeneas is quite justified in considering him to have broken his promise (*rex nostra reliquit hospitia et Turni potius se credidit armis* [11.113] ['it was your king who abandoned his guest-friendship with me and chose instead to rely on the arms of Turnus'], and Latinus, for his part, as soon as he believes that the time has come to put an end to war, summons a council of state and lays the proposals for peace before it (11.234ff.). It is diplomatic acumen that makes him begin his speech by expressing regret that he had not summoned his council before (302), and which leads him, both in the presence of his nobles at this meeting and in the presence of Turnus later, to take the responsibility for the war upon himself. This is constitutionally correct, in so far as he did not persist in exercising his veto to the very end but allowed the others to have their way; because he was still king while his people were fighting a war, he can say of himself *arma impia sumpsi* (12.31) ['I wickedly went to war'], although strictly speaking he had neither done so himself nor ordered the others to do so, but had merely been too weak to impose his will. Psychologically it is exactly right that at the crucial moment he is painfully convinced that it is impossible to resist the pressure of the war-party (7.591), and that nevertheless he reproaches himself afterwards for his weakness (11.471). But in fact it is such an extraordinary state of affairs – an entire nation waging a war against the will of its king and without his participation – and so difficult to portray in detail, that the precise nature of the situation is of necessity less clear than it might be.[4] This also affects Latinus' relationship with Turnus, particularly his attitude towards Turnus' claims to Lavinia. These seem well-grounded at first glance: Turnus has commended himself both by his personality (7.55) and by his services in the war against the Etruscans (423f.), and he was under the protection of Amata – Virgil took this motif from tradition (Dion. Hal. 1.64) and made good use of it; Latinus himself has shown no opposition to the idea, so that his wife, although in deliberately ambiguous phrases (7.365) and with a woman's carelessness for objective truth, can state that the king has already

175

144

entered into an agreement with Turnus. Before the warning omens the alliance had seemed a safe prospect, as is clear from the words of Faunus *thalamis neu crede paratis* (7.97) ['put no trust in any wedding which lies ready to hand']; but it is equally clear that a formal bethrothal had not taken place, and that Latinus himself does not feel that he was bound by one.[5] That is why, when Latinus thinks that Aeneas' arrival is the event predicted by the oracle,[6] he does not hesitate to offer his daughter to him: Aeneas sees this as the fulfilment of Creusa's prophecy. Turnus, on the other hand, his senses confused by Allecto, feels it to be a shameful breach of promise; the main purpose of war for him was to win back Lavinia. But since Latinus, as we have just explained, has allowed the war to take place since he is too old and weak to prevent it, it inevitably follows that he has allowed Turnus to court his daughter again, and in these circumstances Turnus does indeed claim Lavinia as his right (11.359), and, on the assumption that he is her suitor, he calls her father *socer* (440) [father-in-law], as was the custom after a betrothal. Latinus himself is conscious of the fact that by allowing the war to go ahead he has broken his promise to Aeneas that he should marry Lavinia:[7] *promissam eripui genero* (12.30) ['I stole the promised bride from her betrothed']; and yet, as things stood, he was in no position to give either a negative answer to Aeneas, or a positive answer to Turnus. The fact, which is tacitly recognized by both sides, that Lavinia will be the prize of victory, is not explicitly stated until the *foedus* (12.192) [pact] that is concluded before the decisive duel. All this would be much simpler and clearer if Latinus had openly opposed Aeneas from the start, or if he had openly broken an earlier promise. We are now in a position to see how difficult it was for the poet to get around these two problems, and what sacrifices he had to make in his efforts to do so.

2. Expansion

As we have seen, Virgil regarded the condensation of his material as one of his principal tasks; on the other hand, there is one episode that is considerably expanded. There were artistic reasons, and practical reasons too – i.e. political and patriotic ones – for introducing everything that could be discovered about the earliest period of Italian history into the framework of the *Aeneid*. One simple way of doing this was for both sides to call upon all available allies and auxiliary troops. The neighbouring communities could easily be represented as allies of the Latins and Rutulians, and this provided Virgil with an opportunity to weave in many legends about origins and foundations. But it also made it possible to include the saga of Diomedes, still very much alive in South Italy, which could be used not only to increase the prestige of the Trojans but also to introduce the particularly attractive character of Camilla. The same device made possible Aeneas' alliance with Evander, which is so very important for the political message of the poem, and his visit to the future site of Rome, and, what is very significant symbolically, his assumption of command over the original population of Rome's territory. Since Evander's character, which was already well-established, was unsuitable for a heroic warrior, and since he could hardly be presented as Aeneas' subordinate, his place was taken by Pallas. According to a legend invented to explain the name of Palatium, Pallas was a grandson of Evander (the son of his daughter Launa and Hercules) who had died very young and was buried on the Palatine (Dion. Hal. 10.32.43); for obvious reasons, Virgil turns him into Evander's son, and gives him a Sabine mother (8.510); thus he represents the fusion of Greek and Italian stock. His early death, taken from the legend, provides the poet with further useful motifs. Aeneas' journey to visit Evander was important to Virgil in its own right; at the same time he has worked it most skilfully into the narrative, using Aeneas' absence as a vital piece of motivation corresponding to the wrath of Achilles. Less obvious, but still percep-

179 tible, are the reasons which led him to include the Etruscans among Aeneas' troops. In Virgil's own time, the predominant tradition knew only of a battle fought by Aeneas and Ascanius against the Etruscans under Mezentius; however, an earlier tradition, reported by Timaeus, which unfortunately is preserved only in the obscure phraseology of Lycophron,[8] said that Aeneas stayed at Agylla-Caere and made an alliance with Tarchon and Tyrrhenus. Virgil combined the two: Mezentius remains the Trojans' enemy, whereas the Etruscans are their allies, but – and this reveals Virgil's pragmatic intention (i.e. using myth as historical propaganda) – they are represented not as allies of equal standing but as under the command of Aeneas, *gens externo commissa duci* (10.156) [they trusted themselves to the care of a foreign leader], a leader who had been assigned to them by the will of the gods, as revealed by the prophet. Thus in those ancient times fate had already decreed a situation which was only to come about in reality after hard struggles throughout many centuries, the subordination of Etruria to the control of the descendants of Aeneas. From the point of view of the verisimilitude of the narrative it is an advantage that the introduction of this episode considerably increases the forces at Aeneas' disposal, so that we are not faced with the improbable story that a handful of Trojans and Arcadians were able to overcome the united opposition of all the other peoples of Italy. From an artistic point of view, Virgil makes full use of the situation to enrich his narrative with new motifs. There is the catalogue of Etruscan forces, which, as in the *Iliad*, follows that of their opponents, and is in form like the catalogue of ships; Aeneas' journey by sea; the figure of the bold and resolute cavalry-commander Tarchon; but above all there is the highly original characterization of Mezentius and his relationship with his former subjects, a new creation that results from the fusion of the two traditions, which necessitated separating Mezentius and his son Lausus (whom Virgil also took over from the tradition) from their fellow-countrymen.

The main source for the material in the battle-scenes was the *Iliad*. Virgil's ambition was to create a new work by reshaping Homer's most effective motifs to suit his purposes, and by enriching it with new situations, such as those in the Camilla episode.

180 # 3. Arrangement

If the second part was to be equal in length to the first, the poet had six books at his disposal. In deciding what material should go into each book, he was mainly concerned to avoid two pitfalls: shapelessness and monotony. He felt that these were two major faults in the construction of the *Iliad*: on the one hand, the poet handles the chronology quite recklessly, and the action darts here and there, apparently following no set plan; on the other hand, the endlessly drawn-out descriptions of fighting with their mindless repetitions which had held Homer's archaic Greek audience spellbound would certainly have appealed to very few in Virgil's day.

Virgil gave the second part of his work a well-defined shape by using the same methods that he had used in the first part: he allotted one self-contained piece of the action to each book. Thus Book 7 covers the period from the arrival up to the declaration of war; Book 8 contains Aeneas' visit to the site of Rome; Book 9 the events that take place during his absence; Book 10 the first major battle; Book 11 the armistice and the cavalry battle; Book 12 the decisive battle. The books also fall into three groups of two: 7 and 8, the preparations for the fighting; 9 and 10 leading up to the first great conflict; 11 and 12 the events which culminate in the decisive duel. Moreover, the division into books corresponds as far as possible with units of time: 8 and 9 depict simultaneous events, centred on Aeneas in 8, on the Trojan camp in 9; while 10, 11.225 to the end, and 12 each contain the events of one day.

The danger of monotony was greatest in Books 9 to 12, which contain the actual battles. The conclusion and outcome of these battles were obvious as soon as Turnus had been given the rôle of Aeneas' main opponent; his death had to be the decisive event, and artistic logic demanded that he could not simply be killed 'in battle' as in the tradition, but must be slain by the hand of Aeneas himself. The ἀναίρεσις [slaying] of Hector by Achilles was the model that must inevitably have imposed itself on Virgil. Everything that preceded this crucial event could only serve to delay it – the poet's problem was to elevate this series of delays into incidents that were significant and interesting in their own right. The shaping of the whole of the second half so that it would reach its climax in the duel between Aeneas and Turnus entailed only one essential change: regardless of the tradition, Mezentius had to die before Turnus; in all other respects Virgil was free to do as he wished. First, he took advantage of the absence of Aeneas to allow the heroic figure of Turnus to shine 181 forth in all its unclouded glory, in this, too, taking on the rôle of Hector: the attempt to burn the ships, the fighting at the wall, and the fighting at the camp – that is, the three most important phases of the battles described in Books 12 to 15 of the *Iliad* – provide the opportunity for this in the case of Hector, and while the spotlight is on Turnus, the description of the general mêlée of the two armies is restricted to the minimum, in order not to anticipate the later books. The incident in Book 10 of the *Iliad* is skilfully adapted: the ill-fated venture of Nisus and Euryalus interrupts the description of Turnus' exploits, which occupy the beginning and end of Book 9. Before the fighting begins again in Book 10 the assembly of gods provides relief (10.1-117): similarly, there are scenes with the gods at the beginning of Books 4, 8, 13, 15 and 20 of the *Iliad*. There follows in Book 10 the first actual battle, in which, on the Trojan side, Pallas is killed by Turnus – this feat is eventually to cause his own death, just like Hector's greatest achievement in *Iliad* 16 – while on the enemy side, Lausus and Mezentius are killed; the fight between Aeneas and Turnus is postponed by the phantom sent by Juno: this motif is taken from the end of *Iliad* 21. Book 11 also begins with peaceful scenes in the camp and in the city; then comes the second day of battle, in which Aeneas and Turnus play no part whatever; the unique figure of Camilla appears in the foreground; the cavalry battle takes its own distinctive course, and thus provides a contrast to Book 10.

Book 12 does not begin with scenes of battle either; the preparation for the duel by negotiations in the city, the solemn treaty and its violation (these come from *Iliad* 3 and 4), then one more battle, which at last proves decisive (from *Iliad* 20 to 22). Here, too, only a short section (257-310) is devoted to the general mêlée; Aeneas' wound gives Turnus another opportunity for an *aristeia* (324-82); when Aeneas has been healed (like Hector in *Iliad* 15) and appears on the battlefield, seeking Turnus, Juturna's intervention causes another delay; only the attack on the city and Saces' urgent appeal brings Turnus to face the enemy. Before the final scene, the resistance of Juno on Olympus is at last overcome (791-842); then comes the decisive duel.

In this way Virgil did indeed succeed in keeping repetitions to the minimum, in intermixing the inevitably similar scenes of battle wherever possible with scenes of a different type, and in maintaining the tension right up to the end. He did so by selecting and rearranging the traditional motifs, not one of which, however, was simply retold: all of them, as we shall see, were refashioned in Virgil's own characteristic manner.

182

II. *Allecto*

1. Allecto personifying Discord

Virgil introduces the period of renewed sufferings that await Aeneas in his struggle for Latium with scenes which deliberately parallel the corresponding scenes at the beginning of the first part of the *Aeneid*. In each case, Juno is amazed and furious to see the good fortune that her enemy enjoys, and pours out her emotions in a soliloquy; in each case, she uses a minor divinity to destroy her enemy; in each case, her command is immediately obeyed and disaster strikes. But because it is necessary to increase the tension, and because this second and final attempt at revenge has to have a more powerful effect, her plan has to be introduced in a way that is more striking in every respect. This is ingeniously achieved in Juno's monologue: hatred of the Trojans, disappointment at previous failures, her conviction that she has been wronged and humiliated – all this is expressed in stronger terms than ever before.[9] It is precisely because she foresees that her plans will inevitably come to nothing that there are no bounds to her overwhelming desire to exact the greatest possible vengeance while she still has the chance to do so. With the splendid antithetical phrase *flectere si nequeo superos, Acheronta movebo* ['if I cannot change the will of Heaven, I shall release Hell'], she enlists a more powerful ally than before. Instead of the ruler of the winds, the peaceful Aeolus, who had been a guest at the table of the Olympian gods, she summons a monster from the Underworld, hated not only by the Olympians but even by the gods of the world below: Allecto, the Fury who drives men mad. Instead of unleashing the powers of nature she unleashes furious passion, the insanity of mortal men, which causes so much more harm than the powers of nature ever can. It is war that is going to flare up, and Virgil and his

183

contemporaries knew very well what that meant. Hell knows no more fearful plague; anyone who wants to shatter the sanctity of peace must be out of his mind. Only those who share the total abhorrence of war felt by Virgil's contemporaries can fully understand why the poet made it the work of Allecto. Thus the queen raves *lymphata* (377) [in a reckless frenzy]; her companions have *furiis accensae pectora* (392) [hearts ablaze with hysterical passion]; Turnus' lust for battle is *scelerata insania belli* (461) [the accursed lunacy of war]; and Tyrrhus reaches for his axe *spirans immane* (510) [panting with savage rage]. So the mad tumult breaks out almost simultaneously in three different places: Virgil has created a unity out of a haphazard juxtaposition or unconnected series of events by means of the figure of Allecto, so that they are converted into a carefully arranged sequence brought about by the machinations of a single will.

However, Allecto is not really the personification of madness, but of discord, *cui tristia bella iraeque insidiaeque et crimina noxia cordi* (325) [Allecto, who dearly loves war's horrors, outbursting wrath, treachery and recriminations with all their harms] and *tu potes unanimos armare in proelia fratres, atque odiis versare domos* (335f.) ['You know well how to set brothers, united in love, at armed conflict one against the other. You can wreck homes by hate']; her real work is the dissolution and destruction of peaceful agreements: *disice compositam pacem* [shatter the pact of peace which they have made] and when she has done her work she announces *perfecta tibi bello discordia tristi: sic in amicitiam coeant et foedera iungant* (545-6) ['Behold, you have your quarrel, and it has been securely ratified by horrors of war. Now see if you can join them in friendship again and make them agree to peace!']. Thus she is to a large degree the counterpart of Eris, who similarly appears in Hesiod (*Theog.* 225f.) as one of the daughters of Night (cf. *virgo sata Nocte* [331] [maid, daughter of Night]), and whose destructive swarm of children may have been in Virgil's mind when he wrote line 325 (quoted above). So she does not really appear as a vengeful or punishing *daimon*: she is an Erinys to the extent that if she succeeds in her work then madness will result (447, 570), and she is one of the *deae dirae* (324) [dread goddesses], the *sorores Tartareae* (327) [Tartarean sisters], of whom she is the most loathsome. Like the Erinyes, she carries whips and torches (336), and has snakes for hair (cf. *Discordia demens vipereum crinem vittis innexa cruentis* [6.280] [Strife the insane, with bloody ribbons binding her snaky hair]. Virgil may have drawn his inspiration for this creature from tragedy, in which, from Aeschylus onwards, Erinyes and other such daimons had frequently appeared: thus an author as early as Macrobius, in the remarkable passage in which he mocks all these scenes, writes *sparguntur angues velut in scaena parturientes furorem* (5.17.3) [there are snakes everywhere, as on the stage, giving birth to madness]. In surviving tragedies, it is the figure of Lyssa in Euripides' *Herakles* who comes closest to Allecto;[10] an even closer parallel may well have appeared in the attempts of post-Euripidean tragedians to outdo Euripides. They will have supplied Virgil with the basic colours for his picture: but the concept itself came from another source. *Postquam Discordia taetra Belli ferratos postis portasque refregit* [when hideous Discord burst apart the iron-bound doors and gates of War] wrote Ennius in his *Annales*; Virgil deliberately echoes this in *Belli ferratos rumpit Saturnia postis* (622) [the Saturnian queen burst apart the iron-bound gates of War]. It may well be

184

that Ennius also described how Discordia prepared the way for war, and that Virgil is trying to outdo that description; but Discordia was too abstract for his taste, and he preferred to use the well-established and graphically developed figure of the Erinys.

2. Amata

Allecto's first victim is Queen Amata, who is driven insane by poison injected by one of the snakes from Allecto's head. The snake, which is elsewhere no more than a horrible attribute of the Erinyes, here becomes, as a poisonous reptile, a symbol of consuming madness; it injects its poison in many different guises, just as Allecto herself *tot sese vertit in ora* (328) [assumes so many countenances]. The immediate result of Amata's madness is that she tries to induce her husband to act against the will of the gods by means of a sophistic interpretation of the oracle. When this attempt fails, and madness like a consuming disease forces its way even deeper into her very spirit, the queen's collapse into insanity becomes clear to all: in crazed delirium she rages through the cities of the land. And in her ecstatic state she roams even further afield: she becomes a maenad and flings herself into the woods, taking her daughter with her. It is not easy to say in what sense Virgil wishes his portrayal of this βακχεία [Bacchic frenzy] to be taken. *In silvas simulato numine Bacchi...evolat et natam frondosis montibus abdit quo thalamum eripiat Teucris...'euhoe Bacche' fremens, solum te virgine dignum vociferans* [she went out into the forests in her flight, pretending that the power of Bacchus was upon her...and she hid her daughter among leaf-clad mountains...to rob the Trojans of their wedding. 'Ho, Bacchus!' she shouted, and 'None but you' she shrieked, 'deserves the maiden!']. Two things are clear, firstly that Amata is truly in the grip of madness, not acting in a cold, calculating way and feigning madness after careful consideration. Previously she had already been truly *lymphata* [frenzied], then *maiorem orsa furorem* [seized by an even wilder madness], and finally Virgil writes *talem...reginam Allecto stimulis agit undique Bacchi* (404) [so fared it with the queen, as Allecto goaded her now this way, now that and drove her by the Bacchic power]. On the other hand, it is equally certain that in spite of this last phrase, and in spite of the fact that the women are later said to be *attonitae Baccho* (580) [under the shock of Bacchus], it is not a question of true Bacchic ecstasy: for how could Allecto bring that about? After all, the *Bacchi stimuli* [goads of Bacchus] are not hers to command. But Virgil does say explicitly *s i m u l a t o numine Bacchi* (385) [*pretending* that the power of Bacchus was upon her], and just as the description that follows is in many respects unmistakeably dependent on Euripides' *Bacchae*,[11] so too this phrase is very reminiscent of Pentheus' suspicion that the women are gadding about πλασταῖσι βακχείαισι (218) [pretending to celebrate the rites of Dionysus] in the mountains: except that what was a false supposition in the *Bacchae* is actually the case here. And in fact the words that Virgil uses, especially the addition of her intentions *in silvas evolat...quo thalamum eripiat Teucris taedasque moretur* (387f.) [she went out into the forests in her flight...to prevent the marriage ceremony and to rob the Trojans of their wedding], support the view that Amata is pretending to be acting in obedience to the command of Bacchus, rather than that

Allecto drove her to the delusion that she was possessed by Bacchus. Later, Virgil writes *stimulis agit undique Bacchi* (405) [drove her now this way, now that, by the goads of Bacchus]; this must be a case of ἐκβακχεύειν [arousing a *kind* of Bacchic frenzy] here ascribed to the Fury from the Underworld, just as in Euripides' *Trojan Women* (408) Apollo is said to ἐκβακχεύειν Cassandra [fill her with Bacchic frenzy].[12]

Virgil's creation is quite idiosyncratic and can only be explained as an amalgamation of several concepts. At first, Allecto plays a role similar to that of Lyssa in Euripides' *Bacchae* (977), when she is called on by the chorus to incite the maenads against Pentheus. There, too, madness sent by the powers of the Underworld is involved in the action.[13] In Virgil, the god plays no part, although the rites are performed in exactly the same way as, for example, in Euripides' *Bacchae* and in   186 the cult of Dionysus generally. In Virgil, Roman sensibilities are very evident: the god Liber himself cannot desire any kind of dissolute maenadism, in which respectable upper-class matrons forget all morality and decency; that would be an abuse of the name of the god, which would be a serious offence – hence *maius adorta n e f a s* (386) [venturing a still graver sin] – which could only have been prompted by insanity sent from Hades. In a very similar way, the Bacchanalia, where genuine ecstasy certainly did play a rôle, were once regarded in Rome as a criminal deception and banned by the magistrates.[14] But if the intention of Amata with her *thiasi* [troops of Maenads] is to make it impossible for her daughter to marry, on the grounds that she is dedicated to the god – *taedas morari* (388) [to prevent the marriage ceremony] – this is reminiscent of another heroine who falsely claims to be dedicated to the cult of Bacchus, and for much the same reasons: Laodameia, who in Euripides' famous drama tried to evade marriage by a similar pretence: her *thiasi dolosi* [groups of fraudulent maenads][15] may well have been in Virgil's mind. Amata, however, does not persist in her deception; when the other matrons, in the grip of the same madness, join her and she swings the pine-torch in their midst, in her confused mental state she believes that she is carrying the marriage-torch in the bridal procession, and she sings the marriage-song for her daughter and Turnus.[16] But in the middle of her song (this is surely how *repente* [suddenly] in line 399 is to   187 be understood) she breaks off and calls on the women of Latium to join her in resisting Latinus who is guilty of showing contempt for a mother's rights. The result achieved by Amata, or rather by Allecto through Amata is twofold: first, Lavinia, *frondosis montibus abdita* (387) [hidden amid leaf-clad mountains] and allegedly dedicated to the gods, is temporarily taken out of Latinus' hands, and secondly, all the women of the land have been mobilized in opposition to the marriage that he has proposed, and this in its turn affects the male population: *quorum attonitae Baccho nemora avia matres insultant thiasis...undique collecti coeunt Martemque fatigant* (580) [from all sides there gathered the relatives of those women who, under the shock of Bacchus, had gone prancing in frenzied bands about the trackless forests...and they too clamoured incessantly for an appeal to Mars]. Possibly Virgil was borrowing a Greek motif here and toning it down, with the result that it does not achieve its full effect: it is conceivable that in some Greek work, an ecstatic movement took hold of the women and they yielded to it μετ' ἀκοσμίας ἁπάσης [with total abandon][17] and thereby provoked their menfolk to embark on a war. This would be a development of the idea which Aristotle put forward to explain the remarkable behaviour of Odysseus in *Iliad* 2.183: he ignores good manners so that the population will be astounded and will turn to him, 'as they say that Solon behaved when he wanted to gather the people together to persuade them to fight for Salamis'. The incident to which Dümmler (*Kl. Schr.* II [Leipzig, 1896] 405f.) rightly refers in this context, the ἀσωτία [abandoned behaviour] of Elegeis, daughter of Neleus, will have come even closer to the motif as we may suppose it was presented by Virgil's source. Virgil himself seems to imply that the men are anxious to fight in order to put an end to the women's disorderly and giddy behaviour. He has thus found an ideal way of making the mad lust for war spread all over Latium; the women, who are more susceptible to this infectious mania, are the agents whereby the men, who are slower to be moved *en masse*, are all individually inflamed to resist Latinus' plans. We can only regret that this ingenious piece of motivation is not treated very clearly and fails to achieve its full effect.

3. Turnus

188

Allecto has begun her fiendish work with the action which has the least immediate impact, which needs the longest time to develop, and which at first only briefly thwarts Latinus' plan by delaying its execution.[18] She now turns to Turnus, the real motivating force behind the war. While he is asleep she comes to him in the guise of the priestess of Juno, and goads him with words calculated to touch his sense of honour and his manly pride; she herself mentions Juno, and claims that she is acting on her orders. Turnus refuses; then the Fury is filled with anger, appears in her true form and plants her torch in his chest: he wakes up, bathed in sweat, and from that moment on the fire of hell burns in him. In this episode, too, Virgil has blurred the clarity of the one motif by combining it with too many others. The appearance of the dream-figure is based in the first instance on the dream of Penelope in the *Odyssey* (4.795ff.), in which she is consoled by an εἴδωλον [phantom] which is sent by Athena and takes the form of her sister Iphthime. Penelope replies to her in her dream, just as Turnus does (and that is what distinguishes this dream-narrative from the others in Homer) and tells her about her worries: then the εἴδωλον says that it has been sent by Pallas Athena, the personal protectress of Telemachus, and that puts Penelope's mind at rest. Παλλάς...ἥ νῦν με προέηκε τεῒν τάδε μυθήσασθαι [Pallas...who has sent me now to tell you these things]: Virgil has incorporated this straightaway in Allecto's first speech to Turnus, with *ipsa palam fari omnipotens Saturnia iussit* [the Saturnian Queen, the Almighty, had herself commanded me to say this openly to you], and, in fact, Calybe, as Juno's priestess, could indeed have received instructions from her in a dream:[19] though it does appear rather awkward when we find that Turnus rejects this revelation and proceeds to appeal directly to Juno himself, confident that she will not forget him. These lines have not been completed, as is shown by the half-line 439; Virgil probably intended that Turnus should go on to say that he did not believe in Juno's alleged warning, on the grounds that she would not permit events to proceed as far as allowing his bride to be withheld from him. This is followed by the mocking rebuke that inflames Allecto

152

with blazing anger. Formally, the final lines of Turnus' speech (443-4) are modelled 189
on Hector's farewell speech in the sixth book of the *Iliad* (490-2);[20] however, the
motif of rejecting a divine warning, and suffering a divine anger in consequence, is
derived from another source. In his *Hymn to Demeter* (42), Callimachus describes
how Demeter takes on the form of her *priestess* Nikippa,[21] and gives a friendly
warning to Erysichthon, who wants to fell her sacred tree; he dismisses her scorn-
fully, and then she reveals herself in her divine form and stature – ἴθματα μὲν
χέρσω, κεφαλὰ δὲ οἱ ἄψαθ' Ὀλύμπου [her feet touched the ground, her head
touched the heavens] – and utters fearful threats. Either Callimachus himself or
some very closely related source supplied Virgil with the motif. It probably goes
back to the dialogue between Helen and Aphrodite in Book 3 of the *Iliad* (386ff.),
although there are no close echoes of the Homeric passage in Virgil. However, the
result of the goddess' angry speech is the same in each case: Turnus, like Helen,
immediately does what he had at first refused to do. It is this reversal and the
increase in dramatic tension that it creates which caused Virgil to combine the motif
of Penelope's dream with the motif of Helen or Erysichthon, yet it cannot be denied
that the latter motif has no true psychological justification in this context. Whereas it
certainly contributes a good deal to the characterization of Helen, and of Erysichthon, that the former at first tries to avoid Paris, and that the latter very coarsely
repudiates the priestess' reprimand, this is not true in the case of Turnus: at most,
Virgil perhaps hoped to show that to start with he had been a peaceable character,
who had had no inclination whatever to enforce his claims with a mailed fist; but
that possibility seems to be excluded by the fact that he rejected the message simply
because he did not believe the truthful account given by Calybe.

4. Ascanius: war breaks out 190

Turnus commands his Rutulians to take up arms, in order to give Latinus a strong
warning against the newly-made alliance. However, a peaceful settlement was still
perhaps possible; Allecto knows that a breach can be healed if blood has not yet
been spilt, so she puts the finishing touches to her work by means of a third
intervention: Trojans and Latins are to come to blows. At the same time, there were
two reasons why the Trojans had to be made responsible for starting the dispute.
First, everything is arranged so as to pile as much tinder as possible around the
throne of Latinus, since that is where the flames of war are eventually to flare up and
blaze forth. However, Latinus' subjects can only demand that their king should
declare war if they feel that they themselves have been injured; if they were to begin
the war themselves, they would have no occasion or reason to be angry with the
foreign settlers and they would be in no position to come before the king demanding
revenge. Secondly, Virgil could not be indifferent to the fact that this gave him the
opportunity to respect the tradition, in so far as it existed, according to which the
casus belli was some form of encroachment by the new settlers, such as looting or
other incursions into Latin territory. Virgil is operating very skilfully when he makes
the offence committed by the Trojans as slight as he can, yet serious enough to
motivate the anger of the Latin country-folk. The country-folk: that is explicitly

191 emphasized several times (504, 521, 574), and apparently they are very different from the city population that is stirred up by Amata (384); they are the uncivilized, undisciplined[22] bands, who are always prepared to rush to help each other at the call of the shepherd's horn, to drive off robbers and wild animals; it is these men, who act on the impulse of the moment, passionately, and without mature reflection, who are to strike the first blow.[23] But the injustice which incites them to retaliate in this case is not any theft or wrongful raid, but an offence by an innocent offender, Ascanius. Allecto brings it about that Ascanius, while out hunting, fatally wounds a tame stag, which is the household pet of Tyrrhus' large and highly respected family, although of course Ascanius has no idea that it is a privileged beast. It is significant that Allecto does not dare to lay a finger on the boy himself, the darling of the gods; she puts his hounds on the scent of the stag after she has 'flung madness upon them', (*rabiem obiecit* [479-80]), as Artemis had once done to the hounds of Actaeon. Ascanius, who is passionately devoted to hunting (which was regarded as a thoroughly Roman pursuit in Virgil's day), catches sight of the magnificent stag, and possessed by an understandable longing for glory (*eximiae laudis succensus amore* [496]) takes aim. Tyrrhus' daughter Silvia is the first to see the wounded creature; she immediately breaks into a loud lament and calls on the country-folk for help; thus events are set in motion by a woman, who is much more liable to give way to mindless grief than a man. Allecto then sees to it that the affair spreads far and wide (505, 511). All this is undoubtedly Virgil's own invention. We ought not to look for the motif of the ill-starred hunt in any historical version of the legend, since it is far too Hellenistic in spirit. But the tame stag and its accidental death were perhaps borrowed by the poet from the story of Cyparissus, which he knew from a Hellenis-

192 tic poem, as we learn from the combined evidence of Ovid[24] and Pompeian paintings (especially Helbig 219 cf. Ovid *Met.* 10.113). I might almost go as far as to say that we cannot fully comprehend Silvia's sorrow and anger and the other consequences of the fatal arrow unless we know the sad outcome of the Cyparissus story: the Hellenistic poet will have used every one of the many artistic devices at his disposal to touch the reader's heart with the story of the boy's mortal grief. Virgil had to respect the laws of epic and restrict himself to allusions, but he was still censured for it: one ancient critic found the whole motif *leve nimisque puerile* [lightweight and too childish] (Macrob. *loc. cit.*).

How first Silvia's menfolk come running in answer to her call, how Tyrrhus, armed with his axe from his tree-felling, summons his troops, and how someone – it must have been the Fury herself – raises the alarm by a blast on her horn – and immediately men come pouring in from every direction – all this is vividly described by Virgil; and, since Ascanius is apparently in danger, it is also clear why the Trojan warriors immediately march out armed for battle – if it had been some Trojan of no particular significance who was in danger, it would have been necessary to supply some additional motivation to produce this effect. After that, bloodshed is inevitable, and it comes as no suprise that the inadequately armed country-folk are overcome by the Trojans, who are experienced fighters. Blood now cries out for vengeance.

Thus Allecto brings her work to a climax, and Virgil has plotted its progress with calculated artistry: Juno had pronounced *sere crimina belli, arma velit poscatque simul rapiatque iuventus* (339f.) [sow in recriminations the seeds of war: in one breath let their manhood want, demand and grasp their arms], and she can now ascertain to her own satisfaction that *stant belli causae* (553) [motives for a war are established]. Now that disaster is on its way, there is no need for further help from the powers of darkness. Once *discordia* has sprung up between men, its own inner nature forces it to erupt into war. The three separate streams of war-fever unite in Latinus' palace, and the weak old man tries in vain to stem their flood; Allecto has seen to it that he will be alone in his resistance, and the waves pass over him and onward. The actual outbreak of war however still needs to be embodied in some public action; Virgil therefore creates an episode out of something which *may* have been no more than a figure of speech in Ennius (see above p. 149f.): the opening of the *Belli portae* [Gates of War]. By means of the descriptions of the temple, and a solemn reference to the custom that is still observed (601ff.), the event is given the importance that it requires; and since it is not Discordia (as in Ennius) but Juno herself who flings open the gates, we are given the impression that, despite Allecto's help, the war has been brought about by the goddess herself.[25]

III. *The Battles* 193

Four books of the *Aeneid*, a third of the whole work, are devoted to descriptions of fighting. The economy of the work required that they should be allotted a considerable amount of space. Aeneas has to be given an opportunity to display his heroism, particularly because he needs rehabilitation after the defeat at Troy. Also, quite apart from Aeneas himself, the history of Rome is one long story of battles and victories, so Rome's prehistory must also tell magnificent tales of battles and victories. The *Iliad* provided the prototype for heroic battles; Virgil could not even consider making changes to this model, let alone rejecting it in favour of one of a quite different type. However, the *Iliad* had also exhausted virtually every possible variation on this theme (apart from a cavalry battle), and any attempt to think up new forms could only have led to eccentricities. That is why Virgil keeps closer to Homer in these descriptions than in any other part of his poem with the exception of the Funeral Games. At the same time these descriptions are Virgilian through and through.

The difficulties that faced him are not to be underestimated. Virgil found virtually no hints in the threadbare tradition to help him in his characterization of individual warriors and had to rely almost entirely on his own imagination, although he had to take care that his own inventions should not be recognizable as such. A bold departure from the repertoire of characters established in the mythical tradition would have clashed with the overall style. Any obtrusive fictions, or any introduction of obviously contemporary situations, would have spoilt the illusion that all this was age-old material, hallowed by tradition. As for the action itself, that is, the motivation and incidents of the battles, this could easily be adapted from Homer, although great care had to be taken in so doing. Homer's audience loved battles and 194 could never hear enough about heroic single combat. It is clear that the poet himself had a lively technical interest in the vicissitudes of spear-fights and sword-fights, the wounds and different forms of death, and he could presuppose the same interest in the audience for which he was reciting. Virgil's contemporaries had also lived through wars enough, and the style in which they were fought was still comparable with that described by Homer – we should remember that in Roman tactics, too, the decisive factor was still the proficiency of the individual, not of the whole army; but how few of those who heard or read Virgil had ever themselves carried a sword! Above all, how remote Virgil himself was from the cut and thrust of the battlefield! He thus found himself faced with the enormously difficult task of having to invent his own characters, characters who moreover were designed with only one end in view, namely to perform deeds to which neither Virgil's mind nor that of his public could relate in any real way, except insofar as they aroused their general sympathy for humanity.

Confronted with these difficulties, Virgil decided on the following guidelines: he would concentrate the interest on the smallest possible number of characters, and by careful use of Roman and national material, make the battle scenes as graphic as possible and emphasize the overall human interest or psychological aspect of the events. As for the composition, he decided to maintain the listener's interest by means of constant variety and an energetic, dramatic pacing of the action.

1. Types of battle-scenes

If we classify the types of battle scenes under various headings, we see at once that the ἀριστεία, the account of an extended sequence of heroic deeds performed by one man, is by far the largest category. Thus Book 9 is almost exclusively the *aristeia* of Turnus; in Book 10 we have Aeneas in 310-44, Pallas' deeds and his death at the hand of Turnus in 362-509, Aeneas again in 510-605 (606-88, the removal of Turnus, is a later addition), Mezentius in 689-746, and his death from 755 to the end (908), the latter being Aeneas' first decisive achievement. The battles in Book 11 (597-895) are for the most part (647-724, 759-867) the *aristeia* and death of Camilla, interrupted by an exploit of Tarchon (725-58), and concluded by a description (868-95) of the consequences of Camilla's death: the flight of the Latins and their pursuit up to the walls of the city. Finally in Book 12 Tolumnius and the spear, and the subsequent hand-to-hand fighting at the altar (257-310), is followed by the wounding of Aeneas (311-23), and another *aristeia* of Turnus (324-82) and the healing of Aeneas (383-440): then his sortie with his faithful companions, which includes a few lines about their deeds (458-61), the attack by Messapus on Aeneas and what might be described as a combined *aristeia* of Aeneas and Turnus (500-53), up to Aeneas' attack on the city, which then leads to the decisive duel (554-696) that rounds off the work (697-952). Thus the interest is concentrated on five characters: Turnus, Aeneas, Pallas, Mezentius, Camilla; of these, only Turnus and Aeneas appear in more than one book; two books (9 and 11) have only one main character each. If we disregard the episodes concerning isolated feats performed by other characters – Nisus and Euryalus in 9.176-502, Ascanius in 9.590-671, Tarchon in 9.725-59 – and if we ignore the few characters whose only function is to oppose the main heroes and who are given some importance in order to magnify their *aristeia* –

195

Lausus in 10.791-832, Aunus in 11.699-724, Arruns in 11.759ff., and to a lesser degree Pandarus and Bitias in 11.672-716, Halaesus in 10.411-25 – all that is left is a few not very extensive passages which serve to give an impression of the general fighting by naming the victors and the vanquished; and we may observe that Virgil inflicts such a 'butcher's list' on his readers only once in each book: 9.569-89 (though 573-5 makes it belong in part to Turnus' *aristeia*), 10.747-54 (also 345-61, though this is rather different), 11.612-47 (though this includes the very general description of the ebb and flow of battle in 618-35), and 12.458-61. And indeed, it is only exceptionally that Virgil expands his narrative so as to give an account of an actual duel (for example in Book 11, and again in 9.576-89, and in 12.287-310, though that passage is not strictly comparable); otherwise it is merely a case of listing names as in *Iliad* 6.29-36, followed on one occasion (9.576ff.) by a slightly more detailed description of two fights, rather like *Iliad* 14.511ff., where the list is followed by the very sketchy description of the killing of Hyperenor. On the other hand, what is completely absent in Virgil, but fairly common in Homer, is what we might call the 'chain of combats', where the poet tries to bring several single combats fought by various heroes into some sort of relationship with one another – as for example in *Iliad* 5.533ff.: Agamemnon kills Deikoon, the comrade of Aeneas, and then his two brothers, who had joined the expedition against Troy out of loyalty to the Atridae; Menelaus, later joined by Antilochus, ἐλέησε [felt pity] for them; Menelaus and Antilochus then kill two Trojans; Hector ἐνόησεν [observed] this and he avenges their death with that of two of the enemy; Ajax ἐλέησε [felt pity] for them and strikes Amphius (cf. also, for example, 13.576-672, 14.440-507, 15.518-91). Such series have a more tiring effect than plain, rapid lists, unless, at least, famous heroes appear in them to lend interest; and few such heroes were available to Virgil.

196

2. Differences between Homeric and Roman battles. Cavalry. Chariots.

The Virgilian battle-scene, built up from a description of tactics and types of weapon, is modelled faithfully on its Homeric prototype in all essentials, but contains occasional touches which would give the Roman reader the feeling that these are descriptions of battles fought by his own ancestors. There are many passages where it is clear that Virgil has applied these touches above all in connection with the native troops. Military ensigns are mentioned only in such phrases as *signa sequi* [to follow the standards], while Turnus proclaims the beginning of the war by flying the *vexillum* [flag][26] from the citadel. Virgil had introduced Misenus as trumpeter in Books 3 and 6, in accordance with the tradition; he also explicitly says that he had stood at Hector's side in that capacity (6.166f.). During the fighting the *classica* [signals for battle] are often mentioned, given by *tuba, bucina* or *cornu* [trumpet or horn], but without exception in passages which refer to Etruscans or Latins:[27] Virgil is aware that trumpets were thought to have been invented by the Etruscans, and were therefore unknown to Homeric warriors.[28]

Perhaps the most important difference between Virgil's battle-scenes and

197

Homer's is Virgil's introduction of cavalry. He did not hesitate to provide even the Trojans with cavalry, probably because without it the *lusus Troiae* could not have been presented as a tradition derived from their former homeland. Unfortunately we do not know how the Roman antiquarians squared this with their knowledge that there were no cavalry battles in Homer. It is for this reason that only isolated Trojan cavalrymen are mentioned (Glaucus and Lades, 12.343; Thymoetes, 12.364; Amycus 12.509), and none of them are generals, or come from the aristocracy. Although Aeneas himself is depicted as riding on the march (8.552), he never appears on a horse in battle. The actual cavalry in Aeneas' army are provided by his allies,[29] Evander's Arcadians (8.518; 10.364) and Tarchon's Etruscans, who appear again later in Book 11 as the real opponents of Camilla (*Tyrrhenos equites* [504] [Etruscan cavalry], *Etruscique duces equitumque exercitus omnis* [598] [Etruria's chieftains and all the cavalry], *Tusci* [629] [Tuscans], *Tyrrheni* [733] [Tyrrhenians]), although isolated Trojans also appear in this context (Orsilochus and Butes 690, Chloreus 768). The Etruscan king Mezentius also used to ride away from the wars on his battle-horse (10.859), and his son Lausus is called *equum domitor* (7.651) [horse-tamer]. On the Latin side, too, it is the allies who constitute the main contingent of cavalry, although the Rutulians (9.48 but cf. 7.793) and Latins (11.603) do have a certain number. Turnus himself only rides, accompanied by selected companions, when he needs to reach the enemy camp as quickly as possible (9.47); he does not ride into battle. Other mounted warriors include the Faliscans under Messapus, son of Neptune and tamer of horses, whom the poet wishes to impress on our imaginations as the cavalryman *par excellence*, in the same way that Turnus is *the* outstanding chariot-fighter (10.354; 11.464, 518, 692; 12.295; *equum domitor* [tamer of horses], one of Virgil's few stock epithets, is applied to him at 7.691; 9.523; 12.128); also the men of Tibur under Catillus and Coras (11.465, 519, 604), which, as Servius on 7.675 rightly points out, is why they are compared with centaurs; finally, and most strikingly, the Volscians led by the maiden warrior Camilla (7.804; 11 *passim*), who eventually commands the combined Latin cavalry in the battle in Book 11 (519).

As we have already said (p. 148), Virgil inserted this cavalry-battle between Books 10 and 12 so as to vary the character of the fighting as well as that of the combatants, and thus avoid the danger of monotony. The reader does indeed come to the decisive battle in Book 12 with keener interest than if it had come immediately after the one in Book 10, which is of exactly the same kind and which involves exactly the same people. However, so that Book 10 shall not anticipate the cavalry-battle, Virgil has to invent the story that the Arcadians, because of the difficult terrain, were compelled to fight on foot, and this also explains their initial defeat (10.364); no similar motivation is necessary in the case of the Etruscans, since obviously they cannot think of disembarking their horses during the fight to secure a beachhead. Furthermore, the fact that their first task is to attack the enemy camp may explain why the Latin cavalry, and Camilla, do not appear in Book 10,[30] although it is not at all certain that Virgil himself deliberately motivated their late appearance in this way.

For the cavalry-battle itself Virgil could no longer rely on his constant guide, Homer. His account is none the worse for that. Of course we should not automatically assume that everything is Virgil's free invention, for, just as there were many paintings of Amazonomachies, so too there must have been many poetic descriptions which included motifs which could be borrowed for Camilla's encounters: in 659ff. Virgil himself mentions the Amazons by the river Thermodon, and Hippolyta and Penthesilea. However, it is unthinkable that Virgil used the archaic epic, the *Amazonis* or the *Aithiopis*, as a source for his cavalry-battle; it is improbable, in any case, that he had read these epics, as is shown by the fact that he knows of Penthesilea, not as a horsewoman, but only as a woman who fought from a chariot (*seu cum se Martia curru Penthesilea, refert* [11.661] [or else when martial Penthesilea drives back in her chariot from war]), a conception which he must have derived from mythographic compendia and illustrations; and this is further evidence that the Amazons did not ride horses in the archaic epics.[31] But already in the archaic period, certainly by the sixth century BC, the idea of the mounted Amazon had been introduced and was never to disappear; but in the iconographic tradition the opponents of the horsewomen, to the best of my knowledge, are always hoplites, not horsemen as in Virgil; and it is this circumstance which gives his description its individual colour. How the two armies first approach each other in orderly ranks, then, when they are only a spear's cast apart, suddenly break ranks, and the leaders, Tyrrhenus and Aconteus, charge each other's horses, so that one crashes to the ground as if struck by lightning – that is described in as vivid and lively a manner as the subsequent ebb and flow of the armies which leads up to the actual hand-to-hand fighting. We see a wounded horse rear up and beat the air with its front hoofs (638); a rider struggling to stay mounted on a wounded steed as it plunges to the ground, and scrabbling for control of the reins; his companion tries to stop him falling, but both receive fatal wounds (670); by skilful manoeuvring of her horse, Camilla pursues an attacker (694); Tarchon pulls an opponent down from his steed, and, holding him in front of him, tries to kill him with his own spear-point (741); here we see an Etruscan, clad in animal skins and carrying a lightweight spear like a huntsman (677), there an armoured Trojan on an armoured steed (770); and scenes of pursuit and flight of many different kinds (760, 780, 783, 814).[32] Thus our imagination has been carefully guided to visualize all the warriors as mounted, even when this is not explicitly stated (666, 673, 675), and on the one occasion when Camilla, tricked by the cowardly Ligurian, dismounts from her horse to answer a challenge to fight on foot, then every reader who has been alert to the poet's intention will take it for granted that she remounts her horse, which her companion has been holding meanwhile (710), after this encounter (as is implied by 827), without this being explicitly stated; on the contrary, if Camilla had continued to fight on foot, Virgil *would* have had to say so explicitly.[33]

199

200

The war-chariot plays a much smaller part in the *Aeneid* than in the *Iliad*, partly because it is used only on the Latin side. Virgil confines the chariot strictly to them, presumably on the grounds that Aeneas and his followers will not have brought chariots across the sea with them, whereas the auxiliary troops, the Arcadians and Etruscans, form substantial chariot contingents. But even on the Latin side the chariot is a distinction which the common soldier never enjoys; particularly in Books 10 and 12 it is invariably linked with Turnus.[34]

Turnus leaps down from his chariot when he goes to confront Pallas (10.453), drives to a duel the brilliant white horses, a gift from a goddess (12.83), mounts his chariot when the fighting is renewed (326), and fights on, sometimes standing on the platform of his chariot, sometimes getting off to confront his opponent (12.226-340, 355, 370-83); with the help of his swift horses, Juturna, who takes the place of Metiscus as charioteer (468), takes him out of range of Aeneas, and he is able to fight on for some time in the same way (511, 614ff.) until the news of the threat to 201 the city makes him leave his chariot at last so as to go and meet Aeneas face to face (681). Thus the poet takes care that the picture of the king fighting from his chariot is firmly impressed on our minds; he makes this effect more powerful by restricting the use of chariots by others: for whereas his description of the Italian auxiliaries leaves no doubt that he believed that the ancient Italian leaders normally made use of chariots (7.655 Aventinus, 724 Halaesus, 782 Virbius, cf. also 9.330 Remus), in Book 12 no chariot is mentioned other than that of Murranus, who is descended from a long line of kings; in Book 10 the *quadriga*[35] (571) [four-horse chariot] of Niphaeus and the pair that belong to Lucagus and Liger (575) bring variety into the list of Aeneas' opponents; and Rhoetus fleeing in his chariot (399) interrupts the enumeration of the warriors who fight Pallas on foot. Otherwise, no chariot can compete with Turnus'. In these four exceptional cases, the chariot is not mentioned arbitrarily, but serves to give an individual touch to the description of each man's death.

3. Weapons

The weapons in Homer are similar to those which Virgil attributed to early Rome. In fact the weapons of Virgil's own time, too, were still basically the same, although by then there had been great developments in the form of individual items. In his descriptions of battle, Virgil was thus able to equip his men with the offensive weapons of the Homeric warrior. For attack from a distance there were the long, heavy throwing-lances and, if necessary, stones picked up from the ground (10.381, 415, 698; 12.531, 897); and for close combat the sword. In the parade of troops in Book 7 he named a large number of weapons that were especially characteristic of early Italy; but neither *pilum, dolones, veru Sabellum* [javelin, pikes, Sabine spit], which are characteristic of Aventinus' men (7.664) nor the Oscans' *aclydes* (730) 202 [small clubs], thrown from leashes, nor their sickle-shaped swords, nor the Campanians' *cateiae* (741) [boomerangs] are mentioned when it comes to the actual battle. That is all the more remarkable when we consider the care which Virgil took to achieve variety, at least in vocabulary, as for example in the great number of synonyms that he uses for *hasta* [spear].[36] The only weapon which is really different from the *hasta* is the hunting spear, *sparus*, which is mentioned only once (11.682). Nor, while we are on this subject, are the peculiar pieces of armour and clothing that are described in Book 7 ever mentioned again: the wolfskin *galeri* (688) [caps] and the leather leggings (690), the Oscan *cetra* (732) [short shield], the Campanian cork helmet and the crescent-shaped shield (742). Thus what we have here is antiquarian material about ancient Italy juxtaposed with narrative based on the Homeric epics, and Virgil makes no attempt to reconcile them, just as he felt no need to bring the military leaders mentioned in Books 7 and 10 into the main body of his narrative.[37] During the Latins' preparations for war, axes are sharpened (7.627, cf. 184); they are not used in the fighting (for in 12.306 the axe that Alsus snatches up is the one intended for slaughtering the sacrificial beast). Only Camilla and her companion Tarpeia carry battle-axes (11.656, 696), like Amazons in the poetic tradition, and similarly the sons of Hercules' companion Melampus are equipped with clubs. There is only one occasion in the fighting where a non-Homeric, native Roman weapon is mentioned: the *falarica* [heavy missile], with which Turnus kills the giant Bitias (9.705); this illustrates at one and the same time the strength of the attacker, who is able to hurl such a gigantic missile which is probably normally dropped from above – like *pila muralia* [defensive pikes] – and also the gigantic size of his victim, who could only be felled by a missile of this kind; the weapon itself had already been given a place in epic by Ennius (*Ann.* 544 Vahlen); the lightly armed Praenestines generally carry slings (7.686), like the Locrians of Ajax in *Iliad* 13.716; archers are frequently mentioned (9.572; 10.754, Camilla 7.816; cf. 11.654, Chloreus 11.773, Clusium and Cora 10.168); in the description of the battle both slings and arrows, as in Homer, are mentioned in only a very few isolated passages 203 (the arrow shot at Aeneas, 12.319, modelled on Pandarus' arrow in *Iliad* 4.104f., an arrow-wound, 12.651). But during the storming of the camp, Mezentius carries a sling, since even the Roman legions resort to slings in such circumstances;[38] in attack and defence the legionaries will have used bow and arrow, too, like Capys (9.578) and Ascanius (9.631), Ismarus (10.140) and other defenders (9.665; 10.131).

When we come to protective armour we find the same situation. The complete panoply of plumed helmet, breastplate, greaves and shield (as for example Aeneas' armour 8.620, 12.430; and Turnus' 11.487) resembles both the Homeric, or Ionian, and the Roman. If anything, as far as details are concerned, Virgil keeps rather closer to the Homeric model, merely introducing one or two Italian national features. The shield is carried on the left arm in battle; if this is cut off, it falls to the ground (10.545); when Aeneas has finished looking in amazement at his new shield and prepares to march out to battle, he lifts it onto his shoulder (*attolit umero*, 8.731) which must mean that he carries it by a strap across his back like the Roman legionary on the march, and like Odysseus in *Iliad* 10.149: ἀμφ' ὤμοισι σάκος θέτο [he put the shield around his shoulders]. The shield is round (*clipei orbem* [10.546, 783; 12.925] [the circle of the shield]), and protects a man down as far as his groin (10.588) or to mid thigh (12.926), and is large enough for its owner to be able to crouch behind it (*se collegit in arma poplite subsidens* [12.491] [he gathered himself behind his armour, dropping down on one knee]) so as to allow a threatening spear to hurtle past; Virgil must have imagined the shield of Idomeneus in *Iliad* 13.405 as being a heavy, round shield of this kind: κρύφθη γὰρ ὑπ' ἀσπίδι πάντοσ' ἐίση...τῇ ὕπο πᾶς ἐάλη [he hid himself beneath his circular shield...beneath which his whole body crouched]. Virgil does not generally distinguish between *clipeus* and *scutum* [a round and oblong shield], and we must think of the *scuta* of the Trojans (8.93) as including the so-called Argive round shields (for even the *cavalry* of Volcens are called *scutati* [9.370] [equipped with *scuta*]): but when the companions of Pallas carry his body from the battlefield on a *scutum* (10.506) it must be a long shield (cf. 8.662 the *scuta longa* of the Gauls), for which this is the correct term, and it is worth remembering that according to tradition (Plut. *Romulus* 21) it is a weapon of Sabine origin. However, wooden shields are never mentioned by Virgil; he mentions bronze as a material (10.336; 12.541); the shields of Aeneas (8.448: bronze, gold and iron) and of Turnus (12.925) consist of seven layers of metal, just as the shield of Homer's Ajax (ἑπταβόειος, *Iliad* 7.220) has seven layers of bull's-hide, and Achilles' marvellous shield at least five layers of metal. Homer's bull's hides (ῥινοὶ βοός) also provided the model for the *duo taurea terga* [two bull hides] of the giant Bitias (9.706) and the composite shields of leather and metal that belong to Pallas and Mezentius: *clipeum, tot ferri terga, tot aeris, quem pellis totiens obeat circumdata tauri* (10.482) [Pallas' shield, with all its layers of iron and bronze and the many dense-packed coverings of bull's hide] (= ἐπέην ῥινός βοός [there was bull's hide upon it], *Iliad* 20.276) and *per orbem aere cavum triplici, per linea terga tribusque intextum tauris opus* (10.783) [through the shield's domed circle of triple bronze, the layers of linen and the texture of three bull's hides]: Virgil's shields, with their extra layers of iron and linen, are even tougher than Homer's, and, while the iron needs no special explanation, perhaps scholars are right to remind us in connection with the linen that this material was used in early Roman *scuta* [shields] (according to Polybius' description, 6.23).[39] As for the bronze breastplate, *lorica* or *thorax* (7.633; 10.337; 12.381), Virgil found no precise information in Homer; he visualized it as the breastplate constructed of chain-mail and linked metal scales (11.488) of his own time, which was strengthend by doubling the layer of scales (*duplici squama lorica fidelis et auro* [9.707] [the trusty corslet with its double layer of golden scales]) or doubling, or even tripling, the chain-rings: *bilicem loricam* (12.375) [two-leashed cuirass], *loricam consertam hamis auroque trilicem* (3.467) [a corslet of hooked chain-mail and three-leash golden weave]. Such a triple chain-mail tunic is so heavy that only a hero of extraordinary strength could wear it (5.263): it is no doubt a story-teller's exaggeration.

Besides the warriors in full panoply, Virgil also has lightly-armed men, the counterpart not of Homer's archers and slingers (*Iliad* 13.716) but of the Roman *velites* [light armed troops], i.e. they have no defensive armour, and the light *parma* [buckler] instead of the *clipeus*, but they do carry a sword: thus the Trojan Helenor *ense levis nudo parmaque inglorius alba* (9.548) [went lightly armed, with only a bare sword, and with no tale of glory on his still unblazoned buckler], and the Etruscan king's son Lausus, who, not yet strong enough for a full suit of armour, wears only a tunic stitched with gold threads and likewise the *parma, levia arma minacis* (10.817) [buckler, too light an armament for his defiant temper]; such a *tunica squalens auro* (10.314) [tunic stiffened with gold] is elsewhere worn under the breastplate just as the Homeric χιτών [tunic] is worn under the θώρηξ [breastplate]; however it is unlikely that Virgil realized that Homer too has inadequately armed men who wear only a *chiton* and no breastplate. More frequently than Homer, Virgil describes the special armour of individuals, not merely for the sake of a vivid pictorial effect, but generally so as to add a particular touch of colour to the narrative. We are told that the youthful Helenor (9.545) is equipped with only *ense nudo parmaque alba* [a bare sword and unblazoned shield] so as to intensify our sympathy for the despair which drives him to plunge into the midst of the foe *qua tela videt densissima* [where he saw the weapons cluster thickest]; again, we admire

Lausus' self-sacrificing action still more when we know how inadequately armed he is to fight against an opponent clad in bronze armour (10.817). On the wall of the camp stands the son of the Sicilian Arcens, wearing a richly embroidered purple robe (9.582); he is killed and immediately Numanus mocks the Trojans by shouting out a scornful phrase about their effeminacy: *vobis picta croco et fulgenti murice vestis* [your garments are embroidered with saffron and ablaze with purple dye]. With purple crest and purple robe Acron towers above his men; his bride has adorned him, and her love is the cause of his death: Mezentius sees the purple splendour from afar and plunges into the midst of the foe, to kill the conspicuous warrior (10.722). Haemonides, the priest of Apollo and Diana, wears, even in battle, his priestly ribbons and his long priestly robe of gleaming white (10.537): just as Haemonides is accustomed to sacrifice beasts to the gods, so Aeneas now sacrifices [*immolat*] him, but only after he has fled all over the battlefield forgetful of his priestly dignity, and has stumbled and fallen. The gigantic Herminius, who is so sure of his own invincibility that he leaves his blond head and his upper body unprotected, is punished for his pride: his bare shoulder is struck by a spear (11.644). Ornytus fights in hunter's garb, almost insolently, as if he were slaying wild animals; he pays with his own life for provoking Camilla's anger (11.677); but as for Camilla herself, it is the splendidly colourful, gold-encrusted trappings of Chloreus' horse, which she covets, that bring about her downfall (11.768). Virgil was writing for a public which knew how to read between the lines; he never pedantically spells out the implications of these subtle touches.

4. Wounds, death and spoils

As for types of wounds, Homer provided Virgil with more than enough material; indeed he very nearly exhausted every possible variation. Originality, of course, was not Virgil's aim, but he does not abandon his independent approach even here. For his first description of a wound in battle he invents something unusual:[40] Privernus is lightly wounded, and throws aside his shield in a moment of foolish anxiety, to put his hand to the wound; whereupon an arrow pins his hand to his left side and fatally buries itself in his body (9.576). Several times (9.762, 10.700) hamstrings are cut, something which, as it happens, is not found in Homer, although we do know that *poplites succidere* [cutting of the hamstrings] was a wound which the Roman legionaries particularly dreaded. But these unconventional details are much less important than the general nature of Virgil's descriptive technique. The first difference from Homer to be observed is that Virgil as far as possible avoids describing complicated wounds, and confines himself to the simplest and most obvious types. One example will suffice to make this clear: let us compare their descriptions of wounds to the head, which, with the chest, is the main target for an attacker. In Virgil, helmet and skull are hewn through, so that the warm brain spatters over the victim's face (11.696); forehead and jaws are split open with the stroke of a sword or the blow of an axe (9.750; 12.307); a spear is driven through the helmet into the temple (12.537) or the temple is hit by a sling-bolt (9.588); an arrow (9.633) or a spear (9.418) goes right through the head, entering at the temple; a rock hits a man

206

full in the face (10.698) or smashes the head in from the front, so that splinters of bone, with brain and blood adhering to them, fly around (10.415); spear (10.323) or sword (9.442) enters a mouth opened wide in a shout. It is clear that Virgil was seeking variety but avoiding detailed description as far as possible. Everything is very much the same in the *Iliad* too, except that there a sword slashes the forehead above the nose (13.615) or a stone shatters the eyebrows (16.734), so that the skull breaks and the eyes fall out, or the spear pierces the nose by the eye, goes through the teeth, cuts the tongue off and comes out under the chin (5.290), or goes into the mouth and knocks out the teeth, so that blood is forced into the eyes and spurts out of the mouth and nose (16.346), or under the eyebrows, so that the eyeball falls out, and out through the nape of the neck (14.493), or, conversely, into the nape and out through the teeth, cutting the tongue (6.73); also, by the ear (11.509), into the ear (20.473), above the ear (15.433), beneath the ear (13.177), under the jaw and ear (13.677 etc.). In some parts of the *Iliad* (specifically Books 5, 13 and 14 and to some extent Book 16), the poet seems almost to enjoy describing these complex wounds, as if it were some kind of sport. Virgil no doubt took offence at these detailed accounts on the grounds that they were too much like technical medical descriptions for the elevated style of epic. On the other hand, he often made an effort to make a wound more interesting, not anatomically but from the point of view of *ethos*; for example, when Pharos opens his mouth to utter vain boasts, and a javelin comes flying into it (10.322; cf. 9.442; 10.348); or when Alcanor has his right arm pierced by the spear with which he was about to support his falling brother (10.338), or when Hisbo, mad with rage over the death of his friend, leaps on Pallas, and Pallas *tumido in pulmone recondit* (10.387) [buried his sword in his swelling lung]. A brave warrior scorns to kill an enemy in flight, but meets him face to face, *haud furto melior, sed fortibus armis* (10.735) [to prove himself a better man not by trickery but by true valour]; this is why Camilla overtakes the steed of the fleeing Ligurian, grabs his bridle, and faces him as she slays him (11.720). That is why the noble warriors themselves are also killed through the chest (Turnus and Pallas, Euryalus, Lausus and Camilla); but cruel Mezentius is deservedly wounded in the groin first (10.785f.) and then stabbed in the throat (907). However, we are not told where the treacherous arrow strikes Aeneas (12.318), nor does any song name the archer; *mortalin decuit violari volnere divom?* (12.797) [was it fitting that a deity should be outraged by a wound from a mortal man?]. To make it possible for warriors in full armour to be wounded, Virgil, like Homer, often says that a power-ful spear-thrust pierced through both shield and armour (10.336, 485) or, again like Homer, that a careless movement left a man's chest or flank exposed (10.425; 12.374; cf. 11.667; 10.314), or that the enemy's weapon penetrated the gap between helmet and armour (11.691; 12.381): it is not surprising that, since he is no more of a pedant than Homer, he did not spell out every detail, and sometimes mentioned the shield but not the armour. However, when Virgil describes Turnus' first wound (12.924) and says that both shield and cuirass were pierced at the thigh, and then Aeneas proceeds to plunge his sword into his breast (950) with no apparent diffi-culty, we remember how carefully Homer dealt with an equally important event, the death of Hector, making Achilles search out a vulnerable point: he strikes between the helmet and the cuirass, where the shoulderbone meets the throat, in the gullet, yet he does not sever the windpipe, so that, as the poet naïvely adds, the dying man could still speak to his victorious foe (*Iliad* 22.319ff.). To Virgil's mind, details of this kind at such a moment would have robbed the incident of its pathos: therefore, with the utmost simplicity and grandeur, he writes *ferrum adverso sub pectore condit* (12.950) [he buried his blade full in Turnus' breast].

In that passage the fatal wound is described as briefly as possible. In other cases it is not even mentioned. Of the two Trojans who escape with their lives when the tower on the wall collapses (9.545), Helenor plunges into the midst of the foe, while Lycus is attempting to climb the wall with the help of friends within when he is pulled down by Turnus together with the parapet; obviously both men are killed and the poet does not bother to say so; he was only interested in the two situations and the contrast between them. Similarly, there is the incident where Tarchon pulls Venulus off his horse, puts him in front of himself on his own horse, breaks off the point of his spear and tries to find an unprotected place where he can thrust it home, while his victim tries to fend off his right hand (11.741): the outcome of this struggle is in doubt, but the poet loses interest in it at this point, because he was attracted only by the opportunity that it gave him to describe an unusual situation. If Homer had described any of these incidents he would have given much more factual detail; his audience will have wanted to be satisfied that the foe was really dead, the one thing which matters in an actual battle.[41]

The victor strips the weapons from the body of his opponent and regards these spolia [spoils] as his greatest claim to fame. This practice is described both by Virgil and by Homer: in this instance the national Roman tradition corresponded with the Homeric one, and it was a Roman tradition to take the *spolia opima* (10.449) [spoils of honour] from an enemy commander. Thus Arruns, who flees after he has mortally wounded Camilla, forfeits both the spoils and the renown (11.790) and Diana carries away her body and all her weapons with it; on the other hand, Euryalus takes spoils from Rhamnes (9.359), the Rutulians take spoils from Euryalus and Nisus (450), and there are many more scenes of this kind in the other battles. But here too what is really important is something new, the poet's ethical sensibility: to adorn oneself with plundered weapons is at best childish folly, as in the case of Euryalus, who meets his death as a direct result of this folly, or else it is a matter of female vanity, as in the case of Camilla (11.779); for a man it is wanton hybris (10.501) which will be followed by well-deserved nemesis: it is Pallas' sword-belt that makes Aeneas kill Turnus (12.941ff.). By contrast Aeneas, with humble piety, dedicates the spoils of Haemonides (10.542) to Mars,[42] and constructs a *tropaeum* (11.5) [trophy] for Mars out of Mezentius' weapons; he honours the proud spirit of Lausus by leaving his weapons by the side of his body (10.827). Pallas vows to father Thybris that he will hang the spoils of Halaesus on a holy oak (10.423). Perhaps Camilla intended to dedicate Chloreus' gold weapons in the temple (11.778). Mezentius is too proud to adorn himself with booty, and he despises the gods, so when he has killed Pallas, he gives his weapons to Lausus (10.700); and Lausus is to be equipped with the weapons that he expects to take from Aeneas, which the impious Mezentius envisages as a kind of trophy to the god whom he invokes, his own right hand (10.773). In any case, Virgil's warriors do not neglect their other duties for the sake of taking spoils; they do not fight over them, as Homeric warriors so often do, nor does Virgil

209

210

think it seemly that a great hero should strip an enemy's body and carry off the spoils himself. Aeneas delegates the job to Serestus (10.541), Messapus to his soldiers (12.297). But the most important item of booty – and here Virgil differs from Homer – is the *balteus*, the decorated sword-strap or sword-belt, strung across the shoulder and richly decorated with *phalerae* [studs] and *bullae* [bosses]; this is the only item which is mentioned when Rhamnes and Pallas are stripped of their arms, and these are the two most significant instances in the poem.[43] Virgil's preference for a decorative piece of equipment rather than an actual weapon – for in both these cases, the hero does not give a passing thought to the sword itself – surely reflects contemporary attitudes.

5. Characters

Homer's heroes do not really differ very much from each other on the battlefield; they have no special traits of character. One may be stronger or more skilful or quicker or braver than another: all these are attributes that affect the outcome of the battle; it is exceptional for Homer to think of presenting a warrior as a human being with his own individual character. But this was precisely what Virgil regarded as important: even on the battlefield it is the purely human element that concerns him most of all. Much that is relevant here has already been discussed: let us recapitulate. Aeneas is the ideal Roman man and Roman fighter: he is quick to acknowledge magnanimity in an enemy (10.825), he can feel *clementia* (12.940) [clemency] even towards his most bitter foe, he is a model of Roman *virtus* [manly valour] (and, in true Roman fashion, prides himself on this, 12.435) and of *moderatio* [avoidance of excess] (above p. 165), of *fides* (12.311) [honouring of solemn agreement] and of *iustitia* (11.126) [justice], of *pietas* [dutifulness] towards the gods, and towards Pallas, whose father has entrusted him to him, and who is his ally and his guest-friend (10.516). It is only when he has to avenge the death of Pallas that the depth of his sorrow makes him harsh, even scornful, towards his victims;[44] the thought of him stifles any idea of mercy, and in the fury of his grief he kills Turnus despite all his pleas. To have shown mercy on this occasion would have been a cowardly failure to do what duty demanded.

211

His opponent Turnus[45] is his equal in strength and courage; but Aeneas has *vis temperata* [controlled strength] while Turnus has *vis consili expers* [strength unaccompanied by judgement]; the gods deprive him of their support, although he, too, piously respects them (9.24; 12.778). Above all, he is not fighting on behalf of his people and their future, as Aeneas is, but is justifiably reproached for fighting to defend his own personal claims, and it is immoral to provoke a war for reasons of that kind.[46] It was Allecto who drove him to war: possessed by the Fury, he has lost that clarity of vision and that self-control, without which boldness becomes madness; this works to the advantage of the Trojans, as we can see most clearly when he is besieged in his camp and is so crazed with his rage to kill that it does not occur to him to open the gate for his own men (9.760). He is animated by a lively sense of honour (10.681; 12.645, 670), but this too expresses itself as an unhealthy type of extravagance. The plain words spoken by the self-assured Aeneas contrast with

Turnus' loud boasts about his own strength and heroism (9.148; 11.393, 441; 12.360). He, too, respects the courage of the warrior he has slain (10.493); but he does not possess the *moderatio* [self-control] to refrain from decorating himself with spoils, and his elation in victory turns to crude barbarity when he cuts off the heads of the men he has slain and decorates his chariot with them while they are still dripping with blood (12.512). He does not stop to think before charging after Aeneas (10.645), and declares himself ready for a duel as soon as he is challenged (11.434); then, when he is taken at his word, he does not go back on it, in spite of the urgent pleas of Latinus and Amata. However, it is not with calm resolve, but in a mood of savage violence (*violentia* [12.9], *furiae* [101] [madness]), that he prepares for the fight, and it is a finely observed touch that immediately after this burst of feverish excitement his courage ebbs away when he faces the decisive conflict (220).[47] The danger is scarcely over when his rage for battle flares up again (325), but, not altogether unwillingly and not altogether unconsciously, he allows his divine sister to draw him away from Aeneas, until his former sense of honour slowly reawakens, and he realizes that it is his duty to avenge his own people's suffering; this, together with Saces' urgent appeal (653ff.), finally forces him to confront Aeneas: but now his passions are running twice as high (*amens* [622, 742] [crazed], *amens formidine* [776] [crazed with fear], *mixto insania luctu et furiis agitatus amor* [667] [madness and misery blending, love tormented by passion for revenge], *hunc sine me furere ante furorem* [680] ['First, let me do this one mad deed before I die']) – and his fate is sealed. As his enemy is already poising the fatal spear, Turnus snatches up a huge rock, an ancient boundary stone, to fling at his opponent – Virgil here makes very effective use of the Homeric contrast between the strength of his heroes, and οἷοι νῦν βροτοί εἰσιν [those of his own generation], and even increases it – but it is too heavy, his knees give way as he tries to run, and the blood freezes in his veins – and the stone falls short of its target. A striking symbol of Turnus' fate: he has set himself a task which was too great for him, despite his enormous strength. He had not been able to go calmly to meet his enemy in the final duel; neither can he face death with a steady mind now. He does not sink so low as to beg for his life (*nec deprecor* [931] [I make no appeal]), but his last words express a fervent desire to live, and to save his skin he is even prepared to give up his claim to Lavinia (936): Virgil implies that anyone capable of that, has never been worthy either of her or of the throne.[48]

 The figure of Mezentius stands in sharp contrast to Turnus. According to the tradition, he was *contemptor divom* (7.648) [scorner of gods]: he is said to have demanded from the Rutulians the first-fruits which were usually dedicated to the gods; this led the Latins to pray to Jupiter to grant them victory if he wanted the first-fruits for himself, as hitherto, instead of letting Mezentius have them.[49] The tradition also said that Mezentius' son Lausus fell in battle, and that this was the essential reason that led the king to urge that peace should be made. Virgil was not able to make use of the traditional example of the Etruscan king's godlessness – because there was no occasion for Mezentius to make such a demand in the scheme of his poem – but he adapts the motif skilfully to his own ends. Traditionally, Mezentius demanded that the honours due to the gods be paid to himself. In Virgil (10.773) his only gods are his strong right arm and the weapon it bears.[50] It is to

212

213

these that he addresses his prayers: he wants to adorn his son with the armour of his dead enemy and thus erect as it were a *tropaeum* [trophy] to himself, which the pious Aeneas eventually dedicates to the gods instead (see above p. 165); other blasphemous utterances also characterize him as *contemptor divom* [scorner of gods].[51] However, in his account of the Lausus incident, Virgil portrays a particularly close relationship between father and son, and it was easy to develop this relationship so that Mezentius' love for his son becomes the only vulnerable spot in an otherwise granite character, and also to represent this love as reciprocal, and to

214   transform Lausus' death in battle into a voluntary self-sacrifice undertaken for the sake of his father. So as to increase our pity for Lausus, the poet portrays him as a shining, heroic figure, and thus he stands in sharp contrast to his father (7.654). Moreover, Virgil, who had decided to introduce the Etruscans as Aeneas' allies (see p. 146 above), had to present them as independent of Mezentius: he achieves this by inventing the story that he is a cruel tyrant who has been expelled by his subjects because of all his brutal acts. Virgil attributes to him stories which Aristotle, and Cicero after him, had told about the cruel behaviour of Etruscan pirates (8.485). Virgil further exploits the split between Mezentius and his own people by using it as the third motif in the combats in which he takes part: they begin with the tyrant being attacked in hate and fury by his own subjects (10.691f.) – this gives new life to the Homeric simile of the boar encircled by huntsmen; they culminate in Mezentius' cry of misery when he realises that Lausus' death is the punishment for his own actions and for the first time regrets them because they have brought shame and destruction upon his son (851); and they end when he is defeated and begs that his body should be protected from the wrath of his own people (903ff.): here too we have a characteristically Virgilian contrast with Hector's plea that his body should be returned to his own people. It may perhaps seem surprising that Virgil has refrained from illustrating Mezentius' cruelty by making him perform some atrocity during the battle – that would have been easy for him, but effects of this kind were alien to his artistic ideals, which completely rejected τὸ μιαρόν [repulsive behaviour]; it makes a difference whether the poet puts accounts of such behaviour in the mouth of, for example, Evander or Achaemenides, or narrates it himself, thus setting it directly before the reader's eyes. Nevertheless, it is no mere accident that Mezentius plants his foot on his fallen foe while he is still alive, leaning on the spear which has pierced the dying man (10.736); and certainly, although the plot does not demand that Mezentius should order his men in the midst of the battle to raise the paean that the Achaeans sang when they returned to camp after the death of Hector, the picture of the triumphal song reaching the ear of the dying man has a powerful emotional effect (10.738). Similarly, there is a deliberate contrast between Aeneas, who does not take Lausus' weapons as spoil, and Mezentius, who threatens to ride

215   away from the battlefield with Aeneas' severed head on display among the bloody spoils on his horse (862). Furthermore, Virgil has carefully contrasted what we might call the nervous courage of the youthful Turnus with the unshakeable iron calm of this giant with his grey hair and his long beard, who withstands attacks from every side like a rock which remains steadfast amidst the storms that rage around it (693), who has no fear even of Aeneas and prepares to confront him *et mole sua stat* (771) [solid in his own great bulk], and who can be thrown off balance only by the

death of his beloved son. And whereas Turnus at the moment of his death is afraid of dying and is prepared to concede defeat in exchange for his life, Mezentius himself calls on his enemy to strike the fatal blow: life is not worth living if he is vanquished, and even his battle-steed would scorn to submit to a Trojan master (865).

Camilla, the maiden who rejoices in battle, swift of foot, tireless, resolute, with a pride that is easily inflamed (11.686, 709) and an innocence in the face of cunning, fearless and conscious of her duty even at the moment of her death (825), makes a stronger impression on our imagination than perhaps any other character in Virgil.[52] The clearest indication of her irresistible strength is that her enemies do not dare to confront her face to face in open battle: one tries to escape from her by a ruse, another kills her by throwing his javelin at her from the safety of a hidden position and does not even dare to go near her after he has wounded her. But for all her heroism she remains a woman, and feminine weakness brings her death:[53] coveting the gleaming armour of Chloreus she forgets everything else and so falls victim to Arruns, who has been lying in wait for her after trying in vain for so long to find a   216
weak spot: she is so completely intent on acquiring the dazzling prize that she is the only one who does not see and hear the fatal javelin hurtling towards her; her faithful Volscians see disaster approaching but cannot prevent it, and she sinks to the ground before her women can catch her in their arms.

The counterpart of Aeneas, the ideal of the mature warrior, is Pallas the ideal youth. We see his achievements; we see how by word and example he makes his wavering troops stand firm; we recognize in the words that he utters his sense of honour (10.371) and his habitual piety (421ff., 460f.) which relies on supernatural help; at one and the same time we admire and deplore the youthful boldness of spirit which leads him to accept Turnus' challenge, though Turnus is a warrior of over-whelming strength, and he knows very well how much weaker he is (459, cf. 11.153, 174). For him the highest good is not life but victory and a glorious death (450); he himself says so, Jupiter comforts the sorrowful Hercules with the same idea (467ff.), and the same thought is enough to make his grief-stricken father pull himself together (11.166ff.); better to die in victory than to live on in shame: it is this conviction that assuages Aeneas' pity for Pallas' father (55). Pallas, sent out to battle from the future site of Rome, is the first great sacrifice made on Italian soil in the sacred name of Rome; he was fighting not only against the ancient enemies of his native city (8.474, 569), but also for the sake of its glorious future (11.168). His lifeless body is brought back to his father, *dolor atque decus magnum* (10.507) [a source of bitter pain and of high pride] as the poet puts it with the brevity of a graven epitaph; times without number Rome's sons will fall in battle, and she will look on them with the same bitter pride. The lamentations which now rise up around the body of Pallas are lamentations for the generations to come; so too is the solemn pomp of his funeral; anyone who is not aware of this is welcome to make cheap criticisms of the poet for his sentimentality.

Pathos of a very different kind is evoked by the story of Nisus and Euryalus. Here again it is instructive to compare it with its source, the *Doloneia* (Book 10 of the *Iliad*). It is quite clear that both the broad outline and the details[54] are derived from   217
Homer; but it is equally clear that Virgil always tends to reshape his material into

something new. Instead of a long and tedious exposition – Homer takes 200 lines to bring his commanders together for a consultation – Virgil concentrates on the main characters:[55] the narrative begins with them and remains with them, while the council of the Trojan leaders, to which they wish to gain admittance, is described in a few lines only (9.224-30). Whereas in Homer we have an epic narrative that unfolds in one steady sweep, in Virgil we find lively pathos, dramatic movement, a *peripeteia* [reversal of fortune] at the peak of success, an increase in tension leading to the final revenge and death of Nisus. But the greatest contrast is between Homer's portrayal of the deed performed by two bold and cautious heroes, where the reader is charmed by the deed itself and its success, and Virgil's emphasis on the psychological development to which the outward events are a mere accompaniment. It is in Nisus' ambitious and adventurous spirit that the plan for the enterprise is born (186, 194); Euryalus agrees with it (205f.) and his determination overcomes his friend's reservations. But it is precisely this ambition, which is the driving force for their bold enterprise, that leads to their downfall. Even before they set out, they are already intending not simply to perform their mission but also to return *cum spoliis ingenti caede peracta* (242) [with spoils, after wreaking a havoc of slaughter]; they have chosen a route which will bring them safely through the enemy's lines, but they give way to the temptation to turn the enemy camp, where all are asleep, into a blood-

218 bath.[56] The bold deed is successful: Nisus is intelligent enough to restrain Euryalus' childish lack of foresight (354), but not intelligent enough to deny him the pleasure of adorning himself with booty from the men he has killed. As a result, he escapes the enemy cavalry himself, but Euryalus pays the price of his *hybris*: the shining helmet betrays him, the weapons he has looted weigh him down (384), and he falls into enemy hands. When Nisus loses him and then sees that he has been captured by the Volscian cavalry, his only thought is his desire to rescue his friend; he tries to give him an opportunity to escape by throwing his spears to create a diversion, but this is unsuccessful; when he sees his friend in mortal danger, he loses his head: he throws himself forward *amens* (424) [madly] and begs them to kill him and spare his friend. In vain: he can only avenge his friend's death and then, mortally wounded,

219 cast himself onto his body. Thus they both meet their deaths not because of external circumstances, or because of their hatred of the gods, but because of their own passions: *sua cuique deus fit dira cupido?* (185) [or do we all attribute to a god what is really an overmastering impulse of our own?], as Nisus himself had said with unconscious prescience. Their mistake[57] was that they both allowed themselves to be carried away and gave precedence to other passions over their immediate duty; but this mistake arose from noble impulses, and they paid for it with their lives. Who will find fault with Virgil because he does not add a narrow-minded moralizing epilogue, ὡς ἀπόλοιτο καὶ ἄλλος [so perish any other man who shall do such a deed], but gives full rein to sorrow and admiration?

6. Structure

It only remains to look at the structure of the four great battle-descriptions. We shall see that Virgil's main concern in the arrangement of the material in the individual acts and scenes was the same as in the overall plan of the whole narrative of the war (see pp. 146f. above): namely, above all to avoid what annoyed him even more than us in so many comparable passages in the *Iliad* – the lack of organization, and the arbitrary to-ing and fro-ing. His main aims at this level too were clarity of structure and clarity of purpose.

First, where a large number of persons have to be listed, it will help the reader if they are divided into groups. Virgil found precedents for this device in the *Iliad*[58] and developed it systematically. This can be seen most clearly in the battle for the camp in Book 9: first come the contrasting fates of two Trojans (545-68); then a 'scene of butchery'; when the first pair is mentioned each is allotted a single line, which begins with his name: 220

Ilioneus saxo atque ingenti fragmine montis
Lucetium portae subeuntem ignisque ferentem (569-70)

[Ilioneus with a stone like some huge crag from a mountain (brought down) Lucetius, equipped for fire-raising, advancing on a gate]; and then two pairs, with only the victors characterized:

Emathiona Liger, Corynaeum sternit Asilas,
his iaculo bonus, hic longe fallente sagitta (571-2)

[and Liger slew Emathion and Asilas Corynaeus; Liger had a sure aim with the javelin and Asilas with the arrow flying from afar unseen]; then two more pairs, without any characterization, but one is first victorious, then beaten:

Ortygium Caeneus, victorem Caenea Turnus (573)

[next Caenus slew Ortygius, and Turnus Caeneus, in his moment of victory]; the poet lingers on Turnus; first there are two pairs in one line:

Turnus Ityn Cloniumque, Dioxippum Promolumque (574)

[and Turnus slew Itys also, and Clonius, Dioxippus, Promolus –]; thus up to this point the account has become progressively more compressed[59] but now it expands again with yet another pair, whose names come at the beginning and end of the line:

et Sagarim et summis stantem pro turribus Idan

[Sagaris and, as he stood in defence at the top of the turreted wall, Idas], and finally two more detailed descriptions, the death of an attacker (576-80) and of a defender (581-9). The Ascanius episode follows (590-671); then the pair Pandarus and Bitias appear: they kill four men (864f.); their action is then avenged by Turnus killing four in turn (696-702), and in addition Bitias and Pandarus themselves (703-55); then Turnus, rampaging through the camp, kills first Phaleris and Gyges, Halys and Phegeus; then four who are named in one line (767); finally, four more (768-79),   221 until at last the Trojan pair Mnestheus and Serestus put an end to the flight of their men. We can see that throughout the entire account, with a few exceptions, there is an emphasis, sometimes greater, sometimes less, on groups of two or four. The one example that we have examined may suffice; the principle is not, in fact, carried through so consistently in the following books. Rather different, although equally striking in its symmetry, is the structure of the section from 12.500 onwards, which narrates the achievements of Aeneas and Turnus in different parts of the battlefield: the introductory lines (500-4) are followed by Aeneas (505-8), Turnus (509-12), Aeneas (513-15), Turnus (516-37) – in other words the pattern is ABAB. Then comes a simile illustrating the raging fury of the two heroes (521-8); then Aeneas: Turnus (529-37), Turnus: Aeneas (538-41), i.e. the pattern is ABBA. The detailed description of the death of a Trojan (542-7) (at whose hand is not stated) leads into a brief general description of the battlefield (548-53), with which the section comes to an end.

The pace of the narrative is different in each of the four books; but although Virgil avoids monotony, he follows the same artistic principles in each case. This will become evident from a rapid survey.

The storming of the camp in Book 9 begins with a general description (503-24), in which the great contingents appear first: the Volscians, Trojans, Rutulians are named, then other contingents are referred to by the names of their leaders Mezentius and Messapus without any further details. These two provide the transition to Turnus, who is placed emphatically in the foreground by means of the poet's appeal to the Muses (525-9). Turnus begins by destroying one main tower; two Trojans escape from the collapsing debris, of whom he captures one and pulls down part of the wall in doing so (530-66). This leads to a fiercer onslaught by the attackers, which is countered with equal energy by the defenders. This is where Virgil places the scene of butchery that we have just discussed (p. 171); it reaches its climax with Turnus' exploits (up to 575) and concludes with two accounts of individual incidents, of which the last, as we have seen on p. 171 above, prepares the way for the Ascanius episode (up to 658). Ascanius' success and the manifest support of the gods gives new heart to the opposing Trojan forces (to 671), among whom Pandarus and Bitias are the boldest: they open the gate, and kill the men who rush in; the Trojans even advance out into the open (to 690). In doing so, they disobey Aeneas' explicit orders (42): and at this point, the moment of the Trojans' greatest success, a vigorous reversal begins with Turnus' assault. Those who have advanced furthest from the camp fall at his hand; then he kills Bitias at the gate itself. The Trojans retreat, Turnus is shut inside the camp as a result of the carelessness of Pandarus, whom he kills (the combat between the two is given prominence by Parndarus' attack and by their two speeches; it is depicted as the culmination of Turnus' exploits); blind panic seizes the camp. But Turnus (see p. 166 above), in his mad thirst for slaughter, misses his chance to destroy the entire Trojan army, and although he does kill large numbers as they retreat or are taken by surprise, yet he cannot keep going for long single-handed. As soon as the Trojan leaders hear of the situation, and Mnestheus' speech brings the panic-stricken men to their senses, they attack him with closed ranks (788). He is finally forced to retreat, although reluctantly and making further assaults as he does so. Juno withdraws her support, which

222

had protected him at the moment of greatest danger (745) and until now had increased his strength. When he leaps fully-armed into the Tiber and is safely reunited with his own men, his retreat constitutes another heroic achievement.

To summarize: the narrative leads gradually towards Turnus; it first shows him performing an important feat, after which it leaves him occasionally, only to return to him in a most natural way each time, and finally is totally concentrated on him. He is the centre of interest, and yet we are given not just a picture of him, but of the whole battle. Moreover, Virgil devotes the greatest care to maintaining the continuity of the narrative. One of the best ways of achieving this is to mention how the 223 exploits of some individual hero affect the army as a whole, and how this in turn gives rise to further brave deeds by individuals. Furthermore: the narrative does not progress in a straight line, as for example if Turnus had been shown gaining an uninterrupted series of successes; on the contrary, his first successes provoke a counter-offensive from the Trojans, which he has to overcome, and the conclusion is brought about by another counter-offensive. Finally: the narrative is not related at one constant pitch, nor does it rise and fall arbitrarily, but in a carefully planned series of crescendos; and every time that the action reaches a climax, there is a *peripeteia*. Because of the nature of the plot, the most powerful effect cannot be reserved for the final scene, so Virgil gives the end of the episode an unusual form, and avoids a serious anticlimax by creating a final upsurge of interest. There is no repetition whatever of any individual motifs or incidents. One passage which is really a digression, and is characterized as such by the mass of detail lavished on its telling, is Ascanius' shot (9.590ff.); but this treatment is justified by its importance for the plot[60] and it is integrated into the main narrative by many fine threads that link it to what has gone before and what is to come.

These qualities stand out even more clearly if we compare this scene with the corresponding section of the *Iliad*, although the Battle at the Wall (*Teichomachia*, Book 12) is one of the most unified and self-contained parts of the work. It begins with a very detailed account of Hector's strange plan to drive his chariot across the ditch in front of the wall, until he is dissuaded by the sensible advice of Polydamas. The whole scene merely serves as a preparation for Asios' exploit: for he drives his chariot, not however over the ditch to the wall, but to an open gate, which he could 224 obviously have reached just as easily had he been fighting on foot. This gate is defended by the two Lapiths who were taken over by Virgil and integrated into the main action. In Homer we leave this part of the battlefield without learning what becomes of Asios. The other Trojans swarm over the ditch, after Hector has overridden Polydamas' scruples arising from his interpretation of the portent of the eagle. Sarpedon's attack on the wall is described in detail, and Homer says that without him the Trojans would not have succeeded in forcing an entry into the camp. However, we do not see them doing so: instead, after Sarpedon has pulled down part of the parapet and tried in vain to climb the wall, Hector uses a boulder to smash the wall open in a completely different place – something that he could have done anyway at the start. In the following books, 13 and 14, Homer's narrative is much more disjointed. Virgil was compelled by the nature of his subject-matter to invent and to compress. He could not allow the enemy to rush in all at once, as in Homer, since the Trojans' movements are always restricted by the fact that there are too few of them to risk an open battle. Besides, he wanted to avoid anticipating the large-scale fighting that he will have to describe several times later on; so, since Aeneas is absent, he uses this episode as an opportunity to establish Turnus' character from the start in its true light. He therefore depicts him as the only one to enter the camp and escape from it again unscathed.[61] It was not possible to combine this episode with an attack on the ships: Virgil has separated the Battle at the Wall from 225 the Battle at the Ships (*Epinausimache*) and made the incident which corresponds to the latter occur on the previous day.[62]

The structure of the battle-scenes in Book 10 is a good deal more complicated. Here Pallas and Mezentius have to fall in battle, Turnus and above all Aeneas have to take their proper place in the foreground, but they cannot be allowed to meet in combat, since that would anticipate the decisive duel. Virgil begins with the renewed attack on the camp and the desperate plight of the few defenders within (122); then he describes Aeneas' voyage and the Etruscan ships, including a catalogue of them; Cymodocea informs Aeneas about the situation of his men, and we learn at the same time that the Arcadian cavalry and some of the Etruscans have advanced by land and have already taken up their appointed position.[63] Our attention is focussed on the situation on land, so that we can fully appreciate the effect of Aeneas' arrival. The Trojans are the first to catch sight of him, the enemy are bewildered by their joyful cries and fresh courage until, turning round, they see that the ships have already reached the shore. Turnus is not discouraged, but now (285) he has to form a second front with the greater part of his troops. Then Aeneas and his men disembark, and there is a battle at the ships, which, as is only to be expected, involves a series of daring deeds performed by Aeneas. Virgil feels that he should explain why Aeneas does not encounter Turnus in battle immediately; it must however be admitted that his motivation seems somewhat contrived.[64] While Aeneas 226 is engaged in his successful encounters,[65] the enemy commanders, Clausus, Halaesus and Messapus, arrive. The fighting comes to a standstill, and then ebbs and flows indecisively for a long time (*anceps pugna diu* [359] [the fight is long in balance]): this allows us to leave this part of the battlefield.

The poet takes us to another position, to the aforementioned Arcadians and Pallas:[66] here begins the action which leads by a logical progression to the final catastrophe of Book 10. In the first place, Pallas has to die. To kindle our sympathy, he is given his own *aristeia*, which, apart from its immediate consequences, causes the Arcadians to call a halt to their retreat (397, 402f.) and even to force their way forward again (410): here the action begins to turn against Pallas, with the successes of Halaesus, whose defeat forms the climax and crown of Pallas' *aristeia*, and who therefore needs to be characterized as a heroic figure by being given a series of successes. This is the ideal moment to introduce Lausus in a neat piece of plot-construction (οἰκονομία) which prepares us for his later intervention. Abas is the only one of his victims to be mentioned by name, but all that is needed is that Lausus should bring the struggle against Pallas to a halt again (431) – he would not, of course, be able to maintain his position for long without Turnus, who at this point strikes down Pallas, after all his great deeds; in an epilogue (501-9) the poet gives this event special emphasis and refers to the effects that it will have on the distant future, since it is an exception to Virgil's usual practice in having no immediate consequences for Turnus. The news of Pallas' death sets Aeneas' anger most furiously ablaze. We left him engaged in an inconclusive struggle; now he forces his 227 way forward in victory. The second list of his feats, which starts at this point, represents a higher level of achievement than the first (as we have already pointed out, p. 166 above). It comes to a close with the most detailed account, that of the death of the two brothers Lucagus and Liger. The result is that the Trojans have broken through the encircling ring of besiegers, and relieved Ascanius and his men (604). Aeneas' next task ought to have been to wreak vengeance on Turnus (514); the duel could not be postponed any longer, but it would have served no purpose had it been described here. That is why Turnus is lured away from the battlefield by a mirage of Aeneas sent by Juno, and carried back to his native city. In his place, Mezentius steps into the foreground and performs a succession of feats which brings the counter-offensive to the height of its success; his last feat, the killing of Orodes, which is celebrated by the paean, concludes the description of his achievements. In the scene of butchery that follows (747-54) it is almost always the Latins who are the victors, and they seem to have more or less equalled Aeneas' achievements (*iam gravis aequabat luctus et mutua Mavors funera* [755f.] [now Mars pressed heavily on both sides and gave equal share of anguish and equal exchange of death to both]). The moment for the decisive duel between Aeneas and Mezentius has arrived. A new start with a new description of the terrifying Mezentius prepares us for the importance of this last combat (762). The episode does not develop in a straightforward manner. When Lausus sacrifices himself, and thus allows his wounded father to retreat in safety, a decisive outcome seems to have been frustrated; but it is Lausus' death that brings Mezentius back into the battle. Melancholy and tired of life, he mounts his trusty steed, and when it collapses, mortally wounded, he is trapped under it and is at the mercy of his opponent's sword. This is the most effective scene in the book, and it brings it to an end; there is not another word about the further course of the battle or of the day. Every sympathetic reader will of course realize that once the chief commanders of the Latins, Turnus, Halaesus, Lausus and Mezentius have all been removed from the scene and the beleaguered Trojans have broken out, then the fate of the day has been decided; but Virgil would have stated this explicitly only if he had been a historian, or a poet who cared more about factual accuracy and the satisfaction of pedantic readers than the effect that his work would have on his readers' emotions.

The complex structure of this first great battle stands in sharp contrast to the simple cavalry intermezzo of Book 11. This is basically Camilla's *aristeia*; but, in order to provide a general engagement of the troops as a background for her 228 exploits, this is described, first in detail as it gradually breaks out, then with emphasis on individual figures – Orsilochus on the Trojan side, Catillus on the Latin side; and this provides the transition to Camilla, the most distinguished of the warriors. But she too appears first within a general description (648-63), to allow the reader to imagine the context in which her individual exploits will take place in the following scenes: two introductory lines (646f.) arouse our attention. There follows her actual *aristeia*, which ends with her boldest and mightiest deed, which furthermore is described in the greatest detail: it is the crown of her success. In the manner now familiar to us, the counter-offensive then supervenes: Tarchon's speech and bold action,[67] and the consequent revival of the fallen morale of his men (758), one of whom, Arruns, now conceives the plan of slaying Camilla without facing her in the open. Her own carelessness, the causes of which have already been discussed (p. 169), gives him his opportunity: Camilla is slain (759-835). The action up to this point, that is, the whole of the battle in which Camilla is involved, is framed by two scenes in which the gods appear. Beforehand, Diana presents Opis with a bow and arrow, to avenge the death of her beloved Camilla (533-96); afterwards, Opis carries out the mission by laying Arruns low (836-67). Clearly this framing arrangement deliberately marks off the story of Camilla as a separate section, although it does contain threads that link it with what has gone before and what is to come. For, of course, the poet cannot end at this point, with the death of Camilla. We still need to be told what has happened to Turnus since Juno lured him from the battlefield. His rapid return (which rescues Aeneas from great danger) is motivated by the success of the Trojans, and the greater their success, the more plausible is this motivation. There follows an extremely lively description of the pursuit of the Latin cavalry,

229 their annihilation beneath the city walls, and the battle at the gates (868-95). This also forms an effective counterpart to the description of the arrival of the armies at the beginning (597-607). Furthermore, the arrival of the armies was immediately preceded by the account of Turnus' departure from his camp (522-31); so too the final scene of the battle is immediately followed by the account of Turnus' return to his camp (896-902). A description of the new situation brought about by the cavalry victory brings the book to a close. The Trojan camp is no longer far away on the bank of the Tiber, but under the city walls. The Trojans have moved from defence to attack.

The last book begins with Turnus' decision to fight a duel, and ends with this duel and Turnus' death. The poet uses all the means at his disposal to delay this outcome and at the same time maintain the interest of the reader. The first retardation is brought about by Latinus and Amata, and – unintentionally – by Lavinia; it is soon overcome and it is irrevocably decided that the duel shall take place (1-112).[68]

230 But already, while the people are gathering where the oaths are to be sworn, Juno's speech to Juturna paves the way for another retardation; and when the oaths have been sworn Turnus' own behaviour[69] and its effects on the Rutulians who are standing near him cause Juturna to intervene; she causes the restlessness to spread to the Laurentines and the Latins;[70] the ambiguous omen of the eagle transforms hostile feelings into action; Tolumnius, the augur,[71] throws the first spear and strikes one of nine brothers; the other eight are understandably eager to avenge him, the Laurentines advance against them, while the Trojans, Etruscans and Arcadians come to the aid of the brothers. Thus gradually everyone finds himself in the grip of the re-kindled rage for battle, and a tumultous struggle develops around the altar. Aeneas still believes that he can control it, but he is wounded by an arrow from the bow of an unidentified archer. Now that Aeneas has withdrawn, there is nothing to prevent the battle beginning.

It is certainly true that Pandarus' shot in Book 4 of the *Iliad* is the prototype of Tolumnius' shot. Modern Virgilian critics agree on this, but seem to think that this leaves nothing more to be said about Virgil's use of his model. On the contrary, I think that this incident provides an unparalleled opportunity to gain a true understanding of the nature of Virgil's skill in adapting the work of his predecessor. In Homer, Aphrodite removes Paris from the field of battle when he is at the mercy of Menelaus; Menelaus searches everywhere for him, in vain; and none of the Trojans, even, can say what has become of him; they wish that they could, since they all loathe him as much as grim death itself. Agamemnon then demands that the duel shall be regarded as concluded, and the condition satisfied (end of Book 3). Meanwhile, however, Athena has come disguised as Laodocus to Pandarus (there is a detailed description of the scene in Olympus that leads up to this), and has advised him to shoot at Menelaus: this would earn him the gratitude and respect of all the Trojans, and of Paris above all. The foolish Pandarus is soon ready: there are extremely graphic descriptions of the bow, the preparations for the shot, and of the shot itself. Thanks to the intervention of Athena, Menelaus is only wounded, not killed; we are told in great detail exactly how he is wounded. Then comes a long speech by Agamemnon to Menelaus, but the latter reassures him and says that he is in no real danger; the herald is sent to the doctor and delivers his message; the doctor arrives, extracts the arrow from the wound, and applies healing herbs which his father had been given by the friendly Cheiron. Meanwhile, the Trojan troops are advancing. Agamemnon, for his part, goes round the troops to give them advice and encouragement (his great ἐπιπώλησις [tour of the camp], which occupies some 200 lines), then the armies meet in battle. How vividly and vigorously Homer describes all the external aspects of this narrative, both visible and audible! He gives us enough details to try to reconstruct Pandarus' bow and Menelaus' intricate armour; we hear the vibration of the bow, the twang of the string, and the arrow whistling through the air; we see it strike its target and the blood stain Menelaus' thigh, shin and calf with its purple flow; but how little about the emotions and – Virgil would no doubt have added – how tediously the narrative drags itself forward, and how badly its details are motivated! Homeric critics of our own day [1903] have been driven to the hypothesis that originally the Πάριδος καὶ Μενελάου μονομαχία [duel between Paris and Menelaus] had nothing to do with the ὅρκων σύγχυσις [violation of the truce], and that many other inconsistencies are to be attributed to later authors and redactors. Virgil, however, was a practical critic, not a critic of history. In Homer, all the Trojans and their allies, including Pandarus and his Lycians, hate Paris like hell itself, and yet, in order to gain Paris' gratitude, Pandarus is prepared to shoot his treacherous arrow, and the Lycians are prepared to protect him with their shields while he does so. And once the shot has hit its mark, no-one thinks for another moment of honouring the truce; instead of stoning Pandarus, the Trojans advance in battle-order, and Agamemnon, instead of trying to appeal to his troops' sense of honour, orders them to fight against them. The assembly on Olympus, the conversation between Agamemnon and Menelaus, the treatment by the doctor, Agamemnon's tour of the camp to encourage his men, are, according to modern literary theory, delaying devices characteristic of early epic, but in Virgil's view they disturbed and interrupted the main flow of the narrative. That is why he placed the decisive scene on Olympus before this episode, and the healing of Aeneas and the advance of the Trojan leaders and their troops after it. He is most careful to describe the motives which led to the actual breaking of the truce.[72] We see the Latins becoming gradually more and more antagonistic towards the duel, until the

231

232

interpretation of the omen by an apparently well-qualified augur brings their emotions to a head; we see the stages which lead gradually to the outbreak of fighting, and Aeneas trying in vain to enforce the terms of the treaty, until his absence inspires Turnus, too, with fresh courage; after which, of course, it is impossible to call a halt. Thus in Virgil all the emphasis is placed on the dramatic development of the action, and its psychological motivation. Virgil has retained only two lines out of all the detailed descriptions in Homer, those which describe the exact place where Gylippus was hit by Tolumnius' spear.

While Aeneas is away from the battlefield, it is important that the action should not stand still. The gap is occupied by Turnus' deeds (324-82), recounted in an elevated style which is suitable for the heightened emotional mood of the narrative as it approaches its conclusion. Whereas in Book 9 we saw Turnus fighting on foot, against heavy odds, and in Book 11 emerging victorious from a duel, now he drives his chariot across the field like the God of War himself, destroying all before him. The structure of the scene is somewhat different from those which we have examined so far. The main stress is laid on the single combat in the middle of the scene (346-61), which is given special prominence by the speech of Turnus – *en agros et quam bello Troiane petisti Hesperiam metire iacens; haec praemia qui me ferro ausi temptare ferunt: sic moenia condunt* (359-61) ['See Trojan! Lie there, and measure your length in the fields of our Western Land which you sought to gain by war. This is the prize which they win who dare to make test of me by the blade; this is how they establish their walled city'] – words addressed to Eumedes, but in fact aimed at Aeneas. This combat is framed by two lists of names (341-5 and 362-4), which in turn are framed by two general descriptions of the irresistible force of Turnus as he storms against the foe (328-40 and 365-70): the death of Phegeus, who throws himself in vain against Turnus' horses, and is dragged along and finally crushed by the chariot (371-82), serves as an illustration of Turnus' triumphal progress.[73] There is no climax leading up to the end in this case, because Virgil cannot begin to describe the reversal of Turnus' fortunes so early in the book.

233

While the exploits of Turnus keep the action moving, Virgil is able to describe the treatment of Aeneas' wound without giving the impression of holding up the narrative. Virgil has combined the situation of Hector in the *Iliad* (15.236ff.), whose strength is renewed by Zeus and Apollo so that he is able to return to the battle, and motifs taken from the healing of Menelaus by Machaon in *Iliad* 4.192ff., of Eurypylus by Patroclus in 11.842ff. and of Glaucus by Apollo in 16.508ff., and has combined them in such a way that here too the simple epic narrative becomes excitingly dramatic. Iapyx tries in vain to pull the arrow from the wound: all the skills at his command seem ineffectual; already the roar of the battle is coming closer, clouds of dust are darkening the air, enemy missiles are already falling into the midst of the camp: then Aphrodite comes to his aid – not with her own hands, but by pouring drops of the sap of a miraculous herb into the water, and now Iapyx, who bathes the wound with this water, unaware of its new quality, suddenly succeeds: the arrow comes away in his hand, the blood clots and the pain vanishes; there is now nothing to prevent Aeneas from returning to the fight, and his reappearance on the scene together with his faithful friends immediately changes the nature of the situation (447, 463). His mind is fixed on Turnus – it looks as if the duel is going to take place immediately, but then comes the final retardation, Juturna's attempt to take Turnus away where Aeneas cannot reach him, by assuming the appearance of his charioteer Metiscus. Still Aeneas pursues him, and him alone – for he still cannot bring himself to disregard his side of the *foedus* [treaty] – until Messapus' attack makes it impossible for him to observe it any longer (496). Then come the interwoven *aristeiai* of Aeneas and Turnus which we have already analysed (p. 172). The artistic purpose of this unusual structure is clear. From the beginning of the fighting until the end, the two main opponents are gradually brought closer to each other. In Books 8 and 9 they had both been in action in totally different areas. In Book 10 they were fighting 234 in the same battle, but did not meet or have anything to do with each other, apart from their mutual longing to fight. In Book 12 we have been hearing about Aeneas and Turnus alternately, first at fairly long intervals, but now in rapid succession. All this conspires to create the illusion of an ever stronger magnetic attraction between the two heroes, which must inevitably lead them to a final collision.

The poet handles the action in such a way that Turnus is spared the humiliation of being overtaken by Aeneas and therefore compelled to fight, or simply being slain by him. Strong motivation needs to be provided to lead him to the decision to fight the duel that he has avoided for so long – Virgil takes this opportunity to dispose of Amata, the chief opponent of the new alliance, something which, for artistic reasons, had to occur before the end of the work – but finally Turnus' better self gains the upper hand, he goes forth to meet his opponent of his own free will, and the great final scene of the epic can at last begin.

The duel between Hector and Achilles in *Iliad* 22, which was the prototype for the final duel in the *Aeneid*, is described in three scenes; first, Hector's flight and pursuit; second, after the weighing of their souls and as a result of Athena's intervention, each hero throws his spear but misses; third, the close combat: Hector attacks with his sword, Achilles wounds him fatally with his spear. The first scene also includes the conversation between Zeus and Athena which decides Hector's fate. (This, of course, grossly contradicts the weighing of the souls.) Virgil has preserved the individual elements of this narrative, but he has changed their order and transformed them in many ways – although in this case, of course, where his predecessor had created a magnificent and unified composition, disfigured only by trivial interpolations, Virgil could not give his art as much free rein as elsewhere.

Virgil, like Homer, presents the duel in three phases, after he has brought the scene vividly before our eyes by describing the mood of the spectators (704-9).[74] First, after each hero has cast his spear once,[75] we have a long, indecisive sword-fight; then the interlude, which contains Jupiter's weighing of their fates (725-7).[76] The second phase begins when Turnus' sword breaks,[77] so that there is nothing he 235 can do but take to his heels; this guarantees his safety for a while, since, because of his wound, Aeneas cannot run as fast. While Aeneas is struggling in vain to pull his spear out of the tree-trunk, Juturna returns Turnus' sword to him, Venus helps Aeneas with his spear, and they come face to face again, armed for another fight. So the decision has been deferred yet again. But then, because Juturna has returned Turnus' sword, Jupiter intervenes: his remonstrations cause Juno to renounce her enmity at last, and peace between Trojans and Latins is decreed in heaven. It is remarkable that in this passage Virgil uncharacteristically interrupts the course of

'ith a long interlude on Olympus, although he is careful to mention a
'is passage, which relieves the tension of battle – *adsistunt contra*
rtis anheli (790) [they stood facing each other again, panting, but
  ᴏr combat under the rule of Mars] – and is essential for another reason too:
ᴛne assuagement of Juno's anger has to be postponed until the last possible moment,
since once this final cause of delay – which is in fact the only one left – has been
overcome, the action must inevitably come to a close. Juno's anger opened the
poem, and her reconciliation has to end it; what follows, the death of Turnus, is only
her resignation made manifest in the world of mortals. But Virgil has taken care to
make it clear that this intermezzo is no mere technical necessity, but that it is also
essential for the furtherance of the plot: up to this point, all the prophecies have
spoken only of the rule of Aeneas and his family: now we hear that not only Troy
but Latium too will come into its own within the new alliance: we gain the impression that Juno's efforts and struggles have not after all been completely wasted.
The despatch of the *Dira* [dread Daimon] begins the third and final scene. Juturna
leaves her brother; Turnus freezes with fear; he realizes that the gods are against
him. He no longer dares to fight with the sword: Juturna's final attempt to help her
brother has been in vain. Finally, he tries to hurl the great boulder, and fails; while
236 he looks about him in desperation, he is struck by his opponent's spear and thrown
to the ground. Hector speaks his last words as he dies, and he is concerned only with
the disposal of his body: but Virgil does not cease to strive for dramatic tension to
the very end of the poem: there is one more glimmer of hope for Turnus as Aeneas
considers the possibility of sparing his life. But that glimmer is extinguished when
the sight of Pallas' sword-belt reminds the victorious Aeneas of his duty to avenge
his death – *ast illi solvuntur frigore membra, vitaque cum gemitu fugit indignata sub
umbras* (951-2) [and Turnus' limbs relaxed and chilled; and the life fled, moaning,
resentful, to the shades].

Notes to Chapter 5

171   1. For details cf. F. Cauer, *Die römische Aeneassage* (Jahrb. Suppl. XV), although this contains much with which I cannot agree. The author makes no attempt
to throw any light on the aims and methods that are peculiar to Virgil.

172   2. In Cato, Lavinia seems to have played no part at all; Servius on 6.760 claims
that his account is based on Cato, but, as Jordan (*Prolegomena* XXVIIIf. following
Niebuhr) correctly argues, there is no truth in this. Cf. Servius auctus on 1.259,
where the *Historia* is cited for the same account. Cauer's attempt to rescue the
greater part of that account for Cato (op. cit. 117; see also n. 26, 116) fails completely; the only material that can be ascribed to Cato is that which corresponds with
the scholia on 4.620, to which Servius refers with *ut supra diximus* [as we have said
above].

175   3. The narrative of Justin 43.1 is almost identical; in his version Lavinium is
founded only after the death of Turnus and Latinus. Appian's version has survived
only in short, unreliable excerpts (*Reg.*1 fr. I.1), from which however it is clear that

Aeneas was on good terms with Latinus and that it was only after his death that he had to fight against Turnus and Mezentius.

4. Thus Probus already noted that when the Latin army (which he imagines as being inevitably duty-bound to unconditional obedience to its king) joins Turnus, their action contradicts Latinus' refusal to fight (7.600): schol. Veron. on 9.368. Servius' reply (cf. Georgii, *Die antike Aeneiskritik* n. 16 above, 137, 412) shows that 7.600 was the passage which he objected to, not the *regis (Latini) responsa* [replies of the king (Latinus)] of 9.369 which according to the more complete version of Servius was the reading *in omnibus bonis* [in all the good manuscripts]: in his reply he takes no notice at all of this reading (which is certainly wrong in any case). Moreover, it is clear that Virgil wished to motivate the appearance of the cavalry which was demanded by his version of the situation; for Turnus (9.4) has certainly left Ardea, with his foreign auxiliaries (Messapus, 9.27) and the *agrestes Latini* [Latin country folk] (*Tyrrhidae*, 9.28); he has sent out a Rutulian cavalry division under Volcens from Laurentum on a tour to mobilize the infantry of the cities (367ff.); while these are getting into rank and file to march out, the Rutulians go on ahead to their king to report to him.

5. As Servius rightly remarks on 12.31.

6. Here, too, Virgil based his version on tradition: Faunus, who delivers an oracle to Latinus in a dream, corresponds with ἐπιστὰς καθ' ὕπνου ἐπιχώριος δαίμων [a local divinity, standing over him in a dream], who, according to Dionysius 1.57, commands Latinus, who is determined to fight Aeneas, δέχεσθαι τοὺς Ἕλληνας τῇ χώρᾳ συνοίκους· ἥκειν γὰρ αὐτοὺς μέγα ὠφέλημα Λατίνῳ καὶ κοινὸν Ἀβοριγένων ἀγαθόν [to receive the Greeks into his land as fellow-settlers. For their arrival would bring a great benefit to Latinus and an advantage that all the original inhabitants would share]. Virgil puts particular emphasis on this, because it helps us to understand how Latinus can suddenly offer his daughter to a stranger; that is why he strengthens his motivation with the miraculous signs that lead Latinus to consult the dream-oracle. Furthermore, I doubt whether such a thing as Faunus' dream-oracle ever actually existed; it would have been the only trace of incubation in Italy in early times, and in Virgil's account we can see the fusion of three concepts: (1) the prophetic nymph, Albunea, (2) the voice of Faunus resounding in the grove (95), (3) the ἐγκοίμησις [incubation, i.e. sleeping at a shrine in order to receive divine revelation], which is not linked with Faunus' prophecy anywhere else except in Ovid, *Fast.* 4.649, whose account does not seem to me to be genuinely Italian to any extent: the association of Somnus and Faunus is similar to that of Hypnos and Asclepius, the ascetic practices borrowed from Greek ritual etc. Above all, sleeping on the ground would only be intelligible in the case of an oracle of a chthonic divinity: and Faunus was no such thing. Besides, as W. Buchmann, *De Numae regis Romanorum fabula* (Diss. Leipzig, 1912) 42ff., has shown, the idea of a prophetic dream, even without incubation, is alien to Roman religious belief.

7. It is perhaps surprising that at the meeting of the council of the Latins Turnus' opponent Drances (11.343ff.) makes no reference to the oracle, and even Latinus does not mention it to Turnus before 12.27; this cannot be a deliberate concealment after the clear statement at 7.102ff. We might infer that Virgil had simply forgotten this motif during the intervening books: but this cannot be the case, as we can see if

176

177

we compare *fatalem Aenean manifesto numine ferri admonet ira deum tumulique ante ora recentes* (11.232) [the anger of the gods, witnessed by the freshly-made grave-mounds before their eyes, already warned them that Aeneas was clearly by divine warrant a man of destiny], with *hunc illum poscere fata et reor et si quid veri mens augurat opto* (7.272) ['it is my belief, and, if my intuition comes near to divining the truth, it is also according to my wish that it is Aeneas to whom Fate is pointing']: thus Latinus' original belief that the oracle referred to Aeneas is confirmed by the result of the battle *manifesto numine* [clearly by divine warrant]; it must therefore have been in doubt until then. In fact, Amata had interpreted Faunus' words in such a way as to make them refer to Turnus (7.367f.), and the ambiguity of the phrasing (which is not obvious in the oracle) makes it clear that Virgil had envisaged this possibility from the start: *conubiis Latinis* (7.96) [a Latin marriage-union] can refer to Latins in a narrower or wider sense, so it may not include the Rutulians; instead of an unambiguous phrase such as 'over the sea', or 'the foreign suitor will come from Asia', the oracle says only *externi generi* [suitors from another land]. So I think in fact that Virgil felt that this was sufficient to justify not introducing the oracle into that meeting of the council; his real reason was of course technical and artistic, namely his desire to present the opposition between Drances and Turnus in purely human terms, with no supernatural motivation. Another objection that has been raised is that Turnus is not told anything about the oracle until shortly before his death, through the words of Latinus at 12.27, whereas according to 7.102ff. it was generally known throughout Ausonia. However, I do not believe that the words *sine me haec haud mollia fatu sublatis aperire dolis, simul hoc animo hauri* ['let me then speak plainly and tell you my thoughts, however painful they may be to express; and do you take my meaning earnestly to heart'] are to be taken as implying that Latinus was now telling Turnus something completely new; it would be foolish to imagine that he would not have heard anything about the oracle in all the discussions which must have taken place before the outbreak of the war. Servius comments percipiently on 22 *hoc loco intellegimus Turnum dolore voluisse in aliqua verba prorumpere* [in this passage we are aware that Turnus, because of his grief, wants to break into speech], which is confirmed by *ut primum fari potuit sic institit ore* (47) [as soon as he could speak, he began to say]. Latinus points out to Turnus that there are other distinguished Latin maidens and hints (*nec non aurumque animusque Latino est* ['and besides, I, Latinus, have gold, and a generous spirit']) that he himself will provide the dowry: no wonder that the noble youth is furious. Latinus holds him back: *sine me haec* etc. ['Please let me speak to you quite frankly for once'], *simul hoc animo hauri* ['and take this to heart'], and now he states what he believed in the first place, and what he believes even more strongly now after all his misfortunes: 'the gods did not permit me to take you as a son-in-law; I tried to do it nevertheless – and you see the result. It is impossible to oppose the marriage with Aeneas; it will happen sooner or later, whether your life is sacrificed or not'.

179   8. 1245f.; cf. Geffcken, *Timaios' Geographie des Westens* (n. 42 above, 93) 44.

182   9. Compare, for example, *una cum gente tot annos bella gero* (1.47) ['I have been making war for all these years on a single clan'] with *nil linquere inausum quae potui infelix, quae memet in omnia verti, vincor ab Aenea* (7.308) ['after

forcing myself in my failure to shrink from no humiliation, after leaving no means untried, I am vanquished, and by Aeneas']. The piling up of rhetorical devices indicates that her emotions are now stronger: *num capti potuere capi? num incensa cremavit Troia viros* etc. (7.295-6) ['Could they stay in the trap when it closed? Could even Troy in flames burn up the Trojans? No'].

10. See Wilamowitz, Euripides' *Herakles* I² (Berlin, 1895) 123. Lyssa is hated   183
by the gods, as are the Erinyes in Aeschylus (*Eum.* 350, 366); Virgil intensifies this idea by making his Allecto hated even by Pluto and the sisters of Hell, 327f. The reason given for this, besides her horrible appearance, is *tot sese vertit in ora* [so   184
many are the countenances which she assumes], which is precisely what she does in the episodes that follow. That ability is generally ascribed to another spirit of hell, Empusa, but cf. the invocation Τισιφόνη τε Μέγαιρα καὶ Ἀλληκτὼ πολύμορφε [Tisiphone and Megaira and Allecto *of many forms*] *Pap. Par. Wess.* (C. Wessely, *Wiener Denkschrift* 37 [1889] 2798).

11. *omnis...ardor agit nova quaerere tecta* (393) [every heart...now blazed with   185
the same passion to look for a new dwelling place]: cf. *Bacch.* 33-6; *deseruere domos* (394) [they forsook their homes]: cf. *Bacch.* 217-20: γυναῖκας δώματ' ἐκλε-λοιπέναι [the women have forsaken their homes], ἐν δε δασκιοις ὀρεσι [and on the leaf-clad mountains] (*frondosis montibus* [387] [on the leaf-clad mountains]) θοάζειν...Διόνυσον τιμώσας χόροις [they gad about, honouring Dionysus with their dances] (*lustrare choro* [391] [around you she dances]): *ipsa* [*Amata*] *inter... medias...canit...torvumque repente clamat* (397) [in the centre of them Amata...sang...suddenly she roared like a beast]: cf. *Bacch.* 689: ἡ σὴ δὲ μῆτηρ ὠλόλυξεν ἐν μέσαις σταθεῖσα βάκχαις [and your mother, standing in the centre of the Bacchae, raised a cry]; *capite orgia mecum* (403) [take to the wild rites with me]: cf. *Bacch.* 34: σκευὴν ἔχειν ὀργίων ἐμῶν [to take on the clothing of my ritual]; an even closer parallel is the expression τὰ ὄργια αὐτοῦ αναλαμβάνιεν [to take up his wild rites] in the hypothesis to the tragedy. *stimulis agit Bacchi* (405) [drove her by the goads of Bacchus] cf. *Bacch.* 119: οιστρηθεὶς Διονύσῳ [goaded by Dionysos]. Admittedly most of these expressions will recur in more or less the same form in any description of maenads.

12. There have been attempts to explain the apparent contradiction by supposing that at first Amata is pretending, and later Bacchus punishes her by really driving her mad. But there is nothing in the text to support this; it would require at the very least that we should be told at 405 that Bacchus is acting in conjunction with Allecto.

13. Wilamowitz, *Herakles* II² 196. Also in Aeschylus' *Xantriae* Lyssa gave a speech ἐπιθειάζουσα ταῖς βάκχαις [which turned the Bacchae into women pos-sessed]. The transition from Bacchic ecstasy to true madness is of course a gradual, uninterrupted process.

14. In the denunciation of Hispala (Livy 39.13) it was alleged *viros v e l u t*   186
mente capta cum iactatione fanatica corporis vaticinari; matronas Baccharum habitu crinibus sparsis cum ardentibus facibus decurrere ad Tiberim, demissasque in aquam faces, quia vivum sulphur cum calce insit, integra flamma efferre [men were throwing themselves about like fanatics and uttering prophecies, *as though* their minds were possessed; married women dressed as maenads, with their hair

streaming out all dishevelled, were running off to the Tiber with blazing torches; they plunged the torches into the water, and because there was live sulphur and lime inside them, they were still alight when they pulled them out]: in other words, the miracle was exposed as a conscious deception. So too a Christian denies that ἐνθου-σιασμός [divine possession] took place; Arnobius 5.17: *Bacchanalia...in quibus furore mentito et sequestrata pectoris sanitate circumplicatis vos anguibus atque ut vos plenos dei numine ac maiestate doceatis caprorum reclamantium viscera oribus dissipatis* [the Bacchanalia...in which you pretend to be mad and you entrust the sanity of your hearts to the control of another; and then you let snakes wind themselves around you and, so that it looks as if you are possessed by the power and majesty of a god, you tear open the flesh of goats with your teeth, and the goats scream out against you].

15. Stat. *Silv.* 2.7.124; various pieces of evidence, including sarcophagi, show that the traditional version was generally known. The far-fetched theories of M. Mayer, *Hermes* 20 (1885) 123 may be ignored: maenadism seems to be 'totally opposed to the duties and vocation of the female sex' : Rapp, *Rhein. Mus.* 27 (1872) 21. It is worth noting that in Virgil no unmarried girl other than Lavinia joins the *thiasos*; everywhere (393, 400, 580) he speaks specifically of *matres*. This corresponds with historical examples of the Greek practice, which has also left its mark on the descriptions of mythical *thiasoi*: Rapp, *art. cit.* n. 21, 12.

16. Was Virgil thinking of the scene in the *Troades* where Cassandra brandishes the torches βακχεύουσα (341) [like a bacchant] or μαινάς (349) [maenad] and sings the marriage song for herself (308ff.)?

17. The phrase used by Apollodorus 2.27 of the Proetides. It is characteristic of Macrobius' authoritarian attitude that it is precisely the ἀκοσμία [abandon] of the queen and her women to which he took exception: *regina de penetralibus reverentiae matronalis educitur...bacchatur chorus quondam pudicus et orgia insana celebrantur* [the queen is lured out from the inner rooms where a respectable matron should stay...her troop of women, hitherto modest, rave like bacchants, and celebrate crazy rites].

18. That is what is meant by *postquam visa satis primos acuisse furores c o n s i l i u m q u e omnemque domum vertisse Latini* [and now, seeing that insanity was afoot and that the edge which she had given it was keen enough, since she had already contrived to overturn the *plan*, and the home of Latinus...] at 406; this of course does not refer to a real change of mind on the part of Latinus.

19. Nevertheless, the phrase that follows, *placida cum nocte iaceres* (427) [while you are lying in night's kindly peace] would cause total confusion: for it would betray the fact right at the beginning that the dream was a dream, whereas Turnus proceeds to reply to the real Calybe. I regard Klo:uçek's emendation *iacerem* [while I was lying] as self-evident.

20. *cura tibi divom effigies et templa tueri: bella viri pacemque gerant, quis bella gerenda* [your responsibility is to watch over the temples of the gods and their statues. It is for men to wage war and make peace: for it is for them to make war]: ἀλλ' εἰς οἶκον ἰοῦσα τὰ σ' αὐτῆς ἔργα κόμιζε, ἱστόν τ' ἠλακάτην τε...πόλεμος δ' ἄνδρεσσι μελήσει [but go back home, and attend to your own work, the loom and the spindle...for war will be men's concern]. Only someone who had failed to understand the point of the phrase *quis bella gerenda* [it is for them to make war] would propose that it should be deleted; the expression is ambiguous, meaning first 'concern about war (and peace)' and also 'wage war': furthermore, it is only in relation to this phrase that Allecto's final words *bella manu letumque gero* [in my hand I bear war and death] achieve their full effect, for they give it yet a third meaning.

21. So too in Aeschylus' *Xantriae* Hera appeared in the guise of a priestess (fr. 168 Nauck[2]).

22. *duri agrestes* (504) [the hardy country-folk], *indomiti agricolae* (521) [the   190 dogged farmers]. In order to understand the events as Virgil intended, it is in my view important that we should dismiss from our minds all thoughts of the meek and pious shepherds of the *Eclogues* and *Georgics*, and remember rather the suspicious, xenophobic, coarse angry *rusticus* [rustic] of the real world, who resorts to throwing stones or brandishing a sword at every insult, real or imagined (Cassius in Cic. *Ad Fam.* 16.19.4: *scis quo modo [Pompeius] crudelitatem virtutem putet; scis quam se semper a nobis derisum putet; vereor ne nos r u s t i c e gladio velit* ἀντιμυκτηρίσαι [You know how Pompey thinks cruelty is a virtue; you know how often he thinks we have insulted him; I am afraid that he will want to answer our mockery with the sword, *like a countryman*]; this was a type that was certainly well known to Virgil from his own observation and experience. Ribbeck has collected the testimonia on the traditional characteristics of Greek and Roman farmers ('Agroikos', *Abh.d.sächs. Gesellsch, d. Wiss.* 10.1 [1885]), and those that we have mentioned are frequently referred to.

23. By contrast, the rich Galaesus, the big landowner among the shepherds and   191 farmers, keeps his head and wants to sue for peace (535).

24. Ovid may have written *Met.* 10.121ff.: *tu pabula cervum ad nova, tu liquidi ducebas fontis ad undam, tu modo texebas varios per cornua flores* [you led the stag to fresh pastures, you led it to the waters of the clear fountain; at times you would weave a mixed garland of flowers for his antlers] with Virgil 488f. in mind: (Silvia) *mollibus intexens ornabat cornua sertis pectebatque ferum puroque in fonte lavabat* [wreathing his antlers with soft garlands to decorate him, and grooming him, wild creature though he had been, and bathing him in pure water]: but the Greek original must have had something very similar, and also certainly supplied Ovid with the lines that immediately follow, *nunc eques in tergo residens* [now sitting, on his back like a horseman] etc. Virgil has made the tame stag, originally sacred to the nymphs (we should remember Artemis' sacred stag at Aulis), into a domestic pet and therefore has him fed in the house (*mensaeque adsuetus erili* [490] [regularly at the master's table]): Ovid has probably preserved the original version here, when he speaks of Cyparissus taking the stag out to graze.

25. However, Virgil was also certainly influenced by the consideration that a   193 Fury should not be allowed to come into contact with the sanctuary. In this respect he is correcting Ennius.

26. *ut belli signum Laurenti Turnus ab arce extulit, et rauco strepuerunt cornua*   196 *cantu* (8.1) [Turnus hoisted the war-flag on the Laurentine citadel, and trumpets blared out their harsh music]: cf. Lersch, *Antiquitates Virgilianae* (48). Apart from a few useful observations on points of detail, this book is spoilt by the author's

tendency to explain everything in Virgil by tracing it back to a Roman context and saying virtually nothing about Homeric imitation.

27.   7.513, 519, 628, 637; 8.2; 9.394, 503; 11.192 (cf. 184 Tarchon), 424. Cf. 8.526 in connection with the sign from heaven which makes Aeneas decide to turn to the Etruscans for help: *Tyrrhenusque tubae mugire per aethera clamor* [the clarion note of an Etruscan trumpet seemed to bray across the sky].

28. Naturally this was already remarked on in antiquity: scholiast on *Iliad* 18.219.

197   **29.** Virgil has only Italian cavalry divisions (*alae*) [Volscians 11.604, 868, Etruscans 11.730, Arcadians 11.835]; as Servius (on 9.368) already observed, the 300 riders of Volcens correspond in number to the cavalry attached to an ancient Roman legion.

198   **30.** Similarly, in Book 10, Mezentius fights on foot at first, and only mounts his horse when his wound makes it impossible for him to continue on foot; this leads to the peculiar situation where Aeneas on foot fights against a mounted warrior (10.883-94).

199   **31.** On how Graf arrived at this conclusion from the iconographic tradition, in contradistinction to the views of Welcker, Benndorf, Löschcke (*Bonner Studien* 255), see Pauly-Wissowa *RE* I 1780. Unfortunately we know nothing at all about the *Amazonis* of Domitius Marsus, not even whether it was available to Virgil.

32. Compare for example, what Quintus of Smyrna, who depicts Penthesilea as a rider, manages to do with this rewarding subject: Penthesilea mounts her horse, 1.666; she carries quiver and bow, 338; Achilles tries to pull the wounded Amazon off her horse and pierces both horse and woman with his spear, 600; and that is all. The rest of the battle is described just like any other. We are not even told whether Penthesilea's twelve female companions are on horseback.

200   **33.** We have an exactly analogous case in, for example, *Iliad* 8, where Hector descends from his chariot to meet Teucer (320) and soon afterwards (348) is back in it again, without the poet having found it necessary to mention the obvious fact that he had remounted. The phrase used of Camilla, *pedem reportat* (764) [took to her heels], is no more to be taken literally than *circuit* (761) [he moved around] or *subit* (763) [he moved nearer] when used of Arruns, who immediately *celeris detorquet habenas* (765) [swiftly guided his reins]. It hardly needs to be said that Camilla, wearing no armour and protected only by a *parma* [small shield] is not making her way on foot *medio agmine* (762) [in the centre of the battle]. If we must be pedantic we would do better to ask where Camilla gets a sword from (711), since we know that she does not carry one herself, nor does anyone use one at any other point in the whole cavalry battle.

34. In Book 9 he rides to the enemy camp [see p. 160 above), but then naturally proceeds to fight on foot, as in the attack on the camp at the beginning of Book 10. However, when he is pursuing the phantom of Aeneas (10.645ff.), the poet says nothing of his chariot: this sacrifice is imposed by the Homeric situation, for it would have made no sense for Turnus to get down from his chariot before his opponent was ready to fight, nor are we supposed to imagine Turnus in his chariot in pursuit, and unsuccessful pursuit at that, of a phantom that moves on foot.

201   **35.** That is a striking detail; perhaps Virgil was thinking (*pace* Aristarchus) of

Achilles' four horses in *Iliad* 8.185; it is well known that no other *quadriga* appears in Homeric battles. When Latinus (12.162) drives out in a four-horse chariot to conclude the treaty, it is a royal privilege, which was reinterpreted by the Romans and retained in the form of the triumphator's *quadriga*: thus (Dion. Hal. 2.34) Romulus triumphs ἵνα τὸ βασίλειον ἀξίωμα σώζῃ τεθρίππῳ παρεμβεβηκώς [so that by mounting a four-horse chariot he might preserve the dignity befitting a king].

36. Besides *hastile* [spear-shaft] (9.402; 10.795; 11.650 etc.) and the general   202
terms *telum* [weapon], *ferrum* [iron], *missile* [missile], he also has *spiculum* [pointed weapon] (10.888; 11.676 etc.), *iaculum* [thrown weapon] (10.323, 342; 12.354 etc.), *lancea* (12.375) [lance], *cuspis* [spike] (10.484, 733; 11.691 etc.), and, like the Homeric μελίη [ash], referring to the wood from which they were made, *abies* (11.667) [pinewood], *cornus* [cornel cherry] (9.698; 12.267), *robur* (10.479) [oak], cf. *myrtus* (7.817) [myrtle].

37. On this see the section on 'Composition' in Part II, ch. 4.

38. Marquardt, *St. V.* II 344.   203

39. Lersch op. cit. n. 26 above, 69, 186.   204

40. Virgil generally based his similes on those in Greek epic, but the first simile   206
in the *Aeneid* (1.148), on which he lavishes even more artistic skill than usual, in thrice three lines, is drawn from a Roman context (although even in this case there is something similar in Homer: *Iliad* 2.144). When he compares a stormy and a calm sea with a rebellious and a pacified crowd, he is reversing a simile that was popular in Rome: Cic. *pro Cluentio* 138: *intellegi potuit id quod saepe dictum est: ut mare, quod sua natura tranquillum sit, ventorum vi agitari atque turbari, sic populum Romanum sua sponte esse placatum, hominum seditiosorum vocibus ut violentissimis tempestatibus concitari* [it was easy to understand what has frequently been remarked: just as the sea, which is calm by nature, is made rough and turbulent by the force of the winds, so the Roman people is naturally calm, but the speeches of revolutionaries can start them up, like the most violent storms]. Cf. Preiswerk in *Iuvenes dum sumus*, Festschr. (Basel, 1907) 32 (he cites a simile from Demosthenes *Fals. Leg.* 19.136 which is not an exact parallel).

41. In other cases where a death is not described but is left to the reader's   208
imagination, it is clear that the poet has hesitated to put the horror into words. Thus in 2.526ff. he describes how Neoptolemus pursues Polites brandishing his spear and   209
trying to clutch him with his hand, then Polites collapses and meets his death: Virgil passes over the fatal thrust in silence; nor at 2.225 does he say in so many words that Laocoon is killed by the snakes; he passes over the fatal blow which Dido inflicts on herself (above p. 105); and Palinurus does not say that he was murdered on the shore by marauders (6.361) (see Norden *ad loc.*). It would of course be out of place to transfer this principle to descriptions of battle.

42. Similarly (3.286) he dedicates the shield of Abas to Apollo.

43. *immania pondera baltei* (10.496) [his heavy, massive swordbelt] on which   210
the foul deed of the Danaids is engraved in gold: its prototype is the *telamon* [sword-strap] of Hercules in *Odyssey* 11.609ff. It is also called a *cingulum* (9.360; 12.942), but it must not be confused with the real *cingulum militiae* [military belt] which is worn around the waist: see 9.364; 12.941.

44. 10.531, 557, 592, 599, 897. Virgil has taken great care that, in the scene of

fighting before the death of Pallas (310-44), he does not behave in this way. At
10.517 Virgil makes Aeneas take eight of the enemy alive, so that he can sacrifice
them at Pallas' funeral-pyre (11.81); this has been criticized as an imitation of
Homer that is out of character with the *pietas* of Virgil's hero. But Virgil knew that
it had been an early Roman custom (Varro in Serv. on 3.67); moreover during his
own lifetime Augustus had sacrificed 300 Persian prisoners-of-war at Caesar's
funeral (V. Gardthausen, *Augustus und seine Zeit* I [Leipzig, 1891] 209); surely he
would have had this in mind when he included this in his work?

45. For the following cf. H. Nettleship, *Lectures and Essays* (Oxford, 1885)
108ff.

46. *sed ea animi elatio, quae cernitur in periculis et laboribus, si iustitia vacat
pugnatque non pro salute communi sed pro suis commodis, in vitio est; non modo
enim id virtutis non est, sed est potius immanitatis omnem humanitatem repellentis*
[but as for the elation of the spirits, which can be seen to drive a man through toils
and perils, if there is no just cause involved, and a man fights, not for the preservation of his people, but for his own advantage, then that is wrong; for not only is that
nothing to do with valour, but rather it is characteristic of outrageous behaviour that
denies every kind of human feeling] (Cic. *De Off.* 1.19.62).

47. οἱ μὲν θρασεῖς προπετεῖς καὶ βουλόμενοι πρὸ τῶν κινδύνων, ἐν αὐτοῖς δ'
ἀφίστανται, οἱ δ' ἀνδρεῖοι ἐν τοῖς ἔργοις ὀξεῖς, πρότερον δ' ἡσύχιοι [bold men
are headstrong and eager in advance of danger, but at the moment of danger they
hold back; whereas brave men are keen in action, although quiet beforehand]
(Aristotle *Eth. Nic.* 3.10, 1116a7).

48. 'It is most remarkable how closely Virgil imitates Homer in the duel between
Aeneas and Turnus...it is modelled almost *verbatim* on the duel between Achilles
and Hector (*Iliad* 22.248ff.).... At the end Turnus (932f.) pleads with Aeneas for a
decent burial in almost the same words as Hector (*Iliad* 22.337f.)': Cauer op. cit.
n. 1 above, 181. He has failed to perceive how great a difference there is here, and it
was precisely on his readers' familiarity with Hector's last words that Virgil was
relying in order that this contrast should achieve its maximum impact.

49. Cato in Macrob. *Sat.* 3.5.10 (fr. 12P.). There is a rather different version in
Dionysius 1.65.

50. The motif comes from Apollonius where Idas says: ἴστω νῦν δόρυ θοῦρον,
ὅτῳ περιώσιον ἄλλων κῦδος ἐνὶ πτολέμοισιν ἀείρομαι, οὐ δέ μ' ὀφέλλει Ζεὺς
τόσον ὁσσάτιόν περ ἐμὸν δόρυ, μή νύ τι πῆμα λοίγιον ἔσσεσθαι, μηδ'
ἀκράαντον ἄεθλον Ἴδεω ἐσπομένοιο, καὶ εἰ θεὸς ἀντιόῳτο (1.466) ['let my swift
spear, which brings greater glory in battle to me than to any other man – indeed,
Zeus is less help to me than my spear – let it know that I shall suffer no painful
wound, nor will Idas fail to follow it up and gain a victory, not even if a god should
fight against him']; Idmon then reproaches him for θεοὺς ἀτίζειν [dishonouring the
gods]: this *contemptor divom* [scorner of gods] too was later punished for his
arrogance.

51. Another certain example is *nec mortem horremus nec divom parcimus ulli*
(10.880) ['I have no horror of death, and set no value on any god']. More dubious is
Nunc morere, ast de me divom pater atque hominum rex viderit (743) ['Now die. As
for me, the Father of Gods and King of Men will decide']. As Servius correctly

remarks, the fact that Mezentius speaks the words *subridens* [smiling], excludes the possibility that Virgil carelessly allowed his *contemptor deum* to lapse into pious devotion at this point; but the interpretation transmitted by Servius '*viderit utrum Mezentio possit nocere ille quem vos deorum et hominum creditis esse rectorem*' ['let that person whom you believe to be the ruler of gods and men see whether he can harm Mezentius'] is perhaps too artificial. Still, there is, in my opinion, an element of contempt in *viderit*, here as frequently elsewhere; this would define the tone of *divom pater atque hominum rex* [the Father of Gods and King of Men] as 'let him kill me – see if I care'.

52. As we can deduce from Servius on 1.317, the story of Camilla's youth is   215
based in part on the tale of Harpalyce (see O. Crusius in Roscher I.1835; G. Knaack, *Rhein. Mus.* 49 [1894] 526-31, who however presses the comparison too far). Other elements may be derived from a local Volscian legend (see now R. Ritter *De Varrone Vergilii...auctore* [Diss. Halle, 1901] 391ff.). However, Virgil is not completely successful in combining the character that he has derived from this source with that of a Penthesilea: purple robe, golden hair-clasp and golden bow suit an Amazon queen but not a virgin huntress who has grown up in the wild (11.570) and has always lived there (843). Penthesilea rules over a nation of women: but how did Camilla come by a bevy of companions-at-arms (655, 805, 820), when she had acquired her unique character only because she had been brought up with her exiled father in the loneliness of the forest? And how is it that she has become the leader of her people, although her father, the Volscian king Metabus, had been driven out of his country by his subjects, and forbidden to enter any of their cities (567)? On the reason for this discrepancy see the section on 'Speech' in Part II, ch. 3.III.

53. *C a e c a sequebatur totumque i n c a u t a per agmen f e m i n e o praedae et spoliorum ardebat amore* (781f.) [*blind* to all else, in a *girl's* hot passion for plundering those spoils she was ranging *heedlessly* about the battle-lines].

54. It has been suggested that Virgil was reading *Iliad* 10 again when he was   216
composing his own Book 9: Mnestheus' lionskin (306) is derived from *Iliad* 10.177;
Ascanius' sword (303) from 255; Turnus' steed (269) from 322; the detail that   217
Rhamnes' sword-strap had been given in return for hospitality (361) from the leather helmet given in return for hospitality in *Iliad* 10.268; the reference in Nisus' prayer to his father Hyrtacus (406) from the reference in Diomedes' prayer to his father Tydeus (285); and do not the names Rhamnes, Remus and Rhoetus recall the name of Rhesus? There is yet another echo: in the Ascanius episode the young bullock with gilded horns which he promises to Jupiter (627ff.) is derived from Diomedes' vow to Athena (294).

55. It is only on Ascanius that Virgil's narrative (257ff.) dwells longer than necessary; this is to enable us to hear about the *primitiae* [first fruits] which he promises in the council before we hear about his *primitiae* in the actual battle (590ff.). Aeneas' absence is used to good effect in both cases. This maintains the childlike character of Ascanius, see above p. 128.

56. The poet does not make them do this pointlessly, 'merely because Odysseus and Diomedes had done it' in *Iliad* 10 (F. Cauer op. cit. n. 1 above, 180), but for the same reasons as in their case. Diomedes even has to be restrained by Athena from slaughtering still more of the enemy, which would endanger both himself and his

218 friend. Every ancient reader would have understood how he felt. And there is a great difference between the lack of caution of inexperienced youths and the carelessness of an experienced warrior like Diomedes. Nisus' ambition is not satisfied with a single task. The poet has taken pains to prepare us for this (186ff.), and he has also made sure that Nisus shall appear more level-headed than Euryalus (322, 354). If Virgil had decided to provide an additional motive for the bloodbath by making Nisus and Euryalus fight their way through the enemy camp, that would have been unnecessary as well as incompatible with the facts: it cannot be deduced from *lato te limite ducam* (323) ['I will lead you forward along a clear, broad lane'] nor from *via facta per hostis* (356) ['our way through the foe is clear now']. Anyone who goes through enemy lines has to hack his way through them with his sword; Nisus would have thought it shameful to creep through without leaving any trace of his passage. I am even more reluctant than usual to regard this as an ἀβλεψία [oversight] on Virgil's part, for everything in this episode is motivated with special care, almost, we might suppose, in deliberate contrast to the slapdash details which abound in *Iliad* 10. Virgil has already told us about the friendship of Nisus and Euryalus in Book 5 (pp. 126f. above) (and note the contrast!); it is from that book that we know that Nisus is a fast runner, as he is here too (386); his successes with throwing the spear (411, 417) are credible in the light of his passion for hunting (178, 407); and this also explains his knowledge of the surrounding countryside (245). In the moonlight Euryalus' helmet gleams and shows the way to Nisus, while the darkness of the dense wood conceals him but conversely hinders Euryalus' escape (384). And how can Nisus find him again in the wood? *audit equos* (394) [he heard horses]. The author of Book 10 of the *Iliad* had had great difficulty in finding a plausible motive for Diomedes and Odysseus to leave the camp, and it fits rather awkwardly into the context. In this respect too, Virgil was no mere thoughtless imitator. We might find it surprising that not one of Rhesus' Thracians woke during the bloodbath. Virgil had forestalled any objection by introducing the detail that the soldiers are stretched out in drunken sleep (316, 335, 350, cf. 165), and this has already been prepared for by Turnus' words *laeti bene gestis corpora rebus procurate viri* (157) ['See to your comfort, warriors, happy in the day's success'].

219 **57.** However, in my opinion it is unlikely that Virgil and his audience would have taken the same view of Nisus' action as we do. Nisus' fault lies in failing to complete his mission despite Euryalus' death, and we would regard this as dereliction of duty, although we might arrive at this verdict only after a certain amount of reflection. To be carried away by passion is more characteristic of the Mediterranean temperament than our own, but even we northerners hardly realize that in a similar situation, the emotional scene when Max Piccolomini rides to his death in Schiller's *Wallenstein*, it is even more flagrant dereliction of duty. Imagine Nisus in some safe hiding-place watching his friend being killed, too sensible to attempt to fight in vain against overwhelming odds, and going on to obey orders and complete his mission – a Nisus who behaved like that would have been regarded as a character lacking in warmth and lacking in love. Here is the verdict on this episode by a modern writer who was Virgilian in spirit, Bernardin de St Pierre: 'Virgile a renfermé dans une seule action les premiers devoirs de la vie sociale, que les moralistes n'ont mis qu'en maximes isolées' [Virgil has enshrined in a single action the

fundamental duties of social life, which moralists have only expressed in isolated maxims] (*Oeuvres* 10 [1826] 180).

58. C. Robert, *Studien zum Ilias* (Berlin, 1901) 337, pointed out that grouping by 220 pairs is prevalent in the *aristeia* of Diomedes; the origin of this, as he rightly observes, lies in the pairs, warrior and driver, in each chariot. It is the same in the *aristeia* of Agamemnon: in *Iliad* 11.91ff. Agamemnon kills three pairs, including two pairs of brothers; he is confronted by a fourth pair, Iphidamas and Coön, the sons of Antenor, at 221ff. This continues at 310ff.: Diomedes and Odysseus form a pair: they kill three pairs; Diomedes then wounds Hector, but is himself wounded by Hector's brother Paris. At 420ff. Odysseus kills four men; then, with the pair of brothers Charops and Socos, his score matches that of Agamemnon. Meanwhile, at 300ff. Hector kills nine men in three lines of verse, three per line, which is surely not just coincidence. The number three plays a role in the *aristeia* of Patroclus: at 16.399ff. he kills first three single fighters, then three times he kills three together; then at 684ff. he again kills three together three times, and immediately before his death at 785 he three times kills nine. The deliberate crescendo is unmistakeable. There is nothing like it in Books 13 and 14 (apart from the end of Book 14, 508ff.).

59. Hellenistic poets certainly deliberately followed this principle in the case of long lists of names. It is certainly clear for example in Tibullus' description of the Golden Age (1.3.37ff.): first two pairs of lines about voyages, in the first of which 221 *pinus* [ship] is the subject, in the second *navita* [sailor]; then a pair of lines on each of the following topics: animal-breeding – the subjects are *taurus* [bull] and *equus* [horse]; securing one's property – the subjects are *domus* [house] and *lapis* [stone]; nutrition – honey and milk; and finally two pairs of lines each with four subjects, unity and peace, war and sea-travel. Here the increasing compression reflects increasing excitement.

60. Although it has no significance for the course of the battle, it is significant 223 for the general purpose of Book 9, since it shows the ancestor of the Julian *gens* avenging the people's honour. The scornful speech of Numanus (9.598ff.) (which also gives a picture of archaic Latin customs – modelled in fact on Spartan customs, for according to learned Romans [Cato?] ap. Servius on 8.638; but cf. Jordan *Prolegomena*]) a distant Roman connection with the Sabines made πολλὰ τῶν νομίμων Λακωνικά, μάλιστα δὲ τὸ φιλοπόλεμόν τε καὶ λιτοδίαιτον καὶ τὸ παρὰ πάντα τὰ ἔργα τοῦ βίου σκληρόν [many of their customs Spartan, and especially their love of war, their plain life-style, and their austerity in all the activities of their lives] (Dion. Hal. 2.49); cf. the old Lucanian principles of education in Justin 23.1.8, *quibus et Spartani* [*liberos*] *instituere soliti erant* [by which the Spartans also were accustomed to educate (their children)]) and the Trojans' situation is reminiscent of the scornful speech of the Etruscan beneath the walls of the Roman camp in Livy (2.45.3), which is certainly based on more detailed (poetic?) sources.

61. This resembles an incident in the Punic War: *cum refugientem* [*sc. Hanniba-* 224 *lem*] *ad urbem Tauream Claudius sequeretur, patenti hostium portae invectum per alteram stupentibus miraculo hostibus intactum evasisse* [when Claudius followed him (Hannibal) as he fled to the city of Taureas, he was carried in at one of the enemy gates, which was open, and came out through another unscathed, and the enemy were amazed at his miraculous feat], says Livy 23.46, on the authority of 'certain annals'.

62. 9.67ff. So that Turnus and his men can try to set fire to the ships without first storming the camp, Virgil situates the fleet near the camp, but not defended by it, and depicts it as protected on the landward side by a mere wall, not by a proper defensible fortification. Drachmann, *Nord. tidskr f. filol* 14. (1905) 69 is right to correct me by interpreting 9.69f. (*classem quae lateri castrorum adiuncta latebat, aggeribus saeptam circum et fluvialibus undis* [the fleet which lay hidden close under the flank of the encampment, fenced on one side by an earth-pier built round it, but elsewhere by nothing but the river waves]) in this sense. This also explains why Turnus hopes that the attack on the fleet will lure the Trojans out from their walls, and also why the men in the encampment cannot protect the fleet against fire. The poet does not state the topographical reasons that caused this separation of the fleet from the camp. After the Romans land at Aspis, Polybius (1.29) particularly emphasizes that they begin the siege νεωλκήσαντες, ἔτι δὲ τάφρῳ καὶ χάρακι περιλαβόντες τὰς ναῦς [by hauling the ships onto land, and surrounding them with a ditch and fence].

63. But not, as some have believed, that they are already in the camp; on the contrary, Cymodocea says that Turnus intends to prevent them from entering the camp, *medias illis opponere turmas ne castris iungant* (239) ['to confront them squarely with his own main squadrons before they can join the Trojan camp']; nor do the Arcadians play any part in the fighting when they land; see n. 66 below.

64. *turmas invasit agrestis Aeneas, omen pugnae, stravitque Latinos* (310) [Aeneas charged against the levies of country-folk, a good augury for the fortune of the fight, and he struck the Latins down]; Servius connects this with 8.7: *undique cogunt auxilia et latos vastant cultoribus agros* [they mustered their levies from all around, stripping fields of their cultivators over a wide area], but surely it refers to the inadequate armour of Turnus' allies, e.g. the *legio agrestis* (7.681) [levy of countrymen] from Praeneste: 'Aeneas attacks them first, rightly believing that it is here that he will be most successful, and so begin the battle with a good omen', Brosin *ad loc*.

65. Aeneas kills two of the seven sons of Phorcus; the third son wounds Achates; Virgil breaks off at this point, but we can see what is going to happen.

66. The narrative suffers from lack of clarity at this point. The Arcadian cavalry had been forced by the difficulty of the terrain to dismount, and they found themselves at a disadvantage because they were not accustomed to fighting on foot. So it is obvious that they did not take part in the fighting at the ships: so much can be deduced from the strongly emphasized phrase *parte ex alia* (362) [elsewhere on the field], and from the contrast between the Arcadians and Turnus at 238f. But it remains unclear whether Pallas, who has come by sea with Aeneas (190), sees the Arcadian cavalry only from afar – *vidit Latio dare terga sequaci* (365) [he saw that the Arcadians were turning in flight before the pursuing Latins], or whether he has already joined up with them; in either case we ought to be told at some point or other about his fighting his way through to them. *Vidit* [he saw] would appear to support the former interpretation (particularly if we compare it with the passage where Tarchon is trying to restore courage to his companions who have taken flight: *inter caedes cedentiaque agmina fertur equo* [11.729] [he charged on horse-back amid the carnage where the ranks were in retreat]), but the narrative that follows

192

would appear to support the latter. Nor is the topography entirely clear. I confess that I am as baffled by Brosin's attempt to explain it (in his note on 362) as I am by Virgil.

67. This corresponds very well with the picture which we have formed of Tar- 228 chon from his conduct in the battle at the ships (10.290), where he has no patience for careful disembarkation of the troops, and orders his ships to be rowed straight towards the beach, regardless of the danger of damaging them. The words with which he encourages his comrades are reminiscent of Brasidas' words during the landing at Pylos: he orders his sailors not to spare the ships, ὀκείλαντας δὲ καὶ παντὶ τρόπῳ ἀποβάντας τῶν τε ἀνδρῶν καὶ τοῦ χωρίου κρατῆσαι [but to run them aground and disembark in any way possible, in order to gain control of the men and of the position] (Thuc. 4.12). The Thucydides passage was famous as a masterpiece of vivid description: Plut. *De glor. Athen.* 3, cf. Lucian *De conscr. hist.* (How to write history) 49.

68. Once Turnus has sent Idmon with the message to Aeneas, he goes into the 229 palace, calls for his horses, puts on his armour, takes up his shield and sword, and finally brandishes his spear and utters threatening words – *totoque ardentis ab ore scintillae absistunt, oculis micat acribus ignis* (81-106) [fire glittered in his flashing eyes, and all his face showed the fierce heat within, a heat to send sparks flying] etc. All this is modelled on the scene of the arming of Achilles in *Iliad* 19.364ff.; Virgil does not even omit lines 365-8, which were rejected by Aristarchus as spurious, but works them in at a suitable point (but without the gnashing of teeth, γελοῖον γὰρ τὸ βρυχᾶσθαι τὸν Ἀχιλλέα [for it is ridiculous that Achilles should gnash his teeth] schol. A. *ad loc.*). In fact, it is not in the least remarkable that Turnus, who has to go to fight early the next morning, should try out his weapons the evening before (this is Servius' explanation – it would be nice if Virgil had been explicit in the same way here), and brandish his spear (at Apollonius 3.1262 Jason practises leaping and brandishing his spear before battle), and it would certainly make sense to do so while there was still time to make sure his equipment was in good order and to remedy any faults. Furthermore, line 76 makes it quite clear that the encounter will take place the next morning, which prevents the reader from making the false assumption that this encounter will come immediately after line 112. (We should also note how very different this is from the description of the arming of Turnus at 11.486.) Nevertheless, the final arming before the actual combat is so much more important than these preliminary exercises that we must ask ourselves why Virgil did not do the same as Homer and Apollonius and describe that moment. It seems that he was more interested in the character of Turnus than in the factual details of arming: on the eve of the duel, immediately after the decision has been made, he is so consumed by raging lust for battle that he cannot wait to brandish his weapon against the opponent he hates so much; in the morning, just before the fight, his passion has ebbed away (see p. 167 above). Aeneas, by contrast, remains 230 unchanged.

69. See p. 167 above.

70. So as to make this appear plausible, Virgil has avoided saying anything earlier about the general feelings of the Latins, or their hatred of Turnus. Only Turnus himself sees *sua nunc promissa reposci, se signari oculis* (12.2) [that they were demanding that his spontaneous offer should now be made good, and they were singling out him alone] – but who 'they' are is not stated. Previously, however, it was the widows and orphans of the fallen Latins who had demanded that there should be a duel (11.215); only Drances allied himself to their cause. Nothing at all of this kind is ever said of the Rutulians.

71. His intervention has been prepared for at 11.429, where Turnus reassures the Latins after the news of Diomedes' refusal to ally himself with their cause: *at Messapus erit felixque Tolumnius* [sc. *auxilio*] *et quos tot populi misere duces* ['yet Messapus will (sc. aid us), and fortunate Tolumnius too, and so will other chieftains whom these many nations have sent]. That the *augur* Tolumnius is identical with this *dux* [chieftain] Tolumnius ought never to have been doubted: compare Picus, who was both augur and king, 7.187f. (cf. Cicero *De Div.* 1.89), and Rhamnes, *rex idem et regi Turno gratissimus augur* (9.327) [he was himself a king, and also a seer, whom King Turnus loved]; Tolumnius may be one of the princes allied to Messapus. Turnus does not rely on him in vain, as we can see when he casts his spear; but *felix* [fortunate] contains bitter dramatic irony, for Tolumnius is fortunate in that his spear strikes home, but he loses his life as a result, 12.460.

232   **72.** We have already discussed most of this. There is also the phrase *vulgi variare labantia corda* (223) [the feelings of the *multitude* were changeful and insecure]: the *vulgus* [multitude] is fickle and just as quickly moved to sudden anger (11.451) as to sudden sympathy; again, Juturna appears in the semblance of Camers, who is highly respected as a member of a distinquished family as well as for his personal qualities; a further incitement is her appeal to the Latins' honour, love of freedom, ambition, and inveterate hatred of the Etruscans.

233   **73.** The scheme is thus ABCBA.

234   **74.** The poet often reminds us of them later in the narrative: 730, 744, 768, 918, 928. Cf. our comments on the funeral games, p. 131 above.

    75. *coniectis eminus hastis* (711) [while still far apart, they cast their spears]: no Homeric poet would have dared to conclude the essential first phase of the duel in

235 only three words, leaving us to deduce from the silence of the narrator that each spear had missed its target.

    76. On this see Part II, 236f. 'Jupiter and Fate'.

    77. Motivated in 739ff.: *postquam arma dei ad Volcania ventum est mortalis mucro...dissiluit* [but as soon as he faced instead divine weapons forged by Vulcan himself, the mortal blade...flew into splinters]: we might suppose, at the first stroke; but it was sound enough to start with: *crebros ensibus ictus congeminant* (713) [they redoubled their sword-strokes and smote again].

PART II

1

The Creative Method

I. The Sources

The relationship of Virgil to the traditional myths of Troy and Rome was not like that of a modern poet to the material which has inspired him to the creative act. It was more like that of an ancient historian to the traditional history which he was re-telling. The material did not simply serve as a basis for his own invention: the transmission of the tradition was an end in itself, and the poet felt that it was his obligation to state the truth, to pass on what had been passed on to him (in so far as he did not wish to reject something on account of the nature of the material or for artistic reasons). This obligation was an age-old legacy of ancient poetry, but in the course of the centuries the legacy had necessarily been considerably modified to suit the taste of each new generation. In ancient Greek times, the poet, whether writing an epic or a drama, was no more than an interpreter of the myth; he interpreted it according to the meaning that it had for *him*; the myth had its own life and the poet helped it to live on, as generations had done before him. Later, when men had a different mental relationship to the myths, the poems still retained the same external relationship to them. Although the life of men was no longer influenced and permeated by the myths, they had learnt them in their childhood in their traditional form, and it was in that form, and no other, that they wanted to hear them from the epic poet. If any poet found the familiar myths tedious or thought that they no longer had any relevance for his own time, that was fair enough: he was welcome to search for novelties in remote corners, or to collect local folk traditions which had not yet become common Hellenic property; but he had to keep innovation within the framework of the tradition. Anyone learned and bold enough to serve up some particularly surprising novelty would do well to affirm solemnly in his opening words that nothing in his account had been conjured out of thin air. This was how Virgil's contemporaries, and Virgil himself, conceived the task of the epic poet; and, since the story he was about to narrate was the history of the origins of the Roman race and of the Julian *gens*, he would be even less likely to put his own invention in place of the traditional version.[1] 240

Which authors, then, were available to Virgil as representative sources of the traditional accounts? In the first place, of course, the national historians and antiquarians; it was surely in their works, Virgil believed, that the truth was to be found, and he spared no effort in drawing on these sources. But secondly, and especially for the Greek parts of the narrative, he could go to the poets; it stands to reason that they, precisely because they were expected to be faithful to the tradition, could themselves constitute the tradition for later writers. Furthermore, in many cases they were the only source which the conscientious writer could use for the earliest period. It is therefore scarcely surprising that, for his account of the fall of Troy, Virgil makes as much use of Euphorion as he does of Hellanicus or Varro; and he extends this practice to include Roman poets, if, as is very likely, he took the story of Dido not from the historians but from Naevius.

In these circumstances it naturally never occurs to Virgil to attempt to disguise his dependence on the works of his predecessors, any more than his Hellenistic and Roman forebears had done.[2] Apollonius is admittedly exceptional in occasionally referring naïvely to certain persons, 'earlier singers'[3] who have said this, that or the other; generally, poets use the impersonal φασί [they say] or refer to the evidence of φήμη [what people say], which comes to much the same thing. Thus Catullus, no doubt keeping closely to his Greek original, presented the whole of his epyllion

241 (poem 64) not as a narrative but as the re-telling of a narrative;[4] thus, too, Horace often introduces examples from myth and history as 'what people say';[5] in the same way Virgil himself had introduced the Aristaeus epyllion at the end of the *Georgics* with *ut fama* [according to what people say] (*Geo.* 4.318; cf. 286). In the *Aeneid*, too, he often refers to what he has heard, what has been said or reported, *fama*. Indeed, he leaves no doubt that when he calls upon the Muse to inform him about some particularly difficult and obscure point, this Muse is none other than *fama* itself;[6] this relieves Virgil of the burden of responsibility for the truth of what he writes, and at the same time allays any suspicion that he may have invented it. Virgil naturally realizes, and so does the reader, that *fama* is far from being absolutely reliable, *tam ficti pravique tenax quam nuntia veri* [as retentive of news that is false and wicked as she is ready to tell what is true] (*Aen.* 4.188),[7] Such references to

242 'what people say' generally occur in the context of miraculous mythical tales[8] and they are generally confined to stories that have no close connection with Virgil's own account and are remote from it in time and place:[9] it is as though he is only

243 willing to take responsibility for the truth of his own main narrative, and prefers to shift the responsibility for everything else onto others. But this limitation of liability is a matter of poetic tact; it remains true that the poet himself acknowledges the existence of a tradition which formed the basis of his work; indeed, in one place, where he has to recount that an immortal performed an action unworthy of an immortal because his vanity had been wounded, he does not conceal his doubts about the traditional version, any more than a cautious historian would, and as his Greek predecessors had also done in similar circumstances.[10]

In order to discover where Virgil drew the line between tradition and invention, let us briefly survey those sections of the *Aeneid* where our analysis in Part I involved a consideration of their sources.

In our analysis of the Sack of Troy, we saw that the individual details, except for a few which we shall mention in a moment, were modelled closely on the tradition, but that their selection and combination were obviously Virgil's own work. We have to imagine how he set about his task. Before setting pen to paper, he will have let his mind dwell on all the relevant material, and will have re-fashioned it so as to create a totally new episode that was in harmony with his own very individual intentions. In the scenes involving the wooden horse, hardly one detail was Virgil's new invention, but Sinon's act and the death of Laocoon seem to have been presented in a new light, and the artistic structure of the scenes also seems to be new. We found exactly the same in the case of, for example, the scene of Priam's death, where we were able to trace practically every detail back to the earlier tradition. In the narrative of Aeneas' own adventures, we were able to observe a combination of different traditions: on the one hand Hellanicus, for the defence of the citadel and so forth; on the other hand the popular tradition; and finally the help given to Aeneas by Venus; the figure of Panthus seemed to have been combined with the role of some other person, unknown to us; the death of Coroebus was linked with the rape 244 of Cassandra, and the death of Polites with that of Priam, thus creating a completely new overall picture. The rescue of Creusa by the Great Mother, as well as numerous individual characters – such as Thymoetes, and the heroes in the horse – and circumstantial details – the burning of the city, moonlight, the torch-signal etc. – all turned out to have been taken over from previous versions. If we are looking for original Virgilian invention, the limitations of our knowledge make it impossible to be certain, but we would probably not go far wrong if we included the appearance of Hector in Aeneas' dream; the death of Androgeos and Coroebus' plan of disguising himself in his armour; the scene between Aeneas and Venus, and Venus' appearance to him; the scenes in Aeneas' house (which imply an earlier date for the *auspicium maximum* than that handed down by tradition); and Creusa's appearance and her prophecy. We can see that in every case the function of these new details was to fill gaps in the tradition which became apparent as soon as the story was presented from a Trojan point of view and concerned itself with the personal adventures of Aeneas about whom there was little in what we may call the official Greek version. Virgil follows very much the same procedure as Hellenistic poets who wished to present a well-worn myth in a new light: they placed a minor figure in the foreground, and thus made it possible for them to say new things within the framework of the ancient myth.[11] We may observe, incidentally, that Virgil filled most of these gaps with mythical material; furthermore, at no point, as far as we can tell, did he contradict the consensus of traditional opinion, although he did omit a great deal of traditional material.

We also came across another clear example of this abbreviation of the material in the account of Aeneas' Wanderings. Virgil seems to have permitted himself a major departure from the tradition when he located the death of Anchises in Sicily; we have seen what practical and artistic considerations led him to do so. He may have thought that he was justified in introducing a new version when the traditions provided so many different accounts of the event. Elsewhere in the Wanderings too he is filling in the gaps in the tradition: in Book 3, apart from the Andromache scene, he inserts supernatural or fabulous material: Polydorus, Apollo at Delphi, the Penates in Crete, the Harpies, the omen at the landing in Italy, the story of Polyphemus and Achaemenides. In Books 4 and 5 he merely embellished the tradition.

For the events in Latium, Virgil's treatment of the characters and their adventures 245 remains faithful to the sources. But here too we find, first of all, the combination of different sources – the alliance with Tarchon and the battle against Mezentius, the friendly attitude of Latinus and the battle against the Latins. Secondly, Virgil allows himself complete freedom in the manipulation of the chronology – Mezentius' death occurs before that of Turnus (and therefore in a duel with Aeneas, not, in accordance with the tradition, with Ascanius); the events are concentrated into a few days; the death of Turnus occurs before that of Aeneas; Lavinium is founded only after the conclusion of hostilities. Again, the material is expanded by the inclusion of other ancient Italian traditions – Evander and Pallas, Turnus' allies, including Camilla, and again, Diomedes. Finally, Virgil re-shapes the tradition in epic style – he describes battles that include many episodes, but above all, again, mythical material: prodigies, Allecto, various types of scenes and stories in which the gods appear, including some that are manifest inventions, for example the metamorphosis of the ships by the Great Mother and the transformation of the ancient Latin goddess Juturna into Turnus' sister and Jupiter's beloved: this (like perhaps the dream-oracle of Faunus, see above p. 181 n. 6) is a remarkable attempt to contribute to the Hellenization of the native gods of Italy which was to be a constant preoccupation of Ovid. Apart from the chronology and its consequences, Virgil never directly contradicts the tradition.

Some of the minor figures were freely invented by Virgil: these probably include Androgeos in Book 2, Achaemenides (above p. 93 n. 43), Nisus and Euryalus, Drances, and many warriors in the battle-scenes, for which the tradition supplied far too few names; but even here Virgil prefers to keep to the tradition wherever possible, and often it may only be our ignorance of the tradition that leads us to assume that Virgil has invented a name:[12] Venulus, the ambassador sent to Diomedes, is taken from the legends of Lavinium (Servius on 8.9), and Latinus' chief shepherd is named Tyrrhus after the shepherd in whose hut Silvius was traditionally said to have been born (Servius on 6.760; 7.484), etc.

Thus we have established that the general guidelines that Virgil followed in
246 handling his sources are as follows: to accept as much of the traditional version as possible, in so far as it was compatible with artistic considerations; in order to achieve this, different sources might be combined; free invention was permissible to fill any gaps or inadequacies in the tradition; in the selecting of this new material, preference is given to mythical subject-matter, which had only a general link with the tradition, but no connection with particular scenes;[13] he is permitted freedom in the arrangement and combination of different traditions, but he is not permitted to contradict the consensus of the tradition unless it is absolutely necessary.

If we disregard the mythical element, which it is the right, or we might even say the duty, of the epic poet to add to his narrative, then Virgil has, on the whole, transmitted the tradition more conscientiously than the majority of Roman annalists, to say nothing of the novelistic historians of Hellenistic times; we have only to think of what these historians regarded as permissible by way of διασκευή [elaboration]. Thus, as far as we can see, it appears that the ancient critics of the *Aeneid* did comment on those few places where Virgil deviates from the traditional narrative, but that they did not hold it against him. They were satisfied that it was only an oversight if he deviated from the established facts of Italo–Roman history;[14] other-
247 wise he is granted a certain degree of freedom in shaping his own story, and indeed Servius, comically standing a well-known aesthetic principle on its head, says that the epic poet has no right to report the unadorned truth, even, for example, about Venus' star, which, according to the traditional account, guided Aeneas to Latium.[15] However, one thing is obligatory: that the poet should know the traditional version

200

and should not contradict it out of sheer ignorance.[16] Therefore, when he deviates from it, he should make at least a covert reference to the true version in order to reassure learned readers. The ancient commentators succeeded in tracing a considerable number of such allusions in Virgil,[17] though they certainly followed several false trails; but their observations ought not, in my opinion, to be rejected out of hand. As we have already seen (p. 80), Virgil omits the tradition that Diomedes returned the Palladium to Troy, although he hints (5.704) that he is aware that the Nautian *gens* believed that it explained their relationship with the cult of Minerva. He omits the tradition that Latinus presented the Trojans with a specific piece of land, but he makes Latinus express the intention of doing so (11.316). Unlike Cato and others, he does not say that the battle between the Latins and Trojans was the consequence of marauding raids by the Trojans; but Juno's violently anti-Trojan speech accuses them of *arva aliena iugo premere atque avertere praedas* (10.78) [laying a heavy yoke on farmlands not their own and driving off their plunder]; and there are doubtless many similar examples,[18] although it may be difficult to draw the line between learned allusions and the free adaptation of traditional motifs in every case.[19]

248

Finally, we may observe that Virgil handled the traditional material just as Homer was then believed to have done.[20] He, too, had taken the true story of the Trojan War and the return of Odysseus, and made a poetic version of it (διεσκεύασε [he organized]); in other words he had embellished the events as recounted in the tradition, and had made them come alive (διάθεσις [rhetorical arrangement]); at the same time he had interwoven all manner of supernatural and miraculous events (μῦθος [myth]) with the ordinary affairs of mankind, in order to give his listeners greater pleasure, interest and moral instruction than they would have derived from a straightforward historical narrative. Homer, too, has written nothing which is completely untrue (except perhaps here and there out of ignorance); it is rather the case that, beneath the cover of myth, the perceptive reader can discern the traditional account which enshrined the real truth.

II. *The Models*

The fact that Virgil depended on tradition in the way just described has little or nothing to do with the question of his originality. It is not the free invention of new material that constitutes originality – how few great poetic masterpieces would count as original if that were so! – but rather, to a great extent, the successful appropriation or remoulding of tradition. Let us say nothing of the Athenian tragedians; even the Hellenistic poets (who stood in much the same relationship to tradition as Virgil himself) were still able to find, if they were true poets, plenty of scope for the exercise of their own creative powers; and for Virgil, too, the tradition provided little more than the bare bones of the action – as for example in the case of Dido. The fact that the general outlines of his material have been firmly established does not cramp the imagination of a great poet; rather, he is upheld, uplifted and borne along by it; he actually seeks out figures from legend and history to use as

249

vehicles for his own powerful emotions, or as a trellis to support the luxuriant tendrils of his invention as they constantly burgeon forth in all their sweetness from the rich soil of his imagination. Virgil's creative activity is of a different kind: between the tradition and his own imagination stands his *model*. This fact does not need proving, but perhaps it is necessary to define more precisely the how and the why of it.

Dependency on a model affects, first, the outward form, and would seem to make total freedom impossible. A heroic epic written in anything other than Homeric metre and style was inconceivable, and Homeric style in Latin that was independent of Ennius was equally inconceivable. Virgil never translates directly from the Greek, and seldom takes more than isolated words and turns of phrase from his Roman predecessors; but he scatters clear and intentional allusions to them throughout his work. Virgil searches out opportunities to use Homeric epithets and phrases, metaphors and images, and to display stylistic jewels from Ennius in new settings. Of course, he has his own stylistic ideals, and no-one would deny that the personal style that he created was a magnificent achievement; but even in this case he was not creating from scratch, but sorting through the ancient building-stones with infinite patience and tireless judgement to decide which of them could be re-used in his new construction.

External form is closely linked with a second major area of imitation. The world which Virgil depicted in the style of Homer had to be the world of Homer. The inhabitants of his earth and of his heaven were taken from Homer; therefore they must behave and act in a Homeric manner. The great Hellenistic poets had come to the same conclusion; and because they did not on that account wish to be denied the opportunity to take up again the tradition of heroic poetry, they avoided as far as possible those areas which Homer had made his own for ever, such as descriptions of battles; they placed in the foreground characters who had played only minor roles in the tradition; they were fond of depicting passions and emotions, which must have existed in archaic Greece, but about which early epic had remained silent, since they were alien to its elevated style; in short, they transferred the ancient stories from the sphere of myth to a familiar, human setting – yet the result of all these changes was still no more than a compromise. Virgil also made a compromise: he does not suppress his own views about life, the world, the gods and his own emotions, but the means by which he expresses them are Homeric, and, as though he wishes to introduce the modern elements as unobtrusively as possible, he follows his model all the more faithfully in all those details which make no great difference to him.

However, this, too, is basically a question of style which is not inextricably linked with the question of creativity. It is creativity that we will now proceed to consider.

Virgil rarely describes landscape. The few extended descriptions that do appear in the *Aeneid*, however, are imitations: the harbour on the Libyan coast is modelled on the harbour of Phorcys in the Odyssey (13.96ff.); the Gorge of Ampsanctus (7.563ff.) is modelled on the Cave of Acheron in Apollonius (2.736ff.); Etna with its terrors (3.57ff.) is modelled on Pindar (*Pyth.* 1.34). Of course in all three cases Virgil has produced a more powerful effect than his predecessor, and has refashioned the description in his own style; but his starting-point is his source, not personal observation. The description of the storm at sea in Book 1 almost wilfully avoids any detail that might suggest personal experience. The material that he uses in his similes, in so far as they describe natural phenomena, is almost all borrowed; Virgil has no qualms about borrowing such a striking and unusual simile as the comparison of a vacillating mind with the reflection of trembling sunlight on the surface of water in a basin (8.22: Apollonius 3.754). These references to the natural world are not an important part of the epic, but these instances are typical of Virgil's practice throughout the whole narrative. 251

On the whole, then, we may say that Virgil takes the material of his story from the tradition, and in the broad outlines he sticks more or less closely to his models. And we may add that the most characteristic examples of this are to be found, not in the major and most important themes, for which the *Odyssey* and *Iliad* serve as models: the fact that Games are celebrated at the tomb of Anchises as at the tomb of Patroclus; that Aeneas, like Odysseus, descends into the Underworld; that in Latium, too, beached ships are defended, a city besieged, a woman fought for – such things as these are general motifs which tell us nothing about the independence of the poet who is making use of them: but when in the Games in the *Aeneid* there is a boxer who has difficulty in getting an opponent to come forward, as in the Games in *Iliad* 23; when victory in the footrace depends on the slip and fall of one competitor; when a bow-shot hits the cord that holds the dove instead of the bird itself; when Aeneas in the Underworld meets and speaks to a friend who has recently suffered an accidental death, and an unreconciled enemy, and an old comrade-in-arms; when Turnus, like Achilles, is drawn away from his opponent by a phantom, and the decisive duel is divided into the same three phases as in Homer – then it is clear beyond a shadow of doubt that Virgil, far from avoiding motifs used by others, in fact consistently and deliberately uses them as a starting-point, and introduces allusions to them throughout his work. When he reaches some part of his story that he wishes to develop in epic style, then he does not let this scene grow out of the soil of his own invention, either unaided or fertilized by the poetry of others, but, on the contrary, he searches through other works until he finds analogous scenes, and re-shapes them to meet the requirements of his own story.

This practice is not restricted to the broad outlines of the action. When Virgil wants to describe Aeneas' emotions during the mortal peril of the sea-storm he does not invent a vivid metaphor of his own for it, but considers to what extent he can use for his own purposes Odysseus' expression of his emotions in a similar situation. When he has to describe Dido's misery and despair, these feelings do not emerge in a vivid and intuitive form from his own emotional experiences; on the contrary, he looks around for existing images which have been created by other poets and with which he can adorn this particular situation. He does not often go as far as he does in the case of Dido, but there are traces of this process throughout the *Aeneid*. 252

The way in which Virgil imitates his predecessors is very different in each individual case, but it falls between two extremes. The simplest case is when a passage of some other poet, usually Homer, is used as it stands as the basis for a corresponding passage in Virgil: the oath and its violation, or the duel at the end of Book 12, may serve as examples. This technique is used at greatest length for the competitions at the Games. The most complicated case is when we can no longer speak of imitation of the whole of a particular scene, but when motifs and details from a great variety of sources have been woven together so as to form a new whole: I cite as examples of this the adventures involving the Harpies and Polydorus, the scene of Allecto with Turnus, but above all the story of Dido, whose character combines traits taken from a number of poetic models without completely resembling any one of them.

There are of course some scenes in Virgil's poem which we may safely regard as his own free invention; I would count among them, for example, the scene in Anchises' house, a splendid piece of imaginative writing. But when we think of these scenes, we observe that little or nothing actually happens; they describe encounters and conversations rather than actions, situations rather than events or psychological developments: think of Creusa's appearance in Book 2, Aeneas' encounter with Andromache in Book 3, Ilioneus and Latinus in Book 7, Aeneas and Evander in Book 8: in these cases and others the essential innovation is not what is done, but what is said and felt, even in the scenes with Evander, which are depicted with greater liveliness and vividness than practically any other passages that are Virgil's own free invention.

What is the reason for this very remarkable phenomenon? As we have already seen, the answer is not to be found in any theory that a poet was not permitted to indulge in free invention. It is difficult to draw the line between lack of desire and lack of ability in this case; but, in the final analysis, Virgil did not exercise much originality in re-shaping his material simply because, like his fellow-Romans generally, his powers of imagination were not very strong. That is the common factor in the various degrees of imitation which we have been enumerating: they all point to a basic lack of the intuitive ability to conceive things in visual terms, which irresistibly drives other artists to express their emotions in new poetic creation. Of course, like the other great Roman poets, Virgil experienced powerful and overwhelming emotions: he was sensitive to the sorrow of an aged father at the loss of his only son, or the misery and humiliation of a proud princess who is deserted by her beloved, as deeply as he sensed the greatness of the Augustan principate and the blessings of the *pax Augusta*; but his imagination was too weak to give any original expression to these feelings, and that is why he resorted to the works of his predecessors – just as Propertius could only express his burning passion in the traditional forms of Hellenistic erotic poetry, though I have no doubt that this passion was genuine enough; or even like Lucretius, who of all Latin poets had the strongest imagination; his genuine enthusiasm for the philosophical teachings in his poem and for Epicurus, the master of this philosophy, is evident in every line; nevertheless, when he writes a hymn in praise of this master, he adorns it with images taken over from other poets. This characteristic weakness of imaginative power, which must on no account be confused with lack of feeling, is evident not only in Roman poetry: it has left its mark on all the intellectual life, art and science, religion and philosophy, of Rome, and it even had a clear effect on politics and warfare: the *imperium Romanum* [Roman empire] is the work of men whose power of imagination, by comparison with their force of character and other mental faculties, was not strong enough to enable them, like a Napoleon, to seize total mastery for themselves.[21]

253

As a result of this characteristic cast of mind, the Roman people lacked ⁄
the ability but also the appetite for original poetry. It is not so much the phen⹀
of poetic imitation that is surprising, but the fact that continual dependence on
foreign models was not felt to be a weakness, nor lamented as being a shortcoming
which they would try to conceal as far as possible whenever it was unavoidable.
Exactly the opposite is the case. Horace, for example, does not even attempt to win
recognition for his own talent; instead, he takes more pride in his claim that he was   254
the first Roman to interpret the poetry of Archilochus, Alcaeus and Sappho, and he
regards Greek poetry as superior to Roman not because it was original but because it
was more perfect in form. There is nothing in Virgil that suggests that he was
attempting to free himself from the influence of Homer and other models, or to
conceal his dependence on them; on the contrary, he gives the impression that he
wants this dependence to be as obvious as possible to every reader. Nor did his
contemporaries think of criticizing him on this account. They criticized him when he
seemed to fall short of his model; they praised him when he seemed to surpass it. If
an imitative passage was ineffective, they excused him on the grounds that he had
gone too far in an effort to do what was in itself laudable.[22] It seems that doubts were
expressed only over one question, whether it was beneath the poet's dignity to have
taken over numerous passages word for word: Virgil himself openly acknowledged
such borrowing, and did so with pride.[23] In Rome, poetry had never been independent of models, nor was there any concept of such poetry; imitation was not
regarded as a failure to achieve independence, but as an improvement on mere
translation; personal style, not personal creativity, is the boast of the Roman poet
over the centuries. But not even the surge of intellectual activity in the Augustan age
broke away from tradition, and the reason for this may to some extent have been the   255
tendency of all Greek literature during the Hellenistic period to imitate the ancients,
who – at least as far as style was concerned – seemed to have exhausted every
possibility in poetry and prose, and to have achieved the highest degree of perfection
already. It is certainly true that the nature and extent of the dependence of the poets
of the Augustan age on their predecessors varies greatly from one poet to another;
but it is equally true that in seeking to escape the exclusive influence of the Alexandrians and to gain access to the genuine classics of epic, drama and lyric, they
believed that they were only doing what they had seen their erstwhile teachers
doing. The only difference of which they were conscious was that their own task
was much more difficult since they were imitating the creations of a foreign civiliza-
tion and for this purpose they needed to start by hammering their own language into
shape, regulating, enriching and refining it. But in this task and its achievement they
found a new reason for pride: by imitating these foreign classics they Romanized
them, they 'captured' them, so to speak, for Rome. Virgil was too modest and intelligent
to suppose that he could rival Homer, let alone surpass him, but he was certainly
striving to create something which could mean almost as much to a Roman as
Homer meant to a Greek. In so doing he would have thought that it was senseless to
reject splendid passages from Homer simply in order to be original; on the contrary,
he believed that he must imitate the finest and most splendid passages of his Greek
predecessor and so 'capture' it for his own nation. Imitation, in his view, was not a
makeshift to be ashamed of, but a patriotic action and therefore a cause of pride.

III. *Virgil's personal contribution*

This technique of using and imitating sources that we have been discussing would have produced no more than a mechanically derivative piece of work if it had been carried out without thought and feeling, reflection and taste. It would have been a cheap and nasty patchwork with all its joins showing, its colours clashing and its outlines lacking in clarity and in character, expressing nothing but the incompetence of its maker. Countless readers have been well aware that the *Aeneid* is no such clumsy hotchpotch, and, in particular, those whose opinions on questions of literary craftsmanship deserve to be taken seriously have borne witness to it time and time again. The excellence of a work of art can only be demonstrated – if at all – to the extent that the poet's personal feelings, thoughts and artistic inclinations are open to inspection; I have attempted to do this in my analysis in Part I, and in Part II I shall summarize and develop this analysis. For a rigorous scholarly investigation will show that Virgil was no mere mechanical imitator. Of course, there are occasions when he failed to achieve his aim; sometimes the situation which he is using as his model has too little in common with what he has to describe, so that not even all the artistry at his disposal can conceal the incongruity; more often, the fusion of disparate elements into a new whole leads to contradictions or obscurities; finally, and perhaps worst of all, the poet's own intentions suffer because they have been transmitted through a foreign medium, so that only too frequently they do not leap to the reader's eye but only reveal themselves after careful consideration. None of this can be denied, and an objective list of such instances is essential for a proper evaluation of the whole poem;[24] however, we should not pronounce judgement on a poet's failure to achieve his artistic intentions before we have established what these intentions were, and given due credit to the passages that are successful. Let us now briefly list the different areas in which the poet's original contributions are to be sought. In the present context I shall not deal with any matter of style in the narrower sense.

We said above that the broad outline of the plot of the *Aeneid* was taken over from others. We must now formulate this more precisely: Virgil often takes a scene from elsewhere and develops it in his own manner – he develops it, so to speak, backwards or forwards, by giving it either a motivation or consequences that differ from those which it had in his source. For example, in the case of his description of the fight for the camp, he has a striking image at hand in Homer's description of the fight at the wall: one gate of the camp is opened, and on either side of the entrance stands an enormous guard. In Homer (*Iliad* 12.120ff.) they are holding the gate open to allow retreating soldiers to enter; in Virgil (9.672ff.), since those besieged in the camp have been forbidden to risk a sortie, the guards have opened the gate so as to mock the attackers and dare them to enter; with defiant bravado they challenge them to a hand-to-hand fight. Or again, Virgil wants to describe how Aeneas and Dido were first united in love. He drew on Apollonius for the scene: Apollonius describes how Jason and Medea, in a cave on Corcyra, constrained by necessity, consummate

their marriage in secret (4.1130f.). Virgil uses this situation, but in order to give it a new motivation he invents the hunt and the storm (4.129ff.). And now an example of developing the consequences of a scene: in a race, one of the runners slips and falls, and therefore forfeits the prize. This is in Homer (*Iliad* 23.773ff.) and in Virgil (5.327ff.); but in the former that is the end of it; in the latter Nisus makes use of the fall which prevents him from winning, to help Euryalus to victory. Or again: two heroes, sent on a night-time reconnaissance, enter the enemy's camp and kill some of their number; in Homer (Book 10) they come home safely; in Virgil (Book 9) their carelessness brings about their death. In all the examples we have cited, it is not only the outward action which has been remodelled, but its psychological content as well; and this is another extremely important point. We have touched on many instances of this kind already; I would remind you of the last scene of the   258
Aeneid: Turnus pleads in vain; externally this is absolutely identical with the corresponding scene in the *Iliad*, but what happens in the minds of both Turnus and Aeneas is something completely new. Again, when the hero is telling his host about his wanderings, how different Dido's emotions are from those of Alcinous! And from a psychological point of view, the violation of the oaths in Book 12 is totally different from that in Book 4 of the *Iliad*; and so forth. But this remodelling also occurs even where Virgil is imitating not just the course of the action, but also the expression of emotion: the feelings that Aeneas expresses in his speech during the storm at sea (1.198ff.) are quite different from those of Odysseus in the same situation; and in the story of Dido the psychological development which leads from her discovery of Aeneas' betrayal to her death is, in this form, Virgil's own, however dependent he is on others for individual details.

The new and original motivation and so forth that we have mentioned stemmed from the practical requirements of the plot and of the characters. The second important area that we shall explore is the purely artistic one – we might say that it is a matter of artistry of form. Virgil aims at clearly-defined and easily demonstrable artistic effects with the aid of a technique developed with great sensitivity and especially suited to this particular purpose; and if occasionally his intentions as regards the plot are not realised with all the sharpness and clarity that we might wish for, his artistic intentions never fail to achieve their aim. We can grasp them best in those instances where his model is available for comparison; to mention only one of the examples that we have already discussed, consider how he re-shaped Homer's account of the violation of the treaty; we shall encounter many more examples as we proceed. Obviously, here too we can trace the influence of earlier poets on Virgil – when was an artistic technique ever created out of nothing? – but it is impossible to maintain that Virgil was a mere imitator in this respect: he learned from his predecessors, but as far as we know none of them had attempted or achieved what he was aiming at. In the history of narrative art, Virgil's *Aeneid* marks a watershed.[25]

We shall explore both these tendencies in the following chapters, and our dis-   259
cussion should lead to a sharper definition of the aims of Virgil's epic technique. The great impact which his work has made is largely due to another factor which deserves at least a mention in any discussion of Virgil's personal contribution: that is, on the one hand, the warmth of his sympathy with the emotions of his characters, and on the other hand the strength of his moral and religious sentiments and of his

260   national feelings – it is the combination of these two characteristics that forms the central pillar that supports his poem. To describe them in more detail is not our purpose here; our concern is with Virgil's *ars* [art, technical skill], not his *ingenium* [native talent].

IV. *Virgil's working methods*

It is clear that to adopt the working methods that we have described must have been extremely laborious – quite apart from the care that had to be bestowed on the external form of the composition. Virgil must first have made an extensive preliminary study of the sources and of his predecessors;[26] if we think of the echoes from epic, epyllion and tragedy that we can still identify in, for example, the story of Dido, we will almost certainly conclude that, as a foundation for his own work, Virgil made a systematic search through all the relevant literature.[27] It is hardly possible to overestimate the endless process of appraisal, consideration and reconsideration that Virgil needed to undertake before he could work the motifs that he had borrowed from his predecessors into the action of his own narrative.

    We do not know exactly how long Virgil worked on the *Aeneid*. There were ten or eleven years (29-19 BC) between the completion of the *Georgics* and Virgil's death; but it is not very likely that he started on the *Aeneid* as soon as he had completed the *Georgics*; we know from his own words[28] that at that time he had plans for an epic of a completely different nature. At all events, he was already at work by 26 or 25 BC: Augustus wrote from Cantabria in Spain asking him to send him a first draft or at least some extracts (Suet. 61R) – in vain; at about the same date, Propertius announces (2.34.65) that the *Aeneid* is in the process of composition, and he appears to know the poem already, though this does not necessarily mean that he knew anything else about the content of the work; we should think of the poem as being still in its earliest stages at that time. Virgil recited Books 2, 4 and

261   6 in the presence of Augustus and his closest associates; this recital must have taken place after the death of Marcellus at the end of 23 BC.[29]

    As for Virgil's method of working, we have Suetonius' account (59R), which we can be sure is derived from the best contemporary sources. Suetonius says that Virgil made the first draft of the *Aeneid* in prose, and divided his material into twelve books; however, he did not work on the books consecutively from beginning to end but chose specific passages that particularly attracted him and worked on these separately.[30] And his method was not to concentrate painstakingly on details, slowly adding word to word and line to line, but to allow himself to be swept along on the flood of improvisation, even leaving some lines unfinished if necessary. The final polishing, which involved making a considerable number of cuts in the first draft, was done gradually and was never finally completed.[31]

    The most surprising feature of this method is surely that described by the words *particulatim* [in individual sections] and *nihil in ordinem componere* [not composing in order]. Since it was always characteristic of Virgil that he worked towards a total and unified effect, we cannot take this to mean that he tackled various bits and

pieces at random, writing, say, a monologue for Dido one day, and some arbitrarily   262
chosen passage from a battle-scene the next; it is much more reasonable to assume
that he selected short self-contained sections to work on, poems within the poem as
it were, and that *n i h i l in ordinem* [*nothing* in order] is a considerable exaggeration. The story of the childhood of Camilla in Book 11 might be one of these short
self-contained sections, and we might surmise that the same is true of many other
episodic scenes, for example the story of Nisus and Euryalus in Book 9, or of
Hercules and Cacus in Book 8. But generally speaking it is the entire books which
constitute the sections of the poem; and we can prove with absolute certainty that
Virgil worked on *one* of the books separately, and out of sequence, namely Book 3.
When he read out Books 2, 4 and 6 to Augustus, he was presenting him with three
separate poems, each complete in itself, which did not require the linking narrative
of Books 3 and 5. Indeed, Book 6 is connected by an insignificant detail to Book 4,
which had already been written.[32] Thus Virgil wrote these sections not only out of
sequence but also without concerning himself much with what he would have to say
in preceding books which he had yet to write. We would naturally assume that when
he wrote the account of the *prodigia* in Books 7 and 8, and of Palinurus in Book 6,
he must have realized that it would be necessary to refer to them again in Book 3
and Book 5; but for the time being, as a provisional measure, he presented things as
if they were appearing in the course of the narrative for the first time; in other
words, he started by writing completely independent poems, each of which contained its own particular presuppositions, and left the task of working these
individual pieces into a satisfactory whole to some future date. Furthermore, as is
clear from discrepancies between Book 3 and the later books, he wrote the latter
before he had finally decided on the plan of Book 3 in all its details. Of course he
must have laid down the general outlines of the narrative and the order in which the
events were to be described: that is why he began by making a provisional choice of
his material and dividing it into the twelve books. Nor is there any reason to doubt
that he kept to this plan in all essentials throughout, even if he modified many
details, as for example in Book 3. Finally, the fact that each book was completed
separately does not exclude the possibility that Virgil later made changes in and   263
additions to what he had already written; indeed this would have been essential in
cases where when writing earlier sections of the epic he realized that he would have
to change presuppositions underlying later sections.

It is extremely important to bear this method of composition in mind. It will help
to resolve certain difficulties in the narrative and to elucidate a large number of
contradictions and loose connections;[33] and, besides, it is only in the light of this
knowledge that we can properly appreciate the composition of the individual books.
We shall investigate this later; at this point all that we need to do is to ask what led
Virgil to adopt this unusual method of composition.

Perhaps it would be best to make the outward form of the work our starting point,
as Goethe did when he was trying to clarify the difference between epic and dramatic technique. The *Aeneid* was not intended to be read right through like a modern
novel, but to be recited in separate sections. We know that Virgil recited three
separate books to Augustus; he had also recited the *Georgics* to him *per continuum
quadriduum* [on four consecutive days] (Suet. 61R), that is, one book a day. That is

not too little at a time; poetry of this kind should be savoured in small sections to do justice to its fine qualities; if the poet has taken care with every single word, the listener too should appreciate every single word; this requires careful attention, alertness, receptivity, and concentrated involvement, all to the highest degree. Again, it would be wrong to break off at some arbitrary point in a long continuous poem when the listener has had enough, and leave the rest for another day; the best, the cumulative effect of the whole, is then lost. Anyone who ventures to create a great epic must try to compose it of separate parts each of which is a unity in itself and each of which is effective by itself; in other words, the work must combine the qualities of a long 'continuous' poem of the Homeric type with the qualities of a garland of separate poems in the style of Callimachus. But if each book is to be a ἕν

264 [unity],³⁴ then it must have a beginning and an end, i.e. it must make as few presuppositions as possible, and lead to a definite climax. This is the direct opposite of the requirement that has been deduced from a study of Homer, that epic poetry should flow in an unbroken stream, with each section attached to the next like a link in a continuous chain; but Virgil has attempted to overcome this conflict. It would certainly have been more logical, and safer, to write the separate books in the proper order, and a poet who was chiefly concerned with the inexorably logical continuity of the whole poem would have done so had he been in Virgil's shoes; but Virgil worked *prout liberet* [as it suited his fancy]; one whose first priority is the effect of the individual sections will allow himself to succumb to the attractions of any part of his work that suits his mood at any given time. This meant that contradictions and so forth inevitably arose, and were allowed to stand for the time being. We must of course assume that they really were temporary makeshifts, and that Virgil intended to remove them; everyone naturally feels a need for logic and unity, and, besides we know that contemporary theorists believed that logical unity underlay Homer's work too, and that a poet should as far as possible try to achieve it. We cannot say to what extent Virgil would have succeeded in removing the contradictions. He would hardly have been able to eradicate all the infelicitous traces of his idiosyncratic method of composition. Our generation has learnt how to recognize these traces more clearly than readers in earlier centuries, who either overlooked them or invented arbitrary interpretations to explain them away. A modern interpreter is in duty bound to mention them, but we should not forget how insignificant they are in the context of the poet's principal intention. We should also remember that they have not detracted from the powerful effect that the *Aeneid* has had on all those who have been attuned to it, just as the much more serious contradictions and discrepancies in the Homeric epics have never impaired the powerful effect that they too have achieved.

Notes to Chapter 1

240   **1.** It hardly needs saying that Virgil regarded both the fall of Troy and the settlement of Latium by Aeneas as historical facts; in his time the only matter of uncertainty was the extent to which the details were reliable, and even Livy, who is

unusually sceptical about these events, is prepared to believe most of them. Dionysius cites the τεκμήρια [evidence] which still bear witness to Aeneas' visits to different points along all the coasts as proof of the accuracy of his own version of the *errores Aeneae* [wanderings of Aeneas], just as, for example, Strabo 1.2.39 cites similar τεκμήρια as evidence for the historical basis of the traditional voyage of the Argonauts.

2. E. Rohde, *Griech. Rom.* (Leipzig, 1876) 97f.; Norden 112f.

3. 1.59 Καινέα...ζῳόν περ ἔτι κλείουσιν ἀοιδοί Κενταύροισιν ὀλέσθαι κτλ. [for singers tell of Caineus, who, though still alive, perished at the hands of Centaurs, etc.].

4. *dicuntur* (64.2) [they are said], *fertur* (19) [it is said], *perhibent* (76, 124) [they   241 relate], *ferunt* (212) [they say].

5. *Odes* 1.7.23: *Teucer.. fertur vinxisse* [Teucer is said to have bound], *fertur Prometheus* (16.13) [Prometheus is said]; *Epp.* 1.18.43: *putatur Amphion* [Amphion is thought]; *Odes* 3.5.41: of Regulus' return to Carthage: *fertur* [he is said].

6. Just as in the passage from the *Georgics* that we have just mentioned the reference to *fama* follows a question put to the Muse, so too in *Aeneid* 1.15: *fertur* occurs in the account of the reasons for Juno's anger, which the Muse had been asked about; at 9.79 the poet addresses the Muses before the strange metamorphosis of the ships: *dicite: prisca fides facto, sed fama perennis* [tell me: there is only ancient warrant for the event, but the memory (*fama*) of it never dies], probably in the sense of Livy 7.6.6. *fama standum est, ubi certam vetustas derogat fidem* [we must rely on tradition (*fama*) when the passage of time has removed all reliable accounts] and then continues (9.82) with *fertur*; at 7.37 Erato had been asked explicitly only about the situation in Latium at the time of Aeneas' arrival, but when Virgil proceeds to introduce his account of Latinus' descent from Faunus and Marica with *accipimus* [we are told] he does not of course intend us to assume that this is distinct from what is revealed by the Muse. Such a distinction, however, is implied when Virgil imitates Homer's invocation of the Muses which precedes the Catalogue of Ships, ὑμεῖς γὰρ θεαί ἐστε, πάρεστέ τε, ἴστε τε πάντα, ἡμεῖς δὲ κλέος οἶον ἀκούομεν, οὐδέ τι ἴδμεν [for you are goddesses, and you are present, and you know all things; but we only hear what men say, and know nothing] (*Iliad* 2.485f.) = *et meministis enim, divae, et memorare potestis; ad nos vix tenuis famae perlabitur aura* [for you are divine, and you have the gifts of memory and story; but only the faintest echo of the tale has come down to me] (*Aeneid* 7.645); but Homer's contrast between divine omniscience and human ignorance is changed in Virgil into a contrast between established tradition, *memoria*, and obscure rumours. Moreover, in my view it is far from certain that every time Virgil invokes the Muse or appeals to tradition he does in fact use them as his source: on the contrary, it is very likely that the metamorphosis of the ships (9.79ff.), for example, is Virgil's own invention, but he does not wish the reader to be aware of it. The invocation of the Muse with no reference to tradition at 9.525 (cf. 12.500), is purely Homeric imitation.

7. For example at 12.735 Virgil reports a *fama* which directly contradicts his own earlier account (90ff.).

8. It is significant that in the catalogue of the Latin allies it is the unmistakably   242 mythical elements (and only these) which are said to be derived from the tradition:

211

e.g. Caeculus 7.680: *omnis quem credidit aetas* [whom every generation since has believed] to be a son of Vulcan, Oebalus 734: *quem generasse Telon Sebethide nympha fertur* [whom it is said that Telon begot by the nymph Sebethis], *ferunt* (765) [they tell] of the miracle whereby Hippolytus is brought back to life, and similarly, in the second catalogue (10.189) of the metamorphosis of Cycnus. Again, Latinus' descent from the god Faunus is introduced with *accipimus* [we are told] (see above); so too with Picus *is parentem te Saturne refert* [he *claimed* you, Saturn, as his grandfather]; and even Aeneas expresses himself with similar caution on the subject of his and Evander's family-tree: *ut Grai perhibent* [as the Greeks relate] and *auditis si quicquam credimus* (8.135, 140) [if we believe what we are told]; similarly, *ut perhibent* (4.179) [so men say] of the genealogy of Fama. We should remember that Asclepiades τῆς ψευδοῦς ἱστορίας, τουτέστι τῆς μυθικῆς ἓν μόνον εἶδος ὑπάρχειν λέγει, τὸ γενεαλογικόν [says there is only one kind of false, i.e. mythical history, namely genealogy] (Sextus *Adv. gramm.* 253). Other mythical digressions which should be mentioned in this context are the story of Daedalus' flight (*ut fama est* [6.14] [as the story goes]) and the labyrinth (*fertur* [5.588] [it is said]); the city of Ardea is said (*dicitur* [7.409]) to have been founded by Danae; even the characters in the poem use the same phrases, e.g. Helenus (3.416) and Aeneas (3.551, 578). In the Nekyia (the visit to the Underworld) the poet desires *audita loqui* (6.266) [to tell what has been told to me], cf. Norden *ad loc.*; however, in the parallels from visionary revelation-literature which Norden cites, the author usually refers to particularly reliable sources to confirm his account; Virgil differs from these authors, and from Socrates in Plato *Protag.* 524: ταῦτ' ἔστιν ἃ ἐγὼ ἀκηκοὼς π ι σ τ ε ύ ω ἀληθῆ εἶναι [this is what I have heard, and *believe* to be true], since he rarely states his own belief in what he has heard from others; the nearest he comes to doing so is when he feels it necessary to ask the gods of the Underworld for permission to divulge what they have told him; it is only in giving information about dreams – where they live, and the gates through which they leave the Underworld – that he adds *ferunt* (6.284) [they say] and *fertur* (893) [it is said]. The account of young Ascanius' intervention in the battle at 9.590ff. verges on the miraculous and is therefore introduced with *dicitur* [it is said]. Servius comments on *accipimus* at 7.48: *propter varias opiniones hoc adiecit* [he adds this because opinions varied]; this may be true of some instances in Apollonius (Orpheus' descent from Calliope 1.24, Augeias' descent from Helios 172, the death of Tiphys 2.856), but F. Leo, *Hermes* 42 (1907) 68f., rightly denies that this is true of Virgil, including *quam fama secutast* [who has acquired the reputation] at *Ecl.* 6.74.

9. This is true of the great majority of the examples that we have given; we may add *fertur* (9.82) [it is said], which introduces the conversation of the Great Mother with Jupiter which precedes the main action. *Dicitur* (4.204) [it is said] which Virgil uses of Iarbas' prayer to Jupiter is a similar case: it is not mythical, but the poet is with Dido and Aeneas in Carthage, as it were; meanwhile, anything that is happening at a distance is known to him only by hearsay.

10. *si credere dignum est* (6.173) [if we can believe such a deed] of the story of Misenus and Triton; he had used the same words of the story of Pan and Luna which he believed to be equally unworthy of a deity (*Geo* .3.391). Apollon. 1.154, referring to Lynceus' miraculous eyesight, adds εἰ ἐτεόν γε πέλει κλέος [if the story is true].

243

212

On εἰ ἐτεόν [if it is true] in Arat. *Phaen.* 30 (cf. 260, 637) the scholiast remarks ὡς μὲν ποιητὴς παρεισάγει (scil. τὸν μῦθον), ὡς δὲ περὶ φυσικῶν διαλεγόμενος οὐ πάνυ τῷ μύθῳ συντρέχειν δοκεῖ· ἐπήγαγε γοῦν τὸ εἰ ἐτεὸν δή, ὅπερ ἐστὶ δισταγμοῦ, ἤτοι τοῦ ἀμφιβάλλοντος [as a poet he introduces it (sc. the myth), but as one who is discussing natural phenomena, he appears not to be in total agreement with it: so he has added 'if it is true', which is an indication of uncertainty, or of doubt]. This is also true to a certain degree of Virgil's relationship with the myths concerning the gods: we shall see below that, as far as possible, he avoids anything which would contradict religion as interpreted by the philosophers. The painful question *tantaene animis caelestibus irae* [can Gods in heaven be capable of such rancour?] is almost the same as εἰ ἐτεόν [if it is true].

11. Wilamowitz, *Euripides: Herakles* I² 84 note.   244

12. Cf., for example, Norden 252ff. on Polyboetes, the Trojan priest of Demeter,   245 mentioned at 6.484.

13. When Virgil invented some mythical detail which had no precedent in the   246 traditional versions, the critics remarked on it; opinions seem to have varied about whether he was justified. Cornutus (in Macrob. 5.19.1) commented on 4.698: *unde haec historia ut crinis auferendus sit morientibus, ignoratur* [we do not know the origin of this story, that a lock of hair must be taken (sc. by Proserpine) from those on the point of death] (and in this case there was every justification for the question, because the poet writes as if it was generally known), *sed adsuevit poetico more aliqua fingere ut de aureo ramo* (6.136) [but Virgil frequently invents certain details, as poets are wont to do, as for example in the case of the golden bough]; in other words he did not deny the poet the right to invent such details. Others passed stricter judgement: Servius on 3.46 defends the invention in the episode of Polydorus by citing the example of Romulus' spear: *vituperabile enim est poetam aliquid fingere, quod penitus a veritate recedat* [for it is blameworthy for a poet to invent anything that is utterly remote from the truth], and 9.81 (the metamorphosis of the ships), *figmentum hoc licet poeticum sit, tamen quia exemplo caret, notatur a criticis* [although this is a poetic fiction, nevertheless it is castigated by the critics, because it is unprecedented]. That is the theory which Horace follows: *ficta voluptatis causa sint proxima veris: ne quodcumque volet poscat sibi fabula credi, neu pransae Lamiae vivum puerum extrahat alvo* [fictions intended to give pleasure should remain close to the truth, so you should not expect people to believe anything you like to put in your story, nor should you depict a live child emerging from Lamia's belly after she has eaten it] (*Ars Poetica* 338). The rule that the poet must consider probability throughout his narrative (Servius comments on 11.554 [Camilla tied to her spear]: *Probus de hoc loco* ἀπίθανον πλάσμα [Probus says of this passage: 'an implausible invention']) therefore applies also to mythical material: the reader is prepared to accept the familiar but tends to quibble at the unfamiliar. Cf. now E. Stemplinger, *Das Plagiat in der griechischen Literatur* (Leipzig, 1912) 102.

14. See Hyginus in Gellius 10.16 on the anachronism of Palinurus' reference to   247 *Velini portus* (6.366) [harbour of Velia], and the alleged confusion in the lines about the conquerors of Greece (6.838); Hyginus believes that Virgil would have corrected these errors in the course of his final revision. See Norden 112ff.

15. Servius on 1.382: *hoc loco per transitum tangit historiam, quam per legem*

artis poeticae aperte non potest ponere...Lucanus namque ideo in numero poetarum esse non meruit, quia videtur historiam composuisse, non poema [in this passage he touches in passing on a matter of history, which because of artistic principles he cannot narrate plainly.... For this reason Lucan does not deserve to be counted as a poet, because he seems to have written a history, not a poem].

16. Servius on 1.267: *ab hac autem historia ita discedit Vergilius, ut aliquibus locis ostendat, non se per ignorantiam, sed per artem poeticam hoc fecisse* [Virgil departs from the historical tradition at this point, but in such a way as to demonstrate in a number of passages that he has done so, not through ignorance, but for artistic and poetic reasons]. This is just like Strabo's defence of Homer against accusations of ἄγνοια [ignorance] (1.1.2-10, esp. 10).

17. For example, Servius on 1.363, 487, 491, 3.256.

18. Norden rightly observes that the emphatic phrase that Virgil uses of Theseus in the Underworld, *sedet aeternumque sedebit* (6.617) [he sits, and so will sit for ever], indicates that he is rejecting an alternative version of the myth.

248 **19.** Amongst the latter I would include, for example, his use of Pacuvius' version of the death of Priam (see p. 59 n. 71 above); Dido's statement *nec patris Anchisae cineres manisve revelli* (4.427) ['I never tore up Anchises' grave to disturb his ashes and his spirit'] – according to tradition, that is what Diomedes had done; the transformation of Mezentius' demand for the *primitiae* [first-fruits] into a blasphemous prayer (10.773; see p. 165 above); and so forth.

20. The following passages are taken from Strabo's introduction, which anyone who wishes to understand Virgil is well advised to read; it gives us some idea of what Virgil's views on Homer and on epic poetry would have been. His main point is: τόν τε Ἰλιακὸν πόλεμον γεγονότα παραλαβὼν ἐκόσμησε ταῖς μυθοποιίαις, καὶ τὴν Ὀδυσσέως πλάνην ὡσαύτως· ἐκ μηδενὸς δὲ ἀληθοῦς ἀνάπτειν κενὴν τερατολογίαν οὐχ Ὁμηρικόν (1.2.9) [He (Homer) took the Trojan War, which was a historical event, and embellished it with mythological inventions, and he treated the wanderings of Odysseus in the same way; but it is not Homer's habit to attach some idle miraculous tale to something that has no truth in it]. Similarly he refutes Eratosthenes' contention that ποιητὴν πάντα στοχάζεθαι ψυχαγωγίας, οὐ διδασκαλίας (1.2.3) [every poet aims at entertainment, not instruction]. The tripartite division of poetry into ἱστορία, διάθεσις and μῦθος [history, rhetoric and myth]: τῆς μὲν οὖν ἱστορίας ἀλήθειαν εἶναι τέλος...τῆς δὲ διαθέσεως ἐνέργειαν...μύθου δὲ ἡδονὴν καὶ ἔκπληξιν [the aim of history is truth...that of rhetoric is vividness...and that of myth is to please and to astonish] (1.2.17, reporting the views of Polybius) – this is almost identical with the well-known division of ἱστορούμενα [narrative] into ἱστορία, μῦθος and πλάσμα [history, myth and invention] in Sextus *Adv. gramm.* 263, where μῦθος [myth] is defined as πραγμάτων ἀγενήτων καὶ ψευδῶν ἔκθεσις [an account of falsehoods and of things that have never happened]. In Latin this is *historia, fabula, argumentum*: Cic. *De invent.* 1.27 and elsewhere. All this is to be found in Homer; as an example of διάθεσις [rhetorical composition] he cites his descriptions of battles.

253 **21.** See also the excellent remarks of W.J. Sellar, *The Roman poets of the Augustan age: Virgil* [3] (Oxford, 1897) 87ff.

254 **22.** Macrobius 5.13.40: *sed haec et talia ignoscenda Vergilio, qui studii circa*

Homerum nimietate excedit modum [but we should forgive Virgil for this and other such things, since it is his excessive enthusiasm for Homer that has led him to overstep the mark].

23. Even his admirer Asconius was not happy: *quod pleraque ab Homero sumpsisset; sed hoc ipsum crimen sic defendere assuetum ait: 'cur non illi quoque eadem furta temptarent? verum intellecturos, facilius esse Herculi clavam quam Homero versum subripere'* [that he had taken a great deal from Homer; but he said that he was in the habit of defending himself against this particular charge as follows: 'Why didn't they themselves try to commit the same thefts? then they would discover that it was easier to steal the club from Hercules than to steal a line from Homer.'] (Suet. 66). This implies that Asconius' criticism does not refer to imitation in general, only to the *furta* [theft] of various lines. In Virgil's time, after small-scale poetry in the Hellenistic style had reached its full maturity at Rome, and, as the *Ciris* shows, had by no means died out, the opposition that had been expressed by Callimachus and his school against the great Hellenistic imitations of Homeric epic will certainly have been directed against the *Aeneid* as well; and just as the Alexandrians had formerly mocked their contemporaries for their unscrupulous borrowing of Homeric phrases, so too Virgil's 'thefts' from Homer may have been used by his critics to brand his work as 'cyclic' [derivative epic]. The *furta* [thefts] of Perellius Faustus and the *Homoeon Elenchon libri* [Books of Critical Enquiries into Similarities] of Octavius Avitus also had their predecessors at Alexandria: Porphyry (in Eusebius *Praep. Evang.* 10.3) assembled a whole series of writings about the κλοπαί [thefts]   255 of famous authors; the list of examples given there of Antimachus' thefts from Homer is the closest analogy to Macrobius' collection. See now Norden 359, note 1 and Kroll, *Neue Jahrbücher* (1903) 8 and the survey of literature on κλοπαί by Stemplinger op. cit. (p. 213 n. 13 above) 6ff.

24. I have pointed this out repeatedly, e.g. on p. 30ff., 32, 36ff., 74f., 78f., 82,   256 108 n. 8, 117 n. 44, 120 n. 59 etc; it is not the purpose of this book to provide an exhaustive analysis of it. In recent years it has become fashionable for scholars to track down such imperfections in the *Aeneid*. Unfortunately, most of them do so without paying any attention to Virgil's special intentions, which provide an explanation for many of his alleged mistakes: e.g. Georgii frequently in his *Antike Aeneiskritik*; K. Neermann, *Über ungeschickte Verwendung homerischer Motive in der Aeneis* (Plön, 1882); P. Cauer, *Zum Verständnis der nachahmenden Kunst des Virgil* (Kiel, 1885); W. Kroll op. cit. (p. 63 n. 102 above; on which see the reviews by Deuticke in the *Jahresberichte d. philol. Vereins* [1901] and Helm, *Bursians Jahresberichte* [1902], answered by Kroll, *Lit. Zentralblatt* [1903] 746). Virgil's independence in his imitations has been excellently discussed several times by Plüss (op. cit. n. 25 below) e.g. on pp. 38f. (as also by, e.g. Sainte-Beuve); but he is stretching his point too far when at pp. 342ff. he regards Virgil as an imitator only in the sense that every great poet imitates; this loses sight of the peculiar nature of   257 Virgil's creation, and displaces the centre of gravity of his achievement.

25. Plüss in his article 'Das Gleichnis in erzählender Dichtung' (*Festschrift zur 49. Philol.-Vers.* [1907] 53; cf. also Sellar op. cit. n. 21 above, 413ff.) rightly   258 emphasizes that in his similes, too, where, as we have already observed, Virgil frequently takes his material from others, it is not a matter of mindless mechanical

imitation: the poet nearly always re-shapes his material in his own individual
manner. This question deserves detailed examination, but a few examples will illustrate what is characteristically Virgilian in this area. Turnus hastens, splendidly
arrayed, into battle *qualis ubi abruptis fugit praesepia vinclis tandem liber equus*
etc. (11.492-3) [like some stallion which has broken his tether and, free at last,
gallops from his stall]: in its externals the simile is very like that in *Iliad* 6.506ff.;
but in the *Iliad* Paris had to be roused from deep sleep by Hector's reproaches,
whereas Turnus was unwillingly attending the council which was to decide on war
or peace, and he rushes out as soon as the approach of the enemy is announced.
Again, at *Iliad* 15.582ff. Antilochus kills Melanippus and leaps onto his body to
strip it of its armour, but when Hector comes rushing up he retreats to his own side
θηρὶ κακὸν ῥέξαντι ἐοικώς ὅς τε κύνα κτείνας ἢ βουκόλον ἀμφὶ βόεσσιν
φεύγει, πρίν περ ὅμιλον ἀολλισθήμεναι ἀνδρῶν [like some wild animal that has
done harm, who has killed a dog or a herdsman tending his cattle, and takes to flight
before a crowd of men has gathered to pursue him]. At 11.809ff. Virgil uses this
simile for Arruns, who hides fearfully amongst the soldiers after he has killed
Camilla unobserved, as the wolf *priusquam tela inimica sequantur...occiso pastore
magnove iuvenco* [before any threatening weapons can pursue him, when he has
killed a shepherd or a large bullock] runs to the mountains: Virgil greatly enriches
the psychological content of the simile. The helmet and shield of Diomedes shine as
brightly as Sirius, *Iliad* 5.4: so too do the helmet and shield of Aeneas at 10.272, but
here we are told of its effect on the enemy; Sirius is described as *sitim morbosque
ferens mortalibus aegris* [the star that brings thirst and disease to suffering hu-
manity], and Virgil adds the detail of the doom-laden comet: this enhances not only
the visual impact of the simile, but also its psychological content. In this last
instance, without the simile Virgil would not have been able to continue, *haud
tamen audaci Turno fiducia cessit* [but the daring of Turnus never quailed; he was
firmly confident...]; it can often be demonstrated that the context of a simile contains references to the simile itself, even if they might be omitted without damaging
the structure of the narrative; this fact prevents me from agreeing with Norden 206
that Virgil inserted the similes into his finished draft at a later stage; nor do I think
that they are put in merely *ornatus causa* [for decorative effect], or, for that matter –
in the majority of cases – in order to heighten the three-dimensional effect of a
scene, and to make it more like real life. Their chief purpose is to convey either the
passionate emotions of the person to whom the simile refers, emotions which cannot
be conveyed by ordinary means, or to make us feel more vividly the effect that
something extraordinary has produced upon the person who experiences it. There is
only *one* simile in Book 3; this is not, in my view, because the book was never
finally revised, as Norden believed, but because of the unusual nature of its contents
and of its narrative method.

26. Virgil himself wrote to Augustus *tanta incohata res est, ut paene vitio mentis
tantum opus ingressus mihi videar, cum praesertim ut scis alia quoque studia ad id
opus multoque potiora inpendam* [I have started on an enterprise of such magnitude,
that I am inclined to think that it was almost some kind of mental aberration to have
embarked on such a vast work, especially since, as you know, there are other and
much more important fields of study to which I must devote myself in order to

composed without regard to the other books, and so far as subject-matter and material are concerned, more or less finished and brought to completion]. Cf. also Wilamowitz, *Homer. Untersuchungen* (Berlin, 1884) 117 note; C. Schüler, *Quaestiones Vergilianae* (Diss. Greifswald, 1884) 15 etc.; Kroll op. cit. (p. 63 n. 102, p. 148), although I must say that I strongly disagree with both his interpretation of the facts and his views on their consequences.

264   **34.** Callimachus rejects the ἓν ἄεισμα διηνεκές [a single continuous song] for himself, fr. 1.3 Pf.; see C. Dilthey, *De Callim. Cydippa* (Leipzig, 1863) 25. 'The frequently cited phrase μέγα βιβλίον μέγα κακόν [a great tome is a great evil] makes much better sense from the standpoint of the listener than from that of the librarian or the reader,' R. Reitzenstein, *Epigramm und Skolion* (Giessen, 1893) 2.

achieve that work] (Macrob. 1.24.11). However, he was referring not only to research into history and antiquarian matters, but also, and perhaps above all, into philosophy.

27. See also, for example, p. 189 n. 54 above.

28. *Georgics* 3: proem; see E. Norden, *Neue Jahrbücher* 7 (1901) 315ff.

29. Suet. 61R. Servius' comment on 4.323: *cum privatim paucis praesentibus recitaret Augusto, nam recitavit primum libros tertium et quartum* [when he recited it in private to Augustus and a few others; for he recited Books 3 and 4 first] should not be regarded as contradicting Suetonius on this point; Book 6 is not mentioned here because it was irrelevant to this particular passage; Servius himself mentions the recitation in his note on 6.861. It was Book 2, not, as Servius says, Book 3 (this might be a deliberate correction): this is supported by our conclusions concerning the chronological relationship of the two books. But the most likely explanation, to my mind, is that Virgil chose these three books because they were the first to be finished. What other reason could there be for omitting, for example, Book 1? This is also entirely compatible with the information concerning the individual sections *prout liberet arripuit* [he took them up just as it suited his fancy]; it is obvious he was enticed to polish and complete these three books before the others. Of course this does not mean that he had not started on any of the other books at this date; the four remaining years of Virgil's life would hardly have been long enough for nine whole books – but even if Book 1, for example, had in all essentials been completed by then, too much of it would still have been *imperfectum* for it to be recited in public.

30. *Aeneida prosa prius oratione formatam digestamque in X11 latim componere instituit prout liberet quidque et nihil in ordinem* [he wrote the Aeneid in the form of a prose draft, and divided it into 12 books; he began to compose individual sections, taking them up just as it suited him, in no particular order].

31. *ut ne quid impetum moraretur quaedam imperfecta transmisit, alia verbis velut fulsit, quae per iocum pro tibicinibus interponi aiebat ad sustinendum opus, donec solidae columnae advenirent* (ibid.) [and so that nothing should hold up the flow of his work, he left some sections unpolished, and held others together, so to speak, by very unsubstantial words, which, he used to say jokingly, were inserted like wooden props to support the structure until the solid columns arrived]. Note also Suetonius' account of the way in which he composed the *Georgics* (ibid.): *traditur cotidie meditatos mane plurimos versus dictare solitus ac per totum diem retractando ad paucissimos redigere* [the story goes that he used every day to compose in the morning and dictate a large number of verses, and to spend the rest of the day working over them and reducing them to a very small number].

32. See above p. 136 n. 1.

33. Conrad has the distinction of being the first to discuss the structure of the *Virgilianae* (Progr. Trier [1863] XV111: *singulos Aeneidos libros tamquam singula corpora esse suo quodque nomine, ceterorum quemque expertia... quod... quantum ad res et materiam attinet quodammodo absolutum... esse videatur.* It is clear that each individual book is, so to speak...

2

Invention

I. *Mortals*

a) Characters

1. Generic characteristics

Ancient literary theory distinguished very sharply between the characterization of types and the characterization of individuals. In the *Poetics*, Aristotle is most interested in the characterization of individuals, but he does occasionally allude to the characterization of types; he deals with the latter more fully in the *Rhetoric*. It is significant that Horace's *Ars Poetica* lays particular emphasis on this kind (112-18; 156-78), and passes very quickly over the other, in a way that shows that he believes that in elevated poetry a mere handful of conspicuous features will provide sufficient characterization of individuals (119-27). This corresponds exactly with the practice of the post-classical phases of ancient poetry. As early as Aristotle, we find the opinion that 'more recent' tragedy lacks ἦθος [moral character] (*Poetics* 1450b 25): it had been pushed into the background by πάθος [emotion]. In Hellenistic poetry, subtler touches of individual characterization are restricted almost entirely to comedy and the less elevated genres (where, it is true, with a few brilliant exceptions, it became fossilized into 'typical' characterization). Serious poetry was considered to have other aims; it employed characterization, if at all, only in broad outlines or in a general way. Callimachus' Acontius and Cydippe, as the recently discovered papyrus shows, were simply a boy and a girl, a neutrally-coloured ground from which the splendid blossoms of passionate love, with all their rich hues, can spring. Apollonius' Jason is a stereotyped heroic youth – in so far as a man of Apollonius' calibre is capable of conceiving one; his Medea is merely the typical maiden who is overpowered by the strength of Eros; the only way in which a woman like her could plausibly have become a *Medea ferox* [fierce Medea] would have been by means of more individual characterization. Theocritus' Amycus is the stupid, clumsy, foreign 266 athlete, the opposite of the Hellene Polydeuces, in whom mind and body are equally well developed.

Virgil's roots were in Hellenistic poetry; but he was too enthusiastic and perceptive a reader of Homer and Attic tragedy not to attempt, at least from time to time, to rise above the level of the Alexandrians.

The main aspects of characterization according to γένη [types] are, in the first place, the differences between the stages of human life, and between male and female; secondly, the differences that are characteristic of various nations and social classes, though this last category is irrelevant to the heroic world of Virgil's epic.[1]

We have already mentioned (p. 128) the young Ascanius in connection with the *lusus Troiae* [Troy Game]. In the character of Ascanius, Virgil was depicting a typical young member of the nobility, noble by birth and noble by nature, although, since he is a heroic youth, he is mature enough to take part in the hunt and in battle at an earlier age than youths of today. In his case, he had had no mother to care for him during the long years of his childhoood; he had been taken along on a dangerous voyage that had wandered here, there and everywhere. It is understandable that *ante annos animumque gerit curamque virilem* (9.311) [he bore beyond his years the mind and responsibilities of a man]. But Virgil has nevertheless – and this is a delicate touch – made use of the fact that Ascanius is no more than a child, by attributing to him the exclamation *heus etiam mensas consumimus* [Hullo, we are even munching our tables!] on the occasion of the *prodigium* of the tables (7.116), a piece of schoolboy humour (*nec plura adludens* [jokingly; that was all he said]) which Aeneas is immediately able to recognize as a fortuitous omen.[2] Furthermore, I observe that Ascanius' first action in battle, the bow-shot with which he kills Numanus (9.590ff.), is also the last action of his that we hear of; it is as if he grows before our very eyes from childhood to young adulthood.

Next to Ascanius in years comes Euryalus;[3] he is already old enough to take part in the young men's foot-race – although childish tears roll down his cheeks when he realizes that he is not going to win the prize (5.343); and he is already old enough to take part in the dangers of battle – but he does not yet possess the caution and experience of a mature warrior; and it is this that leads to his death. Then come the young heroes Lausus and Pallas, as brave as Euryalus, except that Euryalus' bravery is characterized as mere hunger for action and honour, whereas that of Pallas is characterized as resolute and steadfast courage,[4] and that of Lausus, which is shown in one scene only, the scene in which he meets his death, as self-sacrifice through *pietas*; but the difference here lies in the situation rather than the characterization; these three young men – and Nisus may be added as a fourth – are presented on the whole as ideal types of youthful manliness, full of hope; so that it is fitting that, for the sake of a great cause, they should throw themselves into dangers for which, in the eyes of their more cautious elders, they are still too young.[5]

The mature men, Turnus, Aeneas, Mezentius, are not given the typical attributes of men of their age; more particular traits are mentioned.[6]

Typical old men include Ilioneus, Nautes (5.704), Evander and, above all, Anchises; they speak and act calmly, thoughtfully, dispassionately; they give guidance to the younger men and offer advice from the rich store of their experience, and they enjoy talking about the past.[7] Some of them have been granted the privilege of special insight into the will of the gods and the decrees of fate: Nautes has been given this power by Pallas Athene (5.704); Anchises interprets the omen when the Trojans first land in Italy (3.539); he appears as prophet at 7.123, a fragment that survives from an earlier draft. The portrayal of Latinus is also rich in generic characteristics: but Virgil adds individual touches as well.

As for the women, their generic characteristic is, above all, that they are more easily excited; in their case, every emotion is much more likely to develop into passion, and this passion destroys their psychological balance and drives them mad

– the Trojan women in Book 5, Dido, Amata represent the various stages of madness; and as soon as one woman is seized by madness of this kind, it spreads like an infection (7.392): sorrow becomes despair, and despair brings death, or turns life into a cruel torment (e.g. Euryalus' mother 9.473ff.; Juturna at 12.879). All these were traits which Hellenistic poets were particularly fond of stressing when they portrayed the nature of women, but they were very common in Roman thought too.[8] *Varium et mutabile semper femina* [women were ever things of many changing moods], Mercury tells Aeneas in a dream (4.569): the Trojan women set fire to the ships in their despair and fury, but as soon as they have caught sight of the men *piget incepti lucisque* (5.678) [they were disgusted at what they had done and ashamed to be seen in the light of day]; the women of Laurentum ally themselves with Amata (7.392ff.) to avenge the violation of her rights as a mother, and embrace the cause of Turnus, and in so doing they are largely responsible for the outbreak of war; but after the first defeat they curse the cruel war and Turnus' marriage-plans: let him fight by himself, man against man, to win the kingdom that he claims (11.215). Yet Amata remains a loyal supporter of Turnus; in taking his side she is setting her own life at risk. Her behaviour is not motivated by anything special in her character, but – as Virgil portrays it – it is typical of the way that any woman in her position would react, except of course that not every woman is driven to extremes by an Allecto.[9] She has selected Turnus, that handsome, noble, splendid young hero, who is moreover one of her kin, to be her son-in-law; when things turn out differently and her daughter is to be handed over to a homeless, penniless foreigner, she resists extremely violently, as might be expected; she is an easy prey for Allecto. First she pours out her grievances and entreaties to the king, accuses the stranger of being a 'treacherous pirate', and uses bold subterfuges in an attempt to turn the oracle of Faunus to her own advantage; and all this is *solito matrum de more* (7.357) [as a mother well might speak]. When Latinus remains unmoved she becomes a raging Bacchant; and disaster ensues.

269

Camilla, the maiden on horseback, belongs to a world outside the normal sphere of women and is not to be measured by the same yardstick as the others. But in order to make her perhaps not totally implausible, Virgil has given her one typical feminine characteristic: the gleaming accoutrements of the Phrygian priest catch her eye, *f e m i n e o praedae et spoliorum amore* (11.782) [in a *woman's* hot passion for plundering and spoils], she throws all caution to the winds in her pursuit, and falls victim to her own passionate greed.

unpleasing characteristics are offset by only one praiseworthy
nswerving love for her own family. This is of course an
by honourable men, but whereas in their case it is regarded
v and acknowledged as such, it is thought to be just a
re not to deserve any special praise; for a man it is one
woman it is her whole existence.[10] A woman's love
forms. Love for her children: Venus is the prime
Aeneas, as Thetis is for Achilles in the *Iliad*, but
yalus' mother too, who forgets all troubles and
when she loses him, no longer has anything
Ascanius the resemblance to her own

Astyanax (3.486) and hopes that Ascanius yearns for his lost mother (341), because
270   she feels that if the same fate had befallen her, she would have survived in the
memory of her Astyanax; Creusa, whose last words to her husband are *nati serva
communis amorem* (2.789) [guard the love of the son whom we share]. Love between brothers and sisters: Anna, Dido's *unanima soror* (4.8) [the sister whose heart
was one with hers], whose first thought when she hears of the death of the sister
'whom I love more than life itself' (4.31) is regret that Dido had not thought her
worthy to share her fate; Juturna, whose immortality becomes a torture to her when
her brother dies. Love between husband and wife: Dido, whose greatest pride lay in
her fidelity to her dead husband, becomes unfaithful when she is fatally infatuated
with Aeneas; she hears the voice of the dead Sychaeus calling her, and resolves to
die, so as to rejoin the husband of her youth in the underworld, and to be united in
love with him again, as in days gone by; and, again, Andromache, *coniunx Hectorea*[11] [the wife of Hector] even when forced to be wife to another (3.488), who utters
the incomparable *Hector ubi est?* ['Where is Hector?'] when she thinks that she sees
the shade of Aeneas (312). Finally, when their ancestral home, their fathers, hus-
bands and brothers are in extreme danger, then heroic courage wells up in the hearts
of the women also, and *verus amor patriae* (11.475, 891) [true love of their home-
land] drives them on to the walls to meet the enemy attack.

    In characterizing whole nations, Virgil most often restricts himself to a handful of
outstanding traits which were common currency to his contemporaries and himself.[12] Sinon is the very type of the deceitful, resourceful, wily Greek.[13] Venus fears
danger for Aeneas from the *Tyrii bilingues* (1.661) [deceitful Tyrians]: that is the
conventional Roman view of the Carthaginians, although it is hardly borne out by
the behaviour of Dido and her people. Again, the Etruscans are described by their
own king Tarchon just as the Romans usually imagined them: bent on pleasure,
271   dancing and feasting at lavish sacrifices, *hic amor, hoc studium* (11.739) [this is
their passion, their interest]; this may be historically justified to some extent, but
there is nothing about Virgil's Etruscans that seems to justify these criticisms;
perhaps the point of this depiction is to offer an explanation of the maiden Camilla's
military successes as being due to the inefficiency of her enemy, which consisted
mostly of Etruscans? Another traditional attribute, the terrible cruelty of Etruscan
pirates, is used to characterize Mezentius 8.485 (see above p. 168). The native
inhabitants of Italy are characterized by Numanus, himself an Italian, as being like
the popular image of the ancient Sabines and so forth (8.603); Numanus, also,
surprisingly, characterizes the Trojans as Phrygians, worshippers of Cybele, for this
was how they were best known to the Romans (9.614ff.), and the Numidian Iarbas
has also imagined Aeneas in this way (4.215); of course this description is totally
inapplicable to Virgil's Trojans. All Ligurians are liars:[14] Camilla too has this i[n]
mind when she shouts to the Ligurian opponent who has tried a cowardly trick
her: *nequiquam patrias temptasti lubricus artis nec fraus te incolumem falla[t]
feretAuno* (11.716) ['You were slippery! But it has done you no good t[o]
native tricks, for your cunning will never bring you safe home to Aunu[s]
who is a cheat like yourself'].

2. *Aeneas*

Thus in the case of the Greeks and the Ligurians, Virgil took a single character and portrayed him as typical of his countrymen. In the case of Aeneas, he did essentially the same, although with much richer detail, representing him as the typical Roman as conceived by the Romans themselves – or, more precisely, by the Romans of the Augustan age and of the Stoic persuasion. This type is well-known in its main outlines; and to portray him in full detail and to make him comprehensible as a product of the outlook of the Augustan age would be an important and attractive undertaking, but would be appropriate to a history of Roman morality, not to an account of Virgil's artistic technique. Furthermore, it is impossible to see the significance of this typical Roman in the context of the work as a whole until we come to consider Virgil's treatment of the supernatural (below, 239f.), since the most essential aspect of Aeneas' character lies in his relationship to destiny and the gods. At 272 this point we must concern ourselves with a different but equally important question. It is clear that the character of Aeneas varies considerably from one part of the poem to another. He has so often been held up as an example of the ideal Roman whom the younger generation should try to emulate; and so, precisely because he is such a paragon, he has become an abstract concept without flesh and blood. I must confess that he does not strike me as much of a paragon in the first half of the poem,[15] and I believe that Virgil would have agreed with me. Certainly, the Aeneas who rescues the Penates, his father, and his son, who shows in the night battle in Book 2 that he does not fear death, may be regarded as courageous and devoted to his family; but that is not everything. A man who has so little presence of mind when danger breaks out that he rushes blindly into the fighting, driven by *furor* [frenzy] and *ira* [anger] (2.316), without stopping to make sure that his family is safe; who is so utterly thoughtless during the flight that he even fails to notice that his wife is no longer with him until all the others are gathered at the meeting-place; who – let us not forget his encounter with Venus in Book 1 – breaks out in loud lamentation about his sad lot, and does not have the courage to trust the comforting assurances of his divine mother until he is convinced by the evidence of his own eyes; who allows himself to become so ensnared by the delights of love that he quite forgets his high destiny, and has to be reminded of it by the stern rebukes of Jupiter; who, finally, allows himself to become so discouraged by the burning of the ships in Sicily that, even though Jupiter has obviously answered his prayer, his thoughts revert to the idea of staying there with his good friend Acestes in peace and quiet, *fatorum oblitus* [forgetful of his destiny], and he has to be reminded yet again by the aged Nautes (5.700ff.) where his supreme duty lies; is a man like that, we ask ourselves, really an ideal Roman, a shining example for the younger generation? Did 273 Virgil really have no understanding of what a hero is made of? And did he really believe that the image of his hero would remain untarnished if he kept breaking the commandment which, as he himself consciously acknowledged, ought to have overridden all others – the command to follow the will of the gods with steadfast devotion? It is true that each time Aeneas is over-hasty, or displays weakness, Virgil carefully motivates it from the situation; but a different character would have reacted differently to such situations. And if Virgil was unaware of how seriously his hero fell short of the ideal which Virgil himself had outlined, then how is it that his hero approaches more and more closely to this ideal as the story unfolds, so that by the last books hero and ideal are one and the same? We might imagine that this results from the development of the story, and to some extent this may be true; but the development of the story is insufficient to explain why, for example, Aeneas' reactions to the injustice of Fate in Book 5 are so very different from his reactions in Book 12. I cannot persuade myself that one of the greatest artistic ideas of the work crept into it by mere chance, without Virgil's knowledge or intention; I regard the change in the hero as Virgil's deliberate and considered design. In that case, we should not regard Aeneas as an ideal hero, perfect from the very beginning, but as a man who learns how to become a hero in the school of fate.[16]

During the sack of Troy, Aeneas displays the best side of his character, as far as patriotism, devotion and courage are concerned; but not, as we have just seen, from the point of view of judgement and presence of mind; he himself often says that he has lost his wits when he most needed them; Venus had to restrain him from a desperate course which would have brought about his own death and with it the destruction of his people. During the flight, it is Anchises who takes command and gives the directions which Aeneas is happy to obey, subordinating himself to the will of his father, which in turn is subject to the will of the gods. We cannot help feeling that the episode at Carthage would never have occurred had Anchises still been alive. After Anchises' death Aeneas is the leader of the refugees; after this severe blow, which happens so suddenly, he is fully aware of his obligations, and cares for his people; not only does he look after their physical welfare, but he also consoles them and keeps up their morale. He commends them, just as Anchises would have done, to the will and command of fate (1.205); God will bring their suffering to an end. But – and this touch is very characteristic indeed of Virgil – in the depths of his own heart he does not possess this faith in the gods which he is trying to instil into his people: *curis ingentibus aeger s p e m   v u l t u   s i m u l a t* (208) [he *concealed* his sorrow deep within him and his *face looked confident and cheerful*]. This becomes quite clear in the conversation with Venus that follows: instead of trusting in fate and in divine protection, he complains that he, *pius Aeneas* [Aeneas the true], who has never failed to obey the commands laid upon him by fate, has now been cast into this miserable situation – *nec plura querentem passa Venus* (385) [but Venus would not listen to more complaints from him]. He hardly takes any notice of the comfort which she offers him – his faith is really not very strong; it is not until he sees the pictures on the temple, with their air of compassion, that 'his fears are allayed, and he dares to hope for life and to feel some confidence in spite of his distress' (451). Dido receives him; love ensnares him; he is in extreme danger of 'lying back' *fatisque datas non respicit urbis* [and taking no thought for those other cities which are his by destiny], when Jupiter's command abruptly rouses him from his life of ease and recalls him to his duty (460ff.); *heu regni rerumque oblite tuarum* (4.267) ['For shame! you forget your destiny and that other kingdom which is to be yours'] exclaims Mercury, rebuking him; and this time, on Jupiter's orders, he appeals, not to Aeneas' desire to achieve fame and glory, but to his duty as a father to Ascanius – his speech could hardly be more severe. But at least his rebuke has results: Aeneas suppresses his personal feelings and his heart's desire, remains deaf to all entreaties and lamentations, and guiltily abandons the woman he loves, driving her to her death by his faithlessness.[17] We might expect 275 that by now it would be impossible for Aeneas to neglect the fulfilment of the task for which he has made such a great sacrifice; but he has still not achieved the unwavering trust in fate and the gods that befits a man chosen by the gods. The prayer in which he appeals to Jupiter when his ships are on fire does not display an unswerving faith (5.691); and even though Jupiter responds to it, Aeneas gives way to faint-hearted doubt: the aged Nautes has to assume Anchises' role and offer him advice and – this is another characteristic touch – in doing so, he uses exactly the same words of comfort and encouragement as those that Aeneas had previously used to address his companions: *quo fata trahunt retrahuntque sequamur; quidquid erit, superanda omnis fortuna ferendo est* (709) [we should accept the lead which destiny offers us, whether to go forward or no, and choose our way accordingly. Whatever is to befall, it is always our own power of endurance which must give us control over our future]. This advice makes a deep impression on Aeneas (*incensus dictis senioris amici* [719] [the advice from his older friend set his thoughts on fire]), though it fails to give him total confidence; he only achieves that after Anchises' ghost has appeared, and after the events that follow: the poet wished to mark a turning point in this scene:[18] indeed, a turning point in Aeneas' destiny: Anchises proclaims to his son that Jupiter *caelo tandem miseratus ab alto est* [from high heaven has had compassion on you at last] and *tandem* [at last], which refers back to the vocative *nate Iliacis exercite fatis* [son, disciplined by the heavy burden of Troy's destiny] shows that this does not merely apply to the extinguishing of the fire aboard the ships but must refer to his destiny as a whole. Anchises then endorses Nautes' advice, and adds that Aeneas is to seek him out in the Underworld: *tum genus omne tuum et quae dentur moenia disces* [you shall learn then all your future descendants and what manner of walled city is granted to you]. This has an immediate effect on Aeneas: all at once he appears confident and assured: *extemplo socios primumque arcessit Acesten et Iovis imperium et cari praecepta parentis edocet et quae nunc animo sententia constet* [then, immediately, he summoned his comrades, Acestes first. He expounded to them Jupiter's command, his dear father's instructions, and the decision which he had reached in his own mind]. However, what shows more than anything else that Aeneas has undergone a spiritual transformation and gained a new strength of character, is his speech after the prophecy of the Sibyl. She has prophesied that he must endure still greater sufferings than those that he has already undergone, but instead of complaining and fainting he says with pride *non ulla laborum, o virgo, nova mi facies inopinave surgit; omnia praecepi atque animo mecum ante peregi* (6.103) ['Maid, no aspect of tribulation which is new to me or unforeseen can rise before me, for I have traced my way through all that may happen in the anticipation of my inward thought']. The Stoic Seneca thought that this summed up the attitude of the wise man when threatened by the onslaughts of 276 fate (*Epist.* 76.33).[19] The procession of heroes in Book 6, however, is intended to strengthen this mood – indeed, this is its main function in the general scheme of the work as a whole: Anchises says that he has long desired to show his son the future of his family, *quo magis Italia mecum laetere reperta* (718) [that you might rejoice with me the more in having found Italy]; he wants to tell him of the fame of his descendants (757), and when he has reached Augustus, the most famous of them all, he utters the words which can only be understood in terms of what we may call the protreptic purpose of the whole passage, and which at the same time, when rightly understood, pay a more profound homage to Augustus than could be conveyed by any other method of praise (806):

> *et d u b i t a m u s adhuc virtutem extendere factis,*
> *aut metus Ausonia prohibet consistere terra?*

[can we now *hesitate* to assert our valour by our deeds? Can any fear now prevent us from taking our stand on Italy's soil?].

In the dangers that follow, Aeneas must show that he can convert his newly-won confidence into action. This does not mean that he recklessly rushes towards his goal, cheerfully trusting in the gods to preserve him from every danger; Virgil holds back his climax until the very end. When threatened by war, we see Aeneas, not plunged into doubt and despair, but worried and thoughtful,[20] as befits a leader; and when the embassy to Evander has not achieved the result that Aeneas had hoped for, and a new uncertainty has arisen, Aeneas sinks again into deep thought. But there are great differences between this scene and similar situations earlier in the poem: first, Aeneas no longer needs any human advice and encouragement (as he had done from Nautes in Book 5), and secondly, he accepts with joy and absolute confidence both the message that he receives from Tiberinus in a dream, and the sign that Venus gives him in the heavens. We have only to compare his words at 8.532ff. with his reaction to the appearance of Venus in human form in Book 1. The words with which he introduces himself to Evander (8.131) are also full of his newly-found confidence: *mea me virtus et sancta oracula divum...coniunxere tibi et fatis egere volentem* [my own valour and holy oracles from gods,...have joined me to you and brought me here in willing obedience to my destiny].

277

It is clear that he has now reached the point where he is being led by his fate instead of being dragged along by it. But it is not until the battle itself that the hero shows that he has achieved a height of heroism from which he will not descend again. In the story, this is shown by the way that divine intervention and support retreat into the background: Jupiter knows that he can leave Aeneas to his own resources, to his *animus ferox patiensque pericli* (10.610) [his own proud spirit, dauntless in peril]. In his new mood he can still feel deep sorrow at the death of Pallas, but this does not deflect him from his duty for one moment (11.96); he goes forth to his duel with Turnus, which he believes he has succeeded in arranging at last, with total confidence in the fates, and instils the same confidence into his men (12.110); and when the agreement is broken through treachery and he himself is wounded and has to keep away from the battle-field, and the enemy has gained the upper hand, he does not waver for a moment: he gives orders that the arrow is to be cut out of his wound with a sword, so that he may return to the fight (389). As he does so, he says farewell to Ascanius, in words which display an unsullied peaceful-ness of spirit, such as befits the wise man: he renounces the favours of fortune, he is conscious of his own worth, and he has no doubt whatever that he will succeed in the end; hence he can present himself as an *exemplum* to his son.[21]

If we ask what gave Virgil the idea of portraying the development of a character in this way, it will not be of much use to look among the poets for precedents. Not that development of character was totally unknown in ancient poetry; what other term can one use to describe the mental processes which the heroines and the audience experience in Euripides' *Medea* and *Hecuba*, to say nothing of the greater changes in character found in comedy (and perhaps their Roman adapters are guilty of making them even greater)?[22] But in drama we are presented with the development of individual characters, and in the case of tragedy it is quite clear that the poet's problem was to make a specific and exceptional deed credible. Virgil's problem is different. He did not envisage his task as one of analysing a particular psychological case, and his aim was not to characterize Aeneas as an individual by describing every slight deviation from the straight and narrow, so as to differentiate him from other heroic figures in myth; for it cannot possibly have been part of his plan to depict the man chosen by Providence to achieve great things as a fundamentally despondent and weak character. Rather, just as Aeneas the fully developed hero is a model of the Stoic 'wise man', so Aeneas the developing hero is a perfect example of what the Stoics termed the (προκόπτων), the man who makes progress in wisdom and virtue.[23] Even the man chosen by the gods does not attain the highest level of morality in a single stride. Total control of the emotions, and the ability to remain as steadfast as a rock before the capricious onslaughts of fortune, is something that is achieved as the result of a grim struggle, a struggle in which a man will of course sometimes relapse into his former condition of weakness and 'foolishness', and one which none may win without the help of the gods.[24] The philosophical doctrines concerning the divinity of the world and of the human soul, and concerning the true goal (τέλος) of life and the means of achieving it, had prepared the ground for a moral regeneration; the clear, unshakeable insight into the nature of things which is revealed to Aeneas in the Underworld is the result of these doctrines. This insight is something that must be preserved throughout all the troubles of life: that is why even Aeneas does not have his crown offered to him on a plate by Fortune, but has to prove himself worthy of it by winning it from his enemies in a fair and square battle.[25]

That Virgil has taken the risk of using his portrait of Aeneas to embody the typical fate of a human soul as it struggles towards its goal – just as his portrayal of Jupiter embodies the rule of divine providence as taught by the Stoics – is certainly a matter of great importance; but it must be clear by now that we cannot speak of individual personal characterization in this context. And what is true of Aeneas is just as true of the other characters in the work. Not a single person is depicted with a unique set of characteristics as a man who once walked on this earth, once and once only; nor is any of them drawn from real life. On the contrary, Virgil depicts character by starting from an ideal, and one person is distinguished from another by the degree to which he has progressed towards this ideal; he is characterized not by the qualities which he possesses, but by those which he lacks.

278

279

280

3. Individuals and the Ideal

We have already discussed Dido as the ideal of the heroic queen: she would have attained perfection if she had not succumbed in the face of an irresistible temptation. Camilla represents the ideal of the warrior-maiden: there is only one respect in which she pays the price for her femininity, and it leads to her death. Latinus represents the ideal king: pious, considerate, generous, just and mild of heart; he lacks only one quality, *constantia* [steadfastness]. He is an old man who has reigned for many years peacefully over a peaceful nation; he is already nearing the grave when he is thrust suddenly into a situation where he has to uphold what he perceives to be right against the onslaught of all his entourage, all his family, and all his subjects – and that is when his strength deserts him. Priam is the exact opposite: he has a lifetime of warfare behind him, he remains a warrior right up to the very last moment, and when his son is killed before his eyes, he forgets that he is weak and old, and feebly flings his spear at the enemy. Then there is Turnus, the ideal of strong, decisive manhood in every respect – except, as we have seen above,[26] that he is *consili expers*, lacking in commonsense and moderation. Mezentius, endowed with all the qualities that befit the splendour of a hero, falls short of the ideal only in that he shows neither respect for the gods, nor that *humanitas* [sense of humanity] which is so closely associated with it; this alienates him from his people and drives him into battle, where he is killed. In his case, Virgil adds an unexpected touch, the love that he shows for his son, which results in a conflict within his character that would do credit to Victor Hugo. In the boat-race, Cloanthus is the ideal captain; as for the other contestants, Gyas loses because of his obstinacy, Sergestus because of his frantic impetuosity, and Memmius is overtaken at the last moment because he has failed to secure the support of the gods.

This is sufficient to show the technique that Virgil used to construct his characters. It is clear that this technique will result in a preponderance of generalized figures, and an absence of individual traits; and this is a weakness in Virgil's characterization. The majority of critics, certainly, are distressed not to find any sharply-defined individuals, and have therefore failed to do justice to those aspects of Virgil's characterization that are comparatively successful. Such aspects certainly exist; I hope that my earlier discussion of Turnus, for example, has made it clear that he is a good deal more than a schematized conventional hero; Virgil maintains this simple basic character, with appropriate nuances, in a wide variety of situations, and does so in a lively and consistent manner; and his character is put in a clearer light, with a well-calculated development and many finely observed details, by means of effective contrasts. All these touches are introduced very subtly and could easily be missed by a hasty reader. We should also credit the poet with another merit: he never overdoes things, and never stoops to cheap effects. His intentions would have been clearer if he had described people's characters directly, but he hardly ever does, except when the plot requires it, as in the case of Evander's account of Mezentius; only in the case of a minor figure such as Drances does the poet himself explain the motivation of an action, when it cannot be deduced from the action itself (11.336). Furthermore, he certainly makes no attempt to avoid stock characterizing epithets – *pius Aeneas, Mezentius contemptor divum, Messapus equum domitor*

[Aeneas the true, Mezentius scorner of the gods, Messapus tamer of horses] being content to follow traditional epic practice; but he does not merely fob us off with these epithets; on the contrary, he is careful to illustrate them in the action.

b) The action

Superficially, the events in the *Aeneid* resemble those in the *Odyssey* and the *Iliad*. A closer examination will reveal that Virgil handles the narration very differently. Virgil lays much more emphasis than Homer on emotions rather than events, the psychological rather than the physical.

It is true that the *Odyssey* is more interested in what goes on in the mind of the characters than the *Iliad* is; but it gives almost equal prominence and significance to physical events – bodily pleasure and pain, and bodily suffering and deeds. We enter into the feelings of the companions of Odysseus as they sit day and night at the oars, desperately struggling against weariness and exhaustion, or when they see starvation staring them in the face; we share with Odysseus the sensation of swimming in the open sea, making a superhuman effort to reach the shore, only to be hurled against the rocks by the breakers, and to fall back into the sea with hands lacerated and bleeding. Odysseus, ἀρνύμενος ἥν ψυχήν [struggling to preserve his life] (*Od.* 1.5) as he makes his way home to Ithaca, is presented so clearly that we feel we could almost reach out and touch him: how frequently he escapes some pitiable death by the skin of his teeth! He draws the bow with only the slightest effort, though none of the suitors is able to do so; and then he has to fight against them and overcome them in a bloody struggle. But physical pleasures have their place too: we are made to understand what a meal means to a man when he is starving, and a cloak when he is frozen, and a bath when his skin has been eaten away by salt foam. This effect is even stronger in the *Iliad*: the poet shows us in the most powerful way not only the pain of a wound, but also the enormous physical effort that is required to fight in heavy armour, and with a heavy shield, for hours on end. In the *Aeneid* none of these things gets more than a passing allusion.[27] Only once in the course of the voyage – during the sea-storm in Book 1 – are Aeneas and his men represented as being in deadly danger, and their escape is not due to their own efforts. The Harpy threatens *dira fames* [terrible hunger]; when it actually occurs in Book 7 it sounds as if it is little more than a slight hitch in the catering, which means that the Trojans have to be content with a vegetarian diet. We can hardly imagine a naked, hungry Aeneas who collapses into deep, death-like sleep after terrifying exertions. What Aeneas suffers is emotional pain: the loss of his homeland and of his wife, his fruitless quest for his new kingdom, his separation from the woman he loves, the death of his faithful companions and so forth. The same is true of all those who take part in the battles: the worst thing is not the physical rigour of the fight, nor the pain of the wounds; Mezentius suffers more deeply from the loss of his son than from his wound; Nisus has to endure the sight of Euryalus slain before his very eyes; Turnus is ready to kill himself for shame and despair when Juno lures him away from the battlefield.

We can thus understand why Virgil emphasizes the psychological processes in

282

the action also. He is not so much concerned with the plot and the succession of events as with their psychological motivation, or the emotions which accompany them. Let us imagine how a poet of Homer's time would have tackled, say, Aeneas' departure from Troy. What a wonderful opportunity for an account of brave and clever achievements in the face of physical obstacles! In Virgil, Aeneas' return to his household, and their flight, take place without real difficulty. The important thing is first Aeneas' decision to abandon his city, and then Anchises'. A Hellenizing poet like Tryphiodorus paints a detailed picture of the Trojans pulling the wooden horse into the city, and of their celebrations; Virgil allots no more than a few words to it, but employs hundreds of lines to explain the Trojan decision. In Book 4 we are given only the bare essentials of the way in which the Trojans organized their departure, but very full details about the way in which Aeneas brought himself to give the command to leave. The foundation of Segesta in Book 5 is accomplished in the twinkling of an eye, but the decision to found the settlement is carefully motivated. In Homer's Doloneia our attention is wholly focussed on the bold and clever execution of the dangerous undertaking, which leads to the slaughter of Rhesus and the capture of his horses; in the expedition of Nisus and Euryalus, the psychological processes before, during and after the deed are far more important than the deed itself. In Homer, when a god rescues a favourite hero from the battle, that is all there is to it; Virgil is not content with depicting the event itself, but makes use of it to illustrate one of Turnus' characteristic states of mind. Pandarus' bow-shot and its consequences are very superficially motivated in Homer, but are themselves most vividly described down to the smallest detail; in Virgil, as we have already seen (p. 176f.), it is exactly the opposite. When Virgil, of his own accord, describes external events in detail, he does not do so for the sake of the events themselves, or because he enjoys sharing his own lively visualization of things with the listener, but because he wishes to arouse the emotions of the listener, or (as with the burial of Misenus) to pay tribute to some ancient local custom.

Similarly, Virgil attributes the fate of an individual, his successes and failures in the battles of life and of war far less often to his physical strengths and weaknesses than to the qualities of his character. Furthermore it is clear that the poet was primarily concerned with ethical matters, since these qualities almost all belong to the sphere of morality rather than to the intellect.

This is most obvious in the battle-scenes. In Homer, a man's destiny is decided in a moment; at every moment he faces death from some unlucky accident or because of the superior strength of his adversary. Sarpedon is killed by Patroclus, Patroclus by Hector, Hector by Achilles; each falls to a stronger opponent, who has a god and destiny on his side; the poet's main task is to show how the stronger man beats his foe. There is no question of any guilt on the part of the vanquished or any merit on the part of the victor. However, when Virgil shows Nisus and Euryalus defeated by superior force, that is only to be expected, and to be taken for granted; the narrative lays emphasis, not on the manner of their death, but its cause: that Euryalus ignored the warnings of his older friend and insisted on undertaking the dangerous mission, and that, by adorning himself, in the euphoria of his victory, with the shining helmet, he had betrayed himself to the enemy; that Nisus, who could have saved himself, forbears to do so because of his love for his friend, but plunges into the thick of the enemy for his sake. The way in which Lausus and Mezentius are killed by Aeneas is vividly described; but more important than this is the fact that Lausus is deliberately sacrificing himself for his father, and that the severely wounded Mezentius, who has withdrawn to a safe position, nevertheless returns after the death of his son to risk his own life in an unequal battle. Camilla does not see any Trojan adversary confronting her: she herself brings about her own destruction through her fatal enthusiasm. It is Turnus himself who pronounces the solemn oaths that inaugurate the war to which he falls victim; Juturna tries to prevent him from engaging in the final duel with Aeneas, but he follows a higher impulse, and enters into it of his own free will; he is killed, but would have survived if the victor's eye had not fallen on the spoils which his insolence and impiety had led him to take from Pallas to adorn his own person. And the same process occurs over and over again in the case of less important characters: think, for example, of Numanus, of Tolumnius, of Pandarus and Bitias, of Coroebus and Priam: we are told again and again that they behaved as they did, out of pride or obstinacy or a surge of noble-minded anger, and they had to pay for it with their life. It is the same when the competition is not a military one: we have seen how, in the funeral games in Virgil, 285 unlike Homer's, it is basically moral factors which tip the balance. And this is true of life in general, that every one prepares his own destiny: Dido and Amata, for example, are themselves responsible for the consequences of their own actions. However, actions performed in this world have consequences that extend beyond the grave; judgement on a man's value or worthlessness is not pronounced on earth. Death comes even to the noble hero, precisely because of his noble deed; but his reward is that his name wins a glory that never dies, eternal justice decrees that he and the sinner dwell apart from each other in the underworld: the noble hero may wander in the Elysian fields, while the sinner pays for his sins in Tartarus.

c) Emotions

Virgil generally presents his characters in the grip of some emotion. He does not keep such states in reserve for the climaxes of the action, but, apart from a few quiet passages in which he relaxes the tension, he links one emotional scene to another in an unbroken sequence. It is clear that he believes that only heightened emotional states should be depicted in epic; more peaceful moods, it seems, are suitable only in minor episodes. Let us consider the various emotions which Aeneas experiences in Book 1. When he first appears, he is in the depths of an emotional crisis: he is terrified of dying, and his soul is in torment; after his fortunate rescue, he is anxious and concerned about his companions, and while he is consoling them, he is disconsolate himself; he complains bitterly to his mother; the pictures on the temple at Carthage arouse painful memories which bring him to tears; he is anxious and tense when his companions arrive, and full of passionate admiration and effusive gratitude towards Dido. Now he is safe for a while, but he has not yet achieved peace of mind, *neque enim patrius consistere mentem passus amor* (643) [his love for his son would not let his mind rest]: we see that even his love for his son has become a passion. Or we may take the emotional scenes in Book 1 in which the gods appear: Juno's

indignant opening monologue; the rebuke delivered by the apparently serene but inwardly furious Neptune; and finally the behaviour of Venus in her conversations with Jupiter and Cupid. When Aphrodite intervenes in Homer, he depicts it not as a benevolent act, but as an entirely matter-of-fact one, by a goddess who cares (but does not suffer) for her protégé; but in Virgil Venus speaks like a mother who is in
286 agony about her son; her eyes are filled with tears, she feels his sufferings as if they were her own, and sees herself deprived of the one comfort that remained to her amidst all her grief at the destruction of Troy; and later she is tortured by anxiety again and comes to plead with her powerful son Cupid who has so often 'sympathized with her in her suffering' (669).

Aeneas' emotional states are varied: in the sack of Troy he is possessed by *furor iraque* [fury and anger] or *saevus horror* [wild horror]; in the Nekyia [descent into the underworld], tearful sorrow and the tearful joy of being reunited with those he holds dear are juxtaposed with fear and terror (6.270, 559, 710); in the first battle after the death of Pallas, his sorrow goes together with thirst for revenge, which then, uniquely, gives way to a moment of admiration and pity – *ingemuit miserans* [he sighed heavily in pity] – at the death of Lausus; the funeral in Book 11 is the occasion for sorrow and lamentation; before the decisive duel *saevus...se suscitat ira* [grimly...he whipped up his anger] and when the truce is broken, after the peaceful and solemn scene in which it had been ratified, the wounded Aeneas is at first tormented by agonizing impatience (*saevit...acerba fremens* [387, 398] [he raged...growling savagely]) and then breaks out into a wild rage for battle (12.494, 499, 526) and furious joy (700), until he achieves his victory, and, after a brief episode in a gentler mood, *furiis accensus et ira terribilis* [his fury kindled, and terrible in his rage], plunges the sword into the breast of his enemy. What is true of Aeneas is more or less true of the other characters. We need only think of Dido, who is overwhelmed by one violent emotion after another, or of Turnus, who is in a highly emotional state from the moment we meet him right up to the very end, either with resentment and anger or with jubilant confidence, with feeble cowardice or furious rage for battle, with ardent love or ardent hate, with shame or with scorn.

The whole action of the *Aeneid* is designed to call forth the emotions of its characters, but that was still not enough for Virgil: feelings which generally appear in a much gentler form are raised to the level of passions as well. For example, feelings of gratitude are raised to a passionate level in Aeneas' speech to Dido in Book 1, and in Ascanius' speech to Nisus and Euryalus; similarly Aeneas' love for his son, in the account that we have just discussed, and his love for his father, not only before the flight from Troy, when it was a matter of life and death, but also after his death, when Aeneas stands by his grave and swears a vow of eternal remembrance (5.51). Turnus' behaviour is the most remarkable example, when Juno rescues him from death at the hands of Aeneas by means of a mirage (10.668). In a similar situation in the *Iliad*, Paris had been very happy to be rescued and felt no
287 shame until Hector rebuked him. How tame his emotions are by comparison with Turnus' passionate outburst; he would prefer to sink into some chasm of the earth, or impale himself upon his sword, rather than face his men tainted with the disgrace of cowardice. When every emotion is presented as a passion, then the poet needs to be able to move to an even higher level of passion for special occasions: passion

becomes Bacchic frenzy or madness. Andromache for example is *amens* [out of her mind] when she catches sight of Aeneas; so too is Nisus when he sees that Euryalus is in danger, and Iarbas when he hears of Dido's marrage; *furor* [madness] is the name that Virgil frequently gives to heightened passion, whether love or anger; when Dido hears the rumour that Aeneas intends to leave, she storms through the city like a maenad at some nocturnal Bacchic orgy;[28] and Amata falls into genuine Bacchic frenzy when her plan to marry her daughter to Turnus is frustrated.

Virgil does not, of course, ascribe this kind of passion indiscriminately to every character, but what we find is variation of general types rather than of individuals, and this is consistent with the technique of characterization which we have just discussed. Virgil is aware that it is the young who generally tend towards πάθος [passion] whereas ἦθος [moral character] becomes dominant in old age. That is why Turnus, the youngest of the principal male characters, gives way most easily to unbridled emotion. By comparison, old men are conspicuously gentler. The aged Ilioneus speaks in the presence of Dido *placido pectore* [in calm self-possession], despite the danger and excitement of the situation; similarly (at the beginning of Book 11) Latinus addresses the Trojan ambassadors *placido ore* [with a calm expression], and after he has heard their message, he does not allow himself to be carried away by first impressions, but remains for a long time in silent meditation; when the decision is imminent, he speaks words of appeasement to Turnus, *sedato corde* [mastering his emotions], and even if his defeat, and the failure of his offer of help, fill him with deep sorrow, his speech in the assembly is purposefully shaped by   288
Virgil into a model of thoughtful serenity, which contrasts with the characteristically passionate hatred of Drances and the equally passionate rage of Turnus. And even when all around has collapsed, the queen has hung herself, the city has been stormed, and Lavinia and the others have succumbed to a frenzy of despair, the old king remains gloomy and silent in his grief. Virgil is also aware that women have more direct access to the emotions, and that they express them in a different, more extreme way. Women are very rapidly overcome by emotions; see, for example, how Andromache succumbs to the sudden emotion of surprise: *deriguit visu in medio, calor ossa reliquit, labitur et longo vix tandem tempore fatur* [as she looked, she stiffened; the warmth left her, she could hardly stand, and it was some time before she could find words]; and the emotions have a more devastating effect on them: not only on Dido, Amata, and the Trojan women in Book 5, but also on Silvia (see above p. 154) and Camilla (above p. 169). But the most remarkable example is the contrast between the expression of sorrow by the mother of Euryalus (9.475) and by Evander (11.148), both of whom have lost their only son at a tender age. Euryalus' mother has collapsed in total misery: oblivious of her surroundings, and shrieking, she asks for nothing but a speedy death – in fact she is really mourning for herself rather than her son. Evander, on the other hand, though he too is *lacrimansque gemensque* [weeping and groaning] is still, despite his misfortune, able to praise the good fortune of an honourable death, and is capable of thinking of his wife, whose own early death has spared her the sorrow of this loss, and capable too of considering the reasons which had inevitably led to such a result; finally, although he is weary of life, nevertheless, before he dies, he wants to see vengeance taken for his son's death.

233

Virgil's characters express their emotions for the most part not in actions but in words; very often because of the situation their emotions are not capable of leading to action; this is almost always true with the most common emotion, mental anguish. It is very different in the Homeric poems; there, almost without exception, an emotion is mentioned only if it motivates an action; in other words, it is an integrating component of the narrative. On the other hand, Virgil has in almost every case avoided what certainly occurred in some of the lesser Hellenistic narratives: he has not allowed the action to retreat right into the background, or – especially when an emotion is being expressed – to come to a complete standstill. This is what happens,

289 for example, with Catullus' Ariadne (poem 64), the lament of Carme in the *Ciris*, Horace's Europa, and, in another genre, Gallus in Virgil's own *Eclogue* 10, whose laments are admittedly to be classed as elegy, not as an *epyllion*.[29] In the *Aeneid*, emotion at the very least accompanies the action, even if it does not motivate it; that is, we learn the feelings of a character during the course of an integral part of the narrative, and to that extent Virgil obeys one of the requirements of epic style, that the action should progress without interruption.

The speeches, which in Virgil are largely devoted to the expression of emotion, will be dealt with later in their proper place, where much else that is significant for Virgil's characters will emerge from the discussion. But there is one point that I would like to make now: often, where we might expect the natural expression of pain, anger etc., the poet offers us instead the results of his analysis of the emotion in question: he has thought out its component parts or its underlying causes, and sets them out in great detail and with great care, in a way that could never occur during an outbreak of emotion in real life. The poet asks himself what would make the death of Euryalus particularly painful for his mother, and discovers a whole list of reasons: she is old, he was her only comfort, now she is lonely and isolated; when he left her he did not say farewell, although he was going on a dangerous mission: that had been cruel of him; his body lies unburied in a foreign land, so that she cannot perform the last rites for him; and yet she had been thinking of him day and night, she had just been weaving a garment for him; she does not even know where his body lies, whether it has been torn to pieces and disfigured; so this is her reward for the true love which led her, alone of all the Trojan women, to follow him over land and sea! Virgil puts all this into the mouth of Euryalus' mother the moment she hears of her son's death; not in a lengthy speech in which she gradually comes to mention all these points, but as briefly as possible, compressed into some ten lines. It is clear that it is not the poor broken mother who is speaking: the poet is speaking on her behalf: it is the poet who interprets her feelings and expresses them with all

290 the skill at his command. In our next example the speech is not as improbable as that of Euryalus' mother, but the poet's artifice is equally obvious. He asks himself what causes Aeneas to feel so grateful to Dido that he is moved to thank her with such extraordinary warmth. In fact she has done no more than simple humanity requires. But (1) the Trojans had been in a desperate situation, they had undergone every imaginable suffering by land and sea, they had lost everything, they were shipwrecked on an alien coast. (2) Dido was the only one to take pity[30] on them, and she had not only taken their side, but had led them into the city, into her own house, not merely as guests but as friends and equals. (3) She did that, not for any selfish

reasons, but purely out of *pietas*, from a sense of what was
(4) Aeneas is all the more obliged to feel grateful because he ha'
being able to do anything to repay her. All this is certainly e'
strength of Aeneas' feeling, but, instead of proceeding to a su.
pression of gratitude, appropriate to the situation, to the amazement o.
Aeneas suddenly steps out of the cloud which enfolds him, and the expressio.
feeling itself is preceded by a long justification of it in Aeneas' words. And then,
the actual expression of gratitude, every possible element is included: the wish that
the gods may reward her richly; admiration; the promise to remember the noble lady
in the future with respect and praise, always and everywhere.

On the other hand, we must acknowledge that, although he uses this element of
analysis in the expression of emotion, Virgil does avoid branching off in other
possible directions. He keeps strictly to the situation in hand, and does not deviate
into generalizing declamations. He takes hold of the reasons for the emotion which
belong to the particular situation and squeezes out every possible effect, but he
avoids intellectual reflection on the emotion. His aim is to appeal to the reader's   291
feelings, not to use the emotional situation as an opportunity to make sententious
remarks. But that is not a characteristic limited to the emotional speeches. It is
characteristic of Virgil's style as a whole.

II. *The Supernatural*[31]

Introduction: *theologia physica, civilis, fabularis* [theology – physical, civic and mythical]

The participation of the gods in the action was part of the tradition which Virgil took
as his starting point. We do not know of any ancient epic which failed to meet
Theophrastus' requirement that it should portray gods, heroes and men.[32] But Virgil
regarded the divine as something too serious to use as a mere frill or ornament for
his work. The ancient poets had rightly been criticized for straying too far from the
truth in their portrayal of the gods, and narrating things unworthy of them. Not only
does Virgil wish to avoid this, he wants to use the vehicle of myth to convey as
much positive truth as possible. He regarded the obligation to include the gods as
protagonists not as an irksome constraint, nor as a mere excuse to paint impressive
scenes, but as a welcome means of presenting his views of the final causes of all
happenings, clothed in images which, by appearing to the eye and to the mind, can
present the highest truths much more clearly than can be done by abstract discussion. And the truth which he had to proclaim is the following.

There is one divinity: Fate, which consists of both providence and reason, present
in the whole of creation. This divinity guides men's destinies, no-one can gainsay its
will, at every moment everyone is at its mercy; a man's duty is to follow his destiny
willingly. The individual gods are not separate persons, but merely aspects of the   292
one all-embracing divinity; they represent its powers, which permeate the realms of
nature and of the mind. There has to be a cult of the divinity. For a Roman this is

y imaginable in the traditional forms of the Roman worship of the gods, and irgil envisaged his task as reinstating this worship in as orthodox a form as possible and observing it as devoutly as possible; this is one of the main ingredients of piety. Rome became great because of its piety; all misfortune can be attributed to neglect of the gods; he who pays them due honour is led by them to salvation. The divinity reveals its will to humanity in many ways, through oracles, dreams, omens; its will can also be discovered to a certain extent by the use of auspices.

It was somewhat along these lines that Virgil and many like-minded Romans amalgamated *theologia physica* with *theologia civilis*. Now, in the epic, this belief is to be presented in the garb of *theologia fabularis*; Stoic teaching and Roman national cult join with Homeric myth. The cult was easily dealt with: the oldest discoverable form of Roman worship was transferred to mythical times, and Virgil has spared no effort to make this picture as correct and complete as possible. Moreover, it was completely compatible with the common concepts of the Roman people for the national cult to be embodied in figures of gods which were regarded as Greek in origin. It was much harder to reconcile the myth and philosophy. Here there had to be unavoidable concessions on both sides, and philosophy also had to make concessions to the state religion. One must not expect to find a public confession of Stoic pantheism in the *Aeneid*: the poet can naturally not be the one to destroy belief in the poetic pantheon which he himself has set up, nor can he give the state religion a slap in the face. He must content himself with referring to the truth in allusions and hints. These references are obvious enough in the way in which he portrays the gods, in his attitude to his Jupiter, in the rôle alongside Jupiter which is given to *fatum* throughout the work and in the way in which he pays tactful but unmistakable tribute to the interpretation of myths on physical and moral lines.[33]

293

1. Jupiter and Fate

Homer's Zeus stands among the gods as *primus inter pares* [first among equals]; he is the highest, strongest and greatest, who, it is true, has dominion over the others because of his greater might, but is otherwise equal to them, and, like them, subject to passion and weakness. Virgil's Jupiter is the 'almighty'[34] and this attribute is given to him alone; he is the embodiment of the 'eternal power'[35] which rules gods and humans and their destinies. The poet has no choice but to depict him as a person, like the other gods, but he limits the human aspects to a minimum; he looks down at the earth and mankind, he speaks to the gods, smiles and nods approval, sends messengers who proclaim his will, and decides the outcome of battles; but only once does his person appear to us more clearly when, after the end of a council meeting, he rises from his golden throne and is respectfully escorted out by the gods (10.116). The Homeric Μοῖρα [fate] is an intangible power standing alongside the gods, in no actual relationship to Zeus. Virgil leaves us in no doubt that Fate is really

294 nothing else but the will of the highest god.[36] Understandably, this appears most clearly when the topic is introduced for the first time, in the conversation between Jupiter and Venus (1.229ff.). Venus refers to a promise of Jupiter's: the *fata* (239) [fates] of Jupiter's promise have reassured her until now whenever she worried over

the unhappy fortunes of Aeneas: but now, when things seem to be turning out differently, she asks why Jupiter has changed his plan (237). Jupiter reassures her: his *fata* have not changed; he has not changed his plan. To reassure her completely, he reveals the further secrets of Aeneas' *fata* (262); instead of simply prophesying what is to happen, for once he expresses it as his own will: *his e g o nec metas rerum nec tempora pono: imperium sine fine d e d i* (278) ['to Romans I set no boundary in space or time. *I have granted* them dominion without end']; we see that this will is identical with the predestined future. He also knows that Juno will change her mind and will love the Romans as he does, and adds *sic placitum* (283) [I have decided]: here, too, his decision determines the future. This matches the fact that later, on an occasion when Venus is speaking, uncertainty about one's destiny seems to be synonymous with ignorance of Jupiter's will.[37] As soon as *fatum* is acknowledged by the gods as absolutely unchangeable, they no longer think of working against it.[38] Juno's pride makes her angry at the thought that she, the Queen of Heaven, should be forbidden by *fatum* to wreak vengeance on her enemy, when Athena was allowed it (1.39ff.); she harps on the fact that Jupiter lent his lightning to his daughter, whereas his sister and wife has to fight in vain. When she then tries to get her own way with the help of Aeolus, she cannot hope to break *fatum* (she wishes *si qua fata sinant* [1.18] [if somehow the Fates allow it] to transfer to Carthage the world-dominion which she had heard was destined for Rome); the most she can do is to hope that Jupiter may yet indulge her, which would mean laying down new *fata*. She believes that he has the power to do this. Later she reluctantly assents to the death of Turnus, but still dares to hope that Jupiter will think better of it: *in melius tua, qui potes, orsa reflectas* (10.632) [if only you, who alone have the power, would change the course of your designs to a better end].[39] It is true that she is deceived by this hope, here as elsewhere; Jupiter himself feels that once something is *fatum* he is himself bound by it, and refuses even his mother (i.e. the *Magna Mater*, the Great Mother) a wish which runs counter to the eternal laws: he is capable of turning Aeneas' ships into nymphs, but not of changing them into immortals in their 'mortal form' i.e. ships: *cui tanta deo permissa potestas?* (9.94ff.) [what god is permitted such powers?]. One is reminded of Seneca's words, in which the relationship between the World-ruler and Necessity is given short sharp expression: *irrevocabilis humana pariter ac divina cursus vehit. ille ipse omnium conditor et rector scripsit quidem fata, sed sequitur; semper paret, semel iussit* [an irrevocable course of events carries along human and divine actions equally: even the founder and controller of all things did write down what is fated, but he follows it; he always obeys it, he ordained it only once]. (Dial. 1.5.8). However, εἱμαρμένη [fate] is also πρόνοια [will]: Virgil shows us this, right at the beginning of the work, when he describes how Jupiter has tamed the elemental power of the storms so that they will not destroy the world, and then shows him surveying land and sea *iactantem pectore curas* (1.60, 227) [as he pondered his concerns in his heart].

295

It is true that it was not possible for the poem to show these doctrines in their purest form. An all-powerful and all-knowing god, without whom and in opposition to whom nothing can happen, and who has himself relinquished his freedom to decide about anything and everything, is – perhaps – just about conceivable, but is completely unusable in an epic poem. Concessions must inevitably be made; the only question is, how can they be made as unobtrusively as possible? Firstly, he has to be allowed some kind of freedom of decision. This was easily done by making the same concession to cult which the Stoics had done: only the main outlines of what happens are regarded as laid down by *fatum*, and the rest is left in the balance for the time being, so that it is possible for Jupiter to be swayed by human prayers or divine

296   requests.[40] Thus Iarbas' prayer does move him to decide to end Aeneas' sojourn in Carthage; and the Great Mother does achieve at least a part of what she requested. Thus Jupiter, *victus* [overcome], certainly, but also *volens* [willingly], bends to the wishes of his wife in *nulla fati quod lege tenetur* (12.819) [what is not covered by any law of destiny].[41] And here we have the age-old question being raised: how can an almighty and loving god desire or countenance all the sorrow and misery which is so prevalent in the world? One can understand the cases when he sends it as well-deserved punishment (12.853); but how about the cases when it strikes the innocent? Where the poet speaks in his own person, he can express his painful surprise at the incomprehensible decision of the all-loving god;[42] when he speaks as

297   narrator, he has to motivate the incomprehensible, and invents the story that, against the will and commandment of Jupiter, an enemy god has unchained dissension and war (10.6-9); Jupiter allows it to continue, sure that *fatum* will nevertheless find its way, until things reach a point where they threaten to clash with *fatum*; then he intervenes, and all contradiction is silenced, all resistance melts away.[43]

298   The other gods are all treated by the poet as individual personalities, as in Homer. As a group they are also, on the whole, like Jupiter, raised to a higher sphere. As far as possible they are kept untainted by everything base or cheap or frivolous, everything at variance with the Roman idea of divinity, particularly as it was understood in the Augustan period. We shall say more about this later. But the gods are not entirely free from human weakness. This is essential for characters in an epic: the poet, as narrator, makes use of it to motivate the action; at the same time he speaks in his own person to point out that such weakness is basically incompatible with the nature of divinity (*tantaene animis caelestibus irae?* [1.11] [it is hard to believe gods in heaven capable of such rancour]), or, on the occasion of a particularly ungodlike act, such as that of the jealous Triton, he indicates that he doubts the truth of the tradition (*si credere dignum est* [6.173] [if we can believe in such a deed]). It is worth noting that apart from these cases, the actions of the gods (even if, as in Dido's case, they bring disaster) have as their final aim to help their protégés, not to harm others. Even in the motivation of Juno's hatred of the Trojans, the emphasis is put on her love for Carthage (1.12ff.).

More important than this process of elevating the gods, and changing their status in relation to their chief, is the fact that Virgil, if I am not very much mistaken, has deliberately woven into his work references to the belief that the gods are equivalent to aspects of the physical world. We should add that these references would only be noticed by someone who is familiar with this *ratio physica* [natural explanation]. It is done so discreetly that the gods remain persons. In many cases the hints do not go beyond normal usage. The huntsman Nisus, wishing to pray to Diana for a successful throw, looks up at the moon, and addresses the moon and the goddess as one (9.403). In Homer, Iris is the messenger of the gods, and has no connection with the rainbow; in Virgil, the thousand-coloured bow is the path down which she runs to

earth (5.609), or which appears as she disappears (5.658; 9.15), or there is a description of how, when she flies, a thousand different colours play against the sunlight
(4.700); and so it is not surprising that Turnus addresses her as *decus caeli* [glory of
the heavens]; i.e. as the rainbow (9.18). In Homer, Poseidon is the god of the sea, it
is true, but only in the sense that this is the realm which is subject to him; he also
appears on Olympus or takes part in the battle. In Virgil he is inseparable from the
sea, and during the storm (1.126) when he is called *graviter commotus* [much
moved] and yet *placidum caput extulit undis* [he raised his head serenely from the
waves], it is *possible* to take the first as referring to the element and the second to
the god. But the most significant example is the treatment of Juno. When Aeolus
believes that he is obliged to her for being put in charge of the winds by Jupiter, the
ancients had already explained this belief by a *ratio physica*, since Juno is the air
(Servius on 1.78), and in my opinion this method of interpretation is shown to be the
correct one here:[44] it is significant that it is Juno of whom (7.287) it is said *auras
invecta tenebat* [riding the air on her course], that she is watching the battle (12.792)
fulva de nube [from a glowing cloud] (cf. *gelidis in nubibus* [796] [among the chill
clouds], *aeria sede* [810 cf. 842] [on my airy seat]); that she comes down to earth
agens hiemem nimbo succincta (10.634) [girt with a cloud and driving a storm
before her]; in the same way she sends *nigrantem commixta grandine nimbum*
(4.120) [a black cloud charged with mingled rain and hail], and (5.607) blows winds
to speed Iris on her way. Other closely related matters will be mentioned later.

2. The gods and the action

In Homer, the gods who guide men's destinies participate in the action; they are
individuals like the mortals and are subject to exactly the same laws of psychology.
We are told precisely how Odysseus brings Poseidon's anger upon himself, how
Agamemnon can be blamed for Zeus' ruinous decision; and altogether, particularly
in the *Iliad*, the actions of the gods are often motivated from their psychology. It is
true that now and then unfathomable Fate is glimpsed in the dim distance; for
instance, we are told that Achilles is fated to fall at Troy, that Odysseus is fated to be
free at last of perils at the home of the Phaeacians; but the amount of influence
which Fate has on the action is negligible. In contrast, in the *Aeneid* it is precisely
fatum, or the will of Jupiter, which directs the whole action, and this *fatum* stands
right outside the action. We are not told its reasons, nor are we tempted to ask them;
it has been established eternally, and the contents of the poem show only how it
unrolls. In Homer, we have the impression that man hammers out his own destiny;
even Achilles had the option of living a long, inglorious life instead of a short and
splendid one. A man goes his way according to his own wishes and decisions; from
the gods he receives hindrance or help, according to whether he has made friends or
enemies of them. But Aeneas goes his way, not according to his own decisions, but
as a tool in the hand of Fate, which is using him to lay the foundation for the
imperium Romanum [Roman empire]. This is not a difference of artistic principles
but a difference of *Weltanschauung* [outlook on the world]. It is obvious which is
easier to portray in poetry; but our immediate task is not to evaluate the poetic result

but to show that it is the necessary consequence of the poet's presuppositions – presuppositions that he had to take as his starting-point if he did not wish to tell tales *alieno ex ore* [from another's mouth], but wished to give a poetic garment to the belief of his own age.

It was the will of the gods that Troy should fall, but that Aeneas and his household should escape to found a new empire beyond the seas: that is narrated in Virgil's Sack of Troy. Minerva has lured the Trojans to their ruin; the gods themselves destroy Pergamum – Venus shows this to her son and thus persuades him to accept it, after Hector's appearance in a dream has prepared his mind and given him the desire to save the Trojan gods. Anchises' refusal, which would have prevented the exodus, is set aside by Jupiter's *augurium*; Aeneas comes to terms with the loss of Creusa when she reveals it to be the will of the gods, who have destined a new marriage for him in his new kingdom. It is by divine command that Aeneas and his household go to sea; stage by stage Apollo reveals to him the destination of his journey; he follows the divine directives tirelessly. Only once, a slave to love, is he in danger of forgetting his destiny: but a reminder from Jupiter is enough to make

301 him make the hardest sacrifice; with his heart bleeding he abandons Dido. Soon afterwards, in Sicily, a new assault by Juno brings him near to despairing of his destiny; Anchises' shade, sent to him by Jupiter, encourages him to continue to follow the path of duty; he finally lands on the promised shore of Hesperia. Here, on the threshold of a new and difficult task, he is strengthened by being shown by Anchises what the reward of endurance will be: the goal decreed by *fatum*, the *imperium Romanum*, is revealed in the Parade of Heroes.

In Latium, too, there is provision for the will of *fatum* to become known to men. Latinus has received the command to await a son-in-law from abroad, whose descendants shall be the founders of a universal empire; the Etruscans are directed to a foreign chief, who can be none other than Aeneas. But while the Etruscans, and Aeneas himself, piously subject themselves to the directives of destiny, the Latins allow themselves to be so far led astray as to disregard the directive, and although Latinus himself is more perceptive, he is too weak to prevent their making the wrong choice; they pay dearly for it,[45] and it is over innumerable corpses that *fatum* leads the rebellious ones back to join those who had followed it willingly. That is how the foundation-stone is laid upon which the eternal structure of the *imperium Romanum* shall rise.

It must be clear, even from this brief survey, that Virgil's heroes have a completely different relationship to the gods from Homer's heroes. It does sometimes happen in Homer that the gods command the mortals to do something which would certainly not have happened without this command: e.g. in *Iliad* 3 Aphrodite uses threatening words to order the rebellious Helen to rejoin Paris; in *Iliad* 24 Thetis brings to her son the command of the gods to exchange Hector's body for ransom, something which he had always refused to do previously. But, in general, the gods come to mortals as advisers, or sometimes as seducers, and mortals obey them because the advice seems good, not simply because it is god-given; there is no question of a moral obligation to follow the advice of the gods. In contrast, to the question *quid est boni viri?* [what is the duty of a good man?] Virgil gives exactly

302 the same answer as Seneca: *praebere se fato* [to offer himself to fate] (*Dial.* 1.5.8);[46]

the Stoic requirement (which suits the Roman way of thinking so well), *sequi deum*[47] [to follow god], is clearly revealed as the primary, not to say the only, obligation. Aeneas' greatness does admittedly consist likewise in his bravery, but primarily it lies most clearly in his *pietas*; and this is shown more clearly when it takes the form of submission to the will of god, i.e. when he resigns himself to the fall of Troy, the loss of Creusa, the separation from Dido, because he has recognized it as the will of god. We have seen above that he is by no means a champion of the faith without fear or fault; he has his moments of weakness and cowardice, but he overcomes them, submits to *fatum*, and wins his reward. The Latins resist, and are punished for it: *volentem fata ducunt, nolentem trahunt* [the fates lead those who comply, and drag those who resist].

3. Communication of *fatum*

The most immediate consequence of this state of affairs is that the devices by which the divinity makes its will known have to play a much more significant part in Virgil than they do in Homer. There are consequently oracles in the greatest variety, also prodigies, prognosticatory dreams, omens and the like. Before we pass judgement on the justification for using these devices to help the story along, we must consider the beliefs of the time. We cannot emphasize too strongly that these devices have absolutely nothing to do with the conventional machinery of epic presentation borrowed from older poetry, which were merely stop-gaps in the place of purely human motivation. Nobody would think of confusing with them the countless analogous phenomena in the historians, such as Livy. Has the epic poet, who is dealing with the very beginnings of history, less right than the historian? But we cannot even say that both are narrating in the spirit of the past, that they are putting themselves back (more or less skilfully) into the minds of earlier peoples for the sake of atmosphere. The old ideas loomed large even in the bright light of Virgil's own time; indeed it was precisely then that much which seemed to have been driven out now returned with greater force. For Apollo still gave his oracle by the mouth of the Pythia or by the leaves of the Sybil, or sent it to those who slept in his temple to await it.[48] Auspices and prodigies were still most carefully heeded; people still believed in prognosticatory dreams: the bells on the gable-roof of Jupiter Tonans reminded every Roman that Jupiter Capitolinus had appeared to Augustus in a dream, to complain of neglect.[49] Dead men still returned: before Philippi the shade of the deified Caesar had announced the victory.[50] There can be no doubt that all these things were believed, not only by simple peasants but also by highly educated men; their truth was guaranteed not by ancestral tradition alone but also by the teaching of Posidonius. I see no reason to assume that Virgil himself in the depth of his heart refused to believe in them; but in any case it makes no difference either way; it is enough to know one thing: that for his epic he was drawing on the beliefs of his own time, and when he has the Penates speaking to Aeneas in a dream, or the gods sending a prognosticatory *prodigium*, then that is just as credible a motivation for the action as a purely human motivation would have been. However, for the poet's purposes, as we have seen, it is precisely this supernatural motivation which is of

303

importance. It has to become the actual driving-force of the poem if it is to
e us that the settlement of the Trojan Penates in Latium was performed by
and directed by fate. The poet's task was to make sure that all the ex-
304 pressions of divine will, the manifold communications of *fatum*, should not appear
as accidental, arbitrary or pointless, as would be the case if, for example, the sojourn
in Carthage had been caused by an oracle or something similar. Far from it; Virgil
never uses Jupiter's expressions of his will, or the interpreters of this will, to retard
the action, but always to advance it, to bring it one step nearer to its goal. Also it
might seem unworthy of divine attention if – as so often in late Greek novels –*fatum*
had to concern itself so many times with the course of one individual's private life;
Virgil is dealing not with Aeneas' personal destiny, but with the mission which he
embodies, and the final goal of this mission was the present fortunate state of affairs
visible to every reader of the *Aeneid*: the rule of peace in Augustus' universal
empire.

4. Symbolic scenes featuring gods

The communication of *fatum* was a necessary part of the story. Very different is the
matter of the actual scenes featuring gods – conversations of the gods among themselves, interventions by Venus, Juno etc. which help or hinder, appearances of gods
or their messengers among men. Here we cannot speak of historical truth in the
sense discussed above; it is a question of poetic fiction in the traditional epic style.[51]
The only question is whether, when Virgil portrayed the gods intervening directly in
human wishes and deeds, he was merely playing a poetic game and portraying a
poetic world in which quite different forces are at work from those in our own
world, a world in which all the physical and psychological laws which bind us are
removed to make way for the capricious happenings of fairytale. There is no disput-
ing the fact that Virgil did not completely reject the fairytale elements: he follows
poetic tradition by including Laocoon's serpents, the one-eyed Cyclopes, the ungra-
cious Harpies with their bird-bodies and girl-faces; and perhaps he is freely
inventing along the same lines when he does something like letting the Trojan ships
305 be turned into nymphs in the face of the enemy. But all that has really nothing to do
with the actual intervention of the gods. When we come to that, I am in fact inclined,
much more than most people these days (1903), to assume that Virgil's intention
was to use symbols, that is, consciously to change simple psychological processes
into instances of divine intervention, counting on the fact that the educated reader of
these scenes featuring gods would interpret them 'allegorically'.

That they have to be so interpreted is immediately clear in a figure such as that of
Fama, which has to be described as 'allegorical' in the present-day sense, being no
different from the Discordia of Petronius and Voltaire. Here, Virgil's portrayal
(4.173ff.) puts it beyond doubt that he is not trying to make people believe in the
reality of a goddess called Fama, but merely creating a concrete symbol for 'rumour', which is not itself a visual concept. But is the case of Allecto basically any
different? We have seen above (p. 148ff.) that she is nothing but Discordia personified, and that Virgil used the traditional type of the Fury to portray her. In describing

symbolize what we regard as natural psychological processes. *Rationi se subicere* [to submit to reason] and *deum sequi* [to follow god] as, Seneca, for example, so clearly teaches, mean virtually the same regarded from this viewpoint, and other common phrases – *deus ad homines venit, immo, quod est propius, in homines venit: nulla sine deo mens bona est* [god comes to men: indeed, he comes nearer than that – he comes into men: no mind is good without god] (*Ep.* 73.16) etc. – are extremely close to visual presentation of them in mythical terms.

It is true that we can by no means regard all cases of divine intervention in this light. Venus' appearance in Book 2 could, at a pinch, still be understood as a symbol of sudden 'enlightenment'; but when she appears in Book 1, and explains to Aeneas about Dido and her past history, this is impossible, as it also is in Book 8 when she brings Vulcan's armour to her son. These cases are not very numerous; they also include, for example, the scene in Book 10 where Juno uses a false cloud-wraith of Aeneas to lure Turnus out of the battle and onto a ship, which she then looses from its moorings and dispatches towards Ardea; Apollo's words of praise and warning to Ascanius in Book 9; Juturna's entrance in Book 12. At the same time we should note that, apart from Aeneas' shield, we can speak of a *miracle* at all comparable to 310 the transformation of the ships only in the case of the intervention by Juno. Venus' words in Book 1 could equally well have been spoken by a real Tyrian huntswoman, Apollo's words could have been spoken by the real Butes, Camers could have spoken just as well to the Rutulians in Juturna's place, Metiscus could have steered Turnus' chariot away from Aeneas, and handed him the sword in the duel. Just as, in general, Virgil restricted the gods' part in the fighting to a minimum, so he deliberately omitted or toned down the actually miraculous element, which featured so richly in his model, the battle-scenes of the *Iliad*. To quote only one example: compare the miraculous healing of Aeneas by Aphrodite in Book 12 with the healing of Hector in *Iliad* 15. In Homer (*Iliad* 14.409) Ajax has wounded Hector by hitting him on the chest with a huge stone, which made him plummet to the ground like an oak felled by lightning; his companions carry him away from the fighting; he is laid on the ground by the river and water is poured over him, he comes round, spits blood and falls back again into unconsciousness. Soon after (15.239), he is feeling somewhat better and is pulling himself together; then Apollo breathes μένος μέγα [great strength] into him, and he immediately leaps up and, moving his limbs easily and swiftly, runs back into the fight, like a spirited steed which has torn itself away from the manger; and of course the Achaeans have every reason to be amazed, when they see the man they believed dead now unexpectedly restored to full strength. Aeneas has been wounded in the leg by an arrow, but he can still stand if he leans on his lance. The arrow will not budge from the wound; then Venus drips into the water which the doctor has to hand the sap of a healing blood-staunching herb (not a magic potion) and scarcely has this water wetted the wound when the arrow slips out, the pain disappears and the bleeding stops. Thus the long, vain efforts of the skilled doctor are finally and unexpectedly successful; he can only explain it to himself as divine help, and we know that he is right. Aeneas can return to the fight, although the wound does hinder him a little in walking (746). We see how Virgil has taken trouble to make the miracle closer to a natural event, though without falling into trivial rationalizing.

5. Ways in which the gods appear

The ways in which the gods appear are as varied as in Homer. They work either invisibly (e.g. Juno 10.633ff., Venus 12.411, 786), or they appear to mortals in their own form (Venus in Books 2 and 8, Mercury in Book 4, Iris in Book 9) or disguised as humans (Venus in Book 1, Iris and Somnus in Book 5, Allecto in Book 7, Apollo in Book 9, Juturna in Book 12): then they are recognized in different ways, by the person most closely involved, as they disappear (Venus, Iris, Apollo) or – only in the case of Juturna 12.632 – while they are at work; or, finally, they appear in a dream (the Penates in Book 2, Mercury in Book 4, Allecto in Book 7, Tiberinus in Book 8).[60] In Homer I do not think that one can point to any firm principle for the appearance of gods, nor is one or the other form to be recognized as original or at any rate older.[61] Virgil felt that the appearance of gods in their own form was the option which made by far the greatest demands on the reader's credulity, and therefore only uses it when it is unavoidable; for example, when a command of Jupiter's is to be delivered to Aeneas with the fullest authority, when Venus wishes to show her son the activity of the gods who are destroying Troy, and when she brings him the armour, and, finally, when Iris is sent by Juno to tell Turnus things that none of his own men can; also, here (9.16), it is left in doubt whether Turnus fails to recognize her until she is disappearing. In any case, he recognizes her appearance as a mark of superabundant grace from god, and turns immediately to vows and prayers. The scene between Venus and Aeneas in Book 8 is narrated so briefly that we are not even told what Aeneas said; in Books 2 and 4 the divine apparitions have hardly finished talking when they have disappeared, and only the deepest impression of terror is left behind by the visionary appearance of Mercury (4.279).[62] Similarly, the vision of the Nymphs (10.219ff.) fades like a watery mirage before Aeneas has recovered (249) from his surprise. In each case the visionary nature of the apparition is preserved as far as possible; the divinity never lowers herself to have a comfortable chat with the mortal, as Athena does with Odysseus in *Odyssey* 13, or even, when recognized, to exchange angry words, as with Aphrodite and Helen in *Iliad* 3;[63] nor does it occur to the gods to introduce themselves to the mortals as such, as Poseidon and Athena do in *Iliad* 21. A deliberately archaizing poet would perhaps have emphasized such scenes, taking delight in the old naïve concept of divinity. A poet who was merely thoughtlessly imitating would have used the scenes indiscriminately. Clearly Virgil was doing neither of these things.

Even when the gods reveal themselves in a different (always human) form, their true nature is not always completely concealed. They do not actually change into mortals, they merely put on another shape and clothing like a disguise; in the Tyrian maiden Aeneas thinks that he recognizes the face and voice of the goddess, and persists in this belief even when she denies it (1.327, 372); the false Beroe betrays herself to at least one of the Trojan women (who, it is true, had become suspicious for another reason) by the gleam in her eyes, and by her voice, gait, in short, all the *divini signa decoris* (5.647) [marks of divine beauty]; in the same way in Homer, Hector recognizes Iris (*Iliad* 2.307), and Aeneas recognizes Apollo (17.333),

246

although they appear in disguise and do not particularly reveal themselves to be gods by the manner of their disappearing or in any other way. But Venus and Iris do not intend to remain permanently unrecognized (any more than Apollo does in 9.646): as they disappear they reveal themselves in their true shape, which lends greater weight to what they have said. That is how Achates, 1.585, can appeal to the goddess' promise; that is how Ascanius learns of the god's loving concern, which also confirms his high destiny; finally, the Trojan women did not dare to follow a Beroe although they were desperately keen to do so, but when they realize that it was a goddess speaking to them they truly become 'possessed of the goddess' (cf. 5.679) and rush with wild enthusiasm to follow the example of their temptress.

Amor's appearance in Book 1 is unique; one would like to know whether it is Virgil's own invention. In this case, not only does the god take on human shape, he is put in place of Ascanius, while the latter is temporarily removed by Venus. The device has the disadvantage that it cannot be thought through to the end; we are not told when Ascanius is brought back, whether he or Aeneas ever realizes that the substitution took place, etc. This is totally un-Homeric, and Virgil could only do it because Book 1 is separated from Book 4 by the two books of Aeneas' narrative, so that the substitution can be ignored without its being too obvious that this has been done.

6. Dreams

The dream-apparitions in the *Aeneid* (apart from Dido's dreams, 4.465ff.)[64] are not presented as natural dreams such as anyone might experience, but rather as oracles which have been prayed for or wished for. Also, the person who appears to the sleeper is not, as in Homer, somebody close to him, but a god or – almost the same thing – someone who has died. The choice of who shall appear has always been made after careful consideration of each situation. The dream-appearance of the Penates (3.147) was taken by Virgil from the tradition, where these gods repeatedly announced their wishes in dreams. Virgil selects the most appropriate time; when it is a question of which land these Penates are to be carried back to, they themselves give information about their original home. In this case it is left in doubt whether it is a dream or a vision. Aeneas believes that it is a real appearance of the gods; he rejects any thought that it might be a deceptive dream.[65] Hector has a unique vocation to prepare Aeneas for his mission; no other mouth could speak the deciding words *si Pergama dextra defendi possent, etiam hac defensa fuissent* (2.291) ['if any strong arm could have defended our fortress, surely mine would have defended it']. Mercury's dream-appearance in Book 4 is prepared for by his first appearance, Anchises' night-time appearance in Book 5 (which should surely be dealt with here although it is presented as a vision, not as a dream) is required by the mood of the whole book, as also as preparation for 6.695. The god Tiberinus appears to Aeneas in Book 8 when he has fallen asleep on his banks and will be carried to Evander the next day when his waves have been calmed. Here, too, Aeneas has to be made to trust the apparition unreservedly, although it will cause him to leave his men in a dangerous position: that is why the dream is immediately endorsed by the *prodigium*

313

314

of the pregnant sow (8.81). Allecto appears to Turnus as a priestess of Juno – *et est oraculum quidem*, says Macrobius,[66] *cum in somnis parens vel alia sancta gravisve persona seu s a c e r d o s vel etiam deus aperte eventurum quid aut non eventurum, faciendum vitandumve denuntiat* [and it is an oracle, when in one's sleep a parent or some other sacred or important person openly declares, like a *priest* or even a god, that something is to happen or not to happen, something is to be done or avoided] – in order to convince him of the truth of the dream as oracle; she also thereby proves herself to be a messenger of her divine mistress. But these dreams do not come out of the blue, as it were, with no preparation, but only when the sleeper has gone to sleep full of anxiety about the content of the dream, having, as it were, put a question to the gods in his thoughts;[67] or the dream links up with events which have greatly troubled the subject's mind the previous day; they link up so closely that it is clear that the sleeper's mind is still preoccupied with those events. But what the dream-image proclaims is also psychologically true to the extent that the content which is new to the dreamer is always linked to things already known, it is never
315 something completely new and unexpected. With the appearances of Hector and Mercury this needs no further demonstration; Anchises in Book 5 endorses Nautes' advice and suggests the journey to Hades, which may have already occupied Aeneas' yearning thoughts; Tiberinus advises asking Evander for help (and Aeneas already knows of him, 8.138), and thereby links up with the Sybil's prophecy, *via prima salutis Graia pandetur ab urbe* (6.96) [the first path to preservation which will open before you will start from a Greek city] – it is true that a completely new addition here is the announcement of the *prodigium* of the sow ; finally the Penates indicate their original home, Hesperia, and thereby repeat an oracle of Cassandra's (which was probably invented for this very purpose), an oracle which was given to Anchises and thus need not have lain completely outside Aeneas' knowledge. In all these messages there is sufficient new content to stop one saying that the sleeper could have thought of it himself while awake; they are deliberately presented as supernatural 'inspiration'; however, we should realize how very different it would be if Aeneas were to learn in a dream what Venus tells him about Dido, or if Tiberinus, not Evander, were to direct Aeneas to Etruria and explain the situation there. Also, the ritual dream-oracle of Faunus (7.81) is different from those other dreams: left to himself, Latinus could never have thought of the *externi generi* [sons-in-law from abroad] and their noble descendants.

7. Omens

Omens of many kinds, sent by the gods to warn or to encourage, play a rôle in Homer, though not a very important one. The Roman Virgil had to allow them more space. The *auspicium maximum*, which Anchises receives as an answer to his prayer before the exodus, has been discussed above (p. 32). When the promised land has been reached, Jupiter confirms the fulfilment of his commandment with triple lightning and thunder (7.141), and he also thunders from the left and sends lightning from a clear sky when Ascanius prays to him before his first feat of arms (9.630). Here Virgil is making use of the tradition that this highest *auspicium* [omen] first

came to Ascanius in the war against Mezentius (Dion. Hal. 2.5). Othe
Aeneas as first recipient (Plut. *Quaest. Rom.* 78), and Virgil does not i
tradition either: thunder and lightning from a clear sky, together with th
the *tuba* [trumpet] and the clatter of weapons, are the encouraging signs which
Venus sends to her son before the outbreak of war (8.524). Here we see that the
actual *auspicium* is linked with one of the most common *prodigia*, which otherwise
only indicate fighting or killing, but here receive deeper significance from the
connection with the *arma Vulcania* [arms of Vulcan]. Closely related to the
heavenly signs is Acestes' burning arrow (5.522), of which the significance has
already been discussed (p. 133ff.)

The observation of bird-signs seems to have gone out of fashion by Virgil's day.
The repetition of Romulus' vulture-sign when Octavian first took up the consulate
was clearly something quite out of the ordinary.[68] This fits in with the fact that in
Virgil only Venus, once, in the guise of the Tyrian maiden, prophesies from the
flight of birds (1.393),[69] and that the bird-sign interpreted by Tolumnius (12.259) is
false. *Haruspicium* [inspection of the entrails of sacrificial victims] is similarly (and
significantly) used only by Dido (4.63) and she is also the only one who takes refuge
in the dark powers of magic.

In contrast, prodigies play no small part; this is again in the spirit of Virgil's own
day. The two *prodigia* taken from the tradition, that of the table and that of the
pregnant sow, differ from the others in that they serve to confirm earlier prophecies;
but the accounts of Dido's frightening signs (4.452ff.) and of the divine warnings
relating to Lavinia (7.58ff.) read just like the lists of *prodigia* in Roman annals.
Similarly, Virgil also used Roman beliefs to make other τέρατα [signs] comprehensible to his readers. The voice of Polydorus speaking from his grave (3.19ff.) is
treated exactly like a warning *prodigium* (above p. 81); with the Harpies the Trojans
are not sure whether they are really dealing with goddesses or with *dirae volucres*
[sinister birds]; oaths and prayers are prescribed to gain the *pax deum* [approval of
the gods] as one does after prodigies, and as soon as possible the crowd is purified
(3.261, 279). It is in the shape of a bird of misfortune, that is precisely of a *dira
volucris*, that the *Dira* sent by Jupiter shows itself to Turnus (12.862). When the
wooden horse comes to a halt four times as it crosses the threshold of the Trojan
city-gate, the bewildered Trojans take no notice of the omen (2.242), whereas the
belief in omens is otherwise firmly established (3.537; 10.311).

It is a long way from *fatum* solemnly proclaimed from a god's mouth, to ambiguous omens. As we have seen, Virgil does not ignore any stations along this way;
beliefs in supernatural revelations and influences held by his contemporaries all find
their place in the poem. If it is really true, as ancient commentators already felt, that
δεισιδαιμονία [respect for the gods] was one of the most fundamental characteristics
of the Roman character, then Virgil's art has made the *Aeneid* in this area too the
Roman epic κατ᾿ ἐξοχήν [*par excellence*].

317

249

8. Presentation of scenes featuring gods

The theological basis of Virgil's pantheon, as I have tried to reconstruct it, has not been without influence on the external form of the scenes involving the gods, something which we must now examine briefly before finishing our study of this area.[70] It has been remarked often enough that Virgil's gods do not match Homer's in poetic realism. Virgil is not consistent in his treatment. Sometimes he describes the entrance of a god with a rich abundance of detail – as, for example, in the case of the progress of Neptune in Books 1.142f. and 5.817f., and Mercury's mission in Book 4.238f. – but these are exceptions. On the whole, the scenes with gods are less visual than those presenting the actions of mortals. For example, what a patchy description we have of the situation in Book 1 when Juno is conversing with Aeolus, compared with something like Thetis' visit to Hephaestus; and this despite the fact that the meeting takes place in a defined setting on earth, in Aeolus' stronghold on the Lipari Islands. Otherwise, the scenes featuring gods are set simply 'in heaven';[71] only once does the scholar rather than the poet distinguish between the layer of cloud nearer the earth and the pure ether (12.792); or the setting is 'the house of Jupiter',[72] and here again only one single feature, Jupiter's golden throne (10.116) offers anything to visualize; even when the couple Venus and Vulcan are shown together there is only the simple indication of scene, *thalamo coniugis aureo* (8.372) [her husband's gold marriage-room], and one is almost surprised later (415) to be given the further detail of the god's 'soft couch'. Or there is the final variant when nothing at all is said about the setting of the gods' conversation.[73] Now it is true that Homer is often equally vague; but, in other passages, the *Iliad* has very detailed descriptions of the gods' dwellings and activities, and the reader's imagination is already guided in a certain direction so that it easily supplies its own picture where the poet omits it. In the *Odyssey* one can feel a definite difference: the assemblies of the gods in *Odyssey* 1 and 5 are described with a Virgilian vagueness; there is also a Virgilian inconsistency in the treatment of divine entrances. In *Odyssey* 5 we are told exactly where Poseidon comes from, where he is when he catches sight of Odysseus, and whither he then turns his horses, whereas Athena is simply present, and works not as a person but as an impersonal divine force. There is an equally sharp contrast between the two types of presentation in Virgil: in Book 4 Mercury appears, on the Homeric model, as a divine person, described very visually; in Book 1 he works, we are not shown how, purely as the divine λόγος [word]. When we studied the treatment of the human action, we found that Virgil lays most weight on the psychological processes, and less on physical actions. This is much more clear in the case of the gods: the psychological motivation is given with great care in monologue, speech, and action; but where the gods are not intervening directly in human affairs, so that they have to be treated like humans to preserve the unity of the style, Virgil is not at all inclined to emphasize the physical embodiment of the spiritual forces beyond what is absolutely necessary.

318

III. *The Action*

a) The structure of the action

1. *Purposeful progress*

In order to characterize the way in which Virgil deals with the action, I will now attempt to establish the types of action among which his creative inventiveness prefers to move. The general difference between Virgil's and Homer's treatment of the action could be summed up by saying that Homer's action is only significant in itself, whereas Virgil's always has a higher purpose. Reading Homer, one so often has the impression that the narrator has lost sight of the point of each episode; as A.W. Schlegel put it,[74] 'he lingers over every detail of the past with total attention, as if nothing had happened before or would happen after, so that everything is equally interesting as a living present time'. When this 'epic stillness' does occur in Virgil, it is the exception; the *Aeneid* is generally more like drama, where every scene (in so far as it is aiming at specifically dramatic effects) is directed towards a precise goal; Virgil intends us never to lose the feeling that the action is *moving forward*. Compare the treatment of Menelaus when he is wounded by Pandarus, with the treatment of Aeneas when he is wounded in Book 12. That the reader may be excited and tense about the consequences of the treacherous shot does not trouble Homer in the least (unless one is supposed to credit him with deliberately removing the tension and excitement); nor does it have any bearing on the subsequent events whether Menelaus recovers earlier or later; and yet we are made to linger over the scene as every possible detail is given. In Virgil, everything depends on Aeneas' being fighting-fit again, or else the enemy will gain the upper hand; the scene has an energy which directs it towards this goal and gives it point, and the attainment of this goal is essential for the success of the main action. Virgil does not invent an action like the ἐπιπώλησις 'Αγαμέμνονος [Agamemnon's survey of his men], the τειχοσκοπία [the survey from the walls], or the introduction of the Δολώνεια [Dolon episode]. The apparent exceptions prove the rule. It is true that there are scenes which do not contribute anything to the advancement of the main story, and do not show any forward movement in themselves; but this is when the interest does not lie at all in the action and its portrayal but either (as in the Andromache scene) in the portrayal of an emotion, or (as in the tour of the site of Rome in Book 8) the national history of Rome.

2. *Strong openings*

Virgil loves to start the action with a *sudden strong impetus*, rather than slowly and gradually. He wants to catch the listener's interest all at once, not step by step. How little haste the writer of the *Odyssey* makes to get to his hero, how much time he takes with the broad exposition! And when we do finally meet Odysseus, how

319

320

calmly and dispassionately the events then unroll before our eyes! The *Aeneid* begins, after a short introduction, with a turbulent scene, the tempest. When we see the hero for the first time he is in deadly danger. It is true that the exposition of this scene is comparatively calm (Juno's monologue and the conversation with Aeolus) but Juno's first words already proclaim the doom-laden event and swiftly it speeds nearer. This same pattern is repeated at every opportunity in the course of the narrative; I have referred to it repeatedly in my analysis which forms the first half of this study. In the second book, Aeneas' narrative begins more like a report than a description. The description starts when Laocoon suddenly enters. After Sinon's long tale, the entrance of the serpents and Laocoon's death set the action moving with a sharp impetus. The depiction of the night of terror does not begin with Aeneas being wakened by the clamour and gradually realizing what is happening, but with the pathos-laden appearance of Hector in a dream, which suddenly, and all at once, throws a harsh light on the situation. In Book 4 it is a question of bringing about Aeneas' departure. Another poet might have chosen to show the situation gradually becoming impossible, or Aeneas remembering his higher duty after the lapse of a certain amount of time. In Virgil it is a quite precise event, Iarbas' defiant prayer, which sets things moving; and Mercury's mission strikes the unthinking Aeneas like a bolt from the blue. Similarly when he actually sails away: for the story it would have sufficed for Aeneas to wake up at the first light of day and give the order to sail away, but this would have made too gentle a start for an action so fraught with consequences. Virgil makes Mercury enter a second time, and now Aeneas *subitis exterritus umbris corripit e somno corpus sociosque fatigat* (4.571) [was shocked by the sudden apparition: he leapt up and gave his comrades the alarm]. The real action of Book 6 begins when the Sybil enters; Virgil could have narrated how Aeneas sought her out, told her his wishes etc. Instead, he chooses to begin by describing a state of rest – Aeneas sunk in contemplation before the temple-pictures – which is then rudely interrupted; only a few lines later can he begin to consult the god. One final example: the opening of Book 9 when Iris is sent to Turnus. Basically, the technical reason for this is that the new action should not have a flat beginning.

321

3. Scenes

Virgil knew from experience that a scene presented dramatically has a stronger effect than a scene narrated in epic style. He therefore tries to come as near as possible to composing the separate parts of his narrative as *dramatic scenes*. I select for my first example the treaty and its violation in Book 12, a scene which I have already analysed from a different viewpoint (p. 176f.). As before, we can learn much by comparing it with Homer. In Homer we watch the whole course of the action unroll all of a piece. Paris retreats before Menelaus, Hector upbraids him; Paris himself then suggests the duel; Hector restrains the Trojans from entering the fight, Agamemnon realizes why and does the same with the Greeks; Hector speaks and Menelaus answers; the duel is decided upon. Heralds are sent to Ilium and to the Greek camp. Meanwhile, Helen, driven by Iris, goes onto the ramparts and points out the Greek heroes to Priam; the herald finds Priam there and the latter goes to the duelling-place. There oaths are sworn, sacrifices made, Priam returns; preparations and duel. Aphrodite carries Paris off to Troy, there is a long scene there between her and Helen, who finally returns to Paris. Meanwhile Menelaus is looking for him on the battlefield in vain. There follows a long scene on Olympus, resulting in the abduction of Pandarus by Athena. Menelaus is wounded, there is a long conversation between him and Agamemnon; the herald enters the camp, delivers his message to Machaon, returns with him, Menelaus is tended; meanwhile the Trojans are already advancing to fight, Agamemnon is raising his men's spirits individually. In Virgil the arrangements have been made the day before; the action begins as day dawns, as so often in drama. The scene is the plain in front of the city (116); we only leave this arena once briefly during a break in the action, in order to be present during Juno's conversation with Juturna (134-60). The characters enter one after another, so that the audience has time to get to know them; first servants, who erect turf altars; then the armoured soldiers from both sides; the leaders, clothed in purple and adorned with gold, rush about; at a given signal, positions are taken up, weapons are laid down; on the walls and roofs of the city can be seen women, old men and other non-combatant spectators: everything awaits the main characters. This is where the above-mentioned break comes. Now, when everything is ready, Latinus and Turnus, Aeneas and Ascanius enter; with them are the priests; in the case of these main characters their outward appearance is described, giving a vivid picture of the scene. There follows the detailed description of the oaths and sacrifices. Meanwhile, among the Rutulians a feeling of opposition to the duel has already sprung up; it grows as Turnus approaches the altar praying and showing visible signs of excitement: here, Juturna intervenes in the shape of Camers; things develop rapidly until the spear is thrown by Tolumnius and there is turmoil around the altar; Latinus flees back to the city, Aeneas wants to stay but is wounded and has to be led back to the camp: now Turnus shouts for chariot and arms, and the regular battle develops. One could regard the whole narrative as an exact portrayal of a scene as it would have been acted out in the contemporary Roman theatre, which liked spectacular productions: on the stage the one short conversation between Juno and Juturna would be omitted. A second, very clear example is Aeneas' first meeting with Dido. The scene is set in Juno's temple in Carthage. Aeneas and Achates enter; they talk while looking at the pictures. Soon the queen arrives with a splendid retinue; Aeneas and Achates hide so as to watch the situation unobserved for a time. Dido, surrounded by her guard, takes her place on the throne in the centre of the temple and delivers commands and judgements. Noise and commotion are heard from outside; the excited group of Trojan leaders crowds in, surrounded by crowds of Carthaginians; Ilioneus steps forward and speaks with Dido. Scarcely has she expressed her desire to see Aeneas himself before her when he appears to everyone, resplendent in a halo of light. First he addresses the queen with enthusiastic gratitude, then he gives warm greetings to the companions he had believed lost. Dido recovers from her great amazement and welcomes him and invites him to be her guest; *exeunt* all in a 323 merry festive throng (631). All through the *Aeneid*, at nearly all the high-points of the action, there are scenes like this which are conceived from the viewpoint of a dramatist. They are presented using all the means of epic technique, but they retain as much dramatic effect as possible. I need merely mention the scene by the wooden horse; the scene at Priam's altar (2.512); the scene before Aeneas leaves Troy (2.634); the scene at Hector's tumulus (3.304); or at the *ara* [altar] of Hercules; Aeneas' arrival at Evander's shore (8.102). Lesser scenes are the meeting of Aeneas and the Sybil (6.59), the Achaemenides episode (3.588), Aeneas' return to his men (10.215-75). Finally, I remind you of Virgil's ability to bring the spectators of an action into the same picture as the protagonists wherever appropriate. We have discussed this above in connection with the Sinon scene, the boat-race, and the final duel.

4. Peripeteia

Pure epic style has a calm, steady development of the action in a single direction, although it may be delayed at times by hindrances. Dramatic style has a sudden reversal, a περιπέτεια. Our analysis in the first part has shown that, wherever he has the choice, Virgil always prefers to 'break' the action rather than let it unroll steadily. He starts by making the action apparently head in a different direction from the real one, and then suddenly turns it around; or, in cases where the right direction is taken from the start, he is not content with simple hindrances but intensifies them where possible so that they actually set the action off in a different direction.

Seen from the Greek standpoint, the sack of Troy and its prologue form one steadily unrolling action, in which Laocoon's entry and warning bring only a momentary retardation. But as Virgil tells it, from the Trojan standpoint, the action starts by apparently moving steadily towards the deliverance of Troy. It reaches its highpoint in the joyful celebration after the horse has been pulled in. The *peripeteia* occurs here, and the action rapidly moves in the opposite direction. The night-battle itself is traditionally one long Greek victory; in Virgil, it seems for a while that the Trojans may triumph; but, only a short time after, fortune takes a different turn.

Odysseus strives to reach his home with a steady, uninterrupted effort. The sojourns with Circe and Calypso delay his journey but do not change his destination. In Book 4 of the *Aeneid*, at first everything seems to indicate that Aeneas will stay in Carthage permanently: Juno is working towards this end, Dido's love relies on it, Aeneas himself seems to have completely forgotten his true destiny. Then Mercury enters, the *peripeteia* occurs, and the narrative swings unstoppably in the opposite direction, and Aeneas sails away.

In accordance with the historical tradition, the burning of the ships in Sicily only serves to explain the Trojan settlement there: Aeneas had to leave behind the crews of these ships. In Virgil's narrative, where the burning of the ships follows directly on the funeral games, it is a *peripeteia*.[75] The scenes of happy gaiety are suddenly interrupted by an event which the poet deliberately makes more terrible. It is true that Jupiter soon quenches the fire, but Aeneas' whole enterprise seems jeopardized (700-4) and it is only Nautes' advice, in combination with Anchises' appearance in a dream, which brings the action back onto its original path.

According to the tradition, the settlement of Latium took place at first without any great difficulty. It was only later that Aeneas and Ascanius had to fight repeatedly to assert their right to their gains. Virgil's Book 7 is arranged according to the same plan as the actions we have already examined. At first, everything seems to

324

guarantee the happy outcome. The *prodigium* of the tables makes the Trojans sure that they have at last reached the promised land. The oracle of Faunus has already disposed Latinus to give the strangers a friendly welcome. The embassy is taking its course to the entire satisfaction of both parties. Then Juno intervenes, and step by step everything goes into reverse, until the huge war blazes up and seems to engulf in its flames everything which has been achieved.

The same principle which is at work on the larger scale is also visible on the smaller scale, in the separate parts of the narrative. I need only remind you that comparison with Homer's description of the races clearly showed that the unexpected *peripeteia* is Virgil's own. Similarly, in the description of battles, again and again the plot has the action rising to a definite high point and then suddenly switching direction. Rather than go through the same group of examples again, I will adduce some different, isolated ones.

Before Aeneas and the Sibyl find their way over the Stygian waters to the Underworld itself, they have to overcome the resistance of Charon the ferryman (6.385ff.). It would be simple retardation if, in reply to Charon's speech, the Sibyl had pulled rank as Apollo's priestess and Charon had given way to her. Virgil makes a much more dramatic scene. The Sibyl's reply begins with an attempt to dispel Charon's fears; she tells him Aeneas' name, praises his *pietas*, explains the purpose of his visit – all in vain; Charon persists in his refusal.[76] Then the Sibyl pulls the golden bough from under her robe: *ramum hunc agnoscas* ['you must recognize this branch'] – and there is no need of further words on either side; with quiet respect Charon steers his boat to the bank. This intermezzo is a miniature drama in itself.

The morning after the festival of Hercules (8.470), Evander answers Aeneas' request for help. His answer is as favourable as could be: whatever troops can be raised will be at his disposal; he also holds out the prospect of a considerably larger contingent of Etruscans; Aeneas could then thank him and joyfully begin the voyage to Caere. Instead, Evander's speech is phrased in such a way that Aeneas feels it puts an end to all his hopes, and does not dare to trust the prospect of Etruscan help. Aeneas and Achates sit with downcast looks, miserably considering the harshness of fate (520ff.) – then lightning and thunder from a clear sky give a timely sign of good fortune, weapons gleam and clash in the air. Aeneas knows that his divine mother remembers her promise, and all care has gone, the preparations for departure are taken in hand immediately and joyfully.

In the storm in the *Odyssey*, Poseidon's intervention (5.365ff.) does not appear to be a *peripeteia*: he himself says right at the beginning that the end of Odysseus' troubles waits for him on Scheria, and he only tries to delay this. The counter-action of the helpful goddesses, Leucothea and Athena, splinters into a series of small actions which gradually, joined with Odysseus' desperate efforts, nullify the effect of Poseidon's unfriendly intervention. In Virgil, the action starts with the outbreak of the storm. Step by step, the Trojans come nearer to disaster, one ship has already sunk, another four are already in danger of going the same way, then Neptune calmly surfaces from the deep, the winds depart, the clouds disperse, the sea calms down, the grounded ships float free and make for the safe shore. Thus what we have here is not an often retarded but always straightforward action with many stages, but one that has one single energetic break at the *peripeteia*.

5. Surprise

A sudden reversal, such as we have just described, will generally mean that one or all of those concerned are *surprised*. Such surprise, which results from sudden and unexpected events, and emphasizes their significance to some extent, plays an important rôle in Virgil's action, even in places where we can hardly speak of a *peripeteia*. Consider how Aeneas' appearance surprises Andromache,[77] Dido,[78] Acestes,[79] and Evander and his men,[80] or think of Aeneas' own experiences during the last stages of the sack of Troy: Venus' appearance, his father's refusal, flame-omens, the heavenly auspice, the sight of the enemy, the loss of Creusa, the vision of her – it is clear that he tumbles from one surprise to another, and when he finally returns to his household he is also amazed to face a quite different sight from what he expected.[81] Comparison with Homer again sets this characteristic in a clearer light. In *Iliad* 4, when the Trojans advance to fight after the breach of the treaty, Homer merely says of the Achaeans οἱ δ' αὖτις κατὰ τεύχε' ἔδυν, μνήσαντο δὲ χάρμης [once more they put on their armour and turned their thoughts to battle] (*Iliad* 4.222). How Virgil would have depicted this, one can imagine from a scene in Book 11 (445ff.). The armistice is over, in Laurentum they must realize that the fighting will start again, but the scene is described like this:

> *nuntius ingenti per regia tecta tumultu*
> *ecce ruit magnisque urbem terroribus implet,*
> *instructos acie Tiberino a flumine Teucros*
> *Tyrrhenamque manum totis descendere campis.*
> *extemplo turbati animi concussaque vulgi*
> *pectora* etc.

[and, see, the news now darted swiftly through the palace buildings, spreading intense excitement and striking keen alarm into the city; the Trojans, marshalled for battle, and with them the Etruscan contingent, were bearing down on them all over the plain from the river Tiber. At once the nation was shaken to the heart and thrown into confusion]. In the Homeric boxing-match when Epeius issues his insolent challenge, the others all remain silent. 'Only Euryalus went out to meet him.... The son of Tydeus encouraged him to fight' (*Iliad* 23.676). When Eryx decides to accept the challenge (5.400), he throws two powerful *caestus* [boxing-leathers] into the ring: *obstipuere animi...ante omnis stupet ipse Dares* [all were astounded...but Dares himself was the most impressed]. A whole group of such events is formed by the appearances of gods and their subsequent recognition. In Homer, when Ajax recognizes Poseidon (*Iliad* 13.61), Aeneas Apollo (17.333), Priam Hermes (24.468), no words are wasted on describing the effect. It is unusually explicit when Helen 'is surprised' when she becomes aware of Aphrodite's presence (3.398). In such cases, Virgil never forgets to describe to us the terrible astonishment which befalls the mortal – *aspectu obmutuit amens, arrectaeque horrore comae et vox faucibus haesit* (4.279) [he was struck dumb by the vision. He was out of his wits, his hair bristled with a shiver of fear, and his voice was checked in his throat], or however else it is expressed.

We mentioned something in section 2 (p. 251f.) which belongs here: the fact that characters who are to play a significant part in the action enter suddenly and swiftly. On p. 9f. we looked at Laocoon's entrance from this point of view. There is no better parallel than Camilla's entrance in Book 11, before her *aristeia* begins. One might have expected her to take part in the council; she is not mentioned there at all; Turnus hurries down from the citadel ready for battle (498): 328

> *obvia cui Volscorum acie comitante Camilla*
> *o c c u r r i t, portisque ab equo regina sub ipsis*
> *desiluit, quam tota cohors imitata relictis*
> *ad terram defluxit equis*

[here quickly Camilla rode up to meet him, her Volscian regiment with her, and hard by the gates the princess leapt from her horse; and all her band, following her lead, dismounted, slipping deftly to the ground].[82] We can *see* the scene. How much more effective it is than if Camilla and Turnus had already decided on their strategy in the council-house, and what a bright light it throws on Camilla at the very moment when she steps to the forefront of the action.

6. Contrast

The scene of Neptune's intervention in the storm, which we have discussed above (p. 255), can also serve as an example of how the strong effect of the *peripeteia* (or of any sudden event) can be increased by a further basic device of artistic presentation: *contrast*. In the storm scene the sudden calm is all the more effective because of the contrast with the rough wind and waves which have been described just before – the simile at 1.148f. shows that clearly; elsewhere, too, Virgil likes to create a new situation with a sudden reversal and set it in sharp contrast with the previous state of affairs. It can be a contrast of moods: I am thinking of Aeneas' mood before and after the burning of the ships in Book 5, before and after the lightning *prodigium* in Book 8, before and after Mercury's first appearance in Book 4. Or a contrast between complete rest and frantic activity: Turnus is roused by Allecto from deepest slumber to raging battle-lust (7.413, 458); he is sitting in a 329 sacred grove, i.e. in silent solitude, when Iris makes him jump up: *nunc tempus equos, nunc poscere currus, rumpe moras omnis et turbata arripe castra* (9.12) ['now is the moment to call for horses and your chariots of war. Burst a way through every obstacle; surprise their camp into a panic and swiftly make it yours']. Similarly, it is in the still of the night, when Aeneas and his men are sleeping after the toils of the last few days in Carthage, that Mercury appears urging him to make haste, and this is followed by feverish activity, *rapiuntque ruuntque* (4.554, 581) [they heaved and they hurried]. Contrast is apparent in many different places: Aeneas' pious act, plucking green boughs with his own hands to adorn the altars of the gods, is contrasted with the horrible subsequent desecration of the grave of Polydorus: *parce pias scelerare manus* (3.42) [do not stain your righteous hands with sin]); the Cretan colony is flourishing in every way when it is suddenly destroyed by plague and drought and crop-failure (3.132); the joyful and voluptuous feasting when they finally reach land contrasts with the loathsome and terrifying appearance of the Harpies (3.219); these are three examples which occur very close together. In all these and similar cases, Virgil started with the second situation: to increase its effect he invented the first or, where it already existed, he painted it with contrasting colours.

7. Intensification

When an action consists of a series of similar scenes, the weakening effect of repetition is compensated for by introducing some sort of *intensification*. The prime example of this is the series of battles in the Sack of Troy. There are detailed descriptions of the fights in which Androgeus is involved (370-85), the fight for Cassandra (402-34), the battle for the citadel (453-505), Priam's last fight (505-58). Not only is the pathos more intense in the second scene compared with the first – Coroebus' despair at the sight of his betrothed, whom he has been searching for everywhere; but also, in contrast to the first fortunate outcome, there now comes the first serious defeat. Also, in contrast with the unknown Androgeus we now have on the battlefield the chief heroes of the Achaeans, Ajax and the Atrides. Neoptolemus is reserved for the hardest fighting, which follows, and this in turn intensifies the action, as the partial defeat in the second scene is followed by the decisive defeat when the citadel is stormed. Here, again, the finale consists of the greatest possible disaster, the death of the king himself. We have discussed this above on p. 23ff. In the Dido scenes in Book 4 the climax leading up to the end is provided by the material itself. In the competitions in Book 5, after the highly dramatic and emotional boxing-match it was hardly possible to intensify the pathos any further. Instead, for the last competition, Virgil invents Acestes' miraculous feat, thereby raising the mood to the higher level of the portentous and supernatural. Intensification is carried out most carefully where it is most urgently required, in the battle-descriptions in Books 9-12; I have referred to this repeatedly in my analysis above (p. 142ff.). Comparison with the battle-descriptions in the *Iliad* is particularly instructive here.

Moreover, the principle applies not merely to the individual groups of scenes, but to the lay-out of the whole work; or at least Virgil intended it to. The first half of the poem ends with the most sublime passage of the whole work, the Parade of Heroes and Anchises' prophecies. However, compared with this first half, the second half is supposed to appear even more elevated and more splendid: *maior rerum mihi nascitur ordo, maius opus moveo* (7.44) [a graver sequence of events opens before me, and I now begin a grander enterprise]. In fact, it does not convey this effect, and it is also doubtful whether Virgil was satisfied that he had achieved his objective. He was writing from the contemporary standpoint which regarded the celebration of war as the epic writer's greatest task. Books 7 and 8 are devoted to the preparations for battle; Books 9 and 10 describe the first battles and culminate in Aeneas' first great feat, the fall of Mezentius; after the excitement has dipped a little in Book 11, so that another rise is possible, this leads in Book 12 to the climax of the whole work, the death of Turnus. On this high spot the long road reaches its ending. It can never have entered Virgil's head that he should go on to narrate the peaceful consequences which must have followed Aeneas' victory.

b) Motivation

1. Supernatural and human motivation

Motivation of the action, that is demonstration of cause and effect, is of course demanded of every poet at all times. In real life a person often has to be content not to know the reason for something ('Heaven alone knows'), but in poetry the divine Muse is supposed to be speaking through the poet's mouth, giving the listener the satisfaction of surveying the whole course of events. However, like all poetic techniques, the kind of motivation and the degree of motivation are conditioned by their time, and depend on how much insight that time had acquired into the workings of the world, and of the human soul.

    After what we have said about the role of the divine in Virgil's *Weltanschauung*, it is hardly surprising that the initial motivation of every event of any importance is the intervention of a god. That is also frequently the case in Homer, but Virgil is more consistent about it; one might almost say that he is obstinate in his consistency.[83] One has the impression that he is not doing it because he wishes to give his work the ornaments of epic style, but because he wishes to express a particular doctrine. If anyone had accused him of robbing his characters of their independence by having the gods constantly intervening, so that they are mere marionettes in the hands of the gods, he would probably have replied that this is the true state of affairs, and that he is only depicting this truth. He could point to the truth established by the philosophers which demonstrates that even unhappy incidents (such as in the cases of Amata and Turnus) do not happen without the gods' involvement.[84]

    The rule holds good both for natural events and for human actions. In natural events the divine motivation is of course the only one; this only leaves the question of what motivated the god's decision. This is answered either in a preparatory scene featuring the gods – Juno's monologue in Book 1 before the storm, the conversation between Venus and Vulcan in Book 5 before the unnatural calm – , or it is made clear in the course of the action – crop-failure and plague after the colony has been founded on Crete in Book 3; this is a sign of divine disapproval.[85] In the case of human actions the god is again revealed as supplying the real driving-force, exerted either by expressing his or her will, or by proclaiming *fatum*, which the mortal then obeys. As we have seen above, this is on the same level as purely human motives. Or else the god affects the mortal in ways found in myth and poetry; in these cases, human, psychological motivation is not excluded, but runs parallel to, or is symbolized in, the divine intervention, but in such a way that we can still recognize what it was. For example, when the psychological motivation of Aeneas' change of heart in Books 2 and 4 is replaced by the interventions of Venus and Mercury, this is presented in such a way that we are not faced with an incomprehensible command stemming from the god's caprice, which would be a completely new force interrupting the course of the action in a miraculous way; rather, the *commands* of the gods supply what, in the natural course of events, would be psychological factors bringing about the mortal's decision. This is even clearer in, for example, the case of the effect of Iris/Beroe on the Trojan women in Book 5, or of Juturna/Camers on the Latins in Book 12, because here there is no reversal; all the psychological forces are already present, so that only a spark is needed to start the blaze; but instead of presenting these forces in psychological terms, Virgil puts them into the mouth of a god who gives advice. In other cases, the psychological development is described independently, in great detail, and the divine intervention only accompanies it as some sort of visual symbol: thus Amor in the shape of Ascanius; this is the divine intervention, but there is a separate description of how Dido's love is prepared, springs up and grows, and, before the lover yields to her beloved, the short conversation with her sister gives an exhaustive account of the emotional forces at work, as well as her rational reasons for acting as she does. When the psychological processes are long and more gradual in developing, the divine intervention is restricted to providing the first impetus: all the rest unrolls before our eyes in the human psyche, and the poet takes care to show us every stage in the protagonist's own words. This is how we follow Dido's slowly ripening decision to die, and Turnus' developing resolve which is set in motion by Allecto and continues gathering momentum unstoppably to the end: the speeches (12.620, 632, 676) show how the final decision to face his opponent gradually takes possession of him.

333

It is the general rule in Virgil that the psychological motivation is explained either by the words of the adviser, or by the words of the protagonist. It is only in exceptional circumstances, such as when he is paving the way for detailed motivation, or where it would have been difficult or artifical to create the opportunity for a speech, that Virgil himself gives the explanation: this is the case before the above-mentioned speeches of Turnus (12.616), before Juturna's speech which leads to the breaking of the treaty (12.216), before Iris' speech to the Trojan women (5.615); on the other hand, see, for example, the case of Camilla's fateful hounding of Chloreus (11.778), where Virgil steps out of the role of poet and behaves more like a rationalizing historian, providing a choice of two motives: *sive ut templis praefigeret arma Troia captivo sive ut se ferret in auro* [either hoping to fasten arms from Troy as an offering on a temple wall, or wishing to parade herself in captured gold].

Virgil has this in common with the rationalizing historian – such as Livy – that he tries to give the reader a complete explanation of human actions. The historian is generally supplied only with information about actions and events, and has to provide the motivation himself, often finding that he has to explain mass actions which cannot be traced back to individual characters. He is therefore inclined not to single out just one motive, but where possible to combine all imaginable motives, leaving the reader to judge whether the collective motives or one single one from among them really tilted the balance. If one analyses the motivating speeches in Livy, one comes across the same technique again and again: Livy has imagined the situation and the attitudes of the protagonists and taken trouble not to forget anything which ever influenced or might influence such people in such a situation; the more motives

334

the better, and the more ways in which a motive can be exploited the more effective it is.[86] Virgil's technique is very closely related to this. I have shown earlier (p. 102f.) that for Dido's decision to kill herself Virgil does not take one single motive and deepen and strengthen it so that it has to lead to the deed from psychological necessity, but piles up a number of equally valid motives, and it is their combined weight which overcomes Dido. This was an important event, but less important events are treated in the same way. Here I will point only to the above-mentioned conversation between Dido and Anna at the beginning of Book 4, or to Pallas' *cohortatio* [exhortation] to his men, 10.369; when we discuss the speeches we shall return to this characteristic technique. As in the Dido/Anna conversation, so elsewhere too the motivation frequently works itself out in the course of speech and reply. The behaviour of Entellus before the boxing-match shows two stages: first hesitation, then decision; the decision is motivated by Acestes' speech (5.389), the hesitation is motivated by Entellus' reply; but the poet is primarily concerned with using the decision to show Entellus' character, and he therefore rejects an obvious motivation – desire for the victor's prize – and that is also brought about by the speech and reply. Moreover, the historian feels the obligation to make an unexpected decision seem plausible by presenting its gradual development.[87] How skilfully Virgil does this in the case of the wooden horse, or Dido's suicide, or the breach of the treaty in Book 12, I do not need to repeat here.

2. The structure of the action

Until now we have been examining how Virgil, in Aristotle's words, ἐν τοῖς ἤθεσιν ἀεὶ ζητεῖ ἢ τὸ ἀναγκαῖον ἢ τὸ εἰκός [he always seeks in character either the inevitable or the probable] (*Poetics* 14); now we must do the same for the πραγμάτων σύστασις [structure of the action]. The motivation of the main action can be discussed properly later when we look at the structural composition. However, there are a few things which we should mention at this point. It makes a great difference whether the material which the poet has to reshape into his narrative is already a unity, every part connected to another, or whether it consists of several parts which were originally separate and only later connected. In the latter case of course the poet finds it much more difficult to provide motivation, and it is even more difficult if he feels obliged, as Virgil does in the *Aeneid*, to extend the material by inserting secondary material which has no organic connection with the main thread. Aeneas' journey to Latium, as given in the tradition, consisted of a series of separate episodes which had later been fitted into a geographical context. Virgil added the sojourn in Dido's city, the Games, and the Nekyia [visit to the Underworld], none of which had any intrinsic connection with the main story of the settlement of the Trojan Penates in Latium. He felt obliged to create such a connection, but the difficulty of having to supply it afterwards has not always been completely overcome. We can see particularly clearly that work on this difficulty was a late priority for Virgil because the poem is in an unfinished state, and even when he had long been sure of the events and their arrangement, he had still not completely worked out the connecting motivation. We could point out several attempts to motivate Aeneas' journey which contradict the plan actually carried out in Book 3; the same can be said of the Nekyia. For the second part of the poem the task was considerably easier; here the tradition already supplied a connected narrative which could be used without any major additions; there is one episode, it is true, the description of Aeneas' shield, which has not grown out of the poetic re-working of the material but has been interpolated, and this shows up in the motivation; Virgil

335

was certainly aware of this but was still unable to make it seem quite natural.

It is difficult to establish a general rule for the motivation of individual parts of the action. One may say in general that when the action is progressing normally, with no external influences coming to bear on it, Virgil pays careful attention to the causal linking of the separate parts. At the same time we cannot deny that there is some lack of clarity in minor matters. When Aeneas and Achates, who are walking through Carthage wrapped in mist, wait for Dido in the temple (without any expla-

336   nation) (1.454),[88] one is justified in asking why they did so since they were in consequence not in a position to ask for information; we shall never know whether Virgil himself had a particular explanation in mind. For other examples I direct you to my analysis of the Sack of Troy or the Funeral Games, and here I will only take time to remind you of the battle-scenes of Books 9 to 12. I have already shown how carefully the causal nexus is respected here: naturally not with the technical precision of a military history, but in accordance with the laws of poetic representation; so that, with only a few essential details, it creates the appearance of reality. The basic scheme of the battle-descriptions is that individual feats alternate with crowd-scenes: they are linked by the fact that the splendid deeds of individuals eventually have repercussions in the movements of the larger groups, and the counter-effect is that out of the groups come further individual feats. By the law of poetic causality, every time an action has reached its highest point, the counter-action begins; this does not always require special motivation since it is natural for the greater success of one combatant to spur the other on to greater efforts. The basic situation which governs everything throughout is the opposition of Aeneas and Turnus. Turnus' great successes in Book 9 are caused by Aeneas' absence; from the moment that Aeneas enters the battle we know that their meeting will decide the day, and the poet then introduces more and more delays which postpone the finale. Divine interven-tion in these scenes is reduced to a minimum; when, for example, in Book 9 Juno gives Turnus strength, or in Book 11 Jupiter instils courage in Tarchon, the phrases used are almost formulaic, as if only intended to remind us that the gods are behind

337   everything that happens. It is only very seldom that this divine intervention repre-sents a kind of poetic justice: when (10.689), after Turnus' removal, mighty Mezentius steps forward *Iovis monitis* [by command of Jupiter], this provides a replacement for Turnus, to make up the numbers on the Latin side. As an example of the opposite, an example both of the gods providing separate causation, and of the poet attempting, but not always achieving, convincing causation, Homer's κόλος μάχη [the interrupted battle] (*Iliad* 8) may serve. The battle rages until midday, then Zeus weighs the combatants' fates in his balance; he thunders and sends lightning down among the Achaeans. They are immediately terrified and run away: only Nestor is forced to stay behind, since his team of horses is in a tangle. Diomedes gives him a lift in his chariot, and instead of taking him to the camp, drives at the enemy and kills Hector's chariot-driver; and the Trojans are immediately close to disaster, and would have been cooped up in Ilium, if Zeus had not driven Diomedes off with another shaft of lightning. Now Hector presses on the Achaeans in the camp and would have burnt their ships (*Iliad* 8.217), had not Agamemnon, at Hera's suggestion, encouraged his men with an address and prayed to Zeus, who sends a favourable sign: at that, the Greeks throw themselves against the Trojans and,

mainly because Teucer has killed eight of them, force them back as far as the walls of Ilium (295), until Hector wounds Teucer, and Zeus strengthens the Trojans, at which the Achaeans flee again over the ditch to the ships; and their great distress rouses the pity of Athena and Hera. There follow some long scenes featuring gods, then night falls and fighting is broken off. We can see that the poet's intentions were similar to Virgil's, but when we compare the results we see that Virgil's mature artistry makes Homer's work look like the attempt of a child.

It is a different matter when new material is introduced from outside and requires motivation. Then there are two possibilities: either the motivation has already been mentioned, and the poet can refer back to it, or it is dealt with at the point of entry. Now to prepare unobtrusively for a motive which will come into effect later often requires an effort out of all proportion to the gain achieved; also, Virgil prefers, if possible, not to recapitulate, as we shall see when we examine his narrative tech-   338 nique. These tendencies frequently lead him to omit the motivation entirely in such cases, or abbreviate it if possible; the result is a lack of clarity. It is true that this only happens where the motivation makes no actual difference to the action itself. We saw a very striking example of this at the beginning of the second Laocoon scene (2.201); here are some more examples. When the Trojan delegation appears before Latinus, he addresses them (7.195) as *Dardanidae*,[89] and adds, since they must be surprised that he knows them, *neque enim nescimus et urbem et genus, auditique advertitis aequore cursum* [since we had heard of you before ever you turned hither your course upon the ocean, and we already know both your city and your nation]. For the Trojans that is enough for the time being, they can ask for details later; but we should like to know how Latinus had this information. To motivate it would have required inventing an explanation, which would have interrupted the speech badly at this point, and it would have been difficult to bring it in earlier; Virgil therefore prefers to pass over it in silence. When Nisus and Euryalus have the enemy camp safely behind them, they meet Latin horsemen (9.367), who are on the way from the city to the camp. Virgil does motivate this ride (we have to assume that the troops are already all united), but lest the narrative be delayed by a lengthy recapitulation, he does it so briefly that it can hardly be understood.

Virgil displays a certain carelessness here and there in his treatment of less important characters: they are there when he needs them, without their presence being explained first. Dido speaks to her sister (4.416), although she has not been mentioned in the previous scenes. In Cumae (6.9) Aeneas goes to the temple of Apollo; we only learn later from the fact that *praemissus Achates* [Achates who had been sent before] returns with the Sibyl (34) that he was with him; he is also present during the stag-hunt in Book 1, as *armiger* (188) [arms-bearer], although we had   339 previously seen him making a fire and had been told only that Aeneas went away. There are also other places where one does not have to be a pedantic reader to wish for an explanation. In Book 5 all the men are at the Games and the women are alone by the ships – that is how it is to be imagined from the way the narrative presents it; how is it that a certain Eumelus is also there by the ships (665), to bring the news of the conflagration to Aeneas and his men? The Trojan *matres* have stayed behind in Sicily; when we learn later that Euryalus' mother is the only one who dared to accompany her son (9.217), we will not argue with the poet for not preparing us for this during the departure from Sicily; but when (11.35) by Pallas' bier the *Iliades crinem de more solutae* [ladies of Ilium, their hair thrown free for the ceremony] lament, this does add a finishing touch to the moving scene, and it is possible, since *famulumque manus Troianaque turba* [the company of retainers and crowd of Trojans] precedes, that Virgil, as Servius assumes, was here thinking only of the *ancillulae* [serving-maids] as opposed to the matrons: but one might expect to find this expressed more clearly. If Virgil worried about this at all, he must have relied on the pathos of the scene taking the listener's mind off the discrepancy; and here, as in many similar places, he was probably right, as far as the great majority of his listeners are concerned.

3. Coincidence

For the main action, Virgil totally avoided the use of coincidence to replace proper causation. But otherwise, when he is not laying the basis for the main action but merely aiming at a poetic effect which has no vital importance for the plot, it is characteristic of him to make use of coincidence. At the very moment that Aeneas sees Dido for the first time in the temple, the delegation from the lost ships enters. When Aeneas approaches Helenus' city, Andromache is just at that point making a solemn sacrifice at Hector's tomb: the mood of the scene depends on this. When the Trojans come to the shore of the Cyclopes, Odysseus has been there just a short while before; when they are blown off course from Carthage to Sicily, it happens precisely on the anniversary of Anchises' burial. Sinon has just reached the end of his long tale: that is when the serpents come from the sea. Just when Turnus has given his speech to the assembly in favour of war, the news arrives that the enemy troops are approaching. Just when Nisus and Euryalus believe that they are out of danger, Volcens' riders block their way.[90] In the majority of these cases the action would have progressed in more or less the same way without these chance encounters, but the effect would have been lost. One will hardly ever find anything like it in Homer. The epic does not actually need this device for its specific ends; or if such an encounter is necessary for the action – as with the meeting of Nausicaa with Odysseus – it can be motivated by divine intervention. Drama, on the other hand, with its stricter unity of time and content, frequently can barely manage without this device: Polybus of Corinth has to have died at exactly the right time so that the news of his death can reach Thebes when Oedipus' doubts are at their height; Hercules has to arrive at Admetus' house from the Underworld exactly at the moment when the household have just put on mourning; Aegeus, travelling by chance to Troezen, happens to pass Corinth just when Medea is looking for a refuge, etc. It is from drama that dramatically constructed narrative has taken this device for the sake of heightened effect: when, for example Livy – perhaps using a poetic source – has the dictator Camillus arrive before Rome at the very moment of the weighing out of the gold won by the Gauls by a fraudulent agreement (5.49), that is a genuinely dramatic, or, we may now say, a genuinely Virgilian coincidence.

340

c) Time and Place

1. Timetable. Concentration of the action. Days, seasons, years. General chronology. Description and visualisation of the topography

Let us draw up a table of the action to see how many days it covers and how it is divided into days.

I

1st day: Departure from Sicily, storm at sea, landing in Libya; conversation between Jupiter and Venus: 1.34-304.

2nd day: Sunrise 305; journey to Carthage, meeting with Dido, evening banquet (726), Aeneas' tale in the night (2.8): 1.305-4.5.

?3rd day: Dido's conversation with Anna, sacrifice, another banquet in the evening (77), Dido restless in the night, conversation between Juno and Venus: 4.6-128.

4th day: Hunt and thunderstorm: 4.129-68.

Interval of unspecified duration (*hiemem quam longa fovere* [193] [they spent the long winter together]: 4.169-97.

II

?1st day: Iarbas; Mercury and Aeneas; conversation between Dido and Aeneas, conversation between Anna and Aeneas; erection of the funeral-pyre; in the night (522) Dido's soliloquy, Aeneas' dream and departure: 4.198-583.

2nd day: Dido's death; voyage to Sicily; reception by Acestes: 4.584-5.41.

3rd day: Proclamation of funeral games for nine days later, and sacrifice for Anchises: 5.42-103.

12th day: Games; burning of the ships; in the night Anchises' apparition: 5.104-745.

?13th day: Founding of Segesta: 746-61.

14th-22nd day: Interval lasting nine days of festival: 762.

23rd day: Departure; in the night (835) Palinurus' death: 763-871.

24th day: (daybreak is not mentioned) arrival in Cumae; oracle of the Sibyl; the golden bough; burial of Misenus; in the night (252) sacrifice to the spirits of the Underworld: 6.1-254.

?25th day: Nekyia; journey to Caieta: 255-901.

26th day: burial of Caieta; in the night, journey past the land of Circe: 7.1-24.

27th day: in the morning, landing by the mouth of the Tiber: *prodigium* of the tables: 7.25-36; 107-47.

28th day: building of the camp; delegation to Latinus: 7.147-285.

Interval of unspecified duration: Allecto's activity, preparations for war.

III

1st night: Dream-appearance of Tiberinus (morning 8.67); day: sacrifice to Juno, preparation for the journey.

2nd night: (86) until midday (97) journey up the Tiber; festival of Hercules: 7.86-368. Turnus' first assault 9.1-158.

3rd night: Venus and Vulcan. Nisus and Euryalus: 9.159-458. Day: in the early morning (8.455) parley with Evander; Aeneas to Caere, parley with Tarchon (10.148ff.); Turnus' second assault 8.369-731 (cf. 10.148-56) and 9.459-818.

4th night: Aeneas' journey: 10.146-255. Day: assembly of the gods; a fresh assault by Turnus; Aeneas' arrival; first battle: 10.1-145; 256-908.

5th day: Pallas' funeral; Latins' delegation; preparations for the burial: 11.1-138.

6th day: (Night: arrival of the funeral procession at Evander's house? 139-81) 1st day of 12-day (133) armistice; burial of the dead: 182-224.

18th day: return of Diomedes' delegation; council-meeting; advance of Trojans and Latins; Camilla's feats and death; Turnus' challenge: 11.225-12.112.

19th day: Final battle: 12.113-952.

This table immediately tells us one thing: Virgil has made every effort to squeeze the action into as short a period as possible; apart from the periods when nothing, or very little, happens, there are only about twenty days in Virgil's narrative. In this he was not merely following the example of the *Iliad* and the *Odyssey*; his desire for concentrated effect had to lead to the same result. The faster one event follows upon another, the more the reader's attention is held, the more he has the impression of being told everything, the more he can dispense with filling gaps from his own imagination. Virgil was not able to keep to the unity of time as perfectly as the authors of our *Iliad* and *Odyssey* could; he had to allow a longish period for Aeneas' sojourn in Carthage, in order to give the impression that this sojourn was close to becoming permanent; and a second period for the preparations for the war: not only did the Amata story require more than one day, the spreading of the war across Italy, the gathering of the contingents etc. needed a longish time; however, we have to work that out for ourselves; the poet avoids any reference to it.[91] From the realistic standpoint these would not be the only two places where more time would be needed: another thing that we can see from our table above is that Virgil often makes more happen in the space of one day than would be possible, or probable, in reality. It is improbable that between Aeneas' arrival in Carthage and his union with Dido in the grotto only one day has passed, and although it seems clear that Virgil planned it like that originally he obviously felt unhappy about it himself later, and made additions which suggest that we should assume a longer intervening period,[92] but he has refrained from any direct indication, apparently so that the idea of the continuity of the action should be disturbed as little as possible. It is exactly the same with the day on which Mercury appears to Aeneas. It is certainly highly improbable that all the events leading up to the night before Aeneas' departure should happen on this one day, and the poet does not explicitly rule out the possibility that they are spread over several days; indeed this is made necessary by the mention of the *prodigia* which affect Dido's decision;[93] on the other hand, once again there are absolutely no definite indications, and the narrative runs on in an uninterrupted flow, clearly showing that the poet wanted to avoid the impression of a long delay: he prefers to leave the matter uncertain, not least because he does not wish to spoil the impression that Aeneas is arranging his departure with the greatest possible haste. Of course one could assume that Virgil has simply forgotten to consider the timetabling here, but if so this would be the only place in the *Aeneid* where he has done (except for minor matters), whereas we shall find more examples later of events happening at an impossible speed. Servius (on 5.1) already points out that Aeneas could not have travelled from Carthage to Drepanum in the space of one day[94] and says that it was in the evening that Aeneas saw the pyre burning and he then travelled through the night and part of the following day. Virgil himself – who did not necessarily know the exact distance – gives the distinct impression that the journey was completed within a day, just as in Book 1 he has the Trojans making the same journey in the other direction in one day, and landing in Libya in time for Aeneas to go off on the stag-hunt. Whether the timing was possible or not is ignored, and the poet takes care not to raise the question by giving any indication of the time of day – such as the advent of midday or evening. It is exactly the same at the end of Book 5 with the foundation of the city of Segesta: beforehand and afterwards there are precise indications of the time, so that the reader is led to think of Anchises' command being carried out on the day after his appearance, without stopping to think that this is impossible on account of the distance between Drepanum-Eryx and Segesta.[95] Less noticeable is the fact that the same thing happens on Aeneas' Etrurian expedition. As we shall see later, Virgil has given much thought to the synchronism of Aeneas' adventures and the events in Latium; if we work it out, Aeneas must have left Evander on the same day that he then arranged the treaty with Tarchon and sailed out to sea with his new allies, so that we meet them at midnight (10.147) well into their journey. Again, Virgil does not say anywhere explicitly how long this took, but he is concerned with giving an impression of speed: according to Evander, the armed might of the Etruscans is already assembled, the fleet lies by the shore and everyone is burning to go to war (8.497, 503): when Aeneas comes with his request, *haud fit mora, Tarchon iungit opes...tum classem conscendit gens Lydia* (10.153) [there was no delay, Tarchon joined forces...now the nation from Lydia embarked on their fleet].[96] 345

The landmarks in the story are the sunrises: they are reported regularly in the connected narrative.[97] That the day then ends, night falls, and people go to their rest, is only expressly stated when something important happens during the night – which is surprisingly often in the *Aeneid*; but even then we often only learn in passing that it is night-time.[98] Other times of day are only mentioned during the visit to Evander: there we hear of midday (8.97), evening (280) and nightfall (369): this is characteristic of the idyllic tone of the whole episode, which brings us closer to nature than the usual elevated epic style likes to do. 346

As with the times of day, so with the times of year. They are mentioned where they are needed to motivate the action, but not to lend colour or mood to events. We are not told the season in which the action of the *Iliad* unrolls; it is characteristic of the cosy, bourgeois tone of certain parts of the *Odyssey* that the wintry situation is conveyed.[99] The thing most affected by the seasons is seafaring, and this does cause Virgil to mention the time of year: in Book 4 it is winter, so that Dido has a pretext to keep Aeneas from leaving,[100] and can later complain that he wants to leave her despite the winter storms;[101] Virgil has kept to this idea when he has *Fama* spreading the tale that the lovers *hiemem inter se luxu, quam longa, fovere* (193) [are now

267

spending all the long winter together in self-indulgence]. But outside Book 4 he forgets that it is winter: in both Books 1 (755) and 5 (626) there is talk of the *septima* aestas [seventh summer] which the Trojans have already spent on their wanderings;[102] when Aeneas has founded Pergamum on Crete, Sirius scorches the barren fields; the grass becomes withered and the diseased crops refuse to yield (3.141); that is, it is high summer, to make it possible for the *prodigium* of the ἀφορία [crop-failure] to occur; but when the Trojans set sail and suffer a terrible three-day storm (203), the poet certainly does not mean that the season of autumnal storms has meanwhile started.

This leads us to the much discussed question of the chronology of Aeneas' wanderings. In the case of longish periods where the narrative cannot tell us everything, but only superficial details, it is also best from the poetic point of view that exact lengths of time should not be specified. It can be important that a longish period be felt as long: when Dido speaks of the seven years of wandering, she is only indicating how much she expects to hear, and when the same number of years is mentioned in Iris' speech to the Trojan women, it is intended to explain their yearning for rest. But when, in Book 3, it comes to the description of these wanderings, neither Dido nor the listener wants Aeneas or the poet to measure out how the events took up those years, and it would have been boringly pedantic to have actually worked out a consistent chronology. Thus it is only to be expected that the indications of time will be vague and underplayed, and this is so. It seems almost deliberate when the poet leaves us in the dark about the duration of the various sojourns, and we find that he has made as much effort in narrating the main events as in the detailed linking narrative to give the illusion of short periods of time. Everything which is told of the sojourn in Thrace (3.16-68), could be imagined as squeezed into one day: it remains uncertain – and is intended to remain so – whether the mention of the date of departure (69ff.) means that they have waited for spring, although on closer study this does seem the most likely (see above p. 81f.). It remains unclear how long they remained on Crete: it is only from the above-mentioned *prodigium* that one may deduce that a sowing-season and a harvest-season have passed. One might think that the city of Helenus was well suited for a longer sojourn, perhaps for hibernation, but as if to demonstrate the Trojans' conscientious haste, it is made explicit that only a few days were spent here (356). It is therefore hardly surprising that, of the many attempts to work out the chronology of the seven years of wandering, not one is convincing, and I should be tempted to put the blame on poetic licence and rest content with the thought that Virgil himself wanted to discourage such attempts from the first,[103] were it not that we suddenly come across the unexpected information that now 'the sun has finished its annual course and the icy winter-storm stirs up the waves' (284). This information fits so awkwardly into its context – it is not even clear whether Aeneas then did wait there for the winter to end, or whether he sailed on regardless – that I cannot believe that this passage is in its definitive form, and we cannot decide what Virgil intended with this solitary indication of season; one will hardly assume that this was an abortive attempt to provide a chronological framework for the whole.

As with the seven years' wandering, so with the one full year that, according to 5.46, lies between Anchises' death and Aeneas' return to Sicily. Here, however, what concerns the poet is not the length of time which has elapsed, but the fact of the anniversary; he has no interest in explaining exactly how the year is filled by the 349 events of Books 1 and 4 and the extra events which must be supplied in the narrative at the end of Book 3. Critics have found it a great stumbling block that in spite of this period of about a year which lies between the above-mentioned statements by Dido and Iris, they both name the same number of years – *septima aestas*. This is probably simply due to the fact that in both passages – which were possibly written years apart – the number seven was the one which happened to strike the poet as appropriate:[104] the difficult problem, whether the poet had any regard to the one passage while writing the other, and, if so, whether he noticed the contradiction, and, if so, whether he considered it unimportant or privately planned to straighten it out later, I must leave to others to solve; and until it is solved it is not right to draw conclusions about Virgil's art from this supposed contradiction.

Finally, with regard to the general mythical and historical chronology, Virgil did not let it fetter his imagination at all. He respects the period of 333 years before the foundation of Rome (1.265), but at the same time he takes over a poetic idea which has no regard for chronology when he has Aeneas and Dido meet, which puts the foundation of Carthage at the time of the Trojan War. He includes in his catalogues all the heroes from Italy's prehistory that he knows of, without asking whether it is likely that they all lived at the same time. He has Neoptolemus killed by Orestes before Aeneas meets Andromache, although that death was traditionally placed in the tenth year after the destruction of Troy, and he has Achaemenides wandering in the lands of the Cyclopes for only three months, although Homer tells us that 350 Odysseus had already been there in the first year of his wanderings. All this worries him not a jot,[105] and it was a strange misunderstanding of poetic principles to attempt to base on these synchronisms a chronology for Aeneas' adventures: e.g. to work out Ascanius' age from the fact that Andromache (3.491) calls him a coeval of Astyanax, when the latter – according to Homer – was still a babe-in-arms in the last year of the Trojan War: such a calculation would be mistaken even if we did not happen to know that Virgil thought of Astyanax as definitely *not* a babe-in-arms (2.457).

2. Description of place

We have already dealt with the question of place as far as distances were concerned.[106] Place as the scene of the action has the same unimportant role in Virgil as in ancient narrative poetry in general. Τοπογραφία, the description of fictitious places, had, it is true, faint beginnings in Homer which were developed by the Hellenistic poets; but there it is less a case of giving a local motivation to the action than providing atmospheric background; that is also to be found, though not very often, in Virgil. For the rest, he often has to take account of complicated local connections; it is hard to decide whether he imagined the scene clearly to himself but was not able to evoke it equally clearly in the reader, or if he just vaguely thought of a few isolated features of the scene without combining them in his own mind into a united and definite picture; in any case he does not precede his narrative with a connected description of a locality – which would have been the surest means

of achieving clarity, but incompatible with his principles – but mentions in the
course of the narrative here a detail, there a detail; which means that the reader who
351 wishes to visualize clearly not only the characters but also the scene of the action is
badly served.[107] Two fairly important examples will illustrate this.[108] In Book 5
Aeneas speaks to his men first from a mound on the shore (43ff.) and then goes with
them to the *tumulus* of Anchises (76), the position of which is not given any more
precisely than that. On the day of the Games, the people again assemble on the
shore, and the prizes are set out there *circo in medio* (109) [in the middle of a circle]:
how Virgil imagines this *circus* cannot be known. The *agger* [mound] from which
the signal to start the Games is given (113) may be the one previously mentioned
(44). After the boat-race the festive crowds move to a 'grassy place, surrounded with
wooded hills, and in the middle of the valley was a *circus theatri*': the *gramineus
campus* [grassy plain] seems to be identical with the *circus*, but different from the
previous *circus*. When the ships then start burning, the news is brought *ad tumulum
cuneosque theatri* (664) [to the mound and the rows of the amphitheatre], the
tumulus can only be that of Anchises mentioned earlier, and it would certainly be
most appropriate for the Games dedicated to him to take place near his tomb, but we
are only told about this now, rather late in the day. It is possible that the poet thought
of it earlier, for (329) he had Nisus slipping on the blood of slaughtered oxen: this is
modelled on the same occurrence in Homer, where the oxen have been sacrificed at
Patroclus' tomb: it is also possible that this motivation did not even occur to Virgil.
352 Thus all those separate details do not necessarily contradict each other, and it is
possible that they stem from a rounded idea of the scene, but any reader who was
interested in visualizing it would have to piece it together from chance references.

In the second example we may certainly assume that the poet had a clear idea of
the scene, even though he did not enable us to share it. I mean the Trojan camp by
the Tiber, and its surroundings. The camp lies 'near the shore' (7.158), but not right
by the sea: when the enemy attack they have the sea behind them (10.267ff.; cf.
9.238: *in bivio portae quae proxima ponto* [at the fork of the roads outside the gate
nearest the sea]). But it is right on the river bank, and open on that side, with no
protecting walls: otherwise Turnus would not be able to leap from the camp into the
water (9.815).[109] So far the topography is clear; but now (9.468), when the enemy
approach, Virgil says:

> *Aeneadae duri murorum in parte sinistra*
> *opposuere aciem – nam dextera cingitur amni –*
> *ingentisque tenent fossas et turribus altis*
> *stant maesti*

[the men of Aeneas resolutely ranged their line for resistance along the wall on their
left flank, since their right was girt by the river; and they were sadly lining their
deep moats and taking up their posts on their tall towers]. That is, as Servius rightly
remarks, a preparation for Turnus' retreat: it is supposed to impress on us the
situation on the riverbank. But with a camp, how can one speak of a left and right
side of the walls at all? This is possible with a square Roman camp, which has a
front and a back, and therefore a left and a right side; but here the camp seems to

have only *two* sides altogether, and if a square camp is protected by the river on one side, then three are open to attack. Let us suppose that the wall was a level, bow-shaped area with both ends touching the river: then the side facing the enemy could be called the left side (if one were facing the same way as the Tiber's current flows),[110] and the side by the river could be called the right side (to be exact, the right side of the camp, not of the walls): but it is asking a lot of the reader to think out all this, or some alternative. It is certain that the poet meant something definite by *pars sinistra* [left flank] and *dextera* [right], and wanted to convey it to the reader: but he does not succeed in doing so. This is a weakness, but to be fair we must remember how even historians in ancient times failed to describe the topography adequately, and how even modern writers who pride themselves on their detailed scenic descriptions often leave the reader doubtful and confused, so that the only remedy is to provide a sketch map.

In other cases one is inclined to assume that Virgil did not start by imagining a precise scene, but introduced each feature for a particular purpose as it was needed: an example of this is the torrent (10.362) which forces the Arcadian horsemen to dismount (above p. 192 n. 66), or the extensive marsh which hems in Turnus' flight (12.745). However, here it is a question of localities which may have been well known to both Virgil and his readers, and we have to consider the possibility that he may be linking the action to familiar scenes. If this is so, details which would not help strangers might fit together to build up a clear picture for local people, as we can see from the example of the Etruscan camp in Book 8. Evander has begun (478) his report on Etruscan relationships with the τοποθεσία [topography] of the *urbs Agyllina* i.e. Caere, Mezentius' royal seat; he has given an account of the conquest of the city by the rebellious Etruscans when, immediately afterwards (497), he reports that all Etruria is now burning to pursue Mezentius, and the fleet is lying ready by the shore, *litore*; then every reader who knows where Caere is situated, will also know that this *litus* is that of Palo, and, because of that, he will understand that *hic campus* (504) [this plain], where the Etruscan battle force is encamped, is the *campus* around Caere. Further when Aeneas gives as his destination the *Tyrrhena arva* (551) [Etruscan fields] and the *Tyrrheni litora regis* (555) [shores of the Etruscan king], this reader will know exactly what he means; also he will know where to set the grove *prope Caeritis amnem* (597) [near the river of Caere], in which Aeneas receives Vulcan's armour, and which is not far from Tarchon's camp (603) – not by the upper course of the Caere, which the words could also mean, but in the neighbourhood of Caere.[111] Finally, he will not be at all surprised to hear later (10.55) that the army has embarked without delay; but anyone who was ignorant of the local geography and read the last-mentioned passages in isolation would be inclined to complain that here, too, Virgil has been vague in describing the scene.

Notes to Chapter 2

1. Cf. our earlier discussion of the countryfolk, p. 154.
2. Addison has pointed out (*Spectator* 351 [April 12, 1712]) how skilfully Virgil

has removed everything from the *prodigium* that might detract from the dignity of heroic epic: 'the prophetess, who foretells it, is an hungry Harpy, as the person who discovers it, is young Ascanius.... Such an observation, which is beautiful in the mouth of a boy, would have been ridiculous from any other of the company.' This remark is very much in the spirit of Virgil. Dionysius (1.55) puts the phrase into the mouth of one of the παῖδες [boys] or ὁμόσκηνοι [tent-mates].

267   **3.** *te, mea quem spatiis propioribus aetas insequitur, venerande puer* [you, whose age is not so far in advance of mine, admirable youth] says Ascanius to him at 9.275. When he goes on to add *nulla meis sine te quaeretur gloria rebus; seu pacem seu bella geram, tibi maxima rerum verborumque fides* [never shall I desire to win in my career any fame which you do not share, whether I am at war or peace, and in all that I say or do I shall above all rely on you], Virgil is subtly hinting at a relationship similar to that which existed between Augustus and his exact contemporary Agrippa.

    4. He is introduced as *audax* [daring] on his first appearance (8.110, cf. 10.379, 458).

    5. For details see above p. 169.

    6. Aristotle (*Rhet.* 2.12f.) gives a character sketch only of the νέοι [young men] and the πρεσβύτεροι [older men]; the ἀκμάζοντες [men in the prime of life] are merely the μέσον [mean] between these two, 1390a 29.

    7. As, for example, Evander, who is modelled on Homer's Nestor; this characteristic of his is very suited to the atmosphere of the whole of Book 8. Aristotle, *Rhet.* 1390a 6, mentions it as typical of πρεσβύτεροι [older men].

268   **8.** Livy 3.48.8: *...cetera, quae in tali re muliebris dolor, quo est maestior i n b e c i l l o a n i m o, eo miserabilia magis querentibus subicit* [and other things which grief makes women utter on such an occasion: for, *on account of the weakness of their nature*, women are more inclined to sorrow, and therefore their lamentations are correspondingly more pitiful]; *parvis mobili rebus animo muliebri* (6.34.7) [a woman's nature, which it takes very little to upset]. The laments of Euryalus' unfortunate mother are so heart-rending that the Trojan commanders have her taken to one side to protect the morale of the army (9.498-502). We are reminded of the situation in Rome after the battle of Cannae, where the *clamor lamentantium mulierum* [the noisy weeping and wailing of the women] increased the confusion, and the *patres* had to take care *ut tumultum ac trepidationem in urbe tollant, matronas publico arceant continerique intra suum quamque limen cogant, comploratus familiarum coerceant* [so as to bring the uproar and terror in the city to an end, to forbid women from appearing out of doors, and force all of them to stay inside their houses, and keep family mourning within reasonable limits] (Livy 22.55). Cf. also *Aeneid* 11.147: when the mothers see Pallas' funeral procession, *maestam incendunt clamoribus urbem* [their shrieking set the city ablaze with sorrow].

269   **9.** *quam super adventu Teucrum Turnique hymenaeis femineae ardentem curaeque iraeque coquebant* (7.344) [who was already in a feverish turmoil with a woman's thoughts of anxiety at the arrival of the Trojans and rage at the wedding planned for Turnus].

    10. Euryalus is a loving son, but the idea that he should preserve his own life for the sake of his mother cannot hold him back from a dangerous situation which offers him an opportunity to win glory. Evander is the very type of a loving father, but he values his son's renown even above his son's life (8.55).

11. '*L'Andromaque d'Hector agenouillée sur une tombe vide, gardant un amour* 270
unique et la fidélité du coeur dans l'involontaire infidélité d'un corps d'esclave
[Andromache, the wife of Hector, kneeling on an empty tomb, keeping alive a love that is unique, faithful in her heart even though her captive body is forced to be unfaithful]' – Jules Lemaître, *Les Contemporains* (Paris, 1886) 6.276.

12. The ancients were careful to note the way in which Homer characterized Greeks and barbarians; there are an enormous number of scholia on this topic (R. Dittenberger, *Hermes* 40 [1905] 459-68); so too, for example, Plutarch *Quomodo adolescens* 29d, which is of course dependent on earlier interpretations of Homer. Virgil seems to have played with the idea of drawing a similar contrast between the civilized Trojans and the barbarian tribes of Italy, *populosque ferocis contundet* (1.263) [and shall overthrow fierce peoples], *gens dura atque aspera cultu debellanda tibi Latio est* (5.730) [when you come to Latium you will have to defeat in war a hardy nation, wild in its ways]; however, hardly any of this survived as an active ingredient in the final version.

13. See above pp. 6-7.

14. Servius on 11.700: *Ligures autem omnes fallaces sunt, sicut ait Cato in* 271
secundo originum libro [all Ligurians are deceitful, as Cato says in the second book of his *Origines*]. So too Nigidius ap. Servius on 11.715: *Ligures qui Appenninum tenuerunt, latrones insidiosi fallaces mendaces* [the Ligurians who live in the Appennines are brigands, tricksters, traitors, liars]. Cf. Cic. *Pro Cluentio* 72: Staienus (*qui esset totus ex fraude et mendacio factus*) [whose whole character was a tissue of deception and mendacity] chose *Paetus* out of the *cognomina* of the Aelian gens *ne si se Ligurem fecisset, nationis magis quam generis uti cognomine videretur* [to avoid adopting the name Ligur; for that name might be taken to indicate the race that he belonged to rather than his family]: this shows that it was a widely-held view.

15. It is well known that many readers have sensed this; though none has ex- 272
pressed it more concisely or fluently than Saint-Évremont (in *Réflexions sur nos traducteurs*). But some of the customary criticisms are unjust (for example, that Aeneas does not behave like Odysseus during the sea-storm; Virgil has provided a perfectly satisfactory motivation for this); others are misguided, in that they accuse Virgil of failing to portray a hero when he was not trying to do so. It is a quite different question whether Virgil has succeeded in realizing his actual intention to the full.

16. I am delighted that Leo refers to the view which underlies the discussion that 273
follows as an 'observation which is important for the interpretation of the whole *Aeneid*' (*Deutsche Litteratur-Zeitung* [1903] 595); I hope I may be permitted to mention this since Kroll, *Neue Jahrbücher* 21 (1908) 518, states that 'no support has been forthcoming for this interpretation' of mine.

17. Aeneas is guilty, not because he abandons Dido – for he is obeying a divine 274
command – but because he betrays Dido's trust by entering into a relationship with her when he must know that it neither can nor should become permanent. He is therefore guilty of Dido's death and has to suffer heavily for it: the curses that Dido

calls down upon him with her dying breath are fulfilled (4.652ff.). The chivalrous nature of Virgil's conception of a man's obligations to a woman is clearly seen here; Conway was, I believe, the first to point this out; see above p. 115 n. 40.

276   **18.** Cf. also Plüss op. cit. p. 215 n. 25, 165.

    19. Cf. Norden *ad loc.*, who points out that *praecipere* [anticipate] is a technical term used by the Stoics: Cic. *De Off.* 1.80f.: *fortis animi et constantis est non perturbari in rebus asperis...; quamquam hoc animi, illud etiam ingenii magni est p r a e c i p e r e cogitatione futura et aliquanto ante constituere, quid accidere possit in utramque partem* [it is characteristic of a brave and resolute spirit to remain unperturbed in difficult times...; yet it demands not only great courage, but also great intellectual powers, to *anticipate* what is going to happen, by means of reflection, and to decide in advance what may happen for better or for worse].

    20. *tristi turbatus pectora bello* (8.29) [his whole heart agitated by the horror of the war], where *turbatus* does not mean 'bewildered' but 'agitated', cf. *turbatae*
277 *Palladis arma* (8.435) [arms for Pallas when she is aroused].

    21. *disce puer virtutem ex me verumque laborem, fortunam ex aliis...te animo repetentem exempla tuorum et pater Aeneas et avunculus excitet Hector* (12.435ff.) ['From me, my son, you may learn what is valour and what is strenuous toil: as for what good fortune is, others must teach you that...in due time you must recall in your thought the examples set you by your kindred. Your father was Aeneas and your uncle was Hector. Let that be your inspiration']. He could not have adopted such a tone in Book 2. I am well aware that a modern reader might wish that Virgil had made his intentions more explicit. For example, at the beginning of Book 8, in order to motivate the appearance of Tiberinus he has depicted Aeneas' anxious mood in stronger terms than befits his overall intention. But because Virgil, as narrator, never declares his intention in so many words, we should not assume that he did not have one: he never makes any clear statements of this kind: he tells his
278 story and leaves the rest to the reader's judgement.

    22. E.g. Truculentus; Demea in the *Adelphi*. The material that H. Steinmann, *De artis poeticae veteris parte quae est* περὶ ἠθῶν (Diss. Göttingen, 1907, p. 1) has collected from the scholia under the heading *de morum mutatione* (64ff.) [on character change] refers almost entirely to the origin, growth and dwindling of πάθη [emotions].

    23. I can now add in support of my view the article by K. Holl, 'Die schriftstellerische Form des griechischen Heiligenlebens' *Neue Jahrbücher* 29 (1912) 406 – an excellent piece of work in so far as I am able to judge it. Here Holl analyses Athanasius' biography of St Antony the Hermit as a means 'of illustrating his ideal: the height of the goal that his hero achieves is shown by his ascent to it step by step.' The closest precedent for this ideal is that of the perfect Gnostic in Clement of Alexandria, and this in turn points back 'to a much earlier ideal, the Greek conception of the perfect wise man', in fact to the form in which this ideal was presented by Posidonius – it is clear that it is reasonable to compare Virgil with Athanasius in this respect. Holl regards Antisthenes' Heracles as the supreme example within the literary development of the ideal figure: we may regard him as a precedent for Virgil's Aeneas at least in so far as Antisthenes, like Virgil, cast his hero 'as a standard of moral behaviour for mankind' (Wilamowitz, *Euripides: Herakles* I² [repr. Darmstadt, 1959] 107): the idea that we have attributed to Virgil is therefore not something totally unprecedented.

24. Seneca *Epist.* 41.2: *bonus vir sine deo nemo est; an potest aliquis super* 279 *fortunam nisi ab illo adiutus exsurgere? ille dat consilia magnifica et erecta* [No man can attain virtue without the help of god. Can anyone rise above the whims of fortune unless he is aided by him? It is he who inspires us with splendid and lofty advice]. This 'god' is within us; mythical imagery represents a god as a being with whom a man is confronted.

25. The best illustration of how Virgil intended the 'trials' of his hero to be understood can be found in a passage in Seneca *Dial.* 1 (*de Providentia*). 4: *prosperae res et in plebem et in vilia ingenia deveniunt: at calamitates terroresque mortalium sub iugum mittere proprium magni viri est...deus quos probat, quos amat, indurat, recognoscit, exercet* (cf. 5.725, where Anchises addresses his son *nate Iliacis e x e r c i t e fatis*) ...*verberat nos et lacerat fortuna: patiamur; non est saevitia: certamen est, quod si saepius adierimus, fortiores erimus. solidissima corporis pars est quam frequens usus agitavit: praebendi fortunae sumus, ut contra illam ab ipsa duremur. paulatim nos sibi pares facit. contemptum periculorum adsiduitas periculi dabit...quid miraris bonos viros, ut confirmentur, concuti? non est arbor solida nec fortis nisi in quam frequens ventus incursat. ipsa enim vexatione constringitur et radices certius figit. fragiles sunt quae in aprica valle creverunt.* [Success comes even to the common man, and to men of low intelligence; but only a truly great man can triumph over the terrors and disasters that beset the life of man...God hardens, inspects and disciplines those whom he loves and approves (cf. *Aen.* 5.725 where Anchises addresses his son [son, *disciplined* by the heavy burden of Troy's destiny])...We may be thrashed and tortured by fortune: we must put up with it. It is not cruelty: it is a contest; and the more often we are involved in it, the stronger we shall be. The sturdiest part of the body is that which is kept active by constant use. We should offer ourselves to fortune, so that we may be hardened against her by fortune herself. Gradually she will train us to be a match for herself. Constant encounters with danger will breed contempt of danger...why then are you surprised that virtuous men are tossed hither and thither to develop their strength? A tree is never sturdy unless it is constantly buffeted by the wind. For it is precisely this violent agitation that makes it tighten its grip, and fixes its roots more firmly in the earth. The vulnerable trees are those which have grown in a sheltered, sunny valley].

26. p. 166. 280

27. Cf. above p. 84. 282

28. In her love and longing for Aeneas *tota vagatur urbe furens* (68) [she 287 roamed distraught through all her city], heedless of her *fama* (91) [reputation]; when she hears what Aeneas intends to do, *totam incensa per urbem bacchatur, qualis commotis excita sacris Thyias* (300) [she ran in excited riot through the whole city, like a Bacchant excited to frenzy as the emblems of Bacchus are shaken]; note the intensification of the language; note also the poet's view that the way in which Dido's despair (like Amata's) expresses itself is in her ἀσχημοσύνη [indecorous conduct]: she forgets modesty and morality. In the *Ciris* the love-lorn Scylla, a respectable young girl who would have concealed her love from all around her, is described as being 'like a Thracian maenad or a priestess of Cybele', *infelix virgo tota bacchatur in urbe* [the unhappy maiden roamed the whole city like a Bacchant] (*Ciris* 167). Here is another example which shows how little the imitator understood

289 his model.

29. On the other hand, there is a great deal of action in Theocritus' first *Idyll*,

290 even when Daphnis himself is speaking.

30. Cf. Aristotle's analysis of χάρις, *Rhet.* 2.7.1385a 17-21: ἔστω δὴ χάρις ὑπουργία δεομένῳ μὴ ἀντί τινος, μηδ' ἵνα τι αὐτῷ ὑπουργοῦντι ἀλλ' ἵνα τι ἐκείνῳ· μεγάλη δὲ ἂν ᾖ σφόδρα δεομένῳ ἢ μεγάλων ἢ χαλεπῶν ἢ ἐν καιροῖς τοιούτοις, ἢ μ ό ν ο ς ἢ πρῶτος ἢ μάλιστα [kindness may be defined as helpfulness to someone in need, not in return for anything, and not for the advantage of the helper himself, but for that of the person helped. Kindness is great if shown to someone who is in extreme need or needs something important or hard to get, or who needs it at an important and difficult juncture; or if the helper is the only, the first, or the chief person to give help]. It would not be surprising if Virgil had used analyses of this kind: think of Horace's *rem tibi Socraticae poterunt ostendere chartae* [the pages of the Socratics will provide you with material] (*Ars Poetica*

291 310), and Kiessling's quotations from Cic. *De Orat.* 1.12.53 in his note *ad loc.*

31. I need only refer you to the rightly famous exposition of the religious content of the *Aeneid* in Boissier, *La religion romaine d'Auguste aux Antonins* 1.248ff., and can save myself the trouble of explaining how my interpretation relates to his.

32. Suet. 17 Reifferscheid: ἔπος ἐστὶν περιοχὴ θείων τε καὶ ἡρωϊκῶν καὶ

292 ἀνθρωπίνων πραγμάτων [epic is an account of the actions of gods, heroes and men].

33. A unique case, which stands alone, of clothing philosophical–theological

293 (actually Stoic) doctrine in mythical garb is Virgil's eschatology: for this see Norden's introduction to Book 6, which, to my mind, has established beyond question that Virgil follows Posidonius closely here.

34. *omnipotens* (2.689; 4.220; 5.687 etc.); Allecto uses this epithet of Juno to Turnus, although it is not true (7.428); the inhabitants of Soracte also regard Apollo, their *summus deum* [highest of the gods], as *omnipotens* (11.785, 790): that is an ethnic belief.

35. *hominum rerumque aeterna potestas* (10.18) [eternal sovereignty over men and over all the world]; *qui res hominumque deumque aeternis regis imperiis* (1.229) [disposer, by eternal decrees, of all life human and divine]; *rerum cui prima potestas* (10.100) [who holds first authority over the world].

36. *sic fata deum rex sortitur volvitque vices, is vertitur ordo* (3.375) [so are the lots of destiny drawn by the king of the gods: so does he set events to roll their course]. In as much as the lord of fate is the king of the gods, then instead of *fata Iovis* (4.614) [Jupiter's ordinances] one could say, less accurately, *fata deum* [the ordinances of the gods] (2.54, 257, 3.717, 6.376, 7.50, 239), almost equivalent to 'will of the gods', and then also, but quite exceptionally, of a single divinity: *fata Iunonis* (8.292) [the ordinances of Juno] are said to have imposed the labours on Hercules. It is rhetorical antithesis in Juno's great monologue (7.293) when she says *fatis contraria nostris fata Phrygum* [my will opposed by the Phrygian destiny], where *fata* means first 'will' and then 'fate'. Virgil felt the etymological connection with *fari* [to speak]; this can be seen both from 1.261: *fabor enim...et volvens* *fatorum arcana movebo* [I shall speak...and turning the scroll of the Fates, awake their secrets] and from the frequent equation with *fas* [divine law] (1.206; 2.779; 6.438; 9.96; 12.28) and opposition to *infandum* (7.583) [not to be spoken], *infandum bellum contra fata deum* [an unspeakable war contrary to the will of the gods], cf. 1.251 *infandum* of that which goes against Jupiter's commandment.   294

37. *sed fatis incerta feror, si Juppiter unam esse velit Tyriis urbem Troiaque profectis* (4.110) ['but I am subject to the Fates, whose design is obscure to me: would Jupiter wish the Tyrians and the emigrants from Troy to own a city in common?']. Also *nec Iovis imperio fatisque infracta quiescit* (5.784) [neither the fates nor Jupiter's own command can break her opposition] where both are set on an equal level by the copulative *que*. On 10.31ff. see below n. 43.

38. 7.313 (Juno is speaking): *non dabitur regnis, esto, prohibere Latinis atque immota manet fatis Lavinia coniunx: at trahere atque moras tantis licet addere rebus* ['I shall not be allowed, I grant it, to bar Aeneas from his throne in Latium, and Lavinia, by unalterable destiny, will still be his bride. Yet I may prolong the process, and cause delay in events so momentous']. 11.587 (Diana makes no attempt to rescue her dearly beloved Camilla): *quandoquidem fatis urgetur acerbis* [since fate now bears heartlessly against her].   295

39. The development of Juno's attitude is worth studying. In Book 1 she still believes that she can influence *fata* (i.e. Jupiter's will) by her own actions; in Book 7 she renounces this hope, but makes very little attempt to cool her vengeance, although she must know that this does not comply with Jupiter's will; in Book 10 she attempts to defend her action at first with sophistic argument, saying that it does not contravene *fatum*; 10.611 she gives up all resistance of her own, but still hopes for a change in Jupiter's intentions; at the end of Book 12 she finally abandons that hope and only asks for *nulla fati quod lege tenetur* [what is not covered by any law of fate].   296

40. Seneca *Quaest. Nat.* 2.37: *nos quoque existimamus vota proficere salva vi ac potestate fatorum. quaedam a diis immortalibus ita suspensa relicta sunt, ut in bonum vertant, si admotae diis preces fuerint, si vota suscepta: ita non est hoc contra fatum sed ipsum quoque in fato est* [we too believe that prayers have force if they do not impair the force and power of fate. For some things have been so left in suspense by the immortal gods that they may turn to our advantage if prayers are directed to the gods and vows are undertaken. As a result this is not opposed to fate but is itself also in fate]. Nothing can happen, naturally, which goes against *fatum*; when (4.696) it is said of Dido *nec fato merita nec morte peribat* [she perished neither by destiny nor by a death deserved], this is equal to *fatali morte* [by a fated death] in ordinary speech; see Norden, *Hermes* 28 (1893) 375 n. 1. The opposite is *vivendo vici mea fata* (11.160) [I have outlived my span, victor over my fate], which nobody would take literally.

41. It is very difficult to decide what Virgil was thinking when he interpolated into the last duel (12.725) the *psychostasia* [weighing of souls] modelled on Homer (*Iliad* 10.209f.): Jupiter places in the two pans of the scales *fata diversa duorum, quem damnet labor et quo vergat pondere letum* [the differing fates of the two champions, to decide which one should come happy from the ordeal, and whose weight should bring death swinging down]. It is true that it is not stated that Turnus

is now fated to fall: at 10.624ff. Juno was still allowed to hope that he might live, and at 12.157 she still believes that it is possible; but if we therefore assume that Turnus' fate is now finally being decided by Jupiter's will, then the image is not very suitable, since the most that could happen is for the fight to remain undecided; the total scheme makes it impossible for Aeneas to fall now to *letum* [death]. Nevertheless, that assumption does seem to be the only one possible; as the preceding passage shows, Virgil is striving with all his means to make the reader feel the same excitement and tension as the onlookers, who knew that this was the moment of decision and waited breathlessly; in myth the symbol of this decision is the *psychostasia*, and the representation of this symbol seemed to Virgil so valuable for his purpose that he ignored, or overruled, any reasons not to use it. Whether he had noticed that Homer also had Zeus already surrendering Hector before the psychostasia (167-85) we do not know. In any case here, too, Virgil's concern was to maintain the tension, and therefore he deviates from Homer in not saying which way the balance went; that will be revealed by the result.

42. *tanton placuit concurrere motu, Iuppiter, aeterna gentis in pace futuras?* (12.503) ['Jupiter! Did you indeed ordain that nations who were to live together afterwards in everlasting peace should clash in such violence?'].

297   **43.** When (10.8) Jupiter says *abnueram bello Italiam concurrere Teucris: quae contra vetitum discordia?* ['I had withheld my permission for Italy to meet Trojans in combat of war: why is there this rebellion against my prohibition?'] and then *adveniet i u s t u m pugnae, ne arcessite, tempus* ['the *due* time for battle will come; hasten it not'], and finally *quandoquidem Ausonios coniungi foedere Teucris haud licitum* (105) ['since it has not proved permissible for Ausonians to join in compact with Trojans'], there is no doubt that this contradicts the prophecy given in Book 1 to Venus: *bellum ingens geret Italia populosque ferocis contundet moresque viris et moenia ponet* (263) [he shall fight a great war in Italy and overthrow proud peoples. He shall establish for his warriors a way of life and walls for their defence]; not only because the war was there prophesied as arranged by *fatum*, i.e. by Jupiter's own will – one could, at a pinch, explain this by the fact that Jupiter's knowledge of the future does not always have to coincide with his personal preferences, as in so many theological systems, but also because there the war is teleologically motivated as an integral part of Jupiter's plan: the necessity to force culture on the still barbarous Latins. This motive was later dropped completely by Virgil. There is a contradiction here; we should not try to cover it up, nor should we simply write it off as carelessness. We can explain it as the result of the difficulties described above; even Virgil could not master them completely. The assembly of the gods has often been criticized as a passage which imitates Homer in a mechanical, uncritical way, but I would say that, on the contrary, it is just there that one can find evidence of a great deal of heart-searching about the material and the form: this has been shown splendidly by A.B. Drachmann in his penetrating monograph *Guderne hos Virgil* (Copenhagen, 1887) 130ff., where the only thing that I find lacking is a more detailed study of the actual role of *fatum* in the gods' speeches. Venus refers, on behalf of her protégé, to *fatum*, which he learnt from an oracle, and which she regards as identical with Jupiter's *iussa* [commands]; she regards Juno's actions as an impertinent attempt to lay down new *fata* (34ff.). Juno, for her part, is careful not

to cross Jupiter or attack his plans. She merely denies that *fatum*, which she admits that Aeneas followed to Latium, had any effect on what he then proceeded to do there, and makes him himself responsible for the resulting misfortune. Jupiter, who, of course, is the highest authority in matters of *fatum*, could utter a command, stop the conflict and end the war; but then the poem would be over. That is why Jupiter has to choose to allow *fatum* to be decided by the course of events, as if this could convince Juno of her (real or ostensible) error better than his own word could. For his part, all he will promise is not to interfere again, so that the test can proceed without interference. Of course this also prevents the goddesses from taking a hand 298 in the battle. (Drachmann, [149f.] explains very clearly why this prohibition is not expressly stated.) After Aeneas' successes, Juno declares herself convinced, in answer to Jupiter's ironic question (606ff.). 299

44. It is probably to make this reference clear that *hoc regni* (78) [this power] is explained further by 1.80: *nimborumque facis tempestatumque potentem* [you give me power over storm-clouds and storms]. Ἥρα [Hera] is frequently identified with ἀήρ [air]; Varro does so, and also *Iuno* with *terra* [earth]: Agahd, *M. Ter. Varr. Antiqu. Rer. Div.* 2 p. 215. 301

45. *fatalem Aenean manifesto numine ferri admonet ira deum tumulique ante ora recentes* (11.232) [the anger of the gods, witnessed by the freshly made grave-mounds before their eyes, already warned them that Aeneas was clearly by divine warrant a man of destiny] (cf. 12.27ff.). 302

46. Remember Anchises' words *sequor et qua ducitis adsum, di patrii* (2.701) ['I follow, gods of our race, and wherever you lead, there shall I be']: or *divum ducunt qua iussa sequamur* (3.114) ['let us take the path shown by divine command'], *cedamus Phoebo et moniti meliora sequamur* (188) ['Let us trust Apollo, accept his warning and follow a better course']. Also Aeneas 4.340: *me si fata meis paterentur ducere vitam auspiciis...recidiva manu posuissem Pergama victis* ['If my destiny had allowed me to guide my life as I myself would have chosen...I should have re-founded Troy's fortress to be strong once more after her defeat'] and *Italiam non sponte sequor* (361) ['It is not by my own choice that I voyage onward to Italy']; but then *mea me virtus et sancta oracula divom..fatis egere v o l e n t e m* (8.131) ['my own valour, holy oracles from gods...brought me here in *willing* obedience to my destiny']. So Nautes had urged him, when he was thinking of remaining in Sicily, *fatorum oblitus* [forgetful of the fates], *quo fata trahunt retrahuntque sequamur* (5.709) ['we should accept the lead which destiny offers, whether to go forward or not']. Too late, Turnus goes the right way: *iam, iam fata, soror, superant...quo deus et quo dura vocat Fortuna sequamur* (12.676) ['at this very moment sister, fate is prevailing over us... Let us follow where God and our own hard fortune call'].

47. *intuemini enim horum deinceps annorum vel secundas res vel adversas, invenietis omnia prospere evenisse sequentibus deos, adversa spernentibus* ['Consider the successes and the setbacks of this period of years, and you will find that everything turned out well for those who complied with the gods and badly for those who spurned them'] (Livy 5.51, from a speech of Camillus, one example from many). 303

48. Suet. *Aug.* 94.

49. Ibid. 91.

50. Ibid. 96.

304   **51.** Of course this, too, did have some connection with contemporary beliefs: Apollo is personally supposed to have literally led Augustus' ships to victory at Actium.

305   **52.** Propertius 4.4.68 of Tarpeia: *nescia vae Furiis accubuisse novis; nam Vesta...culpam alit et plures condit in ossa faces* [not knowing, alas, that she has lain down with new Furies: for Vesta...fed her guilt and buried more firebrands in her bones], where Rothstein rightly draws a comparison with the Allecto scene.

306   **53.** Cauer (*Grundfragen der Homerkritik*[2], 339) asks: 'What natural causes? I can't see any.' But they are not hard to see in what Allecto says: if one imagines that her words are a soliloquy spoken by an offended Turnus, and that his answer is his other, calmer, inner voice speaking, Allecto's consequent overwhelming *ira* [anger] and its effect represent the victory of emotion – and all the psychological motivation is present to drive Turnus to fight.

307   **54.** Propertius 1.3.45: *dum me iucundis lapsam Sopor inpulit alis* [until sleep brushed my sinking form with his pleasant wings].

   55. These references to divine intervention, without further details – *Iuno viris animumque ministrat* (9.764) [Juno gave him new spirit and new strength], *Iovis monitis Mezentius succedit pugnae* (10.689) [warned by Jupiter, Mezentius took up the fight] etc. – do not contradict Homeric usage: *Iliad* 16.656: Ἕκτορι ἀνάλκιδα θυμὸν ἐνῆκεν (sc. Zeus) [(Zeus) put a cowardly spirit into Hector]; *Odyssey* 19.479: τῇ γὰρ Ἀθηναίη νόον ἔτραπεν [for Athene distracted her attention] etc.

308   **56.** There is nothing wrong with this as such (see previous note); but if it is only to be a straightforward divine intervention with no detailed description, Jupiter need not send Mercury to Carthage, he could do it himself. Also, this is a most unusual example in that the desired effect is not for the immediate present but for the future.

   57. Plut. *De tranquillitate animi* 465b: καὶ τῶν λόγων, ὅσοι πρὸς τὰ πάθη βοηθοῦσι, δεῖ πρὸ τῶν παθῶν ἐπιμελεῖσθαι τοὺς νοῦν ἔχοντας, ἵν' ἐκ πολλοῦ παρεσκευασμένοι μᾶλλον ὠφελῶσι [so also with such reasonings as offer help in controlling the passions: wise men should give heed to them before the passions arise so that, being prepared well in advance, their help may be more effective].

   58. Cauer objects (op. cit. 337) 'There is no process here which can be explained in human terms', meaning that Aeneas is not persuaded and inwardly convinced as Achilles was by Athena. It seems to me only too human that Aeneas follows the command of the λόγος, or let us say 'of duty', although the inclination of his heart still pulls him in the other direction; in this struggle, the heart's inclination is not won over but suppressed by force, and it could not be better symbolized than by the fact that Mercury achieves his ends by divine authority, not by persuasion.

309   **59.** *Iliad* 1.220: ἂψ ἐς κουλεὸν ὦσε μέγα ξίφος, οὐδ' ἀπίθησεν μύθῳ Ἀθηναίης [back he thrust his massive blade once more into its scabbard, and did not ignore Athene's words]: on which Plutarch *Quomodo adolesc.* 26e comments ὀρθῶς καὶ καλῶς, ὅτι τὸν θυμὸν ἐκκόψαι παντάπασι μὴ δυνηθείς, ὅμως πρὶν ἀνήκεστόν τι δρᾶσαι μετέστησε καὶ κατέσχεν εὐπειθῆ τῷ λογισμῷ γενόμενον [rightly and honourably, because, although he could not completely eradicate his anger, nevertheless before doing anything irreparable, he set it aside and checked it by making it obedient to reason]. That this manner of interpreting

was of much earlier date, even in Rome, goes without saying; for Hermes as λόγος it is enough to refer to Reitzenstein, *Zwei religionsgeschichtliche Fragen* (Strassburg, 1901). The equation is a standard one in Homeric exegesis: λόγος sometimes equals 'speech', sometimes 'reason'. For example, Hermes is sent to accompany Priam on the way to Achilles because λόγος is the best soother of the πάθη [emotions], schol. *Iliad* 24.486; Zeus sends him to Aegisthus: δηλοῖ τὴν ἐκ θεῶν ἀνθρώποις λόγου τοῦ κατ' ἀρετὴν δωρεάν [he indicates the gift from gods to men of reason in accordance with virtue] (schol. *Od.* 1.38); the μῶλυ [moly] which Odysseus received from Hermes is the τέλειος λόγος, ὑφ' οὗ βοηθούμενος οὐδὲν παθεῖν δύναται [perfect reason, with the aid of which he is unable to come to any harm] (schol. *Od.* 10.305).   311

60. There is no parallel in Homer for the way in which the Great Mother reveals herself in 9.110. A wonderful light breaks over the sky, people think they see *Idaeos choros* [Idaean bands], and the goddess lets her voice be heard but does not become visible or give her name. The only comparable feature is perhaps the voice of Apollo which sounds from the *adyton* [shrine] on Delos (3.93ff.). This very thing however, the voice of a divinity making itself heard from its sanctuary, is not infrequently reported by the historians, e.g. Livy 6.33.5, Tac. *Hist.* 5.13, Cic. *De Div.* 1.45.101.

61. Cf. Cauer op. cit. 343f., who here modifies his earlier attempt (disputed e.g. by Robert, *Studien zum Ilias* 353) to establish a chronological order of forms of appearance. He now regards the appearance of the gods in their own form to be archaic in most cases, and later imitation in others.   312

62. So, too, the apparition of the Penates, which stands on the boundary between dream and waking vision, 3.172ff.

63. It is different in the case of Turnus and Juturna 12.631, 676; the two are closer, brother and sister – Juturna was raised to the status of an immortal nymph by Jupiter – and that may be the reason why Turnus recognizes her and speaks to her without her immediately withdrawing from his sight.   313

64. There, as Leo, *Geschichte der lateinischen Litteratur* 1.179 n. 2 points out, Ennius' dream of Ilia has served as a model.   314

65. *n e c   s o p o r   i l l u d   e r a t, sed coram adgnoscere vultus velatasque comas praesentiaque ora videbar* (173) [*This could be no dream. I seemed to recognize, there before me, their garlanded hair, and their lips as they spoke*]: for the ὕπαρ οὐκ ὄναρ [waking vision, not a dream] of so many appearances which hover between vision and dream, see Deubner, *De incubatione capita quattuor* (Leipzig, 1900) 5 etc.

66. *Somn. Scip.* 1.3.8; cf. Deubner 3ff.

67. *curas his demere dictis* (3.153) [relieved my anxiety with these words], *in curas animo diducitur omnis* (5.720) [his thoughts were distracted by every kind of anxiety], *tristi turbatus pectora bello procubuit* (8.29) [his whole heart distracted by the horror of the war, he lay down].   316

68. Mommsen, *Staatsrecht* 1.79 n. 1.

69. However Helenus is probably also an expert in the *praepetis omina pinnae* (3.361) [omens of the bird on the wing].   317

70. See Drachmann op. cit.; there are also some good comments in G. Ihm, *Vergilstudien* I (Progr. Gernsheim, 1902).

71. *aethere summo* [heaven's height] and *vertice caeli* [zenith of the sky] (1.223, 225); *superis in sedibus* (11.532) [dwellings on high]; *caelo alto* (10.633) [high heaven].

72. *Iovis in tectis* (10.758) [in the house of Jupiter], *tectis bipatentibus* (5) [the halls opening in two directions].

318   **73.** 1.663; 4.92; 5.780.

319   **74.** *Werke*, 11.191.

324   **75.** Specially emphasized by *hic primum Fortuna fidem mutata novavit* (604) [at this moment Fortune first veered, and turned treacherously against the Trojans].

325   **76.** This is not described but implied by line 405: *si te nulla movet tantae pietatis imago* [if the sight of fidelity so strong has no power to move you].

326   **77.** *magnis exterrita monstris deriguit visu in medio* (3.307) [unnerved by the shock, suddenly, as she looked, she stiffened].

78. *obstipuit primo aspectu* (1.613) [at her first sight (of Aeneas) she was awe-struck].

79. *procul ex celso miratur vertice montis...occurrit* (5.35) [looking from a distant mountain-crest, he observed with wonder...and came to meet them].

80. *terrentur visu subito cunctique relictis consurgunt mensis* (8.109) [they were alarmed at the sudden sight, and as one man they arose, leaving their banquet].

327   **81.** *ingentem comitum adfluxisse novorum invenio admirans numerum* (2.796) [I was surprised to find their number increased by a great concourse of new arrivals].

328   **82.** It occurred to me that Virgil perhaps thinks of Camilla as arriving in Laurentum only at this moment, which would be all the more fitting because he has not used her in the fighting up to this point; *occurrit portis sub ipsis* [she met him hard by the gate] would fit in well with this, as would the opening words of Diana's speech (555). The Homeric analogy would be the late entrance of Penthesilea. But even if one ignored her inclusion in the catalogue (7.803), I believe that when Turnus speaks of Camilla's support (11.432), he would expressly say that she had not actually arrived yet.

331   **83.** For example, I feel that it was unnecessary to make Mercury prepare for Aeneas' friendly reception in Carthage (1.297), since this reception could be explained satisfactorily in human terms; but one can also feel the same about the motivation of Dido's love by the intervention of a god (cf. Boissier, *Nouvelles promenades archéologiques* 303), and we only notice this example less because we are familiar from other literature with the intervention of Amor.

84. Chrysippus in Plut. *De Stoic. rep.* 47 (fr. 997); the φαντασία [perception], which underlies an unhappy incident, is indeed divine, but not αὐτοτελὴς τῆς συγκαταθέσεως αἰτία [the self-sufficient cause of the intellectual assent of the recipient]; for this the mortal is responsible.

332   **85.** There is no such divine motivation during the storm at the beginning of Book 5, but the participants themselves infer it: *haud equidem sine mente, reor, sine numine divom adsumus et portus delati intramus amicos* (55) ['we have come to land and entered this friendly harbour, and for my part I see in this the intention and the will of the gods'].

334   **86.** The speech of Appius, Livy 5.3-6, is a good example of this.

87. A good example is the reception of Sextus Tarquinius in Gabii, Livy 1.53ff.

336   **88.** The idea that Aeneas could simply look for the queen in her own palace

clearly did not occur to Virgil; he can only visualize the meeting as a ceremonial audience, and for the scene a temple devoted to the *curia* [assembly], like Latinus' building, 7.170ff. Aeneas could guess the function of the temple but hardly that Dido was due to come at that very moment.

89. Virgil wants to show that the new arrivals are not complete strangers to the king (he also knows that Dardanus is of Italic descent [7.205]); this is to prepare the way a little for his rapid agreement and offer of marriage. Aristarchus had found it extremely unlikely that Alcinous would offer Odysseus his daughter in marriage when he hardly knows him: schol. *Od.* 7.311.   338

90. In the Doloneia it is different: there the enemy scouts are bound to come upon the Greeks because they are on the same path; also this is no chance encounter, since Dolon was sent out at this precise time.   340

91. Noack, *Hermes* 27 (1892) 422, puts at least the opening of the Temple of War on to the second day after Aeneas' arrival – this is very unlikely in practical terms; the poet leaves the question open.   343

92. Until line 83 we think that we are hearing about one day only, and I cannot see a different meaning for *instaurat diem donis* (63) [she celebrates the day with offerings]. However, *nunc...nunc* [now...now] in 74 and 77 could refer to repeated actions, and the words *aut gremio Ascanium genitoris imagine capta detinet* (84) [or she held Ascanius close to her, under the spell of his resemblance to his father] cannot possibly refer to the same night on which Dido *sola domo maeret vacua* [she mourned, lonely in the empty hall]: likewise, the statement (86ff.) that the construction-work on the city has been interrupted – apparently because Dido takes no interest in it any more – would only make sense if a longer period had elapsed.

93. Unless one assumed that the *prodigia* – e.g. *exaudiri voces et verba vocantis visa viri, nox cum terras obscura teneret* (460) [she heard cries, as of her husband calling her, when night held the world in darkness] and *agit ipse furentem in somnis ferus Aeneas* (465) [she had nightmares of a furious Aeneas pursuing her] – occur as early as before the first conversation with Aeneas, where Dido *praesensit motus futuros* (297) [divined his intended deceit in advance]. But this assumption finds no confirmation in the poet's words.   344

94. The distance is approximately the same as that between Delos and Crete: that takes three days making good speed (3.117). The even longer voyage from Drepanum to Cumae seems from Virgil's account to have been completed in a day and a night, although here again we can only work this out ourselves because at 5.835 there is an indication of the time which the plot forced upon him.

95. But Virgil is careful not to place Segesta on the coast: at 1.570 and 5.35 Segesta is not mentioned. Uncertainty in geographical matters is illustrated by Aeneas' Thracian foundation (above p. 81): neither he nor the great majority of his readers had any clear idea of this district.   345

96. The greatest haste is also so fully justified by the situation of the Trojan camp that Deuticke's assumption (*Virgils Gedichte* III[9] on line 147) that Virgil has Aeneas spending one night in the Etruscan camp does not seem to me to be required by the plot. Nor can I share his later objection (Appendix p. 287) that perhaps we should not count days at all; the question of how many hours the Etruscan and Arcadian horsemen have taken to come from Caere to the neighbourhood of the

Trojan camp (10.238) will not have been considered by Virgil; but this is not on the same level as the division of the action into particular days and nights.

97. One sunrise is omitted, on the day that the Trojans, as we have to assume, stay in Caieta, 7.1; this is not reported, but is revealed partly by the apostrophe to Caieta, partly afterwards when it is recalled at the moment of departure. There is also no mention of the sunrise at the beginning of 6: that may have some connection with the fact that Books 5 and 6 were not written consecutively.

98. *tum Stygio regi nocturnas incohat aras* (6.252) [now he began the nocturnal altar-rite to the king of Styx]; *adspirant aurae in noctem nec candida cursus luna negat* (7.8) [favouring breezes blew onwards into the night, and a radiant moon blessed their voyage]; *Thybris ea fluvium, quam longa est, nocte tumentem leniit* (8.86) [then did Tiber make smooth his heaving flood for the whole length of that night].

99. Wilamowitz, *Homerische Untersuchungen* (Berlin, 1884) 87.

100. Anna says *indulge hospitio causasque innecte morandi, dum pelago de-saevit hiems et aquosus Orion, quassataeque rates, dum non tractabile caelum* (51) ['Entertain your guest freely, weaving pretexts for keeping him here while his ships are still damaged, and winter and Orion the rain-bringer spend their fury on the Ocean under a forbidding sky'].

101. *quin etiam hiberno moliris sidere classem, et mediis properas aquilonibus ire per altum* (309) ['You labour at your fleet under a wintry sky, in haste to traverse the high seas in the teeth of the northerly gales']. On 3.285 see n. 102 below.

102. This is probably due to the general idea that sea-voyages are made in the summer. Or did Virgil (as Ribbeck thought) extend to an individual year the idiom whereby *aestas* is used to mean 'year'? Sophocles does something similar with ἄροτος [season of tillage] τὸν μὲν παρελθόντ' ἄροτον ἐν μήκει χρόνου [the past season/year as to length of time] (*Trach.* 69), alongside δωδέκατος ἄροτος [twelfth season/year] at 825); but I know no Latin parallels. From 1.535: *cum subito adsur-gens fluctu nimbosus Orion in vada caeca tulit* [when suddenly at the rising of Orion, star of storms, the seas ran high and carried us onto invisible shoals] it has been deduced that Virgil is indicating summertime, in agreement with 755, because Orion rises at midsummer (Ovid *Fast.* 6.719); but *adsurgens* [rising] will hardly refer to the actual rising of the constellation, but rather to its threatening upsurge as in *adsurgit ira* [anger rises] etc.), by poetic analogy with the swelling tide (*fluctibus et fremitu adsurgens Benace marino* [you, Benacus, surging with waves and roaring like the sea] [*Geo.* 2.160]). Virgil was certainly not thinking of a particular date when Orion rises, let alone (as Heyne suggests) working out its time for the latitude of Carthage; all he knows of Orion is that it belongs to the *horrida sidera* [fierce constellations] (Pliny *N.H.* 18.278) and he uses it appropriately, in the same way as other Roman poets do (Gundel, *De stellarum appellatione et religione Romana* [Giss, 1907] 181), when he is speaking of a storm.

103. This is Schüler's view, *Quaest. Verg.* 6 (cf. also Deuticke in his appendix to 3), and he also provides a good rebuttal of Conrads' attempt to fit the wanderings into a mere two years.

104. If he had written *octava* [eighth] this would have indicated that he had actually calculated it; the number seven is one that Virgil uses very often (as does

Homer: Diels, *Festschr. für Gomperz* [Vienna, 1902] 10); seven times the snake coils round the tomb of Anchises (5.85), from seven oxhides the *caestus* [leather boxing-thongs] of Entellus are manufactured (404), seven Athenians had to be sent to the Minotaur every year (6.21), with seven ships Aeneas lands in Libya (1.170), seven layers make up the shield of Aeneas (8.448) and that of Turnus (12.925), seven sons of Phorcus fight against Aeneas (10.329), twice seven nymphs belong to Juno (1.71). After seven, the round numbers nine and twelve are used most frequently; the number eight does not occur in Virgil at all. 350

105. On the chronological liberties that Virgil takes in the treatment of the tradition see also above p. 199f.

106. See also Plüss 81 on the carelessness with which the distances on the Trojan plain are dealt with in Book 2. Tryphiodorus is much more careful in this matter: when the horse is pulled into the city ὁδὸς ἐβαρύνετο μακρὴ σχιζομένη ποταμοῖσι καὶ οὐ πεδίοισιν ὁμοίη (328) [the long way grew heavy, torn with rivers and unlike the plains]. 351

107. Norden (133ff.) shows that the information about the Sibyl's Cave and Apollo's temple which Virgil gives in 6 are quite compatible with the real locality; but unless he knew that locality a reader would hardly be able to visualize a clear picture of it. On the vagueness of Virgil's topography of the Underworld see Norden 207, 215, 266: here too there is nothing to indicate that the poet did not visualize it clearly himself; but he is not interested in helping the reader to visualize it.

108. Münzer has rightly pointed out (*Cacus der Rinderdieb* [Progr. Basel 1911] 22) that there is a lack of clarity in the way that the scene is imagined in the Cacus story: *aerii cursu petit ardua montis* (8.221) is only intended to mean, in my opinion, 'he ran up to the steep high mountain', i.e. in the direction of the cave; but from which point Cacus *speluncam petit* [makes for his cave] we are not told, and the visual aspect of the whole scene suffers from this. 352

109. On the fleet's separation from the camp see above p. 192 n. 62.

110. Left and right cannot of course be meant from the standpoint of the Trojans as they face the enemy. The enemy had surrounded the entire wall in the night (*obsidere portas cura datur Messapo et moenia cingere flammis* [9.159] [Messapus was assigned the duty of posting pickets to watch, blocking the gates, and girding the walls with a circle of watch-fires]: this field-camp is called *Laurentia castra* [the camp of the Laurentines] [10.635, 671, cf. 9. 371, 451]); when they now advance to 353 storm the camp, whichever side they approach is 'in front' of the defenders. Moreover if Virgil, as I assume, did name left and right from the Tiber's current, this was not because he was familiar with naming river-banks left and right as we do (cf. Stürenburg, 'Die Bezeichnung der Flussufer bei Griechen und Römern', in: Festschr. der 49. Philologenvers. [Dresden, 1897] 289), but because he is in Rome and following the course of the Tiber down towards Ostia in his thoughts. 354

111. Of course local historians have succeeded in locating this grove precisely: it lay about one kilometre outside the city on Monte Abetone near the course of the Vaccino. See Rosati, *Cere e suoi monumenti* (Foligno, 1890) 13.

3

Presentation

I. *Narration*

1. The whole action and the detail

A narrator who is striving after clear presentation must try to avoid telling the story of a large number of people at once. The listener can only identify with a crowd if they act as a single-minded unit, not as individuals. Otherwise, being faced with a number of characters will confuse the imagination and blur the picture. Apollonius often speaks of his Argonauts as a group, who have done this or that, without going into details. This cannot be avoided if, like Apollonius and Virgil, one has a hero who is surrounded by a number of followers; but as soon as Virgil reaches such a passage he makes haste to concentrate on individuals. Apollonius describes, for example, the funeral feast of Idmon (2.837): 'there they interrupted their journey; sad at heart they tended the corpse. For three whole days they mourned; on the following day they embalmed him most excellently, and the people (the Mariandyni) together with king Lycus took part in the burial rite; there they slaughtered a great number of sheep, as is right when someone has died. And a monument has been raised to this man in that land, with a sign on it, so that even those as yet unborn will see it, an olive-tree fit for constructing a ship'. Compare this with the funeral ceremony for Misenus, 6.212ff.; Virgil doubtless had Apollonius' scene in mind when he wrote it. Virgil, too, begins with a general statement: 'The Trojans mourned Misenus on the shore, and paid their last respects to his ashes.' But this is
followed by a detailed description of the erection of the funeral pyre and an equally detailed description of the further business, which focusses on individual groups: *p a r s calidos latices...expediunt...p a r s ingenti subiere feretro...* [*some* prepare warm water...*some* raised the great bier on their shoulders], until we come to individual people: *ossa cado texit C o r y n a e u s, idem* etc., *at pius A e n e a s sepulcrum imponit* etc. [*Corynaeus* enclosed the bones in an urn, he also...but *Aeneas* the true imposed a barrow]. It is the same when they land in Hesperia (6.5): the young men jump ashore: some of them strike fire from flints, some fetch kindling from the forest, some look for running water and show others where to find it. It is the same when they land in Libya. The Trojans go ashore and stretch their limbs on the beach: Achates lights a fire etc.: then the preparation of the meal: they dismember the stag, some cut the meat into pieces and stick it on spits, others set cauldrons to boil etc.

These are accounts of peaceful, everyday activities. The same need to concentrate on small groups is more urgent when martial deeds are being portrayed. Here, if anywhere, Virgil has learned from Homer. In the *Iliad*, almost without exception, the narrative moves as quickly as possible from speaking about a group to speaking about individuals. A general description was unavoidable when the Italic peoples rose up in arms (7.623). This begins with only one line to sum up the whole situation: *ardet inexcita Ausonia atque immobilis ante* [Italy, the quiet land which no alarm could rouse before, was ablaze]; then, as in the previous examples, the action divides: *pars pedes ire parat campis, pars arduus altis pulverulentus equis furit* [some made ready to march on foot across her plains, some galloped madly in clouds of dust, riding high on tall horses] (where the epithets set individuals before us, and the detail gives us a precise picture instead of a general statement like 'they prepared to fight on horseback'); then five cities are named, which are manufacturing new weapons, and this is described in great detail; finally, when the signal to advance sounds, we come to individuals: *hic galeam tectis trepidus rapit* etc. [one man seizes a helmet from his house with trembling hands], and this is followed by a list of individually named leaders. Or we may then look at the first assault of the enemy on the camp (9.25): only one line of general description, then we are shown individuals; then only one line about the Trojans collectively, then direct speech from Caicus, calling to arms. Or the situation of the beleaguered Trojans, 10.120ff.: it is important for us to remember the position, and so more space is devoted to describing it; however, it is not a general description but a kind of catalogue of the leaders, which we do not really expect to find here, and which probably would not have come here if the poet had not had this particular purpose. Virgil does the same 357 thing in the battle-scenes; it is significant that the general description is by far the longest in the cavalry battle, 11.597-635 (in which there is only one single duel) and 868ff.: the men storm up and chase back in such a compact group that they appear to be a single unit. But here (624ff.), as in similar cases[1] the very short general description is backed up by a most appropriate simile; here, too, Homer had shown the way – remember the three consecutive similes in *Iliad* 2 when the armies advance.

2. Narrative and précis

A summary description of a crowd-scene gathers together all the simultaneous pieces of action; a précis narrative does the same for a series of events; but clearly a précis does not allow a full exposition of the material, and so a poet must not make too frequent use of it. He can do this by concentrating events into the smallest possible length of time; the more the action is spread out, the more often a précis will be needed to bridge the gaps between the major scenes, if, that is, the poet has any interest in maintaining continuity. The most important means to this end is one borrowed from the *Odyssey*, by which the action is made to start near the end of the period taken up by the story, and letting the hero narrate what has happened so far. We have already seen how, in any case, Virgil likes to squeeze events into the space of a few days whenever possible; and how, when a longer time would be necessary in real life he tries to obscure the fact (p. 266f. above). Brevity can most easily be justified in first-person narrative; the poet can shift the responsibility for it onto his narrator, and he, in turn, can say that he must consider his audience; the reader is less likely to demand total illumination from him than from the poet himself, since the narrator is himself part of the imagined fiction. Also, it is only in first-person narrative that a different treatment can be employed as, for instance, in the adventure with the Cicones in *Odyssey* 9, as compared with the adventure with the Cyclops; the Cicones story in the form in which we hear it from Odysseus would clash with the style of the whole poem if the poet narrated it. Virgil has made good use of this possibility, particularly in Book 3: he has Aeneas giving a quick survey of the seven years of adventures, then selecting a few for detailed narration, choosing those which are sure to interest his audience. This means that he can pass very quickly over such things as his departure from his native land and what preceded it – *auguria divum* [divine signs], construction of the fleet:[2] he can choose to describe from the first stage of their exile (the sojourn in Thrace) only the pathos-filled scene at the tomb of Polydorus; he can pass quickly over their reception in Delos, Anius and his hospitality etc., up to the death of Anchises (*amitto Anchisen* [I lost Anchises]); nowhere else in the whole *Aeneid* has Virgil used anything like so much brief summary.

In other ways, too, he has used précis more freely than Homer did. Homeric style allows itself précis only in the sub-plots which are to be less prominent than the main plot,[3] but they too are often narrated in detail. According to Virgil's artistic principles, précis was essential whenever the listener would otherwise have been told something that he already knew. Thus, wherever a section which is being told in some detail reaches the point where one character has to report to others things which we have already seen take place, they are always summarized. Here it is supposed that the imagination will simply reproduce the picture it has already seen; a full repetition would continue the external action, but Virgil's readers are not as patient as Homer's, who are content even when they are not being told anything new. We therefore find examples of précis when Aeneas tells his companions about things that we already know (his decision to sail away from Carthage, the vision of Mercury etc. [4.288]); when Anna has to carry out Dido's errand (4.437); similarly, after Anchises' dream-appearance (5.746), after Turnus' decision to fight (7.407), Aeneas' decision to visit Evander (8.79) etc.; almost always, the succeeding narrative is also shortened; in the last example, Aeneas' departure from the camp is told briefly regardless of the fact that there are important factors that we should know about (9.40, 172) but are told only later. The reception by Acestes (5.35-41) is reported by Virgil with quite un-Homeric brevity: here, too, a clear, detailed description of what we already know would have run into many words. We should also list here messages of which we already know the contents: 9.692 to Turnus after the Trojans' sortie, 10.510 to Aeneas after Pallas' death, 11.896 to Turnus after Camilla has fallen, 12.107 challenging Aeneas to the duel; in these and countless other cases Homer would not have spared us the full details.

Virgil is totally committed to narrating only things which are important in themselves, which are worthwhile for their own sake, and which produce an effect: he omits where possible anything which is unimportant, which is significant only as preparation for future events or as the result of past events. This is the same artistic principle which led the neo-Hellenistic writers to select from their material only the emotional scenes, discussing the rest with a brief reference, regardless of its importance to the plot. It is a severe infringement of the principle of συμμετρία [proportion], which requires important matters and unimportant matters to be treated with corresponding expansiveness or succinctness.[4] Virgil never omits anything important; on the contrary, he takes care that everything significant shall also have artistic value so that it is worth telling. However, it does happen, very infrequently, that circumstances come up in the course of the narrative that are too important to omit but are mentioned only briefly so as not to spoil the effect of the passage.[5] Even more infrequently he relegates a really important matter to minor status for artistic reasons: I cannot think of another example more striking than *tandem erumpunt et castra relinquunt Ascanius puer et nequiquam obsessa iuventus* (10.604) [at last the young prince Ascanius and the manhood of Troy broke out from their camp. The siege had failed.]. That should really stand at the end of the book: the Latins are forced to lift the siege of the camp, the sortie achieves their complete defeat. But Virgil cannot put anything at the end after the death of Mezentius, so the result is told here in advance, and inserted as a result of Aeneas' fury; but it can only be mentioned briefly here because the poet is in a hurry to reach Turnus, against whom Aeneas' angry rage is principally directed. For similar reasons, the description of the shield at the end of Book 8 must not be followed by anything which might weaken the effect; Aeneas' discussions with the Etruscans and their embarkation are therefore not narrated until later, at 10.148: but nothing is lost thereby, and the poet gains the advantage that, since he is recapitulating, he can be briefer than if he were narrating the events in their proper place; in that case it would have been difficult to avoid tedious repetitions of the first scenes with Evander – the presentation of Aeneas, an account of what had been happening etc.

360

361

Finally, the description of the union of Aeneas and Dido (4.165) really does nothing but allude to it, and stands in a class of its own in that the brevity here does not stem from artistic principles:

> *speluncam Dido dux et Troianus eandem*
> *deveniunt. prima et Tellus et pronuba Iuno*
> *dant signum; fulsere ignes et conscius aether*
> *conubiis summoque ulularunt vertice nymphae*

[Dido and Troy's chieftain found their way to the same cavern. Primaeval Earth and Juno, Mistress of the Marriage, gave their sign. The sky connived at the union; the lightning flared; on their mountain-peak nymphs raised their cry]. That is masterly in every trait; it is true that here 'modern' sensibility had to use a 'modern style'.[6] But who can fail to see that the paraphrase here, far from being merely the handmaid of prudery, truly frees the event from every vulgar overtone, lifting it to the heroic level?

3. Ethos

Total clarity in narrative can only be achieved by giving quite precise and detailed information about the outward circumstances of the action which create equally precise concepts in the reader's mind. Whatever Virgil narrates, he lets us see it more or less sharply. Further examination will show that in this, too, he was influenced by his models, and the clearer the picture in his model, the more he strives after the same effect, although using his own means; a more important, and harder, task would be to show what Virgil's perception of events was and how he perceived them, but that lies outside our scope. One thing needs to be said in preparation for what follows: the outward clarity of the narrative was also influenced by the fact that Virgil was overwhelmingly interested in the psychological side of things, as we established above. He cares more about his characters' emotions and desires than about their visible actions; he would rather give the listener the illusion of sharing the feeling than the illusion that he is physically seeing something. When a host of visual details are given, this is, in most cases, not for the sake of providing a picture, but in order to arouse a particular emotion; Virgil knows that the pathos of pity or fear is most surely aroused when the illusion of reality is achieved.[7]

362

The most characteristic thing about Virgil's narrative is that it is soaked through and through with feeling.[8] It is not like later Hellenistic poetry where the *poet's* feelings continually force themselves on us (although, as we shall see, Virgil is much less reticent than Homer in this respect too); but the feelings of the protagonists are intended to be suggested to us by the narrative, without being expressly mentioned. Homer's narrative generally leaves it to the reader to guess what emotions accompanied the narrated events, with the sole aid of conversations and monologues; Virgil never narrates without indicating the appropriate emotion, at the very least by the tone and colours used, and sometimes by an explicit allusion. He has put himself into the heart of his characters and speaks from inside them; he even projects emotion into insentient Nature; he wants to make the listener share their feelings, whether it is a violent passion flaring up, or the steady warmth of a more restrained mood. I have already mentioned the atmosphere of the Games in Book 5 (above p. 135); as further examples I select, not the narration of exciting and emotional events where the *pathos* is obvious, but comparatively unexciting events, and to this end I must cite some longish extracts.

363

The departure of the Trojans from their homeland (3.1):

> *Postquam r e s A s i a e Priamique evertere gentem*
> *i n m e r i t a m visum superis, ceciditque s u p e r b u m*
> *Ilium et omnis humo fumat Neptunia Troia,*
> *diversa exilia et d e s e r t a s quaerere terras*
> *auguriis agimur divum, classemque sub ipsa*
> *Antandro et Phrygiae m o l i m u r montibus Idae,*
> *i n c e r t i quo fata ferant, ubi sistere detur,*
> *contrahimusque viros. v i x p r i m a i n c e p e r a t aestas,*
> *et pater Anchises d a r e f a t i s vela iubebat,*
> *litora cum p a t r i a e lacrimans portusque relinquo*
> *et campos, ubi Troia f u i t; feror e x u l i n a l t u m*
> *cum sociis n a t o q u e p e n a t i b u s e t m a g n i s d i s*

['The powers above had decreed the overthrow of the Asian empire and Priam's breed of men, though they deserved a better fate. Lordly Ilium had fallen and all

290

Neptune's Troy lay a smoking ruin on the ground. We the exiled survivors were forced by divine command to search the world for a home in some uninhabited land. So we started to build ships below Antandros, the city by the foothills of Phrygian Ida, with no idea where destiny would take us or where we should be allowed to settle. We gathered our company together. In early summer our chieftain Anchises urged us to embark on our destined voyage. In tears I left my homeland's coast, its havens, and the plains where Troy had stood. I fared out upon the high seas, an exile with my comrades and my son, with the little gods of our home and the great gods of our race'].

The lines do not give much of a picture, but they do communicate a great variety of emotions, although only one word – *lacrimans* [in tears] – expressly refers to them. We see the fall of Troy through the eyes of Aeneas as a terrible disaster which has come upon the innocent because of an incomprehensible decision of the gods; we are made to share the mood of the refugees who are being sent into the unknown, to inhospitable far-off lands, into exile; who nevertheless, in obedience to the gods, do not hesitate for one moment and piously accept their fate; we share their sorrow as they pass the site of Troy; their divided feelings are made clear to us in the   364 concluding words: deep sorrow, and yet they find consolation in what Aeneas is taking with him: his companions, his son, above all, the gods; the narrative is rounded off with the weighty spondees *et magnis dis* [and the great gods], something to cling to in an uncertain future.

That was Aeneas speaking, but the tone is not very different when the poet narrates. Let us look at their arrival in Cumae (6.5):

> *iuvenum manus e m i c a t   a r d e n s*
> *litus in H e s p e r i u m; quaerit pars semina flammae*
> *abstrusa in venis silicis, pars densa ferarum*
> *tecta r a p i t silvas inventaque flumina m o n s t r a t.*
> *at pius Aeneas arces, quibus a l t u s Apollo*
> *praesidet, h o r r e n d a e q u e procul s e c r e t a Sibyllae,*
> *antrum i m m a n e petit...*

[A party of young Trojans eagerly darted ashore on to the Western Land. Some searched for the seeds of flame which lie embedded in the veins of flint. Others penetrated the forests and raided the tangled shelters of the wild creatures, signalling when they found a water-stream. But Aeneas the True made his way to the fastness where Apollo rules enthroned on high, and to the vast cavern beyond, which is the awful Sibyl's own secluded place] – on the one hand the happy bustle of the young men – they cannot land quickly enough, to find at last on the Hesperian shore the *aquam et ignem* [water and fire] of their new home; on the other hand, Aeneas' emotions as he approaches a solemnly significant event in pious awe.

Aeneas' journey to Evander (8.86):

> *Thybris ea fluvium quam longa est nocte tumentem*
> *leniit e t t a c i t a r e f l u e n s i t a s u b s t i t i t unda*
> *mitis ut in m o r e m   s t a g n i p l a c i d a e q u e p a l u d i s*

s t e r n e r e t aequor aquis, remo ut luctamen abesset.
ergo iter inceptum celerant r u m o r e s e c u n d o,
labitur uncta vadis abies; m i r a n t u r et undae,
miratur nemus insuetum fulgentia longe
scuta virum fluvio pictasque innare carinas.
olli remigio noctemque diemque f a t i g a n t
et l o n g o s s u p e r a n t f l e x u s variisque teguntur
arboribus viridisque secant placido aequore silvas.
sol medium caeli conscenderat i g n e u s orbem,
cum muros arcemque procul ac rara domorum
tecta vident, quae n u n c Romana potentia caelo
aequavit, t u m res inopes Evander habebat.
o c i u s advertunt proras urbique propinquant.

[Then did Tiber make smooth his heaving flood for the whole length of that night and withdrew the flow of his now voiceless waves, becoming so still as he levelled the ripples on his surface that it seemed like a kindly pool or peaceful marsh, on which no oar need strain. So then the Trojans began their journey and made good speed, encouraged by what Aeneas had been told. Greased pine-timbers slid by over shallow water. The very waves wondered, and the woods, strangers to such a sight, were surprised to see floating in the river the brightly painted ships with the warriors' far-gleaming shields. The Trojans rowed tirelessly till a night and a day were spent. They passed round long bends, and shaded by trees of many kinds they cut between green forests on the friendly river-surface. The fiery sun had climbed to the mid-point of the sky's circle when ahead of them they saw walls, a citadel, and scattered house-roofs; all this Roman might has now exalted to Heaven, but at that time Evander lived there in poverty. Quickly they turned prows shorewards, and drew near to the city.]

365   Here we have animation of Nature: the god of the river, who has told them to make the journey, stops the flow of his current and cannot do enough to help them; the waves and woods stand amazed, like children of nature, at the unaccustomed sight; on the other hand, we have the mood of the oarsmen, joyful eagerness as they notice that their task is being made easier, although it is still difficult and tiring enough; joy at the many kinds of trees growing thickly along the banks; when these can no longer shade them from the heat of the midday sun, they find that their destination is at last in sight, and double their efforts to reach it. There is also another feeling, one that is not shared by the characters in the poem: the great contrast between Then and Now, a favourite concern of Virgil's time. Let us compare this with what is said of the Tiber in other places: how the river invites the Trojans to stay when they arrive and Aeneas *laetus fluvio succedit opaco* (7.36) [happily moved up into the shady river]; how Turnus, yielding to superior force, leaps into the river (9.815):

ille suo cum gurgite flavo
a c c e p i t venientem ac m o l l i b u s e x t u l i t undis
et laetum sociis a b l u t a c a e d e r e m i s i t:

[the river welcomed him to its yellow stream and bore him on gentle waves. It washed the blood away and carried him back, happy, to his comrades]: it is as if the god himself could not help admiring the hero, he receives him in such a friendly way, and something which would endanger the lives of others is only a refreshing dip for Turnus. It is different when the nymphs, who were ships a moment before, swim down to the sea (9.124); the onlookers stand horrified –

> cunctatur et amnis
> rauca sonans revocatque pedem Tiberinus ab alto.

[Even the River Tiber checked with a growling roar and flinched, withdrawing hastily from the deep.]

It is worth examining the coming and going of messengers: the delegation from the Trojan ships, threatened by the Carthaginians, *concursu magno, templum clamore petebant* (1.509) [in a great crowd, they made their way amid shouting to the temple]. Aeneas' messengers to Latinus: since they are going to *augusta moenia regis* [the majestic battlements of the king], a hundred hand-picked men are sent; they go into the unknown, but *haud mora, festinant iussi rapidisque feruntur passibus* [having received their orders they obeyed at once and strode swiftly on their way], with quick and obedient resolve (7.156); they return *sublimes in equis pacemque reportant* (285) [on horseback, holding themselves high, and bringing home the agreement of peace]: the first word gives the entire mood. They were sent *pacem exposcere Teucris* [to seek peace for the Trojans]; the Latins come to Aeneas after the battle much more diffidently, *veniam rogantes* [asking for his indulgence].   366
Finally the men sent to treat with Diomedes (11.243):

> Vidimus o cives Diomedem Argivaque castra
> atque iter emensi casus superavimus omnis
> contigimusque manum qua concidit Ilia tellus:

[Countrymen, we have seen Diomede and his camp of Argives. We completed our journey, surviving all its chances; and we have touched that very hand by which the land of Ilium perished]: first we see their contentment that they have come to the end of a long and difficult journey; then the feeling known to anyone who has been privileged to touch the hand of someone truly great.

Enough of examples; anyone can find plenty more for himself. I should just like to mention here a group of features which belong together and which will allow us to link up with the observation of an ancient critic. Asinius Pollio stated (according to Servius on 11.183) that when describing daybreak Virgil always selects a phrase which is appropriate to the situation at that moment. If the examples given by Servius go back to Asinius, then the latter has read things into Virgil which the poet certainly never thought of;[9] however, the idea is worth pursuing, within limits. Obviously it is not mere chance that Virgil nearly always introduces new turns of phrase to replace the stereotyped ἦμος δ' ἠριγένεια φάνη ῥοδοδάκτυλος ἠώς [when rosy-fingered dawn appeared, child of the morning]:[10] it would go against his usual manner of presentation if he did not strive to evoke a particular mood   367 wherever possible. The idyllic tone of the scene with Evander is matched by 8.455f.:

> *Evandrum ex humili tecto lux suscitat alma*
> *et matutini volucrum sub culmine cantus*

368 [the strengthening light of dawn and the morning song of birds under the eaves roused Evander to leave his lowly house]. Similarly, at the beginning of the day which is to bring the final decision, the magnificent lines (12.114)

> *cum primum alto se gurgite tollunt*
> *Solis equi lucemque elatis naribus efflant*

[when the horses of the sun had just begun to arise out of ocean's depth, breathing light from their high-held muzzles]; on the happy day of the Games (5.104)

> *expectata dies aderat nonamque s e r e n a*
> *Auroram Phaethontis equi iam luce vehebant*

[the awaited day arrived. In fine weather Phaethon's horses were now already bringing the ninth dawn]; on the day of the heat of battle (11.182)

> *Aurora interea miseris mortalibus alma*
> *extulerat lucem referens opera atque labores*

[meanwhile Aurora had lifted her strengthening light for pitiful humanity, bringing back to them their tasks and their toils]. Aeneas, lying awake worrying during the first night on the Libyan shore, sees the new day as a blessing, since he can now establish whither the storm has driven them (1.305):

> *per noctem plurima volvens*
> *ut primum lux a l m a   d a t a est exire locosque*
> *explorare novos...constituit*

[after a night spent in thought, he decided to walk out in the freshness of the dawn to investigate this new country]. The first white light of dawn is mentioned when Dido, sleepless on the watchtower, catches sight of the fleet floating on the sea (*ut primam albescere lucem vidit* [4.586] [when she saw the first white gleam of dawn]); it is in the gleaming rays of the sun that the splendid, happy procession of the hunt forms (*iubare exorto* [4.130] [when the brightness arose]); during a pink dawn full of hope, the Trojans see their new homeland for the first time rising above the horizon (*rubescebat stellis Aurora fugatis* [3.521] [Dawn with its first red glow had routed the stars]); it is in the first full brightness of day that Aeneas and the Tyrrhenian fleet approach the Latin coast: his shield gleaming in the sunlight and his flashing armour will signal to his men from far off that rescue is on the way.

It would be easy to fall into a trap here. Pollio can serve as a warning not to credit
369 the poet with too much calculated intention. But taken as a whole, nobody would

argue that it was mere chance that the nuances in these quotations match each situation. The same is true generally: many of the individual examples are uncertain, but the main principle will be accepted by all who read any part of the *Aeneid* from this viewpoint; and if any hesitation remained, it would vanish if one compared the corresponding passage by someone like Apollonius.[11] We can learn a lot from this comparison because it is very probable that Virgil was consciously trying to be different from Apollonius in this respect. One of the main reasons why the long epic form was rejected by Callimachus and his Greek and Roman successors alike was   370 that they believed that such a broad stream inevitably carried along with it 'a lot of sludge'; since the Homeric epic countenanced no omission, no allusion, no abbreviation, they thought that it could not be copied without 'dead' stretches which arouse no interest or emotion in the listener. This explains why certain writers of short poems then adopted a peculiar technique which did not treat even a small-scale subject in a balanced way. When Virgil, in defiance of warnings from this school of critics and poets, dared to attempt a large-scale epic, one of his major concerns must have been to show that it really was possible to keep it interesting and alive all the way through; in fact he could learn from Apollonius what was to be avoided if he was to achieve this object. Thus, here too, conformity with contemporary artistic theory may have helped to strengthen his stylistic tendencies, although of course their roots drew their main nourishment from the poet's own nature; as the *Georgics* relate to the Hellenistic didactic poems of such as Nicander, so does the *Aeneid* stand in relation to the Hellenistic epic of Apollonius.

4. Subjectivity

The process described above is perfectly compatible with a completely objective stance on the part of the poet: he leads us into the emotions of his characters without forcing his own upon us. This objective stance, which was strictly observed in Homer almost without exception, was also consciously adopted in the earlier Hellenistic epic, as far as I can see; it is very noticeable how completely Theocritus, for example, effaces himself when narrating, in the *Hylas*, *Heracliscus* [young Herakles], and *Castor and Pollux*; even there, in the hymn form, the poet himself does not speak except infrequently when he addresses the person celebrated; it is hardly any different in the narratives of the Callimachean hymns; it is true that Apollonius sometimes steps out in front of the curtain in his rôle as singer; but he very rarely allows himself to utter his own opinions or sentiments, or reveal his reaction as a human being to human events.[12] In the only two poems which can give us any idea of the style of the Roman Neoterics (and of the tendency of the Greek poetry of the   371 time and just before) – Catullus' *Ariadne* (poem 64) and the *Ciris* – the situation is completely different: the narrator pities his heroine, is horrified and worried when he imagines her sorrows, wishes she had not done this or that, tries to excuse her: in short, he displays how touched he is by the story which he has to tell, and takes care that we do not forget him while listening to the story. Virgil has avoided this excited manner from the start, in the Aristaeus epyllion of his *Georgics*, where he puts only occasional indications of his own feelings into the mouth of the narrator Proteus. In the *Aeneid* he consciously strives for the same objectivity; but he seems to have experienced some difficulty in adhering to it. It is significant that the tale of Dido, which is closest to the nature of Hellenistic art, also contains the greatest number of infringements of this rule: one example, strictly speaking, is the repetition of *infelix* [unhappy][13] and *misera* [unfortunate], which anticipates further extensions: *pesti devota futurae* (1.712) [condemned now to sure destruction], *ille dies primus leti primusque malorum causa fuit* (4.169) [on that day were sown the seeds of destruction and death]; we have, completely in Neoteric style, the exclamation *heu vatum ignarae mentes* (65) [how pitifully weak is the prescience of seers]; there are beginnings of comments about love: *improbe amor, quid non mortalia pectora cogis* (412) [merciless love, is there any length to which you cannot force the human heart to go?] (this is a very abbreviated reproduction of Apollonius' apostrophe mentioned above); *quis fallere possit amantem?* (296) [who can deceive a lover?]; and the sympathetic words addressd to Dido *quis tibi tum, Dido, cernenti talia sensus?* (408) [what must have been your thoughts, Dido, when you saw all this?].

Other parts of the story are not completely free of such things; but in general the poet is consistent in suppressing his own feelings, restricting himself as far as possible to the few occasions where Homer permitted a subjective utterance. When Patroclus has begged Achilles to send him into battle, the poet cannot refrain from alluding regretfully to the consequences (2.46): 'So he spoke, pleading, the ignorant fool: he should have asked straight out for his own death and destruction.' Virgil is more elaborate, after Turnus has killed Pallas and taken his spoils (10.501): 'Men are truly ignorant of their fate and of the future, and when they are raised up by good fortune they lose hold of moderation! The time will come for Turnus when he would give a great deal for Pallas to be unharmed, and he will live to curse these spoils and this day!' This example is unique, as is the one in Homer, and can therefore be recognized as a conscious imitation of it. In other places where Virgil feels that he must speak, he uses a different form. After the death of Nisus and Euryalus he breaks out with the cry 'You fortunate pair![14] If there is any power in my song, the day will never come which strikes you from human memory, as long as the sons of Aeneas live around the immovable rock of the Capitol' (9.446). Lausus' sacrifice for his father is announced by the poet (10.791): 'Now I will sing of your heroic death, and of you, unforgettable youth.' In both these examples the poet is speaking as himself; they are generically similar to the phrases which were used in the catalogue, although these had no particular moral: *nec tu carminibus nostris indictus abibis* (7.733) [nor will you go without mention in my song] and *non ego te, Ligurum ductor fortissime bello, transierim* (10.185) [I am not one to pass you over, valiant war-leader of Ligurians], and these, again, are echoes of the formulae of the proem, as in *arma virumque cano* [this is a tale of arms and of a man] or *dicam horrida bella* (7.41) [I shall tell of a ghastly war], and the latter is also linked with the Homeric appeal to the Muses: ἄνδρα μοι ἔννεπε μοῦσα [Sing, o Muse, of the man] and Ἴλιον ἀείδω [I sing of Ilium] are thus the germs of that insertion of a 'parabasis' for the development of which Homer himself had shown the way when he inserted a second proem before the Catalogue and spoke in it about himself and his relationship to his material.[15]

There is also another way in which Homer could provide at least the excuse to deviate from strict 'objectivity'. With the famous phrase οἷοι νῦν βροτοί εἰσιν [the sort of men who live today] he draws a contrast between himself and his own time and the narrated past; like a lightning flash this one phrase illuminates the vast chasm which separates him from that past, since one might otherwise think that his story was set in recent times. The learned epic-writers of the Hellenistic period are   373 never tempted to produce this illusion and never try to make us forget how long ago it all happened; that is why Apollonius, for example, in his periegetic sections, continually breaks the illusion that we are 'living' the story by mentioning later occurrences, or pointing out the survival of a custom, a foundation or a monument. The poet of the Αἴτια must have regarded this as stylistically offensive; he wisely decided against the epic form for his own work linking present and past. Virgil does not go anything like as far as Apollonius; in most cases he is content to let the reader work out for himself the connections between the story and the present time,[16] but in the case of genealogical information, for example,[17] or in order to identify localities, he often mentions later situations: *locos qui post Albae de nomine dicti Albani* (9.387) [the spot later called Alban after Alba Longa] and *a summo qui nunc Albanus habetur tumulo* (12.134) [from a high crest, a hill known now as Alban]; and so in Aeneas' visit to the site of Rome: *Carmentalem Romani nomine portam quam memorant* [the gate which Romans call the Carmental gate]; *lucum quem Romulus acer asylum rettulit* [a wood which the forceful Romulus was to adopt as his sanctuary]; *Romano foro* [Roman Forum] (8.338, 342, 361)[18] and the thought of what will rise from these humble beginnings fills him with such excitement that he lets himself be carried away to speak of the splendid present day (99, 397). Otherwise, there are only two mentions of the survival of old customs to his own time: at the *lusus Troiae* (5.596ff.) and at the solemn declaration of war (7.601ff.): we know that both were particularly closely connected with Augustus' archaistic nationalism: thus here Virgil has sacrificed his artistic principles for political considerations. However, it is obvious that Virgil has allowed this restriction to affect only the form; in reality Virgil regards prophecy as an opportunity to draw rich material from the history of recent times down to the present day.

5. Vividness   374

Apparently closely related to these subjective expressions of feeling, but really quite different, is the striving to use every possible means to draw the reader towards the action, or even right into it. Virgil's aim is not like Homer's, who wanted the listener to experience the action as something past and gone, so that he could remain independent and survey it from a distance; the more successfully he produces the illusion in us that we are actually present at the events, the more perfectly Virgil believes that he has reached his goal. An external feature of his narrative, but a very characteristic one, is the overwhelming use of the historical present. It is not simply a convenient replacement for the ponderous forms of the past tenses:[19] it is intended to paint the happenings for us as truly taking place now. The present tense is also retained when the protagonist has to make a decision: *quid faciat?* [what is he to do?] he says then, or *quid agat?*, as if we ourselves had to decide how to advise him.[20] The frequently interpolated *ecce!* [Look! Lo! Behold!][21] shakes us out of the comfortable relaxed attitude of someone listening to past history, and forces our fantasy to imagine that the events are taking place now. Apostrophe was already used by Homer quite often, but not to arouse pathos; Virgil goes very much further when he – and the listener with him – steps as it were right up to the corpse of Pallas and addresses it: *o dolor atque decus magnum rediture parenti! haec te prima dies bello dedit, haec eadem aufert* (10.507) [O Pallas, the bitter pain, and the high pride, which you will bring to your father when you return to him! This day first gave you to war, and the same day steals you away]. This brings the past into the present; the parallel to this occurs during the Parade of Heroes when Anchises, overcome with emotion, sees the future as present, cries to Caesar *proice tela manu* [fling your weapons from your hands], and calls for flowers to strew on the grave of Marcellus (6.835, 883): that is a vision which would not be surprising in a prophet; but the poet is also a *vates*: he does not only narrate; sometimes, when he is swept away by the story, he has visions.

375

6. Clarity

An essential requirement for *clarity* is that the narrator shall inform his listeners, in good time and completely, of the presuppositions which underlie his narrative; in other words, that he give an adequate exposition of the separate parts of the action and of the characters. An illustration of this from the *Aeneid* is in Book 2 where Aeneas anticipates something which he himself only learned later, so that the following events will be completely clear to the listener (above p. 14f.). We shall see later that Virgil likes to weave such exposition into the action by having one person being told the necessary information by another, e.g. Dido's story told by Venus, Mezentius' history by Evander, Camilla's childhood by Diana. Only rarely does the poet himself provide the exposition, because this holds up the narrative; he was unable to avoid explaining the metamorphosis of the ships; less uncertain and equally necessary was the exposition of the situation in Latium; this acts as a kind of prologue to the second part of the epic and marks a strong division in the narrative. Similarly, at the beginning of the whole work, Virgil explains Juno's attitude in an introductory passage (1.12-33) which one may compare with the prologue to a drama, while the attitude of the friendly gods, Venus and Jupiter, is explained in a conversation inserted after the first act of the narrative (223-96). In comparison, the exposition of the human side of the action at the beginning of the work seems, at first glance, to have been neglected. The proem (1-7) informs us about the subject; from the account of the reasons for Juno's anger we learn that the Trojans are still engaged on the voyage to Latium; at the beginning of the actual narrative we hear that they have just left Sicily, in good heart, and are on the open sea. That is all – but it is perfectly adequate: what they had experienced in Sicily and beforehand, how long they have already been wandering, in fact all further information would only have weighed down the exposition, without furthering the comprehension of what follows; it would also have anticipated things which are to be told in their proper context later. The first of these pieces of information is presented as the result of

376

Juno's hatred, the second gives us the setting of Juno's monologue; this gives the poet the advantage that he can remain with Juno, who conducts the first part of the action, without having to jump about to follow the story: an advantage which he prized greatly, as we shall see. He has the further advantage that he can begin straightaway with the story, go straight *in medias res* [into the midst of events], without delaying the narrative with any introductory remarks: this was an advantage which was already admired in Homer. The *Iliad* achieves it by presuming that everybody already knows the circumstances at the beginning of the story.[22] Apollonius was imitating this when he started his poem by narrating why Pelias sent Jason out; he does mention the fleece, but gives no further details about this fleece or the purpose of the voyage: the listener already knows all this. Virgil makes similar presuppositions about the familiarity of his material in that he narrates nothing specifically about the Trojan War, Aeneas' flight etc., but he does allude to it all, partly in the proem, partly in the prologue about Juno's intentions; the little that is required in order to understand the special situation at the beginning is similarly mentioned only in passing, apparently by chance.

It is even clearer in the case of the characters that Virgil is consciously imitating Homeric usage. Naturally it does not occur to Homer to say who Achilles or Agamemnon was; that the Menoitiades who enters in *Iliad* 4.307 is Patroclus, the reader knows: the poet 'is only following the tradition'.[23] This is how it happens that the poet who wrote the prologue to the *Odyssey* does not even name his hero at first; it is only after 'he' has been mentioned several times that the name Odysseus comes in, as if accidentally (*Od.* 1.21); who the ἀνὴρ πολύτροπος [man of many devices] was did not need to be spelt out to any listener. Similarly, in Virgil's opinion, every Roman would know who the man was, 'who came from Troy to the Lavinian shore and brought the Trojan gods to Latium'; for the rest, he only mentions the Trojans (30), the king of the Teucrians (38), the race hated by Juno: it is only when Aeneas himself enters as protagonist that his name appears, in line 92.

377

This late naming of names occurs so frequently in the case of less important figures that it cannot be mere chance. Latinus' 'daughter' (7.52) is not named Lavinia until she takes part in the action; his 'wife' (56) is not called Amata until Allecto comes to her (343); Juturna is introduced as Turnus' *alma soror* [guardian-sister] when she is as it were working from a distance (10.439); her name is only given by Juno when the nymph herself appears on the stage (12.146); the Sibyl has been mentioned several times in general terms (3.443; 5.735; 6.10) before we meet Deiphobe, Glaucus' daughter, at the moment that Aeneas catches sight of her (6.35). It is as if the listener is not interested in learning someone's name until they appear in person in front of him. Strangely enough, we find the same thing in Homer on occasions. In *Odyssey* 6 Alcinous' wife is often referred to as such and as Nausicaa's mother; it is only when Odysseus is about to meet her that he (and with him the listener) learns the name Arete. Odysseus' swineherd is introduced in *Odyssey* 13.404 and often mentioned thereafter; it is only when he is about to speak himself (*Od.* 14.55) that the poet feels the urge to address him as Eumaeus.

However, in Virgil this phenomenon is not restricted to the simple naming of names; it is almost the general rule that no details are given about a person until they themselves 'appear', or until they have their main scene to play. One might be tempted to attribute this to the fact that Virgil did not write his books in order and so had already given details about a person in later books so that, writing earlier books afterwards, he thought he only had to mention them briefly. But let us start with an example where this cannot have happened. In Book 11 when the Latin delegation is asking Aeneas for an armistice in order to bury the dead, Drances is introduced as their spokesman, an 'elderly man, sworn enemy of Turnus': we need to know that much to understand what he says at this point (122). We are further told (220) that *saevus Drances* [fierce Drances] stirs up rebellion against Turnus in Laurentium; but it is not until the subsequent assembly that he has his main scene. It is only immedi-

378 ately before his great speech against Turnus that we hear further details about him: he envies Turnus' fame, because he himself, although rich and articulate, is militar-ily unfit; his word is respected in the assembly, and he has a large party behind him; on his mother's side he comes from a distinguished family, but not on his father's side. We see that the details are meted out to the listener in the measure that suits the amount of interest aroused by each appearance; without a doubt, this is much better than if the poet were to empty his whole sack of information at the first mention, so that the listener would have nothing to wait for. We should bear this in mind when judging analogous cases. Iarbas is mentioned in Anna's speech only as an unsuc-cessful suitor of Dido's (4.36); we are told more about him when his prayer to Jupiter has an important effect on the action (198). In the Harpy adventure (3.239), Misenus gives the trumpet-signal to attack: to go into his family, his skills, his earlier life, would have been as out of place here as it is fitting during the narrative of his death and burial (6.164ff.): Virgil could not have done anything different here, even if he had written Book 3 before Book 6. Acestes was known to every educated person as a Sicilian of Trojan descent and first ruler of Segesta; but even someone who knew nothing about him would learn enough from the two lines when he is first named in 1.195: *vina bonus quae deinde cadis onerarat Acestes litore Trinacrio dederatque abeuntibus heros* [the cargo of wine-casks which with a hero's generos-ity the kindly Acestes had given them on the beach in Sicily as they embarked]: he had given the Trojans hospitality in Sicily. In Ilioneus' speech to Dido the situation gives rise to the mention that Acestes is of Trojan stock and rules over Sicilian cities (549). It is not until Book 5, when he meets Aeneas, that we see him as a person, with exact information about his descent, his external appearance etc. Virgil deals in exactly the same way with Nisus and Euryalus (Books 5 and 9), with Evander, and many others. For the war-heroes in the second part, the catalogues in Books 7 and 10 supplied a convenient opportunity to introduce them; but here too Virgil wisely restricted himself, and said no more about the most important characters (Mezentius, Camilla) than suited the style of the catalogue: we learn more soon enough, later, when it can have its full effect.

The consistent carrying through of this principle, of which the effect can also be seen in other aspects of the narrative, does not necessarily go back to theoretical

379 considerations; but it is reminiscent of Horace's rule about *lucidus ordo* [lucid arrangement]: the poet *iam nunc dicat iam nunc debentia dici, pleraque differat et praesens in tempus omittat* [he should say at present what requires to be said at present: he should defer much and leave it out for the time being] (*Ars Poetica* 43).

7. Continuity

To keep the listener's attention, the poet has to concern himself with the *continuity of the narrative*; he must not let the thread snap too often. When that happens, when the narrative makes a leap, to start again in a different place, at a different time, with different characters, this is a strain on the imagination, which has to build up a new picture, instead of continuing to develop an existing one. This is most easily avoided in first-person narratives, though not always; when the author is narrating, and the narrative is not restricted to the adventures of one person or one group of people, it is often necessary to jump and make a fresh start, the more often the more the action spreads out. In ancient epic, the action is divided between heaven and earth, which in itself gives rise to frequent changes of standpoint. To make this easier, the poet has two devices which he can use to advantage. Firstly, as far as possible, he will avoid abrupt transitions; instead, he will build bridges to lead the listener easily from one thing to another. Secondly, he will not break off during a 'cliff-hanger', as a novelist does to win the reader's excited attention, but pause only when he reaches at least a temporary conclusion, or a passage where the further development can easily be imagined.

After continuity of narrative, a second important consideration is *continuity of action*. The poet wants to create the illusion in us that we are 'living' the story; to this end, since things in real life continually develop and time does not stand still, he must do the same in the narrative and lead us ever onward; he must not let the action come to a halt while he recapitulates past events, and he will achieve the desired effect all the more surely if events follow closely upon each other, so that he does not have to skip over long intervals where nothing happens.[24]   380

A *bridge* is particularly necessary when there is a rapid succession of changes of scene and participants. Virgil has invented several particular devices to fill this need. In Book 4 there is a danger that between the union of Aeneas and Dido and their separation there could be a gap, since the poet does not want to give a detailed account of their life together; to fill the gap he decides to describe the impression made by the unexpected marriage on those around them – that will be used again later as a motive for Dido's suicide; then Aeneas has to be reminded by Jupiter of his duty; that must be preceded by a scene in heaven. In order to join all this together in one continuous narrative, Virgil introduces the figure of *Fama*, describes her nature (visually, with concrete symbols), reports what she is broadcasting among the people and how she visits Iarbas. There is a pause while he is introduced, then the action strides forward: *rumore accensus amaro* (203) [bitterly angry at what he heard] he addresses his defiant prayer to Jupiter; the latter listens to it, turns his gaze on Carthage, and sends Mercury to Aeneas; this creates a continuous narrative with no breaks. In Book 7 the problem is to describe how the dry tinder of war-lust catches fire in three different places and finally flares up in one huge blaze. It would seem inevitable that the narrative would have to jump about, but Virgil introduces Allecto, who hurries from place to place on night-dark wings and, scheming, kindles rage first in the house of Latinus, then in Ardea and finally over the whole country.

381 Matters are more complicated in the narration of the storm at sea, because it has two parallel actions – the mortals' and the gods' – and one of these consists of several separate parts. The analogous scene in the *Odyssey*, which was Virgil's model, is available for comparison. It falls into two parts: in the first Poseidon leads the action, in the second Athena leads the counter-action; the narrative starts with Odysseus, then passes to Poseidon; but his action is interrupted by Leucothea's intervention, during which we lose sight of Poseidon completely; like Leucothea, Athena is not set in any kind of relationship to Poseidon; she intervenes several times in the second part of the action, but without becoming visible, which would have implied that she was present all through. Virgil, unlike Homer, has chosen to narrate from the standpoint of the gods, and has thus been able to preserve the unity of the scene. We can distinguish three parts in the action: preparation of the storm; storm; pacification. In the first part the action is directed by Juno (Virgil starts with her, and only mentions the Trojans in passing at first, p. 298 above), in the third Neptune is in charge; to lead from the first to the third, the winds are introduced as persons (p. 44 above), and the poet takes time to describe them during Juno's action, so that the listener's attention is directed towards them; they are the real heroes of the second part; what happens on earth is described only as a result of their action: that is why 102ff. specifies what Aquilo, Notus and Eurus do. They then provide the transition to Neptune, who notices *emissam hiemem* [that a storm had been unleashed] (125, cf. *vicit hiems* [122] [the storm prevailed], calls the winds to come to him and sends them home; then he remains upon the scene and, with his helpers, wipes out the traces of Aeolus' rampage.

8. Simultaneous actions

The passage which we have just discussed can also serve as an example of how Virgil chooses to narrate two simultaneous actions, which often impinge on each other: he does not alternate equal chunks of each, but puts one decidedly in the foreground and gives us, as it were, glimpses of the other, making as few sudden leaps as possible and preferring to lead carefully from one to the other. This weight-
382 ing of one action is very significant from the point of view of the composition; here we will mention only the treatment of the transitions. Book 4 is mainly about Dido, but we must not lose sight of Aeneas; how does the narrator manage the many transitions from one to the other? (Only once, 554, does he use simple synchronism.) Or in Book 9, how does he move between the attackers and the defenders? Here the narrative begins with Turnus and stays on his side for all of the first section; we are only placed inside the camp for a short stretch, 33-46; we see there the clouds of dust stirred up by the approaching enemy, *prospiciunt Teucri* [the Trojans look out]; they prepare *armatique cavis expectant turribus h o s t e m* [and under arms in their hollow towers they await the enemy]; this provides an opportunity to return to the enemy. Further, the poet does not show us the Trojans themselves trying to protect the ships; we only deduce this activity from the words of the Great Mother (*ne trepidate meas Teucri defendere navis neve armate manus* [114] [haste not, Trojans, in fear, to defend my ships, neither arm your hands]),

302

which is heard by Trojans and Latins alike, but we are shown its effect only on the Latin side (123-7); we thus remain on that side. The Nisus episode interrupts Turnus' *aristeia*; for this we are taken into the camp, 168 (*haec prospectant Troes* [the Trojans are watching this, i.e. the encirclement of the walls]). The episode ends on the enemy side: once more the result of their action (showing off the heads of the slain) is seen among the Trojans; we hear the lament of Euryalus' mother; while the desolate woman is being led aside, the *tuba* sounds the attack, and now at last the two sides meet, the reader can see them both at once, and no more transitions are needed.

9. Intrusion of a second action

There is a very frequent variant of what we have just discussed: one action is interrupted by another of which the early stages are contemporaneous with the stage we have reached in the first. The poet has a choice of procedure here. He can proceed with his narrative until the second action starts, and then insert a recapitulatory explanation. The disadvantage here is that the action is interrupted while past 383 matters are caught up with, almost like a footnote. Moreover, the additional material has to be told in the pluperfect; the composition easily gets out of hand; recapitulation always reports instead of describing, and the visual aspect is lost. Virgil preferred the alternative: he abandons the first action, switches to the second, and continues to narrate this to the point where it joins with the first. Thus here the continuity of the narrative is broken, and the break is usually covered only with an *interea* [meanwhile] or suchlike; but there would have been a break in any case, even with the recapitulatory method, and making a new start has the advantage that the narrative still moves forward; the listener is not kept waiting in one place while an explanation describes things which are past and gone. An example is the Nisus narrative: we leave Nisus and Euryalus on their way to the king's tent (9.223); here the narrator breaks off and makes an emphatic new start: 'all creation lay in deep sleep and forgot their troubles and cares; but the leaders of the Trojans were holding a council of war etc.: then Nisus and Euryalus asked for an audience.' Similarly further on (366); instead of narrating how the pair suddenly hear and see in the distance enemy horsemen approaching, and then inserting the explanation: 'it was three hundred Latin horsemen, who were under Volcens' leadership and supporting Turnus' etc. – instead of explaining and recapitulating like this and then returning to the two Trojans, the poet breaks off and narrates: 'Meanwhile there rode to Turnus' camp from Laurentum three hundred etc.; they caught sight of the two, called to them and, receiving no answer, divided up to cut off their retreat'; in this way he returns to the fleeing pair in an unforced way.

This process is necessary particularly often in the scenes featuring gods which precede their intervention in the action. It is never reported that this and that happened because in Olympus such and such a decision was made; it is always done by making a fresh start. Thus, for example, at 1.656 we do not accompany Achates to the camp and to Ascanius, only to hear that this was not the real Ascanius but Amor, whom his mother had asked to act as love's messenger; no, we leave Achates on the

384 way and then visit Olympus for the scene which explains the basis for what follows, *iamque ibat Cupido* (695) [now Cupid was on his way].[25]

When the poet decides in such cases to abandon one action and start afresh, instead of interrupting the action with a recapitulation, then the precondition mentioned at the beginning must be fulfilled (and this is also true of the transitions discussed in the previous section), if we are not to feel that abandoning the first action creates a violent and arbitrary break: the action has to be brought to a point where we can see how it will develop, i.e. it must have reached a stage where it will continue in a balanced way, or develop in a predictable way.[26] Virgil does this nearly every time. We have seen in our analysis of the battle-scenes, where the nature of the subject requires frequent changes of standpoint, that Virgil always takes care to lead the action on the one side to at least a temporary conclusion before he switches to the description of what is happening simultaneously on the other side. This is true in every case of a transition from one action to another. In our final passage for discussion, three actions interweave: the preparations for the banquet in Carthage: at 1.637ff. they are described as an action proceeding on an even tenor; then Achates is sent off: we abandon him (656) on his way, *iter ad navis tendebat* [he made his way to the ships], and can thus turn our attention to the third action, the conversation between Venus and Amor. Some further examples: we could not leave
385 the Games in Book 5 without breaking into an action which is fast, changing and unstoppable: the *lusus Troiae*, which unrolls peacefully, with no result expected, provides the suitable moment at which to move over to the Trojan women and the appearance of Iris. Before the solemn oath-swearing in Book 12 we see the two peoples advance and take up positions, waiting for the kings: that is the moment when we can conveniently leave them and listen to the conversation between Juno and Juturna (134-60). In Book 11, Diana's revenge wrought by Opis on Arruns should follow immediately on his deed and flight (815), or at least on the news of Camilla's death (831), but in both cases the action would have been badly interrupted, for the reader wants to know the result of Arruns' shot, and also what effect Camilla's death had on the course of the battle; Virgil therefore continues with the main action until a static situation (*crudescit pugna* [833] [the battle hardened], *incurrunt* [834] [they charge] etc.) permits a quick shift to another place. The scene between Jupiter and Venus in Book 1 has borrowed its motif from Naevius, if what Macrobius (6.2) says is true, that Naevius has Venus bewailing her sorrows to Jupiter during the storm, and being comforted by him. For the plot, this timing is completely justified, but technically it was unacceptable to Virgil, since he already had the gods acting during the tempest and could not interrupt again so soon: our interest has been captured by Aeneas and his men and we want to hear more about them. The scene with the gods is therefore inserted when the action on earth has reached a point of rest with everybody asleep; Virgil does not recapitulate ('While Aeneas was in deadly danger, Venus had turned to Jupiter') but carries the narrative forward, so that we have to imagine the conversation as taking place by night. It is also in the night, in Book 4, the night that precedes the fateful hunting expedition, that Juno and Venus forge their plan (*ubi primos crastinus ortus extulerit Titan* [118] [as soon as tomorrow's sun rises at dawn], *Oceanum interea surgens Aurora reliquit* [129] [meanwhile Aurora rose and left the ocean]). The night setting has a better motivation in Book 8, the scene between

Venus and Vulcan when everything is at rest; that is also the time when the heavenly couple meet in the marriage-bed. In all these examples and countless similar ones, Virgil achieves the added advantage of absolute continuity in the narrative, since it has no gaps even in the nights.[27]

This rule is infringed only once: with the conversation between Juno and Jupiter during the duel between Aeneas and Turnus (12.791-842). The first two bouts are over, the combatants stand ready for the third, which is to be the decisive one: then, at this moment of greatest tension, where if a stable situation has been reached it can only last for a few moments, we have to leave the scene to follow the poet to the gods. Virgil's intention is certainly not to create a 'cliff-hanger'; that would go against his artistic principles: it is just that here these have to take second place to practical considerations, as explained above p. 179f. Since this case is unique, and there were exceptional reasons for breaking the rule, the rule itself holds good.

386

10. Synchronism in Books 8-10

We need to look separately at the treatment of the simultaneous happenings in Books 8-10. This is the only place where Virgil has to narrate two longish simultaneous actions, which converge only at the end, and which otherwise run their course without touching each other; one notes with some surprise how difficult he found it to deal with these simultaneous actions. In Book 8 Aeneas is brought close to Caere, and the events of the book take up three nights and days counting from the appearance of Tiberinus (above p. 265). We leave Aeneas on the third day; after contemplating the shield he seems about to set out (731) to meet Tarchon. Then the beginning of Book 9 takes us to Turnus with the words *atque ea diversa penitus dum parte geruntur, Irim de caelo misit Saturnia Iuno audacem ad Turnum* [while this was happening in a distant part of the country Saturnian Juno sent Iris down from the sky to the fiery Turnus]. According to the normal use of such synchronistic formulae one would take that to mean 'during the events just depicted', and therefore set Iris' visit on the third day, and this fits in perfectly when she says about Aeneas (9.10) *extremas Corythi penetravit ad urbes Lydorumque manum, collectos armat agrestes* [he has pressed right on to those furthest cities of Corythus, where he musters the country-folk and has a host of Lydians under arms]: where this last statement taken literally would take us a little further than the end of 8, perhaps deliberately anticipating events.[28] However it would be strange if Juno delayed her warning for such a long time and did not command Turnus to attack on the morning after Aeneas' departure, and this is what Virgil calculated, as the chronology of the subsequent events shows: on the second day we have the approach of the enemies and the metamorphosis of the Trojan ships, on the third night we have Nisus' expedition, on the third day (459) we have the fight for the camp; 10.256 would refer to the break of the fourth day: thus on that day Aeneas would return and the first great battle would take place. It is true that Virgil has, then, at the beginning of Book 9, obscured the chronology when, in order to avoid a recapitulation, he takes two actions which really happened simultaneously and makes it seem that the second happened after the first.[29]

387

305

If we go on to examine the times given in the first part of Book 10, we come up against more difficulties. When does the great assembly of the gods take place? Book 10 begins with *panditur interea domus òmnipotentis Olympi* [meanwhile the gateway to Olympus, the seat of supreme power, was flung open]: at first *interea* [meanwhile] seems to indicate that it is simultaneous with the end of Book 9, i.e. with Turnus' rescue from the Trojan camp. But that possibility is excluded by Jupiter's words 107f.: *quae cuique est fortuna hodie...nullo discrimine habebo* [whatever the fortune enjoyed by individual men today...I shall make no discrimination], where *hodie* [today] must refer to a new day as opposed to the previous one, and this becomes even clearer in the subsequent description of the encircled Trojans, which is linked to the gods' assembly with *interea* 118, when the phrase *pulsi p r i s t i n a Turni gloria* (143) [the glory of his *previously* repelling Turnus] indicates that since Turnus' *aristeia* a night has passed. In this case, the line quoted above would, as ancient commentators also understood it to do,[30] paraphrase the break of day, and also correspond to the first line of *Iliad* 8, ἠὼς μὲν κροκόπεπλος ἐκίδνατο πᾶσαν ἐπ' αἶαν [Dawn spread her saffron mantle over the whole world], in the same way as the subsequent lines in *Iliad* 8 are also imitated: for Jupiter's decree is analogous to that of Zeus in *Iliad* 8. The *interea* should then, just as at the beginning of Book 11, be taken as a loosely linking 'now':[31] however, here, where it could easily be misunderstood, we can hardly be happy about either this *interea* or the paraphrase of the unambiguous Homeric expression.

If, then, the new, fourth day begins with Book 10, how does one explain the lines which, after the description of the camp mentioned above, return to Aeneas (146): *illi inter sese duri certamina belli contulerant: media Aeneas freta nocte secabat?* [so had the two armies clashed in the close conflict of stubborn war; and Aeneas was cutting the channels of the sea at midnight]? Is this simultaneous? Impossible; battles do not take place at midnight. Nor can it refer to the following midnight: it is obvious that 260ff. is intended to follow directly on from the description in 118-45. The only remaining option is to assume that Virgil is here, in a most peculiar way, apparently narrating simultaneous happenings, but really intending us to understand: 'in the morning they were engaged in battle: (a few hours earlier) at midnight Aeneas was at sea': i.e. before the daybreak mentioned at 10.1, which would then be identical with the one described at 10.256.[32] Why does he venture to do such a thing? Apparently only in order to avoid several interruptions in the narrative. It would have been chronologically correct to report Aeneas' night-time voyage *before* the assembly of the gods; but – quite apart from the loss of the pathos-filled introductory scene – there would then have had to be an interruption after the scene with the nymphs, we would have been led first to Olympus (which would also have destroyed the connection of the gods' speeches with the events of the previous day), and then to the Trojan camp – for the hard-pressed state of the besieged had to be described, so that the thrilling scene when Aeneas' shield flashes out from the sea, reflecting the dawn rays and promising rescue, can have its full effect – and then again to Aeneas. This jumping about is avoided, though by rather drastic measures. However, Virgil now has to turn even further back, to the time before Aeneas' night-time journey: for there is still a gap between this and the end of Book 8, to be filled with Aeneas' discussions with Tarchon and the sailing of the fleet. But here too the poet does not decide on a true recapitulation in the pluperfect, but, with one leap, carries us back to that point in time, and then narrates in the normal way in the present tense: *namque, ut ab Euandro castris ingressus Etruscis regem adit...haud fit mora, Tarchon iungit opes...classem conscendit gens Lydia...Aeneia puppis prima tenet* [for, as after leaving Evander and having entered the Etruscan camp he approaches the king...there is no delay: Tarchon joins forces...the Lydian nation embarks on their fleet...Aeneas' ship heads the line]. Thus here too the continuity of action is preserved, although at the cost of the continuity of narration.[33]

11. Past events 390

So far, we have seen how carefully Virgil sought to avoid interrupting the narrative with recapitulatory explanations, preferring to start afresh with a new continuous narrative. In the case of simultaneous happenings this was achieved by following the new action until it converged with the old; the matter is less easy when past things have to be recapitulated, whether they date back to before the beginning of the whole story, or happened during the story but are only narrated later. Virgil gives such past events, whenever possible, to one of his characters to narrate, thereby preserving the continuity of his own narrative and action. Venus' account of Dido's earlier fate in Book 1 is supplemented in Book 4 by Anna's remarks about the unsuccessful Libyan suitors (36ff.). Aeneas learns from Tiberinus (8.51ff.) of Evander's settlement; he learns from Evander himself of Mezentius' cruel deeds and the situation in Etruria (8.477ff.); Andromache (3.325ff.) narrates her sorrowful history herself, after everything that was necessary to introduce the episode had been given as briefly as possible by Fama (295-7); and in this way we hear from Achaemenides' mouth about Odysseus and Polyphemus (623ff.). Thus it is an established technique, whether it is due to a conscious principle or results from Virgil's artistic tact in each case. This technique is not self-evident; one can contrast it with Apollonius' treatment of the Phineus story, 2.178. First the poet himself speaks of Phineus' guilt and punishment; then the latter speaks of the plague of Harpies (220-33); 391 finally we experience this plague ourselves (266-72). Similarly, when the Argonauts are approaching the island of Lemnos the poet himself freely narrates what has happened there before their arrival, 1.609, and tells the history of the sons of Phrixus before they met the Argonauts 2.1095, although Argus then has to repeat most of this history to them (1125). This is clearly very different from Virgil's technique.

For the stories of the foundation of Italic cities and the legends attached to them, the two catalogues are a convenient vehicle: here it is not the poet speaking, but the Muse. Anything which could not be accommodated here, Virgil weaves in with a special device when the opportunity arises: Venus, speaking to Jupiter, recalls the example of Antenor, who founded Patavium (1.242): the detail she goes into about the circumstances of the foundation is perhaps not fully justified by the situation alone. Diomedes tells the Latin delegates about the transformation of his companions (11.271): that is very skilfully motivated there, as is Evander's long narrative about Hercules' fight with Cacus and the establishment of the cult of Hercules, 8.185. Something different again, not direct speech, but also not simply a report from the poet, is the way in which the story of Daedalus' settling in Cumae, and the foundation of the temple of Apollo, is introduced, as an *ecphrasis* [description] of the sculptures contemplated by Aeneas (6.14).

There are only a few cases where it is not possible to insert past happenings into the present in this way. Book 7 begins with a description of the present situation; this description leads imperceptibly back into the past; and the result of what is narrated, with which the interpolation ends (*Fama per urbes Ausonias tulerat* [104] [Rumour had brought the news among the Italian cities]), is again simultaneous with Aeneas' landing, to which we then return. Nevertheless, the whole interpolation interrupts the course of the action, which carries on at 107 directly from 36; since Virgil was not able to avoid this, he does not attempt a cover-up; on the contrary, he emphasizes it in 37-44 by giving it its own proem, which marks the beginning of the new, second part of the work: in such a position a smooth transition is dispensable, or even not desirable. Similarly in a second case, which should be mentioned here: at 9.77 the prehistory of the Trojan ships is to be narrated, that is, recapitulated; none of the characters in the poem knows of the conversation between Jupiter and the Great Mother, so the poet himself has to report it. By calling on the Muses he indicates that it is something remarkable in every way. One only asks oneself, why does he move the scene back to the time when Aeneas was on Ida felling the timber to build the ships? Why does he not have the Great Mother approaching her son with a request in the usual way, while *interea* [meanwhile] Turnus is trying to start a fire and the Trojans are trying to stop him? The reason is obviously not that he felt bound by any tradition, for he disposes of the tradition quite freely in such cases; but we must confront the question, why the ships have been exposed to the raging waters (in Book 1) and raging fire (in Book 5) without any protection, yet at this particular moment the Great Mother intervenes. The appeal to the Muses, apparently required by the uniqueness of the occasion, has also the technical significance that it makes the interruption and recapitulation seem less intrusive.

The second of the eventualities mentioned above was that something which had happened during the timespan of the action has to be reported afterwards. This may be in the case of events which happened at the same time as the main action but which did not seem important enough for the thread of the narrative to be broken for their sake in the manner described above. We are brought only to the result of the secondary action, which is itself introduced to explain the situation in hand. This is the case with the death of Misenus, which occurred during Aeneas' absence, but which is reported only when Aeneas finds the corpse on his return, 6.162.[34] Outwardly quite similar are the cases in which something belonging to the main action is narrated, after having been omitted at its rightful place: e.g. the arrangements which Aeneas made when he left the camp (9.40, 172): their rightful place would have been 8.80, but it is possible that the need for such arrangements did not occur to Virgil at that point. Similarly, Turnus' exchange of swords, which becomes fatal during the duel with Aeneas, and is therefore not mentioned until then, 12.735, is not mentioned in 326, because it has no consequences at that point and would seem unimportant. But these are extremely rare cases, and Virgil himself will have considered that he was taking liberties in treating them as he did.

Such recapitulation can be avoided here too by the poet having one of his characters mention the occurrence later. We then learn things which the poet could have told us earlier from what they say: this happens much less often in Homer, as far as I can see, than it does in Virgil. At 11.446 we are told very briefly *castra Aeneas aciemque movebat* [Aeneas was moving his camp and his battle-front]: the further details, that Aeneas is sending on the cavalry to an open battle, while he himself will reach Laurentum by a different route and take it unawares in a surprise attack – these we learn from what Turnus says to Camilla (511). That Aeneas has prepared a riding display as a surprise for the Games, we learn from the whispered instructions that he gives to the *paidagogos* (5.547). That, after the embarkation from Caere, the Etruscan and Arcadian cavalry were sent by land and Turnus prevented them reaching the camp – this information would have weighed down the short report of the events in Caere (10.148): the poet tells us about it later, in Cymodocea's words to Aeneas. In these cases there is no doubt that Virgil is consciously narrating κατὰ τὸ σιωπώμενον [by passing over in silence], i.e. letting us deduce from the narrative that something has happened about which we were not told earlier.[35] It is important that we are able to be certain about this, because in other cases where a new motif is introduced at a late stage we might not have been able to tell whether the poet had forgotten to prepare for it in advance, or purposely omitted it earlier, and (in cases where this preparation would have belonged in an earlier book) whether its omission can be attributed to the fact that the books have not been brought into complete agreement with each other. At 4.351 Aeneas, defending himself to Dido, says that Anchises appears to him every night in his dreams, reminding him of his duty – we should have been told this before Mercury's appearance, but there was no opportunity. At 4.421 Dido says that Aeneas has always had confidence in Anna (see p. 114 n. 38 above); to have made that clear at the right place would have required considerable expansion of the narrative. At 6.343 Aeneas refers to a prophecy given by Apollo which applies to Palinurus: the right place to mention it would have been in Book 3; there is nothing about it there, but I do not believe that Virgil would have thought it necessary to change Book 6 to bring it into line with Book 3.

Virgil deals with future events very much in the same way: things which will happen are mentioned in direct speech, and that is sufficient for the poet, who does not bother to mention them when they do happen: *haec in oeconomia praeiudicia nominantur, quotiens negotii futuri exitus tollitur* [these instances in the arrangement are called 'prior judgements', when the outcome of a future action is presumed], Servius on 11.593, where Diana foretells that she will carry Camilla's corpse from the battle-field and bury it in her native land. Servius points very perceptively to Venus' words (to Amor), *tu faciem illius noctem non amplius unam falle dolo* (1.683) [you must for no more than one night assume his shape as a disguise], with which the poet tries to make it unnecessary to give any later statement about the replacement of the false Ascanius by the real one.

This brings us to the treatment of the distant future which lies outside the time-scale of the whole poem.

394

12. Future events

Things to come play a very important role in the *Aeneid*: the significance of the narrated action lies principally in the fact that it lays the foundation for the future. That is why we need prophecies for Aeneas' own fate; we have to learn how, after the death of Turnus, the two peoples are united, who the descendants of Aeneas will be, how Lavinium, Alba and finally Rome, will be founded. But that is still not enough: the whole mighty history of Rome, the development of the *imperium Romanum* [Roman empire] to its recently attained pinnacle is pulled into the contents of the poem, as much as the prehistory of Italy and the prehistory of the Trojans going back to before the Trojan War and their original home in Italy: Homer, too, who only described a few days of the Trojan War, had also understood how to incorporate both past and future events into his poem.[36] Homer also served as a splendid example of how to introduce the future: he did not do it by stepping forward and explaining that history will run on in such and such a way; he puts a prophecy into the mouth of one of his characters, about Achilles' death or Troy's fall or Aeneas' dominion, or whatever else he wants his listeners to learn. The device was extremely useful in Hellenistic times in the writing of short poems: where only one episode of a myth is being narrated, the listener has to be told what the consequences will be: to this end we have prediction, vision or prophecy.[37] We have also seen that Virgil's *Iliu Persis* [Sack of Troy], which was conceived as a separate work, was also rounded off in exactly the same way, with a prophecy which contains everything of significance in Aeneas' later destiny (p. 36 above). It is true that the whole *Aeneid* is really just one episode – granted, one of the most important episodes – from the whole mighty epic of Roman history, of which the final catastrophe was the Battle of Actium, and whose last scene of splendour was Augustus' reign of peace: the episode is therefore extended by the usual means to include these. That is why the poem starts with Jupiter's comprehensive prediction, which touches on only the highest pinnacles and brings us to the poet's own time; in the very centre of the poem there stands the vision in the Underworld, when the heroes of Rome pass by in a long procession; before Aeneas himself goes to fight he is able to gaze on the battle-feats of his descendants, *pugnata in ordine bella* [in order, the battles which were fought], pictured on the shield sent by Vulcan, who knows everything about the future; finally, the end of the real action of the poem, which lies outside the time-span of the narrative, is given in Book 12 in Jupiter's promise for the future. Thus in none of these cases is the continuity broken: even during the description of the shield the action does not come to a complete halt since we have to think of Aeneas contemplating it, who *rerum ignarus imagine gaudet* [having no knowledge of the events nevertheless rejoiced in their representation] and then strides off *attollens umero famamque et fata nepotum* [lifting onto his shoulder the glory and the destiny of his heirs].

II. *Description*

Narrative depicts a sequence of events, description depicts a state of affairs, a collection of concrete objects, or even an event if the aim is not to narrate how the event proceeds but to describe it by a comprehensive survey of its individual features. Ancient critics rightly classified this technique – for example the description of a battle or a fire or a storm – under the heading ἔκφρασις, *descriptio* [description]. The common factor of all kinds of description is that it delays the progress of the action; the reader stands still and examines the details of a picture. From what we have said above about the structure of Virgil's action, it is clear that description cannot loom large in his work; where it does occur, it is made to resemble narrative as much as possible.

This ἔκφρασις of events does not come into full blossom until after Virgil's time; but not only orators and rhetorical historians, poets too must already have used such a thing; the good poetry of the earlier Hellenistic period seems to have refrained from it, as far as I can see, trying to make every description preserve the character of narrative (unless it was explicitly introduced as the description of a picture or something like that). This tendency is unmistakeable in Virgil: if one compares, for example, his description of the tempest in Book 1 with that by Quintus (p. 45f. above), it is clear what an effort he has made to emphasize a sequence of events.[38] The Fall of Troy as a subject could tempt a writer to pile up descriptions of single features, and the later epic-writers wallow in it; Virgil rations himself severely.[39] Dido's passionate love, a very rewarding subject for detailed description, is equipped with a number of descriptive features on the Hellenistic pattern (4.68ff.), but since the passage of time through the day is also described, the progress of the action also receives its due.

The descriptions of localities, as already mentioned, is restricted to a very few cases where a mood-setting background is to be supplied for the action. The most detailed description, eight lines long, is of the harbour on the Libyan coast (1.159); this is an imitation of a description in the *Odyssey* and is intended to be recognized as such; in Virgil, the main purpose of this description is not to help us to visualize the scene but to make us share the feelings of the survivors of the wild tumult of the elements as they find refuge in a place protected from every breeze and the pounding of the waves. The late-Homeric description of Alcinous' royal seat (*Odyssey* 7.86ff.) may be regarded as paralleled by the description of Latinus' palace (7.170); Homer gives the visual and attractive picture of expensive buildings and luxuriant nature, Virgil portrays the original form of a Roman *atrium*, furnished with the images of the earliest Latin kings; this is primarily of historical interest.[40] The sites of ancient Rome are portrayed in Book 8, particularly in 337-61, not in a descriptive τοπογραφία [topographic account], but as the route taken by Evander and Aeneas from the *Ara Maxima* to the Forum, i.e. in the form of action. Similarly in the Underworld, the different landscapes are presented as stations on the way, and described briefly, but given visual characteristics: we see the Stygian marshy

397

398

landscape with its mud and reeds, the secret paths of the shady myrtle-grove in which the victims of unfortunate love linger, the flame-encircled iron fortress of Tartarus, and finally sunny Elysium, with its grassy fields and sandy places, exercise-grounds for gymnasts and wrestlers, its laurel-grove of fame by the Eridanus and, past a little hill, the green valley of the River Lethe: all the scenes stand out clearly, particularly because they contrast with each other, but they are seen only in passing.

Compared with this small amount of nature-description it might seem that too much space is allotted to the description of works of art. Apart from brief depictions of exceptional pieces of armour,[41] we have at 5.250-7 an embroidered chlamys [cloak] depicting the rape of Ganymede; 1.466-93: the images on the temple at Carthage; 6.20-30: the doors of the temple of Apollo at Cumae, which Daedalus has decorated with his own story; and finally 8.626-728: the shield of Aeneas. Here the form is clearly borrowed from the technique of the Hellenistic poets, who frequently chose to describe works of art in this way. But although this custom must have sprung originally from their pleasure in precious and beautiful articles, it had already often become a pretext to narrate the chosen stories in a descriptive manner; Virgil has taken this farther, so that the work of art has no importance in itself, but only in the matter depicted.

If we then look for the reason which led Virgil to include these descriptions, the one in Book 5 is not necessarily connected with the action: the precious nature of the prizes given by Aeneas could have been made clear in other ways. But if anywhere in the *Aeneid*, such a description, arising from joy over a beautiful object, has its place in these scenes which overflow with *joie de vivre* (see 135f. above); the listener is intended to share the mood of the victor who receives this costly artefact. Then in Books 1 and 6 the descriptions are of technical importance: Virgil wishes to compose scenes (p. 253 above) and he has to occupy Aeneas until the queen or the Sibyl enters; that is the purpose of the pictures which he contemplates. Finally, the description of the shield springs from the pressure of epic tradition; the shield of Achilles and of so many other epic heroes must be paralleled, as must the love of Calypso, and Odysseus' journey to the Underworld.

The difficult problem of how to prevent the action from coming to a halt during the descriptions was best solved by Virgil in Book 1: there he is really aiming at giving us the impression that we are not having images described to us but having Aeneas' changing emotions narrated to us. In Book 6 he makes no such attempt; it is said only at the end that Aeneas saw the images which have been described (*quin protinus omnia perlegerent oculis* [33] [they would have gone on to survey everything]); indeed the description, as in Book 5, is so brief that one hardly notices the lack of action. In Book 8, too, the shield is described to us as Aeneas looks at it; but here the contents are unintelligible to Aeneas and he must be disregarded during the description. The poet compensates for the lack of action by making his description itself into a narrated action; in the first part it goes rapidly through the earliest history of Rome, in the second part it gives a connected account of the Battle of Actium and the subsequent victory-feast, during which the shield and its manufacturer are only mentioned for form's sake.[42]

The content of what is represented is always connected with the content of the

399

400

poem. This is achieved most successfully in Book 1, where the pictures even have a rôle in furthering the course of the action (p. 97 above). Here they present scenes from the Trojan War; the embroidery in Book 5 shows a famous scene from Troy's earlier history; the pictures in Book 6 provide an opportunity for us to linger over the story of Daedalus, the founder of Apollo's temple at Cumae, and also tell us the prehistory of this foundation, which may be regarded as part of the history of early Italy. In the same way as these images take us back into the past, the description of the shield leads us into the future: instead of remaining merely a piece of poetic decoration, it becomes a motif which points forward and, together with Jupiter's prediction in Book 1 and the Parade of Heroes in Book 6, shows us the distant culmination of the poem's events, thereby greatly increasing the significance of what is narrated.

It is only in Book 5 that the depiction can be said to be purely descriptive and visual. The images in Book 1 are intended to arouse the listener's pity, in the same way as they bring tears to Aeneas' eyes: that is why the description lingers on the most painful scenes of the war, and passes quickly over the actual fighting, which   **401** contains less pathos. It is very clear that the description in Book 6 is also aimed at arousing pathos; it mentions the pitiful human tribute paid by Athens to Minos, Pasiphae's horrible madness, Ariadne's love, so desperate that Daedalus himself feels sympathy for her; finally, the death of Icarus is *not* depicted but is mentioned to make us share his father's sorrow. The description of the shield serves a different purpose: the journey through Rome's history, from the twins abandoned in the wolf's lair, to Augustus, triumphant in splendid majesty, is meant to impress upon the listener the greatness of the Fate which raised Aeneas' race from simple beginnings to dominion over the whole world.

Finally, the main aim of the way in which the work of art is depicted is not to produce an impression of a real artefact. Virgil comes nearest to this in depicting the separate pictures on the shield, but even here it would be difficult to reconstruct them, particularly the last picture: there we do have the beginnings of a description of a picture, but basically it is a description of a festival with no regard to whether the details can be represented pictorially.[43] It is the same in Book 6: nobody can say how the scene of Ariadne's thread was depicted; we are told the story. Similarly in Book 1, the description changes into narrative.[44] I do not think that this is because   **402** the poet was not skilful enough to maintain the standpoint of someone simply describing. Here again he is more interested in the events than their depiction in the concrete artefact, and he is more interested in reminding the reader of those events than in creating the impression of a visible object; so that even here, where it properly belongs, we do not have pure description.

There are also cases where the poet has other characters describing something, or makes us see something as if through the eyes of others. When Achaemenides describes the horrible diet of the Cyclops, a tiny detail slips in which does not belong to the visual description but has crept in from the narrator's own knowledge.[45] The poet himself does the same thing. When the Trojans sail past Circe's island, we might expect to be told what they saw and heard; we are told to some extent, but other information is added by the poet himself (7.10-20). When Aeneas, on the way to Carthage, looks down from a hill at the activities of the builders, what

313

we are told is basically what he can actually see; but that 'some are selecting the site for their house' (1.425) can hardly be seen, and I therefore doubt whether the following line, *iura magistratusque legunt sanctumque senatum* [they were making choice of laws, of officers of state, and of a consecrated senate] may be regarded as interpolated: Virgil believes that this activity was part of the foundation of every city (3.137; 5.758) and that is perhaps why he had it in his mind here, although it does not fit into the presentation.[46]

Closely related to description, in one sense, is the detailed list, in so far as it, too, depicts co-existing things, and brings the action to a halt. I will look at only one such list, where we can again learn much from comparisons: the catalogue of the Latin auxiliary troops in Book 7. In the Homeric Catalogue, as in Apollonius' catalogue of the Argonauts (1.23ff.), and, as, finally, in Virgil's catalogue, the basic interest is historical. Whereas the Hellenistic poet stops at that, and Homer, exceptionally for him, enlivens the list with description,[47] Virgil deliberately and skilfully appealed to the eye, to make the list come alive: he not only evokes a three-dimensional impression of the leaders[48] but he also describes the appearance, armour and weapons of the men. But, here too, the description is not the most important thing. The Homeric Catalogue hardly ever takes notice of the occasion which gives rise to the catalogue – the need to take up arms and march into battle – and in general Homer is content to name the number of ships which each provides. Apollonius avoids counting the assembly; he says that this one and that one came;[49] and that is that. In contrast, Virgil makes an effort to provide real *action*, as elsewhere; here he describes the troops marching up to marvel at the splendid sight *hunc legio late comitatur agrestis* (681) [he is accompanied by a legion of countrymen from far and wide], *ibant aequati numero regemque canebant* (698) [they moved in regular rhythm, singing of their king], *scuta sonant pulsuque pedum conterrita tellus* (722) [their shields clattered, and earth was alarmed by the tread of their feet], *insequitur nimbus peditum clipeataque totis agmina densentur campis* (793-4) [he was closely followed by a cloud of foot-soldiers, whose bucklered columns clustered thick over all the plain]; there, the leaders setting out or coming in: *agmina in arma vocat subito ferrumque retractat* (694) [suddenly he rallies his troops to arms and handles the sword again], *curru iungit Halaesus equos* (724) [Halaesus yokes his horses to his chariot], *Virbius...aequore campi exercebat equos curruque in bella ruebat* (781-2) [Virbius...drove his horses over the level plain and dashed in his chariot to war], *ipse pedes...regia tecta subibat* (666-8) [he himself moved up to the royal palace on foot]; right at the end, he lays special emphasis on the entrance of Camilla, at whose arrival *omnis iuventus turbaque matrum* (812) [all the young men and a crowd of mothers] come streaming out of the houses and from the fields to marvel at the splendid sight.

III. *Speeches*

Virgil's copious use of direct speech is taken over from his most distinguished model, Homer. They both use direct speech throughout the whole narrative; they both allot to it a rôle which exceeds its real-life one and allows the poet to enter places where, to be true to reality, he should have restricted himself to describing the protagonist's feelings. They both construct their scenes featuring gods so that they consist mainly of direct speech; like Homer, Virgil too has question and answer, assignment and errand, request and grant, prayers and wishes, prophecy and divination, all in direct speech. The similarity extends into the particular: when an errand is carried out and described in almost the same words with which the assignment was given (4.226 and 270; 232 and 272); when people talk in their sleep with dream-apparitions (2.281; 7.435); when fighters mock each other or, dying, put a last request to the victor – that is obvious imitation, intended to give the whole narrative a Homeric colouring. But, however great the similarity may seem at first glance, the difference is equally great: here too, Virgil maintains his own style consistently in the face of Homer's.

1. Comparative brevity of Virgil's speeches

The first thing that we notice in Virgil is something negative: the great reduction in the length of *conversations*. Great conversation scenes, such as that at the court of Alcinous (e.g. *Od.* 11.353ff.), or in the palace of Odysseus (e.g. *Od.* 17.369ff.), or as in the assembly in *Iliad* 1, in which Achilles and Agamemnon, Calchas and Nestor converse, and even Athena speaks – though she is audible only to Achilles – and Achilles himself speaks no fewer than eight times; or lengthier duologues as in *Odyssey* 1, where there are four exchanges between Athena and Telemachus; or complicated series of conversations, such as in *Iliad* 6, where Hector speaks in quick succession with his mother, with Paris and Helen, with the housekeeper, with Andromache, and finally with Paris again – there is nothing like this in the *Aeneid*. The most common kind of interchange is between two speakers and takes the form of only one utterance and one response:[50] often the first speaker then replies once more; 405 the only examples of two utterances and two responses are in Book 1 between Venus and Aeneas, and in Book 9 between Nisus and Euryalus, if Euryalus' short, incomplete final words (219-21) are to be counted as a response. Virgil very seldom goes beyond a duologue, and almost only when depicting assemblies: at the beginning of Book 10, besides Jupiter, Venus and Juno also speak; in the Laurentian senate (11.243) we have the messenger Venulus, Latinus, Drances and Turnus; in the Trojan camp – and this is the richest of all these scenes (9.232ff.) – Nisus, Aletes, Ascanius, Euryalus and Ascanius again. In addition, one may speak of a series of duologues: in Book 1, Dido replies first to Ilioneus, then to Aeneas who has just entered; in Book 2 (638ff.), first Anchises and Aeneas converse, then Creusa speaks to Aeneas, then Anchises and Aeneas speak to each other again; in Book 9, first Pallas and Aeneas, then Aeneas and Evander; in Book 12 first Latinus then Amata with Turnus; later (625ff.), first Juturna with Turnus, then Saces with him, finally Turnus with Juturna again. It can be seen that when Virgil has a series of conversations he also keeps them remarkably short.

This technique is shown to be deliberate by the fact that Virgil repeatedly interrupts a duologue with certain devices to prevent its extending beyond a single or two-fold exchange. In Book 3, Aeneas and Andromache have each spoken once: then (345) Helenus approaches and greets his countrymen. In Book 4, Dido has replied to Aeneas' response: before he can reply again, she abandons him, *multa volentem dicere* (390) [wishing to say much more], and serving-women carry her to her room in a faint. In Book 6, Deiphobus has answered Aeneas and then put a number of urgent questions to him: but the Sibyl cuts short the rest of the conversation (538). In Book 11, Latinus has to break off the meeting of the assembly before a decision has been reached, when the enemy approach and everything is suddenly thrown into confusion.

We need to establish the perspectives which led Virgil to keep his duologues, and all his speeches, so very short; a negative approach will be best here.

Virgil avoids everything which does not directly contribute to the artistic effect
406 or tell the reader anything new, and which would only be included for the sake of completeness. Whereas the main aim of the Homeric poets is to capture the scene which they have before their eyes, in all its changing detail, and to place it before the eyes of their audience, and they achieve this by depicting *everything*, leaving as little as possible to the imagination of the audience, Virgil expects every single component of the narrative to contribute a certain effect, and omits anything which cannot achieve such an effect by itself.[51] This is his governing principle both in the presentation and in the choice of speeches. The intense interest of Andromache in Aeneas and his family, like the amazed admiration of Deiphobus at Aeneas' journey to Hades, finds expression in their questions: Aeneas, for his part, could not say anything in reply except what the listener already knows, and that is why he does not say anything. In Homer, Agamemnon says to the wounded Menelaus (*Iliad* 4.190): 'The doctor will heal your wound and soothe the pain with herbs', then to the herald Talthybius: 'Call me Machaon quickly, to look at Menelaus, who has an arrow-wound', at which Talthybius goes into the camp, looks for Machaon, sees him standing with his men, goes to him and says: 'Get up, Asclepiades; Agamemnon is summoning you to come to see Menelaus, who has an arrow-wound' – there are three direct speeches: the first announces the errand, the second assigns it, the third executes it. The equivalent passage in Virgil (12.391) has only *iamque aderat Phoebo ante alios dilectus Iapyx* [and now there stood Iapyx, whom Phoebus loved beyond all others] – that a messenger has been sent to fetch him, and that the messenger has carried out this errand, can be left for us to deduce. But Virgil does give messages in direct speech, e.g. at 5.548: Aeneas sends to Iulus to say that the Troy Game can now begin; this enables the listener to understand the point of the parade which follows, including the fact that Aeneas has planned it as a surprise for the other spectators. To name only a few examples in Homer, the message which the οὖλος ὄνειρος [dread dream] takes to Agamemnon, Iris to Priam, Hermes to Calypso, has been given to them beforehand by Zeus in direct speech (*Iliad* 2.8, 24.144; *Od.* 5.29); this is clearly superfluous since we hear the message again when it is delivered. In Virgil (5.606 and 9.2), we hear at first only that Juno is sending Iris
407 on an errand; we do not learn what the message is until the same moment when the mortals concerned receive it. On the other hand, at 4.416 we hear Dido's message to Aeneas in direct speech at the point of dispatch, not at the point of delivery: here the more important consideration was to show Dido's state of mind. But on one occa-

sion (4.223), in imitation of the despatch of Hermes in the *Odyssey*, Virgil does tell us a message in direct speech although it is given again in direct speech on delivery: he felt that the detailed depiction of Mercury's preparations for the journey, and the journey itself, required a broader foundation than a simple *misit de caelo* [he sent from heaven], which really covers the journey too. It is normal practice, all through Homer also, for the messenger to receive the message silently; also, when, for example, Iris calls the winds, they follow without replying (*Iliad* 23.212), as when one hero challenges another to come with him, or despatches him, etc. (e.g. *Iliad* 10.72, 148; 13.468); on the other hand, it belongs to the nature of the situation that when a request is directed to an equal or a superior, and its granting is a matter for doubt, the one who is petitioned has to declare his explicit approval (Zeus and Thetis [*Iliad* 1.518], Aphrodite and Hermes [*Iliad* 14.212], Hephaestus and Thetis [*Iliad* 18.463]). Virgil does much the same in such cases: Anna and Barce do not reply to Dido's orders (4.437, 500, 641), nor does Camilla to Turnus' command (11.519); on the other hand, Aeolus replies to Juno (1.76); Neptune (5.800) and Vulcan (8.395) reply to Venus. But Amor's answer to Venus' prayer (1.689) and Allecto's to Juno's (7.341) are suppressed. This was already noticed by the ancient exegetes,[52] whereas they correctly regarded it as only to be expected that, for example, Opis receives Diana's command in silence (11.595). The difference is this: Diana commands but Venus and Juno both request, the latter even in very emotional words.[53] But in spite of the form of these requests,[54] it is clear in both cases that of course they will be granted: the son cannot refuse his mother's wish – in the same way (*Iliad* 21.342) Hephaestus carries out Hera's request without further ado – , the daemon cannot disobey the command of the queen of heaven: that is why the poet is able to dispense with direct speech here. He can also manage without questions, whenever they do not express a particular *ethos* [character], or do not elicit information which we would not otherwise hear; e.g. Agamemnon's question to the embassy returning from Achilles' tent (*Iliad* 9.673) and many similar occasions in Homer. Virgil either passes over where one might expect questions – take for instance Juno and Aeolus, or Venus and Vulcan, as compared with the visit of Thetis to Hephaestus (*Iliad* 18.424) or of Hermes to Calypso (*Od.* 5.87) – or, where the situation makes it essential to have something of the sort, Virgil gives a brief summary instead of having someone speak: *primus Iulus accepit trepidos ac Nisum dicere iussit* (9.232) [Iulus was first to welcome the excited pair, and he asked Nisus to speak], Latinus *legatos quae referant fari iubet et responsa reposcit ordine cuncta suo* (11.240) [commanded the ambassadors to deliver their messages, requiring of them the detailed answers to all that he had asked]; similarly in the visit to the Underworld, when Aeneas has to question his guide repeatedly to elicit explanations (318, 560: here very emotional, like his interrogation of Palinurus, Dido, Deiphobus; 863 to show the vivid effect on the onlooker of the beautiful but melancholy sight of Marcellus); there is one place (710) where he reports speech in indirect and abridged form, to make a strong contrast with the direct question which immediately follows (719), so that Aeneas' great amazement is emphasized. For the sake of variety, Virgil uses indirect speech in place of direct in other places too: in the Games in Homer, Achilles introduces every single contest with the same turn of phrase; Virgil is deliberately recalling this formulaic usage when he uses almost identical words to

408

317

409   introduce two contests, although they do not occur close together;[55] but the invitation to participate in a contest only takes the form of direct speech once: that is on the occasion of the only dangerous contest, the boxing-match, and it enables *ethos* to be put into the challenge; in two other places, indirect speech suffices (291, 485). Other examples of direct speech are: one occasion when Aeneas himself names the prizes (309); one occasion when he adjudicates in a doubtful result (348); and one occasion when he interprets the heavenly omen as signifying victory for Acestes (533).

2. Avoidance of delay

In general, Virgil tries not to interrupt the course of the action with any kind of discursive insertion, preferring the action to advance steadily towards its goal, except when he chooses to delay it for a particular purpose. His striving after concentrated effect is incompatible with any slowing down of the action such as takes place when protagonists converse at length, as happens so often in Homer. The difference can be seen most clearly in the descriptions of battles. While the fighting rages around the ships, Idomeneus and Meriones meet and hold a long conversation (*Iliad* 13.249-94), which contributes absolutely nothing to the outcome of the battle: this is one example among many of something which Virgil regarded as inadmissible. The more important of his warriors, meeting on the battlefield, do exchange words before throwing their spears: but these are brief utterances only a few lines long;[56] nowhere do they go on as long as, say, the famous duologue between Achilles and Aeneas (*Iliad* 20.177-258). More space is granted by Virgil to the pleas from a loser to the victor:[57] but even they are never as long as the

410   interchanges between, for example, Achilles and Lycaon (*Iliad* 21.71-113), where the poet has already said something about Lycaon, and Achilles has also already had the opportunity to speak. It is extremely instructive to see how Aeneas describes the discussions which took place in his father's house before the exodus (2.634ff.). If the speeches had been reported in full, they would have taken up a great many lines. But we do not hear every speech and every response; instead, the three main characters, Anchises, Aeneas and Creusa, each speak once only, and in each case this represents an important moment in the action: first, Aeneas meets unexpected resistance from Anchises; secondly, after trying in vain to overcome this resistance, he resolves to return to the fight; thirdly, when he has armed himself and is about to leave the house, Creusa begs him to stay for the sake of his family: this creates the dilemma from which only the miraculous sign from heaven can rescue him. Aeneas passes quickly over his own opening words (*genitor, quem tollere in altos optabam primum montis primumque petebam* [2.635] [the father whom I had been hoping to find, and carry, my first care, high up into the mountains]), for what he has to say there is already known to the reader, and it would be better to hear his proposals later during the actual departure (707f.). He also passes over the first part of Anchises' speech (*abnegat excisa vitam producere Troia exsiliumque pati* [he refused to go on living in exile after Troy had been razed]), in order to be able to allow full space for the pathos of the piteous final words, without holding up the action with a

long speech. Finally, he passes quickly over his further attempts to make his father change his mind, and his father's replies, because much of it would inevitably have been repetitious. In this way Virgil concentrates our interest on the most pathetic aspects of the action, and strengthens the effect of the pathos.

3. Speech used in characterization

This brings us to another of Virgil's artistic tendencies which causes speech to be used sparingly. Conversation, whether it runs on without any real result, or is directed to some sort of end with a greater or lesser degree of purposefulness, seldom actually furthers the action of an epic: anything required for that could be presented more concisely in other ways. The purpose of conversation is to bring the characters nearer to the reader by depicting relationships, and by developing, estab-   **411** lishing and altering these relationships before the reader's eyes. Conversation is the best means of showing traits, individual qualities, and the differences between people. However, Virgil is not primarily interested in these two advantages: they do not suit the way in which he sees people and wants us to see them. He does not feel the need to use conversation to represent the individual traits and emotions of his characters; he has hardly observed anything of the sort himself, but does not feel that this leaves a gap in his epic which needs filling with borrowed material. His understanding of psychology is enough for him to present clearly what does concern him: individual morals and emotions. Moreover, it is remarkable how 'atomistic', so to speak, is the world of men which Virgil depicts in his epic. Homer shows us countless relationships between his characters; Virgil's characters almost all stand alone. Even in the case of the greatest relationship of all, how little we are told of the inner relationship of Aeneas towards Dido! Virgil prepares their love most carefully, as we have seen, and because of this preparation the reader's imagination can, on this one occasion, create a well-differentiated picture of this love; but the poet himself shied away from doing so: as soon as the pair are united, he leaves them to their fate, and does not bring them before us again until they separate. The mutual relationships between Aeneas and his men are totally summed up in the one word, *pietas* [dutifulness]; just once (12.435ff.) in the whole poem do we hear Aeneas speak to his son, who has accompanied him on all his journeys: and it is to commend *virtus* [manly character]. How little Creusa's farewell words (2.776) tell us about the relationship between her and her husband: nothing, except that he is her *dulcis coniunx* [sweet husband], she is his *dilecta Creusa* [beloved Creusa], and they shared a love for their son (*nati serva communis amorem* [guard the love of the son whom we share]) – that is more or less what an inscription on a Roman tomb would say about any parents. Virgil makes no attempt to establish relationships for Aeneas with Latinus and Lavinia, or Turnus with Amata: and yet the beginning of a friendship could have given him an advantage over Homer here. Finally, towards the companions who accompany the hero throughout the whole story, Aeneas does show his *pietas* in general, but it makes no difference whether it is Achates, Misenus or Palinurus whom he has with him. It is only towards Pallas that, for one moment (11.45), he feels a special responsibility; but the many opportunities which Book 8   **412** supplies to prepare for this moment or to develop it, are neglected, and the farewell speech to the dead youth dwells almost exclusively on his feeling of sympathy for the surviving father. I do not need to extend this observation to cover all the other characters in the *Aeneid*: it is clear enough, why elaborate conversational interchanges could hardly be of any value to Virgil.

4. Instead of conversation

After this, we can understand why Virgil avoids long exchanges of speech and reply even where they would seem to belong to the nature of the subject. Many another poet would have written the farewell scene between Aeneas and Dido in the form of an increasingly emotional dialogue, and the gradual rise in excitement on Dido's part, contrasting with Aeneas' unchanging, calm resolve, would have been extremely effective. One might perhaps have expected something of the sort from Virgil, all the more because it would have had a genuinely dramatic effect, and Virgil favours this so often in other places. But quite apart from the question of whether such a verbal exchange (something like that between Agamemnon and Achilles in *Iliad* 1, or the repeated exchanges between Telemachus and the suitors) would have matched his ideal of heroic dignity, any such conversation would have led to a development, or at least a gradual revelation of the psychological position, which does not even exist for Virgil: his aim is to present two emotional states in as interesting and complete a way as possible, and this purpose is served by Dido's two interconnected speeches before and after her rejection much better than it would have been by an extended conversation. In the assemblies, both those of the gods and those of men, a single exchange of speech and the reply to it is Virgil's norm: an *altercatio* [debate] with its rapid to and fro of statement and rebuttal, accusations and justification, would also be stylised by a historian into a connected account of the arguments on each side: this gives the reader a clearer picture – and that is what the historian is aiming at, not at an exact reproduction of reality – , and it is only in a lengthy *oratio* [speech] that a speaker's skill is displayed in its full splendour. But Virgil did sometimes feel the need to explain why a realistic conversation was not included. When Aeneas listens to Dido's first speech right through in silence, without protesting, that is not from mere politeness; he needs time to recover, because he has been violently affected but must keep up an appearance of calm: *obnixus curam sub corde premebat, t a n d e m pauca refert* (4.332) [he strained to master the agony within him, and *at last* he spoke, shortly]. One might feel surprised that Turnus the impetuous does not interrupt Latinus' speech, which contains suggestions which are almost insulting: that is why Virgil makes Latinus explicitly silence him (12.25, see p. 181 n. 7 above), and Turnus' reply is introduced with the words *ut primum fari potuit, sic institit ore* (47) [as soon as he could speak, he began to say...]. These concessions to realism show that Virgil did stop to consider what he was doing when he selected the forms which suited his style.

Whether Virgil found classical models in narrative poetry for his treatment of conversation I do not know. He would not have found anything like it in Apollonius: the third book of the *Argonautica*, for example, has long conversations between

413

Hera, Athena and Aphrodite (lines 10-110), between Medea and Chalciope (674-738), and between Medea and Jason (974-1144). Apollonius' polar opposite, Theocritus, transfers the semi-dramatic form to heroic narrative in his *Idylls* and presents the conversation between Pollux and Amycus in the form of a dramatic *stichomythia* (12). Virgil himself was still using short fragments of conversation when he wrote the Aristaeus story in the *Georgics* (353, 358, 380, 445), but they are outweighed by long monologues. It is possible that the intensification of the pathetic and rhetorical element in neo-Hellenistic poetry combined with a corresponding development of the form of conversation such as we find in the *Aeneid*; it may have developed from the connected pathetic monologue, which for its part had found a favourable medium for its development in narrative elegy. In Catullus 64, direct speech occurs only three times: Ariadne's lament, the message sent by Aegeus (which Theseus does not answer) and the song of the Parcae. The writer of the *Ciris* does not present the conversation between Scylla and her nurse in the way that realism would require, in the form of short, repeated utterances and responses, but very much in Virgil's manner (and perhaps actually modelled on Virgil): a single long address from Carme (224-49), a single answer from Scylla (257-82) and a   414 concluding speech from Carme (286-339). I have just mentioned another literary source which might be considered as a model for Virgil: the historians, in whose writings one might in fact find the closest parallels to Virgil's assembly speeches and ceremonial addresses.

5. Narrative in speech

Although Virgil avoided the dramatic element in the parts of his work that we have examined so far, he reverted to it when he constructed the individual speeches. Once again it is useful to start with a comparison with Homer. Speech in ancient epic can be characterized briefly as being infinitely capable of extension,[58] particularly when it is a question of incorporating additional epic material. Wherever and whenever the poet chooses, he turns epic speech into narrative, however incongruous it may seem from a realistic point of view. This peculiar characteristic of epic speech does not spring merely from the poet's insatiable appetite for story-telling, as people have been quick to assume; rather, he uses these interpolations as a convenient and conventional means of explaining the facts underlying his characters' emotions, so that their actions appear in a clearer light[59] and their relationships with each other become psychologically deeper. This ability to incorporate extra material is however only the most noticeable consequence of the stylistic principle which governs both the monologues and the whole epic work. 'There is no obvious striving towards a main goal, even when it is present in the content of the speech; each part which prepares for subsequent development seems to stand only for its own sake; progress is leisurely, there are long descriptions which are sensuous and enlivening, sequences are loosely linked, as in the epic in general'. In all of these regards, Virgil's use of speech is the exact opposite. Its guiding principle is concentration: each speech is the expression of a single emotion, a single decision or train of thought. In   415 place of loose links he has strict connections; instead of long descriptions he has basic expressions of feeling; instead of leisurely progress he has an energetic striving towards a goal, or leisurely, but equally energetic, dissection of an emotion.

Virgil is well aware that extension of speech by means of narrative insertions is an essential feature of the epic tone which he is striving to achieve. He therefore does not avoid it, by any means; on the contrary, he seeks out opportunities to use it; but he only considers that the opportunity is there when the insertion can be explained by the context, i.e. when it makes an essential contribution to the purpose of the speech and therefore to the action; and such opportunities are not exactly plentiful.[60] There is one place where such epic insertions serve *ethopoia* [depiction of character]: when Evander, the old king, in addition to the independent tales of Hercules and of Saturn, also weaves in other tales – about his meeting with Anchises (8.157), Mezentius' atrocities (483), his fight with Erulus of Praeneste (561) – this trait is supposed to remind us of Nestor and thereby define Evander's character; but unlike Nestor's all these tales are carefully motivated by the context, with the exception of the last-named, which is intended to make the imitation more

416 obvious,[61] and at the same time Virgil manages to weave in an Italian legend which did not find a place in the catalogues. This is one deviation from his established stylistic rule; another, much more remarkable one occurs in Diana's long tale of Camilla's youth (11.539-84).[62] It is obvious that the motivation for the narrative in this context is inadequate; one cannot justify it as *ethopoia*. Add to this the fact that during the narrative Diana herself, although participating in the action, keeps completely in the background, and, when she cannot avoid being mentioned, even speaks of herself in the third person;[63] and finally, if one considers that the picture of Camilla drawn here bears no resemblance to that given elsewhere,[64] one will no longer doubt that this is merely a provisional version which was never given a final revision by the poet.[65]

417 # 6. Completeness of the speeches

However, this avoidance of digressions is only one aspect of speech in Virgil; its basic character has everything in common with Virgil's epic style as a whole. Virgil's speeches are free of anything accidental, arbitrary or untidy. His speakers do not start from a chance position, to reach their goal by various detours, or to be steered towards it by their interlocutors; he does not select a point arbitrarily, when others could have served equally well; rather he exhausts all possible material; he does not leave the point he is dealing with until it is dealt with completely, so that he does not have to return to it repeatedly; he does not leap suddenly from one thought to another, leaving a gap for the listener to fill in for himself, but places similar things next to each other, or develops one thought from another. The psychological presupposition for this is that each character at every moment is capable of surveying and arranging all the material which has anything to do with his speech: we do not need to spell out how seldom this can ever happen in real life, least of all in moments of great emotion: that Virgil does not depart from his rule even here has already been pointed out above (p. 234); he strives to make his depiction penetrating and convincing by portraying its causes as completely as possible. He makes his

characters use the same means to persuade each other as he himself does to win over
the reader: if a character is to be won over by pleading or persuasion, it is not
enough to take one argument and make it effective by widening or deepening it; as
many arguments as possible are lined up. This is true not only of the longer ad- **418**
dresses, such as that of Venus to Jupiter (1.229ff.) or of Dido to Aeneas (4.305ff.),
but also of quite short speeches. When Magus pleads to Aeneas for his life
(10.524ff.), this is modelled on Homer's Adrestus (*Iliad* 6.46); the latter pins his
hopes entirely on his opponent's greed, promising a rich ransom. Magus does not
forget to do the same, but before he does so he appeals to Aeneas' feelings as a son
and as a father, in order to arouse his pity for his own father and son,[66] and finally he
argues that one dead soldier more or less makes no difference to the Trojans'
victory: all this without using many more words than his Homeric model. When
Somnus, in the shape of Phorbas, wishes to send Palinurus to sleep (5.843-6), he
compresses into a few lines a reference to the calmness of the waves, the steady
winds, the steersman's recent exertions and fatigue, and his offer to take over; and
Palinurus' rejection of the offer also takes only a few lines (848-51), dwelling on the
unreliability of that monster, the sea, the deceptiveness of the winds and of the
bright sky; he mentions his own experience in these matters, and points out the
responsibility of his position, since it is Aeneas who has entrusted himself to him.
The numerous shouts of encouragement given by Homer's heroes to their men as
they fight or hesitate usually consist only of a brief appeal to honour or to the
present favourable chance of victory, or the danger of the situation, or the results of
victory and defeat; or else just a few of these motifs are combined; when Pallas
(10.369) encourages his men, he starts by appealing to their sense of comradeship by
addressing them as *socii* [friends], then his oath *per vos et fortia facta* etc. [by
yourselves and your brave deeds] reminds them of their own honourable record,
their loyalty to Evander and his previous successes; he mentions his own ambitious
hopes, and finally their obligations towards their common homeland and its great- **419**
ness, *vos et Pallanta ducem patria alta reposcit* (374) [your proud land requires you
and me, Pallas your leader]; there follows an explanation of the present situation: we
are fighting against mortals on an equal footing, not against divine disfavour, we are
equal in number to the enemy; in any case we have to fight and win since flight is
impossible as we are completely surrounded. We see that the Arcadians are sho-
wered with a deluge of arguments, each one indicated so briefly yet fully that a
summary of its contents would not be any shorter than the speech itself. Similarly
Anna's persuasion of Dido (4.31-49): all possible arguments against Dido's remaining single, and in favour of the new marriage, are compressed here – in the Homeric
style these arguments would fill several pages – , and one has the impression that
Virgil never gave a thought to the question of whether it was possible for Anna to
think all this out so quickly, and for Dido to consider all the implications immediately; rather, the poet uses Anna's speech as a pretext to motivate the psychology of
Dido's action as thoroughly as possible. Finally, to look at just one more example, it
is instructive to compare Latinus' advice to Turnus (12.19ff.) and Priam's advice to
Hector, to desist from combat against a stronger opponent. Priam dwells on two
points: on the fate of his two sons, Lycaon and Polydorus – here he digresses greatly
from the actual purpose of his speech – and the tragic fate which he himself would

face after Hector's death: that is painted at length in cruelly painful detail. Latinus' words combine the description of what would be left to Turnus after renouncing Laurentum and Lavinia, with a reminder of the will of the gods, and the tragic consequences which his neglect of them has already had; the king then shows why he himself must wish to end the war; finally he refers – obliquely and briefly, cleverly calculating Turnus' character – to the danger of the undertaking (*respice res bello varias* [43] [think of war's shifting chances]) and adduces as a clinching argument the respect due to Turnus' aged father. If all that together has no effect then nothing can.

420

7. Slanting of speeches

When Magus and Turnus (12.933) try to reach Aeneas through his love for his father, when Anna believes that she can round off her speech most effectively with a reference to Carthage's splendid future, when Latinus, in the warning which we have just mentioned, plays down the danger which Turnus himself is in, all these and related cases demonstrate a clever regard for the personal qualities of the one addressed; this is one of the main traits of Virgilian speech: it reveals the character not only of the speaker but also of the listener. It is certainly a deliberate contrast when Pallas reminds his Arcadians, the earliest Romans, of their martial honour, but Tarchon in the same position has to throw biting scorn at his Etruscans to goad them into holding their position (11.732); and when, on the other hand, Androgeus, in order to urge his loitering compatriots to make haste, reminds them that the others are getting all the best plunder (*alii rapiunt incensa feruntque Pergama* [2.374] [the rest are looting and pillaging Pergamum which is in flames]), the poet regards both him and all the Greeks as condemned by this trait.

This accurate adaptation of each speech to suit the character of the person addressed is merely one particularly clear illustration of the extremely calculated nature of each speech as it strives to achieve a particular goal. The masterpiece in this kind is the great speech by Sinon, which we analysed above (p. 7f.). Further detailed examples are unnecessary: the alert reader of, for example, Venus' various requests (1.229; 5.781; 8.374, to which 387f. should also be added) cannot help noticing the numerous individual *artificia* [artifices]. But perhaps we should mention how even in the prayers, with many variations, there are attempts to move the gods to grant the requests by specially adjusting the briefly indicated arguments: an example of this – apart from the oaths (5.235; 9.625 etc.) – is when Aeneas is praying to the Magna Mater and refers to himself and his men as *Phryges* (10.255),[67] and when

421 he reminds Apollo that he has followed his guidance until now (6.59); when Nisus the hunter reminds Luna the huntress of the hunting-trophies he has dedicated to her (9.407), and Pallas reminds Hercules of the guest-friendship he has enjoyed in Evander's house (10.460), and on the other hand Turnus (12.777) tries to win over Faunus by accusing the Trojans of cutting down his sacred tree which the natives had always revered. Likewise it is intended to characterize the boastful king Iarbas with his barbaric conceptions of a god when he uses accusations, containing veiled threats, against Jupiter, the king of Heaven, to try to make an impression (4.206ff.).

A naïve speaker explains the situation as it appears to him, trusting that the person addressed will then see it in the same way and draw the same conclusions which he himself draws and would like to see drawn by others. A calculating speaker does not start by thinking how he can most clearly express his own feelings, but he considers what will move the other person away from their own standpoint to act in the desired way. He therefore tries to present the situation, not in the way that it appears to him, but in the way that he wants it to appear to the other. He is easily led to omit facts, to change them or invent them, if he thinks it will help him to achieve his end.[68] Virgil's speakers are good at such sly insinuations: naturally they are most used by advocates of a poor cause, i.e. in this case by the enemies of the Trojans. The masterpiece of this art is, as is only right, Allecto's speech to Turnus (7.421ff.): how, in a few words, the whole situation is distorted, so that Turnus appears as the one who is being cheated out of the well-deserved reward of his efforts which he has been promised, and Latinus as the unprincipled egoist who is making use of the unsuspecting Turnus and laughing at him afterwards! – that is worthy of the demon from hell. Amata's words inspired by Allecto (7.359ff.) nearly match it: in both cases any direct untruth is skilfully avoided, and yet the result is one big lie. How dangerous this weapon can be in political warfare Virgil had been able to observe only too frequently; it almost goes without saying that Drances, the very type of the political party leader, will use it against Turnus (11.343): with great skill he casts him in the role of inconsiderate, egoistical tyrant, who lets no voice be heard except his own, who is ready to quash by force any resistance, and who scorns the people as a worthless mob: one knows how often in the battles between parties in Rome this insult was hurled back and forth, to the annoyance of good republicans. Turnus defends himself most indignantly against this very *formidine crimen acerbare* (407) [sharpening an accusation with fear]. Such poisoned weapons are allowed even in the gods' partisan skirmishes. It is true that Venus is only trying to arouse pity for the Trojans when, against her own better judgement, instead of crediting Diomedes with an attempt at helping the Latins, she presents Diomedes' repeated rebellion against the Trojans as fact (10.28); when she then renounces any prospect of a Trojan empire in Latium, acknowledges Carthage's dominion in Italy and asks only to be allowed to remove Ascanius to a quiet life without fame, this is all sly misrepresentation intended to make Jupiter realize the point to which Juno's hatred has already brought the situation. She goes as far as to end with the request *iterum revolvere casus da pater Iliacos Teucris* (10.61) [allow the Trojans to trace once more the whole cycle of Troy's misfortunes].[69] But when Juno hints in her reply that the forecast given to the Trojans consisted only of the predictions of mad Cassandra,[70] that is malevolent distortion, just as it is when she presents the Trojans as wicked thieves, who only pretended to have peaceful intentions and really desired war (77-80); and when she holds Venus responsible for the metamorphosis of the Trojan ships into nymphs, that could only have been invented by a poet who in his youth had stood by the orators' platform every day listening to the coarsest of calumnies against political opponents – and had seen them take effect. We know that distortion and veiling of the truth were not even condemned in the theory of rhetoric, so long as they served one's purpose,[71] even if the fact was not expressed as crassly as it once was by Servius (in fact in an inappropriate context): *in arte*

422

423

rhetorica tunc nobis conceditur uti mendacio, cum redarguere nullus potest [in rhetoric we are allowed to tell lies when no-one can contradict].[72] In the last example the accusation of deception is not really applicable in so far as the true events during the transformation are in fact as well known to the whole assembly of the gods as they are to Juno herself: she lets herself be carried away by her feelings, and be led involuntarily to distort and to exaggerate.[73] When Dido is most agitated she even believes that she has not only rescued the Trojans from death but also saved their fleet from being destroyed (4.375); she even believes that she had recognized Aeneas as a wicked liar as soon as she met him (597), and as happens here in Dido's case, so too in others: facts appear distorted to the agitated senses, without there being any intention to impress anyone else. The revenge wrought by Minerva upon the Greeks takes on vast dimensions for Juno,[74] because it feeds her rage over her own powerlessness; here Juno is, as it were, her own audience, *se suscitat ira* [she rouses herself to anger].

8. Arrangement of speeches

After all that we have said, one would expect the *arrangement* of the speeches in Virgil to show a similar amount of deliberation and calculation. One who has found how very much the effect of a speech depends on the arrangement of its parts will automatically follow the rules of the art here too. An example is Numanus' scornful speech (9.598ff.), where one thought follows another very logically: he wants to entice the Trojans out of their entrenched position, so he starts by accusing them of cowardice: 'Are you not ashamed?'. That leads to the scornful utterance: 'To think that these are the people who are crazy enough to want to bully us out of a marriage by force! We, who have much more significance than the Greeks, and *they* have already beaten them.' He proceeds to expand on who 'we' are and describes Italic life according to the different generations: infants, youths, men, old men. 'And what can you offer? You adorn your bodies and live an idle, vain existence.' Logical conclusion: 'Go home to your Phrygian orgies and leave the field to us real men': finishing with the worst insult: *o vere Phrygiae neque enim Phryges* [you who are really women of Phrygia, not Phrygian men] and *sinite arma viris* [leave arms to men].[75] The emotional speeches have the same characteristics. Aeneas' lament over Pallas' corpse refers, in order, to the dead man (11.42-4), Evander (45-57), the future of the realm and its ruler, Iulus (57-8); in speaking of Evander he refers first to the past, then comments on the present, then predicts the future; finally he anticipates the *consolatio* [consolation]. Aeneas does not put himself to the fore, and says nothing about the direct effects on himself of the loss of Pallas: the indirect effect is that he realizes that the dead youth's pleasures which are now made vain were the same as his own (42f.), that he felt responsible to the father for the son (45ff., 55) and – something which goes without saying – that he is deeply concerned about the future of his family. Dido's first speech to Aeneas on his departure falls into two parts: accusation (*indignatio*) (4.305-13) and pleading (*miseratio*) (314-30); the transition from one to the other is very natural: 'You are in such a hurry to run away, that you don't even give a thought to the winter storms, and it is not even as if

you are anxious to reach home – you are going to a strange land', this leads of itself to the thought of what he is giving up: *mene fugis?* ['Is it from me you are trying to escape?']. The pleas are based on the past (315-18), the present (320-3) and the future (324-6); the finale is formed by the lament, arising directly from her thoughts of the future, that she will not even have an image of her beloved in the shape of a little son: if anything might move the hard-hearted man and force him to remain then it would be this last argument.[76] How Aeneas for his part briefly meets the accusations one after the other, and then explains in detail, point by point, that his   426
departure is not voluntary, I do not need to tell you.

In these three examples, which will suffice to represent many others, the poet has arranged his material with a sure touch. At the same time, he has avoided making this arrangement too obvious: he elides the divisions between sections rather than drawing attention to them. It is unnatural for a violently upset person to give vent to his feelings in a well-ordered way; with great art Virgil makes it seem as natural as possible, clothes the skeleton of the speech and smooths out the transitions so that we seem to see not a framework of bones but a living body. He therefore starts not with a cool *propositio* [exposition] but with a leap *in medias res* [into the midst of the matter], starting from the thing nearest to hand; no announcement of, or emphasis on, each new section,[77] no explicit formulae at the conclusion; trains of thought which are psychological rather than logical, perfectly in tune with the purpose of the speech, which Virgil intends should work overwhelmingly upon the feelings, not upon the mind. That is true even of the speeches which come closest to the *oratio* [formal speech] as found in the art of rhetoric, the speeches made in the assembly by Venus and Juno in Book 10, by Drances and Turnus in Book 11: they argue, and on both occasions the reply refers as closely to the previous speech as only a reply in the senate or a court of law does, even quoting *verbatim* from the opponent; at the same time they remain full of pathos, every part calculated to affect their emotions, and it is only in Turnus' speech that one finds anything like a rhetorical emphasis on its arrangement:[78] this is intended to make a clear-cut division between the well-considered *oratio deliberativa* [deliberative speech] and the heated *invectiva* [accusation] of the first part of the speech.

The poet is so accustomed to arranging his speeches in this way that he does not   427
even change completely when, as with the lament of the mother of Euryalus (9.481-97), he wishes to use the form and the content to give the impression of a person completely beside herself; there is only one occasion where he ventures to use broken utterances to express crazed agitation, and that is in Dido's outburst of anger when she sees the fleet sailing away (4.590ff.): but even here the effect depends more upon the form of the speech – loud exclamations and questions – and its content, which is close to sheer insanity – than upon any disturbance of the normal sequence of thought.

9. Monologues

Virgilian *monologue* is very different from the Homeric. Homer[79] uses direct speech all the way through his narrative, to enliven it, and to reveal the inner thoughts of his characters, and he even uses it when a dialogue is impossible because the character is unaccompanied; in such a case, either he puts the speech into the form of a prayer, which can develop into a monologue,[80] or he presents his character's feelings or thoughts, not summarizing their content himself (except in a very few straightforward cases),[81] but in direct speech, which he introduces as an address to the θυμός [heart], without suggesting that there is actually a dialogue between the two halves of the divided self. The formula at the end usually denotes this solitary speech by the phrase ὁρμαίνετο κατὰ φρένα καὶ κατὰ θυμόν [he pondered in his mind and heart] so that it remains uncertain whether we are to think of it as spoken aloud. In the *Iliad*, monologues which present the conflict of two desires and then motivate the victory of one occur only in one standard situation: a hero finds himself isolated during the fighting and wavers between holding his ground and retreating.[82] There are also, very infrequently, monologues which are intended to present the effect which a painful, unexpected happening has on a solitary hero better than the poet could from his own mouth;[83] inner agitation is present here in every case, but the poet makes no attempt to achieve the effect of a sudden overwhelming emotion which bursts involuntarily into a stream of words; the phrase φρονεῖν κατὰ θυμόν [thinking in his heart] includes calm expression of fears and other considerations, as well as explanation of the situation.[84]

In the *Odyssey*, the reason for the monologues in the Homeric style is Odysseus' solitary state in the period between his farewell to Calypso and his meeting with Nausicaa, and then again after waking up on Ithaca; we do not find decision-making monologues here, although reflection may lead to a decision. It also matches the second type in the *Iliad* when Poseidon's involuntary surprise at the sight of Odysseus sailing home is expressed in a monologue – here Poseidon stands alone, away from the other gods: strictly speaking this is the only monologue spoken by a god in Homer.[85] It is just this peculiar type of conversation with oneself that Virgil has taken over, together with the lay-out of the whole scene in Book 1, and repeated in a heightened way in Book 7, as we have described above (p. 148).[86] In both cases, Juno's words are a preparation for the subsequent action: this introductory function is emphasized so strongly, compared with Poseidon's monologue, which is fitted into the narrative, that one could well call them prologues, comparable with the prologues spoken by the gods in tragedy, such as the prologue of the *Hippolytus*.[87] The tone of the two Virgilian monologues is also very different from the Homeric ones: Virgil gives, as it were, Juno's conversations with herself, in which she goes over, not the plain facts, but the reasons why she is angry, and about what, and why she must continue to be angry (*se suscitat ira* [she rouses herself to anger]);[88] in Book 7 he adds the threat, swelling into thirst for revenge, a powerful heightening of Poseidon's words prophesying doom. Drama, and also Hellenistic narrative poetry, has made Virgil so familiar with the pathetic monody which wallows in pain or anger in order to arouse ὁμοιοπαθεῖν [sympathy] in the listener, that monologue must have seemed flat and ineffectual to him.

Apart from this one characteristic development, Virgil refrained from using the Homeric type of monologue.[89] The only other monologues which he gives are those of Dido when she is alone: here there is no connection with Homer, and even if they may have been inspired by Medea's monologues in Apollonius,[90] Virgil has moved far away from his model and closer to the dramatic monologue on the one hand (see above p. 100) and, on the other to the short, emotional poems of pathos of the Hellenistic period.

Otherwise, Virgil makes a sharp division:[91] if there is no pathos exerting a direct effect, he reports his hero's thoughts, sometimes in more detail than Homer allows   430 himself in such a situation; or he makes it obvious that violent emotion is forcing the character to speak aloud. Thus, in place of the partly descriptive and deliberative words of Odysseus at the outbreak of the storm at sea, he puts the much shorter, emotionally heightened speech of Aeneas (1.94-101), an ejaculatory prayer rather than a monologue, which makes it closer to Achilles' groan (ᾤμωξε ἰδὼν εἰς οὐρανὸν εὐρύν [he groaned and looked up to the broad heaven] – heightened to *duplicis tendens ad sidera palmas* [raising both hands to heaven] – Ζεῦ πάτερ κτλ. [Father Zeus, etc.] (*Iliad* 21.272f.) – when he was afraid of drowning in the Scamander, than to those words of Odysseus. The equivalent of Achilles' anxious thoughts when he sees the Achaeans fleeing for a second time (18.5-14), is the short exclamation of surprise which Turnus emits (12.620f.): *ei mihi quid* (= ὤ μοι ἐγώ, τί γὰρ αὖτε... [Ah me, why again...]) *tanto turbantur moenia luctu? Quisve ruit tantus diversa clamor ab urbe ?* [Ah me, why are the ramparts loud with these sounds of confusion and mourning? What means this noise of outcry streaming here from the city, so far away?], but before he can think further, Juturna speaks to him. Aeneas' desire for the promised bough is expressed in a monologue (6.186) but is explicitly designated a prayer, as are the pleas to the doves and to Venus which immediately follow (194ff.); there the function of the short monologue is really technical: it serves as a cue for the doves which appear directly after, since their significance would otherwise not be immediately obvious. Virgil also gives the form of a prayer to the cries of distress uttered by Turnus when Juno carries him away on the boat (10.668ff.): at first, he hurls accusations at Jupiter, and at the end, pleas to the winds; on the other hand, his subsequent anxious thoughts are reported by the poet himself. I showed above (p. 103) how in Dido's case, Virgil likewise sought to avoid plain monologue by using other forms – presenting first Dido's simple thoughts, and then Dido herself speaking aloud, with special motivation.

Lament for the dead, as Homer shows very clearly,[92] is not really monologue, since it is intended to be heard: the original involuntary loud outbursts of grief have become a standard part of the θρῆνος [lament]. Thus in Virgil the laments of Evan-   431 der (9.152), Aeneas (11.42), Euryalus' mother (9.481) and of Anna (4.675):[93] but whereas Aeneas speaks his words of farewell in a composed fashion, and Evander, after lengthy, silent weeping, voices a conventional lament, the words of the two women are intended to portray a genuine outburst of emotion: that, too, is the manner of drama, not of ancient epic. Virgil did the same with the lament of Juturna (12.872), who has to leave her brother struggling with death; she does address Turnus, having stood by him until this moment in the shape of Metiscus, but Virgil cannot have meant that her lament really reached his ears; this is the established standard form of monodic lament used in the wrong place.

10. Rhetoric

⸺⸺ ⸺ most suitable place for a few words on the relationship of Virgil's art to rhetoric; 'a few' because the studies which have been made so far do not provide sufficient basis for a comprehensive survey. Moreover, the most interesting aspect, the amount that Virgil and Horace and their fellow-writers owed to rhetorical training, lies outside our scope: I mean the art of oratory, which consists of care and tact in the selection and placing of words, clarity and precision, brevity or fullness of expression, freedom and regulation of the sentence-structure – all matters which we can now begin to appreciate since Norden has opened the path to this study.[94] As for

432   description, presentation and composition, the influence of rhetoric on the early Augustans has, in my view, been exaggerated rather than understated.[95] It is customary to include under the heading 'Rhetoric' everything which a comparison with other poets and prose-writers shows to be standard usage, and which could therefore be attributed to the observation of precise rules of rhetoric: it is possible to find plenty of examples, particularly among the rhetors of the imperial period, if you set about it in this way. However, at the same time one would find a great deal which could equally well, or perhaps better, be attributed to the rules of poetics, which did draw on the fount of rhetoric but also went its own way, often in advance of rhetoric. I should not trouble to object to this simplistic mode of categorizing it, were it not that wherever 'rhetorical' influences are perceived, one has the feeling that poetry has been estranged from its own nature: whereas a poet who uses observations and poetic rules drawn from classical poetry does not leave his own proper ground. Moreover, scholars frequently undervalue the influence of the poetic tradition, which could lead to technical devices being repeated without the imitator being aware that he is following any 'rules'. Finally, if one takes rhetorical theory as one's starting point, it is easy to suspect its influence whenever a poetic motif more or less fits a rhetorical rule which is known to us, whereas the poet may have been led to it by necessity, from the nature of his material. If we consider all this and whittle down accordingly the number of features in Virgil which might at first glance be claimed

433   to be 'rhetorical', not very many examples of rhetorical technique will remain. Virgil may appear to be influenced by the *schemata* [figures] of certain genres of rhetoric when he touches on the field of epideictic oratory. Thus, after Marx perceived in the 4th *Eclogue* the *schema* of the λόγος γενεθλιακός [birthday greeting], Norden tried to show that the great *epideixis* [display] of Anchises in the visit to the Underworld refers to the τόποι [commonplaces] of the λόγος πανηγυρικός [panegyric] in the eulogy of Augustus (6.791ff.), of the λόγος ἐπιτάφιος [funeral speech] in the lament for Marcellus (868ff.), and of the ἐγκώμιον Ῥώμης [eulogy of Rome] in the epilogue to the Pageant of Heroes (847ff.).[96] Further, in, say, the words of farewell which Aeneas addresses to Helenus (3.494ff.), one may find the rules of the λόγος συντακτικός [departure speech] observed much better than in the Homeric example cited by the rhetors (*Od.* 13.38ff.); the strange interjection with which Turnus interrupts himself in a *cohortatio* [exhortation] (*sed periisse semel satis est* [9.140] [a single destruction of their race is enough]) and proceeds to rebut, may be

traced back to a not altogether timely memory of the ἐλέου ἐκβολή [purging of pity] required by the rhetors; indeed, one could perhaps apply these observations to more than epideictic oratory, and find, for example, in Anna's persuasive reply to Dido the τόποι of a *suasoria* [persuasive speech], find parallels in the Roman senate for the speeches in the Latin assembly in Book 11 (p. 325 above), and analyse Sinon's great speech (2.77-144) as a prime example of a *purgatio* [justification] and *deprecatio* [prayer for pardon]: but one will not get very far in applying these technical terms to Virgil if instead of aping the later Latin rhetors, who illustrate rhetorical devices with examples from Virgil, one proceeds in the reverse direction, trying to explain Virgil by means of the doctrines of rhetoric.[97] More important than these details, and more indicative of the influence which his childhood schooling and the rhetoric-soaked life of his time had on Virgil, it seems to me, is the general nature of   434 his speeches: almost everything which I pointed out in the earlier sections of this chapter as characteristic of Virgil, particularly when compared with Homer, brings them closer to the *oratio* [formal speech] of the rule-book: avoidance of dialogue which develops by means of brief speeches and replies; refraining from deliberate digressions; exhausting all possible arguments; calculation of the effect on the listener; and well-considered, lucid disposition. These are all qualities which are in complete harmony with Virgil's total technique, and which the example of poets or historians may have inspired him to cultivate, but they will certainly have received some of their final polish as a result of these rhetorical influences.

However, Virgil remained well aware of the boundaries between poetry and prose; he was not like Ovid, who did not hesitate, in fact was proud, to show at every opportunity that he was a poet who had been trained in rhetoric. Virgil does not seek out excuses to parade his rhetoric, and the poetic shell which he has built up over his epideictic λόγοι [speeches] allows only the sharpest eye to perceive the *schema* [formulaic character] of his invention; also, as we have seen, he veils the structure of his speeches, rather than emphasizing it. Whereas at the time that Virgil was working on his *Aeneid* the young Ovid was listening passionately to the siren-tones of the modern *declamatio* [declamation], and inaugurating in his *Heroides* the genre of poetic *declamatio*, Virgil remained untouched by this latest trend in rhetoric: as a youth he had already felt irritated by the *inanes rhetorum ampullae* [empty mouthings of the rhetoricians]. Compared with the hysterical pathos of those *declamatores* [declaimers], even compared with Ovid's rather more tasteful tirades, Virgil's pathos even seems moderate to us, although it does go further than we like our modern poets to go – Schiller's time felt differently –, and surely Virgil is, here   435 too, revealing his rhetorical training: that is where he developed the ability to play upon the feelings of his Roman audience like a familiar instrument, so that he always had effortlessly to hand the right form in which to cast his emotion so that it would arouse the emotions; for the arousing of πάθος [pathos], a chief aim of his epic poetry, was also one of the chief aims of trained prose oratory. However, we must be careful not to overvalue the 'rhetorical' element here too: I do not doubt that Virgil's treatment of pathos, far though he was from striving to be realistic or true to nature, nevertheless comes a good deal closer to real life than is acceptable to the modern (particularly North European) reader. Virgil's heroes are ancient Italians, easily moved by emotion of every kind, and not accustomed to bear it in silence but to express it in an easy flow of words. Where that is habitual, certain forms of speech naturally develop and are available at all times to the emotionally excited person, helping him to express his feelings with a completeness, strength, order and clarity which can seem unnatural to a listener who hardly ever lets himself be moved to express an emotion in words. We may be sure that Virgil's public thought they were hearing the natural, if somewhat ennobled, expression of true feeling, in places where modern critics shake their heads over unnatural, unrealistic 'Rhetoric'.

Notes to Chapter 3

357   **1.** 4.402; 7.528, 586; 9.30, 668, 791; 10.96, 264, 356, 405, (714); 11.297, 456, 659; 12.365, 587.

358   **2.** In 9.80ff. on the occasion of the metamorphosis of the ships, there is a report of the conversation which the Great Mother had with Jupiter when Aeneas was building the fleet; the scholia remark *sane haec narratio tertii libri erat, sed dilata est, ut hic opportunius redderetur...potest igitur aut* κατὰ τὸ σιωμώμπενον *videri aut hysteroproteron* [of course this narrative belonged to the third book, but it was deferred in order to be related here at a more appropriate point...it may be regarded as an omission (passing over in silence) or a hysteron proteron]. So this is concerned with reference back, which is very rare; it is not a criticism of the unadorned brevity of the narrative in Book 3, as Georgii thinks (*Aeneiskritik* 394). Of course, Servius' *opportunius* [at a more appropriate point] is an understatement; in the first-person narrative of Book 3 the Olympian scene would have been quite impossible.

3. An example, from the Telemachia, *Odyssey* 2.382ff., which is narrated in great detail: Athena brings Telemachus' travelling-companions together and borrows Noemon's ship.

359   **4.** Diodorus, for example, often refers to the demands of συμμετρία [proportion] when he does not want to go into further detail: 4.5.4; 4.68.6; cf. 1.8.10; 1.9.4. Dionysius finds that Thucydides lacks proportion in his narrative: *de Thucyd.* 13ff.

360   **5.** The boldest example of this is probably 6.40: *talibus adfata Aenean (nec sacra morantur iussa viri) Teucros vocat alta in templa sacerdos* [thus she addressed Aeneas. With no delay the Trojans offered the commanded sacrifice. The Sibyl as priestess then invited them into the temple on the height]: there the sentence is not even interrupted by the sacrifice of the seven bullocks and seven sheep. But Virgil's main concern here was to get the action moving; a long interpolation would have left the Sybil's first entrance isolated; also, in 236ff. there is going to be a much more important sacrifice which would not have made any impression if it seemed to be repeating the first. Less noticeable is 211: *vatis portat sub tecta Sibyllae (ramum)* [he carried it (the bough) to the home of the prophetic Sibyl]. In contrast, the brief allusion *exin bella viro memorat* etc. (890f.) [he next told him of the wars...] clashes with the narrative style completely and would surely have been excised during revision: on this see Norden 44ff., who has not been rebutted by Drachmann, *Nord. tidskr.f. filol.* XIII 128ff. The strangest thing is Drachmann's assumption that Virgil inserted lines 890f. only from conscientiousness, so that the

332

prophecy made by Helenus 3.458ff. should be fulfilled; but it is *not* fulfilled, since it is Anchises who prophesies, and not the Sibyl as Helenus had said. There is doubtless a connection between the Sibyl's oracle at 83ff. and Helenus' prediction; since the Sibyl's oracle is permitted to provide exact information and detailed advice on conduct only on matters of ritual, one may question whether Virgil was right to use for Helenus' prediction, in a slightly altered form, the lines specially written for Anchises' prophecy. On the origin of the doublet 6.83ff. and 890ff. I disagree with Norden: see below, p. 351f.

6. It is significant that Apollonius, 4.1126f., does describe the preparations for the nuptials of Jason and Medea in great detail, and also says what he thinks of it, but skates over the actual event out of modesty, 1168: τῷ καὶ τοὺς γλυκερῇ περ ἰαινομένους φιλότητι δεῖμ' ἔχεν εἰ τελέοιτο διάκρισις 'Αλκινόοιο [and so, although they melted in sweet love, they feared that the judgement of Alcinous might be fulfilled]. 361

7. Quintilian 6.2.32: ἐνάργεια *quae a Cicerone illustratio et evidentia nominatur, quae non tam dicere videtur quam ostendere: et affectus non aliter, quam si rebus ipsi intersimus, sequentur* [ἐνάργεια [vividness], which Cicero calls *illustratio* and *evidentia*, and which seems not so much to state as to show: and our emotions will ensue just as if we were ourselves present at the events]. He then gives examples from the *Aeneid*: *excussi manibus radii revolutaque pensa* (9.476) [the shuttle leapt from her hands and her skein of wool untwined]; *levique patens in pectore vulnus* (11.40) [in the smooth breast the gaping wound]; the horse at Pallas' funeral *positis insignibus it lacrimans guttisque umectat grandibus ora* (11.89) [his trappings laid aside, walked weeping and wetting his face with great tear-drops]. Similar examples, above all in detailed descriptions: Troilus, hanging from his empty chariot-seat, the reins still in his hands, his neck and hair scraping the ground, his lance pointing backwards and drawing a furrow in the dust (1.477): Priam's death: Neoptolemus drags him trembling, skidding on the blood of his slain son, as far as the altar: he grabs him by the hair with his left hand, with his right he plunges the sword into his side up to the hilt (2.550). Compare Achaemenides' account of the Cyclops' ghastly meal with the narrative in the *Odyssey*, or – where instead of a host of details the ἐπιμονή [elaborate treatment] is confined to the description – the lines about Tityos in Virgil (6.595) with those in Homer. Such passages are the best illustration of Lucian's famous remark, *De hist.* 57, about Hellenistic detail: εἰ δὲ Παρθένιος ἢ Εὐφορίων ἢ Καλλίμαχος ἔλεγεν [by contrast with Homer], πόσοις ἂν οἴει ἔπεσι τὸ ὕδωρ ἄχρι πρὸς τὸ χεῖλος τοῦ Ταντάλου ἤγαγεν; εἶτα πόσοις ἂν Ἰξίονα ἐκύλισε [but if Parthenius or Euphorion or Callimachus had been speaking (by contrast with Homer), how many words would he have used to bring the water right up to Tantalus' lips? And how many words to whirl Ixion round?]; (rightly understood by Dilthey, *De Callim. Cyd.* 22). 362

8. Sellar has made some good remarks about this, *Virgil* 410ff.

9. *extulerat lucem* [had brought forth its light] is supposed to have been used at 11.183 because the passage goes on to deal with the *efferre* [carrying out] of the dead; *Tithoni croceum linquens Aurora cubile* (4.585) [Aurora leaving the saffron bed of Tithonus], because Aeneas is leaving Dido; on 2.801 Servius maintains that *surgebat Lucifer* [the day-star was rising] refers to the fact that *de patria discedit* 366

Aeneas i.e. *surgit* [Aeneas was leaving his homeland, i.e. was rising]. More on this in Georgii, *Aeneiskritik* 145, who again mistakenly sees criticism where there is none, and also fails to recognize what is true in Pollio's remark.

10. I will give just a brief note on this subject of variation; more than that belongs to a theory of expression. Ancient epic follows the principle that events which naturally recur without noticeable variation should always be reported in the same way, with the same words. Apollonius already took care to avoid these stereotyped phrases; Virgil goes even further. When describing the making of the shield, Homer always starts with the manufacturer, only varying – yes, Homer does vary with deliberate art – the choice of verb. Similarly, Apollonius varies the standard introductory formula in his description of Jason's garment (1.780ff.) Virgil begins his description of the shield 8.628 with *fecerat Ignipotens.. fecerat et...* [Vulcan had made...he had also made...], *addiderat* (637) [he had added], but then changes to simple description: *stabant* (641) [there stood], *distulerant* (643) [had laid aside], *iubebat* (646) [he ordered], *aspiceres* (650) [you might have seen], *stabat* (653) [he stood], *cernebat* (656) [he saw], and interrupts this only twice by returning to Vulcan (*extuderat...addit* [665] [he had hammered out...he added], *fecerat Ignipotens* [710] [Vulcan had made]), with whom he also concludes the whole (*finxerat* [726] [he had fashioned]). In the Homeric Catalogue of Ships the introductory formula does frequently vary, for no obvious reason, and without avoiding exact repetition. Apollonius (1.23ff.), uses variations wherever possible for all the words of coming and going and amplifies plain positives with negative formulae, also finding unusual forms for both, without aiming at any poetic effect. Virgil is more like him than like Homer when he describes the leaders by their manner of arrival, not by their outward appearance; we shall show below how he tries to make the list more interesting in this way; in the introductory formulae, too, among the verbs of coming and the negative formulae there are also visual images: Aventinus displaying his victorious horses on the grass (655); Messapus' peoples who have not fought for many years are called to arms and once again he handles his sword (691); Halaesus yokes the horses to the chariot (723); Turnus is a head taller than all the others (783); not one introductory formula is repeated exactly, and even when the content is nearly the same the sentence-structure is varied – this is made easier by the small number of participants. However, variation is also sought in the naming of the peoples and tribes; not only is this intended to contrast with the Homeric simplicity of οἳ ναῖον, ἔχον, ἐνέμοντο [who dwelt, occupied, possessed], but it truly helps to fill the reader's mind with pictures instead of loading his memory with names (e.g. 797ff.: *qui saltus Tiberine tuos sacrumque Numici litus arant Rutulosque exercent vomere collis Circaeumque iugum, quis Iuppiter Anxurus arvis praesidet, et viridi gaudens Feronia luco; qua Saturae iacet atra palus gelidusque per imas quaerit iter valles atque in mare conditur Ufens* [those who ploughed vales beside Tiber and Numicus' holy banks, or worked with their ploughshares Rutulian hills, Circeii's promontory, farmlands where Jupiter of Anxur presides, and Feronia, in her green woodland's delight; and others who had homes where lies Satura's black marsh and where chill Ufens seeks out his course low in the valleys till he hides within the sea]). Ancient critics noticed the striving after variation and remarked perceptively that it was not necessarily an improvement on Homer: Macrob.

5.15.14: *in catalogo suo curavit Vergilius vitare fastidium, quod Homerus alia ratione non cavit eadem figura saepe repetita...hic autem variat velut dedecus aut crimen vitans repetitionem...has copias fortasse putat aliquis divinae illi simplicitati praeferendas, sed nescio quomodo Homerum repetitio illa unice decet: est ingenio antiqui poetae digna enumerationique conveniens quod in loco, mera nomina relaturus, non incurvavit se neque minute torsit deducendo stilum per singulorum varietates, sed stat in consuetudine percensentium tamquam per aciem dispositos numerans, quod non aliis quam numerorum fit vocabulis* [in his catalogue Virgil took care to avoid tedium, whereas Homer by a different reasoning did not avoid it but frequently repeated the same formula. Virgil introduced variety, avoiding repetition as a vice or a fault. Some people may judge Virgil's abundance preferable to Homer's simplicity: but somehow the repetition uniquely suits Homer, as worthy of the genius of the ancient poet and appropriate to his catalogue: so that where he had mere names to relate, he did not deviate or make minute contortions in refining his style by varying the individual instances, but like a man conducting a military review, he consistently lists the warriors ranged in line of battle and merely using words for numbers]. However if this is supposed to imply a criticism of Virgil, that would be to overlook the fact that Virgilian *variatio* [variation] is required, here too, by the style of the whole epic, and that *repetitio* [repetition] would have had to be regarded as affected, archaic and unbefitting his style; secondly, and more important, that Virgil is striving after visual effects, i.e. does *not* want to give a straightforward list. How Virgil steers away from identical introductions in the Games was noted above p. 123f. 368

11. I recommend the description of the death of Apsyrtus (4.921ff.); see further, 369 for example, above p. 93 n. 44. One more parallel: we have already compared the funeral of Idmon in Apollonius with the funeral of Misenus; the accounts of each death are equally characteristic of the two writers. From Apollonius we learn (2.817) that Idmon was a soothsayer but that his art did not save him. Idmon was walking by the river when a boar (which is described in detail) dashed out of a reed-bed and crashed into his hip, tearing through sinew and bone; he fell to the ground screaming. The boar was killed by Pallas and Idas; the troubled companions carried the dying Idmon to the ship; he passed away in their hands. The narrative may not be very skilfully arranged, but it is completely clear and factual, displaying no attempt to rouse pathos. In Virgil, the account of the actual event (6.162) is short and in the form of a later recapitulation; all the weight is placed on the feelings of the other participants. Aeneas and Achates had been warned by the Sibyl that they would find a corpse on the shore; sad, and worried as to who it will be, they go to the shore; there they see Misenus lying, *indigna morte peremptum* [dead by an unmerited death]. What is then said in his praise – *quo non praestantior alter aere ciere viros* etc. [excellent beyond all others in stirring hearts with his trumpet of bronze], he had been Hector's brother-in-arms, then the *fortissimus heros* [most valiant hero] had joined Aeneas' retinue – is not intended to stir our pity for the dead man but to make us feel Aeneas' loss; the account of his death, including the word *demens* [in utter folly], shows how Misenus' challenge seems to Aeneas, and with him the poet; he then lingers on the feelings of the survivors: *ergo omnes magno circum clamore fremebant, praecipue pius Aeneas* [so all in loud voices raised the cry, Aeneas the

True above them all]; they then go *flentes* [weeping] to the burial. Apollonius, too, avoids the stereotyped Homeric lines and, like Virgil, coins for example new paraphrases for daybreak; but try and establish a connection between these paraphrases and the situation! See 1.519, 1273; 2.164, 451, 722, 1288: ἠὼς δ' οὐ μετὰ δηρὸν ἐελδομένοισι φαάνθη [and soon dawn appeared to their expectant eyes] (3.827, 1223; 4.183, 883, 978, 1168, 1711).

370   **12.** The place where he goes furthest is probably 4.445ff. in the address to Eros: σχέτλι' Ἔρως, μέγα πῆμα, μέγα στύγος ἀνθρώποισιν etc. [headstrong Love, a great bane, a great curse to men...].

371   **13.** 1.712, 719; 4.68, 450, 529.

372   **14.** This *fortunati ambo* [fortunate pair] is particularly effective as it contrasts with the passage preceding it which has just moved us to pity the pair.

15. Virgil has a similar insertion at 12.500: *quis mihi nunc tot acerba deus, quis carmine caedes...expediat* [what god can now set forth for me in story all the horrors, all the various deeds of death...], to which he adds a personal expression of feeling: *tanton placuit concurrere motu, Iuppiter, aeterna gentis in pace futuras* [did you indeed ordain that nations who were to live together in everlasting peace should clash in such violence?]: here we see his religious sense clashing with his political sympathies.

373   **16.** Naturally this was particularly necessary in Aeneas' narrative, e.g. 3.280, 502; on the other hand, a well-motivated example is the allusion in Helenus' words *hac casti maneant in religione nepotes* (409) [your descendants, if they would be pure of conscience, must stay faithful to this rite].

17. *mox Italus Mnestheus, genus a quo nomine Memmi* (5.117) [he was to become the Italian Mnestheus, and his name originated the family name of Memmius] (also 121, 568, cf. 10.145).

18. That is the custom in Hellenistic aetiology: Norden 193.

374   **19.** Cf. Norden 113.

20. 4.283; 9.67, 399; 12.486.

21. E.g. 10.133, 219, 322, 570. Servius on 4.152: *et bene hac particula utitur; facit enim nos ita intentos ut quae dicuntur putemus videre* [he makes good use of this particle, since he makes us so involved that we seem to see what is being described].

376   **22.** *in medias res non secus ac notas auditorem rapit* [he hurries the reader into the midst of events as if they were already known] (Horace, *Ars Poetica*, 147).

23. ὡς παραδεδομένοις δηλονότι χρώμενος καὶ οὐκ αὐτὸς πλάσσων τὰ ὀνόματα [clearly because he is using the tradition and not making up the names himself] (schol. A on *Iliad* 20.40); see W. Bachmann, *Die ästhet. Anschauungen Aristarchs* I (Nürnberg, 1902) 9f.

380   **24.** The present discussion had reached its present shape when Zielinski's thorough and important work appeared: *Die Behandlung gleichzeitiger Ereignisse im antiken Epos, erster Teil (Homer)*, in *Philologus* Suppl. vol. 8 (1899-1901). It confirms many of my findings: for example, it supplies the Homeric analogy for something which seemed most remarkable to me, the connection of Book 9 with Book 8 (above p. 305). I should have liked to pursue this by comparing Virgil's technique here with Homer's, but since Zielinski has already worked on this and

plans to publish his findings I shall of course refrain from doing so. His expositions have helped me to sharpen my conclusions.

25. Virgil observes a very similar practice when the action moves to a place that   384
has to be described. For example, at 1.158 it does not say: they landed in Libya at a place shaped by nature to be a peaceful harbour: there was a sheltered bay there, etc.; Virgil says: *Libyae vertuntur ad oras. Est in secessu longo locus* etc.: *huc Aeneas subit* [they set course for the coast of Africa. There is a haven there at the end of a long sound etc.... Into it Aeneas moved up]. Cf. 3.13, 73, 210 (here the name of the Strophades is given beforehand: this makes the new beginning in this case all the more striking: *Strophades stant Graio nomine dictae* [the Strophades are fixed, called by this Greek name], 570; 5.124; 7.170, 563; 8.416; 11.522). Also comparable is *limen erat caecaeque fores* (2.453) [there was a secret access through a concealed entrance], *turris erat vasto suspectu et pontibus altis* (9.530) [there was a tower, a dizzy sight from below, with high-level bridges]. Also in 7.601, a new beginning, *mos erat Hesperio in Latio* [there was a custom in Latium, the western land] etc. Cf. Norden 132. A different technique at 1.52; 7.83.

26. I am using Zielinski's terms, op. cit. 412.

27. A peculiarly complicated example is to be found in Book 11, where four   386
actions (or strictly speaking five, but Aeneas' expedition does not come into consideration) go forward in parallel. At 449 we hear that the Trojan cavalry is advancing towards Laurentum. At 520 Turnus sends his men against them, and sets out himself on a different path towards Aeneas: the latter action is followed to its end (530f.): *huc iuvenis nota fertur regione viarum arripuitque locum et silvis insedit iniquis* [hither the young leader hurried by tracks whose direction he well knew. He seized the position and settled down to wait in the confined space of the woods]: and since its later consequences are thus anticipated, it disappears now from the picture. The other two, however, have to be thought of as proceeding further while (*interea* [meanwhile]) the conversation of Diana with Opis takes place (532-96; here the narrative shifts, and (597) returns to its steady advance: *at manus interea muris Troiana propinquat* [meanwhile, a division of Trojans drew near to the city wall]. However, in order not to have to shift again when the enemy is mentioned, we remain on the Trojan side and *see* the enemy advance: *apparent* (605) [they appear]; after that the narrative can deal with both sides (*uterque* [608]) at once.

28. See section III (Speeches) 7, pp. 324ff.   387

29. On similar examples in Homer see Zielinski op. cit. 432ff.

30. In particular the comparison with 1.374: *ante diem clauso componet Vesper*   388
Olympo [the star of evening would surely close heaven's gate, and set the day to sleep, before the end] argues for it.

31. There is no doubt that Virgil often uses *interea* in this sense (cf. Hand, *Tursellinus, seu de particulis Latinis commentarii* [Leipzig, 1829-45] 3.416); e.g. 6.703 certainly does not mean that Aeneas caught sight of the Lethean grove while he was vainly trying to embrace his father, cf. also 3.568; 8.213; 9.159; 11.182 and 12.842 should probably also be understood in the same way. Ovid *Fasti* 3.39: *dixerat (Silvia) et plenam non firmis viribus urnam sustulit; implerat, dum sua visa refert. i n t e r e a crescente Remo crescente Quirino caelesti tumidus pondere* *venter erat: quominus emeritis exiret mensibus annus restabant nitido iam duo signa deo* [Silvia spoke, and lifted the urn with faltering strength: she had filled it while recounting her vision. Meanwhile, as Remus and Quirinus both grew, her stomach was swollen with its divine burden: the shining god still had two signs remaining before the year could complete its months and make its exit]. Here *interea* bridges a space of ten months. Cf. *Fasti* 3.465.

32. Virgil took a different way out in 1.579, but still did not achieve total clarity. The scene can only have been played out like this in the poet's mind: immediately after Dido's words Aeneas and Achates, who had been veiled in mist until then, become visible. Before that happens, however, we have to be told the feelings of both of them; when he says *his animum arrecti dictis...iamdudum erumpere urbem ardebant* [her speech startled them...they had long felt eager to break free from the cloud] he is really recapitulating, and we are doubtless intended to think of Achates' words as simultaneous with those of Dido (to which he makes no reference). But in order to make that perfectly clear, in 586 he should have shown that Dido's speech was ending at the same time.

33. The description which ensues also gives rise to objections. The recapitulation at 10.148-56 had not dealt with everything: Virgil did not let slip the splendid opportunity to insert here the catalogue of the Etruscan auxiliary troops, and he adds to it the description of the night-voyage (156-62); we leave Aeneas and Pallas in an inactive situation: Aeneas worried about the result of the war, Pallas at his side, free of care about the future, looking at the stars and listening to the extraordinary adventures of his new friend. After the catalogue, the appearance of the nymphs should get the action going again; but instead of reminding us of the situation as it was described before, and linking on to it, Virgil makes a fresh start and calmly narrates that day is over, it is already midnight etc.; except that now Aeneas himself sits at the helm, since his worries are keeping him awake, and oversees the manoeuvring of the sails. Of course, doing this, he can neither give himself up to worry about the future nor make use of Pallas' company: the need to describe the same situation a second time has led to inconsistency.

34. 10.148ff., where Virgil avoids a recapitulation in the pluperfect by starting afresh at an earlier point and beginning a new continuous narrative, is discussed above p. 306.

35. Naturally this happens even more often with unimportant matters, such as the coming and going of characters which is made clear by subsequent events; Norden 145 has collected the examples of this in Book 6.

36. Cf. the remarks in the scholia, particularly in Eustathius, collected in Adam, *Die aristotelische Theorie vom Epos nach ihrer Entwicklung bei Griechen und Römern* (Wiesbaden, 1889) 41ff.

37. I remind you of Callimachus' Hymn to Delos and the Bath of Pallas (also, the crow in the Hecale told of both past and future things, Wilamowitz, *Gött. Nachr.* [1893] 734), Theocritus' Heracliscus, Catullus' wedding of Peleus and Thetis, Hera's prophesying in the Hellenistic source of Quintus' Oenone episode (Rohde, *Gr. R.* 110, 5 and above p. 36). This manner is at its most extreme in poems such as Lycophron's *Alexandra*, and the *Apollo* of Alexander the Aetolian; the source of Horace *Odes* 1.15 also belongs here. One may doubtless assume that in countless

poems which eulogized rulers by listing the deeds of their ancestors, or praised cities by describing their κτίσις [foundation], this technique was utilized frequently; it enabled the greatest degree of flattery to be introduced without the speaker seeming to be saying it himself. That is probably why Ennius, in the first book of his *Annales*, made use, like Virgil, of a prediction by Jupiter to show where the action would finally lead. Apollonius, too, often has events being foretold although they lie outside the framework of the poem: thus Glaucus (1.1315f.) predicts the future of Heracles and Polyphemus, Hera (4.809f.) the union of Achilles with Medea, Jason interprets the dream of Euphemus (4.1747); in other places (see L. Hensel, *Weissagungen in der alexandrinischen Poesie* [Diss. Giessen, 1908] 54f.) the poet himself points to the future. All this has to do not with the content of the poem but with the people in it, in fact mostly the minor characters; it is therefore very different from Virgil's technique as discussed above.

38. 84-6: the winds break loose, *insequitur clamor virum* (87) [there follows the   397
shouting of the men] etc.; 88-90: night and thunder-storm, 91: consequences for the sailors, 92: for Aeneas, 94-101: his speech, 102-5: what happened next; 106-7: two lines of description, then the action advances until 123.

39. Look at the short description of the situation which Aeneas finds when he wakes (310-12); also Virgil's refusal to give a detailed description of the scenes of terror at 361.

40. The description seems to have been inserted later, with the sole purpose of   398
introducing the series of kings, who had to be included in the poem in one way or another. The temple is called *Laurentis regia Pici* (171) [the palace of Laurentine Picus], whereas one had to deduce from 61ff. that Latinus was the first to settle the area and had founded Laurentum. According to 177ff. the ancestors of Latinus include Italus, Sabinus, Janus and Saturnus: only the last-named stands in the genealogy given in 47ff., and Faunus, who is named as Latinus' father there, is omitted here. One should note that 194 follows on from 169 without a gap, and 192ff. only repeat what was said in 168ff.

41. 10.496: Pallas' sword-belt: that is meant to be fixed in the memory because it plays a role in Turnus' death later. 7.785: Turnus' helmet (the firebreathing Chimaera symbolizing Turnus' *ardor et ira* [burning anger], the story of Io which shows the revenge of Juno, Turnus' patron-goddess). On the portrayal of outstanding individual pieces of armour, always serving to colour the action in a particular way, see p. 162f. above.

42. Since Virgil laid great importance on the steady advance of the action, I do   400
not believe that he failed to notice the 'fineness of his model', i.e. that the shield in Homer is described in the making, not when complete; but the second alternative postulated by Lessing can hardly be true either ('The things which he wanted to show on the shield seemed to him to be of a nature which did not permit depiction'); even if the shield had been shown in the making, the prophecies could still not have been shown as 'uttered by the god' but would still have to be 'explained by the poet', just as happens in Homer. It remains true however, that Homer narrates and Virgil – so far as *form* is concerned – is describing; that the action advances in Homer and stands still in Virgil; Plüss' objections (270ff.) do not seem to me to meet this point. But it has often been said that Virgil had to portray the shield as

complete principally because he needed this description to round off his book; moreover, as Plüss rightly remarks (284), this connects the depicted scenes more closely with Aeneas than if the shield were shown to us in the smithy of the Cyclopes.

401 **43.** This is even more true of the whole shield, and the many attempts to reconstruct it (yet another in W. Volkmann, *Untersuchung zu Schriftstellern des klassischen Altertums* I [Progr. Breslau, 1906]; see below [p. 366 n. 9] for his other theories) are totally fruitless; one really should face the fact that this is a work of art in a poetic, and not a concrete, sense, as Plüss and others have correctly explained. Virgil himself has stated clearly enough in lines 626-9, particularly in *genus omne futurae stirpis ab Ascanio pugnataque in ordine bella* [all the lineage of future descendants, with the wars which they would fight in due order] (of which only a very few are in fact named in what follows), that the shield contains a large number of pictures which he will not describe in detail. I am pleased to find that Robert (*Studien zur Ilias* [Berlin, 1901] 17) returns to the view that Homer, too, in describing the shield was only vaguely thinking of a real object, so that any attempt to reconstruct that is also without basis. The 'kaleidoscopic' quality of many Homeric images is absent in the descriptions of, for example, Apollonius (1.730ff.) and Moschus (*Europa* 44ff.); the figures and groups described there may not be visual but they are always definite; that is also usually the case in Virgil.

402 **44.** *Daedalus ipse dolos tecti ambagesque resolvit caeca regens filo vestigia* (6.29) [Daedalus himself guided the sightless footsteps by means of a thread and unlocked the building's treacherous, winding ways]. *ter circum Iliacos raptaverat Hectora muros exanimumque auro corpus vendebat* (1.483) [three times he had dragged Hector round the walls of Troy and he was selling his lifeless body for gold]. *Penthesilea...mediis in m i l i b u s ardet* (1.491) [Penthesilea blazed...in the midst of thousands].

45. *vidi atro cum membra fluentia tabo manderet et t e p i d i tremerent sub dentibus artus* (3.626) [I have seen him chew their limbs, all dripping and blackened with clotting blood, and their joints quiver, *still warm*, as his jaws closed].

46. Cf. also the case discussed above (p. 30) where, it is true, the apparition had a different origin, but what we said about it will help us understand why Virgil did not object to a lack of visual quality.

403 **47.** E.g. of the younger Ajax ὀλίγος μὲν ἔην, λινοθώρηξ (2.529) [he was short, with a linen corslet]; ἠΰς τε μέγας τε (653) [brave and tall] of Tlepolemos, κάλλιστος ἀνὴρ ὑπὸ Ἴλιον ἦλθεν (673) [he was the most handsome man to come to Ilium] of Niseus, ὄπιθεν κομόωντες (542) [with their hair in locks at the back] of the Abantes.

48. Lausus 650, Aventinus 666, Catillus and Coras 674, Umbro 751, Turnus 785ff., Camilla 814ff.

49. Kaibel, *Hermes* XXII (1887) 511.

50. Consider the conversations which Aeneas conducts in the Underworld with

404 Palinurus and Deiphobus (and, before the beginning of the second periegesis, with Anchises), and compare them with the lengthy conversations of Odysseus with Teiresias, his mother and Agamemnon.

406 **51.** Horace's judgement (*Ars Poetica* 149): *quae desperat tractata nitescere*

posse relinquit [he leaves aside what he despairs of treating in such a way as to make it shine] would therefore apply to Virgil even more than to Homer.

52. Servius on 1.689: *sane notandum, quod interdum ubi inducit minorem festi-* 407 *nantem parere, maiori respondentem eum non facit, ut hoc loco Cupidinem, ut in quarto, 'ille patris magni parere parabat imperio' et in septimo 'exin Gorgoneis Allecto infecta venenis'* [it should of course be observed that sometimes when he (Virgil) introduces an inferior hastening to obey, he does not present him replying to his superior; as in this case Cupid, and in Book 4 'he prepared to obey the command of the mighty father' and in Book 7 'straightway Allecto, charged with her Gorgon-poisons']. Also schol. Veron. on 7.341: *haec sine ulla lectionis intercapedine pronuntianda sunt, quia* κωφὸν πρόσωπον *induxit hoc ex nocendi festinatione ideo-que illam perfecto officio induxit loquentem* [these events are to be narrated without any interval of speech, because he introduces this 'non-speaking character' because of her haste to do harm and for that reason he introduces her as 'speaking' by the performance of her duty]. Naturally it would not occur to any of the ancient critics to criticize the introduction of 'mute characters' as Georgii (323) suggests: πρῶτος Ὅμηρος πρόσωπα κωφὰ παρήγαγεν εἰς τὴν τραγῳδίαν [Homer was the first to introduce 'mute characters' into tragedy] (schol. *Iliad* 1.322), and there are plenty of them in Homer. No fault is found with these passages; the ancient critics were aware, as we are, that they were unusual, and they were looking, as we are, for an explanation: it is to be hoped that ours is better than pointing to the *festinatio* [haste] of the messenger.

53. *nate, meae vires, mea magna potentia solus...ad te confugio et supplex tua* 408 *numina posco* [Son, you alone are my strength, and all my might is in you...now I appeal to you, and humbly pray to your divine majesty for aid] (Venus, 1.664); *hunc mihi da proprium...laborem, hanc operam, ne noster honos infractave cedat fama loco* [do a service for me, and grant me your efforts, to prevent my worship and my renown from suffering injury and taking second place] (Juno, 7.331).

54. This serves to achieve a definite effect in both cases: when Venus addresses Amor we see not the mischievous boy portrayed by Apollonius but the cosmic power, the god who is mighty despite his youth; when Juno pleads, we see how far her hatred has driven her (*dubitem haud equidem implorare quod usquam est* [7.311] [I am not one to refrain from asking aid from any power, anywhere]): she lowers herself to *plead* with the hated demon of hell.

55. *hic qui forte velint rapido contendere cursu, invitat pretiis animos et prae-* 409 *mia ponit* (291) [here he issued invitation and offered prizes to anyone who might wish to compete in speed of foot]; *protinus Aeneas celeri certare sagitta invitat qui forte velint et praemia ponit* (485) [Aeneas forthwith invited any who wished to compete with the swift flight of the arrow, and he named the prizes].

56. 9.737-9, 741f., 747f., 10.441-3, 449-51, 481, 581-3, 649f., 773-5, 811f., 875f., 878-82, 11.715-7, 12.889-93 (this latter is the longest of these speeches: but here Aeneas is trying to make Turnus stand and fight instead of running away), 894f. The scornful speech of Numanus (9.598-620), is long because of the situation.

57. E.g. 10.524-9.

58. A. W. Schlegel put it very well, *Werke* XI (Vienna, 1822-5) 193f. 414

59. When Hephaestus (*Iliad* 18.394ff.) tells Charis the story of his rescue by

Thetis and Eurynome, it is not because she needs to know about it at that moment, but because Homer's audience needs to be told the relationship of piety in which the god knows that he stands to his petitioner.

415

60. Juno speaking about Minerva's revenge on the Greeks (1.39), Venus' speech about Antenor (1.242), about Dido (1.341), Dido's speech about Teucer's presence in Sidon (1.619), Priam about Achilles (2.540), Achaemenides' speech containing the story of Odysseus visiting Polyphemus (3.623), Neptune about the rescue of Aeneas before Troy (5.803), the Sibyl about the Aloides and Salmoneus (6.582), Charon about Hercules and Theseus (6.395), Latinus about Dardanus (7.205), Tiberinus about the Arcadian settlement (8.51), Diomedes about the νόστοι [homecomings] of the Greeks and the metamorphosis of his companions into birds (11.261). Speeches which have narration as their sole or most important aim – Sinon, Palinurus, Deiphobus etc. – naturally do not belong here.

61. *o mihi praeteritos referat si Iuppiter annos, qualis eram cum primam aciem Praeneste sub ista stravi* (8.560-1) [Oh, if only Jupiter would bring back to me the years which are gone and make me as I was when beneath Praeneste's wall I brought down their front rank] = *Iliad* 11.670: εἴθ' ὣς ἡβώοιμι, βίη δέ μοι ἔμπεδος εἴη, ὡς ὁπότ' Ἠλείοισι καί ἡμῖν νεῖκος ἐτύχθη etc. [if only I were as young and vigorous as I was when strife arose between me and the Eleans]. But the Homeric tale extends over nearly a hundred lines, Virgil's over only seven lines, and as if to make the insertion even less obvious, the sentence is continued at 568 from where it left off.

416

62. These lines cannot possibly be regarded as a parenthesis inserted into the speech by the poet himself; that would be without parallel not only in Virgil but, as far as I know, in the whole of ancient epic; and one will look in vain in Virgil for similar peculiarities. And how was the ancient reader supposed to perceive that this was the intention of the poet?

63. The use of her name in 11.537: *neque enim novus iste Dianae venit amor* [for this love which Diana bears to her is nothing new] and 582: *sola contenta Diana aeternum...amorem colit* [she finds complete happiness in Diana alone...and cherishes unending love] might be acceptable, although in the following examples (such as 12.56: *per si quis Amatae tangit honos animum* [by any regard for Amata which can touch your heart]) the mention of the name is more justified since it creates greater pathos (on this now see Norden 259f.). But we cannot understand it in *donum Triviae* (566) [the gift to Diana], and it is completely incomprehensible that Diana, who has protected young Camilla when she was summoned by Metabus, does not say this of herself in the first person: I regard this as irrefutable evidence that the narrative was not originally written for Diana to speak.

64. See p. 189 n. 52 above.

65. Ribbeck considered from line 537 *neque enim* to 584 *intemerata colit* to be a later addition. He has drawn the wrong boundaries, at the very least, since, as Sabbadini (*Studi critici* 87) rightly emphasizes, the words *cara mihi comitumque foret nunc una mearum* (586) [she could have been one of my companions still, and still dear to me] can never have followed directly upon *cara mihi ante alias* (537) [dear to me beyond all others]. Furthermore, if one did assume that the passage in question was composed later, this would still not explain the strangely impersonal form of the narrative. Thus Sabbadini will be right to regard the narrative as composed earlier than the rest of Book 11. However, the speech can never have consisted only of lines 535, 536 and 587-94; the poet must have intended from the start to explain the motivation of Diana's intervention. As far as I can see, this leaves only the possibility that, because the material particularly attracted him, Virgil wrote this little epyllion at an early stage of his work, before he had visualized   417 Camilla the warrior, the splendidly accoutred Volscian queen; and at that time he did not spare a thought as to how the episode might be incorporated; that later, when he was writing Book 11 and came to Diana's speech, he inserted the finished piece as it was, without adapting it to the new context and to the new character which he had given Camilla meanwhile. That he would not have left things like this can only be a supposition, which stands and falls with my conviction of Virgil's conscientiousness where artistry and technique are concerned.

66. *per patrios manis et spes surgentis Iuli te precor, hanc animam serves*   418 *gnatoque patrique* [by your father's spirit and by all your hopes of Iulus now growing to manhood, spare this life of mine for my son and for my father]. This may be developed from Hector's plea (*Iliad* 22.338) λίσσομ' ὑπὲρ ψυχῆς καὶ γούνων σῶν τε τοκήων [I beseech you by your life and your knees and your own parents], but it is characteristic of Virgil to have developed the simple thought, 'I beg you for the sake of what you hold most dear' into something completely different.

67. This is usually a term of contempt applied by enemies to the Trojans: Juno   420 4.103 and 7.294; Amata 7.358, 363; Allecto 7.430; Turnus 7.579; 9.134; 11.403; 12.75, 99; Numanus 9.599, 617; the matrons of Laurentum 11.484.

68. This observation was also used by the interpreters of Homer, to explain   421 contradictions between what someone said and the rest of the narrative: schol. *Iliad* 18.175: ὅταν...ἡ ῏Ιρις εἴπῃ τῷ ᾿Αχιλλεῖ ὅτι βούλεται ὁ ῞Εκτωρ τὸν Πάτροκλον αἰκίσασθαι, νοητέον μὴ τἀληθὲς ὑποφαίνειν, ἀλλὰ παρορμῆσαι αὐτὸν εἰς τὴν κατὰ τῶν βαρβάρων ὀργήν [when Iris says to Achilles that Hector wishes to mutilate Patroclus, one must realise that she is not revealing the truth but motivating him to be angry with the barbarians]. Hera's dispatch of Iris to Achilles is the model for the scene in Virgil (9.1ff.), the dispatch of Iris to Turnus for the purpose of παρορμῆσαι [motivating]; it is possible that Virgil is deliberately imitating the Homeric ψεῦδος [falsehood] when he has Iris exaggerating the truth: see above p. 305.

69. A real λόγος ἐσχηματισμένος [argument taking up a posture], which seeks   422 to achieve something quite different from what it says, cf. Servius on 33, 42, 60. Servius also regards as rhetorical Latinus' speech (11.302ff.), which conceals an attack on Turnus: on 11.312: *excusatio haec ostendit obliquam esse in Turnum orationem Latini* [this releasing from blame indicates that Latinus' speech is obliquely directed at Turnus], i.e. a σχῆμα πλάγιον [oblique figure]. Similarly at the end of Turnus' speech, on 11.434 he says *utitur ductu* (σχηματισμός): *nam oblique promittit se singulari certamine dimicare velle, cum nolit* [he is making use of a leading argument (posturing): for he obliquely professes to wish to fight in single combat, when in fact he does not].

70. *Italiam petiit fatis auctoribus, esto, Cassandrae impulsus furiis* (10.67f.) [the fates encouraged him to sail for Italy. All right! He was actuated by Cassandra's raving].

423   **71.** E.g. Quintil. 2.17.20: *orator cum falso utitur pro vero, scit esse falsum eoque se pro vero uti; non ergo falsam habet ipse opinionem sed fallit alium. nec Cicero, cum se tenebras offudisse iudicibus in causa Cluentiana gloriatus est, nihil ipse vidit* [an orator, when he substitutes falsehood for the truth, is aware of the falsehood and of the fact that he is substituting it for the truth. He deceives others but not himself. When Cicero boasted that he had thrown dust in the eyes of the jury in the Cluentius case, he was far from being blinded himself].

    72. On 9.136: *sunt et mea contra fata mihi* [I have a destiny of my own]. If in fact this does refer to a particular divine command and not merely to a general belief that right will prevail, then Turnus could well be referring to the command given to him by Juno in a dream: *ipsa palam fari omnipotens Saturnia iussit* (7.428) [the Saturnian queen, the almighty, herself commanded me to say this], as well as to Iris' warning which promised victory (9.6ff.). On the other hand, Servius is perhaps right to see a deliberate untruth in the report of the Latins to Diomedes *multas viro se adiungere gentes* (8.13) [that numerous peoples were joining Aeneas]: though perhaps it would be even closer to the truth to call it a deliberate exaggeration and distortion of what the Trojan messenger Ilioneus said at 7.236ff.: *multi nos populi...et petiere sibi et voluere adiungere gentes* [many nations and races have sought alliance and wished to join us].

    73. Schol. on *Iliad* 1.299: ἐπεί μ' ἀφέλεσθέ γε δόντες [since you (plural) are taking her away after giving her] as against the attempt of Zenodotus to do away with the ψεῦδος [misrepresentation] by 'correcting' to ἐπεί μ' ἐθέλεις ἀφελέσθαι [since you (singular) wish to take her away]: ὀργῇ κοινοποιεῖ (ὁ 'Αχιλλεὺς) εἰς ἅπαντας, ὡς τὸν αἴτιον τῆς ἀφαιρέσεως ἀγνοῶν [in his anger (Achilles) involves all of them together as if he was unaware who was responsible for taking her away] (following the reading of Lehrs and Friedländer).

424   **74.** *Pallas exurere classem Argivum atque ipsos potuit submergere ponto* (1.39) [Pallas Athene was able to gut the Argives' fleet with fire and drown all of them].

    75. For further examples I am now able to refer you to Norden's analysis of the speeches in Book 6. However, I consider that Norden applies the rhetorical *schemata* [figures] too rigorously. I believe that Virgil himself would not have felt that it suited his own style to compose the *sermones* [conversations] of his characters according to the *schema* of the *orationes* [rhetorical speeches]. When, in a conversation, one of the two participants, before giving his own message or presenting his own story, immediately replies to the other's words, as for example Aeneas to the Sibyl (103-5) or Palinurus (347f.) and Deiphobus (509f.) to Aeneas, it can hardly be called a proem in the technical sense; nor do I think that lines 116-23 in Aeneas' speech, which are very closely connected with 110-16, or Palinurus' requests to Aeneas 363-71, can be regarded as separate from the actual λόγος [narration], and called an epilogue. When Palinurus starts by refuting Aeneas' mistaken assumption,

425   and then narrates what has really happened to him and what he is now suffering, and finally adds the plea to be rescued from his misery, this arrangement arises directly from the subject-matter and there is no need to explain it by reference to rhetorical doctrines; nor do I believe that Deiphobus' narrative (509-30) would have turned out any differently if Virgil had never heard of any rules concerning προδιήγησις [prologue] and διήγησις [narration] or περιστάσεις [circumstances]. When I say 'rules'

of the art, I do not mean special instructions about the arrangement and execution of the *partes orationis* [parts of a speech] so much as the general rules, that there must be a *lucidus ordo* [clear arrangement], that the end needs a climax, etc.

76. If Virgil, as Servius reports, recited lines 323-6 *ingenti adfectu* [with great feeling], one can be sure that at the words *saltem si qua mihi de te suscepta fuisset ante fugam suboles* (327) [at least, if I had a son of yours, conceived before you   426 left...] he changed to a completely different tone of voice, softer, more tender, melancholy.

77. When (4.337), after Aeneas has started by expressing his gratitude, he introduces his actual defence with *pro re pauca loquar* [I shall speak briefly of the facts], this exception is well motivated: he was on the point of losing control – *dum memor ipse mei, dum spiritus hos regit artus* [for as long as I have consciousness and breath of life controls my movement] – and is, as it were, reminding himself to keep calm and to explain.

78. When he turns away from Drances; this is the transition to the second part: *nunc ad te et tua magna, pater, consulta revortor* [now, sire, I return to you and to your weighty proposal], and then discussion of three possibilities: *si...* (411-8), *sin...* (419-33), *quod si...* (434-44).

79. See the material in C. Hentze, 'Die Monologe in den homerischen Epen',   427 *Philol.* 63 (1904) 12ff. Leo's discussion of the question ('Der Monolog in Drama', *Abh.d. Gött. Ges. d. Wiss.* X. 3 [1903] 2ff.) has led me to a thorough reappraisal.

80. For example, Penelope's lament (*Od.* 20.61), which is really a soliloquy but is introduced as a prayer to Artemis.

81. E.g. *Iliad* 2.3, 10.5, 14.16, 16.646, *Odyssey* 4.116.

82. *Iliad* 11.404 Odysseus, 17.91 Agamemnon, 21.553 Agenor, 22.99 Hector: the decision is introduced each time by the line ἀλλὰ τίη μοι ταῦτα φίλος διελέξατο θυμός [but why has my dear spirit spoken to me thus?]; this is an indication   428 that a εὑρετής [inventor] was the model for this. This is not the same as cases where the speaker finishes the expression of his feelings by coming to some sort of decision, as in Achilles' expression of amazement (*Iliad* 21.54ff.: ἀλλ᾽ ἄγε δὴ καὶ δουρὸς ἀκωκῆς ἡμετέροιο γεύσεται [60] [but surely he will taste the point of my spear]), and other examples mentioned in the next note.

83. *Iliad* 18.6: Achilles faced with the news of the death of Patroclus; 21.54: Achilles at the sight of Lycaon, believed dead; and, very similar, 20.344: after the departure of Aeneas; 22.297: Hector after the disappearance of the supposed Deiphobus: here the monologue is not explicitly designated as such; he says merely φώνησεν (296) [he said] and φωνήσας (306) [having said]. In *Odyssey* 20.18 the words are explicitly described as an address to the κραδίη [heart].

84. On the other hand, Achilles' words (*Iliad* 20.425f.), introduced with the words εὐχόμενος ἔπος ηὔδα [he spoke these words in exultation] represent a genuinely emotional cry, not a monologue.

85. The necessary words at the end of Poseidon's action are clothed in the form of an address to the distant Odysseus, like Zeus' address to the distant Hector (*Iliad* 17.201), and, shortly after, to Achilles' horses.

86. It is certainly also intended to be regarded as an intensification when in Book 1 we are told Juno's thoughts (*haec secum* [37] [these words to herself], *talia*

flammato secum dea corde volutans [507] [debating so with herself in her fiery
429 brain]), whereas in Book 7 we hear her actual words (*haec effundit pectore dicta*
[297] [she spoke a torrent of words], *haec ubi dicta dedit* [323] [having spoken so]):
Virgil makes a sharper distinction than Homer between this monologue forced out
by emotion, and her calm, reflective conversation with herself.

87. An even closer comparison than with Euripides is with Seneca, for example
in the monologue of Juno which begins the *Hercules*: that probably indicates that
Virgil has learnt something from post-Euripidean tragedy.

88. Here, too, the arrangement is very calculated and schematic, particularly in
Book 7: (1) Establishing the theme of *indignatio*: 293, 294. (2) A backward glance
at what has happened, divided into two parts by the ὑποφορά [the imaginary objec-
tion] *at credo* (297f.) [I suppose]): Aeneas in Troy 294-7, Aeneas on his wanderings
299-303. (3) Result for the present time, with an *argumentum ex contrario* [argu-
ment by contrast]: 304-10. (4) Prediction of the future: 310-22.

89. On the monologue of Aeneas interpolated at 2.577 see above p. 26f.

90. 3.464, 636, 770; 4.30.

430 **91.** E.g. 5.700-3; 9.399-401; using indirect speech and then continuing in the
form of a report: 4.283ff., in imitation of the Homeric ὧδε δὲ οἱ φρονέοντι
δοάσσατο κέρδιον εἶναι = *haec alternanti potior sententia visa est* [as he reflected,
this seemed to him the better course].

92. *Iliad* 24.725 etc. over Hector's body, cf. 19.287, 315 over the body of
Patroclus. 22.430: Τρῳῇσιν δ' Ἑκάβη ἁδινοῦ ἐξῆρχε γόοιο [Hecuba led the Trojan
women in vehement lamentation], 476 (Andromache) ἀμβλήδην γοόωσα μετὰ
Τρῳῇσιν ἔειπεν [with sudden bursts of lamentation she addressed the Trojan
women].

431 **93.** Aeneas' brief words after the death of Palinurus (5.870f.) may also be cited
here.

94. In individual cases, it will still not always be easy to distinguish between
traditional elements in the poetic language, and borrowings from the theory and
practice of fine writing. For example, Norden (386) believes that the influence of
rhetoric on Latin writers is shown by Virgil's frequent habit of putting together
several nouns, each qualified by one adjective, in such a way that two such pairs of
words often contrast with each other, or form a chiasmus. But when I see this
stylistic device used often by Theocritus in his non-bucolic poems (e.g. 17.29, 32,
34f., 37; 18.26ff., 43ff.; 22.40ff.), and never more often – together with chiasmus –
than in the short Aeolic Ἠλακάτη (28), whereas in Latin poetry it is hardly ever
432 used to such an extent as it is in Catullus, particularly in the glyconics of his
marriage-song (61, 9-13, 101-9), it seems to me that a different explanation is called
for. (See now R. Gimm, *De Vergili stilo bucolico quaest. sel.* [Diss Leipzig, 1910]
63). Moreover, as far as I can see, the doubling and piling-up of adjectives serves
quite different purposes in oratory, for example that of Cicero, and in the poetry of
Theocritus and the Roman νεώτεροι [Neoterics]: in the one we find either sharp
antithesis or σεμνόν [gravity], in the other γλυκύ [sweetness].

95. The ancient critics were even worse in this respect; there is nothing more
unsatisfactory and boring than, for example, Macrobius' discussion of Virgilian
pathos from the standpoint of the rhetoric of the schools.

96. However, as time passes I have become very doubtful whether in these cases 433
one should not regard the epideictic poem rather than the epideictic speech as
Virgil's model. But this question cannot be pursued here; I hope to deal with it
thoroughly in another context.

97. I therefore consider it misguided when, for example, Penquitt explains, in the
dissertation mentioned above (p. 112 n. 33), that in writing the speeches of Dido
(4.307ff. or 534ff.) Virgil was following *declamatorum scholasticorum praecepta
de suasoria data* [the rules of scholastic declaimers on the subject of persuasive
speeches], just because the separate thoughts can be listed under the well-known
τελικὰ κεφάλαια [headings concerning ends] of ἄδικον [unjust], ἀδύνατον [im-
possible] etc. One would only be able to say that it follows the rules of rhetoric if, as
is sometimes possible with Ovid, one could show that the whole structure of the 434
speech is governed by these τόποι [commonplaces]; moreover, one could label every
sentence of a *suasor* [advocate] in the present-day German *Reichstag* as δίκαιον
[just], συμφέρον [expedient] etc. without proving anything about its relationship to
rhetoric.

4

Composition

1. Unity: Beginning and ending

Aristotle had taught that unity of action was called for in epic as much as in tragedy; he had removed the misconception that this unity could be replaced by unity of person or unity of time; he had, moreover, defined a unified action as one which is whole, complete in itself, with a beginning, a middle and an end; it may consist of parts, but only of integrating parts, none of which can be omitted or moved around without spoiling the whole. That an epic can apparently fulfil these conditions and yet lack artistic unity is shown by the epic of Apollonius (we will disregard the episodic aspect for the moment): he has selected the unified action of the voyage of the Argonauts; he begins, completely in accordance with the rules, with the reason for the voyage, and ends by returning to the point of departure: he believed that this was a ὅλη καὶ τελεία πρᾶξις [whole and complete action]. What he did not realize was that it is not the voyage itself, but its goal, the gaining and keeping of the fleece, which is the πρᾶξις [action] upon which the reader's interest is directed; and that therefore the detailed description of the return journey, taking up several hundred lines after the fleece has been recovered from Colchis, seems to be an inorganic appendage, spoiling the unity of the whole rather than completing it. Virgil has sought to follow Aristotle's rules, and has learnt from Apollonius' mistake. At the centre of his poem stands the eponymous hero, but it is not he who creates the unity, but an action: the migration of the Trojans, or the transportation of the Penates from Troy to Latium. The announcement of the contents in the proem takes Aeneas as its starting-point: *arma virumque cano* [of arms and a man I sing]; what is said about
him then leads to a mention of the goal which has been set for the action, *dum inferret deos Latio* [to bring gods to Latium]; the final words emphasize the importance of the action: *genus unde Latinum Albanique patres atque altae moenia Romae* [that was the origin of the Latin nation, the Lords of Alba, and the proud battlements of Rome]. The starting-point of the action is the capture of Troy.[1] but the finishing-point is not, as one might perhaps expect from the words of the proem, the foundation of the city of Lavinium, but the removal of the last hindrance which stands in the way of a permanent settlement: the death of Turnus; with that the poetic interest of the material is exhausted. One may doubt whether Aristotle, who abstracted his rules from the *Iliad* and the *Odyssey*, would have thought it justified to end at this point, and whether he would have allowed the action of the *Aeneid* to be called τελεία [complete];[2] in fact we have to realize that what is happening here is the bold transference of dramatic technique to the epic. The *Iliad* and the *Odyssey* do contain references to the future experiences of the protagonists, but the action as such of each poem is narrated right through to its end, including all its direct

consequences. A dramatist is content to have reached the dénouement and to have indicated the result: in very many cases it is impossible to present the actual result, for technical or poetic reasons: it is enough that we know that Philoctetes will go to Troy, that Heracles will die by fire; in *Oedipus Rex*, Sophocles can even allow himself to leave his hero's immediate future uncertain, once he has shown him to be inwardly destroyed, and has thus exhausted the tragic material. This principle is even more obvious in comedy: it is all over once the father has agreed to the marriage, or once other obstacles which stood in the way have been removed. It is in this sense that Virgil set the τέλος [end] of his action where he did: we know what Latinus will do after the death of Turnus (12.38), that Lavinia will not refuse the marriage which her father commands, backed up as it is by divine advice (any more than any Roman maiden could); finally we have heard from Jupiter's own mouth the form which the unification of the two nations will take (12.834ff.): the curtain can fall.[3]

2. The whole and the parts 438

The second requirement is that the separate parts of the epic shall be essential components of the whole. This does not mean that Aristotle forbids the interruption of the action by occasional episodes – he himself (*Poetics* 23.1459a 35) praises Homer's numerous episodes, among which he reckons, for example, the Catalogue of Ships; but he does seem (without saying anything more precise on the subject) to have required that the episode, too, should arise from the action in a probable or necessary way, and contribute something to the whole. In any case, he found fault with any 'episodic' plot (9.1451b 34), that is, one in which the separate sections follow one another in a way which is neither probable nor necessary; or, to express it positively, appear to be arranged completely haphazardly or arbitrarily. This is therefore connected with the requirement of careful motivation, but is not identical with it; a piece of action may be excellently motivated in itself and yet be an unconnected episode which interrupts the whole, standing beside the main action rather than arising from it and leading back into it. If we look at the composition of the *Aeneid* in this light, it is clear that Virgil was attempting to follow Aristotle's rules.

The main action of the *first* half of the *Aeneid* is the journey of Aeneas from Troy to Latium. Book 2 deals with its cause, Book 3 the first – longer but less interesting – part of the journey, Books 4, 5 and 6 its last three stages. The main parts of these three books, Dido's suffering and death, the Games, and the visit to the Underworld, were conceived as episodes; we see this clearly, in spite of all the art which the poet has subsequently devoted to concealing the fact; however, he has also attempted to transform the episodes into essential components of the whole. The love of Dido is the greatest 'temptation' which the hero faces; he is in danger of succumbing to it and of forgetting his goal for ever; but he pulls himself together and overcomes it. So far, the most severe critic would have nothing to find fault with; however, the nucleus of Book 4 contributes to the main action only during its first half, as long as Dido is still making attempts to keep Aeneas from departing; everything else directs 439 the reader's attention away from the main action and the main character. And yet Dido's suffering and death are not narrated for their own sakes: the peak of the narrative is the curse which Dido hurls upon the further destiny of Aeneas and upon the future of Rome; the last words of the dying woman (*nostrae omina mortis* [the evil omen of my death]) take it up again, and the reader knows that it will be fulfilled.[4] Regarded in this way, Dido's suffering and death have an effect not only on the events narrated later in the epic, but far beyond: what might appear to be an episode becomes an essential component, not only of the poem, but of the history of Rome. It is true that it is only the reader of Book 4 who feels this: in the second half of the poem Virgil has not referred again to Dido's curse, but has given a new motivation to the sorrows and dangers suffered by Aeneas, in the form of Juno's hatred; he has even refrained from making Juno refer to Aeneas' offence against Dido, even in her *indignatio* (7.293ff.) [indignant speech] or in her hate-filled speech (10.63ff.). It is easy to see why: Juno herself had arranged the union which became Dido's tragedy, and therefore it could not be she who avenged it; also she herself had much weightier reasons to be an enemy of the Trojans; and yet she was indispensable as an actual driving-force for the whole second half of the poem. So, from a technical point of view, Dido's curse is to be placed on a level with Creusa's prophecy at the end of Book 2 and Anchises' predictions at the end of Book 6: they are significant at the time, opening up the view of the future, but the motifs are dropped later because the narrative requires different presuppositions.

The Games have become, as we have seen, the setting for the burning of the ships, which forms on the one hand the last severe test of Aeneas, and leads on the other hand to the foundation of Segesta, the most important permanent result of Aeneas' wanderings. To this extent the games must be regarded as a necessary component, although they have been treated in greater detail than is warranted by their significance, and have become an independent episode.

The visit to the Underworld has obviously proved the most difficult episode for Virgil to provide with an organic connection with the main action. It is clear that the decision to take Aeneas into the Underworld was quite independent of the provision of a motivation for it: here was an unparalleled opportunity to rival Homer, not only in form but above all in content: in place of the *mythos* [story] of the *Odyssey* he would supply a poetic narrative full of serious and sublime wisdom and full of enthusiastic patriotism; Odysseus had brought all kinds of strange information back to the upper world, Aeneas was to be permitted to see the wicked punished, the good rewarded, to be initiated into the mysteries of life after death, and to gaze upon the splendour of Rome and of her greatest son, Augustus. In this way, this Book was made to contribute an enormous amount to the real purpose of his whole poem; but how could he arrange that it should also serve the action of the poem? Virgil stood in Homer's thrall: Odysseus is sent by Circe into the Underworld to question the spirit of Teiresias, who will give him information about the ways and means of returning home. Teiresias does indeed give him this information, but the whole prophecy remains without results: what Odysseus hears in the conversation about conditions at home has already been forgotten directly afterwards, by the time he speaks with Anticleia; for his homeward journey Circe is able to give much more accurate information; the later reconciliation with Poseidon is not completed in the

440

Odyssey. But the motif did seem to Virgil to be usable: in 6.890-2 we have his provisional attempt at using it: Anchises instructs his son about the wars which lie ahead of him, about the nations and city of Latinus, about the means of overcoming all these difficulties. However, Virgil did not keep to this plan; he could see that the motivation of the future consequences could not be used, any more than it could in the *Odyssey*, for if Aeneas knows precisely what is going to happen, he will have no more doubts, no disappointments, no worries. That is why Virgil transferred the equivalent predictions to the mouth of the Sibyl;[5] her obscure, cryptic words do not anticipate later developments. He then needed a new motive for the descent of 441 Aeneas, one which had probably occurred to him during the writing of the first draft, but which now came to the fore. The new driving-force for Aeneas, which commands him to face even the terrors of the Underworld, is his *pietas*, the wish to speak once more to his beloved father, who has been asking for him; to see him not just in a momentary vision, such as is possible on earth, but to make a real visit and have a proper, loving conversation. This venture on the part of Aeneas would certainly help to show his character, but it would not contribute to the main action: this contribution is made, as I have tried to show above, p. 225, by the protreptic significance of the visit to the Underworld: Aeneas is to be strengthened and confirmed for the more difficult part of his task which awaits him in Latium. In the poet's opinion, the purpose of all eschatological mythology is to support and strengthen mankind in their struggle after the Good; it is no different here, where Aeneas is not merely told, but allowed to see for himself. How far Virgil has succeeded in making this intention clear is not the question here; we are only interested in establishing whether we are right to perceive this intention, and, with it, Virgil's efforts to make Book 6, too, an organic part of the whole.

The action of the *second* half of the poem runs from Aeneas' arrival in Latium to the final establishment of the Trojan settlement. Of the larger component parts, one which we may regard as having been conceived as an episode is the *aristeia* of Camilla; to provide the opportunity for it, Aeneas and Turnus have to be removed from the scene, and the poet returns us to the main action when Camilla's defeat brings Turnus back to Laurentum, which also thwarts the ambush which would otherwise have endangered Aeneas. But the motivation of Aeneas' separate expedition is not carried out entirely satisfactorily, and we are left with the impression that it is merely an episode. Among the rest, episodes in Aristotle's sense in the second half are the catalogues in Books 7 and 10, which are perfectly appropriate at the start of the war; the Evander scenes in Book 8, connected very well with the course of the main action; the Nisus story in Book 9, which is only significant within the book, and will be discussed below, as will the description of the shield in Book 8: here, too, it is obvious that the motivation was added afterwards.

3. Catalogues 442

What we have said so far about the unity of the book referred to the uninterrupted course of the action, the logical cohesion of the whole. We have seen that Virgil strove to achieve this, but could not fully disguise the fact that the separate parts of the poem had not grown organically from a single unified conception. The real artistic unity, which means unity both of conception and of effect, is apparent in the separate parts of Virgil's work; wherever the content of a component part of the poem makes it complete in itself, Virgil has also presented it as an artistic unity.

We see such unity (to begin with the least important) in lists of names and similar catalogues, which would seem to resist artistic shaping; if they contain a great number of items then they soon become monotonous and confused, giving the impression of a shapeless, haphazard jumble. The simplest means of countering this is to group the items systematically to produce an orderly, tidy whole; further, where possible, one can put together things which are related, making it easier for the audience to perceive the whole as a unity. Minor examples of this grouping are the list of the men who climbed out of the Wooden Horse (p. 53 n. 28 above), the long list of names in the *aristeiae* (p. 171f. above), and the enumeration of the Latin colonies, 6.773 (2 x 4); a major example of the principle is best seen in the Parade of Heroes in 6.[6] Nearly thirty names from the history of Rome are given here, and their bearers are mostly characterized, briefly or in more detail; if this list were not divided up it would be monstrous. Virgil creates three groups[7] – the Alban descend-

443 ants of Aeneas down to Romulus, the heroes of the earlier period, what we could call the time of the Roman city state, and the heroes of the developing world-empire[8] – without feeling bound by the chronology in the details; the second group is separated from the first and third, not by unpoetic formulae of conclusion and transition, but by two pictures from the present and the most recent past: after Romulus we see the *alter Romulus* [second Romulus], Augustus; after Torquatus and Camillus, the conquerors of Gaul, we see Gaul's conqueror, Caesar, and his opponent, Pompey. These inserted figures are lifted out of the crowd by their position, and at the same time serve to break up the pedantic chronological order, and to give a touch of haphazardness without spoiling the arrangement of the whole. The youthful Marcellus is the third contemporary to appear, and rounds off the whole, linked to the third group by his ancestor, the conqueror of Syracuse, who forms the necessary complement to the figure named last in the third group, Fabius Maximus.[9]

444 A list in the proper sense is to be found in the two catalogues in Books 7 and 10; but Virgil took care that they should not be mere lists like the Homeric Catalogue. In Book 7, Virgil places Mezentius and Lausus at the head, Turnus and Camilla at the end, so that the less important figures are framed by the few who were to play major roles in the battle. Starting from these fixed points at the beginning and end, he has arranged the rest so that the whole presents the following picture: first the places nearest at hand – Caere and Aventinus, Tibur and Praeneste – then three pairs of related names covering the wider surrounding area – Faliscans and Sabines, Aurunci and South Campanians,[10] inhabitants of Aequicula and Marsians – and we finish by returning to nearby areas: Aricia and Ardea, and finally the Volscian Camilla. We are intended to receive the impression of a line which runs back to its starting-point, encircling a closed whole.[11]

4. Sequences of scenes

The closest thing to these lists are actions which consist of a series of similar scenes in sequence. Such actions become an artistic unity if they can be connected in a logical sequence; where this cannot be done, as for example with the Games, then symmetrical grouping combined with variation and heightening of interest can help to avoid the effect of a mere loose assemblage (p. 123f. above). Elsewhere, Virgil has often successfully overcome the episodic effect that clings to such actions. For example, the *Iliu Persis* in Quintus and Tryphiodorus consists of loose episodes: we are faced with a large number of single events which could be decreased or increased or rearranged without affecting the composition. Virgil replaces this with a tight narrative which strives towards a definite goal, in which the single events – Panthus, Androgeus, Coroebus' ruse, the rape of Cassandra, the storming of the citadel, the death of Priam – are necessary components, none of which could change places with another. Dionysius' account of Aeneas' wanderings is episodic: the only connecting thread is the geographical one, but if there were half as many stops, or twice as many, the composition would not be altered. In Virgil, up to the landing in Italy, each individual stop, with the exception of the brief mention of Actium, is a necessary stage on the way to the goal which was indicated at the beginning. Many of Homer's battle-descriptions are episodic: in Virgil, in each of the four books, each individual part has its definite place in the whole: in each book there is a series of single events, which is well arranged in itself, and forms a phase of the whole battle and causes the action to develop in a particular direction; at the end of each act a definite goal has been reached. Finally, the visit to the Underworld in the *Odyssey* is arranged episodically: the sequence of groups – heroines, heroes of the Trojan War, other dead – appears haphazard; of the great number of conversations which Odysseus had, he selects the most important, but could tell a great deal more; out of the great number of people who have been dead for a long time he sees six – he would have seen many more if he had not run off in terror. What Aeneas sees is not haphazard; his path leads to Anchises, and on his way he has to pass all the different areas of the Underworld, and he sees, or hears of, all the different classes of dead people, from those not yet buried to those who are ready to rise again to a new life. Nor does he converse with an arbitrary number: from the first group he speaks to Palinurus, among the victims of unhappy love he speaks to Dido, out of all those fallen in war he speaks to Deiphobus: in each case the need to speak is motivated in such a special way that we feel that these are the only ones to whom he really *had* to speak.[12] Similarly, in Elysium only Musaeus speaks, in the valley of Lethe only Anchises; we should be clear how very different it would be if not one but two spoke in any of these places – we should immediately feel that it could have been more, or fewer: we would lose the sense of necessity.

445

446

5. Unity of person

In order that an action which forms a whole in itself should also be felt to be a unity, it must have an obvious centre and concentration of interest. In the majority of the examples discussed so far, the poet had the advantage that the action is grouped around one person, Aeneas, and is leading this person to a definite goal. However, Virgil also used this device in other places, deliberately in order to create a unity. In the scene of Priam's death (which is made into a separate, independent action for the reasons given on p. 24), note how skilfully Priam himself is set in the centre, by the fact that this section of the narrative is cut off from the rest of Neoptolemus' deeds, that it has Priam as its starting-point, and that it ends with reflective thoughts on his death; Aeneas himself is left completely out of the picture. Further, we have seen how the battle-descriptions are almost all presented as *aristeiae*: the reader's interest is held for as long as possible by one character, or by an exceptional pair of fighters: in Book 9 it is Turnus, in Book 10, in succession, Aeneas, Pallas, Turnus, then Aeneas and Mezentius, who is replaced by Lausus for a short time only; in Book 11 Camilla predominates, in Book 12 Aeneas and Turnus are kept before the observer's eyes throughout. In this case the interest had to be divided equally between them, for practical reasons; where that is not required, Virgil prefers to let Aeneas step back, rather than divide the interest: in Book 8, all the time that Evander is on the stage he is definitely the main character who leads the action and whose speeches are reported; Aeneas himself speaks only twice, when he greets him, and after the intervention of the heavenly sign promised by Venus.[13]

447 This aspect must be kept in mind above all when the action divides into two parts set in different places. If both are given equal treatment the listener is forced to move continually from one to the other, and the unity of the scene is disturbed. In such cases, Virgil puts one part firmly to the fore; the other is made smaller by perspective. We have already seen this in the case of Book 9 when we studied its narrative form (p. 302f.): in the first part we stand on the Latin side, and see the Trojan side only momentarily; in the second part, the Nisus episode, we set out from the Trojan camp and return to it afterwards; it is only in the third part that the two sides are brought together. In the introductory scenes of Book 4, Aeneas does not appear at all; in the scenes after Mercury's first errand, Dido is the only protagonist, we see her suffering develop, and Aeneas' action, which runs parallel to Dido's, apparently serves only to motivate the separate stages of that suffering. In Book 11 we are led first for a short time into Aeneas' camp, but then the action moves to the Latin side and remains there until the end; we experience the battle and its results from the side of Camilla and her followers. Above all, however, it is the composition of Book 7 which is ruled by this approach. As soon as we have been taken by the second proem to the side of the Latins, the position from which to view everything which is to come has been given. We are not actually told how Aeneas encountered cordial goodwill at first, how a sudden change in the situation then meant that his hopes were dashed, he saw himself embroiled in a fight and, in spite of all his efforts, felt the war gradually becoming inevitable. On the contrary, we are

354

told how Latinus, whom prodigies had made anxious about his daughter's future,
received an oracle from Faunus, which he saw fulfilled by the arrival of the Trojans;   448
how then, because of the resistance, first of his wife, then of Turnus, then of all his
subjects, his marriage plans were frustrated, and he himself, incapable of confronting the attack, retired, so that war flared up in Latium where peace had reigned so
long; *rex arva Latinus et urbes iam senior longa placidas in pace regebat* (7.45f.)
[King Latinus had been ruling over the cities and farms in serenity for many years of
peace, and he now was growing old] begins the narrative; it ends with the Latins
preparing for war. We are only led back to Aeneas once, at the beginning, where it is
a question of narrating the previous history of the embassy which Latinus receives;
we hear later that the ambassadors leave richly rewarded but do not hear the impression which their message had on Aeneas: we do not return to him until the
beginning of the next book. In this case the completeness of the narrative suffers as a
result of the artistic principle; for we should like to know why Aeneas does not take
up Latinus' invitation, why he does not prevent the first bloody clash, etc.[14]

6. Unity of each book

From looking at the scenes and series of scenes, we move up to the unit next in size,
the book; the reason why this is always treated as a unit has been discussed above
p. 209f.

First, the rule of unity of action holds good for the books, that rule which, we saw
above, was striven after as the ideal requirement for the whole; but with the majority
of the books the conception was already unified, and that is decisive for the unity of
effect. Each book is supposed to contain a piece of the action which is complete in
itself and which leads to a τέλος [end] in the Aristotelian sense. However, even the
greatest skill cannot divide a connected epic action cleanly into twelve parts each
complete in itself, without the need for any transitions; these transitions are then
placed at the beginning of the books, as a kind of proem, which precedes the real
ἀρχή [beginning] of the action. In many of the books it is immediately obvious that
they fulfil the requirement: 2: *Iliu Persis*, 3: Wanderings, 4: Dido, 5: Sojourn in
Sicily, 6: Underworld, 7: (with introduction) the outbreak of war in Latium and its   449
causes, 8: Aeneas' excursion (with introduction), 9: Turnus' feats in Aeneas' absence, 10: the first main battle, together with preparatory assembly of the gods, 12:
the duel: it is prepared, temporarily frustrated, and carried out. We should note how
in Book 10, for example, the ending is set up in exactly the same way as we noted at
the end of Book 12, which is also the end of the whole poem: Book 10 finishes with
the death of Mezentius; to make this possible, the relief of the camp is anticipated
(p. 289 above), but the results of this victory are kept back until the following book:
Aeneas' address on the following day (11.14ff.) would in all likelihood have been
given on the same day as the battle. How an episodic effect is deliberately and
skilfully avoided in other places can be seen from the examples which follow.

The narrative in Book 6 had to cover not only the visit to the Underworld but also
the death and burial of Misenus, which had no real connection with the Underworld.
But Virgil makes Aeneas visit the Sibyl as soon as he lands; the death of Misenus

occurs while he is absent; the requirement that the body shall be buried and the men purified is made into a *precondition* of the journey to Hades, along with the acquisition of the golden bough. On their return, Aeneas and Achates do indeed find the corpse: that serves not only as concrete proof of the validity of the Sibyl's power to predict (189), but also leads directly to the discovery of the golden bough; while Aeneas is taking this into the temple, his companions build the funeral pyre, and the funeral has been completed before the summoning of Hecate and, with it, the beginning of the journey to the Underworld: in this way the Misenus story is given the strongest connections with the preparations for it.

The description of the shield did not belong to any one place in the action; a poet who was composing episodes would perhaps have been content to have Venus bring the weapons at the end of Book 8, or during the voyage in Book 10; Virgil prepares for it with the prophetic sign from heaven and makes this into an essential part of the action: Aeneas is disappointed and discouraged by Evander's reply, but the sign assures him of divine help and he immediately starts organizing the new enterprise,
450   the Etruscan expedition.

The Nisus story comes in the middle of Book 9; it is itself an episode like the Doloneia, related to the latter not only in its content but also by the fact that its result seems to have no consequences for the development of the main action. Yet Virgil did strive after – and achieve – a better integration than the Homeric poet. First, the episode serves to connect the first and last parts of Book 9, which would otherwise fall apart: it fills the night between the two days and creates continuity of action. Secondly, the expedition of the pair has a better and much simpler motivation than the ancient epic poet achieved. The latter had great trouble making his heroes set out. First Agamemnon calls an assembly, to find a means of rescuing the Achaeans and the ships (*Iliad* 10.19, 44); then he holds a council to choose between fleeing and continuing the fight; finally, after everyone has helped check that the guards are at their posts, it occurs to Nestor that a spy ought to be sent to find out whether the Trojans plan to stay on the open plain or to return to the city – information which cannot help much in the rescue of the Achaeans. Odysseus and Diomedes do not even ask Dolon about it (or at least do not insist on an answer), and when they return with the looted horses, no more is said about their mission or about the rescue of the Achaeans. Aeneas has left the camp before the enemy has been sighted; but now the camp is surrounded, and the coming day will bring a heavy attack: nothing is more natural than that the Trojan generals should feel an urgent desire to inform the absent king about the situation, so that he can take measures, hasten his return, etc.; they are also anxious to know whether his request for support has been successful. Nisus knows that everyone wants this; in the silent night, when he looks out from the wall and sees that in one place the enemy's watchfire has gone out, the idea comes like a lightning-flash that he could be the messenger. He goes with Euryalus to the generals, who are discussing this very plan; his offer is immediately accepted and they leave at once. The feat of Diomedes and Odysseus passes and leaves no trace: neither friend nor foe hears anything more of it. It is true that we are told how the Trojans lamented over the slain men (523) after Apollo had wakened Hippo-
451   coon, unfortunately too late: but once the two heroes have returned to the camp, have washed and fed, everything is past and gone, and Eos rises from her couch by

the splendid Tithonus as if nothing remarkable had happened in the night. Virgil depicts the Rutulians bringing the fallen Volcens and the looted spoils into the camp; there is general consternation as the bloodbath which has been inflicted on the sleeping men is discovered. But the perpetrators have been punished, and when the triumphant column marches out against the camp at daybreak it carried the heads of Nisus and Euryalus, stuck on spears and lifted high. The defenders, who were already disconsolate as they prepare to ward them off, are pierced to the heart by the sight; the mother of Euryalus fills the camp with heart-rending laments which undermine the men's morale; to prevent worse happening, Iulus has the unhappy woman carried into the tent. We see that not only is the outward continuity preserved, but also the tragic outcome of the adventure helps to convey the mood in which attackers and defenders begin the new day's battle.

In each book, unity of action is often connected with unity of person; the person is not always Aeneas. Book 4 starts with Dido and finishes by her corpse; Book 9 starts with Turnus, and ends with him; similarly, Turnus opens Book 12, and it ends with his death. In Book 5, Virgil has made Anchises the centre of interest; Aeneas thinks of him as soon as the tempest forces them to enter the Sicilian harbour (5.31), it is in his honour that Aeneas makes his memorial speech and the sacrifice for the dead; the Funeral Games are also in his honour (cf. also 550); it is when they think of him that the Trojan women lament (614, cf. 652); finally, it is his appearance which introduces the last phase of the sojourn in Sicily, the foundation of Segesta and of the sanctuary of Anchises.

In the same way as Books 4, 9 and 12 have beginnings and endings which correspond because the same person dominates both, Virgil has also emphasized the unity of other books by giving them opening and closing scenes which are contrasting or parallel. At both the beginning and end of Book 5 we find Aeneas at sea – storm and tempest at the beginning, at the end a most favourable wind and the calmest of seas; at the beginning, the conversation between Aeneas and Palinurus, at the end, Palinurus falls overboard and Aeneas laments.[15] Book 8 is opened (after the introduction), and brought to a close by Aeneas in contrasting ways: at the beginning he is full of cares and doubts, at the end he is wrapped in enthusiastic contemplation of the divine shield, assured of support and victory. In Book 4, after the exposition, there immediately follows the scene of Anna advising her sister to agree to the new marriage; immediately before the end we see the counsellor in despair at the tragic result of her advice. This helps us to understand the composition of Book 1, where unity is not easy to perceive: it begins with the deadly danger of the storm, it ends with the banquet where those who were in peril on the sea are gathered safe from cares: a concrete expression of their escape from danger. This banquet, which also provides the opportunity for Aeneas to tell his tale, must of course follow directly upon the arrival of Aeneas, and not be separated from it by other events, as it is in the *Odyssey*: it would then cease to be the necessary expression of reaching safety, and would also no longer serve as the keystone which crowns the unified structure of Book 1.

That leaves only Book 11, the one book without an obvious unity. Continuity of action is maintained, but the sections do not hang together: it starts with the consequences of the first day's fighting – scenes in the camp of Aeneas, Pallas' funeral

452

453

procession, Evander's lament – then, after the armistice, comes the second day of fighting, introduced by the council meeting in Laurentum. The real heroine of this second day, Camilla, does not appear until after the middle of the book (498). How could Virgil have avoided this? He could either have devoted the whole book to Camilla, putting the consequences of the first battle at the end of Book 10; that book might have been able to maintain its unity even so, but it would have lost the final climax of the death of Mezentius. Or he could have done without Camilla, and made the suggestion of a duel in Book 12 arise directly from the council meeting; Book 11 would then have been much poorer in emotional content, becoming a mere stopgap. Finally, he could have considered cutting all of the first part; in that case he would have lost important details in the portrayal of Aeneas and Turnus, and also the whole προπαρασκευή [preparation] of the duel. The poet chose the least of these evils and, in this one case, broke his own rules of composition, finding that it forced him to lesser concessions in other directions; the principle itself is not obscured by this one exception.

7. Unity of the whole work

We turn back now from the composition of the single sections to the composition of the whole, and consider to what extent this was affected by the fact that the books were each designed to stand separately, in the way that we have shown. Obviously, the tendency to make each component part complete in itself must have detracted somewhat from the unity of the whole.[16] Instead of letting each part develop from the preceding one, so as to provide the basis for the following one, there would naturally be a tendency to cut down on the number of connections between books except for very general ones, giving only what belonged within each book, only what had no effect outside the boundaries of the book. That must have happened most often when the poet composed a book before he had written the earlier one which would have explained it. The factual contradictions which crept in as a result of this working method are not its greatest drawback; they could have been removed, and probably would have been. What was more important was that the poet was forced to omit in later books motifs which had figured in earlier ones, or failed to prepare in earlier books for later ones in the way that one would expect in a narrative with a strict unity; he also let fairly important characters vanish altogether, or be introduced rather late.[17] In these cases it is extremely difficult to decide whether it is an involuntary and unconscious result of the manner of composition, or conscious and deliberate poetic licence. I shall give, first, examples of this treatment of characters. Drances stands in the foreground in Book 11; one may be surprised that he disappears completely in Book 12 and makes no attempt to prevent the breach of the agreement. In Book 1, Amor took the place of Ascanius; in Book 4 we hear no more about it.[18] On the other hand, Anna is very much in the foreground in 4: one might have expected to hear something about her in Book 1. It is true that Camilla is already introduced in the catalogue in Book 7; but she vanishes in Books 9 and 10, then dominates the stage in Book 11.[19] In Book 12, Juturna is full of tender anxiety for her brother; the brief mention granted to her by the poet in 10.439

scarcely seems sufficient preparation for this. In all these cases, introducing the characters earlier, or keeping them in the foreground later, would hardly have been an artistic advantage to the books concerned; it would only have added unnecessary complications to the action, and it is possible that Virgil deliberately refrained for 455 that reason; there is no doubt, however, that it increases the episodic effect of the whole. It is the same with the treatment of motives. The revelations which are given to Aeneas in Book 6 by the Sibyl and by Anchises are completely ignored in the subsequent books: they seem to have no effect at all, either good or bad, on Aeneas' moods. That certainly helps to isolate Book 6 within the whole work; but we must ask ourselves how this motive could have been used further without impairing the interest of the story. When Aeneas leaves Evander, he picks out the ablest of his men, and sends the others back to the camp in the two ships, to take a message to Ascanius from his father (548). We hear nothing more about them;[20] but we must ask when and how this message could have been introduced into Book 9: never mind the two ships, which would have been greatly disappointed on arrival to learn that they had just missed being immortalized as nymphs! If one remembers that Books 8 and 9 were both composed to be recited separately, one can well understand the poet's procedure, even if it was deliberate. It is often more noticeable when preparatory information is lacking. I pointed out earlier, that Virgil often leaves us to find out from what his characters say that things have happened that he could easily have told us himself (p. 308f.); he makes use of this liberty mostly when the event itself happened before the book in which it is mentioned. In the Assembly of the Gods at the beginning of Book 10, Jupiter asks in a rage *abnueram bello Italiam concurrere Teucris: quae contra vetitum discordia?* [I had withheld my permission for Italy to meet Trojans in combat of war. Why is there this rebellion against my prohibition?] That would be quite sufficient, if Book 10 stood alone; but anyone who reads the whole epic through is bound to wonder when the prohibition was made. In Book 8, Aeneas refers to a promise by his divine mother, that if war broke out she would bring him weapons wrought by Vulcan: we are not able to say when this promise could have been given. But in this and similar cases we see why Virgil used each motive in composing the separate books, and we also 456 see that to prepare for them in earlier books would have been difficult, or sometimes impossible, without spoiling the action there. A poet who set great store by a watertight exposition would have mentioned in Book 3 the oracle about Palinurus which Aeneas refers to at 6.343 (p. 309 above); by so doing, he would have given his audience a riddle in Book 3 which would have remained temporarily unsolved; those listening to Book 6 could not be referred to that passage, and would either not understand what he was talking about or would have to be told again in full.[21]

The separate composition of each book has also had an effect on the way in which they are linked. In most cases the poet has been completely successful with the transition from one book to another; in one case – Books 5 to 6[22] – the new book is linked so closely with the previous one that when it was recited by itself either the opening must have been changed, or the recital must have started with the last few lines of the previous book. In other cases there is a brief recapitulation at the beginning of the new book (Books 8, 12), but this does not spoil the narrative when it is read as a whole; in yet other cases however, the link is present, but is so loose that the continuity of the narrative suffers, although Virgil was so keen on continuity within each book: the *interea* [meanwhile] (see p. 306 above) which links Books 10 and 11 with what has gone before bridges the interval of a night which has followed the day just described, although nightfall was not mentioned: in neither case was it possible to do so without spoiling the effect of the ending of the book. Finally, Book 3 starts with a formal introduction (1-12),[23] giving a kind of preparation for the new action, recapitulating the main content of Book 2, the destruction of Troy, but then

457 also taking the narrative forward. The fact that there are some factual irregularities in this link with Book 2 can be explained by the fact that Virgil was already aware of the changes that would be necessary in the latter parts of Book 3; the division between Books 2 and 3 is expressed formally by a pathos-filled (see p. 290 above) proem; Virgil used this for practical reasons: he had to start Book 3 by narrating what had happened between the sack of Troy and the exodus, and if he had started the book by passing over this rather uneventful interval with just a dry report or a brief summary it would have had an adverse effect on the listener's feelings.

8. Organization of the whole work

For a poem to give the impression of being a unity, we must be able to have a clear view of it as a whole.[24] We must never lose the thread of the narrative; at every moment we must have a clear view of the situation; digressions must be avoided; our gaze should not be wearied by a confusing multiplicity of material, nor obstructed by complications in the plot, nor distracted from the main subject by an annoying amount of less important detail. Clear organization on the one hand, simplicity and restraint on the other, are the means which lead to these goals.

We have already seen how, in smaller sections which could easily be confusing because of their content (such things as lists), grouping the items made them easier to grasp. In contrast, the organization to be seen in complete books is simply what was demanded by the subject-matter: Book 2 had to fall into three sections (p. 5 above), and the approximately equal length of these sections followed from their equal importance to the plot, according to the rule of συμμετρία [symmetry] which dictated that things of equal value should be treated in equal detail (p. 288f. above). However, Virgil otherwise refrained from imposing 'symmetry' merely for the sake of symmetry upon the divisions of a book which arose naturally from the material,

458 or from creating artificial divisions where there were none; thus it did not occur to him to devote an equal number of lines to the opening and closing scenes of Book 5 just because they are parallel in content, or, in the long journey in Book 3, to point out the divisions which made the book fall into definite and obvious acts: where clarity is guaranteed by the straightforward advance of the action no external aids are needed. On the contrary, one may say that Virgil kept to the principle of continuity and sought to smooth over the breaks between the sections created by the material, just as a dramatist would within each act.[25]

The division of the whole work into twelve books is a different matter. The fact that the action consists of two major parts, equal in content – this is announced in the proem – had to be reflected in the form. This is done by dividing the material into two groups of six books, which are then further divided into pairs.[26] The beginning of the second part is emphasized by the second proem; the parallel monologues of Juno in Books 1 and 7 and her subsequent parallel actions emphasize their correspondence even more clearly. In a similar way, Apollonius had used his first two books to cover the outward voyage of the Argo, his last two books to cover the adventure in Colchis and the return voyage; and even in the *Odyssey* anyone who is determined to find a symmetrical division of the whole by books will do so.[27]

9. Simplification

Much more important than the arrangement of sections is the second of the qualities mentioned above, simplicity. Simplicity and restraint not only make the work easy to grasp, they also make it great and noble; this is the essential foundation for the individuality of Virgil's epic style. It is true that this is more easily sensed than demonstrated, but I must attempt to analyse what produces this impression.

To start with the most elementary: there is restraint in the number of scenes in each longish section of the action; I am thinking of the Sack of Troy (compared with, say, Quintus), the Wanderings (compared with, say, Apollonius) or the Games and battles (compared with Homer). There is restraint in the number of speeches in a conversation, as we have shown: a single speech and a single reply create a picture which makes a deeper impression than a long interchange. There is restraint in the number of conversations: instead of the many ups and downs of the scenes in the *Iliad* in which the gods discuss the fate of the warring parties, Virgil has Jupiter's promise to Venus at the beginning, Juno's renunciation in Jupiter's favour at the end, and, in between, the great scene in which Venus and Juno meet before Jupiter: with these three scenes the principle is, as it were, sucked dry, and the other scenes featuring the interaction of the gods are only preparation for their intervention in individual cases.

There is restraint in the number of characters, or, when a great number is inevitable, as it is in the battles, a few are selected for ostentatious emphasis, and all the rest are relegated to static or minor episodic roles; the intention is not only that the few select characters shall stand out as being obviously more important, but that the story-line of their actions should remain clean and uncluttered. People have often mocked at the presentation of *fortis Gyas fortisque Cloanthus* (1.222 = 1.612) [valiant Gyas and valiant Cloanthus] who do not manage to come to life. The sharply drawn silhouettes of the participants in the Games, Sergestus and Cloanthus, Entellus and Dares etc., show that Virgil was well able to create characters when he chose to. Thus, when he makes no special mention of any of Aeneas' companions in the first books, and gives very few details even about *fidus Achates* [trusty Achates], there must have been a reason. For secondary figures to be characterized there has to be a sub-plot, or at least a branching and broadening of the main plot; if, for example, in the storm at sea, Virgil had wanted to show the characters of the captains of the ships, or if, after the landing, he had wanted to show their different reactions to misfortune, this would have obscured the clear storyline of Book 1, and weighed down the simple exposition. Anyone who has understood this will find it quite in order that, for example, the nurse Caieta is not mentioned until they come to the place where she died and to which she gave her name (7.1ff.); this, and the fact that she was nurse to Aeneas, is truly all that the reader needs to know about her. He will understand when no attempt is made to bring Lavinia into the foreground, turning her into an active figure; the happenings at the court of Latinus are complicated enough as it is, and the poet happily makes use of the pretext that the early Roman *filia familias* [daughter of the family] had no will of her own, and therefore did not act independently, but allowed her parents to rule her. Lavinia is not supposed to interest the reader as a person but only as the daughter of Latinus, whose hand in marriage goes with the gift of the kingdom.

There is restraint in the use of detail; it is almost exclusively used where it can deepen the emotional momentum of the action. If a tragic drama is to move us, it has to be presented with all the fullness of life: in such cases Virgil does not refrain from painting in every last detail. But whether the bow which fires a fateful shot is of one style or another, whether the sceptre carried by a king previously belonged to one person or someone else, whether the deer which Aeneas shoots for his hungry men is carried to the shore in one way or another way, are all minor details with no relevance to the plot, and therefore felt by Virgil to be an intrusion. If the Evander scenes were an epyllion in the Hellenistic style, as it is sometimes suggested that they are, how many small, neat touches would have been required to paint the picture of the old man's simple household! Virgil has done it with a few bold strokes, making it into a piece of epic action. Of course, the sparser the detail, the more effective is what we have: when the king is wakened by the dawn chorus, when two hounds run at his side, that would go almost unnoticed in the genre of the epyllion: but here it adds a great deal to the atmosphere. And, as with these external touches, so too with the depiction of thoughts and feelings. Of course Virgil was as capable as anyone of painting a complicated state of mind in the greatest detail, on the model of the great Alexandrian miniatures which depict emotions; the *Eclogues* bear witness to this. In the epic he scorned to do so: whenever he has men and gods speaking emotionally, it is always to reveal plain and straightforward feelings. I have attempted above to show how, in the most complicated case, that of Dido, we are not given a complicated picture, painted in all the colours of the rainbow and lovingly shaded; we are presented with a well-arranged series of severe and serene paintings, the epic-writer's fresco, which furthers the action. The Medea of Apollonius, however inventive and charming the description of her maidenly timorousness at the decisive step, and of her fear during the first rendezvous with Jason, lacks epic grandeur by virtue of this multiplicity of tiny traits; when Dido is presented in a similar situation, the poet refrains from decorative detail, and although he does not manage to avoid falling into the conventional, he does preserve simplicity.

The temptation to depict psychological conflicts is resisted by Virgil, both in Dido's case and elsewhere. One may be surprised at this; one might have thought that the poet would have followed the example of drama and of Hellenistic narrative; the contemporary elegy also undertook to express the battle between conflicting emotions. Was Virgil not tempted to depict a battle between love and duty in Aeneas' breast, giving a psychological motivation to the victory of duty? Or to paint in detail the scruples of conscience displayed by King Latinus? Or to show

461

how Turnus' love and wounded honour overwhelm his sense of right and his good sense in the heat of battle? Virgil makes us vaguely aware that such inner conflicts are taking place; but he conceals them by using the symbol of a supernatural intervention or, as in the case of Latinus, showing them to us only in an allusive chiaroscuro. That Virgil was not naturally predisposed to such psychological prob-   462
lems is certain; but the same is surely true of the battle-scenes, and yet he did not avoid these, because he felt that the plot demanded them; one will have to assume that he regarded an intensive study of psychological conflicts as unsuitable for the epic style.

10. Variation

Restraint resulted from another factor in addition to the ones we have mentioned: fear of repetition, or, expressed positively, striving after variety, *variatio*.[28] In the same way as Virgil avoids the monotony of stereotyped turns of phrase in his expressions,[29] and avoids having an errand carried out in the same words with which it was given,[30] he also avoids repeating motifs where possible. Anius, the prophet of Delos, is not allowed to prophesy, because Helenus will; the greeting of Aeneas and Helenus is dealt with in one word, because the greeting of Aeneas and Andromache has just been described; the sacrifice at the consultation of the Sibyl in Book 6 is mentioned only very briefly, because the description of a more important sacrifice is to follow;[31] and in the same way in many other cases too we could establish the reason why something is *not* narrated. However, the old epic motifs of the plot had to be used repeatedly: dreams and divine apparitions, scenes on Olympus and prophecies, storm at sea and hospitable reception; in the descriptions of battles, too, types and typical events recur several times. In these cases, Virgil has only avoided putting the repetitions too close together; instead, he spreads them out fairly regularly through the whole work;[32] also, where he could, he raised each example out of   463
the typical by giving it an individual shaping,[33] which resulted in variety. Variation is particularly necessary where the action consists of a series of similar events. The action in Book 3 depends on repeated prophecy; the process takes place each time in completely different circumstances.[34] The Games in Book 5 are made to vary as much as possible in the number and the kind of participants as well as in the nature of the competition itself and its result.[35] In the battles in the last four books, the *aristeiae* are alternated with general fighting, and culminate in the duels; the situation and the goal of the battle are completely different in each of the four books. Variation is also sought after in the description of wounds: the group discussed on p. 163f. may serve as an example.

Virgil had variation in mind as soon as he began the first draft of the whole work. Books 2, 4 and 6, each in different ways, represent a high point of pathetic or sublime effect; they are separated by the more peaceful books, 3 and 5, and it is obvious how important it is from this point of view that 5 should not follow immediately on 3, and 6 on 4. The pathos-filled Allecto scenes and the preparations for war are separated from the outbreak of war by the peaceful Evander scenes. The battle-descriptions in Books 9 to 12 are regularly interrupted with council scenes, at the beginning of Books 10, 11 and 12. In the same way as confident optimism and anxious worries alternate within books, for example in Book 3,[36] throughout the whole work excitement and calm succeed each other in turns: the excitement is not to be blunted by being sustained for too long.

11. Enrichment

Variation can only be achieved by diversity; restraint requires a corresponding enrichment if it is not to result in plainness. As far as possible, each motif is only to appear in the same form once; but all available motifs are to be used, and the effect of each is to be intensified.

Aristotle distinguished four main types of drama, corresponding to the types of plot (*Poetics* 18): the 'interwoven' kind, which rests on a basis of *peripeteia* [reversal] and recognition, the tragedy of pathos, of character, and the miraculous: he taught that the best was a combination of them all. Virgil probably believed that he had achieved this in his epic: even if it is predominantly 'pathetic', it is lacking neither in *peripeteia* nor in 'recognition',[37] neither in character nor in the miraculous:[38] it combines the characteristics of the *Iliad* and the *Odyssey*.[39] It also combines essential elements of the story of both poems, supplementing it with new motifs taken from drama or from later narrative poems: the result is richer and more varied than any earlier poem. And it does not restrict itself to narrating for entertainment: it also teaches and uplifts, combining the *utile* [useful] with the *dulce* [pleasant]. There is an unmistakeable striving after completeness: one will realize this if one considers, for example, the many different forms in which the supernatural makes an appearance in the *Aeneid*: every possibility is utilized. Minor things are dealt with in the same way. We are shown something simple, the focus is on a narrowly delimited area, but this small circle is then criss-crossed with every

possible diameter. The speeches go straight to their goal, but the single thought which each expresses is looked at from this side and that until nothing more could be said. The states of mind are simple and uncomplicated; but every single mood, every single emotion has all possible value extracted. Think of the state of mind of the Trojans as they leave their native land; it is certainly not made artificially complex, but it is unfolded in every direction;[40] or the various stages of Dido's suffering are exhausted one by one. The actions of the gods and men are simple, the motives are obvious and straightforward; but we are intended to have the fullest possible view of them at every moment.[41] Complicated situations are avoided as far as possible; instead, we are shown a situation from every angle until we know it through and through.[42] Virgil does not remain on the outside of events; he intensifies the effect by revealing the feelings of the protagonists; he enriches the action outwardly by introducing *peripeteia* [reversal] and surprise, and inwardly by depicting psychological processes. One example may suffice: we have seen plenty of others during our examination. Compare the Palinurus scene in Book 6 with the corresponding Elpenor scene in the *Odyssey*: in Homer we see on the one hand the grief of Odysseus, on the other the straightforward account and plea for burial of Elpenor; Virgil starts with the sudden light thrown on the ambiguous oracle and has then, in Palinurus' speech, the *ethos* of the faithful servant (351), the pathetic, piteous narrative and description of his present sufferings, the prayer to take him with them across the Styx; this prayer is refused by the Sibyl, but he is given instead the comforting prospect of burial and eternal remembrance; this brings a change in Palinurus' mood: *his dictis curae emotae* [his cares were banished by her words] etc. One has the impression that every possible aspect of the situation has been utilized, giving an effect of completeness.

Notes to Chapter 4

1. See above, p. 3.   437

2. τελευτή...ὃ αὐτὸ μετ᾽ ἄλλο πέφυκεν εἶναι...μετὰ δὲ τοῦτο οὐδὲν ἄλλο [an end...is that which naturally follows something else...but is not itself followed by anything else] (*Poetics* 7.1450b 29).

3. We should remember the judgement of the ancient critics on the second half of Sophocles' *Ajax*, schol. 1123: μετὰ τὴν ἀναίρεσιν ἐπεκτεῖναι τὸ δρᾶμα θελ-   438 ήσας ἐψυχρεύσατο καὶ ἔλυσε τὸ τραγικὸν πάθος [through his desire to protract the drama after the death (of Ajax) he lapsed into bathos and dissipated the tragic tension].

4. Conway has pointed out the significance of the curse, see above p. 115 n. 40.   439

5. This replaced lines 890-2, which would have had to be discarded during a   440 revision: see above p. 63 n.99. I cannot believe that Virgil ever conceived of having both the Sibyl's prophecy and that of Anchises; one could hardly find another place where he has so brutally killed one motif with another, both in the *same* form. It seems to me most probable that Virgil started by working out the showpiece of the whole book, Anchises' great speech, and wrote the opening scenes later, after the change of plan.

6. Another splendid example is the enumeration of sinners who are punished in   442 Tartarus (6.562f.), analysed by Norden 271f.

7. Deuticke correctly gives the grouping as ABABA; there are some perceptive comments on the choice and arrangement of characters in Belling, *Studien über die Kompositionskunst Virgils in der Aeneis* (Leipzig, 1899) 17ff. Cima's idea (*Analecta Latina* [Milan, 1901] 5) that the Republican heroes of the second group, 824ff., had all made the same patriotic sacrifice as Brutus, is very far-fetched and in the case of the Drusi, for example, the facts would have to be distorted to fit it.

8. Only Cossus actually belongs to the second group; cf. Belling, 21. The time of   443 Serranus cannot be established: Klebs in Pauly *RE* 2.2095.

9. In the parallel piece to the Parade of Heroes, the description of the shield in Book 8, it was possible to have a simpler arrangement: there it is a question of a small number of pictures, each needing to be seen separately and to have its own effect. There is therefore a simple division into two parts, nearly equal in length, showing that they are intended to balance each other: pictures from the mists of prehistory and pictures from the bright light of the present day; the first row is rounded off with a mention of the Salii and the Luperci, the most ancient survivals

of the worship of the early Romans; the other row ends with a picture of present-day worship, Augustus' festival of victory and peace. Homer had presented a picture of the world which was complete in itself; Virgil wants to do the same thing in a different way: the first row of pictures is set on earth, the main scenes of the second row are set in the *arva Neptunia* (695) [Neptune's acres], which therefore have to be described first in a relatively detailed way (in four lines); between the two, to complete the picture, the *Tartareae sedes, alta ostia Ditis* [the habitations in Tartarus, and Pluto's tall gateway] are inserted, understandably briefly and only where they concern Roman affairs (Catiline, Cato). Volkmann's hypothesis (above p. 340 n. 43) that what we see is two descriptions of the shield (626-74 and 626-9 plus 675-728), of which the second was intended by the poet to replace the first, already runs aground on the fact that Virgil cannot possibly ever have considered representing the sea on his shield without including any people in the scene; and anyone who knows Virgil's habits of composition will regard it as equally impossible that he could ever have intended finishing his description of the shield with Tartarus (which of course is not to be thought of as representing 'Air', as Volkmann suggests) and the empty lines 671-4.

444

10. Why are these placed between the close neighbours Sabines and Aequi? Surely only because Virgil believed that it would make the division into pairs more obvious.

11. The Etruscan catalogue in Book 10 is divided differently: eight generals, the first four from Etruria itself (here, too, the geographically most distant are set in the middle), the second four (symmetry requires that *Cinyrus* or *Cunarus* [186] be the name of a general) from outside, two Ligurians and two Mantuans.

445

12. Let us compare the reason for the questions: Odysseus asks out of pure curiosity – the poet needs no better motivation to bring the stories to the hero; in Aeneas' case what is essential always is a strong emotional interest.

13. It is different in the rare cases where *ensemble* scenes of people with equal rights to the limelight are required; then Virgil preserves the unity of the scene by keeping the different groups before our eyes all the time. Look at the scene of the departure from Troy in this light: in addition to the two men, Creusa and Iulus also had to be considered (preparation 597ff., then 651, 666, 673ff., 681ff., 710f., 723ff., 747; it is only in 636 that one might wish that their presence were mentioned more explicitly); or the boat-race in Book 5, which was studied from this viewpoint above (p. 131).

447

448

14. It is true that this lack of completeness suited Virgil very well here; if he had had Aeneas taking part in the action at the court of Latinus, the already none too simple action would have become considerably more complicated.

452

15. The prediction by Neptune: *tutus quos optas portus accedet Averni, unus erit tantum, amissum quem gurgite quaeret, unum pro multis dabitur caput* (813) ['he shall reach the harbour by Avernus, which you have chosen as his destination, and you will mourn one Trojan only lost at sea, one life given to the depths for many'], seems to me to be the heart of the scene. The death of Palinurus was not to be a chance occurrence – that would have gone against Virgil's artistic principles – ; if his death, borrowing from known religious concepts, was to be regarded as a vicarious sacrifice, that could only be stated by the mouth of a god, so Virgil invented

the scene between Venus and Neptune (Drachmann [p. 278 n. 43 above, 133] says the same) and developed it in detail into a kind of parallel-scene to that between Juno and Aeolus in Book 1. A difficulty which resulted from this and which Virgil will have noticed for himself (without being able to do anything about it): the god's guarantee had to be given visible expression, and this happens when he calms the sea; on the other hand, Aeneas would not have set out on a stormy sea; this means that from 763f. to 820f. no real progress is apparent. Moreover, critics keep saying that there is a clear contradiction in the fact that Neptune speaks of only *one* sacrifice, but subsequently, in addition to Palinurus, Misenus also dies in the sea; but, I do not understand how anyone can ignore the fact, established briefly and clearly by Heyne, that Neptune is speaking only of the crossing to Italy (see above), so that the death of Misenus, which happens *after* the landing, has nothing at all to do with it. Heyne, for his part, has then objected (and others have drawn further conclusions from it), that Aeneas and Achates are not certain to whom the words of the Sibyl apply: *iacet exanimum tibi corpus amici (heu nescis) totamque incestat corpore classem* (149) [the body of your friend – alas! though you know it not – is lying lifeless, and defiling all your fleet with the taint of death], instead of immediately thinking of Palinurus: but he had died somewhere in the sea far, far away from Cumae, and they would certainly not expect to find his body on the shore now, a *piaculum* [an expiatory offering] for Aeneas' men and for himself. For the important thing is clearly the need for purification, not that some friend of Aeneas is still unburied: this also removes the contradiction which Norden criticized (p. 177).

16. See above p. 209ff.   453

17. By 'fairly important characters' I do not, for example, mean Achaemenides,   454 whose later disappearance struck ancient critics of Virgil as *incongruum* [incongruous] (Servius 3.667, cf. Georgii), or Caieta, the nurse of Aeneas, who is not mentioned until she dies, 7.1.

18. Above p. 309.

19. Cf. above p. 257.

20. See Heyne *ad loc.* and on 10.238.   455

21. In these cases there is also the possibility that Virgil had Homeric analogies   456 in mind: at *Iliad* 21.277 Achilles refers to a prophecy by his mother, that he will fall at Troy from a shot by Apollo; this has not been mentioned earlier although there was ample opportunity.

22. *sic fatur lacrimans classique inmittit habenas* (6.1) [So spoke Aeneas, weeping. Then he gave his fleet rein]; an imitation, noticed long ago, of *Iliad* 7.1: ὣς εἰπών [with these words] and *Odyssey* 13.1: ὣς ἔφατο [so he spoke].

23. That this introduction is different from the recapitulations in Books 7 and 9 has been shown convincingly by Karsten, *Hermes* 39 (1904) 271, causing me to change my mind.

24. εὐσύνοπτον εἶναι [the ability to be properly taken in at a single view] had   457 been laid down by Aristotle as the criterion for the length of a tragedy (*Poetics* 1450b 50) and of an epic (1450a 33); it is obviously also of extreme importance for composition and was certainly also emphasized by the later theorists of poetry.

25. I can therefore, on principle, give only limited approval to the attempt made   458 by Belling (in the book mentioned above [p. 365 n. 7] and in the *Festschrift* for

Vahlen [Berlin, 1900] 267) to find a symmetrical structure within single books, quite apart from Belling's misguided attempt to lay great weight on the exact numerical equality of groups of lines. On this cf., for example, B. Helm, *Bursians Jahresbericht* 113 (1902) 44ff.

26. On 7-12 see p. 143f. above; in the first part, Books 1 and 4 frame the two books of the Aeneas narrative, while Books 5 and 6 are closely connected to each other.

27. Books 1-12: up to the return home, 13-24: Ithaca; in the first part, Books 1-4: Telemachus, 5-8: from Calypso to the Phaeacians, 9-12: Odysseus' narrative; in the second part, 13-16: up to the plan to murder the suitors, 17-20: Odysseus with the suitors, 21-4: execution of the plan from the τόξου θέσις [contest of the bow]. Vahlen, *Abh. d. Berlin. Akad.* (1886) 1, attempted to show hexadic division in the *Annals* of Ennius.

462   **28.** τὸ γὰρ ὅμοιον ταχὺ πληροῦν ἐκπεσεῖν ποιεῖ τὰς τραγῳδίας [monotony quickly sates an audience and drives tragedy from the stage] (Aristotle *Poetics* 24 1459b 31).

29. Above, p. 334 n. 10.

30. Above, p. 316f.

31. Chapter 3, p. 332 n. 5

32. He does this without pedantic exactness but aims at an almost schematic regularity. Dreams: Book 2 Hector, 3 Penates, 4 Mercury, 5 Anchises, 7 Allecto, 8 Tiberinus. Divine apparitions: 1 Venus, 2 Venus, 3 Mercury, 5 Iris, 7 Allecto, 8 Venus, 9 Apollo, 10 Nymphs, 12 Juturna. Scenes in Olympus: 1 Juno and Aeolus; Venus and Jupiter; Venus and Amor, 4 Juno and Venus, 5 Venus and Neptune, 7 Juno and Allecto, 8 Venus and Vulcan, 9 the Great Mother and Jupiter, 10 Assembly 463 of the Gods; Jupiter and Hercules; Jupiter and Juno, 11 Diana and Opis, 12 Juno and Juturna; Jupiter and Juno. Prophecies about Aeneas' kingdom and his future: 1 Jupiter, 2 Creusa, 3.158 Penates, 4.229 Jupiter, 5 Acestes' shot, 6 Parade of Heroes, 7.98 Faunus, 8 Aeneas' shield, 9.642 Apollo, 10.11 Jupiter, 12.836 Jupiter. General fighting, once in each book, see above p. 156f. Duels fought: 9 Turnus and Pandarus, 10 Turnus and Pallas; Aeneas and Lausus; Aeneas and Mezentius, 11 Camilla and the Ligurian, 12 Aeneas and Turnus. Speeches by the leaders: 9 Turnus; Mnestheus, 10 Tarchon; Turnus; Pallas, 11 Aeneas; Turnus, 12 Tolumnius; Aeneas; this contrasts with seven, for example, in *Iliad* 15.

33. For example, compare the dreams of Aeneas with one another: 2.270; 3.147; 4.554; 8.26.

34. Above, p. 78f.

35. Above, p. 123f.

36. Above, p. 78.

464   **37.** I am thinking mainly of the gradual and slowly prepared ἀναγνώρισις [recognition] of the land destined by fate, which is described 7.107ff.; cf. Aristotle *Poetics* 16.1455a 10: καὶ ἡ ἐν τοῖς Φινείδαις (ἀναγνώρισις). ἰδοῦσαι γὰρ τὸν τόπον συνελογίσαντο τὴν εἱμαρμένην, ὅτι ἐν τούτῳ εἵμαρτο ἀποθανεῖν αὐταῖς, καὶ γὰρ ἐξετέθησαν ἐνταῦθα [and the (recognition) in the Phineidae: for when they saw the place they reasoned that that was where they were fated to die: for they had been exposed there].

38. ὅσα ἐν ᾍδου [things in Hades] (Aristotle *ibid.* 1456a 4): also the Harpies, Allecto, the metamorphosis of the ships, the Dira etc.

39. Aristotle 24.1459b 13: καὶ γὰρ καὶ τῶν ποιημάτων ἑκάτερον συνέστηκεν ἡ μὲν Ἰλιὰς ἁπλοῦν καὶ παθητικόν, ἡ δὲ Ὀδύσσεια πεπλεγμένον…καὶ ἠθική [for of his two poems one, the *Iliad*, is simple and involves pathos, the *Odyssey* is complex and involves character] and, naturally, τερατῶδης [miraculous].

40. Above, p. 290.

41. Above, p. 260.

42. I do not deny that in a few cases the striving for richness has detracted from simplicity and clarity: for example the βακχεία [Bacchic frenzy] of Amata is spoiled by being overworked; see above p. 150f.

465

5

Virgil's Aims

1. Astonishment, pity and fear

The aim of poetry as opposed to other verbal arts is to delight, and 'to shake the reader up', as we say, although Greek aesthetics used a different metaphor: 'to put the reader beside himself': ἡδονή [pleasure], also ψυχαγωγία [literally, leading the soul] and ἔκπληξις [excitement] are the continually recurring key words of post-Ar-

istotelian theory.[1] In tragedy the main weight falls completely on ἔκπληξις, and since the aestheticians – since Aristotle, and even before his time – did not discriminate between epic and tragedy, this also held good for the epic. In itself ἐκπλήττειν [to excite, produce an emotional response] did not perhaps have to be bound up with the idea of violent excitement; serene beauty can also move the spirit very deeply. But one does not generally think of the word as embracing this possibility: one takes it to mean what had been established ever since Euripides as the specific effect of tragedy: the 'emotional, unexpected and surprising', or, as Plutarch once paraphrased it, 'the upsetting and amazing',[2] or, to let Virgil's friend Horace have a word, it is the art of one *qui pectus inaniter angit, inritat, mulcet, falsis terroribus implet* [who torments my heart with illusions, grates, soothes, and fills with feigned terrors] (*Ep.* 2.1.211-12): a definition in which only *mulcere* [soothing] allows any small space for the gentler effects which are necessary for variety and recuperation. That certain basic aspects of Virgil's technique are decisively geared towards this goal is very obvious. In the present study of his epic technique, almost everything which we have had to label 'a dramatic touch' serves ἔκπληξις: the writer of epic is attempting to rival the dramatist in arousing excitement, and therefore studies the secrets of his art. This can be felt most clearly in the structuring of the action: the striving after energetic forward movement, the strong emphasis on decisive moments, the stage-like structure of the smaller units, the preference of *peripeteia* [reversal] to a calmer, regular course, the struggle after surprising effects, the harsh light focussed on particular details by means of contrasts and climaxes – these are

all characteristic of Virgil, and they are all borrowed from the dramatist's box of tricks. I do not need to go further with this (and related aspects) again here; but there is a wider field which does require special attention.

At the centre of his theory of the effect of tragedy, Aristotle placed πάθος, pity and fear, which the poet must arouse in the audience. πάθος then continued to be regarded as the core of ἔκπληξις: as time went on, emotion came to dominate poetry more and more; it became one of the highest aims of Virgilian epic too. There are two ways of achieving this aim: either by narrating events which arouse pity, anger, fear etc. in the audience; or by presenting the characters to us in an emotional state: the more vividly and visually this is done, the more easily we will identify with the character and share the depicted emotion, and, although much less intensely, ὁμοιοπαθεῖν [feel with them]. In many cases, both things happen, when there is a description not only of the exciting event but also of its effect on the participants: Virgil preferred this second, surer way.

The most noble tragic emotion, pity, also ranks highest in Virgil. For example, in Book 1 he is not satisfied with merely emphasizing the piteous aspects of the fate of Aeneas and the Trojans: episodic material, such as the narrative about Dido (above p. 107 n. 7), the images in the temple at Carthage (above, p. 312f.) and the dialogue between Venus and Amor, becomes an extra source of pity. In the Sack of Troy, emphasis is laid on the piteous aspects of Hector's dream-appearance, the rape of Cassandra and the death of Priam; with the *prodigium* at the grave of Polydorus, the meeting with Andromache, the adventure with the Cyclops, where it would have been easy to concentrate on different emotions, the poet still appeals primarily to our pity. The sight of any suffering, such as that of a tortured animal or an invalid in pain, can awaken similar feelings of suffering in the onlooker; these feelings are intensified if they are combined with anger at the perpetrator of the suffering. This association of the ἐλεεινόν [piteous] and the δεινόν [fearsome] was also emphasized by the aestheticians, and turned to advantage in rhetoric.[3] Thus the δείνωσις [fear-   469
someness] of Neoptolemus' coarse cruelty and arrogance is an additional factor which increases our pity for Priam and Andromache; Sinon's perfidy, Pygmalion's criminal tyranny are painted in the blackest of colours in order to make us feel the fate of their victims more bitterly; even Juno's implacable hatred belongs in this category. At the same time, it may sometimes be merely the common pity of a tender heart; the whole person feels involved when not only his pity but also his love and admiration are directed towards the sufferer; it is only then that he really reaches the point of identifying with him. What led Virgil in the first place to ennoble his suffering characters in this way was probably his impulse to sympathize fully with them himself; but it is obvious how close this brings him to the requirement for the character of the tragic hero which Aristotle abstracted from Attic tragedy. It is this above all which distinguishes Dido from the suffering heroines of the most recent examples of pathetic narrative, that she not only appeals to other humans as a human being, but also, as a great-hearted and powerful yet feminine and gentle princess, she has won the admiration of the audience before it is time to win their pity. And Virgil does exactly the same whenever possible, even with figures in episodes: when we see Priam fall, we are not only touched by the disgraceful end of an old man: we have seen him face the enemy Sinon with courage, have admired the old man's heroic spirit, and are finally reminded that this poor unfortunate, whose corpse is not even granted a resting-place, was once the powerful ruler of Asia. Andromache's loyalty to her first husband, Palinurus' faithful care of his master, Euryalus' noble ambition and Nisus' faithful love for his friend, Lausus' sacrifice for his father – those are all features which make the poet's own creations really worthy of his pity in their suffering: they are also, one may add, the features which have continued to   470
make these scenes of pathos effective through all the centuries since. Closely related to what we have just said is Virgil's treatment of the guilt which leads men to destruction. Hellenistic poetry had wallowed more and more in presenting *crimes de passion*, thereby seeking out the unnatural rather than avoiding it, in the belief that

this would add to the pathetic effect. Virgil does allow past crimes to be mentioned, but he himself does not present them; how far removed is something like Dido's ἁμαρτία [fault] from the horrors with which the collection of Parthenius abounds. In other cases it is a question of lesser failings: Camilla, Nisus and Euryalus become the victims of their imprudent desires; the immoderate boldness of Pallas can hardly count as a failing; and in the case of the stupidity of the Trojans who pull their own destruction into the city, there can be no talk of tragic guilt. Here mankind faces the unfathomable decision of Fate, which also makes the innocent suffer; the poet knows the final purposes served by the fall of Troy and the wanderings of Aeneas: *tantae molis erat Romanam condere gentem* [such was the cost in heavy toil of beginning the life of Rome]; and it is just this glimpse of the future which prevents our justified pity from sinking to the agony of one condemned to watch the unnecessary and purposeless suffering of his fellow men.

For centuries, the *Aeneid* has been the paradigm of dramatic style in poetic narrative. To the question whether Virgil should be regarded as the actual creator of this style, a definite answer can hardly be given. This much is certain, that among the surviving monuments of Hellenistic poetry there is not one single poem which could lay claim to having been Virgil's model in every respect, or even in every important respect. To be sure, we have been able to draw attention to many minor points of comparison in Hellenistic literature, both earlier and later; but when Virgil copies Apollonius in one respect, and in another copies the originals of the *Wedding of Peleus* or the *Ciris*, it only highlights how different his aims are; Apollonius is totally lacking in the essential element, the dramatic character of the narrative; the later, extremely mannered epyllion, almost perverse in its composition, is the diametrical opposite of the Virgilian epic, which aims at a unified, harmonious effect; their treatment of the action cannot be compared in any way, since the fragmentary, arbitrary nature of the epyllion prevents us from speaking of a real story-line. As for the earlier short narrative poems of Hellenistic times, Virgil clearly did learn from them, above all in the very polished form of presentation, in the ἦθος [character] of the narrative, and possibly also in the striving for a unified effect; but for the rest, once again, their aims are as different as can be: they strive after ingenious enlivenment of the detail and a noble restraint in line and colour; his aims are a simple greatness, strong emotions, tension, excitement – in short, the ἐκπληκτικόν [astonishing].

There is another genre of polished narrative which may have come closer to Virgilian technique than anything mentioned so far: Hellenistic – or, more precisely, Peripatetic – historiography. Both Virgilian epic and the historiography of Duris and Phylarchus are really based on one and the same theory: the Aristotelian theory of tragedy.[4] The character of these histories is shown (even more clearly than by the surviving fragments) by Polybius in his famous critique of Phylarchus (2.56ff.); he says that the latter's main aim was to arouse the reader and to produce pity and anger; it is to this end that each shocking *peripeteia* [reversal] is presented as vividly as possible: ἐνάργεια [vividness] and πάθος [pathos] are the catchwords of this aesthetic tendency. However, it will hardly have stopped at the crudely ἐκπληκτικόν [astonishing], as one might think from Polybius' critique: we can assume that skilful dramatic technique was widely used both to refine and to inten-

472

471

sify the effects.[5] From this school of historiographers came the narrative-artists, masters in their own field, to whom we are indebted for the stories of Camillus and Coriolanus, and the conquest of Veii, to mention only a few: I do not believe that ancient narrative includes anything which comes closer in technique to Virgilian epic. They have the same concentration of interest, the composition of effective dramatic scenes, powerful *peripeteia* [reversal], careful psychological motivation, even the technique of imitation, borrowing the external structure of the action from ancient poetry or history: I need only remind you of the captured *haruspex* [sooth-sayer], who divulges Fate's precondition for victory at Veii, as Helenus did at Troy.[6] Of the theory itself (the development of which probably stems from Theophrastus), very little survives;[7] but the theory on which Dionysius bases his criticism of Thucydides comes surprisingly close to what we have deduced to have been Virgil's artistic principles: we have there the requirement of unity and clearly-organized action (*de Thuc.* 5.6), continuity[8] and symmetry (ibid. 13, see above p. 332 n. 4) in the narrative, the right choice of beginning and ending[9], pathetic effect,[10] and appropriate use of direct speech at highpoints of the narrative (17ff.)

We know next to nothing about the artistic form of the historical epic of the Hellenistic period; whether, and to what extent, it made use of the technique developed by the historiographers, which would have provided Virgil with even closer models, cannot be established. The little that we are able to deduce about the (Hellenistic) epic about which most is known, the *Messeniaca* of Rhianus, makes it probable that they did not lack excitement and tension and dramatic movement; but that is not sufficient to tell us anything about their presentation and composition. Nor does what we know of Ennius' *Annales* from testimonia and fragments justify us in supposing that Virgil learnt about epic technique from him as he did about poetic speech. We can at least say one negative thing, that both the choice of material and the lay-out in the form of annals allow us to deduce that Ennius remained completely unaffected by the aesthetic theory which underlies Virgil's technique of composition.

473

2. Moral purpose

In the previous section we have touched on aims which no longer belong to the realm of aesthetics, but to the realm of morals and religion, which for Virgil were closely linked with politics and patriotism. To have a didactic, inspiring, elevating effect in these areas would not strike Virgil as a goal which is basically alien to poetry and which would be added as a mere accessory to its real artistic purpose; on the contrary, it is a basic part of his concept of being a poet that the *vates* should also be the teacher and educator of his nation. What I have said so far about character and action, about the gods and the relationship of man to *fatum*, is enough to show that the *Aeneid* is firmly rooted in a unified *Weltanschauung*; every poem in which this is the case is also propaganda for the poet's attitudes, whether he himself intends this or not. The only difference lies in whether the poet is more interested in the discovery of truths about life, or in their practical consequences. Virgil would not have been a Roman if he had not valued practical effect above any theoretical

474

insight; he values the Stoic teaching of morals and religion not as an explanation of the world which satisfies ones hunger for knowledge, but as a guide to right behaviour. It is enough to read Virgil's account of the Underworld after the Homeric one to appreciate the distance between poetry with a purpose and naïve poetry;[11] how out of place the cry of that Virgilian sufferer: *discite iustitiam moniti et non temnere divos* (6.620) [be warned, learn righteousness; and learn to scorn no god], would be in Homer's Tartarus. Hardly anywhere else does Virgil express so directly what he wants to commend to the hearts of his audience; he himself does not preach, he leaves the task to the story which he is telling, and it is only the well-organized and deliberate progress of the story which shows us how intently he is working towards this goal.

In this respect, Virgil breaks completely with the habits of his recent past. As far as we can tell, nothing had been farther from Hellenistic poetry than to serve a *Weltanschauung* in order to influence the lifestyle of its public. Poetry with a purpose existed in plenty, but the purpose always had a political and personal point: the panegyric in its manifold forms serves the glorification of a man, of a race, of a city, also perhaps of a political system; that has nothing to do with what we are pointing out here in Virgil. Narrative poetry which wished to fulfil serious artistic requirements stood as far as possible from all that; the only rival here to the purely artistic was scholarly interest. It was no different in Rome: a Catullus did make use of verses as a weapon in party politics, but the idea that the highest task of poetry was to educate the nation would have appeared to him and his likeminded companions as absurd, if not shocking. If one looks in Rome for a predecessor to Virgil, there is only one, and he himself stood aside from the bustle of literati and poets: Lucretius, the great loner. Virgil was the heir, not only to his artistic method, but also to his conception of the nature of the poet's vocation: the *Aeneid* is a positively anti-Lucretian work, although it does not provide scientific proof for the truth of its assertions but lets them come to life in pictures of the prehistory of Rome. Virgil no longer stood alone in his aims; he was supported by the trends of the Augustan epoch which aimed at moral improvement. The *cura morum* [moral concern] of Augustus is all too often regarded as a personal whim of the ruler; we overlook the fact that this effort from above will have been matched by a strong movement from below, which must have been given its initial impetus in the last years of the Republic. The renaissance of the popular philosophy of the Cynics and Stoics must fall within this period, even if its main blossoming came later; but Crispinuses and Stertiniuses did live and teach in Rome, and had their following which took them seriously because they themselves were serious. This class of man was obviously very common, but we know of it only from the caricatures of Horace, who for his part was, here too, going back to classical writers, above all Bion, as models; but his diatribes are to be understood as only the refined reflection of a strongly moralizing movement which had taken hold of the nation, the lower classes perhaps more than the educated. The linking of morals with patriotism, the attempt to find moral models not in the ideals of the philosophical schools but in the heroic, courageous and pious prehistory of Rome, was also taken up enthusiastically and given great encouragement by Augustus, but he did not begin it: this is clear from the writings of Varro's old age. Thus it cannot be explained as simple compliance with the ruler's wishes when the historiography of this period, more than ever before, places the moral purpose unanimously and decisively to the fore.[12] Previously, except for 476 satisfying the hunger for knowledge and also certain artistic requirements, the historian had probably followed political aims, wishing to provide the statesman with practical and moral guidance, or to provide men with something to hold on to in those stormy times;[13] now history wishes, above all, to improve the man rather than the politician, by presenting him with examples to emulate or avoid. We know what great weight Augustus attached to these very *exempla maiorum* [ancestral precedents]; it is no wonder if not just history but also poetry becomes a schoolmistress, thereby striving anew after an importance which it had renounced for several centuries.[14] Now, Horace reads 'Father Homer' in the same way as the Cynics once 477 did, in the nationalistic spirit of their time, as a most impressive teacher of morals; and he praises poetry because it *recte facta refert, orientia tempora notis instruit exemplis* [recounts good actions and teaches the rising generation with well-known examples] (*Epist.* 2.1 130), certain that he is thereby expressing Augustus' own conviction; the *Aeneid* may have hovered in his mind as a shining example while he wrote this: it is as an *exemplum* – though the word itself may be absent – that Aeneas holds himself up to Ascanius (12.439), and the whole poem is the richest mine of *exempla maiorum* [examples from our ancestors] which Augustus could wish for: he himself stands, as the noblest example, at the centre of the long line of Roman heroes who are shown to Aeneas in the Underworld, just as Augustus displayed their statues to the Roman people in his Forum.

3. Scholarly material

About the national and Augustan tendency, which is closely related to the moral and religious tendency which I have just discussed, nothing more specific needs to be said here; the material content of these tendencies lies outside my field, and I am able to refer you on this matter to Norden's essay, which I have already cited several times. At this point I will merely remind you how closely related the national epic of 478 Rome is to the national history of Rome in this respect: we have seen how extremely important it is, in Virgil's reshaping of the Sack of Troy, for example, that he regarded it as part of the ancient history of Rome; there are parallels in Roman historians with which we could illuminate many aspects of Virgil's selection (or invention) of material: Virgil treads the same paths which the annalists of Rome had always trod, whether they were writing prose or poetry. For our purpose it is significant that this tendency caused Virgil to give a completely new face to an important part of Hellenistic poetry: historial scholarship. The *Aeneid* contains it in plenty; Virgil has drawn freely on what the Roman antiquarians as far as Varro have handed down about Italian, and particularly Roman, history, about the history of races and cities, about constitutions, wars and the worship of the gods. At first glance that might seem to resemble the scholarship of which so much is evident in Apollonius' epic: there, too, there is a rich store of the results of aetiological, geographic and mythographic research. On looking more closely, one perceives the great difference between the two poets and their scholarship. Apollonius pursues truly scholarly interests: he is writing for a public who found the saga valuable and interesting primarily because it provided information about historical events and the conditions of earliest times, about the geography of distant, little-known lands, and about the ancestry of famous families; although a great part of it is really pretentious pseudo-scholarship, at least its basis was a genuine scholarly desire to have a historical understanding of the present. It is true that the alliance forged here between scholarship and poetry is a most unhappy union which is unfair to both parties. They stand together as strangers, unattached; there is no attempt to transform learning into poetry, i.e. to produce an emotional effect from it, and at every turn the flight of fancy is weighed down by the historical ballast; at the same time, the poetic form, however badly treated, predominates sufficiently to make it impossible for the material to be presented exhaustively for discussion, i.e. for

479   scholarly use to be made of it. Virgil's purposes were totally different: by including historical material in his poem he was not appealing to the learned interests of his audience, but to their patriotic feelings, and although the effect thus striven after can hardly count as purely poetic, it does come considerably closer to being so because its effect is on the emotions. Virgil was writing with a view to catching the interest not merely of the city of Rome, but of the whole of Italy,[15] and every mention of a city or of a race which confirmed their claim to extreme antiquity must have brought him enthusiastic gratitude from their descendants; imagine, for example, how Mantua must have resounded with the lines in which the poet honours his own native city (10.198-203). Virgil does not restrict himself to ancient history: the Parade of Heroes and the description of the shield lead the audience through the time of the kings and the feats of the Republic, right up to the heights of the present time: it is quite clear that his aim here is to edify and to elevate, rather than to instruct. Virgil possibly considered something else more important than the historical data: the depiction of the *mores maiorum* [customs of our ancestors], particularly the customs associated with the worship of the gods. The learned scholarship displayed in doing this deserves the recognition which was already heaped on it by the ancient critics; but if this led later generations to treat the *Aeneid* as a mine of ancient wisdom, it had an even greater significance in this role for Virgil's contemporaries; their interest in such matters was not merely scholarly and retrospective but extremely practical and relevant: there was a great desire not merely to know about these *mores maiorum* but to re-establish them in a pure form, to bring old, dead customs back to life; the ancient life-style was regarded as a moral and religious ideal, and their attempts to restore the same conditions, attempts that might appear superficial and hollow at first glance, with no hope of success in reality, did spring from the same roots as the enthusiasm for moral atonement and purification mentioned above. Thus when Virgil supplied details of early Italian rites and cult formulae, they were not learned curiosities but evidence of happier days which deserved respect and were hallowed by age. Here, too, the poet is concerned with the feelings of his audience, not with their hunger for information.

480   In Apollonius, the learned details are not fully incorporated, as can even be seen from the form; their connection with the poetic content (the winning of the Golden Fleece and the abduction of Medea) is not organic, and this is reflected in the way in which they are introduced; the poet speaks frequently in his own person, adding

learned explanations or emphasizing that a name, a monument or a custom, etc. survives to the present day. We have seen above (p. 297) how rarely Virgil speaks in his own person in that way: he makes an effort to incorporate scholarly material in a way which makes it seem essential to the action. For important parts of the early history of Italy, the two catalogues in Books 7 and 10 provided a welcome opportunity to do this; in other cases, the poet makes his characters tell of past happenings (p. 307 above), taking care that the reason for it arises perfectly naturally from the story, by having another character who needs to be told about the relevant circumstances. It is only very rarely that he lets himself be carried away by scholarly interest over and above what is required by the plot,[16] mostly in giving the etymology of names; also the *periegeses* [descriptions] of the coast of South Italy and Sicily which Aeneas gives (3.551ff., 692ff.) are not really sufficiently motivated by the situation in such detail: but compared with the geographical sections of Apollonius their brevity, and the limitation of purely scholarly information, is striking. Giving purely geographical information about areas which were unfamiliar to educated Romans is avoided by Virgil completely; we have seen how the omission of facts of purely scholarly interest even led to confusion, e.g. about the site of the foundation of the city in Thrace (p. 90 n. 34 above). But we do know that even educated Romans had little interest in geography, and therefore little knowledge of it; Virgil presupposes in his audience much more extensive knowledge of mythographical matters, although he does not parade his own scholarship or include recondite facts for the purpose of instruction.

481

4. The sublime

We return to the purely aesthetic aims of the poem. What we assembled under the heading ἐκπληκτικόν [astonishing] only describes one facet of the effect for which Virgil was striving: alongside it, or above it, comes his striving for the ὑψηλόν, the sublime. This is certainly more than a certain solemnity of diction, such as had long been *de rigueur* in rhetoric and poetry for treating certain sublime matters; nor is it the same as the concept of 'seemliness' (πρέπον, *decorum*), which played a large role in Hellenistic poetics, but had little effect on the epic other than the negative requirement that it should avoid anything which detracted from heroic dignity. Rather, the sublime is a thoroughly positive aesthetic quality, permeating both content and form, an aspect of 'style' in its widest sense. We need not hesitate to include it in a description of poetic technique, since Virgil was certainly striving for it deliberately; it is not, as it is in Aeschylus, say, or, in a different form, in Schiller, an integral part of his poetic personality: the *Eclogues* alone, written when Virgil was already mature, are sufficient proof that τὸ μεγαλοφυές [loftiness] did not come naturally to him; nothing has changed, in spite of the very considerable transformation which his *Weltanschauung* had undergone in the intervening period. In spite of this, one does not have the impression that the sublimity in the *Aeneid* is 'manufactured' in order to conjure up feelings in the reader which do not fill the poet's own heart and mind; also, it would certainly be wrong to look for deliberate calculation in every instance; it is rather that Virgil himself felt transported to a

482

higher sphere by the story which he had undertaken to treat, and this mood made him try to create in his poem an ideal of the sublime such as he had built up for himself while being carried along on the currents of his time. The result was a work of art with a completely unified atmosphere, something which made it stand out from earlier and later poems which otherwise had similar artistic aims. Even less than for other areas of technique can an examination of details here be a substitute for the total impression which one can gain only by reading the work for oneself; but we must attempt to establish a kind of standard type of the sublime.

Homer's Hephaestus is a grimy smith of supernatural skill, who sweats at the bellows himself, and when important visitors are expected, lays his tools tidily in their box, has a wash and puts on a clean shirt; Virgil's Vulcan is the god who rules the fire, served by the powerful Cyclopes, and who, when armour needs to be forged for Aeneas, does not turn his own hand to it but orders his slaves to set to work. This is a typical example of the difference between the world of the gods in Homer and in Virgil. Homer's gods are men, except that the bounds of their physical limitations have been extended or removed; Virgil's gods are the supreme powers which rule the universe, who have taken on human form only because they cannot otherwise be made visible. In this form, as active characters in a poem, it is true that they are liable to a certain degree of human frailty: but only precisely as much as is essential for the story, and never in a way that appears petty. Thus their Olympian life-style has little of the earthy about it: they do not sit feasting and drinking and playing the lyre and laughing uproariously; they do not bicker; if they do argue it is in passionate but well-chosen words; they do not threaten each other with insults and jeers, they do not attack and wound each other and therefore do not need to weep with anger or roar with pain. The way in which they intervene in earthly matters matches this. No Virgilian god meets a mortal in battle; even at the destruction of Ilium, in which they have a hand, they are not among the combatants. They do not concern themselves with minor matters: it is beneath their dignity to intervene in the Games, and Cloanthus' ship is brought to the finishing-line not by Neptune but by a host of subordinate maritime spirits. When help is needed, they come to their favourites in person: in this way Venus reveals herself to her son, Apollo comes to warn Ascanius, Mercury to warn Aeneas. When they wish to do harm, they do not dirty their own hands: Juno has Aeolus raise the tempest, Allecto raise the war, Juturna break the treaty; Diana gives bow and arrow to her nymph to execute the sentence on Camilla's murderer, Neptune lets Palinurus be pushed into the sea by the god of sleep, although he himself personally opens the Syrtes with his trident in order to rescue Aeneas. Minerva would certainly not behave like Homer's Athena, who delivers Hector to his doom with a shameful deception:[17] when Juno deceives Turnus with a mirage it is in order to rescue him. As with the ignoble, so they are also kept far from anything teasing or jocular. The scenes in the Olympian nurseries and living-rooms in Hellenistic poetry were the exact opposite of the sublime: when Apollonius has Aphrodite receiving two visiting goddesses as a middle-class housewife would receive two slightly more distinguished friends, and complaining about her mischievous rogue of a son and afterwards finding him when he has just beaten poor Ganymede at knucklebones, Virgil will not have understood how Apollonius could so parody divine matters in an epic. However, his Venus does not display total

483

divine sublimity: love, even in its highest forms, cannot be thought of as always serious. Venus does not behave to her son as gods usually do to mortals; she is freer, one might almost say flirtatious. She laughs with pleasure at the successful ruse, when she anticipates the ruin of Juno's evil plan (4.128), she also weeps, and the king of the gods smiles at her groundless fears (1.228). In her, the personification of love, the sensual aspect of love may also have its due: with her charm she entangles   484 her husband, as Homer said that the proud queen of the gods does, although sensual love does not inflame her, the guardian of marriage (1.73; 4.126).

Thus far, the Virgilian world of the gods would satisfy the severest requirements about avoiding τὸ ἀπρεπές [impropriety]: the sublimity of the gods is expressed positively in its working: where it proclaims itself,[18] Nature shudders; it is not however in the wild disturbance of the elements but in its greatest calm that the poet finds the divine to be most solemn: Neptune does not stir up the sea with his trident but calms the waves and chases away the clouds so that the pure blue sky shines over the motionless water (1.142; 5.820); when Jupiter begins to speak, 'the high house of the gods is dumb, the earth quakes and is silent, silent the sky, the wind dies down and the sea levels its waves to a calm' (10.100). The effect of the divine on the human spirit is equally sublime: each time that a human suspects the presence of the divine (8.349), or hears a divine voice (3.93; 9.112) or the divinity even comes bodily to him (p. 256 above), he is seized by the fear of supernatural power, and is shattered to the depth of his being.

Virgil intensifies the uncanny and horrific aspect of supernatural power, making it frightful and sublime: he mitigates the horror of the appearance of the Harpies with two lines which place these scourges of the gods in the realm of hellish monsters (p. 84 above); the terrifying figures of the Underworld are made both more intense and more sublime: Cerberus *immania terga resolvit fusus humi totoque ingens extenditur antro* (6.422) [relaxing his giant back he sprawled all his length across the floor of the cave]; the fiery eyes of old Charon (300) are a feature which banishes any thought of a Lucianic peasant ferryman; the Underworld itself, as conceived by Virgil, consists of 'the silent fields of the night', the 'hollow house and empty realm of Dis': Schiller felt how the intensification of horror here strives for sublimity.[19]

The sublimity of the gods is reflected in that of the heroes.[20] In Virgil's world of   485 heroes there is no room for anything mean or petty. That great kings might quarrel over the possession of slave-girls, that a king's son like Paris might leave the   486 fighting in order to carry on a love-affair – Virgil would not have believed his heroes capable of anything like this. The crooked, bad-tempered, brawling Thersites changes into Drances the demagogue, driven on, it is true, by envy of Turnus' fame, but standing up for the justified interests of the crowd against Turnus' destructive whims, a man who, as his behaviour towards Aeneas shows, can still perceive and respect true greatness. How noble are the reasons which lead the Rutulians to break the treaty, compared with the selfishness of Pandarus! Even the wicked Mezentius has something of the 'noble transgressor', and his death is sublime. Dido is driven along all the labyrinthine ways of passion, but in death, when a person is shown in his true colours, she finds the sublime words:

Vixi et quem dederat cursum fortuna peregi,
et nunc magna mei sub terras ibit imago.

[I have lived my life and finished the course which fortune allotted me. Now my wraith shall pass in state to the world below]. Finally, the further Aeneas develops into the perfect hero, the more purely he represents the very type of the sublime. It goes without saying that Virgil keeps his image free of every mean or petty trait. However, the conventional and fictitious concept of Roman greatness of soul and strength of character receives a slap in the face when Virgil says of his hero at his first appearance (1.92):

487   *extemplo Aeneae solvuntur frigore membra;*
ingemit et duplicis tendens ad sidera palmas
talia voce refert.

[Instantly Aeneas felt his limbs give way in a chill of terror, and groaned. Stretching both hands, palm-upward, to the stars, he cried aloud]. Virgil most certainly gave very careful consideration to this passage in particular, as also to the words which Aeneas then speaks. He sees death standing immediately in front of him, he knows that no human power can help him now: but he may not express any fear of death or any wish to remain alive, as Achilles (*Iliad* 21.273) and Odysseus (*Odyssey* 5.299) do in similar situations – that would be as unworthy of the hero here as it would be when he has achieved sublimity (9.10); he is only allowed to express the wish that he had fallen below Troy's walls, watched by his own household, as Hector and Sarpedon and so many other brave men had died.[21] In the same way as Aeneas sighs at his misfortune here but does not complain – *conqueri fortunam adversam, non lamentari decet* [one ought to lament one's ill-fortune but not bewail it] Pacuvius had said, and thereby pleased the Stoic-minded Cicero (*Tusc.* 2.48) – he is allowed to weep at the sight of Hector dishonoured (2.279) and Pallas killed (11.29, 41), at the memory of the death of noble friends and heroes (1.459, cf. 465, 470, 485) or at the affecting departure of Andromache (3.492) tears of pity also befit the hero;[22] but even when he would be inclined to despair, he must be capable of putting on a show of cheerfulness if duty demands it (1.208), should not let himself be so carried away by his own grief that he acts in a way contrary to his great mission (4.448), should, after he has paid the tribute of grief when it is due, return immediately to active
488   service (11.96); the sublime spirit shows itself not in the suppression of human emotions, but in overcoming them. Aeneas as lover: it is impossible to think of him billing and cooing; slanderous Fama speaks of a licentious, idle life: Aeneas builds the citadel which will one day protect the deadly enemies of his people (4.260). When it comes to practical details, we find that the same is true of Aeneas and the other heroes as we found with the gods. Aeneas is permitted to slay the stag on the Libyan shore, but not, like Odysseus, gut it with his own hands and carry it to the ships. Also, he does not travel alone like any common wanderer, but has at least the faithful Achates at his side, who carries his weapon or can announce his arrival (6.34). It is totally inappropriate to the dignity of a heroic poem to include unnecessary mention of the details of daily life, eating and drinking, sleeping and dressing;

where they are mentioned, there is a special reason for it: someone is asleep when he sees a dream-vision, the meal symbolizes the return of physical pleasure after deadly dangers (1.174, 210), or it brings the fulfilment of a fateful prediction: and if in this and similar cases a detail such as the eating of the tables has to be mentioned, then at least all the splendour of language is called on, to decorate with words what is lacking in greatness.[23] It is a different matter with festive occasions (1.637, 723; 3.353; cf. also 5.100); there royal splendour is displayed in spacious halls, one reclines on purple rugs, dines from silver and golden dishes and drinks from a bejewelled cup. But even at such moments of leisure the minds of the character are on noble things: Demodocus could serve up as a trifle for the Phaeacians a frivolous frolic from Olympian married life; at Queen Dido's court Iopas sings of the wonders of the universe and explains its mysteries: for Virgil and his contemporaries this is the sublimest content of song. How Virgil deliberately avoids anything base in these matters is best shown by the one exception: the visit to Evander is described in deliberately plain language. There is repeated eating and drinking, the men are pillowed on the grass, Aeneas has the seat of honour, the hornbeam stool covered   489 with sheepskin; Evander's herd of cattle snorts on the pasture; Aeneas enters the lowly hut which serves as a guest chamber, a bear-skin covers his couch of leaves; when sunrise and birdsong wake the king, he puts on tunic and sandals, girds on his sword, puts a panther-skin round him for a cloak and goes to his visitor, two hounds, the guardians of his threshold, at his side. All these plain details are the exact opposite of the sublime: yet they serve it indirectly, for the cosily impoverished still-life of the *Romanae conditor arcis* [founder of Rome's citadel] is intended to make the reader, surrounded as he is by the splendour and the buzzing life of metropolitan Rome, appreciate the present greatness all the more because of the contrast.

In what we have said so far about Virgil's presentation of the human characters there is already much which does not merely avoid τὸ ἀπρεπές [impropriety] but strives positively after the sublime. I do not need to spell out how this dominated Virgil's moral sphere: *virtus*, manly behaviour towards both human enemies and the blows of fate, is the ideal, alongside *pietas*, which shows itself at its sublimest in self-sacrifice. As in the case of the gods, Virgil seeks to carry his audience along with him by describing the *effect* which ideal humanity has: think of the behaviour of Aeneas when Dido receives him, of Drances towards Aeneas, of Ascanius towards the daring pair of friends, of Aeneas at Lausus' self-sacrifice – that all serves, as it were, to show the audience how to feel admiration.

Inward greatness is symbolized by physical size; Virgil sees his heroes as powerful figures of great strength; *ingens* [huge], always one of Virgil's favourite words,[24] is used again and again of the heroes and their deeds. With this concept of greatness, Virgil does sometimes become immoderate, which is very rare with him. It can perhaps be excused by the intentionally mythical character of the boxing-match at the Funeral Games where the *caestus* [thongs] with which Entellus will fight are manufactured from seven huge ox-skins (5.401); but when the boulder which Turnus picks up would not, as in Homer, be too heavy for two men of the present   490 generation, but could hardly be carried by twelve specially selected men (12.899), then the intensification is so exaggerated that it misses its mark. When Aeneas and

Turnus prepare for the duel, Latinus feels the sublime power of destiny, which has led the two huge men from distant parts of the world to meet in battle (12.709): one can understand this feeling;[25] but to compare Aeneas with Mount Athos, with Mount Eryx, and finally with the snow-covered Apennines, is asking too much of the imagination.

The tendency towards the magnificent and the sublime also affects the portrayal of nature in the *Aeneid*. The Trojans' landing place in Libya is the equivalent of the harbour of Phorcys on Ithaca, where the Phaeacians land: the steep promontories on either side of the harbour have been made by Virgil into mighty cliffs with summits that reach the sky; instead of the one olive tree throwing a wide shadow, in the background he has a tall grove, murky and gloomy. No real site is described in anything like as much detail as Mount Etna, thundering, flame-spitting and mighty (3.570-82): it also serves in the περὶ ὕψους [*de Sublimitate*] as an example of the sublime in nature (35.4).

There is one source of the sublime which we have not yet mentioned and which, it is true, does not often come to the surface in Virgil's poem, but is all the stronger when it does, and its subterranean rumble accompanies the poem from beginning to end: the greatness of Rome, of the Roman people and of their ruler, of Roman history and of the Roman empire, the *maiestas populi Romani* [majesty of the Roman people]. The thoughts which would be most likely to make a Roman feel the awe of the sublime were all linked to these ideas: the thought of the strength of destiny and the will of the gods, guiding the Roman people in such a miraculous way; the thought, which Virgil's contemporaries also like to use, that from the smallest of beginnings such gigantic greatness can grow; but also the thought of the endless toil and sacrifice which has been the price of this greatness: as Livy feels, when he comes to the great wars against the Samnites, Pyrrhus and Carthage: *quanta rerum moles* [what mighty efforts]! 'How often the greatest dangers had to be faced, in order that the empire might reach its present almost unencompassable size!' (7.29). And it is just this thought which Virgil puts at the beginning, as if to set the tone which will resound through all the sufferings and dangers that Aeneas will undergo: *tantae molis erat Romanam condere gentem* [such was the cost in heavy toil of beginning the life of Rome]. As well as these general sublime feelings there are also more concrete concepts: the great figures of Roman history whom Aeneas sees in the Pageant of Heroes, the famous deeds of his descendants, which he admires on his shield, although he cannot yet understand their significance: such sublime material was, in Virgil's opinion, more appropriate for the decoration of the armour of a Roman hero than the colourful scenes of human life in general which decorated the shield of Achilles. Just as the person of Augustus is the high point in the pageant of heroes, so the deeds of Augustus crown the images on the shield; Augustus as prince of peace, wearing the crown of victory, a god on earth, forms the high point of Jupiter's prophecy, the essential *pièce de résistance* in the First Book which paints in glowing colours the tenor of the poem which the poet himself has expressed in the opening lines in plain words. Just as Augustus is hallowed among men, so is the Capitol hallowed among all sites on earth: Aeneas still does not guess at this when he first sees the wooded height, but the sublime future soon proclaims itself in the pious shudder which the Arcadians feel at the site where Jupiter appears in the storm-clouds. The sublime concept of infinity is summoned to the aid of these images: the rule of Lavinium and Alba was limited, Rome's rule will have no limit to its territory or to its duration (1.278); *incluta Roma imperium terris, animos aequabit Olympo* (6.782) [illustrious Rome shall extend her authority to the breadth of the earth, and her spirit to the height of Olympus]: Virgil's time saw the fulfilment of Anchises' prophecy.

Virgil's highest aim was to arouse a sense of the sublime in his audience; this defines and limits every other aspect of the poem. Even the ἐκπληκτικόν [astonishing] is only allowed if it is also ὑψηλόν [sublime]: that is its specifically Virgilian colouring. In particular, Virgil's *pathos* is ruled and directed by this. We have seen that Virgil did not merely strive to arouse pity by any available means; he scorned anything depressing or merely worrying or melancholy-making and restricts himself almost entirely to the portrayal of heroic suffering which will not just be a source of pleasurable pain to the onlooker but will also inspire him. He also scorns anything revolting, common or unpleasant, the μιαρόν; the horrific appears raised to the sublimely terrible. Finally, Virgil's striving after the sublime is also the key to the complete understanding of Virgil's presentation and composition. Great, uncluttered contours, organization and clarity on both the small scale and the larger scale, a tight structure, omission of all superfluous detail which might distract the gaze and spoil the unified effect – these were the principles which, as we have seen, rule both presentation and composition; they beget the form which is the only one worthy of the sublime material.

The Romans were receptive to the sublime, in Virgil's sense, as no other people were. They possessed a strongly developed sense of the lowest level of the sublime, the dignity of outward appearance; the national toga is its most eloquent symbol, and was felt to be such, as Virgil himself shows when he speaks of the *gens togata* (1.282) [the nation which wears the toga]. They also had a great sense of the solemn: their manner of celebrating festivals, their funerals and triumphal processions bear witness to this: when Virgil depicts the burial of Misenus, the funeral of Pallas, the solemn procession when the treaty is agreed, he is providing scenes which are not only poetically attractive but which most vividly represent the Roman way of thinking and feeling. However, it would be quite wrong to think of their thoughts as being directed only towards outward dignity and outward show. The Roman moral and religious ideal may have been limited and sober, but none can deny that it contained an element of the sublime, even if in fact very few Romans in the whole course of their history ever made this ideal into a reality; that it was created at all is evidence of their aspirations. Moreover, if the Augustan period and its greatness were a powerful source of sublime feelings for Virgil, it was doubtless the same, to the same extent, for his contemporaries. A great wind blows through their times and dies down all too soon; they breathe in a certain intoxication from the sublime, which infects even such an unsublime nature as Horace; it cannot be mere chance that it was in Augustan Rome that the concept of the sublime was introduced into scholarly aesthetics. No-one desired and promoted this movement more than Augustus himself: countless tiny details still speak to us of how keen he was to re-establish in the Roman life-style the greatness which it was piously believed to have possessed in the good old days: Augustus' own statue is itself the most perfect

383

expression of this, the supreme example of the style. It was the early history of Rome that Virgil was describing, and this meant that he was describing the ideal of contemporary Rome; he did not dream up or construct or imitate this ideal, he experienced it and struggled for it himself; that is why it still lives on for us in his poem.

466   Notes to Chapter 5

1. Of course, Aristotle himself did not express it in this form; his deep-reaching doctrine of the κάθαρσις τῶν παθημάτων [purging of the emotions] was clearly trivialized very soon even in his own school. He does sometimes already use the later keyword: *Poetics* 25.1460b 23: ἀδύνατα πεποίηται· ἡμάρτηται, ἀλλ' ὀρθῶς ἔχει, εἰ τυγχάνει (ἡ ποιητικὴ τέχνη) τοῦ τέλους τοῦ αὐτῆς· τὸ γὰρ τέλος τηρεῖται, εἰ οὕτως ἐ κ π λ η κ τ ι κ ώ τ ε ρ ο ν ἢ αὐτὸ ἢ ἄλλο ποιεῖ μέρος [if something impossible has been represented, this is a fault: but if (the poetic art) achieves its true object, then this is acceptable: and it does this if either the passage in question or some other passage is thereby made more striking] (cf. also 14.1454a 4; 16.1455a 17). This does have a very close connection with his theory of *pathos*: the ἐκπλήττειν [astonishing] leads to ἔκστασις [ecstasy]. References in later writers, of which there are doubtless many more (Kroll, *Neue Jahrbücher* 21 [1908] 521,8) adduce more for ἔκπληξις: Polybius 2.56: ἐκεῖ δεῖ διὰ τῶν πιθανωτάτων λόγων ἐκπλῆξαι καὶ ψυχαγωγῆσαι κατὰ τὸ παρὸν τοὺς ἀκούοντας [there (i.e. in tragedy) one must astonish and play upon the feelings of the audience by the most persuasive arguments in the circumstances]. Similarly in Strabo 1.2.17 (εἶναι τὸ τέλος) ἡδονὴν καὶ ἔκπληξιν [(the aim is) pleasure and astonishment]): [Longinus] *De Sublim.* 15.2: τῆς ἐν ποιήσει (φαντασίας) τέλος ἐστὶν ἔκπληξις, τῆς δ' ἐν λόγοις ἐνάργεια [the aim (of imagery) in poetry is astonishment, and in prose vividness]: Plutarch, *Quo modo adulesc.*, 17a: τοῦτο δὲ παντὶ δῆλον, ὅτι μυθοποίημα καὶ πλάσμα πρὸς ἡδονὴν ἢ ἔκπληξιν ἀκροατοῦ γέγονε [it is obvious to everyone that a mythical fabrication has been produced to please or astonish the listener]: ibid. 25d: τὸ γὰρ ἐμπαθὲς καὶ παράλογον καὶ ἀπροσδόκητον, ᾧ πλείστη μὲν ἔκπληξις ἔπεται πλείστη δὲ χάρις αἱ μεταβολαὶ παρέχουσι τοῖς μύθοις [sudden changes give stories their emotional, astonishing and unexpected features, which produce great astonishment and great delight]: Ps-Plutarch *de vita Homeri* 5: πεποίηκε δὲ καὶ τοὺς θεοὺς τοῖς ἀνθρώποις ὁμιλοῦντας οὐ μόνον ψυχαγωγίας καὶ ἐκπλήξεως χάριν, ἀλλ' ἵνα... [he represents gods conversing with men not only for the sake of pleasing and astonishing the listener but in order...]: ibid. 6: καὶ τὸ μὲν ὅλον παρ' αὐτῷ διήγησις τῶν πραγμάτων παράδοξος καὶ μυθώδης κατεσκεύασται ὑπὲρ τοῦ πληροῦν ἀγωνίας καὶ θαύματος τοὺς ἐντυγχάνοντας καὶ ἐκπληκτικὴν τὴν ἀκρόασιν καθιστάναι [in him the narration of events is deliberately unexpected and fabulous in order to fill the hearers with anguish and astonishment, and to make the account startling]: Eustathius, *Odyssey* proem 1379: δέδοται κατὰ τοὺς τεχνογράφους τῇ ποιήσει καὶ τερατεύεσθαι, ὡς ἂν ἐκ τούτων ἡδονήν τε ἅμα τοῖς ἀκροαταῖς καὶ ἔκπλῆξιν ἐμποιήσειεν [technical writers allow to poetry the recounting of marvels so that they may give pleasure to their audience and also astonishment]. In some Alexandrian circles ἔκπληξις [astonishment] seems to have been considered less important; Eratosthenes names φυχαγωγῆσαι [charming the listener] as the poet's 467 sole aim, and truly one can hardly imagine that he or Callimachus imagined ἔκπληξις to be the aim of their own poetry. Sextus, *adv. math.* 1.297, probably from an Alexandrian grammatical source: ἐκ παντὸς ψυχαγωγῆσαι ἐθέλουσιν (οἱ ποιηταί) [(poets) altogether aim at charming]; in his *Epist. ad Pisones*, Horace dutifully speaks of πάθος [emotion] in connection with tragedy too (although in much calmer terms than in the passage cited in the text, *Epist.* 2.1.211), but when he is discussing the general aim of literature he speaks only of *delectare* (333) [to please]; Horace's agreement with Eratosthenes is probably not a mere coincidence, since he also comes close to him in the *ad Pisones* when discussing the usefulness of poetry, on which see below p. 387 n.14.

    2. *Quom. adol.* 25d and *vita Hom.* 6, both cited in the previous note.

    3. Macrob. (*Sat.* 4.2), most exceptionally, places the two aims next to each other: 469 *oportet ut oratio pathetica aut ad indignationem aut ad misericordiam dirigatur quae a Graecis* οἶκτος καὶ δείνωσις *appellantur* [pathetic speech ought to be aimed either at indignation or at pity, which are called δείνωσις and οἶκτος by the Greeks]; cf. Quintilian 6.2.24; Polybius on Phylarchus 2.56: σπουδάζων εἰς ἔλεον ἐκκαλεῖσθαι τοὺς ἀναγινώσκοντας...πειρώμενος ἐν ἑκάστοις ἀεὶ πρὸ ὀφθαλμῶν τιθέναι τὰ δεινά [eager to inspire *pity* in his readers...trying in every situation to put frightening scenes before the eyes]; Dion. Hal. *de Thucyd.* 15: ὠμὰ καὶ δεινὰ καὶ οἴκτων ἄξια φαίνεσθαι ποιεῖ τὰ πάθη [he makes events appear savage and *frightening* and *worthy of pity*]. They are very frequently combined in this way.

    4. See Schwartz, 'Fünf Vorträge über den griechischen Roman', 114ff., *Hermes* 471 32 (1897) 560ff., P. Scheller, *De hellenistica historiae scribendae arte* (Diss. Leipzig, 1911) 57ff. Among the surviving historical works, Justin reveals this tendency most clearly; see E. Schneider, *De Pompei Trogi historiarum Philippicarum consilio et arte* (Diss. Leipzig, 1913) *passim*. The relationship of Livy's narrative technique to Virgil's has been pointed out several times by Witte in his essay on Livy, *Rhein. Mus.* 65 (1910) 270-305, 359-419.

    5. See, for example, how Phylarchus has portrayed the torture of Aristomachus; 472 he has not shown us the actual torture, which would have been μιαρόν [revolting], but has described the effect which the screams issuing from the torture-chamber at night had on the people living round about: ὧν τοὺς μὲν ἐκπληττομένους τὴν ἀσέβειαν, τοὺς δ' ἀπιστοῦντας, τοὺς δ' ἀγανακτοῦντας ἐπὶ τοῖς γινομένοις προστρέχειν πρὸς τὴν οἰκίαν [some of whom were astounded at the impiety, some were incredulous, and some in indignation at what was being done ran towards the house] (Polybius 2.59).

    6. Cf. the instructive compilation by Ed. Zarncke, 'Der Einfluss der griechischen Literatur auf die Entwicklung der römischen Prosa', in *Commentat. Ribbeckianae* (Leipzig, 1888) 267. Ennius' role in the poetic shaping of earlier Roman history is over-valued here, in my opinion.

    7. There is a good discussion of it in the work by Scheller mentioned above (n. 4).

8. 9 (p. 337.22 Usener): χρὴ τὴν ἱστορικὴν πραγματείαν εἰρομένην εἶναι καὶ ἀπερίσπαστον [history should be a continuous and uninterrupted sequence of events].

9. 10 (p. 338.6): Thucydides has been criticized on this point, οὐκ ἐλάχιστον μέρος εἶναι λέγοντες οἰκονομίας ἀγαθῆς ἀρχήν τε λαβεῖν, ἧς οὐκ ἂν εἴη τι πρότερον, καὶ τέλει περιλαβεῖν τὴν πραγματείαν ᾧ δόξει μηδὲν ἐνδεῖν [they say that not the least important aspect of good arrangement is to take one's beginning where nothing could be imagined as coming before, and one's end where nothing more would seem to be needed] – just the Aristotelian requirements for Epic.

10. 15 (p. 347.5): πόλεών τε ἁλώσεις καὶ κατασκαφὰς καὶ ἀνδραποδισμοὺς
473 καὶ ἄλλας τοιαύτας συμφορὰς πολλάκις ἀναγκασθεὶς γράφειν ποτὲ μὲν οὕτως ὠμὰ καὶ δεινὰ καὶ οἴκτων ἄξια φαίνεσθαι ποιεῖ τὰ πάθη, ὥστε μηδεμίαν ὑπερβολὴν μήτε ἱστοριογράφοις μήτε ποιηταῖς καταλιπεῖν· ποτὲ δὲ οὕτως ταπεινὰ καὶ μικρά κτλ [he often has to describe the capture and destruction of cities, enslavement of citizens and other similar disasters: and sometimes he makes the events so savage and terrible and pitiful that he leaves nothing further for historians or poets to add: but sometimes he makes them so trivial and small etc.].

474 **11.** His period firmly believed that eschatological myth should have a moral effect; for example, Diodorus says significantly 1.2.2: ἡ τῶν ἐν Ἅιδου μυθολογία τὴν ὑπόθεσιν πεπλασμένην ἔχουσα πολλὰ συμβάλλεται τοῖς ἀνθρώποις πρὸς εὐσέβειαν καὶ δικαιοσύνην [for the myths which are told about Hades, in spite of the fact that their subject-matter is fictitious, play an important part in promoting piety and justice among men]. It is true that his purpose of προτρέψασθαι τοὺς ἀνθρώπους ἐπὶ τὸν ἄριστον βίον [urging men towards the best life] would seem to be better served by Egyptian eschatology than by Hellenistic, which had lost all credibility through its unbelievable storytelling (1.93.3). How Epicureanism also in its own way valued τὰ ἐν Ἅιδου [myths of Hades] protreptically, is shown by Lucretius (3.978ff.).

475 **12.** This can be seen most clearly in Livy's proem: *hoc illud est praecipue in cognitione rerum salubre ac frugiferum, omnis te exempli documenta in inlustri*
476 *posita monumento intueri; inde tibi tuaeque rei publicae quod imitere capias, inde foedum inceptu foedum exitu, quod vites* (10) [the most helpful and useful aspect of the study of history is that one can observe the record of every kind of behaviour placed on a clear memorial: and from it one can deduce both for oneself and for one's country what to imitate, and what to avoid as being bad in its inception and bad in its results]. Exactly similar is Diodorus 1.2.8; Dionysius 1.6 wishes to give the ancients the praise due to them, thereby encouraging their descendants to show themselves worthy of their forbears; Strabo 1.1.23 considers his ὑπομνήματα ἱστορικά [historical commentaries] to be χρήσιμα εἰς τὴν ἠθικὴν καὶ πολιτικὴν φιλοσοφίαν [useful for *moral* and political philosophy]; the *Exempla* of Cornelius Nepos have rightly been cited in this context by Norden, *Neue Jahrbücher* 7 (1901) 266. Peter, *Die geschichtliche Literatur der römischen Kaiserzeit* (Leipzig, 1897) II.218, deals with utility as the goal of the historian, but does not discriminate enough between different periods or distinguish moral improvement from practical application for the politican, or from the conduct of life in general: in this sense, and not in the moral sense, history is also called *magistra vitae* (mistress of life) by Cicero, *De Orat.* 2.9.36.

13. The theoretical requirement that historiography should have a moral effect by presenting good and bad examples must go back a long way, as Scheller (op. cit. 74ff.) has shown (contrary to my earlier opinion): it goes back to Isocrates, and is known to Polybius, among others. But when the latter mentions it, he is clearly thinking mainly of the moral effect on the politician (e.g. 16.22a; 30.6), and Sempronius Asellio is thinking of the same thing when (in Gellius 5.18.9) he accuses the annalists that they *neque alacriores...ad rem publicam defendundam neque segniores ad rem perperam faciundam...commovere possunt* [are unable to make people either more active to defend the state or more recalcitrant to act wrongly]. Moreover, this theory had hardly any practical effect on, for example, the history written by Polybius; even less on that of Sallust, who in the proem to *Jugurtha* (45) likewise mentions the role of historiography in providing models, but himself serves completely political, not moral aims (Lauckner, *Die künstlerischen und politischen Ziele der Monographie Sallusts über den Jug. Krieg* [Diss. Leipzig, 1911] 24). About Posidonius' attitude to this question I do not yet dare venture an opinion.

14. Aristotle, who left the moral effect of poetry undiscussed, may have observed correctly for his own time: he was definitely shown to be right for later years. The early Stoa, on the other hand, preserving the legacy of Cynicism, did not renounce the use of poetry in the service of philosophical edification, and the Hymn of Cleanthes is a practical example of his aesthetic theory τὰ μέτρα καὶ τὰ μέλη καὶ τοὺς ῥυθμοὺς ὡς μάλιστα προσικνεῖσθαι πρὸς τὴν ἀλήθειαν τῆς τῶν θείων θεωρίας [metre and song and rhythm approach very close to the true contemplation of the divine] (Philodemus *de Mus.* 4.28.10). The Stoic concept of poetry is given by Strabo in his polemic against Eratosthenes, which recognizes as its goal only ψυχαγωγῆσαι [to charm], Strabo 1.2.3: οἱ παλαιοὶ φιλοσοφίαν τινὰ λέγουσι πρώτην τὴν ποιητικήν, εἰσάγουσαν εἰς τὸν βίον ἡμᾶς ἐκ νέων καὶ διδάσκουσαν ἤθη καὶ πάθη καὶ πράξεις μεθ' ἡδονῆς [the ancients say that poetry is in a sense our first philosophy, introducing us to life from our childhood, and teaching us pleasurably about character and feelings and actions]: as far as I know, this doctrine had no further influence on the practice of poetry (but much on the exegesis of Homer: Diogenes of Babylon in Philod. *Rhet.* 2 p. 111; suppl. XXXII, Krates, Wachsmuth p. 21 etc.). Even Horace, who, in his letter to Augustus, is so eloquent in defence of the moral effect of poetry, seems in his *ad Pisones*, following some grammarian as his source, to place among the *prodesse* [advantages] and *utile* [usefulness] of poetry the effects of single γνῶμαι, or of gnomic poetry in general, rather than the influence of *exempla* [moral examples]; similarly, at a later date, Sextus Empiricus, who himself takes poets to be ἀνωφελεῖς ἢ ὀλιγωφελεῖς [useless or of little use] (ἐκ παντὸς ψυχαγωγῆσαι ἐθέλουσιν [they desire entirely to entertain] [*adv. math.* 1.297]), contradicts the teaching of the *Grammarians*, ὡς ἡ ποιητικὴ πολλὰς δίδωσιν ἀφορμὰς πρὸς σοφίαν καὶ εὐδαίμονα βίον (ibid. 270) [poetry provides many incentives to wisdom and a happy life], and does not take this to indicate the moral effect of poetry in general, but only of τὰ γνωμικὰ καὶ παραινετικά (278) [those poems which are gnomic and hortatory].

15. Wilamowitz, *Reden und Vorträge*[3], (Berlin, 1913) 267. 479

16. For example in Venus' speech about Antenor when she lingers over the 480
mirabilia [wonders] of Timavus; derivation of names: Chaonia in Andromache's

477

narrative (3.334): Pallanteum in Tiberinus' instructions (8.54); Argyripe in the account by Venulus (11.246); Samothrace in Latinus' greeting (7.208); Italia in Ilioneus' address (1.532); cf. 3.702 on Gela. Also, Jupiter's remark about the name Iulus (1.268) belongs here. After all this, one will have to recognize as Virgilian the allusion to the κτίσις [founding] of Carthage and the origin of the name Byrsa in Venus' information to Aeneas (1.367); Virgil did not want to miss the chance of rounding off the story of Dido, but he feels as if it is not entirely appropriate to the situation and makes Venus break off, as if she feels the same, after only a quick reference to the legend of how cunning Dido was when she bought the land. Moreover, the common habit of including the etymology of names in Roman poetry goes back a long way: Naevius explained the names Palatium and Aventine, fr. 27.29B; Ennius cannot refrain, in the prologue to his *Medea* (208R), from burdening the casual reference to the Argo with its etymology, etc.

483   **17.** Schol. BT on *Iliad* 22.227: ἄτοπον θεὸν οὖσαν πλανᾶν τὸν Ἕκτορα [it is extraordinary that she, a goddess, should mislead Hector].

484   **18.** Apollo speaks (3.90): *tremere omnia visa repente, liminaque laurusque dei totusque moveri mons circum* [suddenly everything seemed to quake, even the god's entrance door and his bay-tree; the whole hill appeared to move around us]. Hecate approaches: *sub pedibus mugire solum et iuga coepta moveri silvarum* (6.256) [the ground bellowed beneath their feet, the slopes of the forest-clad mountains began to move].

    19. '*Vom Erhabenen*', *Werke* VII, 276 ed. Kurz (Leipzig, 1885).

485   **20.** Hercules occupies a midway position, since he was a hero and is now a god. Virgil's re-shaping of the Cacus legend (8.185ff.), which Münzer's excellent analysis has now made completely clear (see above p. 285 n. 108), is absolutely characteristic in its tendency towards both the ὑψηλόν [sublime] and ἔκπληξις [astonishing]. The thieving goatherd (Livy) or bandit/robber (Dion. Hal.) Cacus is not an opponent worthy of the god; Virgil gives him divine descent and makes him a *monstrum*, comparable with Polyphemus and other monsters of saga (cf. Münzer 43f.). In the historians, the natives support Cacus against Hercules, and it is only afterwards that Dionysius, to explain the Hercules cult, introduces the motivation that there was joy at the death of the robber; in Virgil, Cacus is the terror of the neighbourhood, a murderous monster (there is intensification of the frightful, particularly in the description of the cave [193ff. and 241ff.]); this puts Hercules' feat of rescue into the right light, this σωτήρ [saviour] deserves divine honour at the *Ara Maxima* [Great Altar]. This new conception of the characters is matched by the action: (1) The cattle-rustling is not a jape carried out by Cacus *captus pulcritudine boum* [captivated by the beauty of the cattle] (Livy), but is seen by Evander as the peak of impertinence and criminal behaviour (*furiis Caci mens effera, ne quid inausum aut intractatum scelerisve dolive fuisset* [Cacus who in his insane ingenuity wished to leave no act of crime or fraud undared or unattempted]): it is a sin against the god, whom the sinful monster wants to harm. On the other hand, if possible, Hercules must not appear to have been tricked, or to be worried about the loss of a few cattle: as a result we are not told how the theft was successful (Dion. Hal.: βαρυνόμενος διὰ κόπου κατακλιθεὶς ἔδωκεν αὐτὸν ὕπνῳ [weighed down by his efforts he lay down and gave himself up to sleep] while the oxen were grazing

untended; even worse in Livy: *fessum via procubuisse. ibi cum eum cibo vinoque gravatum sopor oppressisset* [tired of travelling he lay down: and there when sleep overcame him, heavy with food and wine...]); we do not see Hercules count his cattle like a smallholder, and look in vain for the missing ones (line 212 and *abiuratae rapinae* [263] [the plunder he was forced to renounce]) show that Virgil had before him a version similar to that of Dionysius: it is obvious why he adds the broken oath), and we do not hear of his anger until the sound of the stolen cow lowing in Cacus' cave tells him that a crime has been committed (the trick by which Dionysius has Hercules discovering the deception could of course not be used by Virgil). (2) Virgil lays most weight on describing the fight, in contrast to earlier versions, as Münzer has shown: whereas other versions have Cacus taking up a defensive position and then simply being killed by Hercules' club, Virgil invents an action full of dramatic movement: Cacus flees into his cave; at this point, Evander and his men are introduced as onlookers, and nothing can portray the overpowering stature of Hercules more strikingly than *tum primum Cacum nostri videre timentem turbatumque oculi* [then for the first time our eyes witnessed Cacus afraid and in a panic] (Virgil cares little about topographical clarity compared with pathetic effect, see p. 285 n. 108 above); tension is created by the failure of Hercules' first attempt to reach Cacus, which is frustrated by the work of the god Vulcan (who thus still ranks higher than the god-in-the-making), after which his superhuman strength   486 (233-40) and his courage (256-81) arouse even more admiration; the effect of the sight of the slain monster on the onlookers makes a powerful finale: see p. 127 above. The success of Virgil's reshaping of the story was, as Münzer shows very clearly, similar to the success of his retelling of the Dido legend: the historians reject it; the poets (Propertius and Ovid) do not copy every detail, it is true, but they do drop the human Cacus in favour of the monster. Ovid goes even further than Virgil in connecting Evander with Hercules, by making the hero a guest of Evander before he performs his deed of rescue: Virgil would not have countenanced this, since it would then have been Hercules' duty, even without being personally insulted, to rid his host of the monster: it is only after the fight that *haec limina victor Alcides subiit* (362) [Hercules in the hour of victory bowed his head to enter this door] (Münzer 12, n. 15), before that he had only paused to allow his hungry herd to graze (213).

21. Achilles and Odysseus were the model for this, but the *ethos* is different   487 here: Achilles wishes that he were not dying shamefully in the water but at the hand of the bravest of men; the imitative author of the *Odyssey* says, in coarser fashion: τῷ κ' ἔλαχον κτερέων καί μευ κλέος ἦγον Ἀχαιοί [then I should have received burial honours, and the Achaeans would have carried my renown]. In Aeneas' words, *quis ante ora patrum Troiae sub moenibus altis contigit oppetere* [whose fortune it was to die under the high walls of Troy before their parents' eyes] everyone will hear the sentiment of *dulce et decorum est pro patria mori* [it is a pleasant and a fine thing to die for one's country], which cannot subsist in the οἳ τότ' ὄλοντο Τροίῃ ἐν εὐρείῃ [who died then on the broad plains of Troy] of the *Odyssey*.

22. For tears as a sign of noble humanity, see *sunt lacrimae rerum et mentem*   488 *mortalia tangunt* (1.462) [there are tears for the world's distress, and a sympathy for short-lived humanity]. Anyone who is surprised that there is so much weeping in Virgil, and thinks that it proves a particular melancholy on the part of the poet

should read some of Cicero's speeches or some books of Livy: in this respect we should not judge a Roman by our own conventions.

488   **23.** Schol. B on *Iliad* 18.346: τὸ τὰ μικρὰ καὶ ἄδοξα μεγαλοπρεπῶς ἐξενεγ-κεῖν καὶ σεμνῶς ἀπαγγεῖλαι θαυμασίας καὶ μεγίστης ἐστὶ δυνάμεως [to introduce the petty and the trivial in a dignified manner and to recount it in a noble style requires great and marvellous skill]. Further see Römer, *Die exeget. Schol. d. Ilias im cod. Ven. B* (Munich, 1879) XII.

24. Cf. Simcox, *Latein. Litt.* I.273.

490   **25.** Livy seeks to arouse a similar feeling before the account of the battle of Zama (30.32): *ad hoc discrimen procedunt postero die duorum opulentissimorum populorum duo longe clarissimi duces, duo fortissimi exercitus, multa ante parta decora aut cumulaturi eo die aut eversuri* etc. [next day, the two most famous generals by far, the two bravest armies of the two richest nations go forward into battle, to crown or to overturn on that day their many glorious achievements of the past...].

Index of Names and Topics

Index of Citations from the Aeneid